THE LETTERS OF
HENRY ADAMS
Volume I

1858–1868

Henry Adams, 1868

The Letters of
HENRY
ADAMS

VOLUME I : 1858–1868

Edited by
J. C. Levenson, Ernest Samuels
Charles Vandersee, Viola Hopkins Winner

with the assistance of
Jayne N. Samuels, Eleanor Pearre Abbot

The Belknap Press of
Harvard University Press
Cambridge, Massachusetts
and London, England

1982

Preparation of these volumes was made possible by grants from the
Program for Editions of the National Endowment for the Humanities
and from the Seth Sprague Educational and Charitable Foundation.
Publication of the volumes has been assisted by a grant from the
Publications Program of the National Endowment for the Humanities.

Library of Congress Cataloging in Publication Data
Adams, Henry, 1838–1918.
The letters of Henry Adams.

Publication of the letters sponsored by
the Massachusetts Historical Society
Bibliography: v. 1, p.
Includes index.
Contents: v. 1. 1858–1868—v. 2. 1868–1885—
v. 3. 1886–1892.
1. Adams, Henry, 1838–1918. 2. United States—
Civilization—1865–1918—Sources. 3. Historians—
United States—Correspondence. I. Levenson, J. C.
(Jacob Clavner), 1922–   . II. Massachusetts
Historical Society. III. Title.
E175.5.A2A4   1982   973'.072024   82-14673
ISBN 0-674-52685-6 (set)

Acknowledgments

The Massachusetts Historical Society, which controls the rights to the letters of Henry Adams, decided in 1971 to sponsor this edition. From the inception of the project Stephen T. Riley, then director of the Society, has contributed vision, advice, and indispensable help. The sponsorship of the National Endowment for the Humanities and the Seth Sprague Educational and Charitable Foundation has made it financially possible to bring the edition into being. George Farr of the Research Materials Division of the Endowment has offered sympathetic guidance. Walter G. Dunnington of the Sprague Foundation has shown his faith in the project over a long period. Charles Francis Adams and the Adams Memorial Society have made possible the reproduction of six of the watercolors painted by Henry Adams on his journey to the South Seas. Mary Ogden Abbott gave support at a critical moment. The American Council of Learned Societies, Northwestern University, and the University of Virginia have given individual support to the editors. The University of Virginia, where the project is quartered, has provided not only research facilities but also financial and administrative help over the whole span of the project.

Research for the edition has been assisted by Ray W. Frantz, Jr., Roger Leachman, Margaret O'Bryant, Michael Plunkett, and their colleagues at the Alderman Library, University of Virginia; Carolyn Jakeman, Catherine M. Compton, and the staff of the Houghton Library, Harvard University; Louis L. Tucker, Robert Sparks, Ross Urquhart, and their colleagues at the Massachusetts Historical Society; L. H. Butterfield, Marc Friedlaender, Robert J. Taylor, Celeste Walker, and Winifred Collins of The Adams Papers; Wilhelmina Harris and Lawrence Gall of the Adams National Historic Site; and Susan W. Bluhm of the Smithsonian Institution Archives.

We are happy to thank James Milnes Gaskell, Esq., who allowed us to use the letters of Charles Milnes Gaskell to Henry Adams. For letters of Henry Adams and other primary materials, we are grateful to Dr. Cecil Anrep, George W. Arms, Lady Arthur, Edward Chalfant, Sophie Wallace Clippard, Elizabeth Sherman Hughes, Faith Thoron Knapp, Henry A. La Farge, Henry Cabot Lodge, Lady Alexandra Metcalfe, Nigel Nicolson, the Reverend Patrick O'Reilly, Daniel Sargent. Besides those individuals, our research has incurred debts of thanks to William Dusinberre, Eugenia Kaledin, John E. Little, Samuel Holt Monk, Paul Nagel, Russel B. Nye,

Allen Stokes, Arline B. Tehan, Louisa Hooper Thoron, and Sturgis Warner.

The principal holdings of letters, photographs, and watercolors by Henry Adams and of related documentary and visual sources are at the Massachusetts Historical Society. In addition, numerous institutions have generously made available Adams' autograph letters and various visual materials. The form of acknowledgment that follows, when it denotes a particular collection in which manuscripts are to be found, is intended to serve as an aid to future researchers. The location of manuscript or other source, given after each letter, designates American libraries by their *National Union Catalog* abbreviations. We are grateful to—

The Alabama Department of Archives and History (Joseph Wheeler Collection); the Estelle Doheny Collection of the Edward Laurence Doheny Memorial Library, St. John's Seminary, Camarillo, California; the Department of Special Collections, University Research Library, University of California, Los Angeles; the Henry E. Huntington Library (Samuel L. M. Barlow Papers, Thomas H. Dudley Papers, James Duncan Hague Collection, Clarence King Papers, Raphael Pumpelly Papers, Huntington Manuscripts), San Marino, California; The Bancroft Library; Yale University Library (Baldwin Family Papers, Samuel Bowles Papers, Thomas Davidson Papers, Evarts Family Papers, Ellsworth Huntington Papers, La Farge Family Papers, Thomas Lounsbury Papers, O. C. Marsh Papers, Simon Newcomb Manuscripts, William Dwight Whitney Family Papers, Theodore Dwight Woolsey Family Papers, Records of Yale President Hadley); the Collection of American Literature, Beinecke Rare Book and Manuscript Library, Yale University; the Corcoran Gallery of Art Archives; Dumbarton Oaks Garden Library; the Manuscript Division and the Prints and Photographs Division, Library of Congress; the Diplomatic Branch (Despatches from U.S. Ministers to Great Britain), Civil Archives Division, National Archives; the Smithsonian Institution Archives (George P. Merrill Collection; Office of the Secretary, 1907–1924, Records); the National Anthropological Archives, Smithsonian Institution; Eleutherian Mills Historical Library, Greenville, Delaware;

The Historical Society of Delaware; the Newberry Library, Chicago; Lilly Library, Indiana University, Bloomington, Indiana; the Department of Special Collections, Kenneth Spencer Research Library, University of Kansas Libraries; the Trustees of the Boston Public Library; the Print Department (Ralph Adams Cram Collection), Boston Public Library; the Boston Athenaeum; the Isabella Stewart Gardner Museum, Boston; the Museum of Fine Arts (Archives), Boston; the Department of Special Collections, Mugar Memorial Library, Boston University; U.S. Department of the Interior, National Park Service, Adams National Historic Site and Longfellow National Historic Site; the Fogg Art Museum, the Houghton Library, and the Museum of Comparative Zoology, Harvard University; the Harvard University Archives; the Harvard Law School Library; the

Harvard University Center for Italian Renaissance Studies, Villa I Tatti; The Essex Institute, Salem, Massachusetts; the American Antiquarian Society (Bolton-Stanwood Family Papers, A.A.S. Records), Worcester, Massachusetts; the Milton S. Eisenhower Library (Herbert Baxter Adams Collection, Daniel Coit Gilman Collection), Johns Hopkins University; the Manuscripts Division (Robert C. Buchanan Papers), Maryland Historical Society; the William L. Clements Library (Henry Vignaud Papers), University of Michigan, Ann Arbor; the Minnesota Historical Society (James K. Hosmer Papers); the New York State Library; the New-York Historical Society; the Rare Books and Manuscripts Division (R. T. Crane Papers, Ford Family Papers, R. W. Gilder Papers, Macmillan Co. Records, H. J. Raymond Papers, Samuel J. Tilden Papers, Personal Miscellaneous Papers), The New York Public Library, Astor, Lenox, and Tilden Foundations; the American Academy and Institute of Arts and Letters; the Rare Book and Manuscript Library (Frederic Bancroft Papers, Allan Nevins Papers, Columbiana Collection), Columbia University;

The Hispanic Society of America; The Metropolitan Museum of Art; The Pierpont Morgan Library; the Fales Library at New York University; the Department of Rare Books, Manuscripts, and Archives (Lewis Henry Morgan Papers, William Henry Seward Papers, Thurlow Weed Papers), The University of Rochester Library; Schaffer Library (John Bigelow Papers), Union College, Schenectady, New York; the United States Military Academy Library; the Manuscript Department (John Jordan Crittenden Papers, Bradley Tyler Johnson Papers), William R. Perkins Library, Duke University; the Southern Historical Collection (Battle Family Papers, Joseph S. Fowler Papers), Library of the University of North Carolina at Chapel Hill; the Dartmouth College Library; the Princeton University Library; the Case Western Reserve University Archives (Charles F. Thwing Papers);

The Ohio Historical Society (James H. Anderson Papers, William Henry Smith Papers); the Charles Goddard Slack Collection, Dawes Library, Marietta College; the Oberlin College Archives; the Historical Society of Pennsylvania (Dreer Collection, Gratz Collection, MacVeagh Papers, Wister Family Papers); Temple University Libraries, Philadelphia; the Charles Roberts Autograph Collection, Haverford College Library; the Brown University Library; The John Carter Brown Library, Brown University; the South Caroliniana Library, University of South Carolina; the Humanities Research Center, The University of Texas at Austin; the Virginia Historical Society; the Clifton Waller Barrett Library (Henry Adams Papers), University of Virginia; the Archives Division (William F. Allen Papers), State Historical Society of Wisconsin, Madison;

The Public Record Office, London; the Bodleian Library, Oxford; the Master and Fellows of Trinity College, Cambridge; the Principal and Fellows, Jesus College, Oxford; the British Library; the Trustees of the National Library of Ireland; the Trustees of the National Library of Scotland;

the Pre-Confederation Archives (Baring Brothers Papers), Public Archives of Canada; the Musée Rodin, Paris; Columbia University Press; the Houghton Mifflin Company; and Little, Brown and Company.

At the University of Virginia over a score of graduate students have worked hard and well at tasks of research and proofreading. Jane Le-Compte, Mark Reynolds, and Paul Baerman must be singled out for special thanks. William Jones DeRitter, as researcher, proofreader, and manager of innumerable details, was virtually a fellow editor. For their administrative help, we are especially grateful to Charles L. Flanders, Elizabeth L. Jones, Patricia Hawk, and Joy Shifflette.

Maud Wilcox, editor-in-chief, and Ann Louise McLaughlin, editor for *The Letters of Henry Adams,* of Harvard University Press, have offered wisdom, acumen, encouragement, and patience along with their admirable editorial help.

Contents

Introduction — xiii

Bibliographical Note — xxxvi

Editorial Note — xl

Abbreviations — xliv

1 Berlin and Dresden, 1858–1860 — 1

2 Correspondent at Large, 1860 — 109

3 The Great Secession Winter, 1860–1861 — 203

4 Trials of a Confidential Secretary, 1861–1862 — 235

5 The Slow Shift of the Balance, 1863 — 323

6 "Silent and Expectant," 1864–1865 — 421

7 A Man of the World, 1866–1868 — 503

Illustrations

Henry Adams, 1868   frontispiece
Portrait by Samuel Laurence

Henry Adams, 1860   facing page   86
Courtesy of the Massachusetts Historical Society

Caroline Bigelow   87
Courtesy of the U.S. Department of the Interior, National Park Service,
Adams National Historic Site, Quincy, Massachusetts

Louisa Adams Kuhn   192
Courtesy of the U.S. Department of the Interior, National Park Service,
Adams National Historic Site, Quincy, Massachusetts

Charles Kuhn   193
Courtesy of the U.S. Department of the Interior, National Park Service,
Adams National Historic Site, Quincy, Massachusetts

Charles Francis Adams, 15 April 1861   226
Courtesy of the Massachusetts Historical Society

Abigail Brooks Adams, Paris, 1862   227
Courtesy of the Massachusetts Historical Society

Charles Francis Adams, Jr., and fellow officers   314
From a wet-plate negative by Timothy O'Sullivan, 1864. Courtesy of the
Collections of the Library of Congress

Henry Adams to Charles Francis Adams, Jr., November 21, 1862   315
Courtesy of the Massachusetts Historical Society

John Quincy Adams II   348
Courtesy of the U.S. Department of the Interior, National Park Service,
Adams National Historic Site, Quincy, Massachusetts

Charles Francis Adams, Jr.   349
Courtesy of the U.S. Department of the Interior, National Park Service,
Adams National Historic Site, Quincy, Massachusetts

Mary Adams, 1862   418
Courtesy of the Massachusetts Historical Society

Brooks Adams, London, 1863   419
Courtesy of the Massachusetts Historical Society

Charles Milnes Gaskell, 1877   526
Miniature by William Thomas Barber, 1877. Courtesy of James Milnes
Gaskell

Robert Cunliffe, at Acton   527
Photograph by Francis Doyle, 1870. Courtesy of the Massachusetts
Historical Society

Charles Milnes Gaskell, Robert Boyle, and Henry Adams, before
the Chapter House at Wenlock Abbey   527
Photograph by Francis Doyle, 1870. Courtesy of Faith Thoron Knapp

Ralph Palmer   527
Courtesy of the U.S. Department of the Interior, National Park Service,
Adams National Historic Site, Quincy, Massachusetts

The Adams Family genealogy   page   xlvii

The Brooks Family genealogy   xlviii

Introduction

The letters of Henry Adams make up one of the great records of American experience. Written over six decades, from 1858 to 1918, they cover a period of momentous changes in American and world history. The long span of years is matched by a scene that is literally global. The young man from Boston, whose world was to center on Washington and London and, later, Paris, knew many lands and cities. Some of his best letters were written from Berlin, Rome, Budapest, from the Rocky Mountain wilderness, the Upper Nile, the South Sea Islands. Breadth of scene, in turn, is hardly more astonishing than breadth of subject. Although politics and manners—people in their public and private aspects—were Adams' main topics, he wrote with equally lively engagement of mind about geology, architecture, primitive dance. He was the acute observer of secret diplomacy, business chicanery, the expansion of railroads, the waning of native cultures. He chronicled the rising profession of scholarship, the making of art collections, the breakdown of nineteenth-century assumptions about physics and economics and parliamentary democracy. He made it seem that nothing human was alien to him.

Holding all this together is the story at the center, the life of Henry Adams. The story differs at many points from *The Education of Henry Adams,* the autobiographical narrative which he wrote in his late sixties and by which he is best known. The *Education* was composed to suit his didactic purposes as he approached the end of his life. By contrast, the letters do not look back over events; they record them freshly, along with the hopes, perplexities, and insights that arise immediately from them. Whereas the *Education* focuses on perplexities, the autobiography in the letters—especially in the first three volumes—illustrates in one situation after another the human capacity for growth.

The letters begin with Henry Adams on his first trip to Europe at the age of twenty. The purposes that took him there conformed in their way with family inheritance. As a boy he had sat in his father's library proofreading his father's edition of the works of John Adams and sometimes listening to his father's friends, the distinguished antislavery leaders of Boston, as they discussed their campaigns. He planned to follow a literary, political, and even a legal calling as his father and his presidential ancestors had done. But Henry Adams also departed from the family pattern. After two older brothers had gone from Harvard College immediately to reading law, despite having little taste for it, he became the first of the family to set off after graduation on a grand tour. There was debate at home, as his brother Charles later recalled; their father "held Europe in horror" for new college graduates because a classmate of his (as far back as 1825!) had "chanced to go to Europe, and came home an ass, and remained an ass all the long continuing days of life" (*Autobiography*, p. 19). Difficult passages of another sort were the gale-tossed Atlantic crossing and the journey through England's industrial Midlands, which gave the future author of the *Education* his first lessons in seasickness and in cultural vertigo. Yet neither of these events is recorded in the young traveler's direct witness. He wrote home only after reaching Berlin, determined to master the German language and study Roman law.

Law did not thrive. Discovering that he could not follow intricate lectures in mumbled German at the university, Henry Adams enrolled in a gymnasium where he could practice the language among schoolboys. The *Education* and letters hitherto published tell that tale, but there was a good deal more to the young man's experience of Berlin. Cultivating such non-legal studies as music and art, he exerted himself with more earnestness than the previous record suggests. Going on not-so-wild "bats" with college classmates, he enjoyed more frivolity than readers might expect. The full record discloses a complex and engaging character.

Perhaps the most interesting international episode of Henry Adams' German stay occurred during his second year abroad, when he was living in Dresden. Hitherto unpublished letters show how for the most part he avoided the social life there. He disdained to go to the court of a petty prince who might not recognize that an American president's grandson, although a private citizen, could claim at least an equal rank. But when the young officers who set the social pace in the Saxon capital snubbed and mocked the American Misses Gans because they were Jewish, Adams immediately left his seclusion and, for all to see, made a courtesy call on his compatriots—the first of several. His democratic indignation is especially worth noting in view of his later virulent anti-Semitism, a characteristic not native to his culture.

With studies and sightseeing, ambitions and financial needs to be reported at home, Henry Adams put together a circumstantial and charmingly ingenuous record. But he had not consciously settled on what kind of letters to write. His father and brother, knowing his literary aspirations, suggested travel letters that could be published in a newspaper. In the spring of 1859 he composed such a piece on his Prussian gymnasium, but decided to suppress it. The following spring, however, as he set off on an extended tour to Vienna and then southward through Italy, he promised Charles a series of letters which, if Charles thought them good enough, could be passed on to an editor. The Italian journey turned the literary traveler into a first-rate reporter. When the trip ended at Palermo, newly won by Garibaldi and his Thousand, the smoke of gunfire still hovered over the city, and Henry Adams became the first American journalist to interview the revolutionary hero.

The letters of "H.B.A." (Henry Brooks Adams) began to appear in the Boston *Courier* on April 30; seven of the eight were printed, and they ran to mid-July. (All eight are here brought together for the first time and printed from Adams' manuscript.) These letters written for the press differed in style from letters home, but only a little, for the young Henry Adams used public language by second nature. In the society as in the family from which he came, oratory was the liveliest art and history the leading genre of formal discourse. The Ciceronian period was a basic unit of thought, and perception tended to follow established lines. The fledgling journalist could be sure of his readers' response when he noted the callousness of young Austrian officers or the apparent lack of a Sicilian gentleman-class to step forward (like Massachusetts Sons of Liberty) and mold free institutions for their land. Other, less conventional qualities showed themselves in the direct impression of the low-voiced, simple-mannered Garibaldi—"no stump oratory and no sham"—and the vignette of a Swiss mercenary whose ten years' service in the Neapolitan forces ended with the loss of Palermo— " 'And I'm not sorry.' " But hardly anything in the *Courier* letters comes to life like the private postscript to Charles (June 5), written when Henry had just been given the chance to carry diplomatic dispatches to the war zone in Sicily:

> Old moozer
>
> Off to Palermo bearer of despatches to Capt. Palmer of the Iroquois and the Consul. Ye Gods what an escapade and won't the parients howl. Don't let them know unless you think they can stand the news. It's perfectly safe. Don't be afraid.
>
> > My eye
> > What a guy
> > Ever your
> > Henrye.

Exuberance erupting through convention bespoke Henry Adams' need for a style that could do more than inform and instruct. He had still to master spontaneity.

In the growth of style and character, spontaneity did not come first. Shortly after arriving home from his grand tour, he moved to Washington with his parents, as senior son in residence. Although his father was to play a demanding part in the short congressional session of 1860–1861, Henry Adams' secretarial and household responsibilities were light and left plenty of time for writing. Because the correspondence which he sent to the Boston *Advertiser,* unlike the *Courier* letters, was straightforward political journalism, it is not included in this volume. His private letters also changed. A week after arriving in the national capital, he sent Charles in Boston the first of a promised series on the look of things during the historic crisis: "I

fairly confess that I want to have a record of this winter on file, and though
I have no ambition nor hope to become a Horace Walpole, I still would like
to think that a century or two hence when everything else about us is forgotten, my letters might still be read and quoted as a memorial of manners
and habits at the time of the great secession of 1860" (Dec. 9). Despite the
intent, habits and manners got into his letters somewhat less than congressional maneuvering, political incidents, and the suspense of the long
months until Lincoln's inauguration. Young Adams tended to overestimate
Seward, the Republican leader most in the limelight, and to ignore the
president-elect who waited in the wings. He had not yet become the sea-
soned observer who could correct for the distortions of watching from so
close to center stage. But his account of the "Great Secession Winter," as he
was to call it, is vivid, detailed, and compelling. Most important, it is
founded on his resolve to become the historian of his times and not merely
of himself.

When President Lincoln chose Charles Francis Adams to be minister to
Great Britain, it was decided that Henry would once again go with the
family, though it meant leaving the law behind, and serve his father as private secretary. The mission, as none foresaw, was to last seven years, and
the secretarial duties were to be very real. Going to London in 1861, Henry
Adams for the first time was to be privy to momentous affairs of state. In
London the young man who suffered from shyness, isolation, and "stupidity"—his term for being at a loss for words in society—outgrew them all
and gradually mastered the language and manners of the great capital.
There, too, he read voraciously in history, philosophy, and political economy; and regularly sharing the minister's reflections on developing events,
he gained an immediate practical sense of statecraft. In his relish for these
and a host of other topics, his letters now evinced that play of mind which
was to characterize the *Education,* along with the energy and hopefulness of
youth.

Letters, in contrast to oratory or history or even a philosophical memoir
like the *Education,* are addressed to individual readers, and the implied dialogue gives them a very different interest. The interaction of characters is as
important to the letters of Henry Adams as the growth of the writer's mind.
Even when beguiled by the Walpole-like idea of writing for publication in
a distant future, he addressed his brother Charles. Although he welcomed
the enthusiastic response—"Go ahead, & write through me, to posterity"
(Dec. 18, 1860)—he must have known that Charles, the robust critic, adviser, and sharer of his ambitions, was not likely to be a self-effacing medium. A year later, when Charles enlisted in the 1st Massachusetts Cavalry,
his well-being and morale necessarily took first place in Henry's mind and
the abstract audience of the future receded from view. As with Charles, so
with others, Henry Adams shaped the letter to the recipient. So much so
that his principal correspondents, who are also principal characters of the
personal narrative, need to be introduced along with the letter-writer.

After the grand tour Henry Adams' parents ceased to be correspondents and became figures at the very center of immediate experience. His mother, Abigail Brooks Adams, daughter of the richest businessman in Massachusetts, had been secure in her Boston world, but became worried and diffident when she entered the official life of Washington and London. Although her social success in both places is well attested, her chronic anxiety became more and more obvious to the family. Henry, who began by lecturing his older brothers on the solicitude they owed her, developed in his London years a resigned detachment. Once, when he was in charge of the family trip to Italy in the spring of 1865, it even became comic detachment. A humorous view of his mother's compulsive worrying did not, however, keep him from being fundamentally sympathetic.

Henry Adams' relation to his father, though far more complex, was also one of growing to independence. Charles Francis Adams, the son and grandson of presidents, had led the Conscience Whigs into the Free Soil movement of 1848. A decade later, just as Henry was planning his grand tour, the elder Adams resumed active political life as a candidate for Congress. The New England rigor that made him formidable in public was not unknown at home, but his stern doubts about Europe for Henry were outweighed by affection for a favorite child. When the day of departure arrived and he saw Henry to the station, he noted in his diary: "My happiness is all at home, and he is on the whole that one of my sons who is possessed of the most agreeable home qualities. When we came home to our shortened evening table, I was under greater depression than I have felt for a long time" (Sept. 27, 1858). During the next two years Congressman Adams, besides encouraging Henry's studies and writing, conveyed at various times his sense of practical politics. The gist of the lessons was to avoid oversimplification, to balance pro-Union and antislavery principles so as to sacrifice neither: "You seem to think that, after all, the question is one of the *abolition* of slavery. Undoubtedly you are right in the abstract. But the peculiarity in our government organisation is necessarily a barrier to the agitation of such a question in a direct form" (Feb. 18, 1860). Balance was similarly the lesson that Minister Adams exemplified as he steadily upheld Union interests amid the crosscurrents of British politics. By 1868, however, when Henry was thirty and his father was sixty-one, the paternal habit of caution appeared less like diplomatic coolness and more like timid reluctance to try new ideas in a new age. As the diplomatic mission came to its end, the son was more than ready to go his own way.

Once Henry Adams' day-to-day association with his father began, his brother Charles Francis Adams, Jr., became for a long time the principal recipient of his letters. Second of the four sons—John Quincy, Charles, Henry, and Brooks—Charles was nearest Henry in age, and during his last two years in college they were roommates. As the correspondence shows, Charles felt free, being almost three years older, to administer brotherly advice in generous doses, and Henry as freely retorted. Both brothers believed in the value of criticism, and they obviously enjoyed pummeling each other in letters.

The brothers' difference in temperament was brought out by their war experience. Charles's career as a cavalry officer was outdoor, extroverted, and physically demanding, while Henry's service as an unofficial member of the legation taught him much about being silent, patient, and alone. In the early years of the war Charles endured the dangers of combat and the ordeal of serving under an incompetent and capricious regimental commander, while Henry was exposed to the strains of prolonged diplomatic crisis in a hostile capital. After Charles's detested colonel left for another post in 1863, danger and illness remained constants of military life. Meanwhile, as diplomatic tensions began to subside, Henry had more time for study, writing, and the pleasures of society. These were subjects, Henry knew, that would interest his brother, just as he himself was fascinated by the detailed working out of strategy in every theater of the war. But what Henry knew uniquely, and was sure his brother most wanted to hear about, was the day-to-day conduct of their father's mission.

The Civil War letters to Charles tell in detail the challenges and triumphs of that mission. Even before Minister Adams arrived in London, the British granted belligerent status to the Confederacy. Full recognition and a consequent rupture of relations with the United States might follow at any moment, and it took unusual skill and patience to conduct American affairs under such stress. Henry Adams, as he shared the exciting inside history with his brother, made clear how many elements could affect the diplomatic mission. He kept watch on antislavery opinion in England and anti-British adventurism in America; on the lobbying of British shipbuilders with secret Confederate contracts and the entrepreneurial activities of the American Cyrus Field, whose projected Atlantic cable bound the countries in joint investment long before it became an instrument of communication; on the personal rapport of Minister Adams and Lord John Russell and the intransigent hostility of the London *Times*. The Emancipation Proclamation and the great military victories of 1863 were decisive, as the brothers thought, but the letters make clear how many uncertainties of battle and politics had to be endured between Gettysburg and Appomattox.

The novice private secretary in London was socially less secure than the cheerful flirting cosmopolitan in Dresden, but Henry Adams slowly acquired the art of standing alone at crowded receptions—sometimes as many as three in one evening. His running comment on visiting restaurants and pleasure gardens turned to talk about his having a club and a circle of acquaintances. The high note of his personal life was the beginning of a new friendship, which he scarcely knew how to announce. By November 1863 he was writing with a fresh cadence: "Friends! I have none, and my temper is now too bad ever to make another. Society! I know it not. Laziness, stupidity and self-distrust have shut its doors to me. It is wonderful—stupendous to consider, how a man who in his own mind is cool, witty, unaffected and high-toned, will disgust and mortify himself by every word he utters or act he does, when he steps out of his skin defences." After more mock-melancholy the flight concludes: "And yet I never was so contented since the last time I was in love and fancied like an idiot that man was a social animal" (Nov. 13). Charles Milnes Gaskell, whom he had met in April, was the friend who made him feel it within his reach to be cool, witty, unaffected, and high-toned.

Gaskell, in his last term at Cambridge when they met, was four years Adams' junior but easily his equal in worldliness. They met at breakfast at Sir Henry Holland's. They were very much alike. Gaskell was reading classics at Trinity, would go on to training in law, anticipated a parliamentary career like his father's. He also had literary ambitions. Gaskell took his place in the British liberal establishment with an ease and assurance that contrasted with the chanciness of American careers. But the young Henry Adams was scarcely aware of the contrast, for with his friend he too moved at ease in the gracious, cosmopolitan, intellectual world of the liberal aristocracy. Having begun his years abroad very much as a son and brother, he now had a second life that centered in Gaskell's friendship and a cordial relation with Gaskell's family, whose country house in Yorkshire provided an ideal retreat. Adams responded to Gaskell's good humor and high spirits with good humor and high spirits of his own.

Sociable and worldly as Henry Adams became, he still knew how to apply himself to sustained hard work. Out of his later London years came his first serious articles for the *North American Review*. He began with an essay in historical criticism in which he took apart the legend of Captain John Smith. He produced two articles on public finance in which he examined British treasury policy during the Napoleonic wars and pointed up the lessons Americans might draw for handling their massive war debts and greenback inflation. In yet another area, he undertook a critique of the new edition of Lyell's *Principles of Geology*. He had the advantage of consulting Sir Charles Lyell as he went along, but his own contribution was genuine. He studied closely the work of Darwin, Lyell, and other scientists, so that he could analyze the changes from the first to the tenth edition and explain to laymen how the general controversy over evolution hinged on particular scientific investigations.

The pleasures of friendship brought out new gusto in his writing. With Gaskell, Robert Cunliffe, and a widening circle of his own, he learned to be self-aware rather than self-conscious, eager to share his best perceptions of his work, his play, and his hopes. At the age of thirty he had begun to make his mark as a writer and had become a social creature such as he had scarcely hoped to be.

In the second volume of *Letters,* which includes the years 1868–1885, the story of growth continues, though it turns at the end into a tragic initiation. Henry Adams won exceptional success as a political journalist in Washington and as a professor of history at Harvard; then, having moved back to Washington, he went on confidently to the more than ten years' undertaking that came to fruition in his *History of the United States.* His principal correspondents, besides his brother and Gaskell, were his onetime student Henry Cabot Lodge and his Washington intimate John Hay. With Lodge he shared a long New England background: Cabots and Adamses had been political opponents for three generations. With Hay he shared a special war experience as well as a cosmopolitan view: Hay had been Lincoln's private secretary and, for a few years thereafter, held diplomatic posts. Both Lodge and Hay had a gift for friendship that proved, in crucial moments, to be life-sustaining. Marian Hooper Adams in these years became a major figure in both life and letters, but only very briefly a correspondent. Adams and she were married on June 27, 1872. From that time husband and wife were rarely apart until March 1885 when she returned from Washington to Cambridge to attend her father in his final illness. In the summer after her father's death, Marian Adams entered a period of unrelenting depression. She committed suicide on December 6, 1885. The second volume ends with the close of that disastrous year in which the historian at the crest of his powers had to give way to the private man whose world was, as he said, broken in half. Back in July 1868, however, when Henry Adams returned to the United States from London, all was promise.

At the moment of Henry Adams' coming home, his brother Charles provided strong new evidence that the pen could be wielded as a political sword. As a result of his articles on railroad mismanagement and business corruption, he had just been appointed to the newly established post of Massachusetts railroad commissioner. Thus began a career that led to the presidency of the Union Pacific Railroad. At this early stage the brothers coordinated their efforts, and in Washington, Henry began quickly to accumulate power too. Almost at once he enjoyed heady familiar contact with a new generation of public men. He came to know James A. Garfield, who was then conducting congressional investigations of corruption; David A. Wells, who had been tax commissioner of New York and was trying to rationalize the federal tax system; and Francis A. Walker, whose statistically based studies of finance helped to transform American economic science. He collaborated with Walker on an analytic study, "The Legal Tender Act." The second of Adams' annual critiques of Congress, "The Session," was reprinted by the National Democratic Committee as a campaign pamphlet. His article "The New York Gold Conspiracy" was not only shocking but apparently actionable, so that he had trouble finding a publisher even in England. He and Charles jointly published some of their best work of this period in *Chapters of Erie* (1871).

When Henry accepted a Harvard appointment and returned to Cambridge in 1870, geographical closeness to Charles obviated the need for letter-writing. For the next half-dozen years, while their father had a real chance of becoming a presidential candidate, they continued to work closely together. After the election of Hayes and, in 1877, Henry's move back to Washington, the brothers became less intimate. While Charles's practical energy was being reinforced by more and more conventional opinions, Henry's intellectual energy was being directed toward original research, independence of thought, and sustained literary achievement. The ultimate result, his nine-volume *History of the United States during the Administrations of Thomas Jefferson and James Madison* (1889–1891), seems to exist in a totally different world from the Union Pacific Railroad. The two men did not, however, drift so far apart as the great enterprises of their maturity might suggest. Charles came to regard history as his true vocation, his railroad years as waste. Henry continued to value Charles as a critic, asked him to read the *History* in its draft form, and did not hesitate to revise in accordance with some of Charles's rough comments. Although intimacy relaxed into familiarity, the bond between them was secure. It was at Charles's house that Henry recovered from his stroke in 1912.

Despite the scholarly demands Henry Adams put upon himself when he took the post at Harvard, he did not become noticeably less political. By the terms of his appointment, the new assistant professor of medieval history also took over editorship of the *North American Review*. He made that weighty journal, in its political articles, an instrument of reform. Editorial duties kept him in touch with a widening range of journalists and policy-oriented scholars, civil servants, and political leaders. When he could not take part himself, he managed through his brothers and friends to stay in close contact with the new Reform leagues and the semi-political Social Science Association. Throughout his Harvard years he remained an active leader of the Independents; when that political movement faded, he continued as an individual to work for its ideas.

In his Independent politics Henry Adams advocated a program which had, despite limited sensitivity to American social and economic problems that were then emerging, genuine intellectual substance. The object of reform was to eliminate corruption. Its premise was that government, if it were not for avoidable corruption and error, would work rationally. Thus, the liberal principle of laissez-faire called for eliminating costly subsidies, legal and illegal, whether in the form of protective tariffs or rigged railroad consolidation. Such a program fitted the views of the old middle class rather than those of the railroad's rural customers, the new industrial labor class, the increasing numbers of urban poor, or, most obviously, the entrepreneurial forces that were rapidly and ruthlessly expanding the economy.

Paradoxically, the Adamses signaled the class-bound, time-bound nature of their post–Civil War politics when they universalized their claim to truth, as on the question of the gold standard. According to liberal doctrine, the gold standard guaranteed a neutral pecuniary medium that served to keep corruption and error, chicanery and sentimentality, out of the fiscal process. When Charles Francis Adams wrote to his son in 1868 on monetary policy, he sounded like a doctrinaire abolitionist citing higher law: "My objection to legal tender however goes a step higher than the constitution. It is simply an attempt to establish a lie by legislation; an attempt not infrequently made by that class of men who . . . think it enough for the sovereign power to pronounce the sic volo, sic jubeo, and the expected effect must follow of course" (Nov. 19, 1868). Henry Adams accepted the principle of the higher law, and when it turned out that gold was not a neutral medium but an instrument of exchange controlled by the new powers of industrial and financial capitalism, he reacted violently. His hatred in the 1890s of "gold-bugs," bankers, and Jews was in large part a revulsion from his own spoiled belief.

The Independent program, seen in retrospect, did not come to terms with the anomalies of American two-party politics. In the Republican party the Adamses deplored both the zealots of civil rights and the engineers of large-scale corruption, but when they allied themselves with sound-money conservative Democrats, they sometimes overlooked a tacit alliance with night-riding terrorists who were "redeeming" Southern states from so-called Carpetbagger rule. The election of 1876 put an end not only to Reconstruction but also to the Independent movement. Charles Francis Adams, who might have been a willing Republican candidate for president, became a reluctant Democratic candidate for governor of Massachusetts. Because he was unwilling to campaign for the office, he turned the contest into a sham. But the political fiasco was also the turning point which freed Henry Adams to devote his energies to history.

The letters to Henry Cabot Lodge throw particular light on Henry Adams as a college teacher and historian, for their lifelong friendship began in the relation of teacher and student. The new assistant professor went to Harvard as part of an educational movement that was turning a provincial college into an international university. As a teacher he disdained the daily recitation system that put a premium on rote and conformity. He challenged his students with problems of explaining what happened and soon had them scurrying after the details of medieval history as evidence for analytic argument. None of Adams' students responded more vigorously to his demands than Lodge. The young Bostonian had civic and literary ambitions similar to those of the teacher. Lodge, after allowing himself a honeymoon year in Europe immediately after graduation, returned to Harvard to enter law school and begin graduate study of history at the same time. Adams had offered cool practical advice on how other Bostonians had made history "pay": "To do it, requires patient study, long labor, and perseverance that knows no limit" (June 2, 1872), and as a teacher, he enforced the requirements strictly, especially when it came to the painstaking art of writing well. Lodge was one of the three students in Adams'—and Harvard's—first Ph.D. seminar who contributed, along with Adams himself, to the volume *Essays in Anglo-Saxon Law* (1876). Although in reform politics Adams had immediately accepted Lodge as a peer, in literary and academic matters he was more deliberate. The teacher kept his student revising his thesis on Anglo-Saxon land law even after it had been set in type.

It was not as taskmaster but as task-sharer that Adams was most demanding—and best rewarded. He made Lodge assistant editor of the *North American Review* and imbued him with his hopes for the magazine. In range he wanted it to be at least the equal of the great British quarterlies, and in scholarship superior to British and on a par with the best work of German universities. At the end of his tenure as editor Adams invited Lodge to collaborate in a review (Oct. 1876) of von Holst's *Constitutional and Political History of the United States,* a work of masterly German scholarship which they acknowledged to be at the head of the field but which they faulted for failure to understand American nationalism as a political force. In teaching, as Henry Adams moved from medieval to American colonial to early national history, it was Lodge whom he left as proconsul of the American colonial field. In March 1877 he proposed to President Eliot that Lodge teach a rival course to his own: "His views being federalist and conservative, have as good a right to expression in the college as mine which tend to democracy and radicalism" (March 2). The course never materialized, but the dialogue did.

Adams' letter to Eliot did not overstate the conflict of convictions between the friends. Adams and Lodge had worked closely together in the cause of reform, but with respect to the politics of the past their differences ran deep. When John Adams ended the naval war of 1798–1800 with Revolutionary France, his opponents within the Federalist party, believing that he had made a pact with the devil, helped deprive him of a second term. The quarrel passed to the next generation when John Quincy Adams joined Jefferson's party in 1805. The younger Adams acted not only out of positive conviction but also out of suspicion that the New England Federalists were plotting secession; the Federalists countered by calling him a traitor to principle. The bitter clash might have ended with the Hartford Convention of 1815, for Federalist separatism there so discredited the party that it seemed to be extinguished forever. In 1828, however, old Federalists with long memories again helped deprive an Adams of a second term as president. Yet two generations later, the controversy was renewed as scholarly dialogue. Lodge wrote a respectful biography of his grandfather George Cabot, president of the Hartford Convention, and elicited from Adams, in *Documents Relating to New England Federalism, 1800–1815* (1877), an understated factual defense of *his* grandfather John Quincy Adams. Adams and Lodge then sharpened the issues by reviewing each other's books. The controversy transcended family and region: the next stage, marked by Lodge's life of Alexander Hamilton and Adams' life of Albert Gallatin, Jefferson's secretary of the treasury, was truly national and consistently focused on political fundamentals, but no less personal. In politics Adams may have associated too much with like-minded men; in exploring the past he found that his intellectual battles with Lodge constantly raised critical questions about the way things really were. The running argument between the two men profoundly affected Adams' *History of the United States* so that, despite the disillusionments, fatigue, and heartbreaking experience that intervened before he finished the work, his original affirmative conception of American democracy informed the whole.

As Adams' letters indicate, he had had almost enough of teaching when the opportunity of editing the Gallatin papers precipitated a decision about what to do next. His inquiries in the spring of 1877 about other Jeffersonian leaders whose papers might include Gallatin letters were prelude to accepting the job. But he was making a more momentous decision as well. The editing of Gallatin's papers would, he hinted, be useful to him even if he should not go on to write a biography of the man. What he had in mind, but did not state explicitly for another two years, was that it would be useful in writing the history of the Jeffersonian era. Among the clues to this unspoken intent were his buying the *Annals of Congress* and ordering the Thomas Arnold edition of Thucydides. Although he was leaving Harvard and academic history, he was as a historian more ambitious than ever.

To write the history of the American democracy as it gave shape to national institutions and character, Henry Adams once more chose to live in Washington, the capital that had been built in accordance with the Founders' grand design. He conceived his work on a grand scale also. After he published *Gallatin* (1879), he gave himself a year to search European archives for diplomatic documents. Then, while he worked on the nine-volume history of the crucial years 1800–1815, he wrote as collateral volumes biographies of John Randolph (1882) and Aaron Burr (1882; suppressed, but in some degree reworked into the fabric of the *History*), and as recreation he wrote the novels *Democracy* (1880) and *Esther* (1884). *The History of the United States during the Administrations of Thomas Jefferson and James Madison,* which he expected to require the labor of a decade, began to appear on schedule just ten years after *Gallatin*. It was a monument of vision and energy as well as scholarship and creative intelligence.

Return to the national capital in 1877 brought social change, and Adams' Washington years took on the settled routine of diligence and pleasure. After four or five hours' work at his desk each day, he went riding for two or three hours with his wife. The rest of the day they gave to "doing society." A full and lively record of the Adamses' world may be found in *The Letters of Mrs. Henry Adams,* edited by Ward Thoron (1936). The center of that world came to be the Five of Hearts—the Adamses, John and Clara Hay, and Clarence King. In the late seventies the intimacy of that circle flourished on often daily visits and mutual pleasure in wit, gossip, and serious ideas. By late 1881, they had named themselves and had even printed note paper, with the playing-card imprint of a five of hearts in the corner, on which to exchange private notes. The happiness of one became the happiness of all, as a letter of Adams to John Hay, in London with King, made clear: "More and more as I go on, I see that life is worthless except for what positive and active pleasure can be put into it. I repine at seeing a day pass without a joy. I want my hearts all to jump up like the amiable Wordsworth's when he was a boy. To be in London with five jumping hearts would be very ecstacy" (Sept. 3, 1882). Such closeness among friends defined the social situation in which Adams wrote during his most productive years, and the literary effect was evident in the humor, wit, and wordplay that more and more characterized his letters.

Precisely because King and Hay were practical men absorbed in business, science, diplomacy, and politics, they became Adams' literary friends more easily than if they had been concerned, like Henry James or Howells, primarily with literature. Adams met King, who came from an old New-port, R.I., mercantile family, when he visited the Fortieth Parallel Expedi-tion in the Rockies in the summer of 1871. In 1877 King was completing the multivolume report of that great scientific exploration, and he would be much in Washington in the next few years, even serving briefly as head of the Geological Survey. Adams had read King's *Mountaineering in the Sierra Nevada* (1872) when it came out but, deceived by its apparent slightness, reviewed it casually. When the men renewed their acquaintance in Wash-ington, Adams saw how King's wide learning lightly carried went naturally with the spaciousness and openness of his Western manner. King's gift for story-telling and good living made him remarkably companionable, even dazzling, to friends on two continents. In England he could charm Ruskin into parting with two of his Turner paintings—"One good Turner deserves another"—and in Spain he followed Don Quixote's course through La Mancha, reporting his adventures in "The Helmet of Mambrino" (1885). His romanticism had an entrepreneurial side: he spent much of his life in mining ventures and promotions that eventually left him ruined. King taught Adams something of his sympathy with colonized and dark-skinned peoples and perhaps a little of his antipathy to the pallid sentimental fe-males of genteel culture. (Adams may never have known that King led a double life and, as James Todd, had a Negro wife and children in New York.) The enigmas of King's character seem more obscure because of the dearth of personal record: he was at best an irregular letter-writer. For the most part he appears in the Henry Adams letters as a third party rather than as a correspondent.

John Hay, on the other hand, accounts for one of the longest and richest series of Adams' letters. Hay, like King, was both Western and cosmopoli-tan. He passed his early boyhood in a one-horse town on the banks of the Mississippi, an Illinois variant of Mark Twain's Hannibal. At twelve, for the sake of better schooling, he went to live with an uncle in Pittsfield, Ill., which had a Congregational church and a private academy. A couple of years later he went to other relatives and more advanced schooling at Springfield. After finishing college at Brown, he returned to Springfield to read law in an office next door to Lincoln's. In 1861 he went to Washington as Lincoln's private secretary and met Henry Adams, also a private secre-tary, just before the latter departed for London. After Lincoln's death Hay held foreign service posts in Paris, Vienna, and Madrid, and then became an editorial writer on the New York *Tribune*. In 1871 he published the books that established his literary reputation: *Pike County Ballads* and *Castilian Days*. To Adams, the vernacular flavor of the one and the innocents-abroad republicanism of the other were as authentic as Mark Twain's. Hay's liter-ary qualities stood out in his newspaper world: his colleagues on the *Tribune* appreciated his play of mind, wide experience of men and books, and ready humor. In Cleveland, where he moved when he married Clara Stone, these qualities seemed all the more brilliant. There he entered the world of his railroad-builder father-in-law, Amasa Stone, a capitalist who dealt as a peer with Rockefeller, Harkness, and Flagler. He liked taking part in that world, but he left it readily when, thanks to his wife's inheritance, he could devote himself to public service and to his great literary undertaking, the ten-volume history and life of *Abraham Lincoln* (written with John G. Nicolay). Hay's return to Washington in 1879 as assistant secretary of state and his friendship with King brought him together with Adams. By 1881, when Hay left office with the change of administration, he and Adams had become closest friends.

The friendship throve on certain differences. The Lincoln history which made Hay, in his biographer's phrase, the "Republican laureate" and Hay's anonymous novel *The Bread-Winners* (1884), with its businessman's view of labor unrest, were roughly parallel to Adams' undertakings. They were like enough to elicit admiration and unlike enough to rouse no envy. In politics Hay's Republican orthodoxy contrasted with Adams' reserved but genuine democratic faith, but Hay taught political lessons that Adams accepted from no one else. Hay's strength was a healthy sense of things as they are, for, as Adams put it, "he knows intimately scores of men whom I would not touch with a pole, but who are more amusing than my own crowd" (Nov. 12, 1882). With such a friend, privileged humor might contain light barbs of truth. When the Republicans were turned out of office by the election of 1884, Hay jokingly asked Adams to protect him from the incoming "Ku Klux," Adams' Democratic cronies (Nov. 30). A decade later he could call attention to the gap between Adams' situation and his sentiments, teasing him for being "known throughout the country as a Democrat and an Anarchist, and an Unemployed" (April 25, 1894). Hay very probably hinted to his friend what he did not hesitate to say to others, that when Adams "saw Vesuvius reddening the midnight air he searched the horizon to find a Jew stoking the fire" (March 10, 1898). Adams quietly put up with Hay's political realism and was disturbed only when Hay, under the stress of office, let responsibility and fatigue subdue his humor.

When the Hays left Cleveland in 1885 and returned permanently to Washington, the Adamses were the decisive attraction. The two families bought land together on Lafayette Square and commissioned H. H. Richardson to build attached houses for them. The negotiating and supervising often fell to Adams, and his reports to Hay show how much he enjoyed the joint venture. Hay's being next door helped Adams through the hard years after Marian Adams' death. In time the friendship ripened to yet another stage. When Hay became secretary of state in 1898, Adams did duty as a regular companion for afternoon walks and a bulwark against the pressures of office. On those walks Adams did not advise, he philosophized. He elaborated the theories of changing international order that occupied his thoughts, relating them to the day's events on Capitol Hill or halfway round the world. When they were apart, his letters to Hay kept up the philosophic commentary.

Marian Adams is a major presence in these letters from the moment in

1872 when she is first mentioned. That winter, when his father was at Geneva for the arbitration of the *Alabama* claims, Henry Adams dutifully moved from Cambridge to Boston to stay with his mother. The thirty-four-year-old scholar found it distracting to commute to classes, but after working intensively for so long, he was ready for the rather different distraction of occasional party-going. After two years he resumed waltzing as if he had not missed a beat, and his courtship began without general notice. When the name of Marian Hooper came up at home, his mother expressed favor, but Charles, unaware that the topic was by no means casual, reacted brusquely: "Heavens!—no!—they're all crazy as coots. She'll kill herself, just like her Aunt!" (Memorabilia, MS at MHi, p. 284). Charles did not forget what he called his "brutal prophecy," which later seemed prescient, since all three children of Dr. Robert Hooper and Ellen Sturgis Hooper became suicides. Charles's gaffe may account for his never getting on affectionate terms with his sister-in-law.

The Hoopers and the Sturgises were great mercantile families, active not only in politics and reform but also in philanthropy and the arts. Ellen Sturgis Hooper died when her youngest child, Marian, was five, and "Clover," as she was known, had in young womanhood the independence and the closeness to her father enjoyed by the last child at home. She was widely read, she rode a horse well, she had a lively satirical wit. What Henry Adams saw in Clover Hooper is evident in the letters describing his bride-to-be to family and friends. His glowing words are confirmed in Henry James's disinterested witness to her "moral spontaneity" and "intellectual grace," and they are corroborated amply in her own letters. The couple were old enough to act independently of convention. Henry, instead of going to Quincy when the warm weather came, moved into the Hooper house at Beverly Farms for the month before the wedding. And the ceremony, which the couple worked out themselves, seemed to Charles as "peculiar" as the engagement, since it lasted a mere two minutes.

The marriage was happy, but it had its darker shadings. The climax of a year's wedding journey was to have been a trip to Egypt, but when they arrived there in late November 1872, Marian Adams suffered a month or six weeks of acute depression. Whether brought on by homesickness, fatigue, or cultural disorientation, the collapse manifestly exceeded such causes, and fearful remembrance of it became a part of Henry Adams' consciousness. During the bad time in Egypt, his wife was unable to write letters, even to her father. She never did learn to write regularly to her mother-in-law, to whose anxious and complaining disposition Marian Adams never did adjust. Henry Adams for his part got along well with the Hoopers. That the couple spent their summers at Beverly Farms rather than Quincy was a reminder to the Adams family that there were new limits to the old intimacy. The last significant shadow was the childlessness of the marriage. There are signs in the letters that this affected Henry Adams deeply, but that he came to terms with it. How well is suggested by the distance between his forced joking when he congratulated his close friend Robert Cunliffe on the birth of his first son (Aug. 31, 1875) and, on the death of another child a few years later, the delicacy with which he expressed to the Cunliffes the sympathy that those who have no children can feel (Aug. 7, 1878). Adams at forty, his energies focused on history and his private well-being secure, was more than well adjusted in 1878. Thereafter, the years passed almost unnoticed as Adams savored day by day the ripeness of life.

The fulfillment of love and work was evident in the quiet summer of 1883 at Beverly Farms, where Adams' set task was correcting proofs of the first draft volume of the *History*. He varied the day-to-day routine by working on his second novel, *Esther*. He had written *Democracy* there also, at least in large part, while correcting proofs of *Gallatin*. We can infer where he wrote the earlier novel because he shared the secret of his authorship with Mary Dwight Parkman, an old friend and summer neighbor, as well as with his Washington circle. This time he kept the secret of novel-writing inside his household, but his letters to Hay, whose own novel was coming out, have the tone of one gentleman-amateur addressing another. Assigning Hay to a serious literary place in "our Howell's-and-Jame's epoch," he made invidious comparisons: "Howells cannot deal with gentlemen or ladies; he always slips up. James knows almost nothing of women but the mere outside; he never had a wife" (Sept. 24).

In 1885, when Dr. Hooper was dying in protracted pain and Marian Adams' ordeal was beginning, Adams drew on the knowledge of the married which he had implicitly claimed as a novelist. Commanded to stay at work in Washington till summoned, he wrote daily to his wife. In his letters he mixed matter-of-fact and play, gossip and concern, everything that might hold her to his world. Once, having described his Washington rounds, he went on reflectively: "Perhaps it may be a good thing for the helpless orphan to be thrown upon the world. He may thus be forced to mix with it, and to be of it. I am not prepared to deny or assert any proposition which concerns myself; but certainly this solitary struggle with platitudinous atoms, called men and women by courtesy, leads me to wish for my wife again. How did I ever hit on the only woman in the world who fits my cravings and never sounds hollow anywhere? Social chemistry—the mutual attraction of equivalent human molecules—is a science yet to be created, for the fact is my daily study and only satisfaction in life" (April 12).

The day after Henry Adams wrote thus, Dr. Hooper died. When Marian Adams' grief turned to settled depression, summer plans had to be canceled, and then revised plans had to be curtailed. Moments of respite became briefer and less frequent. To intimate friends Adams gave muted warning that his wife had been "out of sorts for some time past" (Aug. 30) and then, more ominously, that she showed "no such fancy for mending as I could wish" (Nov. 29). The fancy for mending or, in Marian Adams' words, the hope that she could "grow back to life" failed as her sense of worthlessness became absolute. She wrote: "Henry is more patient and loving than words can express. God might envy him—he bears and hopes and despairs hour after hour" (Dec. 6, 1885). Having thus summed up her own and her husband's condition in a note to her sister, she took potassium cyanide, one of her photographic chemicals, and put an end to her life.

Although his world was smashed and he could not explain how he survived, Henry Adams determined to go on as steadily and uncomplainingly as he could. The next five years, covered in the third volume of *Letters*, showed how well he held to this resolve. Recovery was slow. Yet the record also confirms remarkable powers of growth, different from those he had shown before. In his twenties the youthful representative of a vigorous, largely political culture passed the stages of initiation into the world and gradually assumed his mature identity. In his thirties and forties he illustrated the development possible to maturity. The political journalist and behind-the-scenes politician became a committed historian, and as Adams mastered first the profession, then the art, of history, he enjoyed fulfillment such as few people know. In marriage, in friendship, and in style of life, as well as in work, he came to savor the pleasure of each day. When all was catastrophically changed by the suicide of Marian Adams, the knowledge that "for twelve years I had everything I most wanted on earth" (Dec. 16, 1885) both intensified his loss and strengthened his endurance.

The reengagement with life that began in 1886 took hold thoroughly, despite serious setbacks. Adams began to make travel, as it were, a second profession. As he ventured beyond his previously known world—to Japan, to Cuba, to the South Seas—he was surprised by perceptions and emotions he had never had before. He completed his circuit of the globe by returning from the South Seas through the Indian Ocean and the Red Sea to Europe and, after a stay in Paris and London, one more transatlantic voyage. When he sailed for home on the *Teutonic,* in February 1892, he faced the resumption of life with foreboding, but he did not try to disguise the other aspect of his temperament, his appetite for experience and readiness for a new beginning.

Travel, apart from a susceptibility to seasickness, was for Adams an ambiguous pleasure. From the time of his first trip to Germany he remembered, even without reminders from home, that it might be a vice, and he conscientiously sought to make it an education. From it he learned not to fix his intellectual borders within the American or even the larger, but still limited, Anglo-American world. His wedding journey took him for the first time beyond Europe. Thereafter, during the lifetime of Marian Adams, he curbed his hankering for the remote. When he chafed against the "bourgeois ease and uniformity" of life, the disciplined historian warned himself that it was "ludicrous to play Ulysses" (Aug. 21, 1878). After his wife's death, however, his attitude changed. He began thinking of travel as an anodyne of thought rather than a stimulus, an escape from life rather than an exploration of its possibilities. Alienation and ennui, those modern characteristics, entered into the balance against Adams' basic liveliness of mind but, as the letters testify, did not prevail.

The Japanese trip of 1886, made when he was still partly numb with grief, seemed to Adams the least successful of his travels. He had some knowledge of Japanese art and of Buddhism before he went. In Japan he learned a good deal more, from William Sturgis Bigelow and Ernest Fenollosa in particular, about drawings, bronzes, fabrics, and pottery, and he put his new knowledge to use in ransacking art and curio shops. As he learned more about Japanese history and culture, however, his progress yielded little satisfaction, for it led him to regard Japan as but the threshold to China. When he returned to Washington, he began studying Chinese.

Although Adams long cherished the hope of visiting Peking, he came to think that he might learn most by seeking not the center but the edges of civilization. He made his first trip to Cuba in 1888, and he began to think that when he finished his *History* he might go to Fiji rather than China. So in 1890, when the work was done down to the last maps and indexes and he sailed from San Francisco again, he embarked for Hawaii, Samoa, Tahiti, and Fiji. Romantic escape was one motive. More positively, he conceived himself as "an ex-Professor of archaic history" (Nov. 24, 1890) carrying his research into the field, and he made professorial preparation: there were not so many books about the South Seas that he could not read them all.

John La Farge, his companion on the trip to Japan, went with him to the South Seas also, and Adams took advantage of his artist-companion's example and help to begin trying to paint in water colors. Doing so almost immediately increased his sensitivity to color, texture, and shade, both in the world about him and in art. He was learning, he said, to see painting a little from the inside. His skill did not progress as rapidly as his eye: in painting he could not hope to arrive at the freedom that the watercolor sketch especially invites. But an analogous freedom came into his letters, an ability to yield to the pleasures of the eye and follow the track of sense as if the language of perception came spontaneously. His most marked advance was not in landscape, but in life drawing. In Japan, when he first saw a bathhouse full of men and women, he had had trouble writing the word "naked." At Samoa, as he watched the glistening bodies of the siva dancers who seemed to come from the sea, inhibition fell away and his sense of art was transformed: "this was the real thing, and made our ballets seem preposterous" (Oct. 30, 1890). In the South Seas he discovered a world of the senses he had never known before.

The rarity of a slip like the mis-writing of "naked" and the ease with which Adams accommodated new ranges of experience are evidence of a characteristic self-discipline. Control is similarly evident in the way the letters are inscribed. Adams wrote in a regular, distinct, readable hand, and a sure one: there are remarkably few false starts or superimposed corrections and not a single serious crossed-out passage. Stylistically, control did not preclude the spontaneity of word-play or wit, but it did set boundaries. The boundaries are suggested by the only surviving sequence of Adams' diary, printed here for the first time in its entirety. The diary sequence, which runs from February 12, 1888, to July 7, 1889, records some of the grimmest stages of his grief. Where the letter-writer said little or nothing, the diarist wrote frankly, but he maintained clinical detachment in recording "excessive and alarming turns of temper," "jim-jams," and "acute depression" (April 8, May 13, June 17, 1888). The direct utterance of "I have been sad, sad, sad. Three years!" (May 20, 1888) stands out, but the understatement is still in character. Yet the identity which Adams had made from a lifetime of writing was in these years threatened by emotions he hardly foresaw.

The principal new correspondent in the third volume is Elizabeth Cameron, whom Adams in his fifties came to love in ways he could neither control nor suppress. The Adamses first met her in 1881, when at the age of twenty-four she became their neighbor on Lafayette Square. Besides being strikingly beautiful, she showed the freshness of her provincial Ohio background and the dignity of her great connections—her father's brothers were Senator John Sherman and the Civil War hero General William Tecumseh Sherman. At twenty-one she had married Senator J. Donald Cameron of Pennsylvania, a widower more than twice her age. As his wife she claimed a place of her own among the great; her paying the first call on Marian Adams asserted that claim. Both Adamses were charmed by her lively, friendly, candid way and, being almost twenty years older, they particularly prized her youth. For her sake they set aside their reservations about her dour, party-regular husband. In 1883, when the Camerons went to Europe, Henry Adams sent his friends very special letters of introduction for her. That same summer he used her as a model for Catherine Brooke in his novel *Esther,* and the idealized portrait obviously had the approval, and possibly the help, of Marian Adams. The women who were linked in the novel were linked in life. Just two days before Marian Adams' ordeal of depression came to an end, concern for Elizabeth Cameron's health brought her out to call. It was the last time she is known to have left her house.

Adams' friendship with Mrs. Cameron became closer with the birth of Martha Cameron, on whom he came to focus his love for children. He cultivated Martha's love, and she came frequently to visit, knowing she could count on chocolate drops and imaginative play. Each time they renewed their alliance of little people and played Mr. and Mrs. Gulliver, another thread bound him to both child and mother. In 1887, when Adams listed the women who graced his breakfasts, usually set for eight, he set down Mrs. Cameron as the first among equals. In 1888 he ranked her friendship with that of Hay. The following year, when Washington friends thinned out, he noted that his society became "wholly Martha Cameron and her mother" (Diary, March 17, 1889). After yet another year life in Washington became more cheerful and Adams could report: "Our little set of Hays, Camerons, Lodges and Roosevelts, never were so intimate or friendly as now, and for the first time in my life I find myself among a set of friends so closely connected as to see each other every day, and even two or three

times a day, yet surrounded by so many outside influences and pressures
that they are never stagnant or dull" (April 13, 1890). For the word "set"
he soon came to substitute the word "family."

After the *History* had gone to press Adams felt himself cast loose. For
months, as he waited for La Farge to join him on his Pacific travels, he was
free from all ties and yet unable to leave. By summer, the letters reveal, his
feelings toward Elizabeth Cameron intensified to the point of anguish.
Torn by a passion he could not rationally countenance, he finally departed
with a sense that escape was urgent.

Adams carried his emotional perplexity with him. Keeping up the writing habits of so many years, he now made daily journal-letters his occupation. Elizabeth Cameron, to whom most of them were written, remained
constantly in his thoughts. The besetting problem, that he could not be a
"tame cat" (Jan. 2, 1891) and could envisage no other way of resuming life,
got worse with time. When the South Seas sojourn was over and he made
his way back to Europe, a few weeks in Paris when Elizabeth Cameron was
there proved how frustrating it could be to see her only in allotted time and
among innumerable friends. In the letter (not hitherto published in full)
which he sent when she departed for the United States, Adams recurred to
the "tame cat" dilemma and yet declared that "French novels are not the
only possible dramas" (Nov. 5, 1891). When he himself sailed for home in
February 1892, he was returning fully aware that he would have to live
with acute and constant frustration. By then he was ready to accept a future he could not wholly control.

The five years after Marian Adams' death began in an agony of grief and
ended with the torment of passion, but grief and perplexity and passion
were by no means the whole story. Nor did Adams lose his last purpose in
life, as he sometimes thought, when he finished the *History*. Old ties still
held, and new people and places generated new interests and purposes.
Among his new friends were William Hallett Phillips, a Washington lawyer and amateur archeologist, who was one day to be counsel to Cuban revolutionary interests in the United States, and Cecil Spring Rice, secretary
of the British legation, who eventually returned to Washington as ambassador. He cultivated young beauties of Washington society, whom he invited to ornament his breakfast table. Mary Charlton, Mary Leiter, and
Mary Endicott—with light-hearted blasphemy he called them his "Three
Marys"—were followed by a succession of nieces and "nieces-in-wish," so
that youth and grace were as consistently represented in his immediate en-
vironment as wit and learning. The exotic places to which he journeyed
became parts of his experience that also led into the future.

Japan was a case in point. He did not let his new knowledge fall into
disuse. Between his own collecting and gifts and commissions for friends,
Adams surmised that he gave the customhouse at Georgetown more business than it had had for years. But he did more than collect. The figure of
Kwannon, goddess of mercy, stayed in mind after his visit to her temple in

Tokyo. He decided that he wanted an American Kwannon as a monument at his wife's grave in Rock Creek Cemetery, and he commissioned Augustus Saint-Gaudens to make it. He wanted it to be a symbol of serenity, not of assertive supernatural belief but of "the acceptance, intellectually, of the inevitable." Adams was a tactful patron. In a first conversation with Saint-Gaudens, his ideas and the sculptor's visual conception came into harmony. After that he wisely let the artist handle artistic problems without interference from an amateur. The result was the greatest work of American sculpture of the nineteenth century. The project, which was to have been finished while Adams was in the South Seas, took much longer than expected; the architectural setting was not completed until 1893. Japan and Buddhism became most vitally a part of his life in the monument they influenced.

Cuba and Tahiti provided direct experience of a different sort. Influenced by Clarence King, Adams had conceived of Cuba as a semi-primitive country in which imaginative energy and a fierce will to freedom was repressed by imperialist Spanish tyranny. His first trip to Cuba, since King was unable to accompany him, turned out to be little more than a tourist visit; nonetheless, he felt the attraction his friend had promised. More successful visits followed in the nineties, and in time Adams' house on Lafayette Square became a lobbying and public relations headquarters for the Cuban revolution.

In Tahiti, Adams made his closest contact with primitive culture. Because of the catastrophic effect, as he put it, of "gunpowder and missionaries," he found there only the remnant of a disappearing society. He described the pervasive melancholy at length, but more cheerfully he continued as an amateur anthropologist to take measurements and patiently ask questions wherever he went. In Tahiti he became what is now called a participant observer. With his genius for making friends he became an intimate, and literally an adoptive member, of the deposed ruling family. Marau Taaroa Salmon and her brother Tati, children of the old queen and her South Sea trader husband, a London Jew who settled in the islands, were to be his friends for life. But it was with the old queen that Adams became most intimate. From interpreted interviews with the venerable Ariitaimai Salmon, the historian-interlocutor learned lore and legends that even her children did not know. With her he felt that at last he had come to know "archaic woman." After his return to Washington he continued research through Marau and worked up the accumulating record into his book on Tahiti, which he had privately printed in 1893 and revised in 1901. The letters, however, remain the most vivid record of Adams' Tahitian experience, for besides accurate history they convey the writer's passage from curiosity to sympathy to lasting human ties.

Of the old interests that continued into the nineties, two were much changed and in their new form became the intellectual axes of Adams' later life. His old ideas of political economy were shattered by the Panic of 1893.

Suddenly made aware that those ideas had been largely based on misperceptions, he began poring over the data of trade balances, gold flow, and industrial output and compulsively tried to frame a new analytic scheme. The great stimulus to these investigations was his brother Brooks, ten years his junior, who became his most important new correspondent. In 1893, when Henry returned to Quincy to help save the family investments if he could, he found Brooks at work on *The Law of Civilization and Decay* (1895). Brooks seemed to have scuttled liberalism, progress, and capitalist models of economic behavior and to have worked from premises of evolutionary laws and social will. To the brothers' discussions Henry could bring much learning and subtlety, but it was Brooks's drive for all-embracing general truths that prompted his historian brother to reopen great questions which for thirty years or more he had been treating as settled.

Before long Henry Adams was speaking of politics and political economy in new terms, and he began framing his own ideas of a coming world order, based on population, resources, and industrial productivity and centered no longer in Europe, but in the United States and Russia. As a "conservative anarchist" he did not know whether he was on the side of centralization and energy or dispersion and freedom. Either way he needed to follow the track of power. He surveyed vast reaches of the past in the hope of being enabled to peer into the future. In letters to Brooks the inquiry sometimes became obsessive, but with other correspondents it gave point and portentousness to his comments on the current scene.

The second great theme of Adams' later life was a renewed interest in Norman and Gothic art, culture, and religion. He had been away from these subjects for a decade and a half when, in 1895, he made an architectural tour with the Lodges and was almost overwhelmed by what he saw. What lay between his earlier experience and this one was the South Sea voyage, with its opening of sensibility, and his own increased sympathy with archaic cultures, that is, with histories outside the orbit of liberal, progressive, middle-class values. In Normandy and medieval France he found that otherness which he had sought among semi-primitive and primitive peoples—but this was a world he could claim as being historically his own. He went about the study of Romanesque and Gothic like a professional scholar, collecting books and photographs, motoring over much of France to see cathedrals, sitting long hours at his desk with the most recent monographs before him. To this end he made Paris as much a base as Washington and, as he put it, spent half the year in the twelfth century and half in the present.

Adams' dual commitment to the medieval past and the geopolitical present evolved into a second literary career. By 1899 he had begun work on *Mont-Saint-Michel and Chartres* (1904). The book, which he called his "Miracles of the Virgin," presents a Middle Ages in which art and thought, imagination and faith, are interanimated. The *Chartres* volume prompted him in 1902 to begin *The Education of Henry Adams* (1907), his "Study of Twentieth Century Multiplicity." In the *Education* he expounded the reasons for accepting, intellectually, the forces for concentration in the modern world. But, as the man who had written *Chartres,* Adams could simultaneously make clear why he withheld his deepest commitment from the industrialized, materialist age that was coming. Because he imaginatively possessed another world in the twelfth century, he could maintain a moral detachment from the twentieth that made him a profound critic and a wicked ironist.

Adams was sixty-nine when he finished the two great books of his later career, but this time the completion of a major undertaking scarcely changed the tempo of his life. He went on studying, writing, acquiring new interests. He followed, at a distance, the progress of modern physics. He tracked down manuscripts of medieval music and listened to *chansons* which he had never hoped to know except as texts. He helped finance an archeological expedition to the Dordogne caves, delighted that his interest in archaic man could be carried so far into prehistory. Friends brought interesting new people to his breakfast table, which became even more famous for conversation than the Adamses' salon of the eighties. Even after he suffered a stroke in the spring of 1912 he kept sharp watch on the world of affairs and active curiosity for the world of the mind.

The outbreak of war in 1914 put an end to Adams' annual pilgrimage to France. He took no pleasure in having anticipated where nineteenth-century progress had been tragically leading, but he was not overwhelmed by the descent of darkness. As a dying man of eighty, he still wrote with sensitivity, penetration, and wit. Until life flickered to an end in the most unpromising days of 1918, letter-writing remained an act by which he reaffirmed the social bond. In his letters Adams created from the data of immediate experience a world his readers, then and since, have delighted to share.

J.C.L.

Bibliographical Note

In 1860, at the age of twenty-two, Henry Adams hoped that a century or more after the Great Secession Winter his letters "might still be read and quoted as a memorial of manners and habits" (Dec. 9). With these words to Charles Francis Adams, Jr., Henry invited his older brother to preserve his letters. Charles needed no prompting; he already had saved more than a dozen and by the end of his life had accumulated 236.

Forty years later, in 1900, Adams attempted to place a contrary obligation on Elizabeth Cameron. His letters to her had been long and not always discreet, and he therefore wrote: "I count on you to destroy them. Do not leave them knocking about, as a mash for the female pigs who feed out of the magazine-troughs at five dollars a page, to root in, for scandal and gossip" (Feb. 27). She replied: "I promise you that no publisher or compiler shall ever get hold of them. They shall be destroyed" (March 19). Eventually, however, in November 1915, Adams not only released her from her promise but also urged her to "immortalise" their Lafayette Square society in Washington by gathering for publication, with "a mere thread of editing," their correspondence, and her correspondence with Marian Adams, Anna Cabot Mills Lodge, and John Hay. Unable to carry out the task, she deposited her collection before her death in 1944 with the Massachusetts Historical Society—908 letters and notes from Adams.

Two years after Henry Adams died in 1918 his letters began appearing in published collections. *A Cycle of Adams Letters, 1861–1865,* edited in two volumes by Worthington C. Ford, included parts of 74 letters by Henry Adams and others by Charles Francis Adams, Jr., and by their father, Charles Francis Adams. *Letters to a Niece and Prayer to the Virgin of Chartres* (1920) included selections from 26 letters to Mabel Hooper La Farge. In 1930 Ford brought out *Letters of Henry Adams (1858–1891),* with 354 letters, and in 1938 a second volume, with 651 (many in brief excerpt) written from 1892 to 1918. In 1947 Harold Dean Cater's *Henry Adams and His Friends: A Collection of His Unpublished Letters* included 636 letters. Three others had appeared in *The Letters of Mrs. Henry Adams,* edited by Ward Thoron (1936). From 1920 to the present almost 250 more have appeared in small groups in scholarly journals and reviews, and several in various biographies. Evelyne de Chazeaux, in *Lettres des Mers du Sud* (1974), translated 28 unpublished letters and parts of 23 others. Not counting duplications and letters briefly quoted in studies of Adams and his era, just under 2,000 of Henry Adams' letters have previously appeared in print in English in whole or in part.

The number of extant letters is now known to exceed twice this figure, nearly 4,500 for the sixty-year period from November 3, 1858, through March 15, 1918, two weeks before Adams' death. The chief recipients, besides his brother Charles and Elizabeth Cameron, are Charles Milnes Gaskell, 393 letters; John Hay, 248; Mabel Hooper La Farge, 186; Louisa Hooper Thoron, 169; Brooks Adams, 147; Mary Cadwalader Jones, 133; and Henry Cabot Lodge, 83. The remaining 2,000 went to more than two hundred different recipients.

Ford, for his *Letters of Henry Adams,* located enough material for five or six volumes. Besides sheer quantity, consideration of family and surviving friends influenced his omitting letters and parts of letters. He systematically excluded gossip, invective, expletives, references to Adams' income and investments. Adams' most personal letters to Elizabeth Cameron were excluded and intimate passages from others deleted.

Harold Dean Cater started collecting Adams letters in 1938, just after Ford's second volume came out. The list of important correspondents he added began with Marian Hooper Adams and included Charles Sumner, John G. Palfrey, Charles Eliot Norton, James Russell Lowell, Simon Newcomb, George Bancroft, E. L. Godkin, and Edward Hooper. He did not find letters to four of Adams' closest associates—Henry Hobson Richardson, Clarence King, John La Farge, and Augustus Saint-Gaudens—and further search confirms the likelihood that they have been destroyed. A Richardson descendant reportedly burned that family's correspondence in the early 1930s. Of the many letters to King, the peripatetic mining engineer probably lost or discarded all but the two which had been found (but not published) by Ford. La Farge cleaned out his office files each year; assuming that most of his extant letters to Adams brought replies, he destroyed at least 200 Adams letters. One letter and two fragments to Saint-Gaudens survive.

Cater generally published letters in full, except when he supplied the parts of letters to Brooks Adams which Ford had abridged and when he omitted occasional references to private matters: finances, marital problems, illnesses. Apart from omissions, the text of this edition is unreliable, and some of the errors garble Adams' meaning. For example, Adams wanted to temper the tyranny of "majorities" (not "majesties") in 1866 (Aug. 23); his *Mont-Saint-Michel and Chartres,* Adams told Mrs. Lodge (Jan. 3, 1905), would give her toilet-table an air of "dissipation," not "distinction."

In 1948 appeared the first of three volumes of the biography of Adams by Ernest Samuels, who in research for that work, completed in 1964, uncovered new letters. Other Henry Adams letters turned up in the canvass of libraries and archives conducted by L. H. Butterfield and the staff of The Adams Papers. Completion in 1959 of the *Microfilms of the Adams Papers,* which terminate with the year 1889, drew renewed attention to important unpublished letters and passages from letters.

By 1970 the work of Ford, Cater, and Samuels, along with studies such as William H. Jordy's *Henry Adams: Scientific Historian* (1952), Elizabeth Stevenson's *Henry Adams: A Biography* (1955), and J. C. Levenson's *The Mind and Art of Henry Adams* (1957), and scores of articles and shorter studies, had established Adams as an indispensable figure in American thought and a major American writer. Recognizing the need for a comprehensive and accurate edition of his letters, Harvard University Press and the Massachusetts Historical Society undertook the task and asked Ernest Samuels to be editor. Charles Vandersee, who had compiled a census of extant letters and published two groups of letters, joined the project at the initial stage of search and transcription. In 1976, as historical and textual editing became the principal effort, J. C. Levenson became an editor. Viola Hopkins Winner became an editor in 1977. Jayne Samuels from the beginning and Eleanor Pearre Abbot from 1981 have been assistant editors.

Work began with the materials at the Massachusetts Historical Society: the Adams family papers in the Adams Manuscript Trust, supplemented by Ford's and Cater's archives at the Society. Besides the work of transcribing complete texts of these letters, and those in collections at Harvard and Brown universities, the editors recorded new acquisitions at the Society and elsewhere and made their own general canvass as well as specific searches.

Of some 600 letters outside the Adams family collection which had not previously been available for publication, the largest group consists of 230 letters to Louisa Hooper Thoron and her husband, Ward Thoron. Mrs. Thoron had helped Cater in attempts to trace and retrieve other letters, but she chose not to publish the ones to her and her husband. Aileen Tone, companion to Adams in his last years, also withheld from publication 14 letters to her, and the Lodges two dozen which they possessed. Adams' niece Abigail Adams Homans had held back many letters of Henry Adams to his wife.

Forty-six letters to Marian Adams' friend Anne Palmer Fell and 62 to Lucy Baxter came to light, as did 35 to Bernard Berenson, held at the Villa I Tatti in Florence. A few letters to the historian James Ford Rhodes and 44 to Adams' Washington lawyer and friend, William Hallett Phillips, were given to Harvard University in 1972 by the bequest of Joseph Halle Schaffner. Also now available are 133 letters to Mary Cadwalader Jones, Edith Wharton's sister-in-law and a friend of Henry James and John La Farge.

Three especially interesting new series of letters are those to Lord Houghton, to the Virginia historian Hugh Blair Grigsby, and to Mary Leiter Curzon, who became vicereine of India. The Clifton Waller Barrett collection at the University of Virginia yielded letters to Sir John Clark of Scotland, two new letters to Carl Schurz, and one to Henry James. Other newly discovered letters include those to such scholars and public men as Edwin A. Alderman, John Bigelow, Melville M. Bigelow, Richard Watson Gilder, Arthur T. Hadley, Edward Everett Hale, William Wirt Henry, Ellsworth Huntington, John Codman Ropes, Moorfield Storey, and Barrett Wendell. Two in 1906 offer encouragement to the Southern historian David Duncan Wallace. Three to Edward Robinson of The Metropolitan Museum in New York give Adams' reflections in 1908 on the Saint-Gaudens monument. Letters found in British collections include those to John Bright and Richard Cobden and several unpublished ones to Sir Cecil Spring Rice. Two new ones to John Hay, after the death of his son Del, were found in an album given by the Hay family to Brown University. Two important letters of 1867 (July 30, Oct. 22) to Adams' brother Charles were found when the family office on State Street in Boston was closed in 1973. One by-product of the search for letters was the discovery of Adams' 2,300-word biographical sketch of John Hay, written for a college yearbook (see April 1, 1893).

The present edition draws its materials from some sixty libraries in the United States and ten in other countries, as well as from a dozen private collections. For the scholar who desires access to the major archival sources, the Massachusetts Historical Society in 1979 issued a thirty-six-reel microfilm edition of the papers of Henry Adams, produced by its director emeritus, Stephen T. Riley. Thirty-two of the reels gather into one chronological run the Henry Adams material (chiefly letters written and received) from all of the Society's pertinent collections; three of the reels present alphabetically, by recipient, letters to and from Adams at the Houghton Library of Harvard University; and the last reel reproduces those in the Brown University collection.

The number of Adams letters that have been collected exceeds what can fit in a printed edition, even one of six large volumes. The difficulty is sympathetically put by Henry Adams, who wrote to Henry Cabot Lodge of his own editorial problem: "You know how hard it is to decide that any particular letter or episode is *not* possibly important to somebody" (Aug. 31, 1879). For the first three volumes of this edition, covering the period from November 3, 1858, to February 3, 1892, the number of letters that survive in their entire text or in part is 1,519. Of this number 1,277 are published in this edition; 549 of these appear in print for the first time and another 261 appear for the first time in a complete text.

C.V.

Editorial Note

For *The Letters of Henry Adams,* the first rule of the editors was to include letters in full. We could not, however, include every letter; the wealth of the
collection made that impossible. We excluded perfunctory social notes and
business letters. However, we extensively sample Adams' business letters as
editor of the *North American Review.* His correspondence with contributors
represents an important phase of his—and the country's—intellectual history. Similarly, documentary value accounts for the inclusion of letters that
clarify Adams' movements or the activities of other political and intellectual figures. Whenever the biographical or historical record was involved,
preserving the record was a controlling consideration.

Adams' habit of repeating himself to correspondents, especially when he
was traveling, presented a problem. The winnowing of time, and his own
sporadic efforts to burn out the past, reduced the problem for the earlier
years, but after 1890 the difficulty was compounded. When Adams finished
writing the *History* in that year, he only slightly modified his habit of working pen in hand for at least four hours a day. As letter-writing became a
substitute for professional writing, a quantum increase in letters resulted.
To show how he varied his point of view as he resumed his dialogue with
one correspondent and then another required a generous inclusiveness.
Moreover, he provided different information of documentary interest to
various recipients. When a prevailing consideration of documentary or literary interest did not apply, many letters were omitted on grounds of repe-
titiousness. These grounds took priority over our desire to republish all letters hitherto in print—a project that would have forced the exclusion of
much hitherto unpublished material. We have, however, included in the
first three volumes all the letters which Worthington Chauncey Ford chose,
so that up to February 1892 the letters in the Ford volumes have been fully
reedited from the manuscripts. Our final volume will contain a calendar of
omitted letters.

We have tried to make our notes pertinent, succinct, illuminating, and
unobtrusive—like stage directions that enhance the reading of a dramatic
text without getting in the way of the drama.

In the notes, the location of the manuscript is given first; if we were unable to find the original letter, the source of the text is noted. American

libraries are designated by standard *National Union Catalog* abbreviations, separately listed below. For the Library of Congress, we also specify the collection from which a letter comes. For the Bodleian Library and the Public Record Office, we provide shelf-mark identification.

We have tried to identify at first mention everyone named in the letters, except when the reference is merely passing or incidental. In other cases, if someone is not identified, it is because thorough search has turned up nothing useful. For the best-known figures, such as Abraham Lincoln or Queen Victoria, biographical summary is omitted, but we have provided vital dates and noted specific events alluded to in the text. If Adams' principal link to someone was through Harvard, we have included college class, and for the period up to 1860, when his acquaintance was still largely determined by college and family, we have noted all Harvard connections. For British friends and acquaintances we have tried to supply details beyond those of common reference works like Burke's *Peerage,* particularly since for women Burke often omits vital data that are not immediately relevant to the passing of titles and estates. Party affiliation and major offices of political figures of the United States or Great Britain are given, so that the general context of Adams' activities is made clear.

Above all, we have tried to clarify Adams' activities, involvements, and attitudes. Earlier editors have done much of the preliminary work, and we are grateful to Worthington Chauncey Ford, Ward Thoron, and Harold Dean Cater. We are similarly grateful to Philip Blair Eppard, whose "Correspondence of Henry Adams and John Hay, 1881–1892" (Brown University doctoral dissertation, 1979) solved a number of problems that had resisted earlier inquiry. We have received help at every point from Ernest Samuels' three-volume biography of Henry Adams. We have also relied upon Martin Duberman's biography of Charles Francis Adams and Tyler Dennett's of John Hay. Since these standard works were written, the opening of the Adams papers and other collections has made primary sources available with which to supplement them.

Whenever possible we have consulted basic primary sources. Contemporary newspapers from Boston, New York, Washington, and London furnished important details. For the years of Adams' active engagement in reform politics and close association with E. L. Godkin, the *Nation* supplied many clues to political references. The letters of Marian Hooper Adams and the Memorabilia of Charles Francis Adams, Jr., helped illuminate more personal relations; both are to be found in The Adams Papers— Fourth Generation at the Massachusetts Historical Society. Letters to Henry Adams from his family and from John Hay, Elizabeth Cameron, and Charles Milnes Gaskell have clarified many references; sometimes they raised questions to be pursued. The Hay, Cameron, and Adams family letters, unless otherwise specified, are at the Massachusetts Historical Society, which has included these incoming letters in its microfilm of the Henry Adams letters; the Gaskell letters are held by his great-grandson James

Milnes Gaskell, Esq., who has generously made them available and allowed us to quote them.

The literary and linguistic notes are not so inclusive as the historical. We have tried to record Adams' literary allusions, since they constitute an index to his reading and his education. Some were beyond our powers of research, while others are not given because they have become catch phrases and lost their status as quotations. Some literary allusions are masked as factual references, as when Adams mentions details of Scottish history that he knew—and assumed his brother knew—from the novels of Sir Walter Scott. In citing printed works, we give the year of publication and omit place and publisher unless they are pertinent. Works to which Adams alluded when, as an editor, he arranged reviews for the *North American Review,* were usually immediately current; they are not dated when the year of publication is the same as the year of review.

We have translated difficult and deceptive foreign words and phrases, but tried to avoid the obvious. We have assumed the modest acquaintance with French, German, Italian, and Spanish that tourists, schoolboys, or stamp-collectors might have. Three letters from Paris, which Adams wrote in the summer of 1860 and which we have left untranslated, provide a rough measure of what we call understandable French (even with his errors of spelling and usage intact). Our rule was not to gloss words, English or foreign, which can be found in a standard desk dictionary.

Textual editing has been relatively simple since there are but few instances where we were not able to work from the surviving letters. Between the autograph manuscript and any previously published version, the autograph text has the authority of being the author's intention. We have adhered to that text as closely as common sense allows. We have kept Adams' misspellings and special usages. Readers may note his difficulty with *Tennesee* and *McLellan* and his omission of the first *a* from the name of his friend MacVeagh. They may also observe that he follows a common nineteenth-century practice and often puts apostrophes in *your's* and *it's* (as his father did before him).

Inscription errors (for example, *the* for *that*), which are by definition not what the author intended, are categorically different from misspellings. Such mechanical errors have been silently corrected unless they are possible psychological slips. In those cases we preserve the manuscript text or, when correction is called for in order to avoid confusion of meaning, we note the change. Corrected errors in dating, since they might make a letter hard for someone to find in the microfilm edition of Adams' letters, have been noted. As to inscription changes which Adams himself made, we do not note them. He wrote fluently and made relatively few false starts or running corrections. A detailed record of changes, Adams' own and the editors', has been kept for the use of future scholars.

Simple procedures have sufficed for the making of copy text. Thanks to the clarity of Adams' handwriting, the number of cruxes is remarkably small. The original letters are in a state of excellent preservation, and the rare cases of defective manuscript have been noted. Where Adams' autograph contractions abridge words and add superscript letters, we preserve those which are immediately readable when superscript letters are brought down to the line (*Dr Mr &c* and leave-taking phrases like *Yr obt servt* or *Afecly yrs*); where such transcription might not be immediately readable and a standard abbreviation exists, we substitute the latter (*Dec.* for *Dec'*); where Adams points his superscript contraction (*2ᵈ·* or *obᵗ·*) and modern usage does not, we again follow usage (*2d* or *obt*); where there is no equivalent, we expand autograph contractions (*which* for *whᶜʰ*). We have not followed Adams' inconsistent practice, but have normally put commas and periods within quotation marks.

Square brackets in the dating of a letter indicate that the letter is dated by us. The use of a question mark indicates uncertainty.

The letters are printed basically in chronological order. Those written on a single day are arranged according to alphabetical order of recipients, except when a manifest sequence of events would be violated. If letters and diary entries were written the same day, the diary entry is put last. Adams often wrote serial letters while traveling, especially after 1890. These are treated as units and placed at the date of the first installment. Letters written to other recipients on days between the first and last installments are placed after the completed serial, and so there sometimes is chronological overlapping.

Abbreviations

ABA   Abigail Brooks Adams (1808–1889)
BA   Brooks Adams (1848–1927)
CFA   Charles Francis Adams (1807–1886)
CFA2   Charles Francis Adams, Jr. (1835–1915)
HA   Henry Adams (1838–1918)
JA   John Adams (1735–1826)
JQA   John Quincy Adams (1767–1848)
JQA2   John Quincy Adams II (1833–1894)
MHA   Marian Hooper Adams (1843–1885)

PUBLICATIONS

Cater   *Henry Adams and His Friends: A Collection of His Unpublished Letters,*
             ed. Harold Dean Cater (Boston: Houghton Mifflin Company,
             1947)
Cycle   *A Cycle of Adams Letters, 1861–1865,* ed. Worthington Chauncey
             Ford (Boston and New York: Houghton Mifflin Company, 1920)
Education   *The Education of Henry Adams,* ed. Ernest Samuels (Boston:
             Houghton Mifflin Company, 1973)
Ford I   *Letters of Henry Adams (1858–1891),* ed. Worthington Chauncey
             Ford (Boston and New York: Houghton Mifflin Company, 1930)
Ford II   *Letters of Henry Adams (1892–1918),* ed. Worthington Chauncey
             Ford (Boston and New York: Houghton Mifflin Company, 1938)
LMHA   *The Letters of Mrs. Henry Adams, 1865–1883,* ed. Ward Thoron
             (Boston: Little, Brown and Company, 1936)

AHR   *American Historical Review*
NAR   *North American Review*

MANUSCRIPT LOCATIONS

A-Ar   Alabama Department of Archives and History
CCamarSJ   Edward Laurence Doheny Memorial Library, St. John's
             Seminary, Camarillo, California
CLU   University Research Library, University of California, Los
             Angeles
CSmH   Henry E. Huntington Library
CU   The Bancroft Library, University of California at Berkeley
CtY   Yale University Library
CtY-B   Beinecke Rare Book and Manuscript Library, Yale University

DCA	Corcoran Gallery of Art
DDO	Dumbarton Oaks Garden Library
DLC	Library of Congress
DNA	National Archives
DSI-AA	Smithsonian Institution National Anthropological Archives
DSI-Ar	Smithsonian Institution Archives
DeHi	Historical Society of Delaware
ICN	The Newberry Library
InU	Lilly Library, Indiana University, Bloomington
KU-S	Kenneth Spencer Research Library, University of Kansas Libraries
MB	Boston Public Library
MB-P	Boston Public Library, Print Department
MBAt	Boston Athenæum
MBG	Isabella Stewart Gardner Museum
MBMu	Museum of Fine Arts, Boston
MBU	Mugar Memorial Library, Boston University
MCLong	National Park Service, Longfellow National Historic Site
MH	Houghton Library, Harvard University
MH-Ar	Harvard University Archives
MH-L	Harvard Law School Library
MH-Z	Museum of Comparative Zoology, Harvard University
MHi	Massachusetts Historical Society
MSaE	Essex Institute
MWA	American Antiquarian Society
MdBJ	Milton S. Eisenhower Library, The Johns Hopkins University
MdHi	Maryland Historical Society
MiU	William L. Clements Library, University of Michigan, Ann Arbor
MnHi	Minnesota Historical Society
N	New York State Library
NHi	The New-York Historical Society
NN	The New York Public Library, Astor, Lenox and Tilden Foundations
NNAL	American Academy and Institute of Arts and Letters
NNC	Rare Book and Manuscript Library, Columbia University
NNH	The Hispanic Society of America
NNMM	The Metropolitan Museum of Art
NNPM	The Pierpont Morgan Library
NNU	Fales Library at New York University
NRU	The University of Rochester Library
NSchU	Schaffer Library, Union College, Schenectady, New York
NWM	United States Military Academy Library
NcD	William R. Perkins Library, Duke University
NcU	Library of the University of North Carolina at Chapel Hill
NhD	Dartmouth College Library
NjP	Princeton University Library
OClW	Case Western Reserve University Archives
OHi	Ohio Historical Society
OMC	Dawes Memorial Library, Marietta College
OO	Oberlin College Archives

PHC	Charles Roberts Autograph Collection, Haverford College Library
PHi	Historical Society of Pennsylvania
PPT	Samuel Paley Library, Temple University
RPB	John Hay Library, Brown University
RPJCB	The John Carter Brown Library, Brown University
ScU	South Caroliniana Library, University of South Carolina
TxU	Humanities Research Center, The University of Texas at Austin
ViHi	Virginia Historical Society
ViU	The Clifton Waller Barrett Library, University of Virginia
WiHi	Archives Division, State Historical Society of Wisconsin, Madison, Wisconsin

The Adams Family

Henry Adams (c. 1583-1646) of
Barton St. David, Somerset, emigrated in
1638 to Braintree, Massachusetts

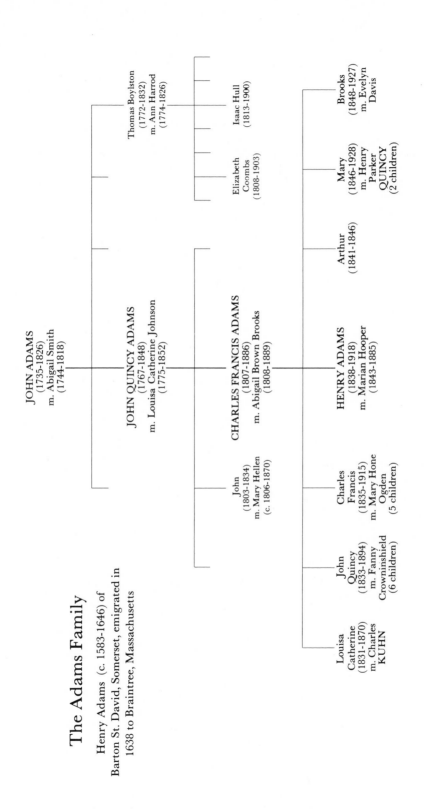

JOHN ADAMS
(1735-1826)
m. Abigail Smith
(1744-1818)

Thomas Boylston
(1772-1832)
m. Ann Harrod
(1774-1826)

Isaac Hull
(1813-1900)

Elizabeth
Coombs
(1808-1903)

JOHN QUINCY ADAMS
(1767-1848)
m. Louisa Catherine Johnson
(1775-1852)

John
(1803-1834)
m. Mary Hellen
(c. 1806-1870)

CHARLES FRANCIS ADAMS
(1807-1886)
m. Abigail Brown Brooks
(1808-1889)

Louisa
Catherine
(1831-1870)
m. Charles
KUHN

John
Quincy
(1833-1894)
m. Fanny
Crowninshield
(6 children)

Charles
Francis
(1835-1915)
m. Mary Hone
Ogden
(5 children)

HENRY ADAMS
(1838-1918)
m. Marian Hooper
(1843-1885)

Arthur
(1841-1846)

Mary
(1846-1928)
m. Henry
Parker
QUINCY
(2 children)

Brooks
(1848-1927)
m. Evelyn
Davis

The Brooks Family

Thomas Brooks (d. 1667) emigrated with John Winthrop
in 1630 and settled in Concord, Massachusetts

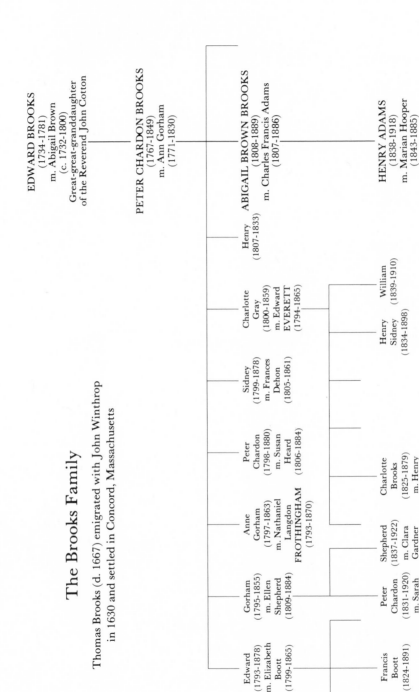

EDWARD BROOKS
(1734-1781)
m. Abigail Brown
(c. 1732-1800)
Great-great-granddaughter
of the Reverend John Cotton

PETER CHARDON BROOKS
(1767-1849)
m. Ann Gorham
(1771-1830)

Edward
(1793-1878)
m. Elizabeth
Boott
(1799-1865)

Gorham
(1795-1855)
m. Ellen
Shepherd
(1809-1884)

Anne
Gorham
(1797-1863)
m. Nathaniel
Langdon
FROTHINGHAM
(1793-1870)

Peter
Chardon
(1798-1880)
m. Susan
Heard
(1806-1884)

Sidney
(1799-1878)
m. Frances
Dehon
(1805-1861)

Charlotte
Gray
(1800-1859)
m. Edward
EVERETT
(1794-1865)

Henry
(1807-1833)

ABIGAIL BROWN BROOKS
(1808-1889)
m. Charles Francis Adams
(1807-1886)

Francis
Boott
(1824-1891)

Peter
Chardon
(1831-1920)
m. Sarah
Lawrence

Shepherd
(1837-1922)
m. Clara
Gardner

Charlotte
Brooks
(1825-1879)
m. Henry
Augustus
WISE

Henry
Sidney
(1834-1898)

William
(1839-1910)

HENRY ADAMS
(1838-1918)
m. Marian Hooper
(1843-1885)

THE LETTERS OF
HENRY ADAMS
Volume I

1858–1868

I.

Berlin and Dresden
1858–1860

The letters begin with Henry Adams settling cheerfully in Berlin in October 1858. When he had to abandon his plan to study Roman law at the university because his German was not good enough, he enrolled instead in a gymnasium. There the teaching covered familiar subjects and was conducted in German he could readily grasp. He stuck to his schoolboy regimen until the term ended in April, but managed also to find time for edifying cultural excursions and less serious private pleasures. In retrospect, however, he found that first winter dismal.

The antidote to his Berlin winter was a spring walking trip that ended in Dresden, where young Adams remained for a few weeks. The contrast had its effect. After his summer travels, he decided that he should spend his second winter not in Berlin, but in Dresden. There he established himself in the Reichenbach household, where James Russell Lowell had lived a few years earlier when he was perfecting his German. Adams' progress in the language can be noted in the various record of serious study and youthful fun. But the letters also show how closely he followed the news from home, where his father in Congress and his brother Charles in the press were taking up new roles in the intensifying conflict over slavery.

To Charles Francis Adams, Jr.

Berlin.
Wednesday. November. 3. 1858.

My dear Fellow[1]

With that energy of expression and originality of thought for which you are so justly celebrated, you have remarked in your last that the pleasures and pains of life are pretty equally divided. Permit me in the particular instance before us to doubt the fact. In the long run it may be so, but as between you in Boston and me in Europe, I deny it in toto and without hesitation.

I humbly apologize to you for the remarks in my last letter, which were written under the supposition that you had forgotten me. Your letter was satisfaction itself. I already knew the main points, but I can ask nothing more complete than your particulars. As to the nomination I am delighted with the manner of it.[2] The election took place yesterday, and a fortnight from today I shall certainly know all about it, if not from you, at any rate from Gov. Wright at the American Legation.[3]

Here I am, then, in Berlin. It is now night; I am writing in my room, which is about ten or twelve, by eighteen or twenty feet; by the light of a lamp for which I paid yesterday two dollars; independent; unknown and unknowing; hating the language and yet grubbing into it. I have passed the day since one o'clock with Loo, who is now here and remains till Friday, and with whom I go about to Galleries and Museums, and then dine at her hotel.[4] As you say, I am not rich and am trying to institute a rigid economy in all my expenses. There is one advantage in this place; if forced to it, one can live for almost nothing. Today I was extravagant. I ordered a quantity of clothes; an inside suit and an overcoat of expensive stuffs. The over-coat is a peculiar beaver-cloth, a sort of velvety stuff; and its inside is thick fur, like sealskin, I suppose; so thick that I can't have it lined. The suit is very strong, fine cloth, as good, I fancy as the man had. But then I had to pay dear. Altogether it cost me fifty one American dollars. Now in Boston perhaps this is not so much, but here it is a great deal.

Then this frightful German! I have had the most amusing times with my landlady who's a jolly Dutch woman and who has a power of clack that is marvellous. If I have her called in and she once gets agoing I can no more hope to make her understand what I want than if she talked Hebrew. So I have recourse to my Dutch teacher, whom I pay very high even for America, and get him to mediate between us and look over my bills and see that I'm not cheated. He comes every morning at ten and I read and talk with him and he corrects my exercises.

What shall I say of this city? Why, Lord bless my soul, I have got things enough to see and study in this city alone to take me two years even if I knew the language and only came for pleasure. The Museums, picture Galleries, Theatres, Gardens; there are enough to occupy one's time for ever-so-long in mere play. I would like nothing better than to go into the Picture Gallery and make the Art a study, and read up in it all the time for the next six months. Then do the same with the half-million or so, engravings. Lord! *such* engravings!

The truth is, in the soberest earnest, I am quite as pleasantly situated as I ever expected to be. Sometimes of course, I feel a little lonely and shall feel more so, I suppose, when Loo goes away and I have no one to think of as near me. Sometimes too I get angry at the excessive difficulty of this very repulsive language, and wearied to death at the continual and fatiguing learning by rote which is necessary for almost every phrase. But on the whole, life here is exceedingly pleasant; there is no relaxation from continual occupation; no excuse for the blues, which always with me come from ennui. Here one is surrounded by Art, and I defy any one but a fool to feel ennuyéed while he can look at the works of these old masters.

Here you have my life then. It will be for the next two months a continual dig at the language varied occasionally by a moment or so of Art. The evenings at the Theatres, concerts or Balls, perhaps, such as they have here, queer affairs I imagine, and the day in hard study.

(Saturday eve. Nov. 6.) I resume my letter where it was broken off, and hope to send it tomorrow. I have just left Loo, who is still here but expects to go to Dresden tomorrow night. She is suffering tonight under one of her fearful head-aches, or I should be with her. She has been very kind to me indeed; very kind; we have been together all the time, going from Gallery to Gallery, and I have almost been living at her expense these ten days, for she would not allow me to pay for my own dinners. I sat with her till ten o'clock last night, and have passed all the afternoons with her (that is, from eleven till six) every day. In consequence I have had to sit up till twelve o'clock to write my exercises.

I have received my clothes, and on the whole they are the best I ever wore. The great-coat is a miracle. I look in it like a veteran. German cloth is, if anything even better than English. However, they ought to be good. They cost enough. Apropos to cost, those bills are right. Apply to papa on my account for the money and let him credit it.

My friends here are all right. I received a letter today from Crowninshield in Hannover in answer to one of mine, in which he represents himself as pretty well except for the fleas.[5] I was very bad that way myself on my arrival here and had a very funny scene with my landlady on the subject, which reached so involved a point at last that an interpreter was called in and as he pretended to speak English but didn't, I'm inclined to think the poor woman to this day doesn't understand. However, I instituted vigorous measures and have not been troubled lately. Anderson is settled here.[6] I went to see him once, but he is a long way off, and I've heard nothing from him for some time. Plenty of Americans are here; one in the next house; but I have had nothing to do with them though I met half-a-dozen at the American Legation last Wednesday. They are of all kinds; some, not attractive. As soon as possible I shall make German acquaintances and in a couple of months I hope to be well enough on in the language, to join the University and make acquaintances there among the donkeys who walk round with absurd caps on their heads; rather more offensive than the soldiers.

Apropos to this, you ask me, what my plans are, here and in life. I hardly know how to follow a plan here, for the way is not at all clear. When I left America my intention was, first to accustom myself to the language; then to join the University and systematically attend lectures on the Civil Law, at the same time taking a Latin tutor and translating Latin into German; and to continue this course in Heidelberg or in Paris or in both. The plan was simple enough; useful enough; and comprehensive enough. But now I see difficulties. I must join the University here in the middle of its term; I certainly can not join to any advantage before January. Shall I be likely to learn much Law by breaking in on a course of Lectures in this manner. To be a student of Civil law I must be an absolute master of written and ordinary Latin; though I need not speak it or write it myself. Now, is it well to study law, Latin and German all at once? Can I have time enough to do all this, or ought I to resign the Law and devote myself to Latin? But supposing I were to do this, devote myself to Latin; I may as well give up the University for it would be mere waste time to attend lectures like Corny Felton's at Cambridge,[7] and, as Carlyle says, these Germans are the worst Dryasdusts on the face of the earth.[8]

These objections will, as I advance further and see clearer, either vanish entirely, or gain strength and finally force me into some new course. I hope it will be the former. I already see very clearly that the two years which are allotted to me here, are not nearly enough to do all that I had hoped to do, or a quarter part of it, and I tell you now fairly that if I return to America without doing more than learn German and French, I shall have done well, and these two years will be the best employed of my life. I am satisfied of this, and though I shall not work any the less hard because I believe it, still I shall feel less disappointed when I return without universal knowledge. At present I adhere to my original plan; and this plan as you see, involves the necessity of my omitting Greek entirely. I am sorry enough to do it, but I became convinced that to attempt the study of Greek now and here, would be hopeless unless I gave up Latin. One or the other I must sacrifice. If I were to include this fourth language in my plan, I should never do anything. Two years will not teach one everything. You may think that as a scholar I should have preferred to sacrifice Latin. As a scholar I should, but as a lawyer I must have only one choice. I take it. And this brings me to the other branch of your question.

As for my plan of life, it is simple, and if health and the usual goods of life are continued to me, I see no reason why it should not be carried out in the regular course of events. Two years in Europe; two years studying law in Boston; and then I propose to emigrate and practice at Saint Louis. What I can do there, God knows; but I have a theory that an educated and reasonably able man can make his mark if he chooses, and if I fail to make mine, why, then—I fail and that's all. I should do it anywhere else as well. But if I know myself, I can't fail. I must, if I only behave like a gentleman and a man of sense, take a position to a certain degree creditable and influential, and as yet my ambition cannot see clearly enough to look further.

In a conversation I had with Mr Dana[9] a few days before I left home, I said all this to him, and the latter part of it he treated with a little contempt. He insisted that I was looking towards politics; and perhaps he was right. There are two things that seem to be at the bottom of our constitutions; one is a continual tendency towards politics; the other is family pride; and it is strange how these two feelings run through all of us. For my own ideas of my future, I have not admitted politics into them. It is as a lawyer that I would emigrate and I've seen altogether too much harm done in this way, to allow myself to quit law for politics without irresistible reasons.

So here you have a few of my thoughts about what I am going to do. Here in Europe, away from home, from care and ambition and the fretting of monotony, I must say that I often feel as I often used to feel in College, as if the whole thing didn't pay, and if I were my own master, it would need more inducements than the law could offer, to drag me out of Europe these ten years yet. I always had an inclination for the Epicurean philosophy, and here in Europe I might gratify it until I was gorged. Give me my thousand a year and free leave and a good conscience, and I'd pass as happy a life here as I'm afraid I never shall in St Louis. But now I am hurried; I must work, work, work; my very pleasures are hurried, and after all, I shall get most pleasure and (I believe) advantage, from what never entered into my calculations; Art.

However, there is no use talking. The Magd has just come in to prepare my room for the night, and her "Guten Nacht" tells me that it is nine o'clock; and I want still to write to John.[10] There will be time enough to despond hereafter. Just now I am sure is the pleasantest time I shall ever see, for there is entire independence, no cares, and endless and inexhaustible pleasures. As for my expences I cannot yet calculate them, but when I square my accounts at the end of the month I shall be able to tell with some degree of certainty how I am to come out. Incidentally you might remark in the hearing of the family circle, that an Englishman the other day said in my hearing that Berlin was an expensive place; nothing was cheap in Berlin.

So farewell. I shall not close this letter on the whole till Sunday night, so that I may say if Loo goes.

H.B.A.

(Sunday night) I have just seen Loo off. She had a bad night, but today recovered and I dined with them as usual. Tonight at seven o'clock they went off for Dresden. They wanted me to go with them and you may imagine I should have liked to have done so. I am now alone here and shall study hard. I shall write to Hollis next week,[11] but probably not home as there will be little to say. Nick came to see me today. He is all right but I shall see very little of him. This letter will reach you about Thanksgiving, when I am to dine at Magdeburg with Crowninshield and the rest. Five of us. Good-bye.

MS: MHi
    1. Charles Francis Adams, Jr. (1835–1915), HA's brother, with whom he had lived during his first two years at Harvard. CFA2 was currently reading law in Boston.
    2. Their father, Charles Francis Adams (1807–1886), easily won the Republican nomination for Congress when his leading rival withdrew in his favor. The Republican ticket swept Massachusetts, and CFA ran ahead of the ticket.
    3. Joseph Albert Wright (1810–1867), former governor of Indiana, minister to Prussia 1857–1861.
    4. Louisa Catherine Adams (1831–1870), eldest of the six Adams children, and her husband, Charles Kuhn (1821–1899) of Philadelphia, formerly a New York sugar broker, were traveling abroad. They were married in 1854.
    5. Benjamin William Crowninshield (1837–1892) of Boston, Harvard '58.
    6. Nicholas Longworth Anderson (1838–1892) of Cincinnati, Harvard '58.
    7. Cornelius Conway Felton (1807–1862), Eliot Professor of Greek Literature.
    8. In his *History of Frederick the Great,* published September 1858, Thomas Carlyle (1795–1881) asserted that "the Prussian Dryasdust . . . excels all other Dryasdusts yet known" (bk. 1, ch. 1).
    9. Richard Henry Dana (1815–1882), Boston lawyer active in Free-Soil politics, *Two Years Before the Mast* (1840).
    10. John Quincy Adams (1833–1894), eldest of HA's three brothers.
    11. Hollis Hunnewell (1836–1884) of Boston, Harvard '58.

To Charles Francis Adams, Jr.

Berlin. December 17–18. 1858.

My dear fellow

Your letter dated Thanksgiving day arrived yesterday, and I give you my word that though I have been having a delightful time here and have enjoyed life to the hubs, still I have never felt quite so glad at being out of Boston as I felt after reading that epistle. There was in it a sort of contented despair, an unfathomable depth of quiet misery that gave me a placid feeling of thankfulness at being where I am. If Boston hadn't been to me what you describe it; if I hadn't felt society to be a bore even while I was yet on the threshold; if I had found one single young woman who had salt enough in her to keep her from stagnating; I believe I never should have thought of leaving home. John and I have already talked on this subject and I know his ideas. For myself, I believe that I can find more interesting women among the very dregs of society here, than Papanti's Hall can turn out.[1] However, at present I can dispense with both. So; Susy Amory has got back, has she? Give her my love, do! She lived in the next Hotel to mine, while I was in London, but I notice her presence didn't have enough effect to induce me to call. Congratulate John for me, and all luck to yourself.[2]

I tell you what, my boy, you don't crow over political successes at home more than I do here. The old Free Soilers, sir, are about the winning hosses, I reckon, just now. What the devil has become of your Seward's speeches I can't imagine.[3] I've heard so much of them that I'd like to read them, but I can borrow the paper here. The Courier's howl I glanced at. It *was* funny, very.[4] As for Mr Sumner I've heard no more about him since he left. He's not written, and Loo has not mentioned him in her letter.[5]

So much for these things. And now for personal matters. You repeat in your letter the kind offer you made before I left, to help me if I needed help. The Governor,[6] too, in his letter which I received with yours, has rather a queer passage to the effect that he is afraid I shall spend here in Europe much more money than my brothers did and that it will be necessary after my return to make arrangements about it. Meanwhile he will keep me supplied, as I send notice. Now this is very well, it is true. I am exceedingly obliged to you, and also to the Governor who seems all of a sudden to have forgotten his original remarks about a thousand a year. But nevertheless I am determined for various reasons to abide by the original sum. If necessary I can live on half of it, even here in Berlin, though not a very pleasant life. I have been making, and am now making steady efforts to reduce my expences at least two hundred dollars within my income, but that cursed journey from Liverpool and the necessary expences of living here, for the first month, have, I'm afraid, brought me hard onto the thousand this year. Meanwhile I am now, for the present at least, pretty well at ease about European expences. The only thing that remains on my mind is Hill, and perhaps I may be able to wipe that out before I return. Apropos, perhaps if you'd like to buy some German books, I can knock off a little of my debt to you so. I can get you what is I believe the best edition of Goethe for twenty five or thirty dollars; thirty volumes, bound; but forty or more, unbound. Lessing and Schiller I shall buy for myself soon. The books here are nicely bound, and very cheap. The Goethe and Lessing higher than the others, though I can get you editions of both for almost nothing. As for engravings &c, I mean to pick some up, but not here. Everything is dear in Berlin. There is nothing that I have heard of, here, that is worth the expence of buying to take home, and I shall only get a few engravings of the pictures in the Galleries, and photographs of the city.

I wrote in my last that I was going to leave these rooms. They are too dear and too many Americans are round. I have taken others quite as good, or rather decidedly better than these, but one story higher, and at least half an hour's walk from the University. They cost with my coffee and bread for breakfast, service, heating, &c about ten dollars a month. My present ones cost about $16.50. The difference itself is not great, but you will know, my boy, if you ever have occasion to live economically, that where one's rooms cost much, everything else costs proportionably. It is not however this expence that will hurt me. But you see, a single bat, a single evening passed as is sometimes done, from six in the afternoon till three in the morning, at the theatre and concerts and wine-shops and bier-locals and balls; a single evening may make necessary a week's economy. And in my new rooms I can economize more easily than here, I think.

Meanwhile I live a quiet life here, occasionally about once a week looking in at a ball, and going pretty regularly once a week to a classical concert and the Theatre. This week I've been three times to the theatre; twice to the Opera Haus to see the Zauberflöte and Fidelio, great German operas which I can't appreciate; and once to the Schauspielhaus to see Hamlet. It was well done; remarkably well done. Setting aside the scenery, which is always perfect here, it was an exceedingly well acted piece. But Dessoir was not equal in stage-effects to Booth and I've seen Mrs Barrow (?) do Ophelia much better than the little Fraülein Fuhr, who didn't at all satisfy me.[7] Then the German spoils it to an Englishman. The speech " 'Tis not alone my inky cloak, good mother," begins in the German, "Gnädige Frau." The whole thing sounds flat to me in German. Othello was given the other night but I could get no seat; I fancy however it was not better. They have good actors here, but no wonders; and as for the singers, I've heard no particularly good one. But the orchestra, the scenery and the ballet in the Opera House are glorious.

As I said, I live a quiet life, usually ending the day with a beef-steak, or some sausage and a glass of bier and a pipe, though this evening I'm on the economical, having dissipated yesterday in taking dancing lessons. Nick Anderson and I took a lesson of two hours. I usually write as much German as possible in the daytime, and read in the evening, but it is desperately slow work, and I expect to be occupied by little else but the language all the winter. The University will be of little use to me, but I may take a private Tutor in Latin. At present I am still at the rudiments. I can't once in a dozen times speak a grammatical sentence, and understand what is said only when very slowly spoken. As for a continued lecture, I can't catch anything at all, and at the theatre very little. But there is certainly a regular advance, and I am desperate in my attempts to talk it.

The great drawback to one's enjoyment here is the weather. Today is the first day for four weeks that the sun has been out, and that we've not had a heavy, muggy fog. Today has been clear and cool and very enjoyable.

And so, my poor boy, condemned to labor in that happy city of Boston, don't you wish you were here? Perhaps Berlin may not be so pleasant as Vienna or Paris, but I think you wouldn't object to be here notwithstanding. Christmas comes off soon and if the fellows from Hannover come on, there'll probably be a pretty loud time, and the masked-balls &c will hear of it. At present, however, I'm drawing back from most of my American acquaintances, but I have not yet succeeded in supplying their places with Germans. There seems to be no place here where German students meet much. Very little student life in Berlin, and what I've seen of that is dirty and fleay.

I have however made one philosophical discovery here; and that is that it doesn't matter where I live or what I do, there will come occasionally fits of crossness and disagreeable feelings. The advantage of living here is however that when one gets bored and cross, there are so many means of driving it away. I myself usually prefer a beef-steak and a bottle of Rhine wine, with a companion, or "vielleicht" two bottles, but I have known a ball to be tried with success, or in fact almost any change of action. One is always doing something new here, if its only discovering a new bier-local, or going to a new concert-room. I mean some evening to set out on a tour of exploration and visit two or three dozen concert-rooms and balls. As yet I know comparatively few.

As for the inhabitants of Boston, I can't say that I feel any very absorbing interest in their affairs, and though it is rather amusing to hear what is going on, still I can't say that I should care much if I didn't hear a word except from the family, while I am away. I am however always very glad to hear from home. Since I began to prepare to wander, I have thought a good deal more of home than I ever did before. I assure you, my dear fellow, one doesn't appreciate home properly, at home. Especially before I started, I had my attention drawn to one thing, to which it ought to have been drawn long ago; how excessively selfish and exacting we children always were toward mamma, and still more, how much she felt it. Before I came away, I had two or three long talks with her, and I came out of them feeling more like a damned selfish, low-minded fool than I ever did before in my life. I determined then that I would at least try not only to show more respect and affection for her in my manner towards her, but also try to get you and John to do so. I spoke to John about it, and he took it as I hoped he would, and as I meant he should. I write now to put the same thing before you, if John has not already done it, not, of course, intending to find fault or interfere, but only to represent that we are now men, grown up and independent or nearly so; that we owe a certain amount of respect and affection to our mother, and that it is not enough to merely *have* this affection; we ought to *show* it more in those little matters that a woman feels most. I do believe that a reasonable amount of delicate attention and *respect* from her sons, would make mamma perfectly proud and happy.

She felt too very deeply the way we treated Brooks, and I think myself that we ought to try our hardest to tolerate the child, who is really a first-rate little fellow, apart from his questions, and we ought not to snub him so much.[8] It will break his spirit, or at all events, can have no good effect. That boy's disposition will either make something of him or kill him. Perhaps our influence, well applied, might give him a start and keep him straight. At all events it will be very bad to make home disagreeable to him, and drive him off to learn all sorts of low things from his companions. That is the very worst that can happen.

As for Mary, I don't know what will become of her.[9] It seems to me that she'll be a great, strapping girl, with as little consciousness of what God made her for, or of what she wants to do besides getting a husband, as any of our other friends. Her manners too will never be good, I'm afraid. She has too many brothers.

I am sure that you'll take as I mean, all that I have written. To me, the first one of us that has left home, the real feelings that existed there were probably shown clearer than often happens. I felt more strongly than ever before that it was an entire mistake for me to suppose that I had only myself in the world to care for; and I appreciated for the first time that there were those who would feel much more for my death or misfortune than I should myself. It made a strong impression on me at the time, and I am not likely to forget it in Europe, where the tone that I hear is so low, so selfish and so irreligious, that it compels me more and more to a love for what is pure and good. I should become a fanatic, I believe, and go into the pulpit if I remained here long.

With this letter I send a list of the letters I have written and the letters and papers I have received. I'm inclined to think some must have missed. Either with this letter or by the next steamer will come a letter for papa, but I shall mail this first, though I've no idea how soon it will go. I'm much obliged to you for your offer about the paper but I dont much care for one. They're at the Legation. Pray send the Atlantic Monthly though, as I wrote papa, and if there's anything in the papers, like Seward's speeches, for instance, I'd like to see them. These had better be sent by Bremen.

I've sat up till one o'clock to write this, and shall close it here as I have a lot more to do before bed-time. I turn night into day a good deal.

Yr's &c.   H.

Letters *to* Home

1.	Chester.	Oct.	10.	To Mamma
2.	London.	”	17.	” ”
3.	Berlin.	”	25.	” ” & John.
4.	”	”	31.	” ” & Papa.
5.	”	Nov.	9.	” Charles & John.
6.	”	”	21.	”
7.	”	Dec.	5.	” Mamma & Papa.
8.	”	”	12.	” John.

Letters Received.

1.	Date.	Oct.	4.	From Mamma & John
2.	”	”	9 & 13	” ” ” Charles
3.	”	”	25 & 26	” ” & Papa.
4.	”	Nov.	12	” ”
5.	”	”	25	” Charles & ”

& one from Hunnewell.

Papers. Traveller. Oct. 8.

2 Advertisers. Nov. 5.

N. Y. Tribune. ” 13.

Your Courier with Seward's speeches is just arrived. Some time ago, Gov. Wright, our Minister, spoke of them to me as very impolitic, and a sort of bravado. *I* think they are exactly what we want, and I never had a higher opinion of Seward than now. The Gov. is getting on; to be made a General of battalion with Wilson for his first ally.[10] He'll have to forget the campaign of '54, and the trading off of the Rupublican party by his new friend.

MS: MHi
1. The fashionable dancing academy in Boston conducted by Lorenzo Papanti and his son.
2. JQA2 had just been admitted to the Massachusetts bar; CFA2 was about to take the examination.
3. William Henry Seward (1801–1872), governor of New York 1838–1842, senator 1849–1861, secretary of state under Lincoln and Johnson 1861–1869. His "irrepressible conflict" speeches at Rochester, Oct. 25, and Rome, N.Y., Oct. 29, made him a leading candidate for the Republican presidential nomination in 1860.
4. The Boston *Daily Courier* was identified with Cotton Whig (proslavery) principles.
5. Charles Sumner (1811–1874), Republican senator from Massachusetts 1851–1874.
6. HA frequently referred to CFA as the "Governor" or "Gov."
7. Mrs. Barrow was a member of the repertory company at the Boston Theatre.
8. Brooks Adams (1848–1927), youngest of the Adams children.
9. Mary Adams (1846–1928), younger of HA's two sisters.
10. Henry Wilson (1812–1875) of Massachusetts, senator 1855–1873. In the party shifts of the 1850s from which the Republican party evolved, CFA and Wilson were usually in rival and mutually suspicious groups.

To Charles Sumner

Hon. Charles Sumner.
Montpellier. France.

Berlin. December. 22. 1858.

Dear Sir

I was exceedingly glad to receive the letter which you so kindly wrote to me, and value it very much, although it does not tell me all that I wanted to know about your own condition. Curiosity, it is said, is an important part of a New Englander's character. My short experience teaches me to believe that it is quite as important a part of the German character. But I hope it is something better than mere curiosity that makes your letter not quite satisfactory to me; that makes me wish to know not only where you are, but also what your physicians have said, and what you yourself think of your present course of treatment. It is not only on my own account either that I would like to know a little more than your letter tells me, but you have many friends here in Berlin who have nearly as much interest as I in your situation, and who often ask me about it.

Pray do not think me impertinent, nor attribute it to boyish forwardness if I ask you why you do not separate yourself from all these questions of American politics wholly for a time. Why not give up at once the prospect of returning this winter to America, and go away; to some place where you cannot by any possibility hear a word of politics; to Egypt; to Jerusalem, and among such wholly new scenes and peoples recover your health and strength.[1] American politics seem to be going on very well; more hopefully than ever yet; why not dismiss them at once. I would even go so far, if I can do it without impertinence, and if you will allow a young friend who speaks wholly from his love for you, without regard for state- or political-reasons; I would even go so far as to say; if you can recover in no other way, why not resign your seat and leave public life for two years; five years; ten years, if necessary, and devote your whole time to recovery. When you do return, I have no fear that the people will have forgotten you. I believe now, as I said to you two years ago, that you have Massachusetts under your hand and will have it so all your life. Your physicians assure you of recovery. Why not make your recovery complete? The great question that you feel so much interest on, is not a question of a day; it will not be settled in one year or five years, and if it would be; if the battle is to go against us, I would nevertheless rather see you once more strong and well than have you go back to that bar-room of a Congress to suffer another relapse on its floor, even though by doing it, you doubled your own reputation.

I don't know whether it's customary to write in this way, but I am sure that you will not be angry with me for it. I am myself rather disgusted with politics. I might have supposed that they had done enough harm in destroying your health and happiness, but here is my father rushing into them and bent upon ruining not only our family comfort, but his own health in the pursuit. Why should you go back to them now? Why not rather send them to the dogs, and try to recover the wealth that they have robbed you of? If you will go and travel in Siberia, I will leave German, Law, Latin and all, and go with you, and take care of you, and see that you don't speak a word of politics or receive a letter or a newspaper for the next two years. And then I believe you would be as well as any man on this earth.

But this after all is, I suppose, of no use, and though I am wholly in earnest in it, you will not care to read it. For the interest which you show on my account, I am exceedingly obliged to you. This is not an easy language and progress is slow, but I believe it is sure. I write exercises in it with much perseverance and read as much as I can, but the vocabulary is large and not easily acquired. I do not know Mr Abthorp,[2] and rather avoid making his acquaintance, on the same principle that I act upon in gradually withdrawing myself from all American acquaintances, Gov. Wright included. I have however sent your message to Mr Abthorp through a young man named Hall, who is, (after the fashion of his family which you probably know,) studying theology, and whom I see every day.

I received a letter from my father a short time ago dated the 25th November. He will not come to Europe and I suppose is fully determined to break himself down with work. The news from home is not great. Gov. Seward's speeches seem to have horrified the respectable old Courier and it's two hundred supporters, to an incredible degree, and certainly they are bold and straightforward. Here, I am in the midst of Americans of all political stripes, but on the first of January mean to leave my present rooms and bury myself in a very distant part of the city where no American ever sets his foot. Berlin and its climate are becoming rather tiresome to me, and in the Spring I mean to leave it and wander far and wide over Europe, or rather over Germany, for I shall not get into Italy or France. I should not object to leave the civilized world entirely and I repeat my offer to you to go to Siberia. The climate, it is said, is remarkably fine and some of the scenery must be superb. I have got several thousand miles away from home orders, and might be in Tartary before my family knew I had left Berlin. That would be a journey worth making.

I hardly dare to ask you to write to me again and let me know how you advance, but I feel so much interest in it that I hope you will from month to month send me a five-minutes note. Meanwhile,

I am Yrs &c   Henry Brooks Adams.

MS: MH
1. On May 22, 1856, two days after Sumner delivered his speech "The Crime Against Kansas" in which he denounced Sen. Andrew P. Butler, he was assaulted at his Senate desk and beaten senseless with a cane by Butler's kinsman Rep. Preston S. Brooks of South Carolina. Sumner was absent from the Senate because of his injuries until Dec. 5, 1859.
2. Robert East Apthorp (1811–1882) of Boston, Harvard LL.B. '43.

To Charles Francis Adams, Jr.

No. 3.   Berlin. January. 18. 1859.

My dear fellow.

Don't crow too quick about the pleasures and pains of life. To prove to you that I am not inclined to change my position, I will merely remark that I should decline for the present any offer of increasing my allowance, if any such offer were made. The deficit must be made up if, or when, it comes, but that is all. I received a short enclosure from the Governor on this subject in a letter dated the 13th Dec. He says that he means to send a hundred pounds more, after New Years, and his concluding passage was incomprehensible to me till I received your last. He says "On the general subject" (that of money affairs) "I shall have some ideas to suggest hereafter, which may have the effect of arranging the affair more satisfactorily." Meanwhile he seems to think that I'm "putting up with privations of all kinds," and he's right too, but I'm happy and what's the odds. All the privations I see won't hurt me, except going without a good breakfast in the morning and having to run to school so fast that I can't enjoy my cigar.[1]

It's rather a good joke that you should blame *me* for not acknowledging what I've received, when to this minute I don't know how many of my letters have reached home. If you'd put off your reproaches till my next letter to you arrived (dat. Dec. 18) you would have received the whole list. Also the directions about newspapers, all of which I have received, that you've sent, but want no more except in case something remarkable happens. I'm exceedingly obliged to you for both your letters and papers. You are altogether the most valuable correspondent I have, and I can tell you, I always gloat over your letters and do them the especial honor of reading them twice; a distinction granted to no others, except perhaps the Governor's—when they come.

Your news too I acknowledge. Bear my greetings to the hub of creation and its society. If any remarkably attractive young woman who is marriageable and has a large property at her own disposal, enquires after me, give her my love. Perhaps you might induce her to enter into a correspondence which may produce the best results. My own female friends haven't, so far as my present information extends, put their affection for me to so great a test as to show it by letter, and so far as I know, there are very few whom I should think would shine in such a demonstration. So much the better. I wish nothing more than to be wholly forgotten by them all.

Your new set are strangers to me. Miss Crowninshield I never spoke to; Susy Amory I knew very little. Georgy Blake, however, I did know, and rather wonder how the devil she has managed to break down the wall of exclusiveness. For my sake treat her tenderly. Add, too, in your next, if convenient, who my successor is with the fair Caroline.[2] I have vacated the place by her side which I held with some obstinacy for two or three years, and now I am curious to know what new Telemachus that truly innocent Syren has caught, for indeed I'll do her the justice to say that she is as innocent a Syren as ever was growed, and never fished for anyone while I knew her.[3] I wish she had. In that case there'd have been more life and spirit in the acquaintanceship.

If there's any message that I ought to send to any one, just be kind enough to make it for me. I give you carte-blanche to say what you will to everyone, and will acknowledge any speech or message that you put into my mouth short of an offer of marriage.

I watch American politics with much interest, and feel disgraced when a German asks about them. By Jove, it is humiliating to have to acknowledge the condition of our statesmanship. I am often ashamed to be known as an American here. Sumner can't return and won't resign, I'm afraid. I received a letter from him and wrote one to him, hinting that I wished and hoped that he would give up all idea of returning until he was really recovered, and rather resign his seat than return to relapse again. I wrote as delicately as I knew how, but of course I could not help implying a wish that he would resign. He has not answered it as yet. Perhaps not received it; perhaps he will not write again though I asked him to.

But how of greater literary works? Could I write a history, do you think, or a novel, or anything that would be likely to make it worth while for me to try? This too is not adapted to me, and yet, rather queerly, this is the only one of the branches of your idea, that has struck me as practicable. I don't know whether you had it in your mind or not when you wrote, but it seems probable that the duty of editing our grandfather's works and writing his life, may fall on one of us, and if it does, that alone is enough for a man, and enough to shape his whole course. I don't think this occurred to you, however, and it is too far off to found any plausible argument on.

Now, my dear fellow, my mind may be pretty but it's not original and never will be, and I shall never get any good out of it if I allow it to sprinkle all its little vigor away in newspapers and magazines. Adams the scholar prefers to live, but Adams the scholar would rather disconsolately die, and let Adams the lawyer do as he can, than make one of that butterfly party which New Yorkers seem to consider their literary world. To become more, the law must be my ladder; without it, you might as well at once press me out into so many pages of the Atlantic Monthly.

My dear fellow, we must make some income; that is necessary. To do it by literature is less to my taste than to do it by law. Behind the law, and with it as a support to fall back on if necessary, I can do as every other man in the same circumstances has done. Without some firm footing we shall go to the devil. With it, God knows what we may be able to do. I hold still by my plan. I hope that you will not succeed in shaking it, for then I shall lose myself entirely, and there will be an end to me. In it I see an object worth fighting for, and one to which I am trying to direct all my resources. Without it I lose my whole life and gain nothing. Stick by the law. Ten years hence we will see how things look, and use our best weapons; not now.

Meanwhile, nevertheless, I acknowledge gratefully your offer to negotiate for me about any article I may care to write. It has occurred to me that as I am here at school, it would not be impossible to write an article on the Prussian schools, which, if thrown into a sufficiantly conversational form, and hashed up with an intermixture of my own personal experiences, might be made as they say, at once readable and instructive. There is no hurry about this, however. I shall remain three months here, and you can give me your opinion of this plan in your next. You see, the subject, as I would treat it, offers a pretty wide surface for anything that I should care to say, whether political, metaphysical, educational, practical, or any other "-cal." If you like the plan pray give me any ideas developing it that happen to come into your head, and I will send you my own to criticise.

I have no more to say just now till receipt of your next. If we don't find out what we want in life, why the devil must be in it, that's all. Meanwhile I wish you or John would either marry or be given in marriage, as it isn't respectable to remain so long single. How much money has John's new "geliebte" got, and why can't he make a good thing of it? It's time he'd finished all this sort of thing and left the little innocents to younger hands. For my own part, I'd almost like to marry a German Markis and live here the rest of my life; not in Berlin, damn it, but round about in spots.

I shall write to Mary as soon as I have time, so I hope she won't be impatient. As I am a school-boy again I am not responsible for delays. By-the-by, I've not given you my reasons wholly for becoming a school-boy and changing my plans again. Never mind! If you find fault I'll justify myself in my next letter. I shall expect to hear in my next whether I shall send you any books or not. They are very cheap here and sometimes very good.

Yrs &c   H.

MS: MHi
1. In order to learn German, HA had enrolled in the Friedrichs-Wilhelm-Werdesches gymnasium.
2. Caroline Bigelow (b. 1840), daughter of Judge George Tyler Bigelow and Anna Smith Miller Bigelow of Quincy.
3. The allusion is to Fénelon's *Télémaque* (1699), not to Homer's *Odyssey*.

To Charles Sumner

Berlin. January 28. 1859.

My Dear Sir

I received your very kind letter the day before yesterday, and should have answered it the same day, but I have now so much to occupy me now that I could not get time. In answer to your kind interest in my progress, I can assure you that though it hardly satisfies me, still it is I believe as fair as anyone else's, and I have given up worrying about it. Your proposition that I should go into a family is superseded by a step which I took at Mr Abthorp's suggestion and with his assistance, at the beginning of this month. You will probably be surprised to hear that I am writing this letter in a public school. If it is occasionally a little disconnected, attribute it to the boys who are continually interrupting me, or the master whom I have to dodge, for I suppose he would object to my writing letters in school hours. A short time ago, perhaps fifteen minutes, I was surrounded by about twenty boys, and as their ideas of America seem to be so perversely wrong, I have given up trying to correct them and amuse myself by giving them original and somewhat astounding ideas of my own. Indeed I expect that in a short time they will really believe that I am an Indian with two squaws and corresponding papooses and live at home in a wigwam adorned with scalps. You may imagine accordingly that I hear and talk enough German, and need to take no more doses of it. I am in school every day from three to six hours, and generally have to come at eight o'clock in the morning. Yesterday I translated into German a page of Xenophon, before the class, and today in Caesar. There are nearly fifty boys in my room, and all very friendly and talkative.

Monday. Jan. 30. On Friday the master was restless and I could not continue my letter. I couldn't carry it home for I left all my books at school in order to go "ohne Gepäck" to a concert and thence to hear the Freischütz.[1] Saturday I was detained in my room by a foot which threatened to be seriously sore; and so I have not been able to conclude. I believe however I have said enough about myself to satisfy you of my probable progress. I am reading Ovid and Kugler's History of Painting, for my own pleasure; and generally am passing a useful and very pleasant winter.[2]

Called on the Abthorp's last night, and sat some three hours, it was so pleasant. Mr Abthorp inquired whether I had heard from you and I gave him your salutation. He made many inquiries about your course of treatment &c &c, none of which I could answer, but told him all that your last letter said. They are a good deal troubled at having this week received letters which speak of a severe attack of illness, which Theodore Parker has suffered, bleeding at the lungs, which will compel him to leave his pulpit and pass a year or two abroad.[3] Probably he will never be able to resume all his labors again. I have received this last week letters from my father, mother and brother John, but mostly on private matters and Boston gossip. There seems to be very little going on either in public or in private life of much interest.

My sister is in Paris, address No 9 Rue d'Isly, I think. I send and receive letters once in awhile, but we have neither of us much to say except to give notice that we are still alive. She writes so voluminously to her mother that I don't expect her to write much to me. In February or March I believe she goes to Italy.

Other news I have little. Life here is very quiet. I have not been near Governor Wright for some time, though he was kind enough wholly unasked, to get me and the Mather's an interview with Humboldt.[4] My duties now however are a fair excuse for my absence.

I am exceedingly glad to hear so good news of your own condition, and no one would be more rejoiced than I to see you back in your seat as soon as possible, provided only that you are well enough to be there. But rather than have you go back too soon, I would prefer that you should leave the Senate altogether. I think your health of more importance than any services or any triumphs which your presence in the Senate could produce either for the party or for your own reputation. The place that you occupy in the Senate is to me a very secondary thing, but the place which is yours in the State and the Nation, everything.

What I say on this point, however, is of course wholly out of my own head, and perhaps influenced too much by personal feelings towards yourself, and by my own rather peculiar ideas about American politics and their present condition and value. Of course I don't hope that they should make any impression on you, but still can't help speaking them notwithstanding. If you choose to consider them merely as the immature ideas of a boy, I certainly will not undertake to say that they are not so; but can only hope that the immature ideas of January 1859 may not be the historical facts of January 1860.

This letter is filled with all sorts of errors, but I hope you will overlook them in consideration of the place where, and the other conditions under which I have written it. I hope that you will not forget the existence of us Berliners, and if not before, will at least when you return to Paris write again to let us know your course.

My Greek recitation begins and I must bid you farewell.

I remain Yrs most respectfully   Henry Brooks Adams.

MS: MH
    1. Opera (1820) by Karl Maria von Weber (1786–1826).
    2. Franz Theodor Kugler (1808–1858), *Handbook of the History of Painting* (1837; English tr., 1842).
    3. Theodore Parker (1810–1860), Unitarian minister, radical Transcendentalist, and abolitionist leader.
    4. Alexander von Humboldt (1769–1859), German naturalist and explorer, a member of the Prussian court at Berlin since 1827 as tutor, privy councillor, and chamberlain.

To Charles Francis Adams, Jr.

No. 4.   Berlin. February. 9. 1859.

Dear Charles

I will pay your last letter the compliment to say that it had effect enough over me to make me feel unpleasantly for two days. Not that I found fault with it. I do not do so, and hope that you will continue to write just so. But it bothered me damnably. For what you say as to my remarks on the Boston young ladies, though your criticisms are rather hard on me, I acknowledge that you are wholly in the right. What one writes is considerably influenced by the accidental state of his mind at the instant of writing, and it is not strange if, among so many letters, when I am hurrying to put down the first thing that comes into my head, and fill out a sentence as quickly as possible, it is not strange, I say, if I say many silly things. Your remark about care in writing what the Gov. is to see, surprised me much more than your criticisms, for possessing as I do a mens conscia recti,[1] I would be perfectly willing to have him see all my thought in reference to my country and believe he would approve them all. If he has expressed unfavorable opinions I wonder that his letters say nothing about them. They, on the contrary, have been very kind and mild, and his last, on finances, the contents of which you seemed to know, was even very liberal, so that I have not a single word to say against his mode of treating me. It is true I shall do my best to make no use of this liberality but am none the less obliged to him, on that account. It is a satisfaction to feel that I *can* spend, and have an ample margin.

What you say about next winter's arrangements I have already heard from mamma. She writes that it's not to be mentioned till next summer but seems to consider the division in just the same way as you. I was surprised to hear of the Melodeon purchase.[2] I know nothing of the size or arrangement of the estate but should think it might be a first-rate thing. Of course I have requested the Gov. to take charge of mine.

Money matters are now very easy with me. I have about six hundred dollars on hand, counting the Gov. late remittance as only five hundred; and this here is equal to eight hundred. I owe not a cent except to you and Hill. This latter I should like to see off my hands, and I'd pay him myself devilish quick if he were here, but as I can't do that nor get the money to him, I'm afraid that I shall have to ask you to see to him. For God's sake, though, don't do it if it will inconvenience you. I feel now that I am perfectly well in condition to pay him myself if I could only send the money, but it is so small a sum that it is hardly worth while to send it by the Baring's.[3]

You surprise me by your admiration of Miss Louisa C.[4] I do not take to her, but perhaps it was an old prejudice that I got when I acted with her two years ago. Society however I will leave for a sheet to John which I shall send with this.

In politics you can judge better than I, but I myself believe that Douglass will win.[5] He is playing a devilish hard game; in fact he is repeating in the nation the operation which was so successful in his own state. We shall see.

About myself I have hardly anything to say beyond what I have said in my last letters. I cannot say that my present life is wildly exciting, nor that the capital of Prussia has as yet shown itself to me in any violently attractive light. But at least if I have not had an exciting time, I have at all events not had an unpleasant one, and if the last month has been particularly quiet, there is at least the satisfaction of knowing that it has been a particularly instructive one. My school is perfectly satisfactory, and I am better satisfied of the wisdom of this step than of anything else I have done. I go a good deal to the Opera, which is a great temptation; to the Theatres not so often for the playing is almost poor and the plays, except when Schiller, Goethe, or Shakespeare is produced, not much. I've not been on a real bat for ever-so-long, being in a very quiet and economical set, and though often indulging after the theatre in a steak and glass of beer or bottle of Rhine wine, this never leads to anything worse. As I have to get up six mornings in the week at either seven or eight o'clock, I have also to go to bed early and not drink too much. I'm virtuous as St. Antony and resist temptation with the strength of a martyr. I've not been to a disrespectable ball for a month or nearly a month, but can't say how long this will last. The way the virtue of the purest is corrupted here is wonderful.

You can imagine that my school lessons don't take up much of my time out of school, though the poor little devils of boys have to work all the time. The master inquires if I can recite, and I say yes or no as it happens. My German is slowly advancing under this pressure, but I must say that I never expect to master it as I once expected. It is terribly long and tedious and my advance can be measured not by days but by months. I read very little German, for most of my time for reading is occupied by my Latin. It may seem to you that this sort of life is not exactly what we usually connect with our ideas of life in Europe, but my experience and observation to the slight extent of four months, goes to show that the American idea of life in Europe, as given by such men as Gus Perkins, the Hammonds, &c &c &c is a damned absurd one and just worthy of them. I've not seen Paris yet but it's my impression that to a sensible person who has no particular object in staying there and is not in French society, it's just as slow as any other city, and except in its Galleries and Palaces, no better than New York. Indeed I've heard sensible fellows who had lived in both places, assert that in its means of enjoyment New York was ahead of any city in Europe that they had seen. I don't undertake to endorse this, but it shows how differently people think on this point, and for my own part I never feel thoroughly jolly anywhere till my whole time is employed.

Lately, it is true I've been rather more out of my room in the evenings than usually, but I hope not to do so much of this after this week. Consult John's sheet for information as to my sights and dissipations.

I will now proceed, my amiable brother, to discuss the last philosophical propositions of yours, and the plan which you propose for my course in life. I confess that it filled me with wonder and general bewilderment. I think in my last I said that you paid me a left-handed compliment, in your idea of my mind. Permit me to retract; humbly apologize. I never made so great a mistake in all my life. I have usually considered myself a conceited fellow. Every one told me so, and I believed 'em. I *had* thought that I set about as high a price on my mental capacities as most other people; perhaps a peg higher. I was mistaken; I've put it's market value up at least twice as high again since your last.

Were you intoxicated when you wrote that I am to "combine in myself the qualities of Seward, Greely, and Everett"?[6] Mein lieber Gott, what do you take me for? Donnerwetter! do you suppose that I'm a statesman like Seward or that my amiable play-philosophy would ever set me up to guiding a nation; do you imagine that I have a tithe of Greely's vigor, originality and enterprise; are you so blinded by the tenderness of your fraternal affection as to imagine that the mantel of Cicero has fallen upon my shoulders, or that I inherit the pride and ample pinion that the Grecian sophist bore? Nimmermehr! What would be the result if I were to return home and gravely and coolly set myself to doing what you propose? Bah! mine brother, you seem to have written under the idea that I am a genius. Give that idea up, once and forever! I never did anything that I should be treated like this. I know what I can do, and I know what a devilish short way my tether goes, and the evening before I received your letter, I had, in my daily lesson in Ovid, read the fable of Phaethon, whose interesting and suggestive story you'll find at the end of the 1st and beginning of the 2d Book of Metamorphoses.[7]

Now a word as to my own condition, and then for our discussion. You know by my last that I have joined a Gymnasium, like our Latin School, only much larger and thorougher. Here I go every day from three to six hours. It is not very good fun; that is of course. But it admirably answers my purposes. Here I pursue my original design of studying Latin and Greek. Here is tremendous practice in hearing and talking and learning German. Here it is very cheap. Here I am free enough and yet must obey the rules where they are not excepted in my favor. I go four mornings in the week at eight o'clock. Three afternoons there is no school and the others are no trouble to me. The boys received me with open arms, and my proceeding caused some noise in Berlin, for every one of the four hundred and odd told it at home, and I became quite famous. One or two of the little fellows I am quite fond of, and you would split if you could see me walking away from school with a small boy under each arm, to whom I have to bend down to talk to. None of them know English, so of course I speak only German, and am familiar enough with it to get along very well. I am stared at as a sort of wild beast by the rest of the school, who only see me when I come and go, for there is no recess, and no outdoor playing, so that I know only the boys in my own room. As yet I only see the boys at school, where they treat me with a certain sort of respect, and yet as one of themselves. They never push me or trouble me in any way, nor play tricks on me. Perhaps they think that I know how to box, and it's as well to let me alone, but anyway they are many of them firstrate fellows, and two especially I cherish with paternal affection. I've not as yet recited in Latin or Greek, but soon shall begin; to translate, that is, into German. I *can* study all the time, or not at all, but I *must* go to school, and that is study enough to satisfy my conscience.

I am also busied during my leisure odd minutes or hours in studying art, and reading and studying theoretically painting. Music occupies me too, during certain hours every week, and more than these certain ones, if there is any that I wish to hear. So you see that I have enough work (or play-work if you prefer to call it so) to occupy me all my time. I seldom do nothing. In my new rooms I seldom see Americans, but know very few Germans indeed. In short I am busy, contented, and only once in a while cross.

Steady application like this implies a harder blow-out than usual when it does come. As for "life" as it is called, it's all humbug. But once in a while one must go on a bat to clear his head, and I can tell you, after a fortnight of school, a fellow feels very willing to kick off the fetters. I very seldom do anything out of the way, and have had only one really hard spree since I came here. This was last Saturday night, at what claimed to be a masked-ball, but if I recollect right, it was to the sober part of the audience, a very dark and dismal failure. I had a pretty high time there, and it took me all the next day to recover. The worst of a bat in Europe is that women are always in it, and a mere drunk is almost unknown. There is an abundance of means of raising the devil, and use one, you must use the other.

So the world wags on here, quietly as possible. The weather is detestable. Formerly it was always bad. For a month we didn't see the sun. Now we have one fine day, and two bad ones. It grows cold and clears, then thaws and clouds up. Still, when one passes nearly all his daytime in school, it doesn't matter much what the weather is.

In money matters I have to be very careful, and this month have rather overstepped my bound as I have bought several expensive books, but I hope to need no more money from home till the first of March, and unless next summer ruins me, I shall get through. It isn't pleasant to have to calculate every cent one spends, but independence is a great thing, and I shall do my best to hold to it. I keep my accounts most rigidly; have no debts except my monthly accounts with my landlady; and always know where I am. As I have always had to be very careful, it is not so hard now. I economize as much as I can, but sometimes can't resist spending too much.

And now as to the last part of your letter, over which I have thought a good deal, and been a little troubled. I acknowledge the force of what you say, and yet I disagree with your conclusions. Let me proceed systematically if possible.

You try to put me on the horns of a dilemma. You attribute to me a certain kind of mind, and argue that if I am to be a lawyer, or in other words, follow my own plan which I have followed for several years, then what I learn in Europe is worse than thrown away. Hence, to be a lawyer I must cease to be what I am. If I acknowledge that my mind is not adapted to my plan, I must give my plan up. If on the other hand I assert that my mind *is* adapted to my plan, I must give Europe up. This I take to be the ground of your letter. I disagree with it, and think that you are mistaken not only in your judgment of my mind, but also in your idea of the necessary result of two years in Europe. But I shall not go into this subject now. Perhaps in another letter I may give you some reasons for believing that what I am learning here in Europe is not in opposition to what I propose to do hereafter. Just now I prefer to attack your position rather than to defend my own. It's easier and there's more fun in it.

I don't deny the truth of what you say, that law is not a pleasant study, and that we are not adapted to make great lawyers. But beyond this I think you lose yourself and run aground. You say that I am not made for a lawyer; but hardly hint at what I am made for. The same things that you say of me, you also apply to yourself. Now let me see if I can carry out your idea to any result that will give a fellow a minute's firm footing.

The law is bad, you say. Wohlan! what then? Why then, you continue, take something that suits you better. And what would be likely to suit me better? What is this kind of mind that you give me? I must say that you pay me a very left-handed kind of compliment in your estimation of me. You seem to think that I'm adapted to nothing but the sugar-plums of intellect and had better not try to digest anything stronger. You would make me a sort of George Curtis or Ik. Marvel, better or worse; a writer of popular sketches in Magazines; a lecturer before Lyceums and College societies; a dabbler in metaphysics, poetry and art; than which I would rather die, for if it has come to that, alas! verily, as you say, mediocrity has fallen on the name of Adams.[8]

But, I suppose, you will deny that your letter leads to this and assert that such men as Mr Everett, Mr Sumner, the Governor, Mr Palfrey and the like, are a wholly different class.[9] I would just suggest that all these began either as lawyers or clergymen; and I merely propose to do the same. But now let's go back to generalities, and see whether something can't be fished up.

In the most general terms then; you would say, I take it, that my mind if not adapted to law, at least *is* adapted to literary pursuits, in the most extensive meaning of the term; and to nothing else. I couldn't be a physician or a merchant, or a shop-keeper or anything of that kind, so well as I could a lawyer. Literary pursuits are very extensive, but I *must* make some money to support me, so we must say, "literary pursuits that produce money." Now literary pursuits that produce money and that I am eligible for, are very few.

To begin with, perhaps, if I were a better man, I might feel inclined to become a clergyman. But as I'm very much a worser man, we'll count that out.

Then you once proposed to me to go into the newspaper line and become an editor. The objections to this are as many and as strong as to law, but if you don't see them, we'll reserve the subject for further discussion.

Of Atlantic Monthly and Putnam and Harper and the men who write for money in them, my opinion is short. Rather than do nothing but that, or make that an object in life, I'd die here in Europe.

No, mein Liebster, this is one of those propositions which would kill any man's chances in America, even though he had all the training of Gorgias (if that was the beggar's name), and all the philosophy of Frank Bacon; (I refer to the Viscount Verulam and not to the young Bostonian of the same name).[10] Yet after all, your idea is not so very distinct from mine, except that it throws out into the strongest relief the object that I proposed to make dependent on circumstances and success in other respects. We are considerably in the same box, brother mine, and what applies to me, applies also, with slight alterations, to yourself. As you say, there are differences between us, and my character isn't your's; in fact, I know many respects in which I wish it were; but still we have grown up in the same school and have, until now, drawn our mental nutriment from the breasts, metaphorically speaking, of the same wet-nurse; indeed we may consider ourselves a case of modern Romulus and Remus, only omitting their murderous propensities. What is still more, we are beautifully adapted to work together; that is, *you* are. I stand in continual need of some one to kick me, and you use cow-hides for that purpose. So much the better. Continue to do so. In other words, I need you. Whether there's any corresponding necessity on your side, is your affair. But it's a case of "versteht sich" that we can work better together than apart. Under these circumstances, let us be very careful how we take a step that will probably knock one of us in the head forever, or so separate us that our objects would become different. I shall hesitate a very long time indeed before I decide to earn my living by writing for magazines and newspapers, for I believe it to be one of the most dangerous beginnings that a man can make. Recollect that thread-bare old Arabian Nights magnetic mountain *that drew all the metal out of the ships* and then sunk them.

I say that our ideas are not far different. The real difference is this. Your's begins by assuming as your ground plank and corner stone that I am capable of teaching the people and of becoming a light to the nations. Mine on the contrary begins by leaving that to develop itself in the future or to remain proved on the other side, without suffering a public disgrace from slumping as I infallibly should do under your idea. I said in my last what I wanted of the law; that I considered it the best grounding in the world for anything that we wish or are likely to do; that it is the strongest point to fall back upon and the best position to advance from; at once offensive and defensive; it gives one a position as literary as if he did nothing but write for periodicals and a good deal more respectable; as a profession it offers many inducements; as merely an occupation it offers still more, and there is much more chance both for you and me to work *up* from it, than there is doubt in my mind that I at least should drop like a stuck monkey from the perch on which you want me to place myself. Perhaps it is my wish and hope that we may do something of the sort you propose, but I do not wish for so large a scale of action, because I know my own weakness; I do not wish to go to work in the way you propose, because in the first place I believe it to be a wrong way, tending to fritter away the little power of steady and long-continued exertion I have, and in the second, it seems to me not to offer that firm and lasting ground-work that the law does. I do wish to adhere to my original plan because, though even that is more, I am afraid, than my powers are up to, yet it seems to me as feasible as any that has yet come before me, and if I can do nothing in that, why let me go to the devil at once, for there's no use staying here. Gott bewahr mich from funny Lyceum lectures and rainbow articles in Atlantic Monthlys with a proof of scholarship as exhibited by a line here and there from "the charming old Epicurean Horace" or the "grand thunderbursts of superhuman strength" from God knows what old Greek trotted out for the occasion. If I was born to be the admiration of girls and Tupperian philosophers, I'll cheat fate and quietly do nothing all my life.[11]

So here I will lay aside this subject and wait for your next. As this letter has been written partly in school, partly here, and is the work of some six or eight different sittings, I'll excuse you for finding fault with it, as with my former one, but you must also excuse the faults. On your theory of my proper plan of life, however, I ought never to say any foolish things but my lips should drool wisdom and my paths should be by the side of Socrates, and Isocrates; (by the way were these two men related and why have they so similar names). I hope your next will take a more practical view of life.

Meanwhile this last week I've been exceedingly dissipated; out every night in one way or another, and able to do very little real work. The last two days too, the weather has been charming. Yesterday Jim Higginson and I took Mr Abthorp out on a spree.[12] He has had us there to dine and gave us some of the best champagne I ever tasted; perhaps the very best; I've dined twice with him and got talking very fast both times. The ladies retired to their room and left us to our wine, and as Mr A doesn't stint the supply and I make it a rule never to refuse a good glass when it's offered, the inevitable consequence is very clear. A bottle of wine is the outside of what I can carry, and in both cases I drank devilish close onto the limit. Yesterday we returned the hospitality by taking Mr A. out for a day of it, to show him the style of our ordinary life. Higginson and I went for him at two o'clock and carried him off to our dirty little restauration, and there dined him and gave him a glass of beer. You know the style of our dinners from my letters, I think. Then we went to a concert till six, and leaving the concert before it was over, we walked down to a little theatre called Wallner's, a devil of a way off, and saw a drama called "Berlin wie es weint und lacht";[13] a thing very popular in Berlin, and has run 137 nights. It's by far the best drama of the sort that I've seen, too. Thence we walked back and sat till twelve o'clock in a Wine-cellar, or Wein-Stube as they call it, which was crowded with exceedingly respectable old people but which, though very clean, yet hasn't the vestige of a table-cloth on ary a table, and was hot as hell and filled with clouds of tobacco smoke. Here we eat and drank and talked and Hig and I smoked, and passed a very jolly evening, drinking two bottles and a half of Rhine wine, really better than I've often tasted at home, for which two bottles and a half we paid something less than an American dollar. This is a dear place for wines too. On the Rhine, I am told, they cost much less. I very often come in here after the theatre and drink a bottle, commonly with Higginson, or if I'm on the heavy cheap, go to a cellar and get a couple of boiled sausages and a mug of beer. The sausages I tell you are good. My supper commonly costs quarter of a dollar or less. My dinner the same. As for cigars, I consider myself extravagant when I smoke really good ones which cost me $15.00 the thousand. They're not proud like yours, but curse me if they dont taste as good as any I used to pay at the rate of $50 & 60 for.

So I will now wind up this letter, which though not so long as yours, has yet the excuse that I've more letters to write than you. I will now proceed immediately, as you say, to put on my paint and feathers (devilish dirty paint in the shape of my old dress suit) for a grand ball in the Opera House, at which I suppose all the Court will be, and which I shall try to tell about in my letter to John. I go from a sense of duty though it costs me three thalers and I'd rather stay at home, but one ought to see these things and I presume it will be handsome and stupid as double-distilled damnation. I don't know anyone except Americans there, and if I did, it wouldn't make any difference. Meanwhile, allerhöchstgeborner Herr, accept the assurances of my deep respect. If I knew enough of this cursed language I'd write you a letter in German, but I don't and never shall, curse it.

Give the tokens of my highest consideration to the family at large. My last letter home was Feb 5th to mamma; before that, Jan. 29th to the Congress man. No letters as yet received this week.

Yrs.   H.B.

MS: MHi

1. *Mens conscia recti:* good conscience.
2. A reference to CFA's investment in a Boston lecture and concert hall.
3. The London banking firm of Baring Brothers.
4. Louisa Crowninshield (b. 1842), daughter of Francis Boardman Crowninshield and Sarah Putnam Crowninshield.
5. Stephen A. Douglas (1813–1861) was reelected to the Senate in 1859 by the Illinois legislature despite Lincoln's apparent success in their popular debates of 1858. He was clearly running for the Democratic presidential nomination.
6. Horace Greeley (1811–1872), founder and editor of the New York *Tribune,* was a popular sage. Edward Everett (1794–1865), professor at Harvard, congressman, governor, minister to England, president of Harvard, and senator, was known for his eloquence; he married Charlotte Gray Brooks and was HA's uncle.
7. Phaethon, son of Helios, persuaded his father to let him drive the chariot of the sun; but losing control of the horses, he scorched the earth till he was stopped by Zeus's thunderbolt.
8. George William Curtis (1824–1892), writer of travel books and familiar essays in *Putnam's* and other popular magazines. "Ik Marvel," Donald Grant Mitchell (1822–1908), *Reveries of a Bachelor* (1850).
9. John Gorham Palfrey (1796–1881), Unitarian minister, professor at Harvard, editor of the *North American Review* 1836–1842; *History of New England* (1858–1875).
10. Gorgias (c. 483–c. 376 B.C.), Greek sophist and rhetorician, central figure in Plato's dialogue of that name; Francis Bacon (1561–1626), 1st Baron Verulam and Viscount St. Albans; Francis Edward Bacon (1836–1909).
11. Martin Farquhar Tupper (1810–1889), whose *Proverbial Philosophy* (1838, in verse) made his name a synonym for commonplace.
12. James Jackson Higginson (1836–1911) of Boston, Harvard '57.
13. *Berlin . . . lacht:* Berlin, How It Cries and Laughs.

To Charles Francis Adams, Jr.

Berlin. 13. March. 1859.

My dear fellow

Yours of the 14th came to hand on the day I expected, just after I had sent off a letter to mamma. I received a letter from mamma on the 24th and one from papa on the 21st. I sent an answer to papa's on the 23d, and to mama's on the 2d. Papa's letter contained as I expected from what you said before, indications of trouble, which were expressed in a manner that irritated me a good deal, and I sat down on the spot and wrote rather an impertinent reply, which may settle the question or may only make him angry, I don't know which. I hope an end will be put to all this stuff. I'm doing my best to do well here God knows, and it's excessively unpleasant to be told without any why or wherefore that I'm becoming a damned fool. Your warnings and advice I've taken readily, and been very glad to take, but you don't deal in enigmas. What the deuce does the Gov. mean by a perfectly Delphian Vaticination in his last, from which all that I could understand was that some one, (of the Abthorps I suppose) had been abusing me, and I'd better be careful? Confound it, a fellow must know a little more than this before he can work straight. Understand, I don't want to be told that I'm a good boy and deserve a sugar-plum in the shape of encourage-ment, but I do want to know the why and wherefore of things in a sensible manner.

I'm glad that you approve my Gymnasium course, and still think myself that it's the best thing I could have done. You estimate the effect of school too highly however. It has enabled me to give method and concentration to my studies, but I have found here that it is impossible to go back ten years in one's life, or graft on to one system the growth of a very different one. I am a man among boys here. They sit on my knee and pull my whiskers and ride on my back and listen to my marvellous tales of home, and yet know five times as much as I do on many things. I too cannot feel their rewards or punishments, nor study except what I please. The mill in which they are placed is forming their minds, but my mind is already formed in a very dif-ferent way, and the process has very little influence on me. However if it teaches me a little German I'll thank God and be satisfied.

Mary Quincy's behavior has astonished and not much pleased every one here. *She* is supposed to have had more sense. For your news of the brave Philo and the fair Caroline, I was prepared through John, mamma and Hollis. By Jupiter, it would give me extreme pleasure to write a congratula-tory letter if she were engaged to him.[1] I don't know how I should ever dare meet his "mother-in-law Mrs Judge Bigelow" again. Hollis is at the soft Catarina, is he? So! After all, I almost wish he'd marry her. She'd suit him very well, I think, and I guess she wouldn't refuse him. I am now patient under the want of woman's society, but I tell you, I'd give something for it.

These are all the points of news you mention, and as I am gradually get-ting out of the circle and feel the want of it, this society tattle becomes pleasanter. Before the two years are over I expect to be an old fogy and all the girls that I knew, married.

My life here in Berlin is in no way changed. I cannot stagnate simply be-cause new ideas are pouring into my mind so fast that I have always some-thing to think of. My only trouble is want of time, and I economize in it as much as I care to. School every day; more or less music; opera or concert every week; study in the evening; or sometimes a call or a blow-out of some sort, which occasionally keeps me up very late. I'm anything but dissipated. Indeed the little tendency I ever had that way has almost wholly disap-peared. I can't say that life is unpleasant, and it isn't certainly exciting, but I hope that I'm learning something, and am waiting patiently till the time comes for me to go down to Dresden. Nothing would tempt me to remain in Berlin later than May, if I could get away.

It seems probable that we shall have war next summer, but no one knows except Napoleon and he won't tell. His behavior is very strange and con-tradictory. His latest declarations look towards peace, but very soon war will be inevitable unless he declares himself plainly and honestly. All Eu-rope except Italy is against it, and yet every one says that all Europe will take part in it; probably France, Russia and Sardinia against Austria, England and the German Confederacy. Italy is in a confoundedly hard position it is true, and so far as Austria is concerned I'd like to see that nation wiped out, but the good that war may possibly do to the Italians is almost sure to be more than counterbalanced by the evil it will do the the Germans.

War however will not change my plans. It isn't probable that any Austrian will shoot me in the valleys of the Tyrol, nor that any Frenchman will chase me up to the top of Mont Blanc. Italy will be the seat of war, and I doubt if the Tyrol feels it at least in the first campaign. However, after all, it seems to me contrary to reason to suppose that Napoleon is going to do so crazy a thing. Every one here is so perplexed; the papers so full of contradictory rumors; all nations arming; ambassadors rushing from Court to Court in hot haste; Stocks rising and falling at every breath; and no one knowing anything about the matter except Napoleon himself; that no fair and cool judgment can be made. We must wait and see, but meanwhile I shall do as I intended. If they chase me I'll run to Turkey like Charles the 12th.[2]

For our discussion I have little more to say. Our ideas are really not very widely separated, and if I didn't feel my own weakness so much, I might perhaps try to change a very little. But I am tired of trying to direct what I have no power over. It's been a great consolation to me to know that these things will work themselves out for us, and that they will come right of their own accord if they come right at all. I shall stick to my present course, which up to a certain point is identical with your plan. When that point comes, I'll be ready to decide.

You have already come to the point and must either decide or leave time to unravel the twist. Even a decision will not necessarily settle the matter if it's against your tastes and wishes. For my own part I feel as certain that I never shall be a lawyer, as you are that I'm not fit for it. If you are cut out for one, why go in, and God help you. I believe myself however that you'll not get far, and I hope you'll not stay long. Yet what else to do just now, I have no idea, unless you beguile the time which your absent clients leave you, by the pursuits of writing, &c which you recommend to me.

As for the family papers I know only one thing; that it is not in *me* to do them justice. I am actually becoming afraid to look at the future, and feel only utterly weak about it. This is no new feeling; it only increases as the dangers come nearer.

I am collecting materials to write an article on the schools. How soon I can do it, or whether I can do it so as to satisfy myself at all, I can't say. I shall adopt the first person in it, and write just as I always did and do. It will interfere somewhat with my studies, but six weeks I hope will change my present arrangement and Dresden will give me more time.

This warm weather and a glimpse or two of clear sky lately, are so extraordinary that it almost makes me homesick, for it seems as if there was no fine weather in Berlin. For nearly five months I have seen very little but clouds, or rather a dead dull sandy sky, and dark, rainy or damp days. The thermometer has only twice fallen below thirty since I've been here. I hardly ever wear a great coat, day or night, yet have never had so little trouble from colds or sickness. The Americans are beginning to leave Berlin. A number went down to Vienna this last week. Nick Anderson goes in a fortnight to Dresden and in June to England probably, to meet his father. Crowninshield leaves Hannover and we expect him here very soon, to abide with us a few weeks before also going to Dresden.

I received yesterday mamma's letter of February 17th and also the March No. of the Atlantic. The Hunnewell's ball seems to have been a great affair. I'd like to have been there. Here I've been to nothing of the sort for a long time, except to a student's ball one evening, where however I refused to do anything but look on. If the girls here would dress better it would be a great improvement.

Now that my time's nearly up at my school, only three weeks more to run before the examinations, I am beginning to find myself in rather a disagreeable position there. Within the last two or three days I have seen indications, very slight, to be sure, but still awkward for me, that the masters don't like me. My own master behaves with the most perfect regularity, and they are all very polite, but naturally they find it very hard to know how to treat me. Tomorrow evening I am to call on Schwarz, the Ordinarius of my Class, to get some information from him about the schools (of course I've said nothing to any one about writing of them) and I mean to find out what the difficulty is. Of course, you know, if I find I am giving trouble, I shall withdraw at once, and perhaps now that my three months are nearly over, it will be as good a thing as remaining, for, you see, by doing this in a polite manner, I can get some claim on Schwarz's gratitude, and make him a friend instead of a master. Now, I want to visit several of the schools here, and also to obtain a large amount of information that I should perhaps not be able to get except through him. So, if I find tomorrow evening that my suspicions are right, I shall strike while the iron's hot and do my best to turn the trouble to my advantage. On the other hand, if I am mistaken, and have imagined all this, I shall hold on at the school, which really is quite pleasant, till the term's over and try to get what I want gradually. More than the three months I cannot remain, for many reasons, a part of which you will see of course in what I said at first about the general result of the experiment. But more directly than that is the fact that after the warm weather sets in I should not dare go there. It would give me the typhus fever or something horrible in a fortnight. You've no idea what a vile hole it is in this respect. So soon therefore as I can get things wound up here, I shall go on to Dresden, taking my same course of study with me.

I was at the Legation last evening talking with Gov. Wright, returned Californians, young medical students &c &c. I see that my visit to Humboldt has got into the papers as I supposed it would, confound 'em. Nick was also at the Legation. He leaves Berlin on the 24th not to return. We expect Crowninshield very soon; perhaps this evening but he may not come for a week. I hear that Billy Howe is at Vienna, Secretary of Legation, I was told.[3] It is possible if I feel rich, I may go down the Danube to Vienna before going into the Tyrol in July or August. If so I shall look for William.

Give my fondest attachments to everyone in Boston and as I suppose by this time one of you has secured Miss Fanny C. just kiss her on account of her distant brother-in-law.[4] Confound you, why doesn't one of you marry. I believe there's nothing particular to be sent, except my particular affection to Miss Eugenia and Miss Caroline, in which latter you can include Philo and also his future mother-in-law, whom by the way I ought some day to write a letter to, for she asked me to do so, and I've never sent the first word to any of them. Trot out the good advice in your next letter, for I'm expecting in the course of about two months a series of siserraras[5] from the paternal hand.

Yrs &c &c   H.

MS: MHi

1. Philo Shelton, probably of Quincy, classified by ABA among the least sober of her son's acquaintances (to HA Oct.5). Caroline Bigelow married George W. Amory in 1870.

2. Charles XII (1682–1718) of Sweden, after his army's surrender to the Russians, took refuge in Turkey 1709–1714.

3. William Edward Howe (d. 1875), of Lawrence, Mass., Harvard LL.B. '53.

4. Fanny Cadwallader Crowninshield (1839–1911), daughter of George Caspar and Harriet Sears Crowninshield.

5. *Siseraras:* violent scoldings.

To Charles Francis Adams, Jr.

Berlin. 6. April. 1859.

Verily, my beloved Brother, thy last gave me pleasure. Thy wit is well-favored though coarse withal, and i' good faith pleases me. For my own part I imagine that my letters for the last few months can hardly have caused much delight, inasmuch as they have neither been written in good spirits nor always in good temper. I received at the same time with your last, one from the head of the family in answer to a particularly cross effusion of mine. The paternal rejoinder was good-natured though with a not unhappy strain of sarcasm; which for a person of his time of life was really not so bad. You know the usual run of the article in elderly individuals. We can only gently pity the weakness and forget it. I answered the letter (omitting the satire) in a dignified manner and hope it will rest there. Really these liberties must be discouraged. We can not allow Congressmen to address us in this familiar way.

Thy own letter, mine Brother, needs an answer in extenso. Our discussion I will let drop. The truth seems to be that your idea is on a large scale and mine on a smaller one. I'm drifting that way and have been all my life. On the other hand you've struck on a snag, but I'm in hopes the Governor's political life will give you something to think of and to do. My path is clear to me for five years yet, and I think, for any number of years.

As for your "hitting me," though one is softer in this damned atmosphere than anywhere else, yet I don't beg off. Hit away my boy as hard as you please and if you're always as right as you were in that matter, I'll stick it out. We're all mortal and all liable to feel cross and blue; especially when one doesn't see a clear sky or a bracing atmosphere more than three days in six months. So peg away as much as you like. I'm expecting a sisserara all round from home in consequence of my last letters, but as I'm a good way off I shall bear it philosophically. There *is* a comfort in getting a blow-up a month old. Independence is a mighty pleasure.

I tell you what, young man, Boston's a little place, but damn me if it isn't preferable to this cursed hole. I don't think I've ever heard more promiscuous swearing than I have from all sorts of fellows within these three months about this sort of life. Such a cussin and a dammin from religious individuals, such a consumption of steaks and Pisporter of evenings to raise one's spirits, such an amount of study from disgust at everything else, is unparalleled in history. Society! Good God, a man might as well try to get into the society of the twelve Apostles as any society worth having here. They're as proud as damnation and as mean as this vile climate. I never saw a flirtation going on, though they've got some jolly places for it. I've no idea where the balls are, that is the fashionable balls, for their palaces aren't any too good for one, and the private lodgings utterly incompetent. The aristocracy all belong to Court and hate everything that smells of America. They seem to have no hospitality, as we do, and as for "making a house one's home," no one but a Prince of the Blood dares to invite any one to dinner. I really believe that there is no society in Germany that would give me any great pleasure, it seems to be so different from all I ever met before. The idea of every one's living in suite's of rooms; cursed holes that at home no man with two hundred and fifty dollars a year would be willing to look at. Then this keeping mistresses is all very well, but from what I've seen of it, I'd rather have one respectably bright girl to talk to if she was as ugly as my German shoes.

Now my good youth, don't air your sarcasm on me for running into extremes in this way. The truth is I've pent up my wrath till I'm tired, and now that I'm on the point of leaving Berlin for six months, I'll just abuse it as much as I damn please. Not that it's worse than other places. Paris is just as bad if I can believe dozens of different fellow's reports. Dresden is infinitely worse and Hannover just ten times worse. Munich may be better but I don't believe it; and so with Wien. But I've eaten German dishes till I'm nearly run to pieces. I've lived in this air till I'm all used up. I've studied the damned language till I'm utterly lost in it, and finally despair of ever becoming a German. For the last fortnight I've been afraid to eat any more of their vile compounds, and have lived on a beefsteak a day. My pleasantest reading has been Cicero de Officiis and V. Rönne, das preussische Schulwesen; my only polite society the Apthorps; my greatest amusement Sinfonie Concerts, Mozart's Operas and Rhine wine, and now, by God, I'm going.[1] So, there you have it summed up nice.

I'm in a jolly good humor tonight, or I should calumniate this city. But as it is, I am rather lenient towards it. I only say, the world is wide; manners are different; and German customs don't suit my ideas. It's got brutally played out. Fellows who can live on music or art or women are all very well here. I've done as well as I could at all three. The two first are good. The last is a damned humbug. But I need something more yet, even if Law is thrown into the bargain.

By jingo, your balls, your canvass-backs (they never saw a decent supper here) your girls, your dancing is tantalization. Of course I don't want to be back, but I'd like deuced well to drop in on you one evening. You blasé dog! Just come to Europe and if you don't get into good trim to appreciate society, then this 'ere child must be rather out of the way. Well, well, well! We can't have all that we want. I'd give fifty thalers for a real piece of roast mutton and caper sauce, and a talk and a walz with a pretty girl. Oh! the wasteful vilyan that I was in old times to go to a ball and be cross. Verily now could I dance like the agile roe-buck and talk words softer than the down of the eider-duck. Which is a rhyme though not meant. Haven't I been staring all the afternoon at a pretty girl across the concert room! And didn't she give the shyest glances back! And *wasn't* her ma a watchin of me! Well you had better believe. No use though. I never shall know her unless I can grind her.

I don't mean to say that I haven't had a good deal of pleasure here and on the whole a good time. But how I have prayed for spring. It's all very well to talk German philosophy with Sauren and drink Pisporter with Higginson, but it gets a little played out in six months I can tell you.[2] So you can retain your "hitting" on this point, for I know just what you can say, and can say it myself. If you could see this damned city you'd appreciate my remarks better.

You ask my plans for the summer. They're not formed yet further than I've described in my last letters home. Cuss me if I don't have a good time though, somehow. One thing is determined. I leave this city on the 12th April. Higginson wants to go off to Weimar for a few days and as my school is up now, I may as well go with him. Thence to Dresden. Aint I glad, though the weather is no better than it was last November, December, January, February and March.

My article or articles on the schools is going on to an enormous length. At Weimar and Dresden I'm going to rewrite it and throw it into the form of letters; three or four; but I long ago gave up any idea of printing them; I write only to keep my hand in, and for future use, after I get home. Don't suppose that this is affectation on my part, and that I want to be urged. I merely don't care to write for publication now.

Crowninshield is pottering round here without apparently any object, and also Cabot.[3] Ben talks unendingly about Hannover which if I hadn't seen it, I should imagine from his account to be a sort of a sixteenth Heaven. He hates it bad though; much worse than I do Berlin. Joe Bradlee is perfectly happy there with his music and the young Unger.[4] I'm a philosopher, and eat beef-steaks, the only things, actually and truly, that are cooked here so that any nutriment remains in them. My God, I wish I could make you eat "erbsen, sauer-kohl and pökelfleisch" or "kartoffelnklos" and if you didn't blaspheme I'm mistaken.

April. 9. I must finish this letter quick and trot it off for I've some six more to write. Received mamma's last, of 22d March. Also an Atlantic Monthly. Also a letter from my classmate Homans which I shall answer as soon as possible.[5]

I'm now busy in packing and taking leave, and as it is always well to provide for contingencies, I will just notify you that in a large box which Higginson and I leave at Anhalt & Wagener's, filled with books &c, is a package addressed to you. In case I should come a Frank Howe game, you must take care that that package does come to you and to no one else, for it contains my journal for five years, and some of my own letters, yours, John's, Hunnewell's &c &c &c. There is also a short letter of directions in it. This providing for unpleasant contingencies seems queer, but can't be helped. I'm sure one has warnings enough that he set his house in order, from the way that fellows drop off.

You needn't show the first part of this letter to the parients nor tell them how I blow up. The great difficulties here are really only three; one that the weather is so bad; the second that the city and country is so flat and unpleasant; the last that one cannot get nutritious and healthy food. Otherwise the place is pleasant and attractive.

You can however tell the congressman that I have just come in from a P.P.C.[6] visit to Baron V. Rönne. He gave me a card of admittance to a debate of the Landtag a little while ago, for which I wished to thank him. He was exceedingly kind. He and I had a quite long conversation, extending over a number of subjects, from the schools, in which I am interested, to the war which he says will surely come though Prussia wants bad to dodge it. Such is fate. Among other things he invited me to call on him at Bonn if I was there, and advises me next winter to be presented at Court. The Baron looks dreadfully unwell but I sincerely hope I shall find him here next winter for he might be of great assistance. I shall call on him at Bonn where I shall be for some time in the fall.

I've bid good bye to my school, the semestre of which ends the day I am to leave Berlin. The boys have always been very polite to me, and I've had not a shade of trouble with any one, scholar or master. It has taught me a good deal, but the two chief things are 1st to understand what is said; 2d to talk with confidence, and not to think I mustn't speak because I can't speak like a German. Lord, you ought now to hear me coolly wind myself up in German conversation. The people laugh, but they understand. At Dresden I am going into a family to try that experiment. The arrangement is all made and my trunks go right on while I stop a day or two round in spots; Wittenberg, Leipsic, Weimar &c &c.

Don't imagine because I blow up at Berlin that it's so intolerable as all that. The truth is I've had a great deal of low-spirits here, and am only now getting really the better of them permanently I hope. (Don't think I've got the pox or am in love; neither is true). Still the winter as I look back on it has been by no means so bad, though I'm devilish glad it's over. At all events it's changed my ideas and course of life immensely. But one of your balls would have been a God-send to me any time last month.

You have my Dresden address. H. G. Bassenge &Co. How long I shall stay there I've no idea; perhaps a month; perhaps two. Puchta and the Institutes and Cicero will satisfy my cravings for literature.[7] You don't know Puchta. Well, he's a cussed old jurist.

Fondest attachment to everyone. I'm in such a devil of a stew this evening that I hardly know what's what. By Jove it's a nuisance to break up an establishment.

Yrs.   H.

MS: MHi
  1. Cicero, "On Moral Obligations." Ludwig von Rönne (1804–1891), "The Prussian School System"; HA presumably refers to von Rönne's *Das Unterrichts-Wesen des Preussischen Staates* (1855).
  2. George Wales Soren (1833–1911) of Roxbury, Mass., Harvard '54, LL.B. '58.
  3. Louis Cabot (1837–1914) of Brookline, Mass., Harvard '58.
  4. Josiah Bradlee (1838–1902) of Boston, Harvard '58.
  5. John Homans (1836–1903) of Boston, Harvard '58, M.D. '62.
  6. *Pour prendre congé:* leave-taking.
  7. Georg Friedrich Puchta (1798–1846), *Cursus der Institutionen* (1841–1847), a textbook on Justinian's *Institutes*.

To Charles Francis Adams, Jr.

Dresden. April. 22. 1859.

My Dear Fellow

Your letter of the 3d arrived to-day. I owe three to the family; one to mamma which I'm afraid must go unanswered except for what you can read for the common benefit in this; one to John, which I shall enclose with this; and one to you. Taking your letter through in order, in the first place if it's all right about the paternal "hints" and my "explosions," I'm contented and let it remain so. In the second, Hill's bill ought to be $50.00, not $63.14. If you haven't paid him yet, you'll find the right bill among the papers I left with you. If you have paid it, it's no matter. Anyway I'm exceedingly obliged to you. You find fault with my wishing that you may not remain long in the law, and if your three alternatives are right, I acknowledge I'm wrong. I wrote however under the idea that there were other branches of development open to you. Society I'll leave for John. Yet I will say incidentally that I agree with you in your ideas about your position in it, and I wouldn't be sorry to see one or both of you married. It strikes me though from my look-out place on this side the Atlantic that we've not been hunting in the best field for wives. I believe that there are better preserves for this article than Papanti's Hall. There's a Miss Agassiz or two whom I've heard a good deal about, out here. I wish you'd try to find out what their weight is generally, and report. I'm getting to distrust myself about young women, from my six months want of practice, and to feel as if I were counted out of society and never should reappear in it. There's a younger set even than I, now coming on; great God where will you be if I'm antiquated two winters hence! I'm not sorry that John's off the Bowditch connection, but I don't know any woman in Boston society who would do much better by him. He'll need an awful powerful team to keep him straight and make him work. If you want to travel, my dear fellow, do drop these damned watering places and go off to the Rocky mountains. That would pay well.

"This house to let" at Mrs Ben Adams's, is it? That must make John feel queer. I fancy that some of his hardest experiences have been in connection with that house, and it must be rather a mournful old graveyard to him.

I know nothing about public and newspaper matters with you. Sickles's trial I had not heard a whisper about.[1] I hope he'll hang though. Whoever told you that an Atlantic voyage salts a letter, never said a truer thing. It gives a most rare and delicate flavor, and you never made a greater mistake if you imagine that your letters don't repay the trouble they give. If all your effusions are read by the public with as much interest as your letters are by me, you'll be a devilish lucky fellow.

Your letter needs so much answering. On the other hand I shall have no difficulty in filling up my sheets this time, for I've been off on a lark and I've more than enough to say.

Well! Gott' sei Dank, I've seen the last of Berlin for a considerable time, and here I am in the good city of Dresden among the Saxons, and also a heap of Americans to all of whom except two or three I've shown and shall show a very cold shoulder. On the 12th, at seven o'clock in the morning I left Berlin in company with Crowninshield, Higginson, and Mr Apthorp with his wife, mother-in-law and small son Willy, who went along with us so far as Wittenburg to perform a pilgrimage to the shades of Luther and partly to bid us adieu. Never mind the particulars. Wittenberg is a dirty, stupid little place, and one's elevated sensations turn into extreme weariness after a couple of hours in it. Mr Apthorp's crowd here turned back, and we, after two hours of slightly stupid waiting at the little depot, took tickets on to Halle. To Halle we should have gone, if some restless devil hadn't inspired us with an admiration for the appearance of Dessau from the car-window, and induced us at forty seconds warning to step out of the car and sacrifice our tickets to Halle. As we had no baggage except our carpet-bags, shawl-strap-contents and travelling pouches, this was easy. The inhabitants of the charmingly neat little Dessau however, who don't see a stranger more than once in a life-time, must have been somewhat bewildered at seeing our procession march through their silent streets. For throughout our trip we insisted on carrying our own baggage and were usually accompanied to and from the hotels by from two to six large men who seemed to think we were mad-men over whom it was their part to exercise a careful surveillance. We used to try all sorts of experiments on them to see what their ideas were; stopping short to see if they also would stop too; walking fast; walking slow; but they never left us at any price. I suppose in Germany no gentleman carries his own carpet-bag. Luckily there were enough of us not to care whether they did it or not.

So we landed at Dessau and rambled round the town till we found a hotel. Never mind Dessau however. I'm not going to copy Murray nor Baedeker, the German Murray, which we always carry. It's a nice, funny little Pumpernickel. Read Fitzboodle for the best idea of these one-horse principalities.[2] We left it the next morning in the same order of march, and went on to Weimar, which is much such another, only they bore you to death there with Goethe and Schiller. Vide Murray for sights, all of which we saw, the funniest sight however being ourselves. Here unexpectedly John Bancroft joined us, as he was removing from Dresden to Düsseldorf.[3] He was a great addition to our party. Modest, equable, good-natured and both able and cultivated, he is a remarkably pleasant companion, and as he talks better German than any of us, was usually our spokesman. We never put up at the best hotels if there was a cheaper one, and I can tell you, if it isn't always so comfortable, it is in the long run a great deal pleasanter. If you were as tired of great hotels as I am, you'd see why this is so, and why I, exclusive of money considerations, prefer to sacrifice a little comfort and get a little something new. We travelled cheaply sometimes, but when we chose we spent as much as we liked. It wasn't much though.

The next day we went on to Eisenach (my plans of work at Weimar were knocked in the head). Eisenach is delightful. The old Wartburg above it is covered with romance and with history until it's as rich as a wedding-cake. The walks and views are charming and I would willingly have remained two or three days, but the next morning we packed every shred of extra-baggage off to Dresden; made a grand immolation of our beavers (except Higginson who clung to his with a love that was more than love, and left it with the baggage master, "to be called for") and taking an open carriage rode through a heavy rain down to Waltershausen, a little place south of Gotha, where we proposed to begin—what! Why a walk in April through the Thuringian Wood.

We carried only our great coats and Ben and I a night-shirt. A toothbrush in one pocket; some collars in another, and some handkerchiefs in a third. I strapped the coat over my shoulders with a shawl strap; the others tied theirs a la militair. We never wore them while walking and though mine is very thick and heavy I never felt it disagreeably. We started from

Waltershausen that afternoon and walked some three hours, stopping once only to drink a glass of beer and smoke a cigar. The scenery was very pretty and, perhaps three centuries ago, wild. The sky reasonably clear, and the weather cool so that we were not too warm. That night we arrived at a little place called Georgenthal when we got a jolly supper and slept in two most romantically large, rickety, cold and ghostly chambers, with the wind outside blowing like fits and creaking the dismal old sign in the most pleasing manner. Up the next morning at about eight and had a delectable breakfast of which honey was the great delicacy, and I never before appreciated how good honey was. Set out under the care of a man who pretended he would guide us through the woods, but he was consummately stupid and we soon found ourselves on the highroad again. So we dismissed the guide and pegged ahead through heavy snow showers which we didn't mind in the least, stopping once at a little dorf where we had a glass of beer and smoked a cigar and Bancroft sketched a dog. Beer is a first-rate thing to walk on and we marched along for an hour up a charming valley with a clear sky and the best of spirits. Crowninshield and Higginson were geese enough to tire themselves by running up a tremendous hill on time, against bets of a bottle of wine, which they won and which like other bets we made, haven't been paid. By and by we began to get deuced tired. The road wound up and up and up and it seemed as if it would never end. We first got into mud, then into slush, then into snow two inches deep, and at last I for one was pretty much used up, and the others not much better. Oberhof appeared however after a tramp of near five hours; a little village perched on the top of the hills, where it was yet dead winter with more snow than I'd seen for a year. It snowed heavily all the afternoon, and as I declared I walked for pleasure and not to get over ground, and wouldn't stir another step that day, Higginson who urged going ahead, was forced to give in and we passed the afternoon as well as we could, finishing by a round talk and a couple of bowls of a compound known as Glühwein; claret punch, hot, with spices and things. The next morning we set off again at eight o'clock in a snow-storm, with from two to eight inches snow on the ground, over a mountainous country. You may think this wasn't much fun, and indeed I believe I was the only one who really enjoyed it, but the glow, the feeling of adventure and the novelty; above all, the freedom and semi-wildness after six months in Berlin, made it really delightful to me. I haven't felt so well and fresh for ever-so-long. After two hours we reached the Schmücke, a couple of houses on the other side of the hills, and here, sir, we indulged ourselves in a real American tipple. We procured the materials and under Ben Crowninshield's skilful direction, we brewed ourselves a real ten-horse-power Tom and Jerry, which had a perfectly miraculous effect on our spirits and set Ben to walking down that hill with the speed of a locomotive. Bancroft and I took it more gently and fell behind. The day cleared; the snow gradually disappeared as we descended and we got to Ilmenau to dinner at about two o'clock. Rode on in an open wagon from Ilmenau two hours to Konigsee through mostly uninteresting country, and at Königsee slept. The next morning, in the most curious manner and without previous concert we all caved in and agreed nem. con.[4] to ride the remaining day's journey. So we did ride it, wiling away the time in an intellectual and highly instructive series of free fights to keep us warm, which commonly ended in a grand state of deshabille all round. The scenery was pretty; one view quite charming, but the day was mostly cloudy and cold and for my part I was so exhausted with fighting and laughing that I hardly cared for anything. We dined at Rudolstadt, the Capital of the little Principality of Schwarzenburg-Rudolstadt or something of the sort. It had as usual an enormous palace, and the Prince I believe is as poor as a rat. Hence we pressed on, hiring a lumbering old travelling-wagon, and after six hours of going up interminable hills and going down interminable hills, we jolted down by the statue of old Wieland into little Weimar and put up zum goldnen Adler as before.[5] So our journey was over. It had been made wholly without plan. None of us knew six hours ahead what we were going to do. It was jolly as could be and the fellows were all pleasant and indifferent to everything except what was pleasant, so that we had a jovial time. Still I did not object to getting through with it. We none of us cared to lose more time. Düsseldorf and drawing were calling Bancroft. Bonn and the Pandects were yawning for Higginson. Dresden and Puchta shouting for me and whatever Ben's plans are, it was time he should begin some application in earnest. So we were not sorry to find ourselves in Weimar again.

So with the exception of a few hours stay in Leipzig, here I am comfortably settled in Dresden, thanks to Higginson who got me my room. Bancroft is already in Düsseldorf. Higginson sets out in a day or two for Bonn. Ben is here seeking a family but I doubt if he gets what he wants. Anderson is here, but unless he changes his set, he'll not see me much. Many other Americans are here, but if possible I shall not go near them. A Mr Stockton is Consul and does the hospitalities, but except under compulsion I shall not go within a mile of him.[6] I mean to leave Arthur Dexter's letter on his brother if he's here, though I don't expect that it will do me much good. Until I get tired, there's no need of seeking this society which, I imagine is confined to the Americans and English whose name is legion.

Puchta arrives on Monday, by which time I hope all my arrears will be done up and I shall set to work to try and make something out of old Herr Justinian's Institutions, which it is quite time I was at. Dresden is a pretty place with much more attractive points than Berlin; as good a theatre and the best Gallery north of the Alps. It's shut now but reopens again soon, when I shall go and learn it by heart. Weather of course bad as usual; the worst ever known, say the Germans. But as yet I don't mind that and have got plenty to do even though in this Holy week every place of amusement is closed and not even a concert to be heard, thanks to their idiot of a King's being Catholic. The change of residence has done me good and I feel better in every way than I did in that damned hole of a Berlin.

So you may count on my remaining here for two months and I imagine that they'll be pleasant ones, although after my Berlin experience I've become confoundedly sceptical about all places, unless there's some absorbing mental application. It's delightful to live a little while in a new city but when the fun is exhausted, it gets played out.

I've received a letter from Loo at Rome in fits about the Dying Gladiator.[7] What she means to do this summer I've no idea. I wrote to her that if she'd settle anywhere in Switzerland I'd bring my books down and walk with her husband. This blasted war which will probably break out within a week if they're not at it already, knocks the Tyrol in the head. Then there will also probably be fighting on the Rhine so that God only knows where a fellow can go, except to Norway, which indeed I would like to visit. Extras are out tonight which indicate that the Austrian troops are preparing to cross the Rubicon, and then all Europe's ablaze: Austria, Prussia, Bavaria, Hannover and Saxony to say nothing of the various other "Bundesgenossen"[8] who contribute ten men and a drummer apiece to the "Reichsarmee."

You'll be out in the country when this reaches you, and can philosophize in peace over it there. But I recommend you if you mean to travel, to do it first in America. You speak of astonishing the relatives, I suppose by trotting off somewhere, but it don't pay to come to Europe and rush over it, and that's just what does pay at home. Go out into the wilds, boy; pass a month round among the Mormons and then come back with a clear head and a little practical knowledge. I don't know how Loo can stand her travels and be in raptures still at everything. I get so bored by all these sights that I only want to get out of their way. A gallery ought to be visited once a week an hour each time, to really enjoy it; otherwise one loses his power of appreciation.

I've abbreviated very much the account of my trip, but it's long enough, and as this letter is mostly about travel it will do for a bulletin, especially as my last was also to you from Berlin. No time to write since. If you see any of my old young lady friends who yet remember me, tell them that I'm alive and hope some time in the dim distance to see them again even though married and settled.

Yrs Affecly   H.

MS: MHi
1. Newspapers throughout the country were covering the sensational trial of Daniel Edgar Sickles (1825–1914), Democratic congressman from New York, for the murder of his wife's lover, Philip Barton Key, son of Francis Scott Key.
2. "Kalbsbraten-Pumpernickel," a fictional German principality visited by Fitz-Boodle, the narrator and central character of Thackeray's *The Fitz-Boodle Papers* (1853).
3. John Chandler Bancroft (1835–1901), Harvard '54, son of George Bancroft the historian, was studying painting.
4. *Nem. con.* (*nemine contradicente*): no one contradicting.
5. At the Golden Eagle Inn.
6. Philip Augustus Stockton (1802–1876).
7. Now referred to as the *Dying Gaul*, in the Capitoline Museum, Rome.
8. Confederates or allies.

To Charles Francis Adams, Jr.

Dresden. May. 15–17. 1859.

My dear Charles

I suppose by this time you've received my letters all square. I've answered everyone of yours most religiously; one arrived April 1st, and was answered April. 10th. Another received April 22d, was answered April 25th with John's. The present one arrived two days ago.

I wish I could write as long as you, and I admire your last exceedingly. You've made a first-rate letter out of common-place materials. But the truth is, though I have probably a thousand things to your one to say, I get so tired of writing them that it comes hard. However I'll do my worst and let her go.

I'm exceedingly obliged to you about Hill's matter, though he's recovered an excellent interest out of the debt in the shape of $13.17 which were wrongly charged and which I made him correct in the original draft. God knows when the time will come when I shall pay you your account. It doesn't look much like it now, though I'm living very quietly, not to say economically and this is not a dear place. I can't imagine what my expenses will be for the year, and am afraid to make a guess when I think of the three months of travel this summer. However I hope the Melodeon may be a perfect California to you and that you will make money to your heart's content. The Governor's last letter to me was a business one, containing a statement of my property which, owing to his liberality in valuing the premium stocks as at par, makes a good round $10.000 and some few hundred over. My first step if I were at home would be to make over to you the odd cash which would just meet that debt, but as it is I believe I'd better let it wait till my return unless you feel in need of it.

As for home matters, I'm sorry mama's so down in the mouth. Lord bless my soul, why is it that we miserable human beings can't enjoy earth without being afraid of Hell! Her letters are cheerful enough and I hadn't supposed she was so badly treed as you say. Society is I suppose now a tale of the past and we'll let it depart. As for Miss Carry, I thought I could guess pretty well how far you'd get. I've trotted over that course a good many times, my boy, and hope I never shall be bothered by doing it again. For God's sake give up horses. You've had the devil's own luck, and will surely get your head knocked open again some day, worse than it was that other time.

For my school-article, I've already written to you about my change of plan. It's now finished in the form of two letters, about the same length, very poorly written and excessively stupid. Don't imagine I'm modest. If you ever see them you'll appreciate that my remarks are not at all unjust. At present they are lying in my trunk, and are likely to remain undisturbed until when years are over, I shall have occasion perhaps to use them. They are now in a wholly unpublishable state, and of no use except as a series of notes and references.[1] The last Atlantic was remarkably good. I passed a whole rainy morning reading it, and my laughter over parts of the Review of Wilson's Mexico aroused the Fräuleins in the next room to the belief that my reason was yielding.[2]

These are the chief points of your letter. I suppose you'll scold me for not writing a good school-article but confound me if I could. I never was a wit and am thoroughly satisfied that I never shall be a genius. Blow you, why don't you write articles yourself if you like it so much? Do you suppose I can do the cursed things here of all places? Bother the thing.

In other words, I'm really obliged to you for your offers but, as I felt here just as soon as I began to write, I can't do anything to satisfy myself or any-one else, and as I have here a very positive objection to making myself uncomfortable, I think I shall let the matter remain in its "trunk-ated" state.

I feel precious little like working very hard here, I can tell you. With the exception of a few pages of Roman law every day, I don't do much labor, unless you call long walks on fine afternoons, and talking nonsense with the Fräuleins labor. This place is a most decided improvement on Berlin and my position here is much pleasanter in every way. In the first place I'm far enough along in the language to be able to feel at my ease among the peo-ple. Then it's summer and we occasionally have a real American day. Then the country round Dresden is delightful. In fifteen minutes one can walk out on any side to very pretty scenery and get a glass of bier in thousands of pretty little restaurations. Then I'm in a family and don't feel lonely. And finally and perhaps the greatest reason of all, it's still new and I haven't yet got tired of it.

You think I suppose of course that one must be happy as pie under such circumstances, and I confess that I do enjoy myself exceedingly and can imagine that it will be tough to come home into an amiable lawyer's-office. But the deuce of it all is that one gets so used to it, and doesn't at all appre-ciate his position. It's only when I think of you and your daily routine and your necessary confinement in Boston that I feel the contrast and see in what a deuced pleasant place my lines have fallen. Still, the longer I re-main here and the more I wander about, the firmer my conviction is that old Milton was right when he talked about the mind's being its own place &c, &c & sich.[3] I believe I enjoyed myself just as much at home as I do here, though of course there were times when it was infernally slow. The differ-ence is that the whole ground is changed. My pleasures and my troubles are all different from what they were at home, and I shall have really to get home and at work before I shall appreciate how much I really have enjoyed myself here.

Society with you is over. With me it is just begun. Perhaps too ended at the same time. Last Wednesday, one of the brothers of my establishment, a

Lieutenant, was married and I was invited to the feast. So at five o'clock I came to my room and costumed myself in that same old dress coat which has seen so many experiences on both sides of the ocean; and then taking one of those nondescript one-horse carryalls which are known through Germany as droschkes, I rode over the bridge and arrived at the Hotel known as the Stadt Wien, or Hotel de Vienne. Here I was shown up stairs and had taken off my coat and was calmly drawing on a pair of gloves, when the servant opened the folding-door and I was horrified at seeing before me an army of white dresses and sternly fixed countenances arranged in order, and all staring, gravely as if it were a funeral, at me as if I were the coffin. With that grace and suavity of manner for which I am famous, I marched up and stormed the phalanx by a series of bows. I did attempt one speech at a person whom I supposed to be the father of the bride, but he looked so alarmed and seemed so thoroughly overwhelmed with his white cravat, that I backed off and took to flight without an answer. Probably I should have remained smirking in the middle of the floor all the evening if I hadn't caught sight of one of my Fraüleins grinning at me. I bolted at her and began chattering nonsense fluently. Admired the bride's dress as in duty bound. She wore all white, as is necessary and a myrtle wreath on her head, fastening her veil and a bouquet of white flowers in her hand. The bridegroom who had just that day received his promotion as Ober-Lieutenant or 1st Lieutenant, was very polite to me, probably because I had presented to my four Fraüleins, his sisters, bouquets all round just before they set off to the church; a piece of extravagance which I had intended should cost me six dollars but which through a stupid blunder of the gardner who didn't understand my German and sent smaller bouquets than I ordered, only did cost one Am. dollar and a half. So here I esconced myself, behind the muslin, and talked idiocy till all the officers and guests had arrived. It is true I found myself alone among the female portion; all the males standing in a corner and talking together. However it wasn't my business. I did know some of the women and didn't know any of the men and they didn't seem to care to trouble me or make my acquaintance, so I didn't trouble them. At last a movement was visible. The alarmed old party in the white cravat paired off with a stiff old lady who had made a bow when I was presented to her. The officers bolted for their partners and I was notified to take the Fraülein Emmeline Strauss into the supper room the which I did. Here we were arranged at table as per diagram. I was placed in a seat which I imagine was not *the* seat of honor and had my partner on my right and a small boy on my left who eat[4] and drank largely and didn't answer my only observation to him. Other small boys opposite who drank too much and eat quite enough. Dinner began (seven o'clock) with soup; then meat, game, all sorts of German dishes, wine (sherry, claret and Rhine). I talked at intervals and the Lieutenant next my partner also talked largely and we had rather an amusing time, making a good deal of noise so that the papa came down and reproved Fraül. E. Strauss.

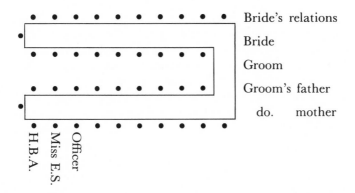

Presently after the first course one of the numerous officers arose and recited a piece of poetry which I couldn't understand very well and which he himself hadn't committed very well. However it passed and ended with a call for a grand "hoch" or hurra, so we all "hoched" and marched round and touched our glasses with the bride and bridegroom. Then another course, another speech, another "hoch" and drinking. And so on till the program was at last varied by quite a pretty ceremony. The sister and brother of the bride came up behind her and took off from her head the myrtle wreath, which only maidens can wear, replacing it with a simple little band of flowers, and at the same time the sister reciting another piece of poetry applicable to the occasion. This again ended with a "hoch" and more touching of glasses, and then another course. In the next interval one of the young ladies appeared as a market woman in costume, with a great basket strapped on her shoulders as the common women wear them here; and standing behind the bride she made her another poetical address producing from her basket the emblems of her household duties, such as a lot of eggs, flour, butter &c &c. I couldn't understand the poetry very well. It was none of it original, but as I was told made for the occasion by poets whose business it is and whose advertisements are to be seen in the papers.

After this the supper ended. The company left the room for a while, and when the tables had been removed we came back and the dancing began. We had had music on and off all the evening. As I was talking with one of the young ladies, the bridegroom came up and asked me if I wouldn't come and take a glass of wine, so I went with him into a smaller room which looked into the supper room and where most of the gentlemen were smoking and drinking. Not to be peculiar I also took a cigar and a glass of wine and made an effort to talk with one of the officers. The conversation naturally fell on the war, and I expressed a regret (which Lord knows I don't feel) that the Austrians should have let their two days start be lost by negotiations. My very modest remark was taken in such dudgeon that I dropped the whole affair and walked off into the dancing room where I took a turn or two in the polka. They dance very fairly here indeed, though I don't like it so well as our own style at home. So the evening passed in variations of dancing and cigar, but I confess that what with the fish &c at supper, I was fearfully and overpoweringly sleepy—towards twelve o'clock. It was all very quiet though. I didn't see any over-drinking as I'd expected. There was no noise nor indeed any very large amount of liveliness that I saw, and at about half after twelve (the married couple having disappeared) we separated and I conducted my large flock over the quiet old bridge in the moonlight, home; for the father is sick and had to retire early and I had the keys.

There may have been about forty or fifty people there. Almost all the men were Lieutenants. The women were as German women usually are, but dressed I think in less bad taste than the Berlinese. German women don't please me; at least those of this class, which is second or third rate. I've not met any of the nobles or first society and probably never shall, but these that I have met, all look too coarse complexioned and dowdy; remind me too much of their diet and want of soap and water. None that I've seen have any ideas beyond their households and little general information. They are good-natured and polite but evidently an American is not the thing here. America is much disliked now in Europe and no one will believe anything good of it. I never allow myself, or very seldom to get into a discussion on the subject for they are wholly incapable as a rule of understanding our ideas on these points. They live in another atmosphere.

This is a good place for engravings if you want me to get some for you. I myself have thoughts of being extravagant in this connection and I want you to do a small commission for me. I want you to go down to your engraving man, I forget his name, and ask him whether he has a good engraving of the Madonna di San Sisto, by Müller, and how much he charges for it.[5] You can also if you will, find out what he calls his best engravings of this picture and send me the engraver's names and prices annexed. I saw last winter at his store a number of these engravings and I want to find out whether the difference in price is enough to warrant my buying one here. Müller's engravings of this picture have the highest reputation here; so I wish you particularly to ask about the prices of the same man's works in Boston.

The world goes on here quietly enough. I know very few persons in this city, Ben Crowninshield being the only American I see much of. We walk together a good deal, if the weather suits, which happens about once a week. I wonder whether they ever have good weather in Europe. I've seen just four days, I think, really clear and bright straight through.

I remain in Dresden pretty certainly till the 1st July. Not having heard from Loo for ever-so-long, I sent off last week a laconical note to her which I think will bring an answer if she's received it. Of course I can't settle any plans till I hear from her and this cursed war, which has already reduced Austrian paper money 50 per cent, and makes me give nearly 5 per cent discount on my drafts on London, they say, though I've drawn none since the war began.

My God, my boy, what a bad affair that Sickles trial was. What cursed fool made that "Sunday morning" opening for the prosecution? How can the people act so like idiots as to treat such a man so? It horrifies these German idiots here and makes me damn mad, for I cant defend it.[6]

Yrs   H.B.A.

MS: MHi

1. His "Two Letters on a Prussian Gymnasium" remained in manuscript until they were printed in *AHR* 53 (Oct. 1947), 50–74.

2. A devastating review of Robert Anderson Wilson, *A New History of the Conquest of Mexico* (1859), in *Atlantic Monthly* 3 (April 1859), 518–525.

3. In *Paradise Lost* (I, 254–255), Satan says: "The mind is its own place, and in itself / Can make a Heav'n of Hell, a Hell of Heav'n."

4. *Eat:* past tense of "eat," pronounced "et," was still standard usage.

5. An engraving of Raphael's *Sistine Madonna,* in the Dresden Gallery, by Johann Friedrich von Müller (1782–1816).

6. The defense argued that Sickles was justified in killing the seducer of his wife by a "higher" law and that, justified or not, he was innocent by virtue of temporary insanity, an innovative defense in American jurisprudence. The opening of the prosecutor's summary for the jury, April 25, was in effect a sermon citing chapter and verse to prove that the Bible did not authorize the punishment of adultery with death. On his acquittal, April 26, Sickles was popularly acclaimed a hero.

To Charles Francis Adams, Jr.

Dresden. June. 7. 1859.

My Dear Charles

You're unlucky. You say in your last that you never took so little pleasure in going out to Quincy as this year. In your first letter from Boston last fall you said you had never been so sorry to leave Quincy as then. Get your mind into a right state again, boy, and forget the young woman and champagne. John I see will be a farmer yet. If he wishes, I'll write a series of "Farmer Letters from Europe" for his benefit, to tell how things are *not* done here. Take the stupidest way possible and you'll know how they *are.*

As you say, the chances of clearing off the old young ladies looks good. I don't want any of them, so don't ask 'em to stop on my account. I am grateful to you however for teaching the new shoots that there is such a person as I am, and trust that they'll remember me.

For the philosophy of your letter, I'm now in such a jovially pleasant and lazy condition that I can't for the life of me discuss it. Work is really out of the question. I've looked for Gibbon but can't find him.[1] Try again next winter in Berlin. Really now the weather is too fine, the country too pretty and the life too lazy to allow of energy.

Why, my boy, this life is regal. I don't recollect to have done a great deal since we began our fine weather, but I lounged lots.

Just this instant the Herr Secretär bolted into my room in his shirt sleeves with a telegram that the French had entered Milan. Luckily the Herr Secretär is himself no friend of Austria, and as I always affirm that "Frankreich und Oesterreich sind mir ganz einerlei"[2] I don't get into arguments. Still it's deuced hard to avoid cheering and kicking somebody's tail when the good news comes. For some time Ben and I tried to remain neutral but 't was no go, Sir. I thank God that as yet I've met no American in Dresden who doesn't side with Sardinia. In conversations with Germans I never mention the subject, not because I'm afraid of the police, for there is little danger of that here, but because it's a disagreeable subject. Just once though I'd like to open my mouth and express to assembled Saxony that I, H. B. Adams, consider them a pack of cowardly, stupid, idiots. Ben has once or twice let out his opinion roundly and quite eloquently, of course not in public nor to everybody, but quietly at home. His host is a republican as are very many people here, but they are all so scared about France that they've lost all presence of mind. Prussia alone keeps cool and knows what she's about. Ben and I have regular old hallelujerums together every night when a fresh battle's won. If Milan's taken, citadel and all, before July 1st I lose a dinner to him at Munich.

You mustn't complain if we talk a good deal about the war. It occupies a very large angle in our thoughts and talk here, and gives zest to our life.

I tell you what, old fellow, I begin to appreciate what the beauty of European life is. In Berlin I had no idea. This is considerably a different thing. The weather is somewhat ahead of everything yet. The city is full of strangers and occasionally a pretty face. One hears Russian on one side, French on the other, English everywhere, German occasionally and samples of every other tongue at intervals. From five o'clock in the afternoon till nine we are usually walking or at concerts. Sun doesn't set till after eight and I tell you, sir, that a sunset concert on the Brühlsche Terrasse at Dresden, sitting under the trees and smoking with a view down the Elbe at the sunset, and a view up the Elbe to the pine hills above, is something jolly. I don't deny it, Sir, I enjoy this life.

We have enough excursions planned to keep us going every day of a stay here. Last Sunday I walked out to a village named Kesselsdorf (where Napoleon fought; one of his greatest battle grounds is almost under my window.) with two of the Fräuleins and the father, to visit that couple whose marriage I described in one of my last letters. They are established there; a battery of artillery quartered on the town. We passed the morning here and dined with them, driving down to a Brewery in the afternoon and remaining here till sun-set. Just imagine a father and two young ladies and a German boarder setting out from Boston on foot at eight o'clock Sunday morning to walk to Quincy and visit a friend. This was a good two hours walk and none of us noticed it in the least, or felt tired after it. Indeed from eleven o'clock in the morning till I went to bed at night I was in a state of continual boozyness from repeated seidels (or töppfchens as they're called here) of bier which I had to drink and which quite opened my heart.

One afternoon Sauren (who is now gone) and I took the steamer and went up the Elbe to a famous fortress called the Königstein, to which, in case of war the King of this great land always packs off the Madonna and some other great pictures, the contents of what is known as the Grünes

Gewölbe³ including the Regalia, and finally his family and himself. I believe the various Royal Majesties have several times had opportunities to see their armies surrender, and yet had the satisfaction to know that there was no getting at their own royal persons. Neither Frederic the Great nor Napoleon could take this place. We didn't bother about the fortress, for which see Murray, but the river was deuced pretty and parts of what they call the Sachsen Switzerland were quite fine.

As for social position it's much as usual. The Fraüleins are well apparently and I am on the best of terms with them all. I strive with giant resolution to do the pretty, but don't effect much on that score. Luckily there's no danger of my affections being made away with, though I like the girls and try always to be polite.

As for sights and all that I've tried to see them but except the gallery it was rather a bore. Goodish collection of armor and weapons; best in the world I believe in some respects. Grünes Gewölbe, lot of old knick-knacks, precious stones and all that; decided bore. Palace, frescoes, rather good but no great. In short sight-seeing is an infernal nuisance and I now cut it down as short as possible.

My German is I believe really profiting by my stay here and has got on quite a step. It is poor enough, Lord knows, but it serves and improves. Ben and I talk it a good deal together and I've worked quite hard on it this last week, writing and committing it. However it's a beastly matter and I never expect to speak it really well. Such a hobbly, hopeless matter I never saw. Only occasionally I feel consoled, as the other day on the steamer for instance when I stepped in to help an Englishman who couldn't even ask for something to eat. It's the set conversations that knock me, especially when I get excited and can't recall words.

No one is here or has been here that I know of. I doubt if I should trouble them if they did come. I read the stranger-list every morning and always see more or less American's names, but as I've not yet troubled the Consul, it does not seem very probable that extra-society will trouble me. One evening at the theatre I sat next to a young fellow whose bill I borrowed and who was polite enough to offer me his glass. Thereupon I made sundry remarks to him in German, sir, that was worthy of a double-distilled native. He didn't answer. Says I to myself he's a foreigner and isn't up to Deutsch. Then I racked my brains to invent a French sentence but all my small stock of French was long since driven out of my head by German. So finally I addressed him in English. It turned out that he was an American, a young fellow named Storrs, from near Worcester in Massachusetts, come abroad for his health; been in Italy and left Milan in the last train that came through. Since then he has left his card on me and I shall call on him. He seems to be a very quiet, gentlemanly "boy," perhaps nineteen years old, and further I know nothing about him.

So much for these matters. I'm sorry to hear you're so bent against marrying. I had hoped that you would have taken that duty on [your] shoulders and should be deuced glad to hear that you'd done it.⁴ One of us must marry, or at least ought to marry soon. You see clearly enough that my chance is out of the question for several years at the least, therefore it lies between you and John. I don't know what John would make of it, but it seems now as if he were degenerating into a superannuating beau. So that as he wont, or *if* he wont, and you can and will, I don't see that's it would be worth while to stick out and lose a greater good to retain the lesser. Go and get in love, boy! Find a strong woman who'll make a team, and has got some real go in her, and marry her if you can. I'll allow you a hundred thalers a year, myself.

Apropos to my money affairs. I've purposely kept the Governor in ignorance of all but generalities, and indeed have written no accounts of expenses home whatever, further than the general information that it cost more than I expected and I have to be economical. This is true enough. I have been pretty economical though not mean nor self-sacrificing. By such cares as I have taken, I have so far bound down my expenses to an average of within ninety American dollars a month, including every cent paid out in any form. This you see is nearly exactly a thousand a year, and if it would last, I shouldn't trouble myself any more about it. But now my travelling will begin and will last three months at least. I shall not return to Berlin till November. God knows what this will cost; I can make no calculation, but I'm afraid it will bring the total up to $1500, certainly. According therefore as my remarks about "strictest economy" &c &c are frequent or otherwise, you may know whether my sum total will come up to $1500 or remain nearer $1100. Of course however, you will not inform the Governor of this explanation. He has been [very] kind and liberal enough so far, but I fear growls unless the greatest delicacy is observed. I am economical, it is true, but I've no objection to his giving me credit for just as much more economy as he will.

About my movements I know only this. Since I wrote to mamma last week I've received a letter from her, from you and one from Loo at Nice on her way to Normandy. From this last I judge that I shall meet Loo at Thun in Switzerland about the 1st August. On the 1st July I leave Dresden for Munich where I remain till the 15th probably; address "Care of Rob. de Froelich. München. Baiern." Thence I shall go on across a part of the Tyrol to Interlaken and Thun. All letters to arrive between July 15th and September 1st had better be sent to Baring's agent in Berne whose name you must get from Mr Ward. I don't have my letters directed "Poste restante" because it's not so safe that I shall get them, and a confounded nuisance to go to the office every day.

Meanwhile give my adoration to all the Frls.   Adieu.   H.

MS: MHi
1. Edward Gibbon (1737–1794), *Autobiography*, first published in 1796.
2. *Frankreich . . . einerlei:* France and Austria are all one to me.
3. *Grünes Gewölbe:* the "Green Vault" of gems and objets d'art.
4. Brackets here and in the next paragraph indicate editorial conjecture where letter is damaged.

To Charles Francis Adams, Jr.

Nürnberg. July. 3. 1859.

Dear Charles

I've just come in from a walk in the dusk alone through this exquisite old city. Ben has gone to bed. I am in a nude state for its hotter than fifty thousand devils and impossible to keep cool. I take this spare minute to begin a letter for Ben is hurrying me to get through this city where I would like to pass a fortnight, and I don't know when I shall have time to write again. Your letter arrived all right the night before I left Dresden but nary catalogue of engravings in or about it so that I can only hope this latter will hit me at Munich.

This week has been a tremendously busy one and at the same time hot as tophet. Last Tuesday afternoon Ben and I visited Tharandt a pretty little town some nine miles from Dresden. The next morning at seven we took the cars and went up the Elbe an hour to Königstein a great fortification perched on a high rock. From here we crossed the river to a place below which is pretty and commands a beautiful view. This country is called the Saxon Switzerland. I tell you what, old fellow, this seeing sights on a flaming July day is tough. However I found it very pleasant, for when at about three o'clock we came down to take the steamer, we fell in with a gentleman and two ladies, one of whom was young and quite pretty. Naturally we entered into conversation with the gentleman who was pretty well on in life. He was a Russian-Swede; spoke six languages but not English; "my daughter speaks English however." Ja wohl! I made a note of that. We continued our conversation; steamer was late; ladies sat a little way off and were unapproachable; steamer at last came and I manoeuvred so as to get a seat by the pretty girl and under the apology of bad German entered into an English conversation with her. She was clever, highly cultivated and interesting. Had just come from Italy and was strong Italian. Spoke pretty English. Was a little taller than I in figure; slim; light eyes; distingué. We talked of travelling, of poetry, of art, of Italy and of many other things. I passed a pleasant, summer afternoon and liked my friend very much. We arrived at Dresden; left the boat; touched our hats; I never shall see the pretty Swede again, but that's a traveller's luck and God forbid that I ever see enough of a woman in Europe to care for her. That would make a fuss. Ten chances to one it makes a fellow unhappy. But now my pretty Swede's in Hamburg; I'm in Nürnberg; we never shall meet again, but I have a pleasant recollection and count myself richer than before by some agreeable hours.

That evening I ordered down some ice-cream and wine and treated my assembled family to an Abschiedsfest.[1] We all got tight; played schwarzer Peter or old maid at cards and as the Frl. Camilla lost, I corked a pair of moustachios on her face. This Frl. is quite nice; we abuse each other and call each other names, but I rather like her; she's bright and not bad looking. What the family think of me I can't say. They seem to think that I'm lazy and selfish. The first I plead guilty to, but the last not. They wanted my photograph but I told them I was far too handsome to give away my likeness in that way and they must wait till all other prior claims were settled. Finally, so far as this family goes I've nothing more to say than that they were always kind, goodnatured, and obliging; I have learned here twice as much German as I knew when I came here and my recollections of this place are all pleasant.

On Thursday morning began packing up in earnest. Ben left a trunk here in which I deposited 10 shirts and other articles in that way and a number of books which will all go on to Berlin. I visited too the Gallery for the last time and the Madonna, the most exquisite of all exquisiteness. After dinner I just managed to get my trunk packed as the time for departure came, and waited for the droschke which ought to have come at quarter past two. It knew better and nary appeared. Waited till the last instant, then rushed off with a carpet-bag and travelling pouch and great coat in a shawl strap. Since then I've had no handkerchiefs, nor drawers nor stockings nor linen shirts nor anything else. Rushed like a mad bull to a droschke station; ordered the coachman to drive as fast as possible to the depot; arrived as the door shut but bolted for a ticket "to Nürnberg." On tearing out my purse to pay I discovered I had only four thalers and the ticket cost eight. My money had gone beyond all idea and I had relied on Ben, who was already in the cars. I said that I had not enough money and wished a ticket to Leipzig instead. No! I had ordered Nürnberg; it was stamped and I must take that or none. With a tempest of choice English and German execrations I bolted towards the glass door to get in without a ticket. No go. Guard forced me back. At this instant as I turned round in despair to leave the whole concern, Ben's host who was there and had learned my position hurried up with Ben's purse which held just enough. I got on board the train which had probably waited for me, and in a state of fever heat I indulged in a general curse to the whole affair, continuing steadily fifteen minutes till I got cool. Then we set to work to calculate our resources. Ben's position was the same as mine and we could raise only four thalers between us. Both of us had however Baring's letters in our pockets and our tickets were already paid to Nürnberg.

So we went on to Leipzig in a heat that made us gasp for air, and amused ourselves by reading, talking with a couple of Cadets, and also by smoking, as I do, but Ben doesn't indulge in the flagrant Bremen. At Leipzig we stopped an hour and attempted to raise money but the fool of a banker wouldn't do it and we had no time to enquire further. Baring has no agent here. At seven or so we started again. In our wagon was a traveller's real set. A Russian with wonderful hair and beard parted across his chin; three Poles who spoke their natywe[2] language which is a mixture of French, German, Italian and Greek; one German who said Ja and Nein and no more; and ourselves. We fraternised with the hairy Russer and the Poles and had quite a jolly time and lively talk till the night came on and towards twelve o'clock at a place called Plauen, the Poles departed. We then had each a seat and it was cooler. We stretched ourselves out and slumbered as well as we could. So we went on all night changing cars at the Bavarian frontier, till towards five o'clock I woke up feeling dirty as you please, and sticking my head out of the window, got some cool morning air and watched the pretty fields of Franconia with their old road-side saints, crucifixes and Madonnas. At six or so we came to Bamberg and Ben and I here got out; we wanted to see the city and the Cathedral. Cleaned ourselves; breakfasted on milk, hard boiled eggs, bread and butter and then rambled up and saw the Cathedral which is peculiar and remarkably pretty. Here again we applied for money but as they said we could certainly get it at Nürnberg we didn't insist on drawing here. We bought a large quantity of cherries instead and went back to our hotel, eat, drank and slept till the cars came at two and we had to go out again into the burning heat.

Two hours on to Nürnberg. A jolly Nürnberger was our only companion, and we were dead of heat. At three we arrived here and came straight to this house, the Hotel zum Strauss. So there are our travels!

Monday, 4th. Our grand American spread eagle has been remembered by us today but not celebrated. We drank a glass of wine and water to him and let him swim.

Ben hurries me on. I would stay here a week but we go tomorrow morning. My amiable brother, what do you want me to say of this city. I hardly know how to express it all. Think me spooney if you will; but last evening as I wandered round in the dusk smoking a cigar in these delightful old peaked, tiled, crooked, narrow, stinking lanes I thought that if ever again I enjoy as much happiness as here in Europe, and the months pass over bringing always new fascinations and no troubles, why then philosophers lie and earth's a paradise. Ben and I have passed the day in a couple of great churches, lying on the Altar steps and looking at the glorious stained glass windows five hundred years old, with their magnificent colors and quaint Biblical stories. So fascinating these things are! Why Charles, damn it, there's no use talking about it. Let it go! Nürnberg is Nürnberg! If I go on I shall be silly, even if I've not been already.

So tomorrow we bid good-bye to Dürer and old Peter Vischer, the churches and the streets;[3] the glorious old windows and the charming fountains and all the other fascinations of this city, and march on to München. The weather bids fair to last forever; we roast and broil in this absolutely cloudless sky, but sleep well and enjoy life. How long München will take us is a problem but not more than a week. Ben wants to get through. As I'm determined at any price not to return to Berlin before the November semestre begins, and hate the very idea of seeing that city, I'm in no hurry.

I've not got your letter by me. As to the lecture you administer in regard to writing and money, I'm obliged but just now can't undertake to discuss it. As for my studying although I still assert the principle that it is well to work I must confess that any slight efforts I've made in that direction have ludicrously failed. Since I left Berlin I've not done a thing except pretend to read a page of law a day, an effort which unhappily never succeeded. In fact I've acted precisely as you recommend, and am quite well satisfied that so far as real work goes I shall do little in Europe. At the same time I do not think that the time could be better employed and believe that what I'm picking up now is of more use than my two years of Blackstone and Carry Bigelow &c would have been at home. Nevertheless you need not scare the Governor by this reflection. Next winter in self-defence I must peg away and probably hard. But as for the law I learn in that way making me a jurist, I doubt it. That it may help to make me a strong man is more possible; that it may be a mere extra-accomplishment kept for show is most likely of all.

Enough of myself. Your letter is in my abandoned trunk which will meet me in München, so I can't answer whatever is there and forgotten. I enclose some old stamps for Brooks, given me by one of the Strauss boys who has himself a collection.[4] The French republic ones I believe are rare and valuable to collectors. I will send him the Bavarian set from München.

So adieu, lebe wohl! I've got an infernal crowd of letters on hand waiting to be answered and have no time. I shall not be able to write every week.

Yrs affectly   Henry.

MS: MHi
1. *Abschiedsfest:* a going-away party.
2. *Natywe:* mock-Polish, native.
3. Peter Vischer (1460–1529), sculptor and bronzesmith.
4. Postage-stamp collecting began about 1840.

To Charles Francis Adams, Jr.

Thun. August. 6. 1859.

Dear Charles

I received your letter of the 2d–9 July the day before yesterday together with a splendid batch of others including one from papa and one from John who seems like the ancient Phœnix to have become young again and this time so devilish thoroughly that I can't begin to keep along with him. When my unhappy conscience will be relieved from this weight of letters Heaven only knows. Some time ago I wrote a line to mamma from Zürich and since then have had every moment taken up, what with mountains and general accelerated motion. Loo however still writes I suppose a la steam engine and she supplies all gaps.

Here I am as you see in Switzerland and have seen this lion or a part of him at last. Very fine he is too but Englishmen have rather injured the primitiveness of the beast.[1] Here in Thun we have been for several days leading a delightfully primitive and lazy life; Kuhn, Theodore Chase, Ben Crowninshield, Loo and I;[2] all economising, and I in particular looking forward to that £100 that should be here in a week, with a firm consciousness that if it doesn't arrive I shall have my movements rather stopped off. Travelling is perfectly frightful. A pound a day is the lowest a man can calculate on. You can see about where I shall be at the 1st of November.

Tomorrow I'm off for Mt Blanc, shall see Fred Hauteville at Vevay,[3] be back here on the 15th and set off immediately with Kuhn, Loo and Theodore over the St Gothard into Italy where we shall visit Turin and Milan and I shall again leave them at Como and come over the Splügen onto the Rhine. This is an innovation on my original plan, but Loo wants me to do it and it will only take about ten days. Then I shall rejoin Ben at Baden and we shall do the Rhine together.

This is the program. Hope they won't find fault with it at home. It will all be done before you receive this letter.

My own conscience smites me at times when I think of what a big plumcake I've got hold of, and what an indigestion it may give me. I wish to God I was not the first of the family who had done all this for it renders necessary all sorts of carefulness and puts me as it were under obligations and bonds for future conduct. Travel as modestly, yes as meanly as I will, it is wholly impossible to keep independent of the Governor's assistance and that will bring it's discount, I suppose, with it, if not in one way then in another. But what can't be cured must be endured.

Further, as for travelling there's not much to say. The women are all ugly here and I'm not vulnerable that way. Besides I've made an oath that if I can help it I'll not fall in love until it's certain I can't get along any other way. I've come to the conclusion that that's a double edged sort of amusement that cuts a little deep occasionally. Moreover no one has taken the trouble to fall in love with me; another good reason for not indulging in this amusement. Then the travelling is very pleasant and unless it becomes tiresome as it may in time, will satisfy my highest wishes. It may seem absurd to you that a fellow should write as if it were possible that travelling should not amuse him. I notice however that Joe Bradlee returns to Hannover in the middle of this month; *the* travelling season.

Your letter wasn't high-spirited my boy. In fact it was anything but it. Your reply to my remarks about marrying may be satisfactory to you but is not to me. Not by a jug-full. Talk about your father's "alms." Why damn it Sir if you marry, your father's bound to help you and there's no "pensioned beggar" about it. Is Kuhn a pensioned beggar because his father-in-law allows his wife so much a year. Gott bewahr! It strikes me you take too low a tone about this matter. The Governor wants us to marry. Well and good. Like other fathers who can afford it, he is willing to allow us so much. I say, take it and if there's any trouble about it, don't back down as if it was your fault. To my mind there's no dependence about it, unless you choose to live as Ned Everett does.[4]

Now, my boy, I don't undertake to criticise your conduct except so far as I know it. But it does strike me that you're giving yourself up to a morbid feeling that will some day swallow you whole, and you'll be a sort of Gorham Brooks.[5] I don't know anything about your proceedings but I have written what I did write on the theory that you was letting your hobby run away with you, and I tell you fairly that I very much suspect it has cost you already just about ten thousand times what it's worth. If you can consider the subject coolly and impartially I would like to have you reason out from the position of a fair umpire whether it's worth while to allow objections like this to play damnation with the best, most natural and probably the happiest course that your life could take. If you satisfy yourself however that it's all right, then of course I've no more to say except that I hope the end won't be the worse for it.

If however the father proposes to rest his hopes of grandchildren on his third son, meaning me, from present appearances I think it probable he'll have to practice the art of patience to a very considerable extent for I haven't seen yet the woman whom I'd marry and until I do I shall not express any opinion about the result. One thing I do know, however. If I want to marry I shall do it and the father may "taunt" as much as he pleases. If I know myself and him it won't last long. He's not unreasonable if he's once shown the right road to travel and this objection of yours would be my smallest.

So much for this matter. I'm glad to hear you are to be at Washington a part of the session. I believe, you know, in a change of society, or of no society if you please, for so far as I know, you live in a world of waste and one person is no more to you than another. A position that I was in until I went to College and thank the Lord never have been in since and never will be again if I can help it. It's bad for the soul and the body. I'll always have a friend if he's only a nigger-boy.

This letter is short and personal. I can't make it longer for Theodore, Ben and I are going off in a moment to Berne to take a "bain complet" of which you'd better not speak to the moral and the European travellers.[6] Life here is deliciously lazy and jolly; Theodore plays and we listen and joke and indulge in all sorts of nonsense of which I suppose Loo tells you. So ponder over this letter and give credit to the philosopher

Henry.

MS: MHi
1. "Lion" in the sense of a thing of great interest or celebrity. The English Alpine Club, founded in 1857, greatly stimulated mountaineering.
2. Theodore Chase (1832–1894) of Boston, Harvard '53.
3. Frederic Sears Grand d'Hauteville (1838–1918), Harvard '59.
4. Edward Brooks Everett (1830–1861), Harvard '50, M.D. '53, son of Edward and Charlotte Brooks Everett and HA's cousin.
5. Probably Gorham Brooks (1795–1855), Harvard '14, HA's uncle.
6. Rooms with private bath were unusual in European hotels and sinfully expensive.

To Charles Francis Adams, Jr.

Berlin. October. 17./59

Dear Charles

Here I am again in this lovely city, lovelier than ever. Have been here some four days or more, Ben, Joe and I and am quite ready to go off again.

Thanks for your newspapers not one of which ever met my eyes, thanks probably to the police. Wiggin's catalogue caught me at Munich and I think I acknowledged it in one of my letters to papa. Received another letter from mamma of 25th Sept. which I shall answer in order.

Meanwhile my dear boy, in spite of the excessively blue tone of your last, I wish I were near enough to have five minutes talk with you. The truth is I'm in a devil of a fix. Here I am in Berlin, a cold shudder running through me every time I think of another winter here; unable to find one trace of such a settlement as could alone make a winter endurable, and yet not liking to finally decide to quit and seek pleasanter quarters. I have through Ben made inquiries about Dresden which I'm afraid won't succeed and have even gone so far as to write to Billy Howe at Vienna to know whether that will suit, but as yet everything is a jumble. Only one thing is certain; I *will not* take rooms here as I did last winter.

But if this were all I shouldn't care a rap. The trouble really is that I don't like to decide on my own responsibility. It has been understood all along that I was to study this winter in Berlin. I don't know how papa will receive this idea that because I dislike Berlin I can walk off to any other place. I have no idea how all that I do appears to you at home. What seems right and fair enough on this side the water, sometimes looks very different on that. Now I don't want to displease papa. He has given me the very widest berth and has never found a word of fault as yet with all I chose to do. I've had a splendid vacation, done all I wished, spent a deuced lot of money and naturally am under some bonds to consult the opinions at home. But I can't get these opinions. I haven't an idea what you think, and only a sort of instinct which a year's absence has made rather dull. So here I am, up a tree.

Ben is just the same. He talks of all sorts of things but I think he'll remain here. For my own part I would rather go to Vienna and so would he, but so much I have about decided, that if Dresden is eligible I shall go there and risk it, rather than sink into a chronic melancholy here.

If there had been any appearance of trouble and thunderstorms in the gubernatorial countenance I suppose you would have warned me. One letter written from Milan to him has not yet been answered and now is out of date. There is no occasion for an answer. Another written from Delft on this very subject, is waiting now for an answer which may decide me if it arrives in time.

The truth is that you at home probably say, I came abroad nominally to study law and how much have I done! It's fair enough to say so but it's fair enough for me to answer that while I was learning German I couldn't learn law and in Dresden I did read pretty steadily. Since then I have not, it's true. I've been always on the move which is inconsistent with law. But now here I am in Berlin. I ought to do something even if the city is unpleasant. I've had my up. I ought to have my down.

If I were certain that you all thought this, I'd stick to Berlin though Hell were in it. But then it looks to me in this way. The one single advantage of Berlin over other cities is it's University. A year's experience in Germany has induced me to believe that for my purposes the University is not worth a rush. German law lectures to an American are of about as much use as a Chinese cannon to a backwoodsman. From books I can take what I want. I can read one chapter on theory and another on practice and know as much about the branch treated as I should if Rudorff or Gneist had slobbered the same subject over five hours a week for the term. The Germans want one thing; I another and I should never get what I want from their lectures though I took five a day for five years and copied every letter of each. You can believe all this or not as you please, but this idea of mine isn't a new one. I made it up more than six months ago. I'm not the only student that thinks so, too. Everyone is nearly of a mind about this.

The probability is that I shall take it easily; shall wait an answer to the Delft letter with some money I hope. Shall hear what the Viennese say, and the Dresdeners and shall try to make acquaintances here with such means as I have. If after the 15th November nothing new turns up and I am still doubtful, I shall take on my own responsability the city that suits me best. If the decision doesn't suit at home I shall be sorry but mean to do the best I can according to the ideas I have.

I've made up this manifesto to you, because I suppose the household will be in plenty of confusion and there will be no necessity of using it unless it's needed. If the Governor doesn't find fault with matters as they are, there's no necessity of my excusing myself. You must use your own judgment and read all or none of this letter to them as you think best.

Meanwhile I've nothing to tell you. We all left Hannover in due course as announced in my last letter to mamma from that capital of the universe. By the way I've come to the final conclusion that it's all nonsense about Joe and the Fraülein. He doesn't care any more for her than I do, at least so far as an affair of the heart is concerned. I saw them together several times and we passed several evenings at the house, and Joe has been with us ever since, and a man less in love I don't know, unless it's Ben or myself.

Since our arrival here we have been occupied in re-examining the lions. Yesterday we went to Potsdam and saw that wilderness of ugly palaces. The old King is dying at Sans Souci so we were not allowed to see the palace but we saw the others.[1] They're all alike; dreadfully ugly. If the King dies it will give us the last knock on the head, for all the theatres and concerts and amusements will be shut off for six weeks. Poor old beggar! It's time for him to go.

The weather here is now very good. One fair day and one foul alternate, a better average than I ever knew here before. Today is the foul and my spirits are down in proportion but I hope tomorrow will raise them.

Bradlee goes on to Paris in a few days. I have had a short note from Hollis and hear that a crowd more of my acquaintances are here. Boston society I'm afraid doesn't mourn over the absence of her choicest spirits as she ought. By the way what young ladies come out this winter. Heavens how I am being left behind. And *will* Philo marry Jephtha's daughter?[2] By Jupiter I'd like to see Jephtha's behavior at the announcement. You may tell her if you choose to do it quick so that I may have time to send her a present from Europe.

Society here looks more charming than ever. We called on Governor Wright the other day who insisted on talking volubly about politics, California elections and God knows what. As I've seen only one American paper in three months I wasn't so well posted as I might have been and displayed a lamentable ignorance as to who the deuce people were and generally what was loose. I'm afraid I lowered myself badly in the Governor's eyes. He wants to know who "we" are going to make speaker. I looked grave and shook my head which he seemed to think had a deep political meaning.

Do keep me posted in a general way on these matters and especially what concerns papa. I have not heard a word about all this for six months and am as ignorant as a German about our politics. More I can't say. Who *will* be speaker; Grow as the Governor suggested?[3]

Just now I must go to the Opera and hear Oberon; Lord such a deep musician as I am, you never heard of. Classic is nothing. I'm climbing up to John Sebastian Bach now whose music few can play, and no one understand. Never mind! I shall come down again some day.

I wonder where everyone is; the Frothinghams and all the other thousand and one old Boston respectabilities who are out here. I'd like to see some of them.

I send Brooks the Brunswick postage stamps. Has he the Prussian or not? What does he want? He yells for more but I don't know what he's got. I'll answer Mary's last letter some day but she must let her lace collar if she ever got it, satisfy her for a while. I have heaps of letters to write and shall be busy a fortnight on them and other writing.

Yrs affectly   Henry.

P.S. 18 Oct. I think to-day I shall settle on Dresden and the Reichenbachs.[4] Ben has received a letter from the Madame that is favorable. My next will probably give my final decision.

Papa's letter of the 15th Sept. has just arrived. According to it I do not see but it's all right and I can pass the winter in Dresden nem. con.

MS: MHi

1. The "old King," long incapacitated with illness, was Frederick William IV (1795–1861). His brother William became regent in 1858.

2. *Hamlet*, II, ii; Judges 11:30–40.

3. Galusha Aaron Grow (1822–1907) of Pennsylvania, representative 1851–1863 (first as Free-Soil Democrat, from 1857 as Republican), speaker 1861–1863.

4. Heinrich G. L. Reichenbach (1793–1879), botanist and geologist.

To Abigail Brooks Adams

Berlin. October. 26. 1859.

Dear Mamma

I have only a little time to write this week so you must make allowance for the shortness of this letter. I wrote last week to Charles and to Ellen,[1] immediately after receiving her letter enclosed in yours of the 5th. I've also received Wendell Phillips' lecture though not Mr Everett's nor the papers Charles sent.

I have at last made my arrangements for the winter. I don't know how you will like them but I have arranged as well as I know how and I at all events believe that it's the best that's to be done. Berlin is too much for me. The city itself, the mode of life here, the American society and the climate have all disagreed with me so much that as I have repeatedly said, I didn't care to go through it all again. On arriving here I did what I could to find out whether I could make it pleasanter. But though circumstances are somewhat changed, the essentials remain as last winter and I determined to try at least whether I couldn't find something better. I got Ben to write to Dresden, to a lady on whom he had had letters and who was very kind to him. I wrote to Billy Howe at Vienna to see what was to be done there, and I kept as a last ressort their old family in Hannover. Madame Reichenbach answered Ben's letter favorably. Billy Howe answered mine very kindly but from Dresden where he has come to pass the winter, having been unable to find in Vienna just what I am looking for. Things looked no brighter here in spite of the attempts of some of my friends to find me what I wished; and so I concluded to wait no longer but to close with the Dresden opportunity. In three days I shall go down there and begin the winter.

Of the Reichenbachs I know something. The Madame is I believe an aesthetical lady, given to Shakespeare, Goethe and Schiller. The Professor is devoted to Botany and a shining light in it. There is a daughter, eighteen years old and pretty, whom I shall probably fall in love with if she gives me a chance. There are two sons, I think, but they are not always at home. A week hence I shall be able to say more of it all. As it is, I don't expect a paradise but hope to be comfortable and be able to devote myself with some pleasure to books and exercise and German.

Ben will not go to Dresden, and as the accounts from Vienna are all unfavorable he proposes to find some family here, the best he can, and stay a month at least on trial. If he likes it as he very possibly will, he'll remain longer. If not he'll go to Vienna and thence to Italy.

I am now pretty busy getting my things in order and arranging for the winter. Our room is a small chaos which would drive you crazy, but I suppose it will get clear in time. At all events I shall leave here on Saturday.

There is nothing particular to tell you of. I have a lot of writing arrears to do up which keep me pretty busy. Berlin is as usual and so is Germany in general and porcellain stoves in particular.

Don't make John or Charles write if they don't want to. My conscience reproaches me more and more that they should be so hard at work and with work too that can't be pleasant to them, while I am dawdling here in Germany. Still I must work too this winter and hope to learn something positive. You too will soon have too much of your own to do to bother about letters to me. So long as everyone is well and all goes right I can do without letters. So don't be afraid to drop one if you're too busy to write, or to send only a line if you've no time for more.

Loo wrote to me a little while ago a very pleasant letter from Paris. I said a few words in my last letter to you about Loo and her appearance to me. I liked her better this summer than I ever did before. She petted me and seemed to try hard to make everything as pleasant as could be. On the Stelvio she behaved like a trump under pretty rough trial too.[2] She mediated beautifully between Kuhn and Theodore and soothed their ruffled feathers as if she were a queen reconciling her ministers. Hotheaded she always was and always will be, but that's no great fault that I know of. I like it, at least for a change.

Whether she's very happy or not I won't undertake to say, and am getting rather inclined to believe that no one who takes a position so hard as hers is likely to be very happy. But still I do think that on the whole she's as happy as she's capable of being. I saw her once or twice very unhappy though she didn't say much about it. Kuhn is wilful and has always had his own way and doesn't perhaps regard other people's wishes so much as he might, but she is so used to this now that the struggle is nearly over and it's done her good too. What a pity it is that a person can't be "improved" except by being made deucedly uncomfortable. This has tamed her and made her a useful working member of society, and on the whole I think her marriage was a good thing, and though I don't like to be trained myself still I believe it's good for people and improves them wonderfully.

As for coming home, we agreed between us that we should be awful bores and make ourselves generally very disagreeable at first. I don't suppose we shall either of us take very kindly to our old life, but the new train of affairs will soon busy me, and let us hope that it will be the same with Loo. If she has children she will be all the better for her European experience; if not—it would have been bad enough any way and at all events she'll have had two years of pleasure. I don't think it will make matters much worse. At least I hope not.

I am very glad about Ellen's engagement. It is brave and honest and sensible and I've no doubt she'll be happy; the more happy as the less ambitious.[3] I wrote to her at once as well as I could though I felt stupid and talked solemn. This letter is solemn and stupid too and so was my last, but when I get settled I'll write better. Everything is straight here. We're all well and thriving and I hope to receive a letter from home today to make us still more so. Papa I will try to answer next week though I hardly like to bother him with my business letters when he must be so busy.

So goodbye and remember me to everyone, the children, Rebecca and all.

Henry.

MS: MHi

1. Ellen Hedge Lunt (b. 1838), daughter of the Quincy Unitarian minister William P. Lunt.
2. The highest Alpine pass, 9,005 feet.
3. Benjamin Warren Munroe, whom Ellen Lunt married in 1861, was described favorably by ABA, though he had the drawback of a different "standing in life" (ABA to HA, Oct. 5).

To Abigail Brooks Adams

[Nov. 2?, 1859]

Dear Mamma

The Fraülein is a perfect duck. What'll you give me if I won't ask her to marry me. Come, we'll make a bargain; I'll give up Carry Bigelow and take Fraülein Augusta; or vice-versa, as you please. She's about sixteen years old; looks dreadfully like Nelly Lowe, whom I always adored; is very bright, with lots of fun; knows everything from coins up to Natural history, and every date since the first recorded in the Bible; she amuses me immensely and almost made me die laughing at the description she gave of the young men at her dancing class yesterday. I tell you, you'd better get me down into Italy pretty quick or there'll be trouble.

Madame is immense. Just get hold of Frank Brooks or Russell Lowell and get them to describe the Herr Professor Hofrath Reichenbach and the Frau Professorin Hofräthin ditto.[1] They are very kind and tell the funniest stories about Frank Brooks and the Coolidges. I have tolerably good rooms only cold as thunder, and am generally well contented. Am strong on the exercise. Bounced an hour this morning round on a horse, without stirrups, making tremendous struggles not to fall off, and presenting a very graceful appearance generally. Begin soon a course of fencing lessons and may also take dancing ones. These all will come on alternate days so I may be sure to get my hour of work.

No letters have arrived since my last home. I got Everett's Oration from Billy Howe and read it. It's very good. Wendell Phillips is an ass to make such a speech as that. What does he want to cut off his own and his friends' heads for. It does no one good and hurts us all.[2]

Billy Howe is just as ever so far as I see. He seems devoted to some American young ladies here and I doubt whether he does anything with German. He dislikes Germans as much as I do; more indeed for he doesn't see them so much, and says, what I believe to be true, that so far as society goes, there's nothing that's so pleasant as our own. I've only seen him once but expect to again soon.

I forgot in my last to ask you about giving Ellen a marriage present. As I'm here in Dresden I can easily send her over some china if she will; I could get a pretty little tête-a-tête service, for instance, for from fifteen dollars up to as many hundred. Just let me know what you think and when the time will come.

Ben is in Berlin. Talks of going to Italy at Christmas and wants me bad to go with him. But I'm convinced that by that time the Fraülein will have said "Ja" and I shall be under the necessity of saying to him "Nein." I don't think Ben is over contented, at least when I saw him last he wasn't. Berlin is a nasty hole.

Yes, I am now much jollier than last week and wish I could lend you some of my good spirits for I know you'll want them. However I'm looking forward now to coming home. More than half of my time is up, so you will soon have the pleasure of receiving me, the height of all that is perfect, again at home.

I enclose Brooks an Austrian newspaper stamp. What countries has he not got? I will do my best to get them for him and tell him something about them in some letter some day.

Where are my letters? My last date is October 5.

Yrs affectionately   Henry.

MS: MHi
1. Francis Boott Brooks (1824–1891), son of Edward and Elizabeth Boott Brooks and HA's cousin. James Russell Lowell (1819–1891), poet, editor of the *Atlantic Monthly*, and known directly to HA as a much admired professor at Harvard, had lived with the Reichenbachs from October 1855 to July 1856 while preparing himself for his professorship.
2. On Sept. 17 Everett, dedicating a memorial statue at the Boston State House, delivered a 1¾-hour eulogy of Daniel Webster. He scarcely mentioned slavery, except to praise Webster's pronouncement that "free labor would ultimately prevail" and that "nothing is to be hoped from external interference, whether of exhortation or rebuke." Wendell Phillips (1811–1884), as an abolitionist, identified Webster with the Fugitive Slave Law, campaigned to remove the statue from the State House grounds, and scorned Everett's speech: "No matter what act Webster did, no matter how foul the path he trod, he never lacked some one to gild it with a Greek anecdote, or hide it in a blaze of declamation" (Oct. 4). As much as any proslavery man, Phillips held that union and antislavery were incompatible; he therefore denounced cautious antislavery Republicans (like CFA) as temporizers in a class with proslavery Whigs.

To Abigail Brooks Adams

Dresden. November. 8. 1859.

Dear Mamma

Since my last to you and papa I've received your's of October 12, and have expected another every day. As I've remarked several times before, I shouldn't be sorry to receive some money too, for I'm on the frightfully respectable here, and my dress suit after three winters severe labor has received a final quietus, having been swallowed pretty nearly whole by moths. As it's been used up a good while, it's final departure doesn't distress me, but I don't care to order another till I know where the money is that's to pay for it. I enclose to you a likeness of your beloved son as he usually appears to the inhabitants of Germany. I think it's flattering, especially the moustache. Ben had one taken at the same time and perhaps he has also sent his home. His was however frightful; at least the one he sent to me.

At No. 4, Kleine Schiessgasse we're getting on as well as could be expected. Frightful kindness overwhelms me from all sides, and I am put to my trumps to be polite. I daren't even joke except in my letters, and ever have a benign smile on my face. Certainly if I don't become as stiff as a German it's not because I don't try. You would scream to see me contest with the Herr Hofrath which of us shall enter a room first. I open the door and stand back with a bow; he says with a gesture towards the room; "bitte recht sehr; apres vous"; to which I smile deprecatingly and remark, "bitte, Herr Hofrath, wollen Sie so gut sein";[1] if he still insists, I yield and precede; if not, he enters and I close the door after him with the highest respect. He is frightfully learned and buried in science so that he seldom comes out but is a good old soul and very kind. This afternoon he's been showing me all over the royal natural history collection of which he has the care. He wants a stuffed swordfish and a lot of American sea-weeds. I should like to help him but hardly know who to apply to.

The Frau Mutter is benign as ever. Yesterday afternoon we all went to a concert; that is the Professor, the Mother, the Augusta and I. There *we* met two of *our* friends, a Countess Rodolorowowski or something that sounds like that, and her mother. Goodness gracious, the formalities, the bowing and scraping and hopping up and down, the air of majesty with which those corpulent ladies swelled about and visited their acquaintances at the other tables. My eye, wasn't it rum. Meanwhile I sat next the amiable Fraülein (who looked deuced pretty and all the Lieutenants envied me) and I think, take the four hours through, I may have spoken about ten words an hour; in the interval sitting still and looking at my kid gloves. The Countess too was particularly gracious and addressed several remarks to me. Only think!

As for the Fraülein, ain't she a one-er, that's all. She reminds me all the time of Nelly Lowe; in fact I call her "Miss Nelly" now. She's a will of her own and gives me the most immense delight. A perfect little Tartar, and smooth as a cat. I'll do her the justice to say, however, she doesn't seem to have any designs on my person, and it's only within a few days that she has begun to recognise my presence at all, for I don't talk a great deal and haven't paid her any profuse attention, seein' as the German girls never know what to make of it when a person takes any notice of them. So I laugh at her nonsense and avoid personal contact.

With the brother, Theodor, about twenty four or five years old, I'm better acquainted. He has a large collection of coins and is passionately fond of all sorts of antiquarian rubbish. If papa wants any particular German coins I might perhaps be able to get them, through young Reichenbach. The other day we went off on a foot excursion and from nine o'clock till nearly four we hardly stopped. Visited a lot of villages, old churches, graveyards, and pretty walks and views. The neighborhood of Dresden is as you know, remarkably pretty, and as the Theodore knows every foot of it and it's history, and the local legends in which Saxony abounds, it is very pleasant to wander about, though I was pretty tired when I returned. Just now I am in hopes of getting up a still more interesting excursion. You must know Saxony has lots of ghosts, ruined castles, haunted churchyards and the like. Madame Reichenbach is superstitious and in her heart, if she only dared say it, believes them all. Indeed I believe every man in Germany, high or low, has more or less of this, and they gravely assert that the White Lady who is said to haunt half the royal palaces in Germany, and announce by her appearance the death of the King or the birth of an heir to the throne, has been seen so often and the fact so clearly authenticated that it is impossible to doubt it, and they tell a lot of ordinary ghost stories to prove it.

When sensible people talk this way, I can only make a face, shrug my shoulders and politely smile. Of course I believe that it's all stuff and nonsense and wish I could see one of their white ladies. But as this is impossible, I have set to work to see if we couldn't hunt up a ghost, and just as sure as I can find a promising one, I'm going after him; and we propose (to Madame's horror) to select some haunted ruin and sleep there a night to see if the spectre will be hospitable. Of course it must be really romantic; otherwise it'll be only a bore.

I'm pretty well settled now for the winter. Three mornings in the week at nine o'clock I go down and take riding lessons; three others my fencing master comes and teaches me how to use a rapier. This secures a tolerable amount of exercise and regularity. At eight o'clock in the evening I am summoned to tea and we talk till past nine, but then usually to bed. At one we dine. Madame is horrified that I don't eat anything. She's accustomed to German appetites and seems to think that a man must starve if he doesn't swill sauerkraut and pickled potatoes. Still I will say she does spare me the saurkraut as much as possible, and her table is the best I've yet seen.

Billy Howe carried me to the Consul's, and also to visit a couple of Miss Lawrences of New York; they have a house at Newport and pa Lawrence is a friend of uncle Sidney's; wanted to know where uncle Sidney was and I hadn't the remotest idea.[2] The elder Miss Lawrence whom I had the pleasure of walking with, while Billy was very tender towards the younger, amused me for an hour during a ramble one morning round the city, and amused me in the real New York style. She's clever enough, knows enough, talks like a patent, high-pressure, thousand-horse-power steam engine, isn't pretty nor young, and is to me a severe bore. Doubtless she holds the same opinion of my valued self. The Consul, pa Lawrence and Billy all called on me the other evening. If I weren't so lazy and to say the truth so stupid (for I don't know how it is, I *can* not support a fashionable conversation ten minutes now) I might go in and have a jolly time in the American society here. It's said to be very pleasant and certainly I've been urged enough all round to have flattered the vanity of an F.P.[3] Besides, the Frau Hofräthin scolds me like a criminal for every word of English I speak. Really I'm afraid to say that I must visit an American; she is so powerfully set against it. Hang me! I believe the old lady is bound to force German down my throat whether I like it or no.

All this about society and amusements. Other occupations I'll leave for another letter. I suppose just now you'll be satisfied to know that I'm all right and having a good time. I expect to gratify you in about a year with the sight of myself and wife; who the latter will be I can't say. Augusta is good, but there's a Cecilia some-one whom I'm to know soon, and Madame says she's a rusher. So I won't make up my mind at once.

I'm anxious to see your next letter. It will probably arrive just as this is off. You ask whether I found my trunk at Strasburg. I said in John's letter that I had received it after waiting in all five days in that stupid hole and forcing Ben to wait a week for me in that other stupid hole Frankfurt. I couldn't have lost my trunk. It had all my wordly possessions and if I'd had to return to Luzerne for it I couldn't have gone on without it. The stupid custom-house officers had detained it at Basel. They picked the lock to examine it, but were honest enough not to steal anything.

I have no more news that I know of to tell you. Politics I'm a good deal interested in, here. You don't know perhaps how uneasy Germany is. On one side everyone says there will be an insurrection and revolution in Austria as bad as that in France in 1789. On the other hand war with France and ten thousand perplexities which makes everyone anxious and restless. Many talk of going to America and inquire about it of me. That, they say now, is the only quiet country in the world.

American politics too interest me very much, only I've no means of learning anything about them. This slave insurrection will complicate matters and make it bad enough. I wish I could learn something about it but the German papers of course tell an American almost nothing.[4]

Remember me to Mrs Henshaw whenever you see her again. I suppose when the time comes you'll send me your Washington address. I shall wait with great interest to hear how your new move will succeed. I don't see why you can't have a very good time when the roughness is worn off and you're used to it. Perhaps however I've been knocked about so much this last year that I don't appreciate how hard the change is for those less used to it. At all events I hope you'll have a good time and find some decent acquaintances.

Love to all and a pleasant Thanksgiving dinner. I'd like to eat it with you. Oh *one* home dinner.

Yrs affectly   Henry.

MS: MHi
1. "Please go ahead; after you." "Please, Herr Hofrath, will you be so good."
2. William Beach Lawrence (1800–1881) of New York, lieutenant governor of Rhode Island 1851–1852, and his daughters; Sidney Brooks (1799–1878), a brother of ABA, partner in a New York importing firm, U.S. agent for the sculptor Hiram Powers.
3. Francis Winthrop Palfrey (1831–1889), Harvard '51, son of John Gorham Palfrey.
4. John Brown and his followers seized the arsenal at Harpers Ferry, Oct. 16, hoping to incite a slave rebellion.

To Charles Francis Adams, Jr.

Dresden. 23 November. 1859.

My dear Charles

Your letter arrived this morning and I will try to answer it at once though I can't make my answer so long as yours. I've too many letters to write for that. But I do what I can.

To condense then. As you seem to begin by wishing to force me to eat my own words, I will grant you that pleasure without an argument. I'm not the first nor likely to be the last whose ideas on subjects of which he is ignorant, have turned out to be silly. I acknowledge therefore, as broadly as you wish, that so far as my plan went, I have failed and done little or nothing. At the same time I feel for myself convinced that this last year has been no failure, but on the contrary is worth to me a great deal; how much depends on the use I make of it; but the worth is there. You say you think I'm a humbug. That implies that you once believed I was something. I don't pretend to know how far you're right or wrong, but I protest against you're judging about the advantages of a few years in Europe from my case. The problem is in fact just this. I have acquired here great advantages; if I am a humbug, they wont help me; but I shouldn't have done any better if I'd remained in Boston; if I am not a humbug, we shall see; but in either case the advantages are there, and the failure, if failure it is, will be in me and not in the European experiment which may be of immense use to a capable man.

As to my occupation for the next year, I am now going on in a general course of German reading mostly on the constitutional history of various countries and desultory light reading, but the German is still the main object. This means you see in point of fact that I'm doing nothing. So far as learning a trade goes, idle I am likely to remain until I return home. So far as education goes, I consider these two years as the most valuable of my life. Indefinite, you will say. But so far as I can see, it is what you yourself recommend.

You recommend me to write. My dear boy, if I write, I must write as I think. Amusing, witty and clever I am not, and to affect the style would disgust me and bore you. If I write at all in my life out of the professional line, it will probably be when I have something to say, and when I feel that my subject has got me as well as I the subject. Just now this is anything but true, for I can't seem to master any of the matters that interest me. So don't ask me to be sprightly and amusing for that is what I never was, am not, and never shall be.

The Gov.s letters have so far been excellent and have, or had, made me think even more of him than before. He seemed really to open in a new light. But your little remark about my having spent £100 in four weeks opened my eyes. I forgot my accustomed philosophy and for fifteen seconds felt almost angry. But this was probably because I'd been up very late at fights[1] for two evenings and had a headache from the—salmon. The truth is his last remittance of £100 lasted me from the 15th August to the 15th November. Three months I think. In that time I traveled in Italy and the Tyrol, saw the Rhine, visited nearly every city in Belgium, traveled over Holland as you know, returned indirectly to Berlin, lived there in a Hotel three weeks and then established myself here. Perhaps the Gov. supposed that innkeepers in Europe keep their establishments for nothing; or will he make the attempt himself; if he does it for less I'll pay the expenses. I've already written to him some correct statements on the subject; he had got some crazy idea that he had sent me 2300 dollars. I proved that passage; money before I left home, and all, I had spent in 13 months just 1800 dollars. Of this he's no right to count a part, for it was a present; and reckoning from Nov. 1st to Nov. 1st every cent I've spent in Europe is £300. If he'll consent to do the same that I've done, for that, damn me if I wont make him a present of it, poor as I am.

Your suggestion about rouge & noir is therefore a mistake, though not uningenious. The money I won paid my hotel bills several days and I have never seen a gambling table since. As the Gov. has been kind enough to leave me here without money I've had to write to London to ask an extension of credit which I got and the Gov. may send when he chooses.

This contest of purpose; this argument about aims, you began against, or if you will, for me. You blame me very fairly no doubt, and try to protect yourself from retaliation by pleading guilty; a sort of Yankee Sullivan tactics, hitting a lick and going down.[2] Face the music yourself. I acknowledge I've failed but I believe I've discovered a treasure if I can but use it. But you; why do you plead guilty to the "tu quoque" before I'd said it! Why do you recommend writing, to me who have been hurrying around Europe like a steam engine and am so busy with learning that I can't spare a second for teaching; why recommend this to me when you yourself are smouldering worse than I, when you have never published a word so far as I know. Busy you are, no doubt, and have worked and studied hard; I believe it; but physician, heal thyself. Nearly three years older than I; plead guilty to a "tu quoque" and pass the 5 + xth winter dancing with little girls just out of the nursery. The Governor's last letter warned me against writing magazine articles on the ground that they are ephemeral. Is that your objection too. Or why have you, who urge it so on me when I am busy with another language and haven't properly any right to talk, think or write English, why have you in these three years of law not broken the path yourself. You haven't even used the chances you have. Of the society of Boston outside of Beacon St, I don't believe you know a soul. Of the distinguished men there who could air you a little and change your course of thought, I doubt whether it ever occurred to you to make the acquaintance of one. There is a very good literary society whom it would be well worth while to know, beginning with Waldo Emerson and going down and its from able men that one learns; not from talking old wornout nonsense with girls, however good fun that may be. You talk about being stifled in Boston and I don't believe you know anything of Boston except half a dozen drawing rooms and bar ditto. You haven't or hadn't a friend in it, worth having. You try to be a society man and yet want to do work that would necessarily cut you off from that Society.

Do as Frank Palfrey does, according to Mr Hillard.[3] "Oh, he's very well; getting along quite encouragingly. Works hard. Only he is *such* a favorite in society that he has to go out more than he ought. It distracts him but among the young ladies he is *so* liked that the temptation is too much."

You mention the position I shall have to take when I come back as if you expected me to return a complete lawyer or a Professor or something. Of course I shall stand to all appearances as you stood on entering an office. I don't see how *you* can expect anything else, though I am fully prepared to hear the Governor lay the fault of every failure and every error in my life to Europe. God Almighty could not get an idea out of his head that had once got in. I shall return and study law; when that's done I shall call my preparations finished, and shall toss up for luck. What I have learned here is a part of my capital and will probably show itself slowly and radically.

I have dived into your letter and hauled out these few points to answer. If it pleases you to criticise the answers, do so. No doubt it's good practice, this fencing with each other and I certainly, as it concerns me, am the very last to find fault. If I had more time and could dilate more, I should like to do it, but home letters come round so fast now that I have to hurry them off as fast as I can.

You mention politics. It's my own opinion, my boy, believing as I do in an "irrepressible conflict," that I shall come home just in time to find America in a considerable pickle. The day that I hear that Seward is quietly elected President of the United States, will be a great relief to me for I honestly believe that that and only that can carry us through, even if that can. We've set our hands to the plough and wouldn't look back if we could, but I would thank God heartily to know that comparatively conservative men were to conduct this movement and could control it. If the Governor weathers this storm he has a good chance of living in the White House some day. All depends on the ability he shows as a leader now.

But if things go wrong as they easily may; if a few more Sumner affairs and Harper's Ferry undertakings come up, then adieu my country. I wouldn't give a bad groschen for the United States debt. We shall have made a brilliant failure with our glorious Republic and the prophet can't say what'll turn up. If our constitution stands this strain, she's a stunner, that's all.

What effect all this may have on our lives, we can't calculate in any way. I mean to come home prepared as well as I know how for luck or unluck, and not to be frightened if I can help it. In America the man that can't guide had better sit still and look on. I recommend to you to look on, and if things don't change within a year then I'll eat my head. If all goes right, the house of Adams may get it's lease of life renewed—if, as I've various times remarked, it has the requisite ability still. Till then we needn't compromise ourselves and will watch what comes.

So much for philosophy and that sort of thing.[4] In reference to life here I have a good deal that I *could* say, but this letter would then be the size of yours and that I can't allow myself who write a letter a day almost. So I'll digest.

My family satisfies me and gives me all I want. They are kind and very German, poor as you say and proud in proportion. I think Frank Brooks needn't have been so delicate in his ideas about writing to them; on the contrary I think a short letter on the occasion of introducing me, would have pleased them if written diplomatically enough. Luckily I never mentioned having asked him for a letter, so his refusal didn't embarrass me at all.

They rather spoil me here. German politeness is a cumbrous affair consisting chiefly in elephantine compliments and profuse lies. The Frau Hofräthin is master of the art, but I have learned to watch the countenances of her son and daughter as indexes, and can now nearly tell when there's a deviation from truth. The daughter, the Fraülein Augusta, is a brick. She might be dangerous if—well, if it only weren't that to me she isn't. I don't know why. One can't explain these things.

Billy Howe is in great feather here. He got disgusted with Vienna; you ought to hear him cut up Glancey Jones; and is now living here waiting Sidney's arrival. A few evenings ago he gave a stunning little card-and supper-party in his rooms. Governor Lawrence, two daughters and that amiable son who was your friend and messmate in College and who has just arrived here; Mr and Mrs Stockton, the Consul; and myself. Just enough for two whist-tables and a pleasant sit-down supper. Of course it was stylish and very jolly; I didn't get home till three o'clock. The next night there was a little blow at the Biddles, son of old Nick Biddle; at least so says Billy.[5] This was rather slow but Billy, the Miss Lawrences and I had our whist and heard an Italian woman whom Billy designated quietly as the "boss whore" sing. Afterwards we smoked and drank punch in his room and I got home at two.

On the 22d Shep Brooks walked into my room.[6] He was from Paris for Vienna and leaves on the 25th he says. I kept him that day to dine with me, and family and all went out to a concert in the Grosser Garten in the afternoon, at which he seemed to be pleased. I did what I could to make his stay agreeable; introduced, or rather got him acquainted with Billy Howe and the Lawrences and we all went under Billy's care to the Biddles.

Mr Robert C. Winthrop and his family has also arrived and we three Bostonians sent our cards in to him yesterday, as we happened to be all dining at the hotel.[7] This morning his courier brought his card to my house, so he lost no time about it. It's queer how the Americans are piling in here now just when the season's over. The Gans's are here; I believe either you or John knew Miss Bertha at Sharon; I don't care to be introduced to her; in the first place I should feel as if I were flirting with my aunt, to follow in your elderly footsteps; and then Madame objects to my talking so much English and I don't go out more than is absolutely necessary. I myself prefer a quiet life at home with a fight about once a week and a flirtation now and then, but lately I've talked more English than German.

Wiggins' catalogue as I have already twice written reached me in Munich and I've had no time to attend to it as I wanted to. As my own expences will be this year larger than last I shall probably spend as little money for myself as possible though I have no objection to paying off my debt to you in this way. I mean to devote a few hours to engravings this winter and shall get the Hofrath to introduce me to the overseer of the royal collection. If I see any good heads in the shops, I will buy a few, though not without advice as to their state, for I know nothing about these things as yet.

Beecher's sermon has not yet arrived.

Yesterday was Thanksgiving I suppose. Shep, Billy and I drank to the health of those at home. Last night we saw Dawison, a famous German, as Hamlet.[8] It was a very remarkable rendering, something entirely new and very striking, but repulsive and painful. I don't want to see it again and yet it showed more genius than any I ever saw.

Yrs affectly   H.
November. 25.

MS: MHi

1. *Fights:* colloquial for parties, as in "tea fights."

2. Yankee Sullivan, a British boxer, lost to the American champion, John C. Morrissey, in 1853 by default in the 37th round.

3. George Stillman Hillard (1808–1879), Boston lawyer, scholar, part owner and an editor of the *Courier.*

4. HA resumed here on Nov. 25.

5. John Glancy Jones (1811–1877), U.S. minister to Austria. Albert Gallatin Lawrence (1834–1887), Harvard '56. Mary Ann Remington Stockton (1816–1908), of Philadelphia. Edward Biddle (1815–1872), son of Nicholas Biddle (1786–1844), president of the 2nd Bank of the U.S.

6. Shepherd Brooks (1837–1922), Harvard '57, HA's cousin, son of Gorham Brooks and Ellen Shepherd Brooks, was traveling in Europe for two years.

7. Robert Charles Winthrop (1809–1894) of Boston, former representative and senator.

8. Bogumil Dawison (1818–1872), well-known character actor.

To Abigail Brooks Adams

Dresden. December. 7. [1859]

Dear Mama

I received no letters last week so am without news later than the 8th November. I suppose it's those confounded German steamers; it's happened so twice before. I sent a long letter to Mary last week, directing at random to Washington. Yesterday I suppose Congress met. I've not forgotten to bear it in mind.[1]

Since I wrote last, everything has gone forward as usual. Last week was a particularly quiet one and very pleasant. As the weather is now disagreeable, I don't go much out; depend for exercise mostly on my riding and fencing, which gives me more than I ever had any other winter; and do a tremendous amount of reading and writing. My health is admirable. I'm perfectly contented and in short it's all right. So your own peculiar anxieties at home can have a sort of comfort at least in knowing that one of your children is in no need of care. On the contrary, I don't think I was ever in my life more thoroughly satisfied with my position.

The Winthrops came through here a short time ago, as I believe I mentioned. I left my card there twice and finally had to go to the picture gallery to meet them. Miss Eliza looked to me all right; a little pale perhaps but not much so; and very jolly. We went through the Gallery and did it all thoroughly up. The small Well's boy was very sick in Vienna with typhoid fever I believe, and still looks pale.[2] This detained them there six weeks. Old Bob was blandly urbane and courtly; desired to be remembered to my family; inquired with interest as to their movements &c &c &c. They are now in Paris, I suppose and winter there.

As for my other American acquaintances I've not seen them since I last wrote; not even Billy Howe, but must call tonight. I lead a very domestic life and dread the coming Christmas because some sons are to come down here; and festivities &c.

We are not without our dissipations however in a quiet way. We go to concerts once a week, usually Monday afternoon, and it is wonderful to see what a dispensation of Providence this is for the old ladies. For me it's often a fearful bore and vexation to be obliged to sit three or four hours in a disgusting atmosphere and listen to a lot of bad musicians, and a lot more of old women's double-distilled, super-refined extract and essence of wishwashy clack and gossip, when I want to be at home and have better things to do. The Herr Hofrath is worse than I am; he can grumble but I have to be polite and with a pleased countenance affirm eagerly that it's the height of human enjoyment. Last week we all went as usual and the Frl. Augusta, who is a good deal of a child, didn't behave herself well; laughed and made a great noise and made remarks about people in a very foolish way. I understand that since then an anonymous letter arrived to the effect that the next time, she'd better behave herself; but what the wording was, I can't say. So the young lady had to mind her eye yesterday. She's a good deal of a girl; has considerable quickness, and not at all German except in not being clean, but I must say I don't like to go to concerts with her.

The day before yesterday (Sunday!) she and two of her schoolmates acted a little play for us. I heard the preparations for some days before hand but asked no questions except to chaff her a little as to the price of admission in order to learn whether I was to be admitted. Knowing German propriety and etiquette I supposed it would be only another bore and wished it were over. All of a sudden I learned that the Augusta had to appear in it as a young man and was getting her costume ready. I had the toughest work not to express my feelings, and to look as if it were a matter of course, for the Madame was a little shakey about it, and if I had expressed surprise, it might have made trouble. Sure enough Sunday afternoon before an audience of six persons, the Hofrath and I being the only males, the play was acted and Miss Augusta appeared in costume to my enormous amusement though I didn't dare to express it. For Germans, I thought this was pretty well, especially as they are to play it again to a much larger audience in another house, "and there there will be several young men" as the Fraülein naively remarked.

So we get on very well in every way. I am diving into German literature in a way that astonishes myself. In the evenings after tea if there is nothing prevents, we read German aloud, something from Göthe or Shiller usually. The Hofrath has read parts of the second part of Faust at my request, but one doesn't make much headway in that. Sometimes we take a play and each reads one or two characters. This is rather slow work but it's good practise. Every afternoon when we're at home I read an hour or read and talk with the Frau Hofräthin. This is my lesson; this is the "instruction" included as a part of the contract under which I pay her so-much a month. Very good German practise indeed but rather a bore. I don't see much society outside of the family, and don't much care to, for I don't think it pays.

I hear occasionally from my friends. Hollis is flying round in Paris under the Marquis Lavalette's patronage. He writes very seldom and I don't know how he likes it. I received a letter yesterday from Nick in Munich announcing his departure from that city for today. He returns to Berlin. Ben Crowninshield is in Berlin doing much what I do here. He is in great spirits for his father in a sudden fit of good-nature seems to have given him carte-blanche, and he is at liberty to make the trip we used to talk of, to Sweden and Russia, besides having a prolonged leave of absence. I doubt whether he'll return for eighteen months yet. Joe Bradlee is in Paris but according to accounts doesn't find it very pleasant there.

Dresden isn't the same now as in summer. It isn't so gay nor so pretty; the Elbe is covered with floating ice and the gardens are stripped, even the statues boxed up in little houses. But the weather is a great improvement on last winter, and we have occasionally very fine, clear, cold days. Altogether there's no comparison between Berlin and Dresden to my mind, though I suppose of course before Spring comes, I shall be very glad to get off, for one gets tired of such a continual restraint as I'm under, in time, no matter how busy one is. Very definite plans for next summer, I haven't, but I hope to see Loo in Italy unless she clears out too early or there's another war. This last is not at all improbable. Hungary is getting very uneasy, and they're very anxious here, and everyone knows how Italy stands.

This letter's short because I didn't receive one last week. Tomorrow I hope to get something.

Love to all.   Your affectionate son   Henry.

MS: MHi

1. CFA and his family had moved to Washington for the new term of Congress.

2. Eliza Cabot Winthrop (b. 1838) was the daughter of Robert C. Winthrop and Eliza Blanchard Winthrop. After his first wife's death, Winthrop married in 1849 Laura Derby Welles (d. 1861), a widow with a son.

To Abigail Brooks Adams

Dresden. December. 22. '59.

Dear Mamma

Your letter of the 24–27 November arrived several days ago, but I completely forgot to write last Tuesday as usual so my letter will be a little late. However, you will be so busy I suppose that you'll hardly notice it. I have given up expecting letters now; they come so irregularly. None this week so far and it is Thursday.

It's only a fortnight since I wrote to you, but it seems much more. And yet I never was so quiet. I am laboring under a perfect avalanche of German books on history, law, art and fiction, and one day is very much like another. That is, I very seldom leave my room and then mostly only for a little fresh air. It's cold enough. The Elbe is frozen over. Everyone except myself wears fur coats and wraps himself up as if it were ten degrees below zero. The streets and squares are full of booths, for the Christmas fair is in full blast and the city is livelier than I've seen it since last May. Altogether the fact is, it's the middle of winter and everyone feels it.

I am contented as ever in my domestic bliss. I've managed to get on pretty friendly terms with my family and even the cat has taken a liking to me and the ugly little creature insists on sitting in my lap while I write, as now. My hosts if they have German faults, have German virtues too and spoil me dreadfully. As I get more used to them I get to like them better and we are quite united now. Billy Howe I see every now and then but not much. He is about as quiet as I.

Excitement doesn't abound. Some time ago we gave a party, we did. My goodness gracious, if it wasn't about the toughest piece of work ever I had to do. At four o'clock in the afternoon I was arrayed in the usual garments and pretty as possible in the horrid ugly German-cut dress-clothes. I went up and presented myself. The room, which is *the* state room and resembles somewhat one of our kitchens polished, adorned with flowers or rather with plants, and filled with chairs and sofas, was lighted and gay as might be. A number of haggard-looking old ladies were seated around, drinking tea or coffee and talking with one another. A number of unhappy gentlemen, the essence of boredness, were standing up, drinking coffee or tea and conversing with each other. I was presented all round as "the American." My first faint effort to be lively, died away before the third presentation. I stood in the middle of the room and wondered what I could do. One or two of the gentlemen I knew, or had seen before, and these I fastened to as the Ancient Mariner did to the Wedding Guest. Luckily they were as badly off as I and we managed to appear to talk at least. Presently the Frau Hofräthin comes and requests me to follow her; conducts me into a smaller room and there presents me one after another to six young ladies all sitting in a circle around a table and all silent. Ye Gods! imagine my position. One against six. I thought that hour was eternal. Such a dribble of conversation I never listened to or joined in. Upon my word, what with six young German girls and no help, it's a wonder to me that I still live. Don't imagine that I kept up the conversation. I rested when I could and only came in when my silence became more painful than speaking. But, by Jingo, in future take my life but spare my reason.

At last this was broken up by our all being called into the next room. And what do you think it was for? To listen to Herr Hammer who read us some of his unpublished translations from Turkish poetry, accompanied by an introductory lecture on the poet-sultans; the whole took an hour or an hour and a half, and was greeted with much sympathy from the haggard old ladies. As the room was crowded I stood up, by the door and listened. I would have run but the door was shut. But it was bliss after the six young ladies; *that* was a trial that an American can't conceive of.

This melancholy sacrifice, this hecatomb of innocent comforts, lasted till ten o'clock. After the Turkish sultans were dished, people seemed to feel that the worst was over and brightened up. I fastened on the men again and didn't return to the Syrens. Punch was brought in and poetry in honor of individuals present was recited; healths of course at the end. The refreshments had been sort of walking round all the afternoon; cake and coffee and tea and flummery, punch and at last ice-cream, all of which and each of which I declined one after another.

Towards ten o'clock, when I was in a state of final and hopeless pulpiness, a sort of soaked rag, metaphorically speaking as to the condition of my mind, the last guest departed. The next time there's a party I'll be sick and lay in bed all day rather than go to it.

But this perhaps was the hardest of all my experience. We lead otherwise a retired life and we don't go willingly into society. We've a daughter too whom we have to take care of and who is yet too young to go out much. So the rule is usually as follows. I don't see the family before dinner unless Madame and I go to the gallery or have some other occupation to bring us together. We dine at about one o'clock, and Madame regularly has a battle with me because I don't eat so much as she likes. That's the only point where we can't suit each other. Some time in the afternoon, usually at about five o'clock, I am summoned. Miss Augusta sits on one side of the table, I take my seat opposite, and Madame sits between us. This is my German lesson. Miss Augusta and I read Schiller's plays, she the women, I the men. The Frau Hofräthin sees that we behave ourselves.

At eight o'clock usually we have supper. After it, I request Miss Augusta to take her book, and she reads English to me; my business being to correct her mistakes. As you may imagine, after muddling my brain all day over history or law or what-not, it's not bad fun to teach a pretty young lady English after tea.

I like the Augusta lots. She's a good deal of a girl, and the more I see of her, the more I think of her. She's a real girl, you know. I always adopt the paternal tone to her, for if I treated her as an equal she'd be frightened. As for flirting, they don't do it in Germany. And as for falling in love, she reminds me of our Mary every day in that. Doesn't know what it is. So I amuse myself by trying to get her to like me, but don't think I'm very far ahead yet, and am not absurd enough to press matters. Under proper treatment she'd have made a stunning woman in every way, but it's too late now. She's no joke either in looks; sometimes I've seen her when she was remarkably handsome.

So you see it's getting dangerous. You'd better get papa to double my margin of expenses and let me go to Constantinople and Jerusalem, or I shall do something silly. Six months more in Europe, Constantinople, Holy Land and the Nile and the winter in Italy, or a German daughter-in-law with bad teeth, who eats with her knife. Choose for yourself.

There's a confounded brother here now of whom I spoke in my first letters; Theodore; the most disagreeable creature I've often seen. I'm convinced I shall slap his face some day. As yet he's reserved his miserable temper for his mother and sister, but he won't get far. You used to be unhappy and fairly about your son's behavior, but there's a little, mean, contemptible smallness about this fellow's behavior that beats anything I ever saw. However, it all helps me. The worse he is, the more I take his place, and of course I let him break his own nose if he's fool enough. Just now he and the preparations for Christmas have rather interrupted our quiet but he will soon go off again and Christmas is very near. I'm rather in a box about Christmas. They'll all make me presents and Lord knows how I'm to return them all. Flowers will have to fill the vacuum.

Good, silly, fat old Frau Hofräthin. She lets me into all the family affairs, consults with me about her daughter and her sons and her husband. I hold secret consultations with her and advise and plan, and shut my eyes tight to all the disagreeable little odds and ends that stick out; the poverty and the pride and the trouble of one kind and another. Her stories about Frank Brooks and the Coolidges and J. R. Lowell, I know all by heart and listen with profoundest attention without hearing a word. The Hofrath is sick; tooth-ache and cold; so that he's rather shut up just now. In fact Theodore's presence and the Hofrath's sickness make our meals silent now. Every one reads newspapers.

What on earth has put it into Uncle Sidney's head to write to me. I feel highly honored, but as the relations between us hitherto have been of the slightest, I'm rather surprised that he should recollect me at all, far more that he should write to me. He offers me a letter of introduction to a Mr & Mrs de Cramer here. This is embarrassing for I don't want to know them or anyone else where the acquaintance will require visiting, but I can't well decline the letter. I have been meditating my reply.

No news from Loo for a month and from that suppose she's all right. I am waiting for a letter from Washington anxiously. I've directed my letters there for more than a month and hope you've received them. News here there's none. The Lawrences are off and Billy Howe's occupation's gone. I called on my friend Mrs Biddle the other day. She's jolly.

Love to all.   Yrs Affectly   Henry.

23d. Yours & Mary's of the 4th are just arrived. I can appreciate your feelings. I recollect my arrival in Berlin. I'm astonished at your laughing at my portrait. *I* think it's very imposing. But the moustache is gone and in the Spring I shall start him again. So, you don't like the cockroaches. There's no accounting for tastes. Where abouts is your house; at which end of the avenue? Who are the Markoes? don't know the gentleman.[1] Remember me to Mr Sumner; also to Seward and Wilson and our other political brothers and cousins. I suppose you are hand-in-glove with them by this time. Great thing to be servants of the people, isn't it? Well! I sympathize and wish I could help you but as I can't, a Merry Christmas to you and a Happy New Year.

MS: MHi
1. CFA rented the 20-room brick house at 2017 I St. N.W., the residence of James Monroe as secretary of state and briefly as president, bought in 1840 by Francis Markoe, Jr., president of the Columbian Institute.

To Abigail Brooks Adams

Dresden. January. 6. 1860.

Dearest Mamma

Your and papa's letter of the 16th arrived on Monday (2d). I suppose there was no letter between that and Mary's of the 4th. Don't give yourself any extra inconvenience to write to me. I can go without a letter once in a while; besides I see the New York papers pretty often and in that way have a certain amount of knowledge of what you're about. I wish I could help you in your troubles; I can imagine what they are; but even if I were in America now, I couldn't be in Washington. Papa objects to my extending my absence six weeks beyond the two years, so that I shall, under the same train of reasoning, have to be awful good on my return and lock myself day and night in a lawyer's office in Boston.

I'm glad you have Mr Elliot there.[1] I like Mr Elliot very much and know that he's a gentleman, which one can't say of all one's political friends and acquaintances. Pray remember me to him and tell him that a variety of young Americans have lately met here and held the "Dresden Conferences" in which it was determined to go ahead at any price and not rest till *Seward* is made President. Remember me to Mr Sumner too. It's my own belief that as things stand, you can have more indirect influence on politics than the whole State delegation has direct. Perhaps you can save the Union. But I wish for your sake you had more refined articles to work on.

As for me, after the "bust" of dissipation mentioned in my last, I have retired into my eggshell again and potter till midnight over obsolete formalities of the Roman law. This life just suits me. It seems to me as if within this last year, 1859, I had become a wholly different person from what I was before. And it's true. There is hardly a subject on which my ideas, if I have any, have not more or less changed. And it's very enjoyable to carry on the process and study quietly by oneself in this little icicle of creation.

The flirtation with Miss Amis rests therefore, and I've returned to the Augusta who is much more interesting to me because I can't get the least hold on her. There's no such thing as flirting with Germans. If they're unmarried they think you want to marry them and if they're married you have the chance between seduction and a duel with the husband. On the whole there are a large proportion more seductions than duels, as might be expected under such institutions.

By the way I was dreadfully amused last Saturday evening. We were all at Mrs Butterworth's who is the aunt-mother of the Misses Amis; that is, they are with her and consider her as their mother. Mrs Butt. was making eggnog and I was helping her and talking. She discoursed about her nieces, how good they were; how accomplished; how affectionate &c &c; but they liked each other so much that she was afraid they'd never marry; they never took to any man; she was sure if any young man tried to separate them, he'd have a hard time of it for they'd all be at him and he'd be terribly treated and in short Mrs Butt. continued in this strain till I began to consider what she meant, and came to the conclusion that my delicate attentions to the elder Miss Amis must have induced the young ladies to fear that I was really stricken and must be discouraged. Now I don't set up for a captivator but hang me if I'm so easily captivated, and though I'm much obliged to Mrs Butt. for her kind warning, I consider it only in the light of a compliment that my assumed devotion should have looked so natural. Madame Reichenbach on the contrary insists that I have a fiancé at home. She takes that ring which you gave me, for a proof of it; and as I have always declined to dance in German society, she thought it was for that reason. I have taken particular care not to deny it.

Ben Crowninshield and Nick Anderson and six other Americans from Berlin, Heidelberg, Düsseldorf, Vienna &c were down here last week and only left yesterday morning. Ben goes down to Vienna and Italy in ten days, and will probably visit Sweden and Russia next summer. I am looking out for a companion through Italy. I intend to leave here on the 1st of April.

At home we are as usual. The miserable Theodor is still here to make us all uncomfortable but he goes off again next week and then we shall have rest. As far as acquaintances go, among the Germans I've not made any to speak of. Madame occasionally drags me out to pay a visit but as I declined to go into society or be introduced generally, I'm not bored much in that way. Uncle Sidney's offer to send me a letter to a family here connected with the Russian Legation, I answered by telling him how I was situated and leaving it to him to decide whether it would do for me to present a letter under the circumstances. It would be equivalent to forcing me into society and then I should have to be presented and go to the Court Balls and all that. If I were in Berlin I should do all this merely as a matter of family pride and consider the expense and trouble as a duty which in self-respect I ought to pay to my own name. That is the way Europeans consider the matter, and that is the reason why among Europeans I dislike to have them know anything more about me than my name. They're not great enough to understand and appreciate the state of society in which the equals of their princes are only private persons, and they cannot conceive how a person whose ancestors have held in succession every position of dignity and power which their nation could give, can consider himself as their equal. But in this little one-horse kingdom I coolly set myself above it, and if anyone asks me why I'm not presented at Court, I answer that it's because the Court isn't worth it. Only the Great Powers are great enough to entertain me.

No letters this week; only a newspaper from Charles. I expect a letter from Charles or John with a good deal of curiosity. Is another winter going to pass over their gray hairs and leave them where it found them? Last winter I had hopes that John was struck deep and would begin life again with a purpose. Write me, do, how he is getting on now. What do you or should you think of Miss Fanny as a daughter-in-law? As a single man John will never do anything. Whether he will as a married man or not, remains to be seen. But anyway it would be worth trying and if he were to settle on his last winter's devotion, I for one will toss up my cap for the eldest-born and love his bride though she were the witch of Endor. I wish this the more because since Charles broke with S.B. or she with him, I don't think he's likely to be drawn so far again until he is ready, which will be many years yet; and as for me, I have other things to get which marriage will have to yield precedence to.

Loo seems happy as you please in Florence. Loo is a person whom, if I could, I'd let remain in Europe all her life if she wanted to. She was not meant for America. She ought to have been an English aristocrat and perhaps in such a position might have found herself happier than she ever could in New York. I don't think she has made a mistake in her marriage or in her life since, for I don't see how she could have done better. The mistake was born in her and her education has increased it till it must destroy her happiness, and till now the only happiness that I know of for her is this life in Italy. Children might give her employment and busy her in that way, but even this would never make her happy. She's out of her sphere everywhere except where she now is; and yet it's easier to say where her sphere doesn't lie than where it does. I'm satisfied of one thing and that is that she is not a person for America, for she has there no field and doesn't even herself know what she wants.

(Jan. 9th.)   Billy Howe leaves here today to go up to Bremen and meet his brother. We dined together yesterday and in the evening called on Mrs Biddle. Billy is the only young man I know here and I've of course become pretty well acquainted with him here where age doesn't count. I was curious to see what sort of an influence he'd have on me, for he is himself a fellow of very strong character and decided opinions and is apt to influence much more than be influenced. We've talked freely enough on lots of subjects but we stand so far apart that there's no room for influence on either side. He has been misplaced too. He ought to have been a European and either an officer in the army or a diplomat. As the latter he would have distinguished himself certainly for he has every requisite. His life here is as quiet and respectable as my own. He doesn't do anything in particular but he does no harm and studies or amuses himself with German, art, and literature. He stays two years longer certainly and I hardly think he'll ever live in Boston which he has a great dislike for. On the whole I've a higher opinion of him now than formerly. There's much more good and less bad in him than I had supposed. I've seen so many people who are worse in principles and more disagreeable in manner that Billy's blasé ideas seem slight in comparison.

I've no news to give you. In my family we are as quiet as can be. Occasionally Miss Augusta has a friend or two and we amuse ourselves as well as we can. The other evening one was here who comes from South-Germany, from Bamberg, and has the pretty Bavarian accent. She was perfectly ecstatic; told stories about geese and hens with a naiveté that was unique and that I never met with before in a German girl; I laughed till I was almost suffocated and have implored Miss Augusta to bring her friend lots of times to pass the afternoon and talk about her "kleines Brüderli" or her little brother. Meanwhile Miss Augusta and I read Schiller's Don Carlos;[2] she tolerates me now, and her brother is such a beastly cub that I have more freedom than if he were a gentleman. Madam has once or twice spoken of my "historical name" &c so that I suppose some one has told her my grandfather was president. She has tact enough however to leave me alone. She's a good old woman but in many respects a awful prosy old fool. Excuse the strength of the language.

A newspaper of the 21st from Charles is all I've received this week except papa's and yours of the 15th.

Love to all.   Yrs affectionately   Henry.

MS: MHi

1. Thomas Dawes Eliot (1808–1870) of New Bedford, Mass., Whig representative 1854–1855, Republican representative 1859–1869.

2. Friedrich von Schiller (1759–1805), *Don Carlos* (1787).

To Abigail Brooks Adams

Dresden. Jan. 23. 1860.

Dearest Mamma

Two days ago I received your letter of December 28; the same afternoon came yours and Mary's of Dec. 20; and to-day yours and Mary's of Jan. 4th. The two first came over Bremen. I receive them quicker and more regularly when they come over England "closed mail."

Your letters excite me more than you would believe. That of the 28th came like a cannon-ball into my quiet, and I didn't get over it all day. You have got the excitement and novelty now. My life is without a ripple. I'm glad that John and Charles are so thoughtful and kind. Europe has taught me one thing, if not more; and that one thing is that the only perfectly reliable friends a man has, are his own family, and outside of that circle, certainty ceases. So long as we all stick together, we're invulnerable.

After, or rather, in all your worry and trouble, you will rather like, I fancy, to think of the perfect rest and quiet here. My excitements consist in my fencing, the engraving gallery and the Fraülein Augusta who is gradually expanding to me and who I am getting to be very fond of. For a good while I've seen none of my American acquaintances and Billy Howe hasn't reappeared yet though I expect him every day. I go to the Theatre a good deal and read a good deal, but the time seems to be gliding away without an idea that I'd rather have it stand still. Meanwhile I'm acquiring all sorts of faults and follies here which you will have to scold me out of when I return.

The great excitement of the last week here has been an American one. Perhaps when you were at Sharon you may have seen a family named Gans. At all events Charles Kuhn, and Theodore and Billy Howe and I believe John too, knew them. A Mr and Mrs Gans and two daughters, of whom Bertha, the eldest, is more or less renowned for some rather steep flirtations. This family is here and has been here since October. Billy Howe of course called on them and promised to bring me, but I wasn't anxious to make their acquaintance and dodged it again and again. You know Billy's tongue. He was indignant that old Gans who was a Hamburg Jew and has made his money in stockgambling in New York, should come here and as an American gentleman, force himself into society. So Billy used quietly to express his opinion of old Gans till among Americans the matter was understood. You see, we Americans here are rather proud. We don't lick boots like the English nor court notice. Not one of us have asked to be presented at Court nor have either sought or avoided society. Gans on the contrary leaves America without the intention of going back; he's a German except in his money and his daughters who are more Americans; he brings letters from Mr Belmont formerly our minister at the Hague,[1] to the master of ceremonies here, and accordingly is duly presented at Court with his family; the only Americans except a weak-minded New Yorker named Delaplaine who wants to be a dancer at fifty and apes English manners and talk, and came here on purpose to be presented.[2] It all went very well till about a week ago I met Delaplaine in the street and he showed me a piece of poetry which had just appeared in one of the papers; it was about the German geese (Gans means goose in German) who had found golden eggs in America, gilded their beaks and tails and clothed themselves in down, and come back to their native land thinking themselves swans. But by side of the real nobility they wanted manners and polish and the goose-foot and jewish look discovered them &c &c &c.

This made a perfect howl and cry in the city. The German or rather the Dresden bourgeois families who are excluded from Court, were delighted that the jewish shoemaker should have humiliated or excited the miserable pride of the court nobility, and every day I hear from Madam Reichenbach (whose breath was taken away at the discovery) new stories about it; how low an origin Gans is from; how his wife is very doubtful character; how the daughters have bought $600 muffs; how von Gersdorff, the chamberlain, is wild about his mistake; how the girls were insulted at the court-ball; how they were *not* insulted at the Court-ball; how one sister laid her hand on an officers arm at the Court ball, to call his attention to what she was saying; how the other sister took a fan out of the elder sister's hand at the theatre; how the King is angry; how the King is *not* angry; how the Gans's will have to leave the city; how they will *not* leave the city &c &c &c till I shout over it all.

For various reasons I had rather dodged an introduction, as I have said. But after the appearance of this poem, I was disgusted at the meanness of it, and begged Delaplaine to tell the girls that I had expressed a particular desire to be introduced. Accordingly, after my vigorous announcement of this intention had silenced Madame Reichenbach's deprecations, I called at the Hotel and Delaplaine introduced me. I did this because I wished them to understand that if they cared for my opinion, I thought the song was a very mean way of treating people, and as a sort of quiet protest against it. Delaplaine told me that they had mentioned it to him and spoken of it in a very fair way, as a thing which they couldn't resent and that was only to be left unnoticed. I found the family just as I had expected; the father and mother speaking broken English and the daughter, Bertha, the one I saw, rather nice looking and quite pleasant.

So stands the great goose-question now. You can scarcely imagine what an excitement it has made in the best society, and how famous the Ganses have become. The whole city is accurately informed as to every article of their clothing, their whole pedigree and all their acquaintances. They meanwhile are quiet as possible, go to all the royal balls, know lots of people, and so far as I am informed, are very well treated. The Americans however know as little of them now as before.

This has been the gossip of the week. Otherwise we are quiet as ever. I must soon begin to make calls again and go to parties; periodically one gets little spells of dissipation and then stops. My friend Miss Amis, I've not seen since my last to you, but I understand from Miss Biddle that she (Miss B) had repeated to Miss A. some remarks of mine and as these were followed by devotion and flowers on my side, it may perhaps account for the mistake I mentioned; namely they're supposing me to be in love. I imagine that the matter now stands in the extreme opposite direction, as Miss B. by this time undoubtedly has repeated with additions other remarks which I made with the intention of correcting the mistake.

I however am happy and contented at home and my desire for lady's society is mostly satisfied by chaffing the Augusta who retaliates so well as she can. The good old fat silly Madame Reichenbach, that female Polonius, looks in and laughs or pretends to. They seem to like me well enough and that is all I want.

Love to all. Yrs &c Henry.

MS: MHi
 1. August Belmont (1816–1890), German-born banker of Jewish descent, minister to the Netherlands 1853–1857. In 1837 he came to New York and founded his own firm. In 1849 he married Caroline Slidell Perry, the daughter of Comm. Matthew C. Perry.
 2. Probably John Ferris Delaplaine (1815–1885), heir to a New York shipping fortune, who in middle age began his European travels and in 1866 became secretary of legation at Vienna.

To Abigail Brooks Adams

Dresden. January. 31. 1860.

Dearest Mamma

Your letter of the 11th arrived yesterday and this time tolerably accurately. Your letters interest me exceedingly; perhaps the more because just now all my correspondents seem to have forgotten me and I look in despair at my table every time I come into my room.

Not much has turned up here since my last. Billy Howe has returned with Sidney but I have seen little of them as in the last week I've hardly spoken to a soul outside of my family. The law has progressed so much the faster and really I almost flatter myself I've been tolerably industrious. Sidney Howe never was a favorite of mine; he's one of those fellows, however, whom one must to a certain degree be able to meet on his own ground, and as that ground is usually whiskey straight, I prefer to have those meetings rather seldom, myself not drinking spirits with pleasure nor in large quantities. Billy intends to wean him of this taste if possible and so far as I can help him I shall do so. I was agreeably disappointed in Sidney's appearance; not that he looks like a gentleman in my conception of what a gentleman should look like, but that he doesn't look very like a bad blackguard. I think Billy will have a good influence on him, for vice in losing all it's grossness, loses half it's evil, and so long as the world remains in its present condition I don't mean to take offence at a man's morals so long as his manners are unobjectionable. There are too many persons who have neither morals nor manners whom one has to put up with nevertheless.

The Gans's are making the town cackle still. To give you an idea of the degree of polish and courtesy among the German nobility and best society, which boasts of pedigrees nearly as old as the Christian era, I can repeat to you some of the performances here. What the Gans girls have done, I don't know, but I'm certain that their *real* offence is their low birth. But I do *know* that they are well behaved enough to pass muster, and though I refuse to accept the family anyway as Americans and think they had no business to force themelves into Court, and wonder that their presentation ever was permitted, still that's no reason why the nobility should become blackguards. Noblesse oblige, but hang me if anything can oblige Germans to be gentlemen.

As I remarked, the Gans's went to the Court Ball. But I didn't know that they came home with their dresses torn off their backs. It is now asserted and on the best authority that in coming away the officers trod on their feet and hustled them, and tore their dresses till they were literally in fragments. Of course the Gans's themselves don't tell this, but it comes from people who saw the operation. A few days after this the song appeared in the papers, of which I spoke in my last. This was a sort of thing that I, in the barbarism of an American education, held then and still hold to be simply contemptible; as it came probably from some of the officers, I naturally consider him contemptible and informed my family so, at which the old lady looked frightened and the young one said she didn't think it contemptible at all. If anyone disavowed these demonstrations or even hinted that they were at all contrary to good breeding, I shouldn't be so disgusted, but on the contrary, not a soul that I know of, has expressed the slightest disapprobation, and a few days ago the Commandant of the city, General von Frederici, really a gentleman, gave a large mixed dinner and this Gans affair became the subject of conversation; finally the General made the thoroughly well-bred remark that if these young ladies in his time, ten or fifteen years ago, had appeared and behaved towards the officers as they have, they would have had their faces slapped. And this remark was repeated to me by Madame Reichenbach, a most intimate friend of Madam Frederici who is herself one of the Court ladies, and repeated with every appearance of triumph and approbation as proving how improperly the Gans's must have behaved. It proved to me nothing but what I knew long ago; and that is that the Germans are still a semi-barbarous people and the ideas of the middle-ages are alive and kicking in the nineteenth century.

Meanwhile what the Gans's themselves think, I don't know. I've not been there since my introduction. But in consequence of the death of some princess the Court has gone into mourning four weeks and perhaps in that time the Officers and the old women may get some new subject to blow about and forget the Gans's. The Americans seem to hold themselves perfectly neutral and as the Gans's know very few persons here, we, as a class, are not mixed up in the affair at all.

The amount of gossip that goes on here is frightful. Upon my word, if I were a native, I'd try and give them something really to talk about. I don't wonder that the Princess Metternich who was here before her husband was sent to Paris, cut up such rummy rigs as she did. She kept the good old city in gossip. She joked the King and chaffed the Queen and there wasn't a day passed that she didn't horrify the whole city. The respectable old last-century stupids here called her crazy. I see that she's now leading the fashions in Paris and have no doubt she's looked on there as a wit and a beauty. I can imagine how the air of this little place must have bored her.[1]

You see there's got to be a revolution here. '48 didn't do it's work, and while France, quiet itself, is setting Germany on fire, these little Princes look on to see what that rascal Napoleon is doing with his torches.[2] All the signs point one way. If there isn't a blow-up next summer there will be one later. And yet these stupid Kings with their Dei Gratiâ can't be either led or kicked into common sense.

My friends are as usual. As I've withdrawn myself from the lists in regard to Miss Betty Amis and Billy Howe succeeded to the position, Sidney being considered as the attendant on Miss Sally, I am now as it were floating, and reserve my attention for Miss Augusta whom I stand very well with now. I find it a bore to make visits and believe I must have grown old since I left home for I cannot for the life of me take pleasure in dancing attendance on a pack of girls merely for the fun of submitting to their whims. It emphatically doesn't pay. However I suppose I shall be hooked again some day and work willingly in the traces again. If my brothers are still under the yoke, I don't suppose I can call myself safe.

At home all is as usual. Madame puts my politeness to awful tough trials; she won't allow me to go anywhere without her. I can't take a walk, visit a gallery or go to the Theatre without her inviting herself to be of the party and the result is that I am more apt now to be worried into rudeness than at first. This eternal clack and potter in one's ears is occasionally too much, especially when one is busy. However I try to keep my mouth wholly shut when I feel cross. The Augusta on the other hand is amusing as usual. Such a child; splendid study of human nature. With a taunt I can drive her in any harness. She plays to me sometimes now; a great triumph on my part for she never would play before to please even her father, but I told her that she was afraid of me and didn't dare to have me listen, and she bolted for the piano and hammered away till I was tired. Then I make her read English to me, and occasionally worry her to be really angry, but she's a good child and is all the pleasanter the next time we meet. It's amusing to sound the keys of a person's character in this way, and as I am particularly careful never to assume an intimate tone (except in matters of utter indifference) and never to insinuate a hint at more than a fatherly interest and care, it isn't probable that either the Augusta or I will be seriously damaged in the process.

Meanwhile I begin tomorrow to take French lessons in preparation for my start in April. I shall never know German much better than I do now, not that I speak it perfectly or even fluently, but well enough for my purposes. So I am contented or tolerably so with what I've done and shall be still more so if I can ever do as much in French. This is to be sure a new expense and just now I'm trying to economize, but there are two things I must spend money on without being afraid; tuition and books. As it is however, please inform papa that I leave Dresden April, 1st and on or before that day at latest, shall be obliged to him for more money. I shall not leave Dresden till I've received it.

Ben Crowninshield is in Vienna with grand plans of travel from Naples to St Petersburg. He wants me to go down to Italy with him now and God knows I'd like to, but it won't do. Joe Bradlee goes with him to Sweden. Joe is said to be unhappy in Paris and to be on the point of returning to Hannover.

I had the pleasure of informing Billy Howe the other day that his father's mill had tumbled to pieces. The German papers gave the general particulars and since then we've received the details. As yet no letters speaking of it, have come. It seems to have been a bad affair enough all round. The newspaper accounts are horrible; I should think cannibals had written them. But besides the loss of life, I suppose the whole insurance is lost to Mr Howe; and besides that I suppose Capt. Bigelow will catch it severely, which won't please the Judge, will it? As Billy remarked when I told him what had happened "it's always been a rotten concern, that mill."[3]

No letter from Loo this month which rather disturbs me as she was laid up and just getting well when she last wrote. However, no news is better than bad news, and I hate to feel nervous; I don't think I ever knew what it was till I came abroad. I write all about myself and things here because I suppose you have enough of Washington as you are. Your letters are very exciting to me. I'm glad you're so well situated as you are. Things might be worse.

Love to all, Moll, Brooks, Margaret & Bridget. Stamps will some day appear.

Yrs affecly   Henry.

MS: MHi

1. Princess Pauline von Metternich (1836–1921). Her husband, Prince Richard von Metternich (1829–1895), the son of the famous Austrian statesman, was minister to Dresden 1856–1859, ambassador to France 1859–1870. She became an intimate of Empress Eugénie and was renowned for her wit, dress, and eccentric behavior.

2. Napoleon III (1808–1873), emperor 1852–1870.

3. On Jan. 10 the roof of the Pemberton cotton mill in Lawrence, Mass., collapsed, destroying the building and killing 88 workers. The building had been poorly constructed, but the coroner's jury held that the owners "had no reason to distrust its insecurity."

To Abigail Brooks Adams

Dresden. Februar. 7. '60.

Dearest Mamma

I begin another letter this week without a word to say. I haven't even seen anyone. The last week I went almost every evening to the theatre to see classic plays, and had no time to pay visits or call much on my friends. I sat an hour or two with the Howe's and left a card on the Miss Amis's. This week I am unwell; that is, I have requested the Howes to say they had heard so. I prefer to remain at home. Of course among the Germans there's no news to interest you or me either for that matter. My family remains much as usual. It's a curious question to me, worthy of a moment's attention, whether Madame Reichenbach really thinks she's doing me a favor by presenting me with so much of her company, for she does cut it precious fat and I have had to hint once or twice that I am of age and can go alone. Thank Heaven, the sanctity of my room remains inviolate as yet, but everywhere else she must be by my side, and the truth is, she is so *damned* weak that Job himself would have cussed and swore rather than stand it; biles was nothin' to it. If I didn't have an opportunity to blow out in my letters home, I really believe she'd stifle me with sheer weakness. I daren't call her names here in Dresden for the chances are ten to one she'd hear of it within twentyfour hours. Indeed I'm not sure she doesn't read my letters when I'm out, for I leave them pretty loose on principle. At the same time, you know, she's as obliging as possible towards me; a deuced sight too much so, and it's the cruelest ingratitude on my part to call her names. But I can't help it. I am of a patient and longenduring disposition; what's more I am very well satisfied with my position and the quiet and leisure suits me exactly; when I have an opportunity to check the mother off against the daughter I am also very well satisfied in this respect, but to have the mother alone for three or four hours is enough to make a marble statue tear its teeth and gnash its hair. I'm getting tired of humoring her; I can't stand her twaddle much longer; I've heard three times over a full and accurate account of all that she ever did in her life, or ever saw, or heard, and all that all her relations and friends and acquaintances ever did, saw or heard or had said or thought they had heard or seen and a deuced lot besides that no human being ever did do or see, and no one but a muddle-headed, soft-brained old woman could conceive of; so that now, when the round is beginning for a fourth time, I feel like being counted out of the fight and handing over the stakes; she has beat me and I might as well own up. I have seen some little of the world and of human nature and though I don't pretend to know either well, I have yet some bowing acquaintance with them. Yet I must say until I came here, the old-women species of the genus homo was only known to me through fairy tales and nursery rhymes. If Germany boasts many such as Madame R., then I don't wonder that the German men consider them inferior beings. Dear me. Dear me! I sometimes meditate during her long stories while I keep my eye fixed on her in a hopeless vacancy, "Old woman, if human nature boasts of you as an average product of its creations, does it and can it pay to advance the cause of civilisation in the world. Whats the use of teaching an idiot to read?"

Enough of her. Yet, oh, that you could see her. See her as she appears at a concert, waving her head and gesticulating her hands in time with the music and expressing in a loud tone her approbation of the performance. See her as she appears at the Theatre in the most conspicuous seat in the house, an air of ineffable hauteur on her face, her peppermints and her bottle of salts before her. See her as she appears at home, looking exactly like one of those big cotton bales rather burst out, stuck on end, and a round bundle on the top; no crinoline; Heaven forbid; and I would like to cry sometimes when I see her style of head-dress. Then she's such a flunkey, and she thinks she isn't; I know I worry her when I laugh at the King's shocking bad hat, and that's why I do it. I suppose of all gossips in the city, she doesn't yield to many, and yet when I let out on Dresden gossip and this "provincial" clack, she acquiesces as readily as if she were utterly innocent. Since the death of the last King, she's been thrown very much into the shade, and her pride and poverty, her past and her present, her silliness and her sense, make altogether a most extraordinary mixture; to say nothing of her art and her idea that she can feel art; can appreciate the works of others. Lord bless her, if the King and her husband said that the Madonna di San Sisto was a blotch, she'd believe it unless somebody helped her to the necessary self-confidence to deny it.

Still her devotion to herself and to her family, especially to her daughter, make up for many short-comings. She isn't selfish, and she believes in educating the mind. She thinks her mind is educated and I sometimes meditate whether her love and admiration of art is self-deceit, or whether being naturally weak-minded, her calibre grasps as much as it can and is really master of that. But what troubles me most is that the Augusta must degenerate into this; you must know I like the little Princess; there's something in her, such as we call spirit and Europeans call nobility because common citizens don't often have it. She's plucky and headstrong and will insist on running her head against all the walls that come in her way. But I see how she's got to be kept inside of the modelling maschine till she comes out according to the rules. That's just the difference between America and Germany; we are all for standing on our own feet and not being like other people; at least that's what we ought to be for; but here an originality is a crime.

Here I've written ever so much without telling you anything in particular. What is there to tell? That the weather's beastly and that I feel it as I always do feel bad weather? That I'm reading law-books which leave precious few ideas in my mind? That I'm devoting two mornings every week to the engraving gallery? that I'm taking French lessons? in short that I'm industrious as the busy bee and in spite of my industry don't seem to get ahead any great? Among other things I'm expecting a letter which doesn't

Henry Adams, 1860

Caroline Bigelow

come; however papa's of the 16th arrived and so did one from Loo which I was glad to have. Crowninshield writes from Vienna that there's no doing anything with Shep; he won't leave his room at any price; the story ran that he went to the theatre and fell asleep in the most exciting part of a very exciting play; usually he doesn't go because he can't understand it. Billy Howe wishes to be remembered to you. At last accounts, I've not seen him since Friday, he had received no letters from home; only a New York Herald which a friend lent him contained an article recommending that the owners of the Pemberton Mill should be imprisoned for life or something of the sort. Also speaking of the "white slaves" of Lawrence and other remarks which made William speak in terms of affection and endearment of that lovely sheet, the New York Herald.

Love to all.   Yrs affectly   Henry.

Letter from Charles just come. Loo. Crowninshield's engagement. Is'nt it extraordinary. I *expect* a letter from Ben.

MS: MHi

To Charles Francis Adams, Jr.

Dresden. February. 10–13. '60

Dear Charles

Your letter was interesting—very. It told me just what I wanted to know. As the engagement is the latest piece of news, I'll take it first in order. So far as I have heard, there's only one opinion of it, out of the family. Ben wrote to me about it, however, astonished as you please, but giving it his entire approval. I should think more highly of Ben if I supposed his approval was diplomatic, compelled by circumstances and merely assumed towards others; but I have no doubt he really does approve it. After all it's only a repetition of the old Hammond story; two cousins married hogs; why shouldn't a third? Ben likes the Hammonds and he's right in doing so; his weakness is in not appreciating their faults; but family unity must be preserved. Mr Crowninshield is much pleased with the young man? And what does Mrs. C. say in her heart of hearts? She's such a severe stickler for aristocracy and breeding that I should think her dear son-in-law would occasionally startle her.[1]

I'm sorry for Carry Bigelow, but I know her so well that all your reports don't surprise me. I wasted a good deal of superfluous philanthropy on her. It was my last and longest hit, that. Lasted me a matter of three years and might be still hanging round me if I'd remained at home, though I had pretty much found her out the Spring before I graduated. It cost me the hardest heart-aches ever I had before I could sit quiet under the conviction that she is—what she is. It changed me entirely in one respect for I used to go on the principle that all women were perfect until they'd proved themselves the contrary and now I believe that all women are fools and playthings until they've proved the contrary. By God, I grind my teeth even now to think how easily I let myself be led by that doll, who didn't even have the brain or the heart to exercise her power. Much happiness to Philo. He caused me then some miserable hours the like of which I pray God I never may have to stand again, but he cured me. A nasty medicine but I'm grateful for it.

If I supposed Miss F.C. were a person of this sort, I should not be in favor of her as a sister-in-law.[2] But I judge from your own letters; if your account of her was influenced by your own liking for her, I can't help it. So far as I know she's the most acceptable of any of John's attachments. I think that John ought to marry her as a matter of policy; not that I think that marriage is wholly good for him but because a bachelor's life is worse. My dear Charles, in all secrecy, I'm losing respect for John. There's a want of ballast about him that doesn't seem to decrease with time nor sober off with age. I know too that you have the same feeling; at least if the tone of your letters proves anything. Now you may question whether our respect for him would be increased by his marriage, but it seems to me that so far as human foresight is capable of judging, John's marriage with a thoroughly ladylike, loveable, and capable girl is the only prospect of steadying him enough to carry him respectably through. I've said often that I don't think he *is* respectable now, and your last letter makes me certain of it. You feel it yourself. What would be gained by his remaining bachelor a year or two longer. Do you think it would improve him, for I'm quite sure it wouldn't? Do you feel so certain that his next love may be as acceptable as this one? for the chances are against it. Do you expect that he'll be richer than he is now? for I don't see how he's going to do it. Do you see any signs of a change for the better in him which marriage would crush? for you've never hinted at anything of the sort. You look only at the objections to the match, and you may be right; but it seems to me that you're postponing buying the Sybilline books. John has worn out his old clothes and must have new or go naked. If there's any way in which he can get out of his present mire except by marriage, let him try it. But to my mind his life of man-on-the-town has lasted long enough.

He's in love with her bad and as you seem to think, she too with him. He has come to the leap; if he takes it, so far, so good; but if he doesn't take it, then he has finished himself—at least with me and when one's brothers are forced to think in this way, the world isn't far behind.

We can tell one another what we think without hurting any one. I don't assume any superiority over John because I think he is going wrong and tell you so. Very likely I shall do the same thing myself and if not that, perhaps worse. Still as I expect to hear, yes and hope every day to hear that he is engaged, the subject had better be fairly aired in time. Pray keep me posted up in affairs. It's more than six months since John himself has written.

As for news or talk here, you might as well look for clients on the third-story-iron-front in Court Street. We haven't it to show. At the beginning of the winter I withdrew myself from German society and declined once and for all every invitation. It was too damned slow. You haven't an idea of it. For a little while I visited the Americans here, but they invited me to tea-fights that were enough to make one puke, and so latterly, I've declined all invitations when it was possible. Billy Howe goes however and so does Sidney who is quite a favorite among the young women and who has behaved very well so far. Indeed so far as rum goes, he can't do much here unless he sogs alone, for I am no drinker and told him that I neither could nor would drink nor bat, and Billy never loses an opportunity to insinuate in the quietest way that he considers bar-rooms and drunks low, and in Europe that sort of thing is not done. If there's anyone else who can lead him off, I've not seen him and he'll run the risk of Billy's throwing him out the window or kicking him out the door. On this point Billy is firm. So far as women go I suppose he has the run of the city, always of course under general companionship from Billy. I think he'll be tamed at last. I see them two or three times every week and smoke a cigar with them occasionally, but as they know that I don't have any time to spare and as my room is not fitted for lounging, they seldom call on me and I don't know how they pass their time. It's only within two days that they've received letters about the Pemb. Mills though they've known it a fortnight. We had all the papers and the fullest details.

I don't often leave the house myself. I've just got fairly into my winter's work and devote all my time to regular occupations. I've made a regular study of engravings and have looked over heaps and heaps in the Gallery. I've ordered your "le Parche" from the man here and expect to receive it very soon. It will come home with my other things this spring when I must send a box.[3]

Feb. 12. Last night I went to a blow given by a Mrs Kearney here to the Misses Gans. You know perhaps that I don't dance any more now, having given it up because I don't dance well enough; modesty was always my weakness; so, as for the life of me I can't hash up a regard for any of these girls, I usually try to get up or join a card party. One doesn't have to talk so much then and whist amuses one. So last night Billy and I and the two Miss Ganses for whom the party was given, sat down to whist and our devotion was very touching indeed. I suppose John has heard of the row their presentation started up here; Gans is an old excrement and the Germans are hogs; so they've had it out between them and I've heard it all from both sides. The young ladies however are unmoved by all this; they are aristocratic and condescending and seem to know nothing of the horror with which the Germans regard them. They are really nice girls enough and well-behaved enough; it's only these damned stupid Germans who make such a row about them and make brutes of themselves to show that

Gans is a German-Jew-shoemaker or was one at first. Miss Bertha and Miss Fanny were all ready to play whist; it was "so nice" and "papa was so fond of it." So papa sat by and directed his two daughters what to play while Billy grinned satirically at him from across the table. Miss Fanny wanted to know all about the German Fraülein I was in love with; she was sure it was something of the sort that kept me always at home; was it true that we read German together; and Wallenstein;[4] and was she really so pretty; and what was she like &c &c till she was convinced that I was a Hamilton and she a Hildegarde and oh it was so funny. You must know that my little concerns as well as every one else's are the talk of the town and all the young ladies ask me as their first question how Thekla or Hildegarde or the Frorlein or Froulein as their fancy and acquaintance with the German tongue may be, for under all and still more than these titles does the poor Augusta labor among my friends; how, I say, she is; and I of course never deny anything. It's now an understood thing that I've paired off with her and have re-signed my position under Miss Betty Amis to which the common report at first promoted me. The Miss Ganses were in raptures at this idea and smiled and lisped worse than when they told me my "brother John wath the funniest man they ever thaw; they never had laughed tho in their whole lives as one morning at Nahant."

Played Euchre and drank champagne and smoked till two o'clock in the morning (party being ended) and the consequence is I've a damned head-ache today and almost swear I never'll drink anymore as long as I live. It doesn't pay. I get more and more of this opinion every time I try it; especially since one night at Hildesheim near Hannover I got awful drunk with Ben and a Lieutenant, and some respectable Lady found me on a trunk in her house from which I refused to move; how I got there; where it was; and who the person was, I can't say nor any one else; the kellner carried me to a neighboring hotel, put me to bed and told me this the next morning.

Remember me to the young women; and to one old one too, Rebecca. Kind words cost nothing and are deuced useful often. I hope you'll go on to Washington soon. I'm afraid the parients will need a little backing up for they've a heavy work.

Yrs always.   H.

Thanks for the photograph; I wish I had one of Miss F.C. I'm dreadfully curious to see what she looks like.

MS: MHi

1. Louisa Crowninshield was engaged to Francis Edward Bacon, described by CFA2 as an "unlicked cub" and by ABA as wanting in conversation and dancing (Mary Adams to HA, Jan. 22).

2. Fanny Crowninshield.

3. Engraving of *Le Tre Parche* (The Three Fates) by Francesco Salviati, then attributed to Michelangelo.

4. Schiller's trilogy, 1798–1799.

To Abigail Brooks Adams

Dresden. February. 13. 1860.

Dearest Mamma

Your letter of the 24th arrived this morning, and as Mary's letter is intended for you as well as to her so far as news goes, I shall take this for private matters. The news of the engagement startled me some if not more; on the heels of it came a letter from Ben officially announcing it. Ben is considerably astonished but swallows it like a good boy and gives it his entire approval. Under these circumstances I answered the letter in the same spirit, and wish him joy of F.B. The family Mifflin-Warren-Crowninshield has the monopoly of the hog-trade.

I'm glad you're entertaining. I wish you could make your "salons" the first in Washington. You know I'm ambitious; I needn't remind you of it; not on my own account, but as a family joint-stock affair. Now papa has got to make himself indispensable; not only in the wild-beast pen, but out of it too. So far as ability, courage, strength and bottom goes, that is, so far as public business is concerned, we'll all bet heavy on him and give odds; but his weak point is just where you can fill it; he doesn't like the bother and fuss of entertaining and managing people who can't be reasoned with, and he won't take the trouble to acquire strength and influence that won't fall into his mouth. People can be lead by their stomachs as well as by their understandings, and the opening is now a magnificent one. I don't see why you can't make your drawing-rooms as necessary and as famous as you please and hatch all the Presidents for the next twenty years there. Gov. Seward knows well enough how important this is and if he says so much as your letter mentions, and went so far as to bring his daughter-in-law to you without a previous call from you, all I can say is, the Governor knows what he's about and I believe in him more than ever. As for having the "Presidency in view" I hardly think it's desirable with the present occupant's fate before one's eyes; I aspire to the leadership in the lower House and the Departments. Be ambitious, Mrs A. You're young yet! Just begun life! Principle is an excellent thing; very; but it belongs at the bottom and not at the top; it makes the foundation of life but the upper stories are lighter material; one can't eat and drink and live on principles, as you justly say. It's all infernal nonsense, you and papa sacrificing yourselves for the good of your country; I tell you, you're doing nothing of the sort, at least if I can help it; you must take just as many honors as you can get and what's more, you must work to get them and be glad that the paths of duty and of ambition combine for you; for most people they lie in contrary directions.

You just mark what Seward says; he's the man of the age and the nation; he knows more in politics than a heap; he's a far-sighted man and yet he's got eyes for what's near, too. I aspire to know him some day. Pray tell him so if you ever lack matter of conversation. Keep him allied with papa, the nearer the better. If he comes in as President in that case, we shall see fun. Don't scold because I advise so conceitedly. I want you to know the views of a European, and I don't see the use of shutting our own eyes however much we may wish our neighbors to close their's.

More next week.

Yrs Affectly   Henry.

MS: MHi

To Abigail Brooks Adams

Dresden. February. 20. 1860.

Dearest Mamma

So you've a Speaker at last.[1] After that vote for Smith, I knew that it must come soon and that the Republicans must yield or be beaten. Of course we must be sorry that the straight-out ticket doesn't carry it, but so far as I can see it's neither to be hoped nor to be wished that the next President should be a Republican, and unless Seward can be elected with a reliable House and national majority behind him, I think it's about as well to yield for the present the straight ticket in the House and if the next Democratic President does as well for us as Buchanan, I think, my dear madame, there's hope for the family A. yet. Which political and philosophical considerations will probably be worth large sums to you who know considerably more about it than your obedient son.

In my last letter or fragment of a letter inclosed with one to Mary, I commented on your views of your future political course. Now I want to say a word about your other affairs, for I see by your letters as I expected that you're at times not over happy in your new position. For myself, when I feel low-spirited, I usually try to cure myself with reflecting how much worse it might be; but I'm afraid it won't raise your spirits much to remind you that there are perhaps out of three or four hundred million inhabitants of the world, by a high estimate ten thousand whose blessings have been so many and whose troubles from without are so few, as yours. I won't therefore insist on this point of view for I know that when a fellow feels miserable all the philosophical reflexions that ever were made, from Confucius down to Bowen, Professor in Harvard College,[2] won't help one much. Now I don't mean to assert that you haven't had a pretty tough trial of it; your entrance into political life hasn't been smooth sailing, not by a good deal, and I don't blame you for thinking it's a pretty mean sort of prospect. But then I recollect my entrance into Berlin some fifteen months ago, wasn't such jolly fun that I'd like much to repeat it; I felt for two months or so much as if metaphorically, some one were pouring buckets of cold water at short intervals over my spirits. But just think; you've all your acquaintances to make, and they'll come in time and pleasant ones too. You're no more separated from your family, or little more, than you would have been if you'd remained at home. So soon as you get used to it, you'll feel the excitement of the life and politics as well as the rest of us. I've already observed that if you labor under the idea that you're martyrizing yourself for your faith, it's only making yourself unnecessarily wretched. I don't labor under any such idea; not by a jug-full. To take a similar case in many ways, do you think Loo was much happier than you, during her first year in New York, much younger as she is and therefore bearing transplanting easier. I guess she was tolerably wretched. And yet she got to like it very much, and I doubt excessively whether she would or could go back to her former life. In short what I want to say and if possible to raise your courage and spirits by, is this. You've risen into a higher life, and of course a higher position demands more care and effort to maintain, but it gives strength to the strong, and I'm not afraid of your wanting there. But it's not going to make you unhappy, not a bit; it's only the first plunge that makes one shiver; and it's not going even to separate you from your family for, just believe me, it is much more likely to draw your proper family closer round you. In summer you are the same as ever, and I must confess that I am no such great friend of Boston exclusiveness and Beacon St society as to be sorry for the step that will loosen it's hold on us. I look forward to sunny weather for you in Washington when we shall stand on the top of the ladder and life will have rather a wider prospect than from the blue-room windows of 57 Mt Vernon St.

To leave this subject for the present. Life here does not vary at all. Only the other evening I went to call on my friends the Miss Amises and their aunt, with Sidney Howe. We took tea and played whist with the young ladies till after twelve o'clock. On the way home I stopped in Howe's room to smoke a cigar; and at about one o'clock some accident reminded me that it was the 16th of February and my birth-day. Properly the day was over as the 17th had already come, but we calculated the eight hours variation of time and so made it all right, and Billy produced a bottle of Champagne that was for an entertainment the next evening. So we sat a couple of hours longer and drank in my twenty-third year. I've no doubt you recollected it though it had entirely escaped from my mind.

The evening of the 17th the Howes had a little card-party in their room, at which the Consul and his wife, Mrs Butterworth and the two Miss Amises were present. Mrs B. has come down on me severely because I've not called there but once since she returned from Paris about a month ago. In fact I get scolded all round for not being more sociable and so far as I know, Billy goes round saying that, it looks very queer; I laugh about it and don't let anyone into my affairs; but he himself thinks that there's something serious between me and the Fraülein. So this serves for my excuse and they try to run me about it, but I have announced that I've got your consent, and Mrs Stockton who knows more of other people's matters than any one else, and who has already announced me as in love with Miss Betty Amis and Miss Edith Biddle, is now considerably confused about it.[3] Billy informed me that he'd been spreading the report, and I'm willing. I've only five weeks more here.

I've got postage-stamps enough for Brooks to fill a wheel-barrow, though you mustn't tell him so. I'll prolong his pleasure by sending them in weekly instalments which I suppose he'd better not expect, else he'll get impatient. The boor, Theodor, had a heap of duplicates and gave me a number of German ones, and Brooks must himself enclose a slip of paper in the next letter, thanking him. Quick, or it won't be in time.

—— Your letter of the 2d has just arrived, interesting as your letters always are, but needing no particular answer. Papers later than the 1st, I've not yet seen. I'm glad that Charles is with you. I expect a letter from him soon with all sorts of news. So far as I can see you're doing firstrate and I think it couldn't well be better. As for Pennington, where's the necessity of keeping him there after the contested elections are decided. Let him resign if he feels, or his party feels, he's unsuited to the place.

Love to all and the enclosed stamps to Brooks.

Yrs affectly   Henry.

MS: MHi
   1. William Pennington (1796–1862) of New Jersey, Whig representative 1859–1861, was a compromise candidate whom CFA reluctantly supported.
   2. Francis Bowen (1811–1890), Alford Professor of Natural Religion, Moral Philosophy, and Civil Polity 1853–1889, with whom HA studied.
   3. Edith Biddle (1844–1924), daughter of Edward and Jane Craig Biddle, later wife of Philip S. Van Rensselaer.

To Abigail Brooks Adams

Dresden. February. 26. 1860.

Dearest Mamma

My weekly despatch will this week be stupider than ever. Since ten days I've not seen an American, not even the Howes, and have received no letters whatever and my latest American accounts reach only to the 2d.

You'll want to know what I've been doing with myself all this time, just like my American friends here who can't conceive why I don't show myself. Indeed, I hardly know, myself, except for absolute want of time. Every day is parcelled out like clockwork, and though a little while ago the bad weather made me feel cross and unwell, it's now clear and cold and I'm as jolly as a sand-boy.[1] So as yet, and partly because I look forward to leaving on the 1st April, I'm as contented as ever.

The days go by as fast and regularly as ever. My mornings are still taken up with French and Fencing and the Engraving Gallery. For as I'm averse to all extremes, I don't usually get to work till nine o'clock; that being the proper medium between the German hour of seven, and the fashionable one of eleven. At one o'clock we dine and read the newspapers; that is, the Hofrath always reads them all through dinner, and I too when I feel cross and there's no political discussion to wake us up. Augusta has decided Austrian sympathies and gets dreadfully pitched into for them. After dinner we either go to walk, Madame, Augusta and I, and on coming home have our lesson; or else I go up at about three o'clock and we read and talk. I read German half an hour or so, and Augusta reads English for about the same time, with intervals of talking and quarelling, and then lately, within a few days we've begun to play games; as for instance I'm teaching Augusta chess; dangerous, isn't it. It strikes me as slightly queer and risky that Madam should smile so beneficently on all this, for I acquit her of any design to hook me for her daughter. But the truth is, she knows Augusta all to pieces and I suppose she's justified in giving her string in the matter. But how does she know that I am not to be the sufferer and what justification has she in putting me to such a test. As it is, it's all right. The very fact that I'm allowed so much liberty; almost directing the whole family, even Augusta, who has been and still is the most independent of all, and has to be treated very carefully; is proof enough that there's no danger of sentiment on either side; and yet I'd like to know whether Madame in her fancied wisdom, when she laughs about my quiet and imperturbability, can be completely at ease about it. I'm beginning to have great confidence in myself, really; I consider my tactics in this family to have been admirable; even Augusta now makes faces at me behind my back and when I catch her and laugh at her for it, she is as confused as possible and acknowledges in every way that she thinks it best as a general thing to pay considerable regard to my opinion. An immense study of human nature, she is. I never had an opportunity before to study such a transparent case of impulse and complete girlishness that knows next to nothing of the world. But I'm glad I'm not three years younger, for at that time I fell in love without half the provocation I've had here; and yet as Charles remarks of a young lady in his last letter "it's the only one I ever met who interests me without a touch of sentiment." I'm a cold-hearted beggar and become more so every year.

So we wander on. My work is mostly evening and night work, reading and writing. We occasionally go to the Theatre, but that has rather died out lately as the best actors and singers haven't appeared. I take walks as long as possible to keep my spirits up in bad weather, for I do hate bad weather. In short, the winter is coming to an end and with it my connection with Germany. I'm not sorry. My longing for Italy is as great as ever.

A little while ago Uncle Sidney sent me a letter of introduction to a Mr and Mrs de Cramer here, of the Russian Legation. At my wish Howe was included. I've not presented it yet, but I mean to do so at once, perhaps this week, though I rather want to post-pone it as far as possible that it mayn't interfere with my present occupations.

The great event of the week was my appearing one day with my whiskers off; the first time since the 27th September 1858 that I've shaved. The look of horror that appeared on the Frau Hofräthin's face was inimitable, as I entered to dinner a day or two ago. Flattery was forgotten and she didn't make the least attempt to conceal the fact that she had *not* supposed I looked like that. She informed me I looked four years younger, and has lamented ever since, the loss of my ornamental appendages. No one knows me any more; my acquaintances all cut me on the street and I'm almost afraid to appear before American young ladies for fear they'll hurt themselves for grief. However, it's only for a time and soon I shall appear more blooming than ever.

27th.   Your letter of the 8th arrived this morning punctually as ever. I'm glad that Charles is with you. I hope he'll succeed, as you say he tries to, in devoting himself to something besides sugar-candy young women and dancing. Just remember, when I come home, if I devote my best time and strength to flirtations and walzes, I hope you'll snub me and sneer at me and worry me till I learn better. Such an utterly non-paying way of passing one's time is seldom met with; at least I know to me the pleasure was about counterbalanced by the pain, and further there was nothing. My gracious, if I'm only as good when I get home, as I talk good now, sha'n't I be a model for well-behaved young men.

As for Carry Bigelow, if she's going to be engaged to Philo at all, I hope it'll be soon. I can write a congratulatory letter, but hang me if I could congratulate her to her face; at least, I could do it, but it would be embarrassing considering little remarks I've made to her about him, and I don't suppose two years are an eternity to make her forget such slight compliments. However, if she kin stan' it, I kin, and lie with a steadiness unsurpassed since the devil was a very small boy; if you'll excuse the lowness of the illustration.

I send Brooks another relay of stamps of various sorts, which I hope he'll like. It's time to begin to think of a new direction for my letters. All that come after the 1st April; that is, all letters that leave home [*The rest of the letter is missing.*]

MS: MHi
1. Boys who hawked sand for scouring or for floor cover (as in butcher shops and pubs) were proverbially happy, but as sawdust replaced sand on floors, they were a disappearing class.

To Abigail Brooks Adams

Dresden. March. 4. 1860.

Dearest Mamma

I've not much more to say this week than I had last. I've described my mode of life here till the subject is threadbare and as there is no change in it, I have nothing new to say. On the other hand a look at some American papers the other day announced to me the formation of the Congress

Committees, and papa at the head of that on Manufactures. I had expected something of the sort, and yet was much gratified at this first national recognition of him as a power. It's pleasant to feel that we're going up the ladder still, and that nearly a hundred years hasn't exhausted the family yet. Meanwhile I wish the other political news from Washington were as encouraging. From the lucubrations of the New York Herald it seems as if my supposition in my last letter were right, that Seward must hold on four years more. Still, perhaps it's all for the best, and as I have pretty much made up my mind for anything and everything, I don't see but what the best thing one can do is to shut his eyes and follow the current without troubling himself for consequences unavoidable.

Since my last I've been dissipated enough to make one evening visit at Mr Pelton's, who was to depart the next day for Paris with his family. The Howes, Mr Stockton the Consul and I went down and played cards, smoked and drank champagne, by way of a farewell visit. Indeed all Dresden is furling it's tents now and preparing to drive it's flocks to other regions. My friend, or Billy's friend Mrs Butterworth is gone and the Biddles go this month; so the Howes and I. The winter is breaking I think and I'm doubling my application to get through my books. There are so many interruptions however that I don't progress very fast. I am still always at home and never make visits as it's a bore, and I like the long quiet evenings. Indeed it's only then that I get ahead, and tonight, or last night for it's now six o'clock and the day-breaking, I've not been to bed, having just received a new book which interested me exceedingly. It is a volume of Humboldt's letters to a friend of his in Berlin, and from distinguished characters to him, and it is making a great talk in the world.[1] They say it's to be suppressed by the Government, but the cat is already out of the bag. The letters are personal to the tip-top, and there's hardly a public man or interest that doesn't come in for a notice. Half the Princes in Germany are ridiculed in it and Prince Albert of England comes in for a scorcher. All Berlin is ridiculed and abused, to say nothing of the very strong political opinions and religious ideas which will set the stupids into a howl. And yet it does more honor to Humboldt and shows more what he was than fifty biographies, for this is all in short, formless, scribbled notes, without connection and hardly to be understood by a non-Berliner. I can't understand half of it. How it ever came to be published is a wonder to me, for it certainly cuts dreadful close, and the letters reach to within two years. However I've sat all night reading it and as it wouldn't pay to go to bed now, I mean to write till sun rise and then take a walk.

My chess goes on, except that I've played lately with the Hofrath to pass the time. I don't play well, I know, but unluckily he plays worse than I, and by Jove I can't *make* him beat me. I tried the other evening by sacrificing all my pieces but the game was a drawn one. Under these circumstances it is naturally rather a bore and I propose to return to the daughter.

March. 6.   Mary's letter arrived punctually. How comes she to be fifteen years old. Billy Howe asked me how old she was the other day and I said her next birth-day would be her thirteenth; he said he knew better, it was her sixteenth. Lord bless me, she's almost a young lady. Has she got long dresses yet? I should think you'ld take her away from school this summer and educate her under your own eye. I don't like schools for girls of that age, and as they never learn anything at all either there or at home, they might more profitably learn it under your care than in such a mixture as a school is. The pleasantest girls I know were not allowed to remain at school; so Miss Fanny Crowninshield and her cousins; but Carry Bigelow *was* and much good it did her, for in the first place she got *no* good from school; in the second, it counteracted the good she might have got at home, *but not the bad,* and in the third place it gave her Hatty Shelton for a friend and Philo for a—husband. All which, you will say, Mrs B by a little character, might have prevented. Some of it she certainly might, but the mass was only preventable by separating her at fourteen totally from her old habits and bringing her back at sixteen fresh. Mary is in many things something like Carry Bigelow, particularly in a want of depth of feeling; I am so too myself and think I understand her character from my own. So she catches all sorts of habits and ideas and the nearest one lasts longest. If I had a child of that age and could do it, I should do as the J. L. Gardner's did, bring her abroad and educate her here where no one can get at her but those you choose.

Just received a letter from Loo who seems happy as ever and whose happiness provokes me because I am so stupid here. However, patience. The days are flying away and my nose is held closer to the grindstone just now than ever. It's aggravating to have to sacrifice the carneval and even the Easter week at Rome which I regret more than all the rest. But it will be worse if war comes, and Napoleon is playing Villa Franca over again, and the deuce knows what may happen.[2] People say there'll be no war. I think they are crazy. War or revolution, or both; and it's my belief that if Napoleon hopes to turn conservatist now, it'll only make the troubles worse and the success less. I should think the statesmen and premiers in these days would go crazy with the responsibility and more than that, with this uncertainty and swaying to and fro. To us who stand so far on the extreme left that all European parties and party fights seem matters of the last century, this doubt about the present is irritating to a degree.

Humboldt's book or letters are suppressed in Berlin and also here. Apropos, American slavery comes in for it's notice; a letter of Baron Geroldt's is in it; anti-slavery but not up to our points; Humboldt's own ideas were ours. A letter of "the great American Historian Prescott," is in it; not political.[3] I send Brooks a new relay of stamps and more next week.

Yrs affectionately.   Henry.

MS: MHi

1. *Briefe von Alexander von Humboldt an Varnhagen von Ense, aus den Jahren 1827 bis 1858,* ed. Ludmilla Assing (1860).

2. In July 1859, at Villafranca di Verona, Napoleon III signed a preliminary treaty with Emperor Franz Joseph of Austria ceding Milan and Lombardy to the Kingdom of

Sardinia (Piedmont) but tacitly ending French support for nationalist movements elsewhere in Italy.

3. Friedrich von Gerolt, Prussian minister to the U.S. 1843–1871; William Hickling Prescott (1796–1859) of Boston, whose *Conquest of Mexico* (1843) won him Humboldt's admiration and friendship.

To Brooks Adams

[March 4? 1860]

King Friedrich Augustus died (or was said to have died) on a journey in Tyrol in the year 1854, having been thrown out of his carriage.

The three pfenning stamps are the same now as then, but I send you two more; that is in case I didn't send them before. The half Groschen stamps have the head of the last King. Of course since 1854 they are no more used and not often to be had. I send two examples.

Also two samples of the one groschen and one of the two groschen stamps. As these are all now rare, the extra ones may be valuable for a trade.

Besides these old Saxon stamps I send all the Saxon post-couverts, which you have not yet had, and three Prussian ones which you haven't got I believe. There are only five Saxon ones.

You must write a few words of thanks to Mr Theodore Reichenbach who gave me the old stamps for you as well as a few more which I will send presently. Tack on to mamma's next letter a few words to him, saying that you thank him very much and will keep his present with the greatest care.

Write me or let me know if there are any particular stamps you want and I'll try to get them.

Yr affecte Brother.   Henry.

MS: MHi

To Abigail Brooks Adams

Dresden. March. 10. [1860]

Dearest Mamma

Billy Howe has just given me a Boston Advertiser, which contains a letter from Washington partly filled with papa and his action in the matter of the House Printer.[1] My opinion one way or the other is of course of no account but as I can imagine how disagreeable and vexatious the affair is, and how many hard words it must have cost, and as I see how very cautiously and treacherously the Advertiser correspondent expresses himself, I think I can allow myself a little word about it. Papa may not be much encouraged by knowing that his son ever so far off, and without much acquaintance with the matter, thinks as he does and enters with all his heart into his view of what are his duties, but at least it will spare him the doubt as to whether I can appreciate the position he has taken. I am too far away to know how public opinion stands on the matter, but I feel sure that whatever the momentary impression may be, his action can in the long run only give him strength and position, and as for me myself, if that can be of interest to him, I'm ready and willing, in perfect coolness and common-sense, to lay all my hope and ambition for the future, on the same stake. I have not an instant's doubt that every one whose opinion we value, feels as I do about it, and as for his constituents if there isn't enough honor left in the Third District to back up such a position as this, then so much the worse for the Third District. Thank God we're not reduced so far as to truck and dicker off our principles in that way, even though much more depended on it than a seat in Congress. But in spite of the hint of the Advertiser, I have enough faith in morality still to believe that this affair far from weakening papa's strength in Massachusetts, will increase it ten-fold, and if he can maintain himself on the floor of Congress, and hold to this beginning, he'll soon be the most popular man in the State as his father was before him. So far as I can judge from the various papers I've seen, the spectacle of an honest man in Congress seems to be something wonderful and beyond all calculation. No one seems to know what to say to it; whether to praise or blame; and I think I can imagine the various newspaper articles as clearly as if I had them here. Luckily it's not the first time we've been in a minority of one, and if the campaign of '48 hasn't broken us in to sneers and abuse, it's time something else did it. Sneers and abuse have got to be taken; there's no help for that; we must only get callous to it; but at least there's one comfort and that is that we needn't be afraid of it. There's no "spot on our scutcheon" that I know of, where anything can take hold.

We must all feel the importance of this start. It's the first declaration of the colors we sail under, and whether successful in it's immediate object or not, it cannot fail to have a good result and make an impression on the honest part of the people. I know it's a hard trial for you and papa; even at this distance I feel it; but it must have come sooner or later, and on this matter as well as another. We young ones don't count much now, but it may at least please papa to know that those who are nearest and dearest to him, go heart and soul after him on this path.

Your affectionate Son   Henry.

MS: MHi

1. Feb. 25, 1860, secretly written by CFA2. CFA and a small group of Republicans opposed the party choice for House printer because it was based on a promise of future campaign funds. CFA2 denounced as even more corrupt a Southern "reform" proposal which would have divided the spoils. CFA and his allies forced the issue to multiple ballots and eventually defeated both corrupt candidates (Feb. 27).

To Abigail Brooks Adams

Dresden. March. 25. 1860.

Dearest Mamma

Your letter of the 4th arrived last week, and also some papers. I read Seward's speech with the greatest interest. It's just what I expected from him; the most able State-paper I've seen for a long time. It's effect on the country of course I'm not in a way to judge of, but posterity will do it justice if the country doesn't.[1]

Only one week more here; at least if money comes. Still no great change. Last week we were a little livelier. On Monday we all drove out to a little village about an hour's drive below the city, to the house of the artist Retsch who made the celebrated outlines to Shakespeare.[2] Retsch himself died about four years ago but his widow has a number of his drawings which she shows and sells to strangers. All the good ones however have been sold, and the rest are precious weak and poor, so that I was utterly disgusted. However, art aside, the excursion was quite a pretty one; day pleasant though the snow still lies on the hills and by the road-side. Augusta was lively; we amused ourselves by snow-balling each other, and quarreling as we usually do. The Professor got huffy because his wife called him back when he was going the right way, and returned to the tavern where he stayed until we were through; some two hours. The old fellow has a way of ambling on before, and botanising and grubbing up weeds and plants, in which occupation he forgets himself and everyone else. He never says anything to anyone. Indeed generally my opinion of him has changed considerably since I came here, and I incline now to think he's about the most selfish old wretch I ever met with. His fits of stuffiness would aggravate me who am now unaccustomed to anyone's ill-humor but my own, unless he had the grace to be silent all the time, so that one can't always tell when he is stuffy and when not. Poor old fellow; he must have been handsome and entertaining once. The revolution of '48 broke him down; he lost his whole property and what was for him worse, his collections and the work of his life. It almost made him crazy.

Wednesday morning we all took the steamer and went down to Meissen to visit the old city and the porcellain manufactory. I had seen it once before, last June, but wanted to see it again and Augusta had never been there. So we made the excursion. On starting they all retired to the cabin, rather to my surprise, for I had expected to sit down in the sun and smoke a cigar on deck and talk with them. But I had to finish my cigar alone, and on joining them in the cabin found the Professor in one corner reading; he had brought a small library with him; Madam was sitting on one side of the cabin, meditating, and Augusta looking out of the windows as well as she could. It's my policy to encourage rebellion to every authority but my own. But too open rebellion would put my own authority in danger of question, so I didn't dare to encourage Augusta to go on deck alone, for that wasn't proper and would have made trouble. I attacked Madame however and in spite of the Professor I managed to get her on deck and seat her and Augusta in the sun, where the wheel-house protected them from wind. So we did make the trip on deck, and enjoyed it too for the Elbe is a lovely river, to my mind just as pretty as the Rhine, though without ruins. On arriving at Meissen we had to take some dinner; it was twelve o'clock, and Madame conducted us to the hotel where as she repeatedly assured us, she had dined with the present King as Prince; if his dinner was as bad as ours, he didn't enjoy it much. Then we visited the Cathedral and the man-ufactory and finally the Professor disappeared to make a visit and we three descended into the city again where we amused ourselves by buying Meis-sen Nauf Fummeln, a sort of pie-crust rather stale. Also a small boy to whom I gave a ninepence to buy a pair of pantaloons, which he did on the spot; at least he came back grinning with delight and said he had bought them; then a lot of children surrounded us at whom I made faces, to Ma-dame's horror. There is a frightful poverty here; the workmen are paid very little and now business is very dull.

On the return the Professor retired to his den in the cabin. Madame and Augusta resumed their seats and we all munched the Fummeln while I drank a big glass of beer and smoked a cigar. It became coolish towards sunset, but Madame stuck it out as long as she dared and at last as Augusta declined to go down into the Cabin, she left us on deck. The Fraülein went to sleep, and I meditated. This you understand was in the highest degree improper. If I had been a German it would never have been permitted, but I'm a very steady young American and perfectly trustworthy. Moreover there were no acquaintances nor many people on board. Still Augusta got her scolding afterwards as I knew she would.

Altogether I'm pretty well satisfied with the position I've had here. Many things I've done haven't pleased my family. There was always a passive opposition between us; they wanted always to keep me in control and I al-lowed them to do it more than I ever allowed anyone since I went to Col-lege. But still I did usually what I pleased and occasionally was brusque in my ways, which I defy anyone to help, in such a position where one meets no open resistance. Then I've laughed a good deal at Augusta which she didn't know what to make of and used to get furious. She's now trained and minds better. If you've been at any time alarmed about her and my posi-tion to her, you can now breath free. She doesn't care any more for me than she does for Julius Caesar, and I am and have been no more in love with her than with Julius Caesar's wife. I like her though and think she's a trump. Lately another offer of marriage has been made to the mother for her; a very rich Hungarian Count wants her; Madame is very thick with some of the noblest Hungarian families. But we don't think it's advisable to engage her yet. Madame to my delight called me to counsel, and I'm the only person except herself, the Professor, and the lady who acts as negotiator, who knows of the offer. I shouldn't tell of it to you if I thought there were any chance of it's returning here. None of the children of the family have been consulted on the subject.

Augusta ist the only one of the family who is straight-forward towards me, and while Madame and her husband let me alone or lay all sorts of round-about nets to get me to do what a simple plain request would have served at once to make me do, Augusta like a trump never disguises her opinion or hesitates to express it. She tells me there's no hope of getting the truth out of me; I tell lies frightfully; as is partially true, though to her I've always told truth enough. We have pitched battles which she by no means always loses, except when she loses her temper and I keep mine. But still as a whole I've done wonders. She reads English to me and talks it if I choose, which she doesn't like to do; she plays the piano for me, which her mother at the beginning of the winter told me she never would do; she isn't angry when I call her a good child, and when I praise her, I can see an instantaneous rise in her spirits. Yet as I say, she doesn't care a copper for me and except in a perfectly paternal way, neither do I for her.

Madame expresses great regret at my departure. How much she feels I can't tell, for her very shallowness makes her hard to understand. I suppose she is sorry that I'm going for my presence has been an excuse to her for anything she wanted to do. She must go to the theatre, a concert, the gallery, to walk, because Herr Adams wished her to. She must not receive a visitor because Herr Adams was reading German to her; she could not make calls because Herr Adams detained her at home; she could not give parties because Herr Adams was in the way; she could not accept invitations because Herr Adams couldn't be left alone; and she only knows how much worse actions and omissions poor Herr Adams has been made the scapegoat of. The Hofrath Professor is on the other hand probably rejoiced that I'm off, because he'll be left then in peace and not be dragged to the concerts and theatres where he catches cold and loses time. And Augusta probably is more or less sorry, because I was the cause of more or less liveliness in the house.

Uncle Sidney's letter of introduction for me and Billy Howe on Mr & Mrs de Cramer, former Secretary of the Russian Legation at Washington, we presented a little while ago. They seem to be very pleasant people; Mrs de Cramer is pretty and more of a Christian than any woman I've seen for six months; that is, in her manners, and dress. We took tea there one evening, frugal and alone.

I've just received a letter from Charles. He seemed delighted with his Washington experience and with your and papa's success. I was prepared for it. I tell you, Mrs A, you're just beginning life. There's no end of prospect before you, and it's hardly even up hill work. In a year or two you'll be famous without an effort, and will be happy as pie in all the bustle and excitement and fight of a life which isn't measured by inches any longer. I'm not afraid. Just you pitch in and you'll cut papa out quicker'n thunder. I shouldn't wonder if you were elected in his place.

Money has arrived too. A week from to-day I leave Dresden for Vienna and hurry on to Venice. My letters mayn't come so regularly but I shall try to keep them tolerably straight. I send Brooks his last relay of stamps; Swedish, Danish, and Russian; the white one is a local stamp used only in Stockholm. I hope he's satisfied with all I've sent, for I shall probably not get any more; indeed he has about all.

Give Moll my love. I owe her a letter. Nick won't go with me to Italy, confound him. Pleasant prospect alone. However I hope to pick some one up on the way.

Yrs ever.   Henry.

MS: MHi

1. Although the *New York Times* reprinted Seward's Feb. 29 speech under the head-line "The Irrepressible Conflict," Seward now avoided that phrase. As a presidential candidate, he backed away from divisive rhetoric and gave a history of the Republican party designed to reassure the nation that no issues were beyond peaceful settlement.

2. Friedrich A. M. Retzsch (1779–1857) spent his life in Dresden; his reputation rests mainly on 80 engravings he made for Shakespeare's works (1827–1846).

To Charles Francis Adams, Jr.

Dresden. March. 26. 1860.

I received your letter of the 5th or thereabouts, this morning, my dear boy, and hurry to answer it, not because it's in need of an answer so much as because I have a good many things to say that won't wait. I hereby acknowledge moreover various papers from you for which I am much in your debt. Of these presently.

You send me a draft-receipt; God knows what for; I never saw one till now, and shall keep it unless the Baring's keep still and don't notify me. Papa's a rum one in money affairs; he writes me at New Years that he makes me a present and mamma too; I buy articles of "luxe" to the amount expecting a remittance of at least £115, as last year; and so count myself nearly $100 out of pocket. I *must* receive another remittance by the 1st June at Florence. Papa will say he's credited me the amount of his present, which is all devilish good but we know, credited or not, it will count in point of fact against me as current expenses.

I have packed and sent off today a box addressed to you. It will go in a sailing vessel to Boston and probably arrive in the month of June when you will be notified through the Custom-house. The box contains mostly books; some pictures by my hostess here, of which the uppermost one I think is for Mrs Putnam; it can wait till my return; a package addressed to D. Crouse, contains a photograph; forward this at once; a box wrapped in oil-cloth and sealed with my seal, contains somewhere near a hundred dollars worth of engravings; among them your Parce; be careful of these; in an old beer-jug down in one corner you'll find among other things a porcellain medallion, angel's head; I'd be obliged if without ruining me you'ld have it set as a breast-pin and give it to Rebecca as a memento; it's not very costly but pretty. You will I hope be careful with all the things as well as with those which have gone home with Ben Crowninshield's things, and I would be immensely obliged if you'ld put them all together to wait my return. That is, use them as much as you please but don't let them get scattered.

I leave Dresden this day week and notify you of this box so as to have it off my mind. I hope to God it will arrive safe for even the insurance wouldn't represent half it's value to me.

Your letter is healthier than usual. It doesn't smell of Boston Common and State Street and I was devilish glad to get it. I'm glad you had a good time in society. There is no society in Europe as we understand it, so I can't imitate you. Your first letter about the printing-affair I happened to see through Billy Howe; without knowing who wrote it; I executed a pas seule with variations and warhoop accompaniment in my appartment on reading it. Then I sat down and wrote a florid letter to mamma in which I honored your epistle with the epithet "treacherous." A few days afterwards I was rather taken aback by receiving a package of papers with your initials as "Pemberton."[1] The game is a risky one; take care of your incognito or else it may react and people think it was a political trick of the Governor's to help himself. Putting this aside, it was a great success. Indeed I'm inclined to believe that papa's "coup" owed a very considerable part of it's success to that letter, and not a small part to it's low tone. Even the Courier's "Giant among Pigmies" was quite as much a hit at the Advertiser as a bonbon for papa.[2] The Courier fell into that trap beautifully. Anyway I congratulate you on your success which is in it's way quite as decided as papa's. As none of my home letters have mentioned all these letters as your work, I've said nothing about it either, nor to anyone here, and shan't till I hear that you've avowed them.

Seward's speech is a great thing. I think there are as few assailable points in that speech and yet as broad a position, as is possible. Even the New York Herald will blunt it's dirty teeth on that. As a statesmanlike production too I'm proud of it, and we shall do well to take a lesson from it. The Senate in it's best days never heard anything better done.

I took a hint from your last and have been lately writing a series of letters to mamma to do at least all I can to fix her out. She complains in all her letters of the nuisance of going out and that it'll be the death of her, but somehow they're all written in the best of spirits, and for all her protesting that she hates the life, despises the President and is acting a wholly self-sacrificing rôle, I think the attention she gets pleases her as much as it does us, and as I recollect she never could be happy at home without something to worry her, I hope that this present worry is only the old chronic one in a new shape.

You come down in your political philosophy to the principle of education; from different grounds I did the same here some time ago. It's the main idea of all progressists; it's what gives New England it's moral power;

Horace Mann lived in this idea, and died in it.[3] Goethe always said that his task was to educate his countrymen; and that all the Constitutions in the world wouldn't help, if the people weren't raised; and he and Schiller did more for it than anyone else. Our people are educated enough intellectually but it's damned superficial and only makes them more willful; our task so far as we attempt a public work, is to blow up sophistry and jam hard down on morality, and there are as many ways of doing this as there are men in the country. This idea was at the bottom of my letter of the 21st Jan. and it's only the manner in which we can invest our strength to the most advantage in prosecuting this idea, that can trouble us. For I for one haven't the courage of Horace Mann. As for the Union, our field of action remains about the same whether it stands or falls.

However because we are virtuous we'll not banish cakes and ale.[4] I've been trying this winter to make my path clear to myself but haven't quite succeeded. I still waver between two and shall leave fate to decide. In the meanwhile I mean to have as good a time as under the circumstances will do, and shan't interfere with others. This apropos to John. Ye Gods, I would like a pretty sister-in-law. I would love her and cherish her and be kind unto her. Damn the odds. Who can tell what the morrow will bring forth? Let us eat, drink and be merry!

Your Washington letters, my boy, have stirred me up. As you know, I propose to leave Dresden on the 1st of April for Italy. It has occurred to me that this trip may perhaps furnish material for a pleasant series of letters, not written to be published but publishable in case they were worth it. This is my programme. You may therefore expect to receive from week to week, letters from me, beginning at Vienna and continuing so long as I don't get tired of it. What the letters will be about depends of course on circumstances. Now, you will understand, I do *not* propose to write with the wish to publish at all hazards; on the contrary I mean to write private letters to you, as an exercise for myself, and it would be of all things my last wish to force myself into newspapers with a failure for my first attempt. On the other hand if you like the letters and think it would be in my interest to print them, I'm all ready. In any case you can do just what you choose with them so long as you stick by your own judgment. But if, under any absurd idea that I wish to print, you dodge the responsibility of a decision, and a possible hurting of my feelings; by showing me up to the public's amusement without any guarantee against my making a slump, you'll make a very great mistake. I could do that without your help. But it needs a critic to decide what's copper and what silver and I suppose you have courage enough not to be afraid to tell me in case my coinage should turn out copper or copper-gilt. So gird on your sword and don't be idiotic enough to bother yourself with family affection or brotherly sympathies.[5]

The life here doesn't change a hair. I feel like a snake thawing out after being frozen in all winter. My family here bores me. Once or twice I've sat up all night playing cards with the Howes. That was my only excitement. I never make calls for they're slow. My books are now all sent off so I've nothing to do but write. The Howes leave this week; the gambling-shop in the Prager Strasse is to be closed, and there will be another winter a closed book. In the whole of it I've not had one good-time. I've digged like a Freshman; hardly once has my pulse beaten faster than usual except at news from home or over plans and thoughts of my own. On the other hand my health has been excellent; my spirits uniform; I've never been unhappy; hardly felt the blues; not been discontented; and usually been more or less amused. So there's pro and contra. The life has been a pleasant life enough and very useful and such as it is, I'm satisfied with it.

Billy and I presented a letter on a Mr de Cramer of the Russ. Leg. which the Mogul (Uncle Sidney) sent me. At my request he included Billy's name. What on earth induces the Mogul to notice me for the first time in his life. Very kind indeed; very; but quite a new trait. He doesn't intend to remember me in his will, does he? No such luck. That's all for his name-sakes.

Give my love to all the little goslings, especially Miss Eugenia who by the way is about the only one of all my acquaintances whom I still recollect with amusement. *Do* get Philo engaged before I return. Mrs Frank Bacon in spe[6] is I hope well. Expect another letter within a fortnight.

Yrs ever   H.

MS: MHi

1. CFA2 published a second Washington letter in the *Advertiser,* Feb. 28. On March 9 he wrote HA, sharing the secret and his satisfaction with his efforts.

2. An editorial under that title, praising the course of CFA, appeared in the Boston *Courier,* Feb. 22.

3. Horace Mann (1796–1859) of Massachusetts, school reformer and founder of the first U.S. teachers colleges.

4. *Twelfth Night,* II, iii.

5. The next letter begins the series.

6. *In spe:* in hope, in expectation.

2.

Correspondent
at Large
1860

Henry Adams' career as a journalist began in 1860. Spurred by his brother's example, he promised that on his journey through Austria and Italy he would write letters which Charles, if he judged them good enough, might submit to a Boston newspaper. So, with a letter from Vienna, April 5, "H.B.A." began his series of travel pieces for the Boston *Courier*. In the newspaper letters, as in the less self-conscious letters to his mother, the neck-craning tourist and amateur art-critic gave way to the observer of a national revolution. As he traveled south from Venice, he reported on city after city that had just overthrown Austrian or papal rule or seemed about to do so. The climax of the series was his dispatch from Palermo with its vignettes of Garibaldi and of humbler participants in the Sicilian campaign. No other American paper received eyewitness reports like these.

After his Italian journey, Adams traveled to Paris, where he spent three months before returning home. His chatty, informal letters—least inhibited when he wrote in French to Charles—show his lighter side. But diligent practice of French was not the only sign of seriousness. As the electoral campaign of 1860 got under way, he kept close track of events at home. It was time to return to the United States, and he was more than ready.

To Charles Francis Adams, Jr.

No. 1.¹   Vienna. April. 5. 1860.

My dear Charles

At last Dresden is fairly passed and gone. The last evening there, that of the 1st, I passed in the Theatre listening to two pieces of music so tremendously classic that it is as good as high-treason to say that the first one exhausted me so much that I could hardly enjoy the second; for the first was Mozart's Requiem, and the second was Beethoven's Ninth Sinfonie, chorus and all. Royal Orchestra, one of the best in Europe and a chorus of between two and three hundred voices. To a real lover of classic music who has never been in Germany, I suppose the idea of listening to a concert like this, leaves about the same impression, as to the real lover of art who has never been in Italy, the idea of seeing Florence. To me it felt considerably like reading Homer with a very small knowledge of Greek and no dictionary. All Pumpernickel was there however to listen. The miserable-looking old King sat with his daughters in the royal box, and the daughters used their royal lorgnettes very condescendingly. Altogether it was a very successful concert and I was very glad to have heard it.

The next day I took final leave of Dresden and of the family who have treated me for five months with real German kindness. It was a beautiful day; the first really Spring weather we've had; but all the way from Dresden to this city the country was under water; at least so far as I was awake to see it; and the Elbe, Moldau and Danube are all a mere succession of shallow lakes more or less nearly connected. The journey wasn't very exciting for seventeen consecutive hours in a German railroad car aren't precisely the most amusing hours of life, but still there are rats and spiders even in prisons and in this car there happened to be an Austrian Lieutenant. An Austrian Lieutenant is sure to be worth talking to. Not that they're cultivated fellows, for that they never are; nor intellectual, for that no Austrian is, as a general thing; nor witty, for, Heaven knows, wit is no failing of the German race, and of all Germans who want wit, the Austrian officers want it the most. This particular specimen was however a favorable one. He was a Saxon by birth and spoke a number of languages; had been in Italy at Magenta, Montebello, Solferino; played the piano, and hadn't smoked for six months; a long list of accomplishments.² He spoke among his other languages a little English, and of course insisted on using that tongue toward me. He was engaged as he told us immediately, to an English girl; very nice girl; had a "bad foot"; nice-looking girl; not very pretty; he was going to leave the army next year and go to England with her. From all which I concluded that he, like other Lieutenants, who are all poorer than poverty and drowned in debts, was marrying for money. His naïf catalogue of her personal charms was enough to prove that there wasn't much love in the matter. He also informed us and the car, with the usual running fire of "Sapperments Kr-r-r-reutz-donnerwetters" &c &c, that the last campaign was only lost through treason; that the Zouaves were cowards; that Napoleon was on his very last legs after Solferino; and that the war was to break out on the Rhine within six weeks from present date. Also that he had shot two French officers at Magenta with his own hand; had fought nine duels with pistols, consequences not stated; and at school had beaten an English boy at fisticuffs; "I-have-gave-him-many-strike-and-I-was-not-satisfied. I-think-I-would-have-killed-him." Further, various accounts of what a Don Juan he was, with statistical statements in regard to practice, and theoretical statements in illustration. Further his views as to politics and the present state of things, not advanced as views but as indubitable facts. Further various adventures he had had; robbed by banditti in Italy, shot down Heaven knows how many, and then had feigned dead, &c &c. In short I listened to this innocent prattle which was mostly in German delivered to an audience of four persons in our compartment of the car, till I got tired and concluded that the show was over, so took a novel and read. We came to Prag at about dark; our two fellow-travellers disappeared, but the Lieutenant remained to entertain me till midnight by a hot political discussion with a Prussian, who didn't show much respect for his opinions and still less for his facts; not that this made any difference, but produced more curses after the Prussian had got out; and now a Hungarian Jew backed the Lieutenant up with two positive statements which I know to be false and several hundred which I believe to be; that is, the two were historical; the several hundred were personal. Finally the Lieutenant did the only sensible thing he had done since our acquaintance began; he went to sleep; and I, who had only mixed occasionally in the conversation, went to sleep also.

So we rolled on, hour after hour, stopping at every station and sleeping an unhappy sort of sleep, stretched out at full length on the seat. The good Lieutenant left us; he was going to Cracau and thence to Galitia where he is now stationed with a probability of remaining there indefinitely. Gradually daylight came; at Brünn three new passengers broke up my sleep finally and smothered me with Austrian cigar-smoke till I felt as though my face were coated an inch-deep with it. At nearly eight o'clock we came to the end of our journey and brought up in Vienna.

I'm very unlucky in the season of my visit here. This whole week is holy in the Catholic faith. Not a theatre is open, not a place of public amusement of any sort, even the imperial picture gallery is closed, though the private ones luckily are more liberal. Concerts too are not to be had, which I'm sorry for, in this city of Strauss and Lanner.[3] All this destroys evening amusements, but the rest of the day is lively enough.

There are a number of Americans here. At dinner there were six of us together, all acquaintances. So there is no want of companionship, the most disagreeable of all wants. We set to work and visited picture-galleries; the Esterhazy gallery has a great reputation and is certainly a jewel. We wandered about the city; admired St Stephan and it's blackened old columns

and walls; and wondered at the smallness of Vienna streets and at the utter
and hopeless impossibility of ever finding one's way in them. For this it
beats any city I've yet seen. But there is a life and gaiety here that is really
pleasant to see. Poor little Dresden, which in winter is like Saratoga out of
season, has made me forget what a really gay place is, and the first impression of Vienna is all the more vivid on that account. The streets here
are immensely amusing. Small as they are, the carriages go through them
at full speed; turn corners on the run with two inches to spare; drive up on
the sidewalks, or crash along within an inch of one's heels; but still accidents seem tolerably rare. The foot-travellers go where they can, in the
middle or on the side of the streets indifferently; and such foot-travellers!
The Austrian army of course is the most prominent figure; the natty white
jackets, which didn't look so pretty after Magenta, enliven the city immensely. Dapper little lieutenants wander up and down, looking good-natured and stupid, and dressed in uniforms where white mingles with every
color ever heard of. Officers of the line, infantry, cavalry, engineers, artillery; Germans, Tyrolese Jägers, Hungarians, Croats; every rank, from Field
Marshalls to drummers; every complexion from the dark Italian to the
blond German. Every one is in a costume of some sort. Yet of the whole
tribe, there is not a soldier who looks so military and so dangerous, as any
common little French private of the line. They are brave certainly; no one
has asserted that the Austrian army wants courage; but there's an immense
deficit in brain. Still here in Vienna they crow loudest, and one would
hardly think that they'd been thrashed out of their wits last summer, to see
and hear them now. To do them justice, however, it is certain that their
uniforms do look uncommonly pretty on a pleasant day.

Besides the army, the city is gay with crinoline which is still strong here;
Hungarians, who are tolerably numerous; Turks, who are more rare; fine
horses, which are not rare at all; handsome equipages; and all the other
thousand and one sights and scenes of a great capital. The Hungarians attracted my attention, for all Americans are prejudiced in their favor.[4] Their
national costume is all very well; as a political demonstration there's nothing to say against it. As a matter of private taste, looking upon it as a mere
fashion, it strikes me that the caps are vulgar; the braids superfluous; the
boots questionable; the whole thing somewhat childish, and by no means
practical. It may be excellent for Hungary, but for gentlemen who don't
masquerade, it is to say the least rather suggestive of jockeys and drum-
majors. I like to see it here however, because here it has a right to display
itself, and it varies the appearance of the streets. In Vienna all costumes are
at home. The grave Turks, Greeks, Armenians, with fezzes and flowing
robes as well as very Jewish faces; the Tyrolese with broad hats and belts
and leather breeches; Russians with beards and queer old hats, and any
number of other semi-barbarisms excite no remark here; not even the famous American black frock in the morning.[5]

After dinner on the day I arrived, we took a carriage and drove out to the
Prater. It is now too early to see the Prater in it's gaiety; very few carriages

were there, and my only wish was to see what it looked like. I was rather surprised to find that it was much like most other straight avenues through parks. It threatened to rain and we turned to go back. An officer and a lady with four servants came by on horseback. As they passed, the coachman turned round to us and said it was the Empress and Graf Grüne.[6] We all jumped as if galvanised, ordered the man to turn and catch them at any price. We followed them till they too turned and came back. I'm not in the least ashamed to confess that I stared at them with all my power of stare. If any man says as I've heard it said, that he thinks a person, who goes out of his way to see an Emperor, is a fool, I answer that I think a person a fool who in such a case does not go out of his way. So long as I have good health and am no misanthrope, I mean to satisfy so far as I can a healthy and harmless curiosity. As I was saying, the party came by us, we took off our hats and stared. Since then I've been dreadfully in love with the Empress. She didn't look at us but inclined her head a shade in recognition; Graf Grüne didn't notice us, and he was right. Our admiration was certainly not intended for him. But the Empress was charming. Such an exquisite little figure I've not often seen in Germany at least, and a pretty, good-humored, girlish face, so far as I could see it. The simple black English riding-habit and little flat hat, became her admirably and displayed her pretty figure in great contrast to Graf Grüne's thick, strong build. We followed them slowly some distance; groups of people collected along the course; she recognised them all as she had us, and the Graf still rode on like a statue. Finally it began to rain and we had to hurry back to the city without waiting to see what became of the riders.

Tomorrow I must hurry off to Venice; thirty hours hard work. I'm sorry to leave Vienna so soon, but the summer is coming and no time to spare, and after eighteen months of Germany even Vienna is little attraction against Italy. It is gay here certainly. I would like to visit Pesth too, but, once for all, I will not rest on this side of the Alps. There is a great deal here to be seen and done. It's politically very interesting too. I have seen American papers which seemed to consider the dissolution of this empire as rapidly approaching and inevitable. Now, this view may have authority that I know nothing of, but the case seems to me a little different.

The truth is, very few persons know enough about the state of things here, to be capable of judging. I confess to knowing only what the German press has told me in the last year. I don't undertake to say that other persons are wrong in expecting Austria's fall; only that, as a matter which admits of hesitation, there may be different opinions about it; this particular opinion does not prevail here. That the dissatisfaction is universal is true; that Hungary may rebel is possible; that it acquires independence is also possible though highly improbable; whether it's independence would be in the interest of Europe and of mankind is a matter on which opinions can afford to differ very widely. That Venice may rebel is possible; so too that the rebellion may be successful; but the opinion in Europe is that Austria can and will maintain Venetia for the present. That the bad government here is excessive is certainly true. Yet in alleged cases of personal violence and cruelty, it would be as well to reserve judgment till both sides have been heard. You may be sure that the Government here feels it's danger too keenly to adopt such measures without strong provocation. The proof of this fact is the eagerness with which the government papers contradict and try to disprove such stories. The people here so far as I have talked with them and heard them talk, are satisfied with their personal liberties much better than with their commercial ones. They complain bitterly of restrictions of trade, vexatious taxes, senseless forms, subjection of schools to the church, antiquated law, irresponsibility of Government &c &c, but I have not heard that there are complaints of personal and wanton injuries. In Venetia it is another thing. There a reign of terror certainly exists. It is also certain that Austria has no choice between this reign of terror and a revolution. We think she is making a mistake in holding on to Venetia; but if she will hold on she must hold with all her claws.

All this proves nothing except that there is a great deal of very bad government here. At the same time I have little doubt that the Government is better than it ever was before, and that it will go on improving gradually all the time. Whether it is advisable to hurry the process by rebellions, is a matter which I for one, am really incapable of forming an opinion on. Unless however these rebellions are more successful and more real than in '48, the evil in them will always balance the good. But under any circumstances it is not considered probable here among the well-informed that Austria's existence is in much question. I myself think that the real danger was last summer, and that now, the empire is likely to last as long as any other.

This is the only sort of politics which it's possible to discuss. No man knows anything more than every one can know if he will, by reading the papers. No revolution here will amount to much which rests exclusively on the cities. The German part of Austria, however discontented, is and remains faithful to the Kaiser though he were a devil. Hungary alone can hardly make herself independent. Bohemia will not try to do so. And the loss of Venetia would strengthen rather than weaken the Empire. This is a German point of view. I don't say that it's the right one, but leave it to time to show.

At all events, in Vienna there is no apparent sign of poverty or discontent. They're as gay here as ever; cheer the Emperor and Empress when they drive; crowd the theatres; cram the concerts; swarm the streets; in short are as usual the gayest of all Germans. It is by no means clear yet how things are to turn out, but one thing is certain; that the Austrian Government will do all the mischief it can, and history proves that it is obstinate enough to do a good deal.

If a person is to set up for a judge in any matter under Heavens, the first requisite is that he should be fair and unprejudiced. If it's a mere matter of special pleading, he can give the reins to his fancy as much as he will. Austria is sound enough at heart. The Emperor is probably not a villain and acts as well as he knows how. Hungary does not probably labor under

greater hardships than Bohemia and Tyrol, as a nation, and it's exiles cannot complain of hardships, for undoubtedly they committed high treason.
The Austrian government is a mass of faults and evils, but even republics
are not always wholly pure. It is fairer and pleasanter to trust that under
the long and steady pressure from within and without, the nation and the
government may gradually be forced forward step by step without marking
it's course by more blood; and that in ten years, or fifty, or a hundred, Austria will have caught up with the rest of the world. Fifty years ago Prussia
was about where Austria now is.

I shall soon write again from Venice. What a great idea, to see Venice for
the first time.

Yrs ever.   H.

MS: MHi
1. HA's numbering for the first of the *Courier* series. It appeared April 30, signed
"H.B.A." Except for omitting some of HA's racier and more personal comments, the
newspaper published the letters essentially as transcribed here. CFA2 may have made
the deletions.
2. France and Piedmont routed the Austrian army at Magenta, Montebello, and
Solferino in the Italian war of 1859.
3. Johann Strauss, the elder (1804–1849) and the younger (1825–1899), and Joseph
Franz Karl Lanner (1801–1843), creators of the Viennese waltz.
4. That is, in favor of their movement for independence from Austria.
5. In polite European society, the black frock coat worn by American men throughout the day was considered unsuitable for morning wear.
6. Elisabeth Amelia Eugenia (1837–1898), empress of Austria; Count Karl Grünne
(1808–1884), a general and Franz Joseph's close adviser.

To Abigail Brooks Adams

Venice. April. 8. 1860.

Dearest Mamma

Here I am, sure as eggs is eggs. It's only with considerable difficulty that I
can persuade myself it is really I who am wandering up and down before St
Marc's and letting myself be gondoliered round under the Rialto and the
Bridge of Sighs. In all my travels I've never felt anything so strange as this
being in Venice. But it's a fact and I'll tell you how it comed about.

I left Dresden last Monday (2d) as determined. The next morning at
seven I was in Vienna. Here I passed the 3d, 4th, and 5th. There were a
number of fellows there whom I know, so I managed to discuss three days
with tolerable appetite. But Vienna rather bored me. It was holy week too
and everything was locked up. Nick wouldn't accompany me to Italy, for
which I told him he was an owl. I take it, the least prejudiced will agree
with me there. So, after doing up Vienna I hurried off. By the way, I missed
Shep. He went off to Munich two hours before I arrived in Vienna. How-

ever I don't suppose he cared much or he could have waited a few days longer.

Accordingly at nine o'clock on the morning of the 6th I left Vienna, travelled all that day and the night till at seven o'clock the next morning I arrived in Triest. I was alone so far as acquaintances go. The people in the car I don't count. The steamer to Venice left at twelve o'clock at night so I was under the necessity of passing all yesterday alone in that mean place, Triest. How I can't say, but somehow or other the time did pass, and at twelve o'clock last night I left the last remnant of Germany blessing the Lord with considerable fervor that I was done with it. At seven o'clock this morning we arrived here. I was landed in a gondola and the gentleman who had the honor to row me ashore made a disgraceful use of my imperfect acquaintance with the language of Dante, and cheated me out of twice his fare; me, who sympathise with Italy!

Is it of any use for me to say that I'm delighted with this broken-winded old hole? that it's the rummiest of all rummy places I ever was in? that it's delicious? splendid? stunning? that it's the only city I've yet seen which made me perfectly happy though I've not an acquaintance within hundreds of miles? Of course it is. Lord bless you, my valet (one can't do without a guide where one can't speak a word) is enough society for me. He gives me long lectures on history and art, on both of which subjects as regards Venice I'm disgracefully ignorant. Just let me have sunshine, a gondola, and a cigar and I don't care who's king.

I'm bound to have a real good time in Italy. I've lived of my own accord like a hermit all winter and I'm coming home in the fall; if I'm not happy now I'm never likely to be, so here goes, and if anyone scolds, I shan't answer it.

We passed all today in examining the churches, that is, some of them. It's great fun to paddle round in these black boxes and turn corners and go under bridges. I enjoy it just like a child. Then one is carried right up into a place and landed on the front steps. As for the churches I hardly know what to say; in short I've been in a sort of semi-drunken condition all day, and up in the skies all by myself.

April. 9th. Bad weather, bless it. Moreover, it's a holiday; everything closed up; my man said there was nothing to see, so I dismissed him to come tomorrow. The bellowings of exuberant Italians under my windows rather disturbed my slumbers last night. Today I shall remain in my room or lounge in the coffee-houses. I've enough to do in various ways to last me. But I sincerely trust that these infernal holidays which spoiled my stay in Vienna, will end soon and ordinary life begin again.

April. 10th. A rain-storm is a stunning thing; even in Venice. I admire it greatly and hope it will come again some time when it can't stay so long. Jove! it's about as cold here as in Dresden, and for the matter of that precious little gayer, though there is more or less liveliness on the quays spite of everything. However I've resumed work again today and visited the Doge's Palace, went over the Bridge of Sighs, examined the treasures in St Marcs, looked at several square leagues of pictures, and generally have laid out a considerable deal of work. I've examined with some care the occupants of the hotel, but have not as yet thought it worth while to urge closer acquaintance with anyone of them. There are some powerful Americans, some tough English, and an old beggar of a Russian with a pretty daughter. I have dined at table d'hote and was at once fearfully impressed by it's vivid naturalness.

For a long time I've been accustomed to seeing people talk to each other, no matter whether they were acquainted or not. I myself, when I'm tolerably good-humored and not so modest as usual, like to enter into conversation with practicable looking strangers. But the view of some twenty people who sit at table d'hote at Danieli's struck my very soul with awe. Such a set of turtles. Not one stuck his head out of his shell except to feed. I did like the others, and my next neighbor looked dreadfully surprised when I bowed to him at leaving table.

As for the people of Venice, I know precious little about them. In bad weather they stay at home. They're not a very fine-looking crowd so far as I've seen them. In fact, there are precious few people of any count, in the city.

So I shall send off this short letter only to let you know that I'm all right. I shall probably leave here and go to Bologna over Verona in three or four days. But if fine weather comes and I enjoy myself, I may make it a day or two more. Loo has not written, so I suppose she's nothing to say. I shall be in Florence in a fortnight at most and see what's become of her. There I shall receive my first home letters. I've ordered everything to be sent there.

I owe a number of letters to Mary and I assure you I'm as anxious as ever to hear everything that is going on politically as well as privately. Seward's speech hasn't yet come to hand. I expect to see it in Florence where it'll have followed me. Don't be anxious if my letters are not punctual.

Yrs ever   Henry.

MS: MHi

To Charles Francis Adams, Jr.

No. 2.[1]　　　　　　　　　　　　　　　　　Venice. April. 11. 1860.

My dear Charles

I wonder whether I shall ever see Venice again. Is it possible that my associations of this splendid place, have got to be connected all my life with a week's storm and rain? I can't think that even the worst luck can be so bad as that.

It looked favorably enough the day I left Vienna, and though the clouds were rather gloomy as we climbed up into them on the summit of the Semmering, they cleared away as we came down this side and I thought it was certainly the influence of Italy. I enjoyed the Semmering immensely. It's the greatest piece of engineering I ever saw; even the Stelvio doesn't come up to it in that, though of course in scenery there's no comparison.[2] Moreover it's decidedly the easiest way of seeing an interesting pass, I ever tried.

I was alone the whole distance from Vienna to Triest, except for an Austrian Naval Captain and his wife and her maid. They were persons of position, and great improvements on the "Herr Oberleutnant." The Captain, who was as polite and agreeable as an Austrian Officer knows how to be towards strangers, informed me that he was on leave of absence from Pesth where he was stationed to look out for the flotilla on the Danube; but he seemed to think very little of his duties, and I rather imagine from what he said, that for several years he has drawn his pay without doing any duties at all; or only nominal. His wife was charming; much more so than her husband. She was the means of my getting quite a quantity of Hungarian wine, for the Captain wasn't inclined to ask my assistance to use up his stock. He looked at me with a sort of Gorgon look as his wife urged glass after glass upon me, and I, aware that he wouldn't allow it again, yielded as modestly as I could, to the kind entreaties. If you know how good a glass of good wine tastes after twelve hours railway-travelling, you can perhaps calculate in what proportion my regard for the lady increased; who moreover was very pretty and twenty years old.

We went on steadily all night and at dawn the next morning I looked out on about the most desolate country I ever saw, except on the tops of the Alps. For hour after hour we saw nothing but fields of rock and harvests of stones. This lasted all the way to Trieste and we only escaped it when the train seemed to turn a corner and suddenly the Adriatic lay right under us. The change was very effective indeed. It would have been much more so to me if we could have taken the steamer at once for Venice, but the steamer didn't leave till twelve o'clock at night and kept me therefore wandering about Trieste for sixteen hours. I suppose "Lloyd Austriaco" knows what the object is in reversing all ordinary rules, and turning night into day. He managed very successfully to make me very uncomfortable and I hope he has to travel on his own steamers; punishment enough.

As for the seven hours of passage, I know little about them. After a short conversation with the Captain, who was busy with the last remnants of his wine and did not invite me to join him, and his wife, who was very unconscious of her master's displeasure, I stretched myself out in the cabin, with my boots in an Austrian Lieutenant's face, and a Hungarian Hussar's spurs very near my nose, and there I went to sleep. I have an idea that it was rather rough, but don't think it amounted to much. It had been some time light when the Hussar kicked me on the head which woke me up and as everyone seemed going on deck I followed them. Venice was right before us and we were bringing to just opposite the Place of St Marc.

My impressions were a good deal confused. The gondoliers made a tremendous amount of noise, and quarreled as badly as Irish hackmen. The Captain too and his wife were going ashore, and he shouted "Addio" from his gondola to me as I leaned over the steamers rail. I haven't seen him or his wife since, but I'm sure I wish her all the luck in the world and hope the next time we meet, she may have twice as much Hungarian wine and no Captain at all with her.

After all that's been written and that's being written every day about Venice, you won't care to hear me repeat much more than is absolutely necessary. I find it just what I had expected, except the weather, which is detestable and of course takes away nine tenths of the pleasure. I have gratified my ambition of going in a gondola under the Ponte Rialto, but it was in a driving rain and I felt cross and dismal. I have wandered up and down the Place of St Marc and drunk my chocolate at Florian's under the arcades, but without a great-coat and umbrella it was wet work. This destroys the beauty of the city. Still, Venice as she now stands, is an object calculated to make one gloomy rather than gay, and in some respects the gloomy sky and the driving rain rather heighten the effect. In these old palaces, large enough to bivouac armies, half in ruins, all in decay, it seems well enough that everything should be solemn and mournful. I visited one such today; the Palazzo Pesaro. The family has lately died out. The estate is waiting to be sold on account of the debts attached to it. The magnificent halls which were once lined with famous Veroneses and Tintorettos are now ornamented with cheap paperings.[3] In one of the rooms two portraits of old Doges of the family, were still hanging on the walls. The old splendor, which makes one ashamed of all modern gilding and papier-maché show-work, is as impressive as ever here. Three centuries have left it firm as ever. One whole side of the building is still sealed up by government; the other open for show to the public, and the whole for sale for two hundred thousand dollars. Some Russian may buy it, or some exiled Prince may take it and add his troubles to the complaints of the Duchess de Berri and the Count de Chambord who have each a handsome palace in the neighborhood; but no Venetian, whether in or out of the Libro d'Oro, has that amount to spare in these days.[4]

I don't suppose you care much to hear again about this, which you must have heard over and over already. Venice is so well known to all travellers and it's present position is talked about and journalised about all the time. Still I can't help groaning about it. There, for instance, I visited the tomb of Paul Veronese in a church filled with his works;[5] ceilings, walls, altars, all covered with paintings from his hand, except one Titian at a side chapel;[6] and all blackening, mouldering and dropping to pieces in the cold, damp air, till now the greater part are valueless. The law forbids their sale out of the city, and the church is too poor to take care of them.

To leave this and take to life which interests most people just now more than to know what is the fate of pictures and palaces. So far as I can hear and judge, I should think that the condition of matters here was as bad in every way as bad can easily be. The accounts do not seem to have been exaggerated. The theatres are closed still, fast as ever. Much as I sympathise with the Italians and wish them success, I must say that I think in this affair of the theatres they have bitten their own noses off, as they certainly have mine. As a demonstration it has undoubtedly made a great effect everywhere, but is there any use in holding so tight to it?[7] However in this matter I wont pretend to judge, for I'm a severe sufferer by the dullness and find the evenings so heavy on my hands that even patriotism sometimes seems a bore when it interferes with amusement.

There must be a large number of soldiers in the city; how many I can't say; some one told me five thousand, but the streets are always full of them and I should have thought there were more. These are partly Italians; at least I hear many of them, officers and soldiers, speaking Italian to one another. The old system of non-intercourse continues I believe in the society of the city.[8] The officers have got up a Casino of their own and associate only with each other. I have myself however seen no signs of trouble. Not knowing how Venice ought to appear I can't say whether she is now particularly gloomy. People tell me that she is so. I only know that in the intervals of rain the juggler or the puppet-show begins on the quay under my window, and the crowd collects and doesn't seem to get tired, for I hear roars of laughter, and it goes on for hours. Still the Piazza is never really gay as they tell me it ought to be, and as for the canals, they're empty as the streets of Thebes. Indeed I have been a good deal enlightened on the subject of gondolas. I came here with the idea that they were the usual and legitimate conveyances of the Venetians of all classes. I find that they're an expensive luxury corresponding to our hacks and private carriages, and that for the people the narrow passages and crooked alleys still form the only road. The gondolas and the conveyances by water of all sorts, take the place of horses and waggons with us, except that no omnibus lines exist besides a rail-road gondola.

Pretty much everyone who can emigrate, seems to have done so. Indeed I can't understand how anyone can well remain. The city exists in some way, but how a hundred and twenty thousand people can get their living here is a wonder to me. Perhaps ten thousand are well enough off to do without labor. But the rest must live from hand to mouth. There are very few manufactories, and on a small scale. Commerce is dead or nearly so. So far as I can see, everything is consumption and nothing production. The army and the strangers must support the place now. How far the annexation would alter the state of things, or Napoleon's idea of an Italian Confederation, is a matter of guess-work; no doubt, very much; but Venice can never well be much more than the shadow of what she was. Trieste on one side and Genoa on the other must hold her down.

As for a rebellion here, it could hardly amount to much, even if the people had the spirit and the means for it. Emigration must have drawn off the most dangerous of the population, and the city is so garrisoned and so commanded by forts at every corner, that there couldn't be a chance of success. You can depend upon it that Austria will not have to yield this province except of her own free will, or possibly in case of another war with France. All Italy combined couldn't, or at least wouldn't be likely, to tear it out of her clutches now.

I was mistaken in saying that all the Theatres are closed. There is one little Italian theatre open, and plays I believe on alternate nights with a German company at another theatre. The division too between the military and the people is not so striking as I had supposed. I see the white coats everywhere and in all company. They have their own cafés but the line is not so marked as I had expected, for I see sometimes uniforms at Florian's on one side of the piazza, and black coats at the officer's café, Quadri, on the other; mostly Germans no doubt, but still there is a German-Italian party here, though a small one. To a stranger who didn't know the circumstances, everything might appear perfectly natural.

April. 13.   The Gods have been gracious and have kindly answered my prayers. It cleared off yesterday beautifully and I have now all I could ask. Early in the morning, that is at ten o'clock, I took a gondola and went out over the lagoons to the little Armenian cloister on the island San Lazzaro,[9] and thence over to the Lido, to see the Adriatic and to satisfy my curiosity as to whether the French in the last war would have been successful in an attack on these fortifications if they had tried it. For if they had gained the Lido, Venice would have been in their hands. The Lido is a long sand-bank stretching along the coast outside of the city and protecting it from the sea. During the war it was protected by thirty thousand men and sixteen redouts with cannon, against the French fleet which couldn't come within gun-shot on account of the shoal-water. I'm about as much puzzled now to know what the result of a fight would have been as I was before. One argument however is tolerably satisfactory; if the French had thought such an attack would have turned out successfully, I suppose they would have made it. It would have been a hard piece of work I imagine, for every advantage would have been with the Austrians.

From the Lido I returned to the city. It was delicious to glide along over the water and bask in the sun, and the islands and the lagoons looked so charmingly that it seemed almost a crime to go back to the six-feet-broad, and very unpleasantly smelling alleys of the city. But I wanted to get the view from the Campanile, or the church tower if you prefer the English, on the Place of S. Marc. It was a grand day for it. The Tyrol mountains all along the north were covered with snow, and the atmosphere was clear as the Adriatic was blue. The city itself looked very ragged, and two solitary chimneys and one dyeing establishment were all that showed of any productive spirit. There are a tolerable number of coasters and one or two larger vessels at the quays and in the stream, but the greatest life is in the gondolas which looked pleasantly lively.

Then I walked out to visit the Rialto. Here there is always life and a stream of passers-by. The narrow lanes too make it look much livelier than it is, for one is always being jammed or jostled. The idea that I got from this walk was that every man in Venice keeps a shop, and every one of them loses money by it. And this must be tolerably near the truth.

At two o'clock there was music on the Piazza and I came back to sit in the sun, and drink chocolate, and smoke cigarettes, and look at the people, and listen to the seventy two musicians, a regimental band in white coats as usual. There was a pleasant variety about all this. The officiers were wandering up and down, looking their very prettiest; the beggars were as dirty and as interesting as ever; the ladies' dresses were more or less pretty, and the faces, many of them, considerably more so than less. I should say that the German element and the beggars were very much in the majority as to numbers, but there was no apparent want of Italians too. The Place was quite gay to my eyes, accustomed to the gloom of north-German cities, and I saw no demonstration whatever. Those that were there before the music began were in no greater number than those who remained through it all, so that, if any went off, their absence was unnoticeable.

A pleasant sun and a warm day does certainly make a wonderful difference in the appearance of things. Not only the Piazza but the whole city looks gay. From my window which looks out over the whole length of the quay, the Riva dei Schiavoni, I can see nothing but a swarm of people, mostly sailors or beggars or both, I suppose, on occasion; all hard at work doing nothing. Greeks in red caps and gondoliers in striped shirts; boys playing or sleeping on the stone pavement in the sun; here and there a uniform, army or navy; people walking up and people walking down; and people occasionally scolding very shrilly in very choice Venetianish; all lazy as they well can be, and live; and presently that eternal puppet show will begin again and there will be a swarm of people before it till nine o'clock at night; with intervals of juggling by a popular master a little way off. Gondolas are always going to and from the Piazza, and across to San Giorgio maggiore, and now and then a coaster hauls up to the quay or out into the stream, or a steamer comes or goes; as happens twice daily. It isn't the Venice of the fifteenth century perhaps, but it's a very pretty Venice, and lively enough, though a useless, ragged sort of liveliness.

There! that puppet-show has begun again and as I've had about enough of it in this last week, I will close this letter now and go to dinner. Tomorrow I leave this great city, the most interesting place I ever was in; and shall make my way over Padua and Ferrara to Bologna. I hope they won't cut my throat there for an Austrian spy.

Yrs ever   H.

MS: MHi

1. Published in the Boston *Courier* May 9.

2. The Semmering Pass in the Austrian Alps is crossed by the first mountain railroad in the world, completed in 1854.

3. The Palazzo Pesaro, on the Grand Canal, built in the seventeenth century by Longhena, now houses the International Gallery of Modern Art and the Oriental Museum. Paolo Veronese (1528–1588); Tintoretto (Jacopo Robusti, 1518–1594).

4. Caroline Ferdinande Louise (1798–1870), duchess of Berry, mother of Henri (1820–1883), count of Chambord, the legitimist pretender to the French crown. *Libro d'Oro:* the Golden Book, a register of noble families.

5. San Sebastiano.

6. *Saint Nicholas* (1563), by Titian (Tiziano Vecellio, 1477–1576).

7. Venetians closed their theaters in 1859 as a demonstration against Austrian rule.

8. In the agitation preceding the Revolution of 1848, Venetians adopted a policy of having nothing to do socially with Austrians, refusing even to sit in cafés in their presence.

9. The Mechitarist monastery, founded in 1717 by Mechitar, the leader of a congregation of Roman Catholic Armenian monks, became in the early nineteenth century a center of Armenian learning and cultural preservation.

To Charles Francis Adams, Jr.

No. 3.[1]   Bologna. April. 16. 1860.

My dear Charles

I was determined at any price not to lose the Romagna on my journey. It's now one of the important squares on the chess-board of humanity, and may before long become still more so.[2] Accordingly, though I could find no one who was going in this direction and might have supplied my shortcomings on the part of the language I set out from Venice the day before yesterday morning, ready for anything that might turn up. The rail-road carried me as far as Padua in company with quite a number of Americans who were going on to Milan. By the way, the travelling for pleasure in these regions seems to be nearly monopolized by Americans now. The English haven't recovered from the war, and are anxious about disturbances.

The diligence to Santa Maria Maddalena, the last Austrian town on the road, left at ten o'clock in the evening, so I had a superfluity of time to examine Padua. I found it dreadfully mournful there. Under the best of circumstances the city must be an ugly one, dark, dirty, flat and provincial; but now it is intolerable. All the inhabitants looked to me like seedy bankrupts; that is, except the beggars, who are above fortune. The old University is now closed, the students having taken to politics; and thus one great support of the place is cut off. The bust of that famous old Professoress Helena Lucretia Cornaro, looked down at me from the walls as if it were a comfort to know there was even one person there to be sorry that her reputation was gone.[3] Instead of students a regiment of Hungarian cavalry is stationed in the city and one hears at every corner the jingle of spurs and the clank of sabres along the pavement. The largest church is turned into a magazine, and around the sarcophogus which holds the ashes of St Luke, are piled sacks of oats and hogsheads of biscuit. Only the shrine of St Antony of Padua is as magnificent as ever, and I had the pleasure of listening to part of a service as I examined the splendid carvings and ornaments about it.

I was soon tired of Padua. There was an oppressive atmosphere about it that weighed on me. Glad enough I was when at last ten o'clock in the evening came, and I was shut up in the diligence, the only passenger. I had it all my own way here, and really rather enjoyed it. I stretched myself out, and dozed and slept as we rumbled along over the road, and if it hadn't been for the postilions who at each post woke me up to beg for a present, I really might have passed a comfortable night. At any rate morning came at last, and before six o'clock I was drinking a cup of coffee on the banks of the Po.

My passport was examined four separate times in ten minutes, apparently by every man in a uniform who took a fancy to make my acquaintance. A half a dozen men in the Tyrolese Jäger uniform, with rifles slung over their shoulders, watched me into a boat, to see that I didn't smuggle any of the Kaiser's precious subjects off with me, and on this side of the river I was snapped up by a Piedmontese officer before I had fairly landed, to make sure, I suppose that I shouldn't attempt a counter-revolution in favor of the Pope. My passport however has about every visa under Heavens on it, and so nothing was said and I could open my trunks and let a dirty rascal pull my shirts about.

The diligence stops on the Austrian side. I had to hire a waggon and driver and go on to Ferrara the first post town, some forty minutes ride. Here I happened to hit a vetturino who was returning to Bologna, and after some tough interpreting, I took possession of the coupé of his carriage, leaving the interior to four very dirty Italians. This was a piece of luck for I escaped a crowded diligence and saw the country at my leisure.

Having half an hour to spare I wandered about Ferrara. It's a strange old place and has a cathedral built before the flood, I believe; a most extraordinary piece of work. The people interested me though, more than the city. The tone of the crowd seemed many degrees more self-assured than on the other side of the river. National-Gardists were strutting about in magnificent independence. The cross of Savoy was everywhere, and occasionally the tricolor, red, white and green, would be flying, out of shop-windows and on public buildings. Almost every door had a placard pasted on it. "Evviva Vittorio Emmanuele II. nostro legitimo Re."[4] There was a grand crowd on the market-place, and that eternal and confounded puppet-show was making more noise than ever. In short there was a total change of appearance in the people and they didn't seem to reflect at all that they were every soul of them excommunicated and eternally damned.[5] At least if they did, they kept up appearances very well.

However, I had no great amount of time to give to Ferrara, and at eight o'clock was off again. The day was pleasant, the trees just budding out into leaves and blossoms, and the dust not too great. But I can't say that, at this time of year at least, the country here is particularly interesting. It all forms part of that great rich plain which extends, flat as a prairie, from the Tyrol mountains to the Appenines, and Bologna itself lies just on the edge, where the plain ends and the hills begin to rise. So there was no varied scenery at all, and not much to look at except canals, ploughed fields and here and there a farm-house with thick walls and windows to which the invention of glass has never been applied. Queer old men and women on still queerer old donkey-carts ambled along by us, and generally specimens of mortality such as Count Cavour might be shy of trusting the right of voteing to.[6] Otherwise there was nothing to look at till as we came near Bologna towards two o'clock or a little earlier, the groups became more frequent and livelier and the donkey-carts quite a drug. Just outside of the city we passed the line of the new fortifications. They were not very far advanced, in this place at least; indeed little more than marked out, and the outlines dug out, but they're hard at work on them, and to judge from their position I should think they'd be about ten miles round on a rough guess. But as I only got a glance at one point I can't say what is to be turned out when it's complete.

I'm charmed with Bologna; that is, not with the city which I haven't fairly become acquainted with, but with the present population. There are, I am told, twenty five thousand soldiers here, and of course it is prodigiously gay. As a travelling philosopher I've amused myself by wandering up and down the most frequented promenades and watching the military which is as yet a sort of cross between militia and regulars. The uniforms too are many of them new to me. I don't think I saw them last summer, for I wouldn't have forgotten such striking affairs.

Of all conceited, affected, ridiculous fops, I suppose a French officer is the perfection; which doesn't prevent his being the best soldier in the world. But the Piedmontese affect the French in all military matters, and in consequence many of the Piedmontese officers are as funny objects as I ever looked at. Now it may be imagination on my part, but I think the army here has not yet settled into it's uniform; every thing looks new and unused; too pretty by half. All the soldiers I saw, officers or privates, seemed to me to be trying to look military; they had their beards artistically arranged to be ferocious; their caps a shade too much on one side; their salute was a shade too formal or too informal; their walk a continual effort to do it right; their waists laced very nicely and tight enough, but not exactly the thing. All this is French, but as yet the Piedmontese are a little behind hand and want practice. When I see a French captain gotten up in this wonderful way, with his crinoline trousers, his tight corsets, his little boots, his jaunty cap and wiry imperial and moustache, I always laugh, for he walks with his arms at a wide angle from his body, and with dainty steps, for his boots are tight, but still I always feel that if he chooses to make an ape of himself, no man dare say a word, for he knows his duties and has done his work. But it isn't so with these Italians and I'm sorry to see such tom-foolery where they ought to feel what their real duties are. No doubt they'll fight well, but they're not yet an army as an army ought to be, and with equal leading I'm afraid the Austrians would beat them. As for hatred and passion, it's about equal on both sides. Still these troops here are I suppose new and untrained. One successful campaign might make them matches for the French. At any rate, though it's a pity that there must be a large Piedmontese standing army, it's still more a pity that this army should be formed on

the French cockney-fatalism rather than on the old Cromwellian, Napoleonic principle of religion and patriotism; fanaticism if you like. The uniform is quite pretty and the silver lace and epaulettes charmingly bright,
but if the officers wear those epaulettes into battle, they'll never come out
of it alive. In the Austrian army the mark of rank is a star on the collar, one,
two or three as the rank rises, and of cloth, silver or gold, so that one sees at
a glance when one is near, but in the distance officer and private are alike.
I've forgotten how the French manage it. But epaulettes are unpractical
and only a childish love of display can hold on to them.

The fortifications here are to be on a scale somewhat like the great wall
of China. My guess of ten miles was low. I might have said twenty I believe,
for I've been up to the Church Madonna di San Luca, from where there is a
most glorious view over the plain, I've no idea how far; and from here I
could partially make out the new lines. They don't amount to much as yet,
but are on a tremendous scale in extent. It will need at least a hundred
thousand men to maintain them. I could only guess at the whole idea, for
the ground is only broken here and there, and my only guide was the
swarm of white spots which a careful examination could detect here and
there in the plain; the shirts of the workmen, digging and wheeling the
earth; for as yet I've seen only low earthworks; no masonry whatever. The
height too round the church was being levelled off and cleared for action,
but of course I can't judge what it's all going to look like. There must be a
good many thousand men at work there now.

Of course I don't pretend to offer you in these letters any statistics whatever. I'm not in a condition to get sure information, and so I do without
any except what my eyes give me. As a resumé and end of all I've seen here,
I can only say that everything seems to me in the best condition possible.
The people look contented, happy and are quiet and peaceable; the country which is one great garden, will soon be opened by rail-ways, and the
population raised up by schools, a free press, and liberal institutions; the
churches of which there are or were a hundred and thirty and twenty cloisters, will be shaved down, I suppose, and the restrictions on trade removed.
The military point of view is the troublesome one, for there's not a tenable
fortification in the whole land and one lost battle may put everything
where it was two years ago. However, sufficient unto the day is the evil
thereof. We'll hope the best till the bad comes and even if the bad should
come, the thing has gone too far now to be wholly wiped out. Austria can
say what it will, but in these days the choice of the people does and must
count for more than that of the Kings.

You won't care to hear about the gallery and churches here which have
taken up the pleasantest part of today for me. There are some grand pictures here and a lot of very wretched ones besides. The gallery is a delightful relief after all the uniforms and the bustle in the streets, and as I detest
soldiers, even the best of them, as such, and am envious of them besides because they have pretty clothes to wear, and a sword and epaulettes, while I
have to dress like other people, I am always glad to get into a gallery where

I'm quite sure there will be no uniforms, officers not taking to art. This morning I had it all to myself and luxuriated in not being interrupted.

Tomorrow I go on to Florence, just missing the King's reception I'm afraid, but I never heard till yesterday afternoon that he was on his tour. Still, I shall see him which is something, and Cavour too, I hope. It's a whole day's journey and the diligence starts at five o'clock in the morning so I will take my sleep while I can get it.

Yrs ever,   H.

MS: MHi

1. Published in the Boston *Daily Courier* June 1.
2. Romagna, a former Papal State, Parma, Modena, and Tuscany voted overwhelmingly by plebiscite March 11–12 for annexation by Piedmont—a major step in the unification of Italy and challenge of the Pope's temporal power.
3. Elena Lucrezia Cornaro (1646–1684), poet and scholar, who received a doctorate of philosophy at Padua in 1678.
4. Victor Emmanuel II (1820–1878), king of Piedmont-Sardinia 1849–1861, first king of Italy 1861–1878, styled the "second" to keep the numbering of the House of Savoy.
5. In late March the Pope had excommunicated all who had promoted or aided the rebellion in the Romagna, including Victor Emmanuel and Cavour.
6. Camillo Benso Cavour (1810–1861), count of Cavour, prime minister of Italy 1860–1861, advised the holding of plebiscites based on universal male suffrage to show that enthusiasm for Italian independence was widespread, even among peasants.

To Abigail Brooks Adams

Florence. April. 19. [1860]

Dearest Mamma

I enclose an unsealed letter to Mary to you, though I suppose she's in Boston again, that you may read it in place of a longer one from me, and seal it and send it to her. I'm sorry about Seward's speech. I'd read it long ago in the news-paper, but would have liked a copy from him very much. Perhaps you might send it to me at Florence care of E. Fenzi &Co.

Here I am with Loo. Your complaints and fears about her may be, in my opinion are, perfectly just. At the same time I will not put my finger in the matter at all. Let every man wear his own boots. It would be another thing if it were likely that I could seriously influence her, but any influence I could exert must be only for a time. Then it might only make matters worse; I think it would. Then further, I acknowledge fairly that I do not myself feel certain enough of what is best for Loo, to undertake to advise her. For God's sake though, if John marries, don't let him come abroad if you can help it. I am really almost anxious about this, especially as I think it not impossible that Kuhn may try to prolong his stay here indefinitely. Loo, I think, would as a matter of duty prefer to go home. As a matter of pleasure of course both she and I and everyone else would prefer Europe. I don't undertake to give you their plans for I don't think they know themselves, but I do not believe they will return this year; perhaps not the next either.

For one, I am free to acknowledge, I think it's just as well they should stay here. I mean that they will never be happy anywhere else, and Loo's object in life is now so far as I see, pretty much reduced to that of being happy. New York would only be Europe for her, on an unsatisfactory scale. Of course if she has no children. I've thought all along that Europe is the best place for her, and though I have and shall express no opinion to her about it, I can do so to you, and even go so far as to say that I shall be glad, things being what they are, if she can remain here, and if she can't lead a useful life, at least lead a happy one; for I have no doubt she is and always will be happier here than anywhere else, not because it's gay or because it's amusing, but because one is free and one's own master.

She looks well and is just as ever, so far as I've seen. Impetuous as ever, and good-hearted as possible. For me they are a little too old. My set is a younger one and I feel always under a cloud where I'm not on an equality. They've charming rooms, and seem to have acquaintances in abundance. I'd like to stay here with them and see a little society, something I've not seen for years, but I've no time and no money. I think I shall go to Rome and take rooms till money comes as I hate to borrow of Kuhn and don't care to forestall at Baring's.

Rather a solemn letter, consequent on my having got up early to write it, as I'm pressed for time. Your message to the Reichenbachs I will send with pleasure. We expect a letter, as our latest date is March. 24th.

Yrs ever   Henry.

MS: MHi

To Charles Francis Adams, Jr.

No. 4.[1]   Florence. April. 23. 1860.

My dear Charles

As I feared, I lost the grand show. I climbed up on the top of the diligence which left Bologna at five o'clock in the morning of the 17th, and there I remained with a few intervals until we arrived in Florence at nine o'clock at night. The journey was among the stupidest I ever recollect to have made. From Bologna the road enters at once into the mountains, or hills rather, for there's no grandeur or beauty to them that I saw, and once there, it seems as though the end never would come. My two companions on the top were Italians from Milan who spoke no language except their own, and whose society was not remarkably interesting. The conductor was better, a jolly, good-natured, lively fellow who talked French and was always laughing with the drivers, which enlivened the scene a little. Inside of the coach was a promiscuous crowd of rather queer characters including a woman whom I take for an opera-singer or ballet-dancer, and a lively little Frenchman who was paying marked attentions to her and who informed me from time to time in German as to the success which he was attaining; which appeared to be very satisfactory to him as it was very amusing to me. As we began to climb the hills, oxen were harnessed on before the horses and as Italian oxen are not much quicker in their movements than those of other countries, you can imagine that our time wasn't quite up to the racing mark. I walked two or three hours of the up-hill work, and so had at least an opportunity to see the country well; a sight, by the way, which, as the weather was cloudy and cold, the hills brown, with streaks of snow on the tops, and the trees leafless as if it were January, I don't care to have again. So it went, up hill and down hill, for fifteen endless hours. A stop for dinner at a precious place whose name I've forgotten, was the only interruption. Morning, noon, evening, came and passed; we saw the sun rise and we saw him set, and it grew dark, but at last we cleared the final hill and as we came down on the run on this side, the conductor turned round to me and pointed to some lights a long way off, with an "Eccola Firenze." There it was, certainly, but as it was then pitch dark and raining, I couldn't see a great deal of it, and my only sensation was joy at finishing the day's work. I bade my friend the Frenchman who had taken the opera-singer now wholly under his care, good-bye, and having rescued my baggage, I rambled off to the hotel, a few doors distant, after a night's lodgings.

The next day everything went beautifully. I felt as though I'd lived in Florence all my life. Half America is here, I believe, and a very pleasant half, at that. There were races that afternoon in honor of the King, and as I had lost his grand entrance into the city two days before, I was anxious to see him all I could. The race-course is just outside the city, and of course there was a great crowd of carriages and people lining it, and a very pretty show of much of the Florentine world. The King and his suite who came in three state carriages with the usual show of postillions and out-riders, were received with clapping of hands and "Evviva Vittorio Emmanuele"; a pretty reception enough and neither very warm or very cold; the heavy shouting had I suppose, taken place on Monday; though indeed the Tuscans do not seem to be a noisy people under any circumstances. At all events, there was "il nostro Re" large as life, and I was jammed in a very dirty but very quiet crowd before his box, in order to get a sight at him. My first impression was that "il nostro Re" looked like a very vulgar and coarse fancy-man, prize-fighter or horse-jockey. He was in civil clothes, and wore a sort of glossy shooting jacket; at least so it looked to me; and as he stood in the front of the stand, with his head thrown back and his hands in his coat-pockets, I began to think that my admiration for him, not only as a soldier but as a King, must have sprung from some mistake or false information. At all events there he was, looking as though he wished the people would not make such a bother, but since they wanted it, he would stand still and be looked at as long as they chose.

The races were pretty poor; I suppose there have been poorer races, but I don't see how there could ever have been much poorer ones. There was the usual amount of bon-bons, gloves and Napoleons lost and won, and as the day was cool and cloudy, no one was sorry to get through. We crossed the royal cortège returning to the city surrounded by a great crowd of people shouting and clapping their hands.

Strange how this bad weather persecutes us. I've now been a week in Florence and it has rained every day and been as cold as ever a man need wish, but still the trees are all green as in summer, the camelias have bloomed by thousands, and are now faded, and the roses will soon flower. All the time the sun is as unseen as ever he was in Dresden or Berlin and the air often really cold and raw.

The evening of the next day, the 19th, was set apart for the Opera. It was immensely amusing and interesting. The house which is very pretty, was lighted in gala style, and all Florence was there in grand costume. I never saw anything like it for prettiness and taste. As however the Florentines seem to make the smallest part of the society here and as Russians, English, French, Americans and Sicilians and Poles, everyone except Tuscans, furnish the rest, the house this evening was certainly no very popular demonstration. Flowers were not the order of the evening; still nearly every box had bouquets and two or three had large ones with the Cross of Savoy in red and white camelias; which was all the fashion in the winter, I believe.

The King was received as usual; it was enthusiastic and did not exceed enthusiasm, for the boxes were filled with ladies, and the pit very respectable in white cravats, which tend to repress too great agitation and rather quell and subdue people, I think. At least that's my own experience. The truth is, in dress clothes, white-kid gloves and a white cravat, I cannot afford to be enthusiastic. Royalty itself looked as usual as if it were a bore. Royalty bowed and continued bowing so long as the pit continued shouting and the boxes waved their handkerchiefs. Finally our King sat down and the whole company proceeded to sing the National Hymn; followed by more enthusiasm.

There was a ballet and an opera; I saw one dance in the first and heard about three minutes of the last. The fashion being to wander about in the boxes and talk, it's slightly hopeless to expect to look on or listen, except in the pit. Some one said that both opera and ballet were miserable, and to the best of my knowledge, he spoke the truth. I do know however that I got a first-rate view of Cavour across the Theatre and examined him through my glass for five minutes steadily, as I always wanted to do. He's a most quiet, respectable-looking middle-aged gentleman. From his appearance I never could have guessed that he was the greatest man in Europe. He seems, too, very modest and retiring, and is said to hate to be displayed for show. At all events, he sat quietly there in a stage box with his face as much from the house and towards the stage as possible, and holding a handkerchief up to shade his eyes from the light or his face from the pit, I can't say which.

The Court retired amid more shouting at the close of the second or third act, and it is said that the King is always more ready to leave than he is to come on such occasions. In fact he prefers his cigar and has sworn that he'll hear no more music at any price. He's said to be not fond of music and they've rather bored him with it here. He rushes about at five o'clock in the morning and if reports are to be believed, is delighted with Florence and with his reception here. He well may be. It's not every King who can have a Tuscany fall into his hands. The prettiest, pleasantest, quietest little Kingdom it was ever my fortune to meet with in Europe.

It was a very lively, pleasant evening; like the Savoy colors, all pink and white. Everyone looked pretty and was mildly excited. I was at first a little alarmed at finding myself in the middle of a theatre—full of princes and counts and famous characters; it's not often that one has the chance to see so many famous men together, and men with names more famous than themselves.

The next day there was another race, beating the first in poorness. Half the course was under water, and I waded about from carriage to carriage in a perfect swamp. There was to have been an illumination of Pisa that evening but the weather was too bad and it was postponed. So I've lost that, said to be one of the sights of the world.

On Sunday, the 22d was the grand show, the prettiest of all. At four o'clock in the afternoon there was the race of Roman chariots on the Piazza Sta Maria Novella, which was surrounded by seats in the style of the Roman amphitheatre. It's a queer custom, this race; ancient, I suppose. The chariots which are ancient chariots in shape, with four wheels instead of two; and very clumsy, are driven by charioteers with Roman helmets and costumes, so that the effect is classically ludicrous. They are precisely like the illustrations of Gilbert A'Beckett to the Comic History of Rome.[2] It is understood to be all arranged before-hand as to which was to win, and the order of the race. A tradition says that once a charioteer, indignant at the subordinate position assigned to him, tried to really contest the race, but only succeeded in tipping himself over and his two companions on top of him while the fourth, the original winner, drove triumphantly over the course. We had no such spectacle as this must have been, for the race was over in a very short time and the relics of antiquity restored to their stables. But now the riding on the Corso began, and I saw the Florence equipages which are famous. The first equipage we met was that of the King. He came right by us so that our wheels almost touched, and I had a chance to see him face to face. It was a great improvement. He did not look so rowdy, and did look much more intellectual than I had supposed at first sight. People say that his brains are supplied by Cavour, but it must need a tolerable amount of brain to appreciate and be willing to follow Cavour. I think for myself that he looks like something better than a mere soldier and father of a hundred and eighty of his subjects.[3]

The equipages are charming. In fact, though I've seen a good deal in Europe, I never saw any show equipages before, worth the name. There is a taste in the liveries and a nattiness in the whole effect of some of the private carriages here, that was wholly new to me. They belong nearly all to private persons, noble or not as may be, and are peculiarly unostentatious; that is, if a state equipage can be unostentatious. Ostentatiousness is unavoidable with four horses and liveries, but as a rule the gold was here less conspicuous than the taste. Perhaps however I ought to make an exception of the American gentleman who has amused Florence this winter by driving a waggon and ten horses through the streets, like a circus-master. How long the line of carriages was, I can't say. It was democratic enough. Any one joined in who could get anything to carry him, and those who couldn't or wouldn't, looked on at the side or out of the windows. Such a quiet, orderly crowd, I never saw or heard of. Tuscans don't quarrel or fight, Tuscans don't get drunk, are not rude or ill-mannered, are not restless or impatient and are infinitely capable of being amused. They make accordingly the most attractive crowd I ever met with. The streets were filled with spectators and the houses looked gay and pretty with all the available carpets and rugs hung out the windows. Still it was all quiet as could be and there was no trouble and very little stoppage during the two hours or more I was there.

These gaieties are all out of season; they are given for the King, and come along as the weather allows. Otherwise the city goes on as usual. There was a crush ball given at the Pitti Palace the other evening, and the accounts of the crowd and heat are something impressive. But the strangers who give a good deal of gaiety to the city, are beginning to leave fast, and only the residents are left here. It's still the gayest little place however I've ever seen. There are troops of carriages at the Cascini every pleasant afternoon, and I see toilettes occasionally that my long abode in the quiet and patriarchal Germany makes me regard with wonder and admiration. It's in comparison with all this show and liveliness that I begin to appreciate how dead Venice was.

I was very sorry to have lost the entrance of the King, for it must have been charming. When I arrived I found the streets and piazzas lined with faded flowers and blocked up with triumphal arches. To our ideas the amount of flowers used on such an occasion as this, is something marvelous. The city in the first place was filled with them; all along the streets and on each side of the course which the procession took, were trees of flowers; camelias fastened ad libitum to green branches; then, as the King passed along, there was a steady, heavy rain of flowers from the windows on each side, so that, if accounts are to be believed, it seemed at times as if there was a solid mass of them falling. Bouquets were forbidden as they frighten the horses; as it was, the King's horse got frightened and was unmanageable, so that unless the King had been a splendid rider he might have had his neck broken. He had to let the horse run, and leave the rest of the suite to follow as they could.

I don't think the Florentines trouble themselves much about politics. They are contented and not inclined to be turbulent. The truth is, they're entitled to a good deal of credit for the unselfish way in which they've acted, for the annexation can't well benefit them immediately nearly so much as it hurts them. As for the misgovernment of the Grand Duke, I fancy the people would never have complained of that, if he had only yielded to them in other respects.[4] Even the most patriotic Italians, so far as I've heard, agree that they have nothing against the Grand Duke except that he was hopelessly stupid and behind the age. I rather fancy that the Government was on the whole an exceptionally good one, and the people among the most happy and honest in all Europe. The annexation will double their taxes, if not still worse, and at the same time makes them provincials. So that it could have been only pure patriotism which should induce them to give up their independence. Among the resident strangers here there's a tolerably strong party of adherents to the old Grand Duke, and they speak openly enough. How large his party is among the people, it would be hard to guess. At all events it's not large enough or not courageous enough to do anything.

All my previous ideas of the Italians have been knocked in the head here in North Italy. Especially the Tuscans seem to me to be the pleasantest people I ever saw, and neither lazy, nor dishonest, nor revengeful, nor ignorant. I'm now going down to Rome and Naples, rather at the risk of getting my head knocked off, and shall see how it all looks there. I'm rather afraid that it will grow darker as I get south. That's the way of the world.

I'm sorry to leave Florence. It's a great place, especially for scandal and art. It's so long since I've seen a really gay place that it's an immense amusement to watch these people here and learn the history of the distinguished characters, one after another, with usually a strong flavor to each. Everyone has some history or other, and all are worth hearing. But the eternal city can't wait for Polish counts and Russian princesses.

Yrs ever   H.

MS: MHi
1. Published in the Boston *Daily Courier* June 1.
2. The illustrations to Gilbert à Beckett's *The Comic History of Rome* (1851) are by the *Punch* caricaturist John Leech.
3. The king's sexual exploits prompted the saying, "No sovereign has been more successful in becoming the father of his subjects."
4. Leopoldo II (1797–1870), grand duke of Tuscany 1824–1859 (deposed).

To Abigail Brooks Adams

Rome. April. 30. 1860.

Dearest Mamma

I arrived here yesterday all right, and hope tomorrow to be able to say that I'm settled here for three or four weeks. Florence I left some five days ago after passing a real pleasant week with Loo. I'd have stayed there with all my heart but the season hurries me up and I'm late as it is. Two days, confound them, I was detained in rain and storm, at Leghorn because the weather kept the boat back. Here the weather is no better; always rain so that one can do nothing. The first thing I did was to look for acquaintances, for I arrived here alone. But it seems as if my arrival had sent everyone off with a rush. I found Mrs Hooker's address;[1] she was out; today I called on Mr Apthorp; he and his family had left at six o'clock for Civita Vecchia and Marseilles direct. I saw my class-mate Billy Milton's name on the list of arrivals a few days ago; I called at the hotel; he had gone thirty six hours before, to Florence.[2] The Winthrops were yesterday in the same hotel. Fanny died here.[3] Last evening I sent a card up, as I heard they were to leave this morning. They went before I was up and I've not even caught a glance at them. Not that I much cared to, under the circumstances.

Today however I did find Mrs Hooker who was jolly as ever; improved, I think. Her husband had accompanied the Winthrops to Civita Vecchia to see them off, so she was alone. I sat with her some time. I assure you, I thank my stars that she is here, for otherwise I should feel dreadfully adrift in this old grave-yard of a city. It's the mournfullest hole you ever conceived of, and at my table d'hote everyone is dying and talks about it, while in the hotel there have been four deaths in a month. People come here for their health. The city is colonised with consumptive people; asthma is the order of the day. The consequence is that the tone is depressive to the best of spirits. The city itself is a dismal, dirty, mournful old place, sort of hobbling along to it's grave.

After my call on Mrs Hooker, the rain drove me home and finding that nothing was to be done, I had a fire made and took to reading books that she had lent me. This is gay work for the first day in Rome. But really I don't care to see a thing today in a drizzle that I can see tomorrow in the sun-shine and I'm not going to do anything except a few churches till fair weather comes.

I feel utterly lost here. I never can hope to see one quarter of what there is here that is interesting. It's a dreadful place for a traveller, it makes him work so. I shall not think of leaving till a new remittance arrives and when that comes, we'll see about it. There are pleasant people here if I can get at them.

I suppose you'll have already heard all about Fanny Winthrop's death. It was very sad and so far as I know, unexpected. She had been going backward here little by little ever since she came. One day she went out horseback riding, and that aggravating her cough, pulled her down. She had one hemorrhage, and then was doing better, so that Mr and Mrs Winthrop went up to Florence leaving Eliza here with Bob and Mrs Adams.[4] They nursed her all the time and no other nurse was allowed. A week ago the others came, as I understand it, in quick succession, Saturday or Sunday and Monday and carried her off at once. Mr Winthrop posted back as fast as possible and arrived two hours before the funeral. The day before yesterday I was told, the body was sent on to Marseilles. Bob is going on to Paris. I suppose he will take Mrs Adams back to America. She meanwhile, with the Winthrops has gone on to Florence. This is all I can tell you now, but tomorrow I'm to dine with Mrs Hooker from whom I have this, and then I can perhaps tell you more.

May. 1st.   Of all my travelling experiences this is the rummiest and among the pleasantest. This morning I called on Hooker at the office as I promised Lizzy (we're cousins now and thick as you please) I should, and he said there were rooms in the same house he lives in, which I could take if I liked. So I came down and with Lizzy examined the appartments which are in fact properly a part of hers but always let separate and happening just now to be empty. The queerest old garrets you ever saw, four or five small rooms and countless passages between them, on the third story and opening out onto the flat roof of a part of the house as a promenade, so that I can walk straight into the Hooker's rooms and they right into mine while we have the same outside door for both. To-day I dined with them and took possession of my new abode. After dinner we arranged that I could always dine with them; as in Rome the custom is to have dinners furnished and keep no cook or kitchen, this is perfectly easy. I have merely to club my dinner to theirs and pay my share. So you see I am in a manner taken into their establishment and feel rather more at home, if anything, than I did at Florence, little as I ever knew Lizzy Winthrop and though I never saw Hooker till to-day.

You can imagine that there could not very easily be a more satisfactory arrangement to me than this. I am perfectly delighted with it, for I've had experience enough of wandering about alone. Hooker is always in his office apparently, and his wife can't have much to occupy her further than her own amusement.

Today was a lucky day in more ways than one; except that it brought no letters from you and I'm getting anxious for my last date is March 24th. I went over to visit the Vatican and I met there a young lady whom I used to know at Dresden, and she introduced me to two more, so that I'm in a fair way not to want pleasant acquaintances. I shall go there and call tomorrow evening, so that they mayn't forget me, which moreover is the less likely as I'm the only available young man in the city. Then there are the Stories to be visited too,[5] and no doubt once begun there'll be no end.

Hooker told us about his trip to Civita Vecchia. Mrs Adams and the Winthrops all except Bob, left here yesterday morning by post for Florence where they're arrived by this time. Hooker went with Bob down to Civita Vecchia and accompanied him on board the steamer to Marseilles. The body was also on board. At Marseilles it's to be shipped for America. Bob goes on to Paris, after attending to all this. In June his family joins him there and I believe they travel in England a time before returning home. Bob is badly cut up; he's been devoted to his wife; nursed her all the time and feels I suppose now a good deal as if he were lost and life had no object. He's had a hard time of it and seems to have gone through it admirably.

As far as gaiety goes, Rome seems rather behindhand now. But then Rome is so big that gaiety doesn't show as it does in Florence. I expect to be tolerably busy. From noon till four o'clock most of the galleries and sights are open; from four to six is the driving, shopping and calling time; at half past six we dine, and in the evening there are visits or the opera or the Colosseum by moonlight, or Heaven knows what. As for the sights, the very thought excites and worries me. I was to-day wandering about in the Vatican and all up in a heap, hardly knowing what to make of it. I really passed over the Apollo Belvidere, the Laocoon, and several other such things, with hardly a look. I felt all lost in the oceans of art there. I wandered into St Peter's and never appreciated where I was, any more than if I were in Boston Music Hall. Indeed St Peter's in effect disappoints me. It doesn't approach in grandeur and dignity, to my mind, to any of the great Gothic cathedrals nor even to St Marc at Venice. The truth is, my German education sticks out in Italy. Loo used to take my views of Italian music and painting and architecture quite to heart.

You can accordingly be very easy about me for some weeks to come. I'm well taken care of, and hope to have a real good time. I'm much obliged to you for your message to Madame Reichenbach and shall send it in my next letter. I shall get them some presents here in Italy. It will not be hard to pick up something appropriate.

I hope to get letters every day. As I dislike anxiety I wont think over your silence but hope it's all right. Very strange though. Here I see lots of American papers and am quite posted up on things. It's well I didn't pass the winter here. I never should have done anything.

Love to all.

Yrs ever   Henry.

MS: MHi

1. Elizabeth Winthrop Hooker, wife of James Clinton Hooker (1818–1894), long-time American banker in Rome, unofficial secretary of the legation to the Papal States. They lived in the Palace of the Bonapartes.

2. William Frederick Milton (1837–1905), Harvard '58.

3. Frances Adams Winthrop (1837–1860), wife of Robert C. Winthrop, Jr.

4. Robert Charles Winthrop, Jr. (1834–1905); Mrs. Ben Adams, Frances Winthrop's mother.

5. William Wetmore Story (1819–1895) of Salem, Mass., son of Justice Joseph Story, was an expatriate sculptor and poet. He married Emelyn Eldredge (d. 1894) of Boston.

To Abigail Brooks Adams

Rome. May. 6. 1860.

Dearest Mamma

At last two letters from you of the 4th and 11th of last month have arrived over Florence. Loo sent them on to me and was in a dreadful taking because none had come for herself. One from Mary also, enclosed. I see too heaps of American papers now.

You mention Charles's Advertiser letter about the printing affair. When I wrote to you I called it "treacherous" without knowing that it was his, till a copy from him arrived a few days afterwards. That changed the case entirely. As the matter stands, I think it couldn't have been better, and papa owes to that letter a good half of the credit he has got from his action. It was an admirably clear and even partial statement of the case, and the more effective on account of it's lowness of tone, and appearance of impartiality. You could see that from the noise it made, and the way it was quoted and attacked. There was a force in the statement independent from the force of papa's position. I am watching from here with a sort of sickness at heart, the course of American politics. These Connecticut and Rhode Island elections and the contemptible tone politics take with us, are no very pleasant forerunners to an election like next Fall's. Not that I feel discouraged; but that each postponement of the final victory confuses matters so dreadfully. However I hope we shall do better as we go on and as long as there's no dodging or begging the question on our side, I'm not afraid.

Here in Rome I'm happy as the day is long. It is utterly delicious here. I wander about and poke into churches and ruins and do what I please and don't care a rap for any man. The Hookers are immensely kind to me. I almost live on them and know hardly anyone else. There are a few young women here whom I know but I believe they think I'm wicked or improper company; at all events I find it rather hard work to know how to manage them and though I go about once a day to see them I don't find that I get ahead much. Unless some one new turns up, I'm afraid I shan't bring home a wife from Rome. By the way, I don't quite understand about John and his troubles. What objection *could* Mrs C. have! If the thing really stands so, I'm contented and trust most sincerely it may so remain; but it would be funny to have a Boston Capuletti and Montrechi arrangement.[1]

The weather here for two days has been something worth seeing. Upon my word it is intoxicating. I feel as if I were in the uppermost of the Heavens. The air is filled with the perfume of the roses, and that sort of Spring sensation that makes everything so delightful. The sky hasn't a cloud. Rome looks it's very prettiest. I wander about the city from noon till four o'clock seeing sights; then Lizzy Hooker usually picks me up to ride till six, and at half past six we dine. You can imagine what a life for the Gods this is. I have all Rome to choose from; it's all new and all beautiful and interesting; I can pass one hour up in the Vatican and lounge before the Apollo or the Laocoon or in the galleries which Raphael painted or the Sistine chapel which is as ugly a place as you need to see, or in Saint Peter's, which doesn't come up in interest to St Marc or in beauty to the Milan Cathedral to my mind; then I can take a carriage and drive over to the Capitol and look a minute at the Dying Gladiator and the Antinöus and the Venus; right behind the Capitol is the Forum with all the ruins; just beyond that is the Colosseum; then when I'm tired here, it's time to meet Lizzy and take a drive out over the Campagna or in the Borghese grounds or along the

Corso and on the Monte Pincio; and after a day's work like this, one's dinner tastes like a feast served for Emperors. I've not made a beginning on the sights yet. I'm dreadfully confused to know what to do. There seems to be no hope of seeing all that I ought to see. This morning I was three hours at Saint Peter's to see the ceremony over the manufacture of some new Saints, but I was sold. The Pope was not there, and makes his appearance first at five o'clock this afternoon, but I'm too lazy to go over again and be jammed two more hours against dirty Capucin monks and fleas. One part of the church was lighted up to-day with candles and this was quite fine. The rest was as I say, a sell.

Last night I went with Hooker to a Cardinal's reception, to which he got me a card. Of course I knew no one there and didn't seek any introductions as I'm not up to talking French yet. What I wanted was to see the people and this I did very well. Everybody was there. The whole College of Cardinals, Antonelli and all.[2] General Goyon and the Duke de Grammont, the French celebrities, and a heap of French officers not of any very polished appearance. All the Corps Diplomatique. Heaps of spiritual dignities in red legs, purple legs and black-legs. The Italian nobility were also there. I saw a Colonna, and a Barberini; the host was an Altieri; and if you could only have seen the diamonds the women wore. Such a flash and a glitter I never saw yet. Of course it was not gay; only a crush reception and every one looked bored; but curious to me and interesting to my philosophical train of mind. The women were not striking in any way, I thought. The dresses were no very great. General Lamoricière was not there as he is busy forming his new army with which he says he'll reconquer the Romagna in four months, alone.[3] The atmosphere here is just not the same as in Florence.

May. 8.   Lord bless me! I never enjoyed myself so much in all my life. I never felt so well and happy as I do in this splendid weather and this delicious climate. Yesterday after a hard day's work over at the Vatican and a ride with a party including the young women I mentioned, out to the Pamfili-Doria Villa in the afternoon, I escorted the same young ladies down to the Colosseum at eleven o'clock at night to see it by moonlight. We went all over it with a guide and a torch, and stayed a long time up on the highest platform listening to an owl and some nightingales, and as the clock of St John Lateran struck twelve, we watched hard to see the ghosts of the gladiators and of the old Roman crowds come out of the shadows and have a fight in the moonlight but it was no go. Everything was as still and peaceful as if the eighty thousand Jews who were killed in building the old place, had never had any ghosts.

On the way home we stopped at the Fountain of Trevi, a magnificent, famous thing, and here we drank a glass of water from the fountain to our return some day to Rome again. The story or legend or whatever it is, says that anyone who has drunk at this fountain by moonlight will some day come back to it. If that's the case, the three young women and myself can look forward to seeing it again for we drank religiously out of it.

Today I'm going to begin horse-back riding. In such weather I feel always restless unless I'm in the open air enjoying it, and so long as it lasts I mean to have my rides out on the Campagna where everything is so beautiful that it keeps even me, who am tolerably phlegmatic and prosaic, perfectly intoxicated with the mere sensation of beauty and enjoyment. It's no use talking about it. I can't make you feel how exquisite this Italian climate and this life in Rome is, unless you've seen it yourself. Some day I hope you will, and if you can forget the fleas, which is hard, you'll enjoy it as I do.

The Hookers are unending in their kindness to me. Lizzy's health troubles her. She suffers a good deal from bronchitis and seems to have continual and uninterrupted difficulty with it. But she's always the most goodnatured, goodhearted creature that ever lived and is just as jolly and loud as ever. I've taken to her immensely and our dinners of three are as jolly as you please, Hooker insisting on my drinking his wine which we daily get pleasantly tight on. They live very happily together; she is as she always is, goodnatured and easily pleased; and he seems to be also good-natured and lets her do as she pleases. I wish the American society here was all in so satisfactory a way, but it seems to be nothing but quarrels and jealousies. The Stories, the Stocktons, the Crawfords and the Hookers seem to be all at swords point; that is, the wives.[4] I believe just now the two first and the two last are in opposition; that is it's two to two instead of being a four-cornered arrangement. Of course I don't care a copper for all this. I think it very probable that if Mrs Story and Mrs Stockton know that I am here, they will put me down as belonging to the faction opposed to them, but that's tolerably indifferent to me as it can't hurt me a great deal. I've called on Mr Stockton as our minister, and whenever I have an hour to spare I'm going to Mr Story's studio. If they either of them choose to invite me to their houses I shall go. If not, I shall stay at home. There's a little fool of a Consul here too, named Glentworth.[5] He belongs I suppose to the Stockton crowd.

I hear that papa has not been well. Your letter of the 11th didn't mention anything of any importance so I don't feel worried. I hope to get a letter tomorrow, though I ought to have had one yesterday or even last week. Lord knows what has got into the letters.

Yrs ever   Henry.

MS: MHi

1. A reference to the Capulets and Montagues (Montrecchi) of *Romeo and Juliet*.

2. Giacomo Antonelli (1806–1876), secretary of foreign affairs of the Papal States.

3. Christophe Lamoricière (1806–1865), commander of the Papal forces, was defeated at Castelfidardo in September.

4. John Potter Stockton (1826–1900) of New Jersey, minister to the Papal States 1857–1861, and Sarah Marks Stockton. Louisa Ward Crawford (1823–1897), daughter of New York banker Samuel Ward (1756–1832) and widow of the sculptor Thomas Crawford (1812–1857), married the painter Luther Terry in 1861.

5. Horatio de V. Glentworth, consul at Rome 1858–1861.

To Charles Francis Adams, Jr.

Rome. May. 9. 1860.

My dear Boy

Your letter dated 8th April has just arrived. Loo sent it on from Florence and took it out of the envelop "to save postage." I hope to God she read it. There are some remarks, not forcible but couched in elegant language, in it, relative to returning home and behavior there, which it would have done her good to see. I shouldn't wonder if she had. I don't believe she can be so damned uncongenially honest as to resist such a temptation.

Your criticisms on my letter of Jan. 13th have been read and considered. I sha'n't cuss you for them for two reasons. One is that I'm having such a damned good time here that I can't have the heart to cuss anyone except the fleas; and the other is that so far as I know, you're about in the right of it, and I never said you weren't, that I know of. The letter was written a good while ago, but I think I recollect reflecting at the time that it wouldn't need a great deal of exertion to seriously damage it's good looks. Your principal error, putting aside a few small ones which I wont criticise because just now I don't feel up to any heavy sparring, is in your inferences as to my intellectual condition as developed in that epistle. I reckon it isn't so werry awful. I'm not such a tremendous high-flyer and ground-and-lofty tumbler as you seem to think Germany has made me. I think you won't find me so badly changed as all that, on my approaching return. "Übrigens" as the Germans say, I'm not sorry that the letter was written for it seems to have inspired in you at least for the time, a more cheerful view of life and a more satisfactory state of mind generally. Go on, my child. I'm soon coming back to help you. Ye Powers of Hell; how funny it will be to come back and be a boy again. I wish you would look round you and hunt me up an office to enter. Consult with the M.C. about it.[1] I don't feel up to the Law School and would rather have a good office where I can work like a horse.

As to the remarks on my bearing, when I again enter the natal city, couched in rough language though they are, I accept them in the spirit in which they are given. I have some confidence still in my own common-sense. When that fails me, I hope to endure the arse-coppering process mentioned, with equanimity and success. You see I'm cultivating largely the spirit in which alone I can hope to meet the aggravated M.C. whom my expences have, I expect, by this time aroused into a state to which that of the Nemean Lion was a trifle.[2] I feel here in Italy a good deal like a truant school-boy and have half a mind to burn the Governor's next letter without reading it and say it never came. As you may have heard tell, his letters are a little apt to sour the best of cream, even Roman. As for Loo however, there *will* be a howl. Just you hold on a bit, and haul close for about the toughest nor-wester you ever heard about. I don't know whether Loo has written as yet about her prospect of *not* returning home. She must soon if she has not already. Still I don't wish to forestall matters, so don't repeat to *anyone* the remark that I don't believe the Kuhns will ever live in America again. Loo has not got so far as this yet. She merely thinks of an indefinite postponement of their return. She's dreadfully afraid of the row the parents will raise about it, and I'm under oath not to trouble her in any way. The truth is, my dear boy, this last winter has as you've supposed, finished the matter. You know, I like Loo; she is always very kind to me; very; too much so. She was no less so the week I passed with her in April. But I think Loo missed her fate in marrying Charles Kuhn; indeed must have missed her fate in America, almost inevitably. She was built for Europe and society. When I arrived this last month and saw how things had gone and were going, I must say I felt relieved when I heard that they proposed really to cut the last cord and become Europeans. If Loo were to come back it would be one eternal howl on both sides, on hers for Europe, on yours, at her absurdity. She would make you angry; you would make her more unhappy than ever. If I could see that she had any particular duties or claims on her in America, I should not be so clear. But as it is, I say, let them stay in Europe, I'm glad of it, I hope only that they'll never come back for that would spoil all.

Those are my sentiments. To her I expressed no opinion, one way or the other. I suppose she must by this time have written to announce Kuhn's return without her in June, or she will announce it soon. In either case you had better use your discretion in softening over to mamma the part that will trouble her, and in preventing any scenes or family divisions. When Kuhn comes, he'll of course visit you at Quincy. I suppose the Governor will be stern. Loo, I think dreads his anger more than anything else. You boys will of course be able to help at least in appearance, the trouble off.

If one of you would only get engaged, it would do it beautifully. I hear through a letter of Aunt Susan to Lizzy Hooker that Mrs C. objects to her daughter's engaging herself, as too young. What does this mean! Does she object to John? In that case she's likely not to get much good out of it, if your remark as to taking John's place is in earnest. Well! Peg away. It seems pretty well made out that Miss F.C. is to be my sister-in-law in some way, unless it hangs on long enough to allow of my offering her my own hand and broken fortunes. It's so long now since I've seen a girl who has disturbed my selflove, that when I next do, I shall probably be struck deep and kick bad. Perhaps a nice sister-in-law would protect me, for the young woman who marries one of you, will, if she's nice, in much probability marry the family, for some time to come. We're all watching on tip-toe how this is going to turn out, and large amounts of money are to change hands on the result, I suppose. It's a pity that I can't hear in time to send her a little present from Rome. It strikes me you two fellows take a devilish long time in hooking one poor fish.

As for me, I'm having a jovial time all alone; that is, except so far as Mr & Mrs Hooker are concerned. Lizzy Hooker has acted like a trump by me, and so has her husband for that matter. Thanks to them I'm enjoying myself here immensely and doing absolutely nothing. Heaven knows why it's all so pleasant. Sufficient unto me that it is. I refuse here to bother myself with any ideas at all except the general one that I'll do as I please. No one is here, to speak of. No pleasant people that I know of. I have not made an attempt to know anyone, for I've not heard of anyone whom I care to know. One part of the day I amuse myself by making plans which during the rest of the day I don't carry out. I ramble about ruins and churches and galleries and talk Italian to shop-keepers and guides, and generally do a power of lounging. The hardest work I ever attempt is occasionally a chapter of Gibbon's Autobiography, which, after having searched for it at your recommendation over half Europe, I picked up the other day at a book-store here. I've begun horse-back riding in the afternoon, and perhaps you can guess at the pleasure of galloping around on the Campagna; Tusculum, and Mt Soracte, ruined acqueducts, old tombs, flowers and a good horse all joining to help one out, to say nothing of an unlimited range of open country and magnificent views in all directions. My only want is a Miss F.C. to go with me. There's where you have me. That's what I can't hunt up here, for my preserve is now small and the hareem nothing but bread-and-butter ones.

11th. Your photograph I've given to Lizzy Hooker for her collection, supposing that you would have no reason to be discontented at my leaving your likeness in the eternal city. As to engravings, I shall buy any that I take a fancy to, if they're cheap. If I get any and you want them, we can settle about it easily enough. There may be something you'll like in that box I've sent home from Dresden. I'm travelling now more decently than I used to, and though economical as a whole, I have given up acting like a miser as I get neither credit nor advantage from it. I expect to hear grumbling enough about me on my return; I may as well give some reason for it.

There's no gossip that I know of. I met Mrs Pete Ronnels in Florence who patronised me beautifully. She has been making a damned fool of herself there this winter at masked balls and a deal of scandal. Pete is thought to have a hard time but to be master. She's gone to Paris now probably to drop a foal.[3] Some other American girls scandalised even Florence last winter; a place as improper as most. I suppose you know even more about poor Fanny Winthrop's death than I, so I shan't discourse on it. I arrived after everything was over and didn't see any of the family.

Philo, for once in the right, suffers for it. Poor boy! Miss C.B. can't well hold on that tack I think. Give Mrs B. my regards and don't forget it.

Yrs ever   H.

MS: MHi

1. Member of Congress (that is, CFA).

2. Wrestling with the lion of Nemea was the first of Hercules' twelve labors.

3. Pete Ronnels: Pierre Lorillard Ronalds (1826–1905), of the snuff and tobacco family, a noted whip credited with starting the sport of coaching in America. Mary Frances Carter (1840–1910) of Boston married him in 1859; they had four children and were separated in 1867.

To Charles Francis Adams, Jr.

No. 5.[1]   Rome. May. 17. 1860.

My dear Charles

My last letter was from Florence three weeks ago. I was afterwards detained two days at Leghorn by a storm, on account of which the Lombardo, the boat that Garibaldi has lately made famous, could not leave Genoa.[2] Of all stupid places to a passing traveller, Leghorn is the stupidest, and the only excitement which the city could furnish was a visit to the English burying ground where I saw the first Spring roses hanging over Smollett's grave, and then a walk along the sea-shore where the gale was throwing the spray about like a fountain, and the sun was setting in grand magnificence.[3]

The Lombardo arrived at last. I had the satisfaction of being alone, and except an ancient Frenchman whom I hardly saw, no one came near my solitary reign in the first cabin. The sea was very quiet, but as it was cool on deck, and as it seemed a pity to make no use of my dignified solitude, I slept nearly the whole time, some thirteen hours, excepting dinner and about an hour at night when I wandered on deck and stumbled over some sleeping peasants who were lying about anywhere and everywhere. The moon was shining as well as clouds would let it, and I could see an island in the distance on our right, which, after a short search for some one awake enough to be rational, I learned from the man at the wheel, was Elba. The next land I saw was the harbor of Civita Vecchia.

The period of time between leaving the steamer and arriving at the hotel in Rome, is a disagreeable part of life to think about. Annoyance which in other countries is only an incident, becomes here the system; a completed science; and the word patience is a satire on human nature. I can't renew my torment by describing it.

The first day or two in Rome were gloomy. The weather was bad; the city appeared deserted and in ruins, and even before the grandeur and immensity of Rome, a stranger may excuse to himself a day's want of attention and interest when Death in it's most mournful and touching form comes to meet him at the gates, as it did me.[4] Add to this that the season was over, and nearly all the friends whom I had expected to find here, already gone, and it's not very strange that the city seemed to promise very little in comparison to what one expects of it.

Since then I've passed a fortnight here; on the whole the happiest fourteen days known ever to have existed for a person who was neither in love nor given to over-drinking. I hardly know where to begin to describe it. I hardly know how it came about that gradually after those first few days I became drunken with the excitement, saturated with the glorious atmosphere of this divine old place. Mr Hillard has described it, and I know from his description that the sensation is no monopoly of my own, but a part of the land and of human nature.[5]

From ruins, from palaces, from history and art, I am just waking up again to the course of life. In the Belvedere, or among the fragments of the Forum, one forgets who he is and what he is living for. At midnight watching for ghosts in the deep shadows of the Coliseum and trying to imagine oneself a young Roman betting with his friends in the next box as to the time in which the next pair of Christians would be eaten up; or at midday panting over the baths of Caracalla with a full consciousness of the inferiority of our own times and fervent wishes that one were a pagan and could have only one of the sixteen hundred bathing-opportunities which those happy generations once enjoyed in this building; or on Sunday afternoon at St Peter's where they have celebrated for three successive weeks the creation of three new Saints; and at six o'clock the Pope enters and walks with his suite, between the lines of bayonets, up to the High-altar. He blesses us all, as the crowd, soldiers and all kneel, and I confess that I do not consider myself so perfect, but that the good old man's blessing might improve me, Catholic blessing or no; though the New York Herald, if I recollect right, does call him, with sublime self-complacency, a "decrepid old fanatic in the Vatican," because he naturally objects to having half his property stolen from him. In law it *is* a theft, though as a solitary and exceptional case, I'm glad of it.

But of all enjoyments, my rides all alone out on the Campagna have been the greatest. I have found and hired a horse, and I never mount him without a serious doubt as to the probability of my existing more than three hours longer. This horse has an embarrassing habit of stopping short, walk, trot, canter, or full run; wheeling round and trying to return home. His weakness is a buffalo or a ruin, and as both are tolerably frequent around Rome he has a glorious chance to display his genius at wheeling round and standing on his hind legs indefinitely.[6] Luck has enabled me to get the better of him in a steady fight, but if he were to get me down once on the first round I'm afraid I should stand no chance.

Of all glorious things here I think a ride on the Campagna in the morning or the evening sun is the most beautiful. There one has Rome and Italy, the past and the present, all to oneself. There the old poetic mountains breathe inspiration around. There one sees the acqueducts in their grandeur and beauty, and the ruins stand out on the landscape without being wedged in by a dozen dirty houses, or guarded by a chorus of filthy beggars. The whole country lies open, unfenced and uncultivated, and as one rides from hill to hill, the scene changes with the ground and St Peter's or the Lateran, an acqueduct or a tomb, Mt Albano and Frascati or Soracte and Tivoli almost bewilder one with their different charm. The Campagna is now green and fresh, the flowers are blooming on it and the poppies are redder than blood; the little lizards fly about with their green backs that glitter in the sun, and when one is glowing with heat after a quick gallop, there's always a pleasant breeze to comfort one. This is the Rome that delights me, and in all Europe as yet I've seen nothing so beautiful and so pleasant.

You will call this poetical and laugh at it. In Rome one has a right to be a little extravagant. The only class of people quite intolerable here are those who will not be extravagant; the Englishmen who curse the fleas and beggars and see no beauty in the "Hantinous"; the Americans who honor Raphael's Stanzas with three minutes of their time and think the Pope an imposter and a hypocrite and discourse largely about the "Yewnited States."[7] The French and Germans are just as disagreeable in their way, and the latter abuse the dishonesty and villainy of the Italians when I can swear to having been just as badly cheated in Dresden and in a much unpleasanter way; just as badly troubled by beggars in Switzerland and the Tyrol, and almost as badly fleabitten in the grand Opera house at Berlin.

To come down to actual life. If you are curious as to Roman politics, I'm sorry that I can tell you next to nothing. Since that "terrible massacre" some three months ago, more or less, which the Times correspondent frightened the world by coloring, Rome has been quiet. The merits and demerits of that affair are now pretty fairly understood. There were perhaps two hundred or less, wounded and a very few killed. It was a bad matter. The gendarmerie were very rough and unnecessarily so.[8] On the other side may be said, fairly, it seems to me, that in such a position as Rome was then in, such a demonstration was a fair object for the armed interference, and that this is best excused by the perfect quiet ever since. We all, of course, wish luck to the "rissorgimento" and I would if I were an Italian, hang tight to the coat-tails of Count Cavour, but that is really no reason why the Pope or the King of Naples should allow his people to riot or rebel.[9] People pretend that this was not a riot, and it's true, but those same people would have made it one if the beginning had gone better. This sort of thing is all well enough if it's successful; if not, people must take their punishment and submit. In the March riot in Boston which began our war of Independence, there was the usual cry of barbarity, as there is now here; there it was much more unreasonable.[10] That hurried the revolution; you may depend that this will check it here. I don't like the government; I wish it were reversed or at least altered; but if the people are not strong enough to throw it off, I'm glad to see the pope strong enough to check street disturbances and disorder.

General Lamoriciere has not shown himself here so far as I know, since I've been here. He seems to be the last hope for the Pope. I am told that he promises to reconquer the Romagna in four months alone and without foreign aid. If he says this, and I was assured he had, it is perfectly incomprehensible to most people how he means to do it. Still, he would not say it without a reason and his strongest reason, as I have heard them given, was, next to his foreign troops, the trust to aid from the inhabitants themselves. There is, no doubt, a strong party both in the Romagna and in Tuscany, friendly to the old state of things and this party no doubt, is growing every day, as the people feel the pressure of the doubled taxes and the levies for the army. But most people seem to think that the Romagna is pretty safe where it is, for the present; and some question whether a serious attack is really thought of. At all events the General is said to be very hard at work and plenty of stories are about as to his way of treating "the force of Cardinals," which he is thought not to understand so well as the force of rifled cannon.

We in Rome see none of the new levies. They are sent to Ancona or Perugia and there they remain. The French swarm here and no one hears yet of an approaching move.[11] The streets are filled with police, gendarmes with sabres, handsome fellows who wander in squads of four or five up and down the Corso; one meets them everywhere in strong force.

Any number of rumors have prevailed for four days about Garibaldi, but further than that he had left for Sicily, we hear nothing certain. Now it is said that there has been a sea fight and two of his vessels and fifteen hundred men sunk, which of course is false. Now it is said that he has landed in the Roman territory to revolutionise Rome and attack Naples on this side, but of course this is incredible. News goes slowly in Rome and perhaps we shall hear in time.

But politics are out of place here for a mere visitor. Here one lives in history and in art, and needs nothing more. By the way, I must say one word of the studios, and discourse as shortly as possible of a few of the new works in which I have begun to feel a personal interest. Perhaps others will disagree with my opinions, but at least it can hurt no one.

The studio of Mr Rogers, the sculptor, is the first for an American to visit.[12] If the visitor has any feeling for art, or interest in the advance of American art, he will go there again and again. Mr Rogers is now putting the last touches to the designs for the bronze doors which are to be placed in the Capitol at Washington, at the entrance of the House of Representatives. The casting is now going on at Munich and he hopes that the doors themselves will in a year, be in their place.

It is hopeless to attempt to disarm cavils or to avoid faultfinding, especially in this case of a new work of art. Not even Raphael was genius enough for that. But if others are as much delighted with these doors as I have been, criticism will never hurt them much. To me they seem more than a success; they seem an honor to the country.

On the panels of the doors are bas-reliefs drawn from incidents in the life of Columbus. Some of these are perfect gems. There is one which represents Columbus laying his plans before the Council; if ever you see it, look at and admire the group of three monks examining a plan, on one side. Peter Visscher never did anything better. There is another which represents Columbus who has just entered the yard of a monastery; he is seated on a mule, and talks earnestly with one of the monks while another has brought hay for the mule to eat. There is a vivid reality in this relief; the figures are so earnest and life-like, and yet the quiet and peace of the cloisters, and the very spirit of the cowled monks, is caught with a happy effect that softens even the dark bronze. It may be that such works can never be popular, but let those who wish to see a work of real art and genius, go and study that. It is too large and complex for a minute description, however, and I am afraid to attempt one. Mr Rogers' other works are all here too, in plaster. One, which he calls Atala and Chactas, a young Indian warrior taking a thorn from the foot of an Indian girl who sits on his knee with her arm round his neck, is my endless delight; a flash of real genius, it seems to me.[13]

Mr Story, too, is here and at work on the art which is to him an amusement and a profession at once. He is and has been for a long time, busied with a statue of Cleopatra, and it is something so original that I cannot help dilating on it a little. He has gone to the East for inspiration, and has broken loose from the whole tribe of senseless, traditional Cleopatras whom Guido and men of Guido's stamp, fastened on the world as the type of the character.[14] His Cleopatra is an Egyptian woman, not a Grecian or Italian girl. He has sought for the pure eastern type, believing that that type contains as much that is grand and beautiful and attractive, as the European, which artists have produced and reproduced for centuries. His statue represents Cleopatra seated; her head leaning on her hand; a figure thoroughly Egyptian in costume as well as feature. She is meditating apparently her suicide. To me, apart from the rich sensualism of the face and form, there is a great charm in the expression that she wears; it seems to be the same old doubt at God's great mysteries of life and death; a scornful casting up of accounts with fate and a Faust-like superiority and indifference to past, present or future. Mr Story has tried to breathe the mystery and grandeur of the sad and solemn old Sphynxes and Pyramids into his marble. I shall not undertake to say whether he has succeeded or not. I only know that his Cleopatra has a fascination for me, before which all his other works, charming as some of them are, seem tame and pointless.

This is life in Rome. I am helpless against the charm of it, and remain without daring to think how the time is going and how the hot weather and the fever are coming on. The weather varies day by day, but as yet there has been no severe heat and occasionally it is really almost cold. The city is empty and dead. The Villa Borghese is as empty every afternoon as though there were no such things as a Colonna, a Corsini or a Doria, and the faces one is familiar with, disappear every day "to Marseilles, direct."[15]

Since writing all this, the news has come that Garibaldi has taken Palermo.[16] This grows interesting. You will hear from me perhaps from Naples where I shall go about the 1st June unless all communication is stopped.

Yrs ever.

MS: MHi

1. Published in the Boston *Daily Courier* June 29.

2. Giuseppe Garibaldi (1807–1882) and his Thousand embarked for the Sicilian expedition from Genoa, May 5, in the steamers *Piemonte* and *Lombardo* and landed at Marsala, May 11.

3. The novelist Tobias Smollett (1721–1771) died at Monte Nero near Leghorn.

4. An allusion to Frances Winthrop's death.

5. George S. Hillard, *Six Months in Italy* (1853, 21st ed. 1881), a vade mecum of Americans in Italy.

6. At that time the European buffalo still grazed on the Campagna, the plain surrounding Rome, and the countryside extended into Rome itself.

7. Statue of Antinoüs in the Capitoline Museum, described by Hillard as "not merely

beautiful, but ... beauty itself" (1858, p. 183). Raphael's *Le Stanze* (1508-1517), allegorical frescoes covering four palatial rooms in the Vatican.

8. The London *Times* was strongly pro-Italian. Figures on the number wounded on March 19 by Papal gendarmes, who were dispersing demonstrators and Sunday strollers indiscriminately, varied from 200 to 50; not even the official Papal newspaper denied that the troopers charged on the unarmed populace without warning.

9. Giovanni Maria Mastai-Ferritti (1792-1878), Pope Pius IX (1846-1878); Francesco II (1836-1894), Bourbon king of the Two Sicilies (Sicily and Naples) 1859-1860.

10. The Boston Massacre, March 5, 1770.

11. Papal troops were expected to replace the French garrison scheduled to depart from Rome on July 1.

12. HA's interest in Randolph Rogers (1825-1892) probably began with Rogers' statue of John Adams (1859), commissioned by the trustees of Mt. Auburn Cemetery, Cambridge, Mass., in 1854.

13. The statue depicts an incident in René de Chateaubriand's *Atala* (1801).

14. Guido Reni (1575-1642), painter of the Bolognese school.

15. In winter and summer months the park of the Villa Borghese was a fashionable promenade where Roman nobility such as the Colonnas, Corsinis, and Dorias congregated. Travelers leaving Rome for points north often took a steamer from Civitavecchia which proceeded directly to Marseilles.

16. Garibaldi did not enter Palermo until May 27.

To Charles Francis Adams, Jr.

Rome. May. 19. 1860.

Dear Buffer

I send the 5th of my regular letters. Your's of April 24th at first rather alarmed me at the threat of publishing these letters with my initials. On consideration however I concluded that you would hardly be likely to publish them at all after once seeing them; certainly not without corrections and changes which I should have made myself if I'd had time. What I said to you at first is literally carried out; the letters are private letters which might be published, but anonymously.

The photograph enclosure was delicious to my thirsty soul. It has been my morning study and my evening contemplation. The truth is, if that young woman is not to be my sister-in-law I shall be seriously disappointed for I've set heavy wishes on it. It arrived safely and no one knows or shall know that I have it. I needn't say that the face satisfies all my hopes and wishes.

I hope that damned German box has arrived safe by this time. Guard the engravings as you would my life. I will get your photographs. You will see by the enclosed that I have spread a little on art. This short criticism is the only part of these five letters that I'd like to have published; it might make me friends. In my last Washington letter I gave them a dab about your printing letter; mamma seemed to write as if she thought I thought you had made a botch of it. I set her straight.

A letter from the M.C. distantly growling. What a splendid opposition member he does make. He says I'm living at the rate of two thousand a year. What a damned fool I was not to have made it three. I'm going to hint as much in my next to him.

If you see Uncle Chardon,[1] mention that I am here with Mrs Hooker. You can pile on my praises of her kindness as heavy as you choose. Say that I express the greatest'gratitude to her and her husband &c &c.

Expect soon to hear of the nominations. But damn the thing without Seward. I shall reserve all my penny-whistle for him.

Everything is as usual here. I heard only yesterday from Mr Storey of Theodore Parker's death.[2] Beacon Street and Mrs Grundy will call it a judgment, mais nous autres keep our mouths shut and our heads thinking. Did you ever read anything doctrinal of his?

I read Gibbon. Striking, very. Do you know, after long argument and reflexion I feel much as if perhaps some day I too might come to anchor like that. Our house needs a historian in this generation and I feel strongly tempted by the quiet and sunny prospect, while my ambition for political life dwindles as I get older. This came up once before in our discussion. What do you think? Law and literature.

This letter is as large as one of your biggest. Give my love to my sister-in-law and Cousin Eugenia. For God's sake do it this Spring.

Yrs ever   Henry.

MS: MHi
1. Peter Chardon Brooks (1798–1880).
2. Parker died in Florence, May 10.

To Abigail Brooks Adams

Rome. May. 22. 1860.

Dearest Mamma

I wrote you no letter last week because I was so busy and had to write to Charles instead. No letter came from you too, so I call it square. I never had so little time as here and yet hang me if I know what I do. A letter from papa arrived however, and one from Charles. From now on, direct to me care of John Monroe &Co at Paris.

The papers come though the letters are long on the way. I've read the Charleston convention all through. Naturally it was one of the pleasantest flavored nuts that ever Republicans had to crack. I was on a broad grin during the whole lecture. It restores a part of my confidence in the power of men to see; even though through a glass darkly.[1] Still I want to know who the Republicans are to nominate. I'm glad I've not got to take part in that responsibility. Here in Rome politics are suggestive, for precisely the same battle went on here between the aristocracy and the people as there is now with us; here in Rome more than two thousand years ago, the people, the plebs, in spite of several victories greater than we Republicans ever got, were kept disunited, by intimidation, bribery and the other usual means, and were beaten, which beat and an aristocratic government for a century and a half, brought Rome down to anarchy and brought a military despotism in. It is wonderfully striking how close the parallel can be drawn between that fight and ours. The right, or the wiser policy, did not conquer there.

I've been getting along on the contrary as peacefully and pleasantly as possible and Rome gets more and more round me every day. But it's almost up, this game. The Hookers move on the 26th to their new Palazzo, and I am to be left alone which is not indeed so very hard but that I might get along, but it's a good signal for quitting and I may as well accept it. They have been very kind to me. I hope you will manage to express to all persons interested how much I feel indebted to them and I wish I could manage to express it to them, but I don't know how. Their moving however is now vigourously progressing and I shall feel alone here when they're gone.

Lizzy and I executed the other day an order from you for breast-pin and ear-rings. We executed it as given; of course in the midst of orders one does what one can best and quickest. I would only remark that of all things in the world Roman jewelry is the most expensive next to diamonds. There is absolutely nothing to be seen at Castellani's, even the simplest pin, under twenty five dollars, and one necklace will cost fifteen hundred and two thousand with only gold in it; no diamonds or precious stones.[2] The other jewelers though not so dear, are still not cheap. Gold costs money everywhere. Pray do not suppose that one gets these things cheap in Italy. Rome is as dear a place as I know. I only say this in order that if you are disappointed with what you receive, you mayn't blame us for it.

I am dreadfully tempted in every direction. Roman jewelry, mosaics, cameos, silk scarfs, bronzes, to say nothing of photographs, engravings and now and then a pretty picture, and all dear as one's life-blood. Living and sight-seeing cost heaps. Then one has the pleasant sensation about economy of knowing that one will regret it on getting home and wish one had bought lots of beautiful things.

Rome itself is lovely as ever. My health is admirable; never was better, and the heat is not great. Indeed there has been no really bad heat; always plenty of air and coolness in the shade. I wander round as usual, poking my head everywhere and endeavoring to make myself understood in Italian of which I only know a few words. One favorite lounge of mine is now the artist's studios which are always cool and where one has clever conversation, pleasant company and cigarettes. I'd give my new hat for another month here. It's the only place yet that I feel really discontented to leave; so imperfectly done. I feel sometimes like breaking the traces and staying as long as I choose.

As to when I shall get off I can't say. Certainly by the first of June and my stay in Naples will not exceed ten days back to Leghorn I think. Whether or no I shall hit Loo I can't yet say for all is in a heap and between my unwillingness to leave here and my wish to see her, I hardly know what I'm about.

May. 24th. Your letter of April. 29th just come. As for what you say about Loo, I suppose the cat's now out of the bag and you see why she is or was so explosive. About her husband I've no doubt it was only a momentary vexation and imagine she's sorry she ever complained. Kuhn is no angel but she's used to him and fancy there is no real difficulty there. But you see, you've been at cross-purposes all winter. She wished to stay in Europe, but didn't care to write about it until her plans were settled, nor to give you the pain of thinking and fearing a longer separation that might not take place. No doubt too, she feared a scolding or perhaps worse, and didn't care to hurry matters. Still she was always wishing to go one way, and you always supposing she wished to go another. Being an explosive character, she naturally was chafed by everything that implied that her real wishes were wrong. As I wrote before, I'm glad the thing is now settled; glad that she's to stay in Europe and hope that future visits will be on your side and not on hers. In other words I hope you'll come abroad; you must, some day; but I don't see why she should be benefitted by coming home. She is not otherwise changed that I know of. By the way, she has sent me a photograph; a hideous thing. If she sends it to you, I just warn you that it's all frightful and looks no more like her than it does like you. I can't say what she is in society, but to me she looked and was the same as ever.

My departure from this village takes place on the 30th. I shall be in Paris on the 15th. I grudge leaving Italy, and except for learning a little French, would just as leave come home now as in the Fall. Paris I don't care for except as a necessary sight. I feel as though I'd had my fun, and as I can't stay here, would just as leave go home. I've written to Charles about looking round for an office for me. When papa gets home to Quincy perhaps he may be able to look round for me. There is nothing else in the way of preparation needed I believe.

May. 26. I must finish this straggling letter now for the post. It is very hard to find time to write, for one works at sightseeing all day and goes to bed early, tired out. Yesterday for instance at eight o'clock in the morning I was on horseback and off for Frascati. It's twelve miles off across the Campagna, a ride all alone, but the weather was exquisite and the Campagna utterly beautiful. At Frascati I left my horse and took another to climb up to Tusculum, as it was too hot to walk. On the way I picked up my family of young women of whom I've spoken before, I think, and who had driven out here about an hour earlier than I. We explored together all the ruins of Tusculum, which I must say I never should have recognized from that engraving of Cicero's Villa there, which hangs in the dining room at Boston; Cicero's villa being on the top of a hill without a sign of a river or pond near it.

But the modern villas are something to enjoy. There are several that look out towards Rome and the sea, most glorious views, the whole Campagna, dotted with ruins and shepherds huts, underneath, and Rome in the distance with the dome of St Peter's just rising above the haze; that same dome by the way, a great disappointment to me. And such pretty, cool fountains and waterfalls round these enormous palaces, and splendid groves. I think on the whole I never saw anything which so completely satisfied every sense and sensation as the view from the Villa Torlonia.

We came back over the Campagna at sunset and I saw for the first time how it was done. But the sunset wasn't so pretty as I'd wished; it left the landscape cold and misty. Still it was splendid and I enjoyed it very much. It was nine o'clock when we arrived in Rome. I had been on horseback about seven hours altogether, to say nothing of climbing about. But I rushed home, dressed, and before ten was at the Story's. Mrs Story asked me to come up, for the Brownings were to be there.[3] So up I went and found a mixed crowd, twenty perhaps, of poets and priests, English and Americans. I talked a little while with Mr Browning; a quiet, harmless sort of a being. Mrs B. is a great invalid and I wasn't introduced. As I know how celebrities talk, I contented myself with looking, and didn't ask an introduction. You can imagine that when I got home at about twelve I felt as if I could sleep. And so I did.

Love to all.   Yrs ever   Henry.

MS: MHi
1. The Democrats split over their presidential nominee: the Northern wing put up Stephen A. Douglas, the Southern, John C. Breckinridge.
2. Augusto Castellani (1829–1914) specialized in reproductions of ancient jewelry.
3. Robert Browning (1812–1889) and Elizabeth Barrett Browning (1806–1861).

To Charles Francis Adams, Jr.

[Rome, May 29, 1860]

Dear Charles

Your last letter has arrived. The first two lines made me feel as if some one had poured a bucket of iced water over me. As I recollect my letters they are not such as I should care to publish as mine, and I shall disavow all part and parcel in it. At the same time I appreciate your kindness and trouble though I'm afraid it won't benefit me much.

I send you the concluder from Rome. Probably I shall write only two more letters for in a fortnight I shall be in Paris. Address to me to John Munroe &Co. Your Courier has not arrived and probably will not.

You say you don't alter. Pray do so as much as you like.

Mamma's last letter was very groany. American politics are funny but the Gods are immortal. I swear I can't decide whether Seward is the man or not. Against Banks, Wade, Chase or Cameron, yes.[1] But some Fremont who could run.[2] If lost now, we may lose forever.

I've no time to write more for it's late and I leave early tomorrow morning. A package of ten photographs will arrive in Boston for me in the summer. Your's are there. They will come to the Boston house.

I have no news and no letters. Money goes like Hell.

Yrs ever   H.

MS: MHi

1. All were possible candidates for the Republican presidential nomination: Nathaniel Banks (1816–1894), governor of Massachusetts; Benjamin Franklin Wade (1800–1878), senator from Ohio; Salmon Portland Chase (1808–1873), governor of Ohio; Simon Cameron (1799–1889), senator from Pennsylvania.

2. John Charles Frémont (1813–1890), Western explorer, former senator from California, Republican candidate for president in 1856.

To Charles Francis Adams, Jr.

No. 6.[1]   Rome. May. 29. 1860

My dear Charles

This is a great age. One may congratulate himself, I suppose, on living in stirring times, indeed, to a certain degree, in heroic times, which will some day be looked on as a golden, or at least a silver age. And here am I directly in the centre of it all, and what good do I get of it? I might as well be in Pekin as here, so far as there is anything to be seen of the course of the time. Rome is externally quiet as death. As I said in my last, mere demonstrations are at an end. There's a deal of seething and boiling in quiet, but to me the eternal city is more than ever only eternal in it's ruins, it's priests and it's beggars. I meet one day a high-churchman, or feudalist or whatever you may choose to name the apologisers of things as they are, and he tells me that Garibaldi is defeated, that the Piedmontese are deserting in swarms and enlisting under Lamoriciére, that the Romagna is growing more and more dissatisfied with it's position, and that the democratic party in Piedmont is getting the better of Cavour and trying to bring back the anarchy of '48. The next day I talk with a warm liberal and learn that Garibaldi has taken Palermo, that Lamoricière has been defeated near the Tuscan frontier by a band from Tuscany, has lost two hundred men, two cannon and half his army deserted, and that nothing can help the country till the Pope, the Cardinals and all are hunted off once and for ever. If I happen to fall on anybody who is a little cooler or more indifferent in the matter, he tells me that no one knows anything in Rome, no one ever was known to do anything in Rome; that the Pope is just as much in the dark as his subjects, and that the Neapolitan Minister here has been posting about to all his associates of the diplomatic body, praying that somebody will tell him something for he for his part knows less about the affairs of his own country than any of the others. This has gone on for a week and even what occurs within fifty miles of the city is a mystery. Today however I saw a couple of riflemen with extensive sword-bayonets before Lamoricière's quarters in the Piazza di Spagna, so I suppose he has cleared off the intruders on that side and has come down here to rest a day or so.

A man more copiously abused than this good General, I've seldom heard of. Of course all the liberals hate him with a really cordial hatred. The French officers sneer at him for his want of success which they take for granted, pity him for the loss of his reputation, and detest him because he is the opponent of their divinity, the Emperor, and the French army.[2] The Cardinals frown at him for cutting into their privileges and kicking their prejudices out of doors. And the officers who have luxuriated in thirty years of faithful service in the Papal army, are utterly disgusted at being ordered up into the country without a week's delay to have their spare shirt washed and leave cards on all their acquaintances. That is the way things are done in Rome. Meanwhile little is heard of the recruits who were promised. The Irish were announced as having arrived. One gentleman declared he had seen them, but his only proof was that early one morning he met a body of ragged-looking fellows marching in file, each with the neck of a bottle sticking out of his coat-pocket, from which he supposed they were Irish. Enthusiasm seized some members of the nobility on one occasion, as you may have heard, and they entered the army as private soldiers. It appears that the other morning they, or two of them, left the city to join their regiments. The departure was described as quite fine, they driving off in a carriage with a number of admirers, of the lower orders, kissing their swords, or trying to. No doubt they would cut their throats too if there were a revolution. The gentlemen in question are young, and one was described as looking decidedly as though he would like to resign his post of honor, while the other kept his spirits up very well.

This you see is all the merest gossip, but it is what we all live on in Rome; that is, those of us who are interested in it. Our news, that is, the really authenticate news, we get from Galignani, and I cannot think that the Papal Government is so illiberal as many persons describe it, when it allows Galignani and the American papers which contain often ludicrously abusive articles about the Pope, to come every day to the public reading-rooms.[3] I think at home I've heard of illiberality worse than that, even in our own enlightened land.

So, as I've said, I feel a sense of personal injury and wrong that everything here should be so quiet. One might just as well live on the Sandwich Islands. Garibaldi and his three thousand might just as well have fought at Thermopylae. Cavour and "il nostro Re" might just as well have ruled a century ago, for all the part that we, who are right in the heart of the country, can take in their troubles or their efforts. There has been only one exception to this rule, I believe. Our well-known gentlemanly Consul here in Rome narrowly escaped being hurt in the affair of last March, when a trooper made a dash at him as he was getting into his carriage. This is a sort of thing quite unpleasant, and our Consul applied for redress for the threatened injury. Cardinal Antonelli, with a quaintness of conceit and a dryness of humor that one would hardly expect from a Cardinal, is said to have replied that it would give him great pleasure to reprimand the trooper in question, if the American Consul would be so kind as to point him out. I really cannot say whether our Consul has taken further steps in the matter or not.[4]

While the world is thus standing at gaze, and watching Sicily, we Romans are making excursions out to Tusculum and Tivoli, or rambling about in the catacombs or lounging and smoking cigarettes in artist's studios. Thanks to the late Spring and cold weather, the Campagna and all the mountain scenery near Rome is looking magnificently. The Villas at Frascati are the very idea of loveliness in nature. I rode out to Frascati the other morning on horseback, passed the day there and at Tusculum and returned in the evening. It is about two hours ride out there, and when that is done, one desecrates the classic ground by riding over it on donkeys. When the party is tolerably large, it's strange how one forgets what one ought to feel. I think we raced our donkeys over the ground that was once a part of Cicero's Villa, and we lay and eat luncheon in the shade, by the side of an acqueduct that was older than Rome. That was one of the sunshiney days of one's life. And then the sun-set as we started back to Rome was one of those sights that make one melancholy to think about.

By the way, in my last letter, speaking of artists here, I mentioned Mr Story's statue of Cleopatra. At that time I did not know that Mr Hawthorne had introduced it into his new novel, and to this moment, in spite of all my efforts, it has been my misfortune not to have been able to get hold of that book.[5] It is not to be found in the bookstores and of course every owner of a copy has pledged it already months deep. When Mr Hawthorne describes or praises anything, it is time that other people should hold their tongues. Yet he saw it only in plaster and I'm surprised that he admired it so much. Placed side by side at least, there is as much difference between the plaster and the marble as between a chalk sketch and an oil painting.

The truth is, it is a great deal too dangerous to attempt to criticise a work of art, else I would try and give you some of the results of my lounging in the studios of Rome. Of course all artists are unequal and a good many are bad. It is rather peculiar that the bad artists sell as many or more works than the good ones. It is naturally amusing to stand by and listen to the comments of visitors on works that have no prestige and on others that have, fairly or unfairly, got a reputation. To be sure, I wonder in the same way at the man who goes into raptures over the Venus de Medici, so that my taste may be just as questionable as theirs, but it certainly seems to me as if people took pains to seek out the weakest and poorest of all an artist's works, and have it reproduced again and again.[6] Every one seems to have a rage after Venuses, from painted ones to fettered ones, and yet it is tolerably safe to say that a statue of Venus, especially a naked one, in one's parlor, is bad taste, and still more, that, usually, a Venus is the most insipid and meaningless work an artist ever makes.[7] Then there is for instance a work here in Rome called a Boy mending a Pen, that has achieved a considerable success. I've never heard any one say that this statue was good; I have heard many people say that it was very bad. Yet it is a favorite work among buyers and has been reproduced several times. The truth is that popularity is no test. I don't believe for instance that the Cleopatra will ever be popular unless Mr Hawthorne has made it so. So among Mr Rogers' works, the least good seemed the most sought. By the way I am told that Mr Rogers is or will be three thousand dollars out of pocket on account of his bronze doors. Some one was laughing here at a proposal in Congress to appropriate fifty thousand dollars to a statue of Lafayette. People seemed to think that if three thousand of that fifty were passed over to remunerate Mr Rogers, there would still be enough left to make two equestrian statues with.

The studios are a great feature in Rome. It's delightful to take one's luncheon towards two o'clock and then smoke an hour and watch the clay take form or the sketch fill out into color and life, and meanwhile talk nonsense or sense as it happens. The range is enormous. It stretches from art to prize-fighting; and men talk equally well about the Apollo and the Dying Gladiator, or about Heenan and Pryor.[8] Politics as developed in America produce curious effects on Americans who have lived a little while abroad. There is a general sensation or suggestion of bad Bourbon whiskey about American politics that is not pleasant. The Charleston Convention for instance was a crowd to whom I should have thought the red-nosed Mr Stiggins might have remarked "This meeting is drunk; Mr Chairman you are *all* drunk"[9] to, with tolerable truth. Just imagine if you can, such a convention meeting in Piedmont or a Pryor and Potter affair coming off in the Turin Parliament. The world would say that Italy had better remain disunited till Italians learned to behave themselves decently. In fact the world would call it barbarism and the world would be about right. Art must exercise a refining influence, and a man who comes here to pass his life, drops Bourbon whiskey and takes to lemonade or Bordeaux at best. Americans who live abroad read the American papers with a sort of groan. To foreigners New York is the Eureka of vice and villainy, and I assure you in all Europe I have never yet seen so much open and unmitigated wickedness as I have seen in one night in that city.

Of course society here is not perfect. The artist world was always famous for jealousies and troubles, and there are plenty of them here. The tone is tolerably low as a whole, in spite of the art which ought to elevate it. But people don't get drunk, for Bourbon whiskey here would be death and if there are jealousies and unfair play, at least it is quiet and not paraded through the streets.

This is my last day here. I leave half Rome unseen, and go away half ruined. You know I suppose, the Roman jewelry and are aware that it's remarkably fine. You know the Roman cameos, that they are very beautiful. You are also aware perhaps that Roman mosaics are pretty, to say the least, and Roman scarfs not unpleasing in their way. Roman photographs are a popular institution, but cost money, and if a traveller is wildly rich he can buy works of art from American artists. For myself, since Castellani showed me his jewelry and named the prices, I've been indifferent to all smaller things. The innocence with which I selected a little thing that I thought I'd like to have, and the utter disgust at hearing the man suggest that the price was "trois cent piastres, Monsieur" cured me of any further desire of possessing any of his objects of art. But if one has three or four gold mines and a rich wife, I should think he might like to have some of Castellani's things.

I feel sad and solemn at leaving Rome as I never have felt about leaving any place before. Partly out of piety towards an old superstition and partly from a belief in it. I have been this evening to the fountain of Trevi and there in the moonlight, in solemn solitude, have drunk of the water and bathed my face in it, for the story goes that he who does that on the last night of his stay, will surely return some day to drink those waters once more. It's hard to think that one will never see the grand old city again. And then the kindness and hospitality that has met me here is something that makes the leave-taking twice as hard.

The Romans seem to think as I do about it and value me on a scale very flattering to my self-esteem, for I had to pay four dollars and a half for my passport. That passport costs a small fortune in one way and another, and the prospect of Civita Vecchia and Naples is anything but bright. One of our gentlemanly Democratic Ministers abroad once crossing a frontier in his normal condition of crazy inebriation, refused to show his passport, and when finally persuaded to do so, flung it with all his force in the officer's face. The principle was correct but the manner faultily suave.

Yrs ever.

MS: MHi
1. Published in the Boston *Daily Courier* July 6.
2. Lamoricière supported Chambord, the legitimist pretender.
3. *Galignani's Messenger,* an English-language daily newspaper published in Paris since 1814.
4. Two other American citizens were assaulted in a separate incident on March 19. The consul, Glentworth, and the others let the matter drop after a diplomatic apology from Antonelli.
5. *The Marble Faun* (1860) by Nathaniel Hawthorne (1804-1864).
6. The *Venus de Medici* in the Uffizi museum at Florence.
7. The painted ones were by the English sculptor John Gibson, and the most famous of the fettered was Hiram Powers' *Greek Slave.*
8. The *Belvedere Apollo* in the Vatican museum. The American champion John Carmel Heenan (1835-1873) fought the English champion Tom Sayers to a 42-round draw on April 17. Also in April, Roger Atkinson Pryor (1828-1919) of Virginia, Democratic representative 1859-1861, challenged Republican representative John Fox Potter (1817-1899) of Wisconsin to a duel. Potter's choice of bowie knives as the weapon was unacceptable to Pryor, and the duel was canceled.
9. Charles Dickens, *The Pickwick Papers* (1837), ch. 33.

To Charles Francis Adams, Jr.

No. 7.[1]   Naples. June. [4?, 1860]

My dear Charles

On the morning of the 30th May I bade good-bye to Rome and my funny old wilderness of rooms on the Via della Croce and after a long struggle and immense good-nature, I succeeded in getting my place in the cars. My companions happened to be several Americans and an Irish priest. Two of the Americans were in a state of extreme exasperation and among other things were applying good set terms to our gentlemanly young Consul in Rome for having made them pay a dollar apiece for his signature. I represented to them that this matter of visas was not a matter of choice with the Consul but was regulated by act of Congress, and that the money did not, as they supposed, go into the Consul's pocket to support his monopoly of flirtation among the Signorinas, but was accounted for to the Government at home. At least, so various Consuls have told me. In fact, I was rather inclined to laugh at the whole thing. But lately on sending for my passport here in Naples, I was utterly disgusted at finding that there was another spread eagle on it and as usual another dollar to pay for that eagle as well as three more for other expenses. Now, as a justly indignant traveller I would like to know whether our Consuls are put here to rob us or to help us. There's a Minister and a Consul in Rome who, beyond passports and procuring tickets for sights, have about as much to do as if they were accredited to Cyrus the Great and resided among the ruins of Niniveh. But they must sign their names about thirty thousand dollars worth in a year or so. Since last September I have paid three times for Consul's signatures, while other people who live under less enlightened Governments can have their Consuls visas everyday in the year for nothing provided they pay for the first. Will you be kind enough to present my compliments to Mr Cass and inquire whether this visa matter is a piece of his or of Congress' wisdom.[2]

This was only an episode in the trip, however. We all got cool and went to sleep before we came to Civita Vecchia and then girded ourselves up for new labors. But the place was not so bad, this time. We had some six hours to spare and so I saw my luggage carried off, my passport disappear, several dozen porters fight over my body and an army of beggars exhibit their nakedness and cutaneous troubles, with an indifference that was worthy of Cato. A stupider place than Civita Vecchia I have only once or twice seen. But my fate was a happy one for I was going to Naples and my boat had arrived. The passengers for Leghorn could do nothing, for their boat had not yet come and at the office there was no information to be obtained as to whether it probably ever would come. So we all sat down philosophically, eat ices, drank coffee, smoked cigars, abused the beggars in their native tongue, and made bargains with the little shoe-blacks to polish our boots. There were about five hundred French soldiers parading too, and very well they looked. I believe you Bostonians are all military now, and no doubt parade much better than the French, but I in my ignorance of what is correct, admired the neatness and quickness of this corps very much.

After we had waited some four hours, the second train came down from Rome with a host more passengers for Leghorn. This furnished a new excitement and I went to enjoy the scene and to inform the unhappy travellers so far as I could that their steamer had not arrived and that they would probably all have to sleep in Civita Vecchia. Whether they did so or not, I can't say. It was now time to go on board, so I left them looking as anxiously from the battlements towards the south as if it were a belagered city and they expected a friendly fleet.

This was a day at Civita vecchia, interesting because the common lot of all travellers in Italy. As for the voyage to Naples, it was uninteresting; particularly so to me because as there was a strong swell, I went to sleep at six o'clock and with only one interruption in order to go to bed, remained asleep till eight o'clock the next morning. Perhaps one reason of this capacity of slumber was that I had slept only three hours the night before. But since leaving Germany I rather prefer to sleep while travelling. There we had always some little adventure; there the people are sociable and one needs only to talk to others and they talk in return and are always queer or interesting. But where can I find in Italy another little Countess who will give me Hungarian wine and tell me her family history! Or another splendid old Russian Major General, like the one with whom we travelled through the Salzkammergut and climbed up the Schaf-berg! The best I could do on this steamer to Naples was to get hold of an English clergyman, but even that only lasted till we landed.

The first thing I heard in the morning was a lady's voice calling some one on deck, as we were just passing Capri, and it was necessary to see it. Rather alarmed at this information and thinking that during my long slumbers, they might perhaps have landed at Naples and be carrying me off to Sicily, I persuaded myself to get up and dress, but on arriving on deck I have reason to believe that it was only a slight geographical error on the lady's part, for we had not yet entered the bay of Naples. It was a pretty morning, but not quite clear enough to be Naples. We had a fine view of the coast and Ischia and at last caught an indistinct outline of Vesuvius but covered with thin clouds.

We were four hours at the landing. I don't wonder that the Italians pray for a united Italy if it is only to prevent such nuisances as this and passports. The only alleviating point was that they gave us an excellent breakfast on the steamer. When we did land I entrusted myself to the courier and the boat of the Hotel I wished to go to, and committed my fate to chance. Still on the whole it was not so bad as at Civita Vecchia and we were soon through.

Naples was an agreeable surprise. There is life here and in comparison with Venice or Rome it's a London. As for the beggars, they are to be met everywhere and prove little as to the welfare of a country. At least I know that the worst place I ever saw for beggars, real decrepid, miserable beggars, was Bruges in Belgium, a country which is certainly prosperous enough. Here people beg because they're too lazy to work, not because the country is in decay. But Naples is interesting in another way just now. It looks as if it had enough energy to rebel, which Rome and Venice do not look like. Indeed it seems to me as if it were all up here with the Government. The city looks very martial. One sees soldiers at every point and a small army around the palace. Patrols are continually passing through the streets and troops of dragoons as well as single gendarmes, riding up and down. This may all be customary here but it is something I never saw in any other city to such an extent. It's hard to get news, but in place of it we get rumors to any amount, and I think within a short time there will be trouble here. All the reports are exciting and disturbing and if Garibaldi is not soon driven out of the Kingdom, it's reasonably safe to believe that the King will be. Still I will say that the army is a very good looking one and well dressed, if it will only fight; and I believe too that the Swiss Guard is strong as ever.

So soon as the landing was fairly effected, I set to work and with an energy unheard of in Naples, went straight to the Royal Museum. This Museum is a magnificent one and it has been a grand point of mine to see it. But I am delighted naturally at discovering that of two of the particular objects of my pilgrimage, one, the famous group of the Farnesian Bull, is like Brown, Jones and Robinson's description of Wallenstein's horse in Prague: head, neck, legs and a part of the body are new, as well as the other three figures; the rest is antique.[3] My second object, the Capuan Venus, is locked up, as you may have heard. The good old King locked up the Venuses and put petticoats on the dancers.[4] Now I pardon him the petticoats, for really, though not prudish, the ballet in Italy is apt to be somewhat al fresco even for me. If the dancers prefer it, it is merely a matter of taste to return to the old Roman dancing girl's costume which really had some sense, but if there is to be any dress, a few inches on the end of it make it a reality and not a farce. So the old King and his petticoats are justifiable, but why on earth he should have locked up the Venuses is a question that is quite beyond me, for as I recollect the cast of the Capuan Venus it was, next to the one of Milo, the finest and most dignified I ever saw.

In the course of the afternoon, as I was wondering at the exquisite view from the convent of San Martino on the height behind the city, luck brought in my way a young German who was like myself alone and wanted a companion to share his expenses and his amusements. He was clerk in a house in Messina, and had just left his work to visit Germany and his family. He wanted to see everything and as I was only too glad to find some one to drag me about and make bargains for the party, I was ready to join him at once. We celebrated our partnership by going to the San Carlo that evening and hearing the Opera that you call La Traviata and that Italians call Violetta. With my friend the German I have seen Herculaneum and Pompeii and ascended Vesuvius and visited Paestum. He has been worth a fortune. The exemplary manner in which he has done everything for us both, merits my highest praise. He has made all the bargains, paid all the bills and arranged all the plans. I consider him the genius of economy. When he pays for anything I always stand off a few yards and light a cigarette with an air of unconcern, for I know that there is to be a howling fight for at least five minutes, and I have several times prepared my mind to see him assassinated and perhaps myself with him, but each time he has emerged and risen superior to the occasion. I see his red whiskers and his green spectacles and I hear his "che diavolo" from the middle of a dozen porters, beggars and carriage-drivers all violently yelling and gesticulating, and once or twice I have really stepped in to help him, thinking there was to be a free fight, but it always came out straight and the enemy had to give it up and retire. The best of it is that though as a rule he is right and pays no less than is fair, several times he has been wrong and has actually succeeded in making these cheating Neapolitans take less than they ought fairly to have had. To be sure, in order to be economical, I have had to be very uncomfortable. Our expedition to Paestum was a curiosity in this way. We arrived at Salerno one evening and I went to bed at ten o'clock leaving him to arrange for the next day, which indeed, what with the necessary chaffer, took the poor man as he told me afterward, till midnight. Considering that we had been up Vesuvius and seen Pompeii that day, and were to start at half after five in the morning, I was sorry for him. But start we did, to my horror, on one of those Neapolitan carts which you may have seen in pictures with a dozen people on them, without a top, the driver standing behind us. It was cool till we were about half way; then the sun nearly burned one half my face off. We arrived all right and saw the ruins and the landscape; the most soft and delicately beautiful sight that ever made me feel how near we may be to a Heaven, just as that horrible chasm of Vesuvius with it's clouds of sulphur smoke driven about by the gusts of air, down in the dark hollow, gave me the first idea of a chaos worse than a Hell. Some English people were wandering about the ruins finding fault with Murray[5] for having counted one too many columns. I should just as soon think of their finding fault with the Pope because at the first sight of the Dying Gladiator they discover that he has a dirty nose. Who cares whether he has or not, or whether the ruins at Paestum have eight or a dozen columns.

But to return to our journey. On starting back to Salerno I fashioned a covering. My friend had a woolen shawl with him which we drew over our heads and which kept off the sun and the dust. The effect was admirable. In spite of a sun like a burning glass, we were cool the whole way. But the effect from without must have been curious for we caused great merriment to the peasants, a large part of which belonged fairly to the green spectacles and red whiskers.

June. 5. On board his Neapolitan Majesty's steamer Capri. An original idea, a glorious idea puts an end to my letter and I am only hurried to get it to the post. I thought of something new, something splendid; I would see a great drama in the world's history; I would take at last a part in the excitement of the day. I am going to Palermo. This is what I call a glorious lark.

You may hear again from me for I must see something worth telling. Till then

                                        Adieu   Yrs ever.

Old moozer

Off to Palermo bearer of despatches to Capt. Palmer of the Iroquois and the Consul.[6] Ye Gods what an escapade and won't the parients howl. Don't let them know unless you think they can stand the news. It's perfectly safe. Don't be afraid.

My eye
What a guy
Ever your
Henrye.

MS: MHi
1. Not published in the Boston *Daily Courier.*
2. Lewis Cass (1782–1866), secretary of state 1857–1860.
3. Richard Doyle, *The Foreign Tour of Messrs. Brown, Jones, & Robinson* (1854), a comic picture book.
4. The autocratic Ferdinand II (1810–1859) was to European liberals the antithesis of the "good."
5. Murray: standard guidebook from the firm of John Murray; in this case, *Handbook for Travellers in Central Italy* (4th ed., 1857).
6. HA was carrying dispatches from the American minister at Naples to Capt. James Shedden Palmer (1810–1867), commander of the American warship *Iroquois,* and to Consul Henry H. Barstow.

To Charles Francis Adams, Jr.

No. 8.[1]   Palermo. June. 9. 1860.

My dear Charles

I thought it was a most royal and magnificent lark, this excursion down to Palermo, when it first came into my head. At Naples we knew next to nothing about the state of things, and there was a delicious uncertainty about having one's head knocked off or losing some of one's legs that was gloriously exciting. Here from my room looking out over the harbor and the bare old Monte Pellegrino, it all seems easy and simple enough and quite a matter of every-day life, but in Naples the prospect was like looking down the crater of Vesuvius. Then on the morning of the 5th I had to fly about from Department to Department and never could have taken the first step if it had not been for the kindness of my friends who pushed me along and worked like beavers for me. After six hours of driving about in a sun that positively singed one, I got it all straight and was put on board the steamer Capri in a state of grand excitement, feeling a good deal as if I were going to an unknown world and might never come back.

The Capri is originally one of the Neapolitan line of steamers that run from Naples to Marseilles, but is now taken by Government to carry supplies to the garrison at Palermo. We took two brigs in tow, one of them laden with nothing but water. You can form an idea of the management of affairs from that one fact that even the water for the troops had to be brought from Naples.

Three long hours we had to wait for the Captain who was at Portici getting despatches from the King. Unluckily the King forgot him and went to dinner, so he had to wait till dinner was over. When he did come aboard he was as jolly a little fellow as I ever saw, flying about and chattering all the time like a whirligig. He spoke very fair English too and as we had the whole ship to ourselves, it was as comfortable as any one could desire. This was the captain of the royal navy to whose care the convoy was given.[2] The captain of the Capri itself was also on board and had the direction of the vessel, but he was very much of a brute.

The weather was exquisite and the sea calm and as the sun set, we steamed slowly down the bay of Naples with the two vessels in tow. Towards ten o'clock when I went on deck to take a last look before going to bed, the moon was rising and I could see the island of Capri still on our left, and way behind us the great fiery blotch on the side of Vesuvius.

I was tired and though I recollect having had several times a lively contest with hungry vermin, I managed to sleep tolerably well, but found myself badly scarred the next day. One must submit to such little trials in Italy as well as in other countries. We went slowly for the two vessels delayed us and it was nearly sunset before we came in sight of Palermo. There was nothing to do all day but sleep or smoke under the awnings on deck, or talk with the little Captain who gave me his card to be presented to General Garibaldi with his respects, as I afterwards faithfully did. The Captain is liberal as most of the navy officers are said to be, and he made rather too little of a secret of his opinions. This was none of my business though, and there was no injunction of secrecy hinted at. As we came along into sight of Palermo, we heard the reports and saw the flashes and smoke of a quick cannonading. I watched it with a feeling of decided discomfort. The idea of being shot, occurred to me with new and unpleasant force. The Captain however consoled me with the assurance that Garibaldi had no cannon and that this was probably an admiral's salute from the war-ships in the harbor. So we drank a bottle of beer together and told the anxious old gunner that he might leave those four precious six-pounders of his unshotted. It was nine o'clock at night when we entered the harbor and passing a number of great ships of war, we came to anchor near the British admiral and there we lay all night.

The Captain's brother came to take supper with us and give us the latest news which all parties seemed tolerably indifferent to, so when we had finished eating, we sat on deck smoking and talking and listening to a band which was playing waltzes on board the Hannibal.[3] There was just moon enough to show how silent and calm and black everything was, just as if no Garibaldi were within a thousand miles. I stayed on board tonight, going to bed in quite a solemn frame of mind. After trying for about two hours to get to sleep, I was fairly beaten out of my berth and had to get up and light a candle which showed me a large collection of the very most colossal bedbugs that ever grew. I wanted to catch one of the biggest with the idea of pressing him and sending him home to you in a letter, but I was rather more afraid of the brute than he of me, for while I was looking for a weapon, they quietly rambled away, so I dressed and passed the rest of the night on a chair in the upper cabin. Excuse these little particulars. They are the soul of travelling.

The next morning, the 7th I went on board our war-steamer the Iroquois and presented the papers I was charged with, and from here to an American merchant vessel to find our Consul. I found him bearing bravely up, though he had been some three weeks penned up with several other families, on this temporary boarding-house living from hand to mouth. The deck as I saw it, was paved to some depth with dogs, chickens, pigs, fleas, babies, trunks and other articles. His spirits were good however under all this weight of trials and he was preparing to return today to his house on shore. The English, by the way, were luckier than the Americans during the troubles, for their line-of-battle ship the Hannibal was turned into a hotel and baby-house, price nine shillings a day, bed and board. We have no large ships in the Mediterranean now so paid famine prices for accommodations on board the merchant vessels. Now however all was quiet again and the day I arrived, the whole of the refugees were striking for shore.

I took a boat and landed. Numbers of men and boys, nearly all armed and looking very disreputable were lounging and talking on the quay and round the Porta Felice. Here and there a red shirt showed itself. They make a very good uniform; rowdy but pugnacious, and now that Garibaldi has made them immortal, all young Sicily is putting them on and swelling about in them almost as vulgarly though more excusably than New York firemen.

I climbed or passed four or five barricades to reach the Hotel, perhaps two minutes walk from the landing. No one asked me who I was nor inquired about the contents of my carpet-bag, which made me more of a friend to revolutions than I ever was before. But on ordering a bath at the Hotel, as the first and necessary step, the servant coolly told me that I couldn't have one. I expressed in terse but elegant Italian my opinion that he was a block-head, and went straight to the landlord. Signore Ragusa declared that "if I give him twenty pound" it couldn't be done, for the insurgents had cut all the water pipes and he had hardly enough left to drink. So I had to take a boat and go off and swim in the harbor among possible sharks. This done I set out on an exploring expedition.

Of course you know the whole story of the campaign by this time, and as I'm not writing a history of events but only an account of a flying visit to the city, there's no use in my repeating what everyone has heard. But just to show you how I found affairs, I will note a few of the dates again.

At about three o'clock, the morning of Sunday May 27th Garibaldi dismounted from his horse at the Porta Termini and coolly puffed away at his cigarette while he urged on his fifteen hundred men into the city. All Palermo rose at once. The street fighting and barricading lasted all that day and that night Garibaldi slept if he slept at all, in the Senatorial Palace, the very heart of the city, directly cutting in between the royal palace at one end of the straight main street, the Toledo, and the harbor and the castle at the other end, and isolating the royal troops in several separate positions. This was a real Garibaldian move, which ought to have cost him his life and the Sicilians their cause; but as it didn't, it put the whole game in his hands. The next day and Tuesday the barricading and bombarding continued; a good deal of property was destroyed and a good many old people, women and children killed, but Garibaldi was the stronger for every bomb that fell.[4] On Wednesday the 30th the Governor yielded to a cessation of arms which on Saturday was changed into a capitulation and evacuation of the city; a most ludicrously disgraceful proceeding, for which the King would, I think, be justified in blowing the General's brains out with his own royal revolver.[5]

So you see already more than a week had passed since the grand fight when on the morning of the 7th we watched from the Iroquois the long line of Neapolitan troops wind along round the city with drums beating and colors flying, to their temporary quarters at the Mole. Two hours afterward when I went on shore, the whole city except the Castle was fairly evacuated and his Majesty's twenty three thousand troops had shown themselves worthy of their reputation.

So, when I arrived, the lively part of the campaign was over. The shops were still shut and the city still in arms, but there was no more fighting nor was it likely there would be any more in Palermo. Of course the first explorations were towards the main street, the Toledo, which the royal troops could have raked up and down, at one end from the palace, and at the other from their frigates in the harbor. There were barricades at every five or six rods, higher than my head, and mostly cannon-proof. Swarms of people were hurrying about but no one was doing any work that I saw, except a few Piedmontese on guard at important points. Almost everyone had a gun on his shoulder and the peasants who had come down from the interior in crowds, looked about as dirty, as lazy and as degraded as the best conservative could wish. They were sleeping in the squares or lounging in groups round the guard-houses, their guns in their hands, and in costumes very suggestive of brigands and cut-throats. It was a strange collection of arms that the insurgents had. There were guns of every shape and length from the short, fat blunderbuss suggestive of stagecoaches and highway robberies two centuries ago, up to long-barreled, thin affairs such as the Arabs might have shot with when Mahomet was a boy. There were plenty of Neapolitan muskets about too, which deserters had brought, or the cowards had thrown away to run better. All the towns-people seemed to have a rage for cutlasses and dirks which were half the time tied over their shoulders with twine. Among other armed individuals there was a priest in his black robes rushing about day after day with a gun in his hand. A large average of the arms were too old and rusty to be dangerous to anyone but the owner. Providence seemed particularly kind to the city, for though everyone was carrying his gun loaded and capped and sometimes at full cock, and jamming against the stone barricades in the crowds at the narrow passages, and gesticulating as only these Sicilians and Neapolitans can gesticulate, we heard of no one case of an accident, though it's hardly possible but that there must have been a few. Still to do the Sicilians justice, for all their laziness and brutish looks and dirt, it was a peaceable, good-natured crowd, and I've seen in all only one drunken man and no fighting nor violence. Perhaps it might not be so well behaved if Garibaldi was not dictator.[6]

I passed barricade after barricade till I came to the Senatorial palace where the head-quarters of the insurgents are. This is not directly on the Toledo, but a little to one side. Before it, there is a small square, and what the naval officers call the improper fountain; improper because there's half Lempriere's Classical Dictionary on it, but a copious insufficiency of costume. Here I found a still greater confusion and chaos, and crowds of desperately patriotic Sicilians were sleeping, eating, chattering and howling under the windows of the General-in-Chief. I stopped a minute here to look at five cannon of all ages and sizes, mounted on waggon-wheels and looking like the very essence of revolution, rusty, dirty and dangerous to the men that used them. These were new arrivals under Colonel Orsini, for Garibaldi had none in the fight.[7] It is curious how the cannon make their appearance in the city. I met today, the 9th, with a splendid new barricade towards the castle, and in it two heavy iron cannon apparently ready for action at any instant, for there was a strong guard of red-shirts there, to say nothing of a crowd of armed ragamuffins. Garibaldi must have a dozen now, at the very least, and some are good little field-pieces. They say that these are old cannon buried in '49 and now dug up again.

A little way above the head-quarters, the other great street of Palermo crosses the Toledo at right angles and from this spot one can look out of four gates at four quarters of the compass. Can you imagine a general with two thousand foreign troops and twentyone thousand native ones, who could lose a city like this. Still a little way further and I met a high barricade with two heavy cannon which commanded the Toledo straight up to the royal palace and the city gate. Some red-shirts were on guard there, armed half with muskets and half with rough pikes. Just beyond this I met another guard of Piedmontese who stopped me and turned me back by "Excellency's orders." As they apologized and were deeply pained, as they declared, to have to do it, I felt rather flattered than otherwise, and turning back took the first side street to the left. There's no use describing the looks of the thing, for by this time you probably know more about it than I do myself. It was now comparatively respectable to what it had been, and the dead bodies and disgusting sights had all been cleared away. After a long detour and a very indefinite idea of my whereabouts, I made my way through all the particularly nasty lanes and alleys I could find, back to the Toledo. For dirt Palermo is a city equalled by few. I don't know whether I ran any danger of being robbed; indeed it hardly occurred to me that it was possible. I never dreamed of going armed, was all alone and looked I suppose a good deal as if I'd just stepped out of the Strand in London so far as dress went, but no one spoke to me or interfered with me in any way. Possibly Garibaldi may have exercised some influence on the robbers and rascals, for he has them shot as they are taken, and the people occasionally amuse themselves by kicking and stoning them to death. I believe about a dozen have kicked their heels at Heaven already by the Dictator's orders.

After fairly seeing it all, I came to the conclusion in the first place that Garibaldi was all he was ever said to be. He and his Piedmontese are the whole movement; the rest is not enough to stand by itself even now. Put a weaker hand than his here and see how long these wild brigands would keep order and hold together. I don't pretend to judge of a country where I've only been three days, but my own belief is that Sicily is a bad lot and it will take many years to make her a good one.

In the second place, let people say what they will, it is utterly inconceivable to me how any sane general with twentythree thousand troops, cannon, fortified positions, ships of war and uncontrolled powers, could have had the brazen face to surrender the city. Disaffection in the troops does not account for it. You can depend upon it that no honest General could submit to such a disgrace as that and live after it. It is one of those things which I could never have believed, and which in any country but Naples would be impossible.

Dreadfully hot and tired I eat some ice-cream and came back to the Hotel. Here one's time is agreeably divided between hunting for fleas and watching the fleet in the harbor which is always firing salutes and making a most hideous noise with them. Almost every nation has it's flag here. People are a good deal surprised that we have only one war-steamer and that a small one. We ought to have some line-of-battle ships round Sicily and Naples now.

At dinner we had quite a famous party. The celebrated Colonel Türr sat at the head of the table, next to him, the correspondent of the London Times, then another of Garibaldi's Colonels, then the correspondent of the London Illustrated News, then I think Colonel Orsini and so on. Bixio is also in the same hotel and a number of other celebrities.[8]

That same afternoon at six o'clock I was taken to see the Dictator. The party was five in all, officers and civilians, and the visit was informal; indeed Garibaldi seems to discourage all formality and though he has just now all the power of an Emperor, he will not even adopt the state of a General. Europeans are fond of calling him the Washington of Italy, principally because they know nothing about Washington. Catch Washington invading a foreign kingdom on his own hook, in a fireman's shirt. You might about as well call Tom Sayers, Sir Charles Grandison.[9]

We walked up the Toledo and found the little square before the palace even rowdier than usual. A band of musicians had been raked together and they were marching about making a great noise and looking very dirty and ragged, with a most varied collection of instruments. Of course the louder they played, the louder the people howled Viva Italia, and the more chaotic the crowd became. The effect was quite striking except that it was rather laughable.

We didn't stop to look at this long, for the crowd made way to the uniforms and the sentries at the steps presented arms as we passed. It was nearly the same scene inside the palace as outside. One saw everywhere the head-quarters of revolution pure and simple. On the stair-case and in the ante-rooms there was a chaos broken loose, of civilians, peasants, priests, servants, sentries, deserters from the royal army, red-shirts, and the blue ones too of Orsini's artillery, and all apparently perfectly at home. We had no time to look carefully however but passed straight on, everyone showing us the greatest respect until finally the third door opened and there we were.

Garibaldi had apparently just finished his dinner and was sitting at a corner window talking with four or five visitors, gentlemen and ladies of Palermo. He rose as we came in, and came forward shaking hands with each of the party as we were introduced. He had his plain red shirt on, precisely like a fireman, and no mark of authority. His manner is, as you know of course, very kind and off-hand, without being vulgar or demagogic. He talked with each of us and talked perfectly naturally; no stump oratory and no sham. Just as an instance of his manner, there was one little action of his that struck me. I was seated next him and as the head of our party remarked that I had come all the way from Naples in order to see him, he turned round and took my hand, thanking me as if I had done him a favor. This is the way he draws people. He talked mostly in French, for his English is not very good. As for what he said, it was of no particular interest to anyone, at least as far as it was said to me. The others can report the conversation if they think it's worth while to report what was not meant to be reported.

But this was only half the scene. At a round table in the middle of the room, a party of six or eight men were taking dinner. These were real heroes of romance. Two or three had the red shirts on; others were in civil costume; one had a dirty, faded hussar jacket on; one was a priest in his black robes. They were eating and drinking without regard to us, and as if they were hungry. Especially the priest was punishing his dinner. He is a fine fellow, this priest; a slave to Garibaldi and a glorious specimen of the church militant. I've met him several times rushing about the streets with a great black cross in his hands. He has a strange, restless face, all passion and impulse.[10] The others were Garibaldi's famous Captains; a fine set of heads, full of energy and action.

Here I was at last, then, at the height of my ambition as a traveller, face to face with one of the great events of our day. It was all perfect. There was Palermo, the insurgent Sicilian city, with it's barricades and its ruined streets with all the marks of war. There was that armed and howling mob in the square below, and the music of the national hymn, and the five revolutionary cannon. There were the guerilla captains who had risked their lives and fortunes for something that the worst envy could not call selfish. And there was the Great Dictator, who, when your and my little hopes and ambitions shall have lain in our graves a few centuries with us, will still be honored as a hero, and perhaps half worshipped, who knows! for a God.

And yet Heaven knows why he of all men, has been selected for immortality. I for one think that Cavour is much the greater man of the two, but practically the future Italy will probably adore Garibaldi's memory and only respect Cavour's. As he sat there laughing and chattering and wagging his red-gray beard, and puffing away at his cigar, it seemed to me that one might feel for him all the respect and admiration that his best friends ask, and yet at the same time enter a protest against fate.

As we came away he shook hands with us again and took leave of us with the greatest kindness. As we made our way through the crowd across the square, we stopped a minute to take a last look at him. He was leaning on the railing of the balcony before his window, quietly smoking his cigar and watching the restless, yelling crowd below. He seemed hardly to be conscious of the noise and confusion, and looked in his red shirt like the very essence and genius of revolution, as he is.

We walked up the Toledo to see the part which I had been refused admittance to, in the morning. The uniforms opened the way for us everywhere, so that we examined the whole ground at our leisure. I suppose you know all about it so I shall not waste my time by describing it. Only take care of believing all that the English reporters say, not that they tell lies, but that they are artistic in their work; in other words they throw a glare of light on their own point of view and leave the rest of the picture all the darker. The Neapolitans are about the most contemptible nation I ever happened on, and the bombardment was of a piece with their character, but as for a fight between Neapolitans and Sicilians, it seems to me that it's just about nip-and-tuck between the two. Putting principles out of the question, the only sympathy I can feel with any party is with the Piedmontese. The Sicilian common people are famous ever since the Sicilian Vespers and especially in the cholera troubles of 1837, for being the most brutal and savage crowd known in modern Europe.[11]

So ended my first day in Palermo; a day which on the whole is the most interesting and suggestive I ever recollect to have passed.

The next morning there was still more wandering about the streets. The amount of red, white and green colors displayed is quite astonishing. Everyone has a cocade, or almost everyone, except perhaps some of the foreigners. I couldn't find a pretty one, so I never got any at all. Placards are beginning to make their appearance just as before the annexation in the Romagna and Tuscany. "We choose Victor Emmanuel the II. for our King." Garibaldi is bound to force that through if he can, but I think his work here will be of the hardest. However, you are as good a judge of that as we are.

We had quite a funny little "looting" expedition that afternoon, up to the Royal Palace. Some English officers from the Hannibal and an American from the Iroquois, with some civilians, nine of us in all, went off to walk and as the only walk is up the Toledo, we brought up finally in the palace. The Neapolitan troops had evacuated it the day before and it was now held by a guard of fourteen Piedmontese. We had the run of the whole place except the state-rooms, and of course made any amount of noise and satisfied our curiosity by going everywhere and examining every thing. Of course a building which has had several thousand Neapolitan troops quartered in it for some months, keeps little enough of it's good looks and still less of it's objects of value, even if there ever were any there, which I doubt. The rooms were full of boxes, beds, scraps of uniforms and soldier's accoutrements, fragments of manuscripts, books about religion and war, indiscriminate dirt and fleas. It was perhaps as dirty a hole as I ever saw, even in Palermo. Still plunder is plunder, or "loot" as the Englishmen called it, and the party loaded itself with old woollen epaulettes, braid, books, hand-cuffs and so on as mementoes. In the stables we found an army of hungry rats and a dead horse. In the guard-house a wretched man who was to be shot within twelve hours for an attempt at assassination; this was a sight that I could have spared, for the people had pretty much made the shooting unnecessary. When we came out again on the square, we had a grand flea-hunt, for the beasts were all over us by dozens and they were the biggest and hungriest specimens yet discovered. The Illustrated News correspondent who was one of the party, is to make a sketch representing us dancing about and diving at each other's pantaloons. The officers' white duck showed the game beautifully, but our woollen ones only gave them a shelter, and the consequence is that I am never free nor quiet, for my clothes bagged the most and conceal them the best.

Loaded with the plunder we marched back again, the grinning red-shirts presenting arms to us everywhere. Only one of us could speak Italian, but no one cared for that and a crowd of the natives had something or other to say to us, good-natured and even liberal. One old brigand whose portrait has already figured in the News,[12] insisted on paying for our ices and treating us to Maraschino all round, which was very generous indeed but the stuff was enough to make one sick even though it was taken to Garibaldi's health. After it we marched down to the harbor with the romantic old bandit and his gun, in the middle of us.

I had now been two days in the city and had only one object more to detain me here. It's always better and pleasanter to look at more than one side of a question, and I was curious to see how it went with the royal troops, and as I had brought with me from Naples a letter to an officer of the Swiss legion, I didn't care to leave the city without presenting it. So, towards evening today I walked round the harbor to the quarters of the royal army, perhaps half an hour from the hotel. They still have their barracks and are packed away in a great prison, a cloister and so forth. These lines of guards stand across the streets towards the city, but I passed without question and so did everyone else so far as I could see. The troops were just forming for the rappel as I crossed the great parade ground, so I delivered my letter to the officer who was already at the head of his command, and sat down myself before the guard-house to watch the performances. The troops came on the ground with their music and all their equipments, looking as fresh and as effective as any troops I ever saw. There seemed to be no end to the numbers. They poured in, thousands after thousands, and packed the whole great space. I don't think I ever saw so many troops together before; there must have been hard on twenty thousand on the spot, all well-armed, well dressed and apparently well-drilled.

As they were forming around the square, a small guard came in on one side passing me, and had in charge an old grey-moustachiod Swiss, either drunk or a deserter or both, who seemed terribly excited and was talking in a half-scream. The Major looked very grave and disappeared as they brought the man in, but he kept on his screaming as they locked him up and I could distinguish an endless repetition of; "Do with me what you will. Life and death are all one now." Poor old fellow. I wonder whether they shot him. The King is in a bad way when his Swiss desert, for whatever faults the Swiss may have, they have proved themselves faithful at least.

After about half an hour the troops were marched off again and my friend came back to me and took me into his quarters. It's a queer place, now, this city, for strange sights and scenes. Here was a battalion of foreign troops quartered in a Franciscan monastery and the cloisters were all alive with busy, chattering German soldiers. We went up the stair-case and into my friend's room, a monk's cell, furnished with half a dozen chairs on which a torn and dirty mattrass was laid, a table on which there were some lemons and oranges, and a lamp. A couple of glasses of lemonade were ordered, and we sat down and sipped it, and smoked and talked.

It was a strange place for a chance traveller to hit on, and I must say the general effect was gloomy to a degree. The evening was heavy and dull with the clouds hanging low on the mountains, and as the little white-washed cell got darker and darker and the hive of soldiers down in the cloisters grew more and more indistinct, while the officer was telling his story, full of bitterness and discontent, I really sympathized with him and felt almost as gloomy as he.

Of course one ought to hate a mercenary soldier and especially one of the King of Naples'. Very likely I should have hated him if he had been coarse and brutal, but as he was very handsome, young and well-bred, in fact quite an extraordinarily gentlemanly fellow, the thing was different. His ideas were just what I had supposed they would be. He and his division had arrived on the second day of the fighting and had not even been in fire. He had personally nothing to brag of and nothing to be ashamed at. But he declared solemnly as his own belief and that of the whole corps that the King had been betrayed; that the city might easily have been held; and that though the greater part of the Neapolitan troops were cowards rather than traitors, there were still excellent regiments and generals among them who would have been more than strong enough under a capable general. The feeling among these troops was that they were all sold out, and the commanding officer of the Foreign legion had felt so strongly about it that when ordered just before the armistice not to stir a step nor to fire a gun, he had gone to the Commander-in-Chief and with tears in his eyes, offered him his sword, protesting against taking any share in such a burning disgrace. The bombardment was just as bad as all the rest of the performance, as cowardly as it was ill-judged. The soldiers had been badly treated and were deserting in crowds, and even the Swiss and Germans were disgusted with the want of faith kept with them in not fulfilling the terms of enlistment, and were deserting like the rest. He asked me what people said in the city about Garibaldi's plans and the immediate prospect and I replied that no one knew anything except the General himself. "Well" said he "I will tell you the universal belief among us. It is that the embarcation of our corps is to be purposely delayed until there's a rising in Naples, so that we mayn't be there to put it down. You will see, we shall not get back to Naples till it's all over there." Don't suppose that I believe all this myself. I only want to show you what the condition of the royal army is. Yet he said that even now, demoralised as the troops were, there were still enough good ones left, with the help of the eighteen hundred Swiss, to hold their position and drive Garibaldi out of the city in spite of barricades and all. Indeed he didn't seem to believe much in the Sicilians or their barricades and called the Piedmontese the only real force that could do any fighting, speaking of them and their General as brave men and honorable enemies.

It was dark when I came away, and he came with me to the shore to see me on board a boat. We had literally to force our way through the thousands of Neapolitan soldiers who were wandering about, chattering and laughing and playing. We shook hands on parting and I wished him happily out of the whole affair. "Yes" said he; "I think indeed the whole matter is now nearly ended; at least, for us. And I'm not sorry. I'm tired both of the people and the service." A tolerably mournful conclusion of ten years duty, and a gloomy yielding up of a long struggle against fate. But we liberals may thank God if the battle ends so easily.

MS: MHi

1. Published in the Boston *Daily Courier* July 10.

2. Marino Caracciolo of Torchiarolo (1829–1884).

3. The ship of Rear Adm. George Rodney Mundy, commander of the British squadron in Palermo.

4. The bombardment committed reluctant Sicilians to Garibaldi and, as the Neapolitan troops were inactive while it lasted, allowed him to occupy most of the city.

5. Historians agree that General Ferdinando Lanza (b. 1788) was incredibly inept, but he was old, deaf, and viceroy only since May 17.

6. At Marsala, Garibaldi had proclaimed himself dictator of Sicily in the name of Victor Emmanuel.

7. As a ruse to pull Neapolitan troops away from the main body of Garibaldi's army as it moved to attack Palermo on May 24, the cannon were taken by a small artillery force under Vincenzo Orsini (1817–1889) to Corleone, in the interior of the island.

8. Stefan Türr (1825–1908), Garibaldi's adviser and diplomat. Ferdinand Eber, war correspondent and one of Garibaldi's officers. Türr and Eber were Hungarian exiles of 1849. Frank Vizetelly (1830–1883?), artist correspondent for the *Illustrated London News*. Nino Bixio (1821–1873), second-in-command of the Thousand.

9. The English prizefighter Tom Sayers (1826–1865); the model gentleman of Samuel Richardson's novel *Sir Charles Grandison* (1754).

10. Giovanni Pantaleo (1832–1879), Garibaldi's chaplain, a Franciscan friar from Salemi.

11. In the uprising which began with the ringing of vespers on Easter Monday 1282, Sicilians massacred the French garrisons and ended the reign of Charles of Anjou. During the cholera epidemic of 1837 rioting against the French Bourbon regime was put down only with the introduction of Austrian troops.

12. Vizetelly dispatched his sketch of Giuseppe La Masa (1819–1881), the Sicilian revolutionary leader, on May 27; it appeared in the June 16 issue of the *Illustrated London News*.

To Charles Francis Adams, Jr.

No. 9.[1]   Sorrento. June. 15. [1860]

My dear Charles

My last letter, dated from Palermo, the 9th, announced that I should come off as soon as I could. It grew stupid there to one who was only a looker-on and not in the secret course of things. There was little or no society, and still less variety of amusement. Barricades are interesting at first, but one gets very soon angry that they're not taken down. It provoked me to see some fifty thousand men roaming about with guns in their hands which nine tenths of them wouldn't dare use against an enemy unless from behind a wall, and all the time the acqueducts were cut and no one thought of repairing them, and the communication from street to street was as good as wholly interrupted. Of course, this was all right enough and it was not to be expected that respectability should get the upper hand again so soon, but I speak naturally as a traveller, not as an insurgent.

From my window I used to watch the ships every day, and the dirty little boys on the quay who were making targets of the marble statues of their Kings. Bomba's head was already stoned back again into a rough block of marble and he had lost all his fingers at the time I left.[2] This was the only wanton destruction I saw, and under the circumstances, it speaks well for the Sicilians. But the greatest reason for moving from this place was that old trouble that I've mentioned so much. Palermo was the Paradise of fleas. It was positively intolerable. My body presented at that time, from head to foot, an irregularly mottled appearance, the brilliant colors of today dying off gradually into the purple and black of last week. There is no exaggeration in this. I was actually martyred, and if you want to enter into the spirit of the excursion, you must always bear this running accompaniment in mind.

Besides, I felt sure that the first act of the melodrama was over and that the second would not have Palermo for it's scene. The most that could be hoped for was a popular vote on the question of annexation to Piedmont, and they seemed to be preparing for this when I was there. But the very idea of this rather hurt my feelings. It is to be sure a great compliment to the strength and life of Americanism that both Napoleon and Victor Emmanuel and Garibaldi think it necessary to go back to our foundation principle as the source of their authority; but do you know, to my mind these European popular elections have a little too much demonstration in them; they are a sort of continental squatter sovereignty, and very like a satire on our theories. I do not pretend to be a philosopher, but I do know that if I were a conservative I should wish nothing better than these elections for an argument against and a sarcasm on popular governments in their whole length and breadth. It's a sword with two very sharp edges, this, and is apt to cut the wrong way as well as the right.

The Capri was still in the harbor on the morning of the 10th and I took a boat and went off to her. The little Captain was flying about in a crowd of officers, busy as could be, but shook hands with me as if I were his dearest friend and we had been separated for years. He was to leave for Naples that same afternoon and would be most boundlessly delighted to have the pleasure of my company. Perhaps you'll appreciate this Italian profusion of politeness better, if I tell you that the Captain is a Prince and belongs to an old and famous Neapolitan family.[3] If you think it's indiscreet in me to quote his opinions and liberal ideas so openly, all I can say is that he talks much more openly than I've written and that all his brother-officers and the whole Kingdom of Naples talk pretty much in the same way.

We were to leave at three o'clock. At four I came on board. Everything was in an Italian confusion. Everybody was screaming and gesticulating or else lounging and sleeping. Some hundreds of soldiers with their wives, children and baggage, as well as some horses, were being embarked, and of course the scene was much like a pitched battle. On the shore among the soldiers there were a number of the famous policemen, the Sbirri, whom the Sicilians have such a love for. Those men must feel happy, very; for if they were accidentally caught, the Sicilian mob is not gentle, and they might find themselves skinned alive, or going through some other process of the kind. An officer of the Iroquois told me that only the day before I got here, he had seen one of these fellows lying in the middle of a street, his head cut off and put between his legs and a cigar stuck in his mouth. Whether he deserved his punishment or not, of course, we can't know. But as a matter of pure curiosity I would really like to know how many of the men who served him up in that elegant way, would have been policemen themselves if they had been offered money enough for it. There is, to be sure, a great deal that's admirable in this Sicilian revolution, but a great deal too that reminds one very much of a servile insurrection. Where is the Sicilian nobility and the gentlemen who ought to take the lead in a movement like this; or is there a single Sicilian competent to sustain Garibaldi or take his place. If not, of course it's the fault of the Government they've been under so long, who have crushed out all developement; but what sort of a people it must be, if a foreigner with an army of foreigners, supported by "native chiefs" and their clans, make the only great force of the whole movement. One can't always control his ideas and prejudices. I can never forget, in thinking of Sicily and the Kingdom of Naples, that under the Roman government these countries were the great slave-provinces of the empire, and there seems to be a taint of degradation in the people ever since. It's not good stock.

It was past six o'clock before we got off and left Palermo and Sicily behind us. The first cabin was not at all full. A few officers of different ages and one girl, the daughter of one of them, were all who sat down to supper with us. On deck it was different. The men were wedged together there and every inch was covered. Among the soldiers were some few Germans and I talked some time with one of them, a good-natured Viennese, who had served fourteen years in the Austrian army and altogether had had quite a glorious career; Hungary in '48 and '49; Magenta and Solferino in '59, and now at Palermo. That's a curiously happy list for anyone who seeks the bubble reputation.[4] He told me all the story of his wrongs; how they had promised him thirty dollars bonus; cooked meals twice a day, and generally the life of a Prince; and how on coming here he had found himself most outrageously sold; never received a cent of his money; lived like a dog, and for ten days since he landed at Palermo had eaten nothing but hard biscuit and raw pork. He was very good-natured under his troubles though, abusing Naples and the Neapolitans terribly, but seeming to think that nothing in the way of bad management had ever been known in his dear Austria. "They didn't do things so there," he thought, and I didn't try to convince him that they hadn't done things much better. He was on the sick list, down with fever, and returning to Naples with some other sick and wounded. He said there had been a great many desertions in his battalion which is new and not wholly formed yet. Indeed I think he seemed if anything rather sorry that he'd not deserted too, and though he scolded loud enough at Neapolitan cowardice, I don't think he seemed any more eager to storm the barricades than his betters had been. Such men as these are nothing to supply the place of the old Swiss regiments. His great hope now was that the report might be true, of the determined disbanding and dismissal of the whole corps, so that he might get back to his dear Vienna. Indeed, whether he stays or not, his military spirit is for the time gone. And so it must be with the whole army, all demoralized.

The captain was amusing as usual at supper. He chattered away as fast as ever, interpolating frightful remarks in English into the conversation, which he intended for our quiet appreciation, while the Italians, not understanding it, supposed that it was very proper, I hope. We drank the King's health with a proviso for his improvement, and discussed the political affairs largely. Everyone is disgusted, or says he is. Half the army says it is rank treason that did the business; the other half says it was incompetence. I believe myself that if those generals had been fighting for themselves instead of their King, they would have done much more than they have done; in other words, as royal generals they deserve to lose their heads. As men their behavior may have been highly praiseworthy perhaps; though it's at least a question, whether a man does well in accepting his ruler's favors and rewards, and then betraying him. To us Americans all these Italian troubles reduce themselves simply to a single process, by which one more of the civilized races is forming itself on the ground that we have always stood on, and taking up as its creed the same list of ideas that we have always declared to be the heart and soul of modern civilisation. Feeling sure of the result as we must, we can afford to be a little cooler than other people, and being so strongly prejudiced, we can almost be impartial. So about the King, I feel more pity than pleasure at his troubles. I never heard anything bad of him except that he is stupid and governed by bad influence, but people who ought to know, have told me that he was a very good sort of a man as men go. It's the fashion to abuse him, just as it's the fashion to abuse the Pope and the Grand Duke of Tuscany, but you would probably find that these are all good men enough; just as good and very likely a great deal better than you or I or the writers in the London Times who tear a passion to rags so splendidly.[5] We, who are so far ahead on the winning side, can afford to try to be fair to the losers. The King of Naples is probably one of the few men in the Kingdom who has done nothing that he ought to be hung for.

It was curious to see, that night, how people can sleep. At about midnight, after finishing supper and smoking, and while everyone was looking up their berths, I went forward to see how the soldiers managed to get along. They were lying all over the deck, tumbled down anywhere, and all snoring like hogs. They lay so thick and it was so dark that I trod on three or four who were in the way, but they didn't mind it, and when the engineer who was passing, kicked them out of the passage, they dragged themselves a few inches on one side, with a groan, but never woke up.

I was not so lucky. Recollecting my last night on board this boat, nothing could persuade me to go down below again, and so I appropriated a sofa in the upper cabin, and with gloves on my hands to keep off the fleas, passed the night as well as may be; but little sleep enough came near me.

The next morning all was still bright and clear. The poor soldiers' wives on deck looked very unhappy, and some, who had fine dark eyes and pretty, olive-complexioned faces, looked so pale and patiently sad that they might have made beautiful studies for Magdalens or Madonnas. Certainly sea-sickness is one of the trials of life which brings us all down soonest to our common humanity; these women seemed absolutely refined by it, and their husbands and friends were as careful and gentle towards them as if they were all a set of refined and educated heroes and lovers.

We were crossing the bay of Naples at eight o'clock and it seemed as though we were coming home, it all looked so pretty and natural. Thanks to the Captain's politeness, we passengers were put on shore at once, and were not stopped long by the police, whose great curiosity was to know how it all looked in Sicily. Our information made them look all sorts of colors, as we had no particular motive to soften the story.

So my excursion to Palermo ended, happily as possible. Nothing could have been easier or more successful. It is something to have seen the raw elements at work, though one is no element oneself; and though before making a demi-God of Garibaldi, one had better wait until it's fairly settled what he's going to make of all this, and whether he is not going to do more harm than good by the whirlwind that he's riding; still, a life has not been wholly uninteresting even if the only event in it were to have talked with one of the most extraordinary of living men on the scene of his greatest success.

Naples is much as ever. It's the gayest and liveliest place in Italy. The Chiaja is swarming with carriages every afternoon, and the common people lounge about, useless to Gods and men, but happy as life is long. Everything is military, but no one believes now in the army and I have sometimes been dreadfully tempted to whisper "Garibaldi" and "Palermo" in the ears of some of these uniformed rascals just to see what they would do. I don't believe they've self-respect enough to feel insulted. There have been rumors enough of intended demonstrations, but nothing has happened, and it's better so. They can't do anything without Garibaldi and had better not try. There's a great deal of anxiety here; endless rumors of constitutions, insurrections, demonstrations and so forth, and just now the two vessels said to have been captured under American colors, are making a good deal of uneasiness in our part of the city.[6]

One of the predictions of my friend the Swiss officer has already turned out false. He has come back and so has his corps, and I suppose his ideas as to the extent of the treason, are now modified.

By the way, one of the first pieces of news that met us on our landing, was from America; the Republican nomination for the Presidency. This is really admirable. We Neapolitans, without distinction of parties, congratulate you. The Americans are certainly a great people. Filled as we are here with Italy just now, will you forgive a comparison that is not so very far-fetched but that it might be worse. The Italian liberals have two great men at their head; Garibaldi and Cavour; and the whole nation has given itself for years with a bitterness of devotion that we Americans think not so bad, for Italy, to the support of their two leaders; and they've held them up so high and so steadily that half the world is now standing still to wonder at it. In America we've changed all that. The heart doesn't beat on that side any longer. We can afford to fling pearls away, richer than all our tribe.[7] In '56 we had the satisfaction of rejecting our Garibaldi, and now in '60 we have done still better; we have deserted our Cavour.[8]

This letter is rather more stupid than usual. You will excuse it, for it is the last. I've tried to show you Italy as I've seen it, and now I have finished it all. It would be interesting to stay this struggle out here, but it will take a long time, and after all, the essential points of interest for us Americans are now tolerably secure. Recollect that Garibaldi and the Italians are after two separate objects; one is a Free Italy; and the other is a United Italy. These are two separate things, and though we all sympathize with their struggles for the first, we can afford to hold our own opinions as to the value of the last. That is purely a question of Italian politics and interests us only as identically the same struggle now going on since fifty years in Germany, interests us; that is, as a minor question of local importance. Of course many people won't agree with this statement of the case, but I'm contented to follow on this question the lead of Napoleon the Third. If you prefer to hold to Garibaldi, we can agree to differ amicably.

I have accordingly come over here to Sorrento to have the pleasure of passing the last day and night in Italy, alone and in quiet among the orange and lemon groves. If you ever come here and smoke your last cigar and watch your last sunset with the waves of the bay breaking under your window, and take your final leave of a book of life that has been all rose-color, you will probably feel as solemn as I do, and will finish with Italy by reflecting that our good God is really good, but that we have ourselves something good and immortal in us, which Italy calls out and strengthens.

Paris. 22. June.

Dear Buffer

I arrived here two days ago and found Theodore here, and no one else. I expect a letter from you soon, scolding me violently for the poverty of these letters. I plead guilty beforehand. They have been poor enough but think how I had to write them. The Governor finds fault on the other side because they're not essays politico-economical. Thank God they're done, and I'm only sorry to have put you in such an equivocal position, as authorising the publication. I don't want to see or hear anything more about them.

My box ought to have arrived in the ship Laura, Captain J. Willmsen, at New York, damn 'em. I said Boston. A. Moeller, 65 Liberty St. New York is to forward it to Boston.

All well and spry.

Yrs ever   H.B.A.

MS: MHi
    1. Published in the Boston *Daily Courier* July 13.
    2. King Ferdinando II, called Bomba after his relentless bombardment of Messina in 1848.
    3. The captain was of the Caracciolo family but "Prince" was probably an honorific title.
    4. "Seeking the bubble reputation/Even in the cannon's mouth"; *As You Like It*, II, vii.
    5. "Tear a passion to tatters, to very rags"; *Hamlet*, III, ii.
    6. The American clipper *Charles and Jane* and the Piedmontese steamer *Utile*, taking some 900 Garibaldians to Sicily, were captured by a Neapolitan cruiser on June 11 and brought to Gaeta. The three other ships of the same expedition were nominally under the U.S. flag.
    7. A near quotation from *Othello*, V, ii.
    8. Frémont lost the presidential election of 1856 to Buchanan; the Republican party nominated Abraham Lincoln in May instead of Seward.

To Abigail Brooks Adams

Paris. 1. July. 1860.

Dearest Mamma

It's a long time since my last letter to you, I believe. I think it must have been from Rome. You know I suppose, the whole course of adventures though.[1] By the way speaking of Rome, I want to remind you again to take care to express my obligations to Lizzy Hooker so that there'll be no doubt about it. The truth is Lizzy couldn't well have done much more for me if

I'd been her brother. The greatest part of my pleasure in Rome is owing to her. The Storys were very kind too.

You know all about my passage from Rome to Naples, then to Palermo and back to Naples. I left on the 17th by the steamer for Marseilles. At Naples the Minister, Mr Chandler, was very kind to me. He gave me first my despatches for Palermo at my simple request, knowing me only by my name and a letter of introduction from Rogers, the banker, to whom Hooker had recommended me. After I came back from Palermo I dined there and called several times. He is the only one of our ministers that I know of, who represents us creditably abroad, and he's the jolliest little man I know. I got quite an affection for him.[2]

The passage from Naples to Civita Vecchia and from there to Marseilles was not over-pleasant. I was alone and after fighting desperately against being sick from Saturday night to Monday noon, I at last caved in and gin it up. It wasn't very bad though, and if I'd stuck it out four hours longer I should have been safe; but I got tired and yielded to the agonies. At midnight we reached Marseilles; landed at five o'clock, after a sleepless night; at ten I started for Paris, travelled all day and night, and at six o'clock on the morning of Tuesday the 20th I was in Paris. So you see I lost no time.

Here I met Theodore and there are two other fellows here whom I know. But it's slow. If it weren't for the absolute necessity of getting some knowledge of French, I would pack up tomorrow and come home. Not that it's not pleasant enough here. I enjoy it very much, or parts of it; but as a whole it's heavy and unsatisfactory. The weather is like winter. There is no society. Theodore is low-spirited; tired of Europe and bored with Paris, and talks to me in the most ludicrously grave way of going home, getting some occupation and marrying. It's queer how fellows change their ideas. Billy Howe used to say just the same thing last winter. Then as I'm here to learn French I have to devote myself to it; read and write all the time, which is not inspiring, and go to the theatres every evening which is first-rate fun but costs mints of money. Thank Heaven the weather is cold and rainy. If it weren't I should be home-sick for the country. Crowninshield, Hunnewell, Bradlee and Shep are travelling in Norway and Russia and it's long since I've heard from them. I don't know when they come back, but as we are all going home at about the same time, I suppose they can't stay more than another month. My own plan is to leave Paris about the middle of September, and in that case I shall be with you about the middle of October. I should be very glad to put it ahead a month and come back in September, but three months is the very shortest time I can hope to get any knowledge of French in, and as October is just about the time every one is coming back, it will be a saving to me to have the extra month for my French. I have rooms here which don't please me excessively and Paris costs frightful sums. However, I don't mind that so much now, as so little time is left.

Your last letter was dated June. 3d. I suppose there's another for me somewhere, but as they all have to go to Florence and come back, its hard to keep the account. You have seen Kuhn I suppose by this time, or will see him before long. He left Paris the day before I got here. I've written to

Loo a letter lately, but not heard from her for a month. Theodore has, however, and says her letters seem rather triste. I dont wonder; her position on the top of a mountain, without society, must be anything but cheerful. Theodore is as sorry that they mean to stay, as we are, and he thinks it's a great mistake. I hope the boys and the family in general wont visit on Kuhn the punishment for the proceedings. It wouldn't be fair to suppose that it's his work any more than Loo's, and I wrote you some time ago that though she might perhaps as a matter of conscience and duty return home unless he wanted to stay, still there's no doubt whatever that, putting the conscience aside, she is as glad to stay as he is. Besides, above all things, the worst is a family quarrel; that would finish the whole matter and by driving Kuhn off, you would make their permanent residence in Europe a matter of certainty. It seems I was mistaken in supposing it already so. I never discussed the matter much with either Kuhn or Loo, as I didn't consider myself the person to do anything in the matter. I'm altogether too young to have much weight and I should only have made her hate me, which I thought a very bad policy. I know your disappointment. As you say, however, it will have one good effect and draw the rest of us the closer. Indeed, since the outside pressure has increased so on us, it seems to me that there has been a good deal of change in this way, and the tone now rings very differently in the family from what it did when I came away. I hope too that John's engagement will be announced soon, so that that will be another great pleasure. I wrote to John last week inclosing a letter for Fanny which I hope she'll take in the spirit I wrote it.

I'm waiting patiently for papa's speech to arrive. The sketch I've seen of it and the papers which Charles sent me, gave me the general idea, which was precisely what we would expect.[3] It's all right. This session has gone off admirably for him, and couldn't be better. As for you, I know that in many ways you must feel homesick, but have there never been times at home when you felt homesick and unhappy too? For my own part, I'm getting dreadfully old and cautious. I find that people are unhappy everywhere and happy everywhere. Charles writes me a plan according to which I should study law in Washington and stay with you always. I never knew before this how I liked Quincy and Boston and how sorry I should be to cut loose of them altogether; but this course which certainly is the one I should choose and follow, if it will go, finishes setting me afloat. I shall make up my bed in Washington, and no doubt it will be just as pleasant as anywhere else. At all events, whether it is or not, it's the place that my education has fitted me best for, and where I could be of most use. So if papa and you approve this course and it's found easy to carry out, you can have at least one of your sons always with you. For my own part, it's the only idea I've yet met with as to my own course that satisfies me entirely.

July. 2.   Today I got yours of the 13th June announcing your return to Quincy. You will have a pleasant summer I hope, though not very quiet. Of course what with John's engagement and your own visits and position as a politician, you can't expect to be very lazy, but you'll have the cows and the pigs and the children and if you're not happy it only proves my remark above that one is never completely blessed. I wrote to papa last week at Quincy and I suppose it will be just right. Your own letters still go to Florence and return which must soon stop for I wrote from Rome to direct to John Munroe here.

I got a letter from Loo to-day, very unhappy at what she seems to think her fault at exposing Kuhn to your displeasure as the cause of their movements. Poor girl, she always was and always will be the most impulsive and unhappy of beings. Where on earth did she get her disposition from? The rest of us are cool-blooded enough. Here she is, crying her eyes out on the top of a Swiss mountain and nothing on earth will ever convince her that she is not the most unjustly treated of women. I wrote at once as soothingly as I could to persuade her that we weren't all trying to tyrannise over her and her husband, but it won't do much good. Provided this lesson teaches her wisdom, I'm glad she feels it, but if pushed too far, it may only make her wholly detest us, and, without wishing to interfere in any way, I would only suggest that if possible it would be as well to keep the tone both towards her and her husband the same as it always was. For my own part, I say to you just as I do to her, let her seek her fate where she finds it pleasantest, for, hard as you may think it, to me hers seems a life thrown away. That is, she has no object to it, and would have no more if she came home now than if she never came home at all. But even now she doesn't face the music properly and I think she knows herself and her own mind as little as she knows Sanscrit.

Papa's speech has not yet come. Sumner's has made more ill-blood than ever.[4] It's queer how much weight people give to him. Tomorrow's post will bring the Democratic nomination I suppose and that will settle things.

Yrs affecly   Henry.

MS: MHi
  1. From his letters in the Boston *Daily Courier.*
  2. Joseph Ripley Chandler (1792–1880) of Philadelphia, Whig editor, minister to the Two Sicilies 1858–1861.
  3. In his maiden speech in Congress, May 31, CFA affirmed that the republic was founded on rights not limited to white men only, and he cautioned the South that secession would not solve its problems.
  4. On June 4, in his first Senate speech since returning to service, Sumner attacked the barbarism of slavery—"Satan is Satan still"—and gave detailed attention to the effect of slavery on the character of slave masters.

To Charles Francis Adams, Jr.

Paris le 9 Juillet. 1860.

Eh bien, mon chèr Mentor, me voilà à Paris! Cette langue du diable ne me laisse pas tranquil, ni le jour ni la nuit, et je ne me permis pas même d'écrire une lettre sans que je me tourmente de ces sacrés idiotismes. Mais ça ménage mon temps, et quant à la qualité du Français, on ne doit pas attendre une parfaite connaissance d'une langue aprés quinze jours d'application.

Ta lettre, renfermante aussi cela de Jean, arrivait ici voie de Florence, et j'ai repondis à Jean sur l'instant même. Mais voilà maintenant quelque chose, pas inattendue, mais bien amusante! D'abord, il faut te remercier de tout mon coeur de ton offre d'argent, mais il-y-a longtemps que je ne fais plus cela. Tu sçais bien que mes dépens en Italie n'ont pas été sur le piéd de $1000 par an. Tu ne trouveras rien d'extraordinaire dédans, n'est ce-pas? En effêt depuis le 1er Janvier j'ai dépensé exactement $1000; c'est à dire sur le piéd de $2000 par an. En arrivant à Paris j'ai écris à notre père, en annonçant l'etat de mes finances. Par un régard pour ses sensibilités vraiment filial, j'ai transmis dans une lettre l'état de mes finances jusqu'ici, et dans une autre une évaluation des probables dépens jusqu'a ma débarquement à Boston. Cette évaluation arrivait jusqu'à la somme de £150, inclusif mon retour le milieu d'Octobre. C'est vrai £120 serait peut-être assez, mais aussi peut-être il ne le serait pas et je ne l'aime pas, la pauvreté dans l'Europe. Eh bien! La dernière de ces lettres a été expediée il y a quatre jours, et je m'ai bien félicité que ce sujet serait enfin tout-à-fait fini. Voilà donc une lettre qui vient d'arriver de mon chèr papa qui m'a vraiment électrisée. Je ne dirai pas qu'elle m'a donnée pour un instant un affreux doute sur l'état de la cervelle de notre père. Il sçait bien que je suis parti de Dresde le 1er Avril avec de l'argent assez seulement pour m'apporter à Rome. J'ai écrit de Rome que j'attendai de jour au jour l'arrivée d'une novelle lettre et c'est vrai qu'avant cette arrivée je m'ai eu forcé de tirer sans aucune lettre, seulement par la politesse de M. Hooker.

Eh bien! il y a deux mois et dix jours depuis ce temps-là. Je suis resté un mois à Rome, j'ai vu Naples, Palerme; je suis venu à Paris avec trente livres sterling dans ma poche, presque assez pour trente jours dans cette ville, et voilà aujourdhui une lettre qui annonce la prochaine arriveé de £50 dont £30 ne sont pas à moi, et qui "attend" que cette somme me suffira pour le reste de mon séjour en Europe. Mais, mon bon diable d'un père, "cette somme" ne suffira même de payer le prix de mon passage à l'Amérique! Qu'est-ce-que-c'est donc, que l'idée, la conception de ce pauvre bonhomme des dépens nécessairs de l'Europe? Il sçait que je suis venu pour rester deux ans; ces deux ans expirent le 1er October, et je serais à Boston le quinze de ce mois probablement. C'est à dire, j'ai encore trois mois en Europe, et monsieur nôtre père avec un sang-froid qui me fait vraiment l'effêt d'un bon-môt, m'annonce qu'il faut vivre trois mois à Paris à trente livres sterling. Eh bien! Je n'ai pas l'intention de faire un emprunt à vous, mais il faut faire comprendre notre pére qu'une idée comme ça est nettement bête. J'ai écris et j'écrirai, moi, avec le plus grand respect du monde, mais il faut avoir de l'argent, et sans délai, car je serais contraint d'emprunter aux autres avantqu'une réponse à cette lettre peut arriver. Si nôtre père ne voudrait pas envoyer la somme de £150, il se pourra je me trouverai contraint de lui autoriser la vente des rentes appartenantes à moi. Mais c'est cela une ménace que je n'aime guère. Tu sçais donc comment l'affaire est située à présent, et tu pouvais peutêtre rendre encore à nôtre pauvre pêre la raison qu'il vient de perdre.

Ton projet que j'entre dans un cabinet d'avocat et fais mon droit à Washington, me plait fort. Mon Dieu, je me trouve triste, ici, à Paris. Il me semble une chose bien indifférante, ce que je fais, ou l'endroit de le faire, mais ce projet est le mieux qui jusqu'ici s'a présenté. Si tu peux trouver une position convenable avant mon retour, fais-le sans me consulter. Mais si tu penses que je ferais mieux d'attendre l'élection, soit! Nous avons du temps.

Tu es à present á Quincey, je suppose. J'attends une lettre chaque jour, mais la seule nouvelle doit étre l'aveu public de l'engagement de Jean. Braggiotti qui vient d'arriver à Paris, m'assure qu'elle est une chose bien entendue et maman a déja écrit qu'on l'avouerait aprés sa retour de Washington. Embrasse ma nouvelle soeur pour moi. Il y eut, dans la lettre que j'écris à Jean, aussi une lettre pour elle. Assurez la de mon affection éternelle.

Paris est amusant—assez. C'est à dire quesi j'aurais cinquante mille livres de rente et si je connaissais parfaitement Français, il serait trés agréable. À présent je travaille de dix heures à quatre heures chaque jour, la plupart du temps en suivant le plan de Gibbon que tu te souviendras d'avoir lu dans sa biographie. C'est fatiguant mais je fais chaque jour de progrés. À six heures nous dinons, Théodore ou Henry Higginson et moi à quelque restaurant, et le soir nous allons presque toujours aux Theatres. Voilà la vie! Je ne puis pas entretenir une maîtresse; en effêt je ne le veux pas. Mais je me léve à neuf heures et je me couche à une ou deux heures, et j'essais de m'occupais de la langue, sous une forme ou l'autre, sept ou huit heures par jour.

Notre oncle et tante sont ici; Sidney. Le dimanche passé ils m'ont invités de leur accompagner en voiture au Bois du Boulogne, et aprés j'ai diné avec eux. Ils partent demain pour l'Allemagne. Notre oncle m'a chargé d'envoyer ses regards à notre pêre et mère. La petite Rodman est aussi à Paris. Par un coup de diplomatic vraiment digne de mes meilleures jours, je m'ai fait introduire, à la fête champêtre à Neuilly, le 4 Juillet, et je suis devenu amoureux comme fou, mais je n'ai pas l'energie ni le temps de la poursuivre.

Théodore vit dans une tranquillité vraiment admirable. Il a des petites chambres au quatriéme de son Hotel et se propose de rester encore un mois ici. Pas plus de maîtresses, pas plus d'absurdités. Je le vois presque tous les jours et nous dinons souvent ensemble à un restaurant le plus bon marché que nous avons pu trouver. Fred Lyman est aussi à Paris mais je ne l'avais pas vu.[1] On dit qu'il démeure dans un Faubourg trés eloigné et qu'il entretienne une maîtresse qui du reste a beaucoup d'influence sur lui. Mais je n'en sçais rien. John Bancroft est venu ici de Dusseldorf et a pris un logement pour l'été dans une village prés de Paris. La belle Ronnels vu devenir une mère, mais je ne l'avais pas demandé quand arrivera cet heureux événement. C'est affreusement evident.

Je viens de recevoir une lettre de maman de Quincy, le 25 Juin. J'en juge qu'elle n'est pas plus parfaitement contente à Quincy qu'à Washington. Elle parle d'une lettre que tu devais avoir écrit la semaine passeé. Probablement tu ne l'avais pas mis à la poste; du moins je ne l'ai pas reçu. L'affaire de Loo semble faire autant d'amertume que jamais. Loo m'a écrit une lettre de Glyon aprés avoir reçu la première notification de la sensibilité que sa conduite a provoqueé. Elle regrette cette conduite amèrement et s'avoue prête de prendre sur elle toute la responsabilité, et cetera. J'espère que cette affaire-ci n'ira plus loin. Moi, je sçais bien que sera l'effêt inevitable de sa résidence prolongeé en Europe. Mais crois-moi, ça a été déja longtemps une "chose accomplie." C'est à dire, le mal est vieux, et ne se laissera pas guérir par son retour à l'Amérique. Je préfere, moi, qu'elle resterait tranquille en Europe jusqu'au temps qu'elle saurait apprécier son erreur, s'il y en a. Loo m'inspire d'une pitié veritable. Je ne la juge pas d'aprés les même regles auxquelles nous autres sont responsable, tu et moi. Elle est femme; elle n'a pas d'enfants; elle est d'une santé toujours douteuse; son mari, toutefois bon garçon, et bien indulgent pour elle, n'a rien d'élevant, rien qui peut rendre ni un objêt à la vie, ni une espérance au dessus de la mort; elle a eu toujours un esprit que ne se laisse pas régler, même par son père, et du reste elle ne sçait pas ni qu'est ce qu'elle veut ni même avec clarté qu'est-ce qu'elle se propose. Qu'est ce qu'il-ya en Amérique hors de sa famille qu'y peut attirer une femme come celle-ci. Mon Dieu, qu'elle dirige ses propres affaires; je reste son ami toujours.

Le père a fait un bon discours à la Congrés. Ça va bien! N'est ce pas curieux comme les journaux et la Chambre sont délicats envers lui! Ils ont peur de l'attaquer à présent, mais attends un peu. Nous verrons! Il se pourra je serai bien nécessaire à Washington. Il n'est pas possible qu'il échapperait toujours comme ça.

le. 12 Juillet.) J'ai reçu ta lettre du 19 Juin. Je te remerçie encore une fois pour ton offre d'argent mais c'est mieux que je l'aurait du père. Il en a plus que toi; il sçait ce que je veux, et je n'ai pas à présent et à cette distance tant de peur de lui comme autrefois. Crois-moi, notre père est un peu en retard de son siécle dan ces choses-ci, mais c'est toujours mieux de suivre une franche marche, dans nos communications à lui. Du rest je n'ai aucune raison de cacher mes affaires de sa vue, et je ne suis pas encore assez lâche pour mesquiver derrière toi. Il grondera; moi, je garderai mon sang-froid et le respect qu'on doit à son père; et enfin il le payera. Mon Dieu, s'il ne le paie pas, je ne puis pas revenir.

Quant aux achats, je ne serai pas assez riche d'acheter une chose quelconque à Paris. La vie demande tout mon argent et je ne puis pas faire des dépens qui ne sont pas absolument nécessaires.

Ce n'est pas la peine de m'envoyer les jiournaux avec mes lettres. J'ai reçu déja cela de Bologne et de Florence, mais il ne me fait aucun plaisir de les lire et je suis bien content de les laisser aller. Personne ici, à part Théodore, n'en sçait rien, ou du moins, personne m'en a dit rien, et j'y suis bien content. Je te remerçie des abréviations que tu y as fait. C'est bien mieux comme ça et m'a oté une grande peur à cause de plusieures passages dont j'ai retenu un souvenir rien moins que flattant. Enfin je te remercie du tout mon coeur pour la peine que tu as pris à cause de ces lettres. Je sçais bien qu'elle ne peut pas avoir été un rien, de corriger et de faire publier toutes ces choses-là, et elle doit étre aussi une affaire de l'argent dont nous pouvons arranger la compte à mon retour.

Tu veux voir la nomination de Lincoln de son meilleur point de vue. Moi aussi. Mais j'en ai grande peur. Tu veux faire le même combat en grande, que nous avons faits il y a deux ans, en Illinois, et avec les mêmes candidats. Nous n'avons aucune raison à croire que Douglas est moins fort en Illinois maintenant, qu'il a été à ce temps-là; et tu te souviendras avec combien de certitude, tu a attendu au temps de mon départ, la victoire de Lincoln. Au reste, je doute toujours si on a raison en mettant à la tête d'un mouvement comme ceci, un homme qui n'a jamais été mis à l'épreuve. Seward est fort et sage; Lincoln aussi peut l'etre, mais aussi peut-etre il ne l'est pas. Et les conséquences d'avoir un homme faible pour Président, seront beaucoup plus graves que celles d'avoir un impotent pour président de la Chambre des Représentatives. Mais enfin, nous autres, qui servent une principe et pas un homme, n'ont en tout cas, qu'une chose à faire.

Je ne sçais rien des Morgans. Théodore dit qu'ils sont trés agréables, mais ça n'importe à présent, car ma dernière lettre de Loo annonce son départ pour Interlaken. Mon Dieu, je ne l'aime pas, tout cela. Mais je ne peut rien faire, moi.

Mais que fais-tu donc? toi? Ce n'est pas possible que tu as resté si long-temps paresseux. Est-ce que tu as des clients, ou est-ce que tu es amoureux? L'un et l'autre doit étre vrai. Ou est'ce que tu travailles en secrét, et personne ne peut savoir qu'est-ce que tu fais? Pour moi, toutes mes efforts sont nécessaires pour le Français, et vu que jusqu'au 1er Juillet je n'ai jamais essayé d'écrire un mot de cette langue, je pense que mes efforts n'ont pas été parfaitement sans succés.

Eh bien! voilà assez! Deux Cuttings, Bob le gros, et son frère sont arrivés.[2]

Tout à toi Henri.

MS: MHi
 1. Presumably Charles Frederick Lyman (d. 1880), Harvard '55.
 2. Robert Livingston Cutting (1836–1894), Harvard LL.B. '59. Heyward Cutting (1837–1876), Harvard '59.

To Abigail Brooks Adams

Paris. July. 19. 1860.

Dearest mamma

Your letter of the 25th arrived last week or thereabouts and since it, two from Charles. You seem to be happy in Quincy and so I congratulate you. Give my regards to all the cows, the pigs, hens, horses, servants and children and any residents of the good town of Quincy who still know me, including Ellen Lunt, Mrs Bigelow, Carry and Charles Miller, particularly the last, and ask him with my compliments how he does and whether his wife's as usual. Give Charles my love and tell him to buy a horse and charge it to me. Remember me to John the married man and my love to his wife.

Paris is quite as usual, thank you, and though slow, rather, to me, who have been rather on the move in summer usually, is still better than it might be if it were stupider. I'm committing a high crime and flagrant misdemeanor by writing in English, as my nose has been held down to the French grindstone for the last month with a pertinacity unparalleled in the history of humanity. We are gay in Paris, we are! I committed the indiscretion yesterday of calling on some Cicinnati people and left a card on Mrs Pete Lorillard Ronnels and her husband. That's what I call rather heavy work for one day.

It's a great life, varied, exciting and elevating. I take a French lesson and my breakfast at the same time. I write English into French until I'm tired when I take to reading and finally at about three I go up to John Munroe's and read the Newspapers. Then a walk; dinner at six at a restaurant where I usually meet Theodore or Henry Higginson or Braggiotti or a fellow named Brown, commonly known as Ned Brown, or all of them, and we dine together.[1] This is tolerably pleasant for one gets a good dinner and really I enjoy it more than all the rest of the day. Then at seven or eight I go to some Theatre usually with Higginson, and never get out much before midnight, or else we wander about and look into the shop windows till it's time to go to one's room. This is certainly not an excruciatingly violent labor, all this, but I'll bet a good deal I work a good deal harder than most people do in July at Paris. It's pleasant, too, in it's way. I enjoy it a good deal; but it costs lots of money and though my pantaloons are getting indecent and there's no lining left on any of my coats, I daren't order more, for I should probably have to pawn them in a week. So I avoid society and go in bad shoes. Do you know I've discovered a grand piece of philosophical economy. I wear bad clothes and a smashed hat but fly cravats and kid gloves (Naples; 30 cts.). In this way I calculate that the extras carry off the essentials, just as good wine will carry off a poor dinner. Isnt it a clever idea.

Uncle Sidney has been here; very kind to me as usual. He has lately departed on his annual tour over his dominions, accompanied by his royal Highness' sister-in-law the Princess Dehon. The health of his majesty is not so bad for a man of his time of life, considering that he's taken so much care of it. I shall probably have the pleasure of seeing his Grace again before I leave Paris.

Theodore is settled here till August. I've pretty much lost sight of him except at dinner occasionally. He says he's blue. Braggiotti says the same of himself, but manages to be pretty jolly at dinner. They're always visiting and dining out, and as I dodge that sort of thing like a very considerable fool as I always was, we don't often hit. I'm becoming a boor for want of good society and am no more of a gentleman than I was four years ago, but so it goes.

I don't like the way Loo is living in Switzerland. I don't think it's the right thing for her at all; she seems to be unwell and unhappy. If this is not changed by the next letter, I am going to write to propose her coming to Paris and living quietly with me. If she were to accept, I should go down at once and bring her up here and we could keep house together. I should like to have her with me very much, and if she is to be sick and miserable in Switzerland, I think the move is highly advisable. Still I've no idea that she will.

Braggiotti and I called to-day to see little Miss Rodman who is here. I met her at the blow-out on the 4th and having remarked her brother whose face I had often seen in college, I at once seized him, expressed intense delight at meeting him and desired to be introduced to his sister. He accordingly introduced me and I became passionately in love at once. I hadn't seen her since then, but as Braggiotti wanted to call, I counted myself in. So we went to-day to the house, climbed up to the fourth story and in a state of extreme exhaustion, rang the bell. Bragi doing the French and being the pretty man, stepped forward as the door opened, to inquire as to the lady of the house, but I saw his face assume an agonised expression and he began to stammer incoherently. The fair Rodman herself had answered the bell and as she seemed about as taken aback as we were, and did not appear inclined to ask us in, Braggi remarked deprecatingly that he thought perhaps we'd better leave our cards, the family being out. As I never saw Mrs or Mr Rodman and as the daughter was thar, I thought it rather a waste of paste-board but submitted and amid tender inquiries, adieus and so on, we backed down the four flights. I call that a profound and painful sell, especially as the family leaves Paris this week. Braggiotti departs too at once and will be home soon after this letter. I've just passed the evening with him and Theodore in Theodore's room. T.C. has a piano and played to me all the evening. I think it's all nonsense to talk about such men being of no use in the world. I'm sure they make it infinitely pleasanter and don't do any harm that I know of; not half as much as most men who are in a working point of view out of sight of them.

John Bancroft and Henry Higginson set out tomorrow on a three weeks trip to Brittany, there and thereabouts. I thought of going with them and writing a pastoral description of the tour which couldn't help being jolly. But as I came here to work I suppose I'd better stick it out and keep Brittany for my next trip fifty years hence. Theodore and I will be alone in Paris again soon and he leaves about the first of August. Then I shall be monarch of all I survey and feel lonely as a solitary duck on the north pole. As for Crowninshield and those fellows, Heaven only knows what has become of them. If I hadn't a supreme confidence in their luck at always coming out straight I should be anxious, for no one, not even Hollis's small brother, knows anything about them. Ben who generally writes regularly hasn't answered my last letter, nor Hollis either.

I got a letter from Lizzy Hooker the other day, who is at Ems, going through a course of treatment for her bronchitis. I suppose of course you'll think it's funny that she should be there and her husband in Rome. But you're all wrong if you imagine that she doesn't get on well with him. I lived in the family a month and I thought they got on admirably. I suppose she married him to be more independant than she could be at home, and as he can't leave his business, she's not the woman to be tied down to him, and he is too fond of her to oppose any commonly possible plans she may have. At all events Ems is the slowest hole in creation and she must be bored to death there. She proposes my running down to see her. If I had the time and the money I might have a jolly summer what with Brittany, the Rhine and Loo in Switzerland.

Still I enjoy Paris very much. It's the pleasantest city I ever was in, for a stranger. The life here is jovially independent and no one bothers me so long as I don't bother them. The theatres are something utterly slap-up and beyond the very highest time known. I have never seen such utterly cheesy[2] acting as here, though in Dresden I saw better actors in single great rôles; there are no great tragedians here. But I can go night after night and enjoy the plays just as much all the time. It costs money—rayther—but when all mine's gone I mean to knock off theatres, cut down my dinners, and be blue as I used to be in Berlin. Till then I mean to be jolly.

The French gets on step by step but next month I'm going to change my plans a little, take two teachers, and hire a small nigger-boy extra to talk to. As time gets short one must increase the pressure.

Love to all.   Henry.

MS: MHi
1. Henry Lee Higginson (1834–1919) of Boston had been in Europe almost four years, much of the time in Vienna studying music until he was persuaded that he could not have a major musical career. Ned Brown is probably Edward Jackson Brown (d. 1907), Harvard '55 (which would have been Higginson's class had he not withdrawn in his freshman year).
2. *Cheesy:* slang for "fine" or "showy."

To Charles Francis Adams, Jr.

Paris le 25 Juillet. 1860.

Mon chèr Charles

Encore une lettre est arriveé de toi aujourdhui. Ça fait deux qui attendent une réponse. Eh bien; c'est bien égal si je traduis Pascal en Anglais et le retraduis alors en Français, ou si j'écris une lettre à toi. Je sympathise, mon ami, à tes souffrances et à tes clous; lequelle est, je crois, le Français pour boils. Tu sçais bien, j'ai été toujours, moi, le victime d'une peau invincible ou d'un sang pas assez pur, et je sçais, moi, les tourments dont tu me parles. Mais pour toi c'est un ennui passant; pour moi c'est une véritable supplice de l'enfer. C'est vrai, depuis un an, la trouble est devenue moins forte, et m'afflige seulement tous les trois ou quatre mois; en Italie je m'ai trouvé parfaitement guéri; mais je l'attends encore ici, et tout ce que je peux opposer à cette misère, est parfaitement inutile. La vie, les femmes, la nourriture, rien ne l'empèche. Mais je crois et j'espere qu'elle devient moins forte chaque anneé et qu'avant peu je me trouverai libre encore. Achète-toi un cheval; promène-toi une heure ou deux tous les jours et tu iras bien.

J'ai reçu aussi deux pacquets de journaux, dont l'une contenait les orations de M. Everett et de notre père;[1] l'autre mes deux lettres de Rome et de Sicilie. Quant aux autres lettres et journaux que tu m'as envoyés en Italie et ici, je t'assure ils sont tous arrivés, tant que je sçais. C'eut été difficile de les perdre, parceque chaque banquier sçait mon addresse, et mes lettres me suivent quelquefois par-déssus la moitié d'Europe. Mais je n'ai tenu aucun compte régulièr de ces lettres et pacquets pendant me voyage, et je sçais seulement que je viens de payer vingt cinq francs à Munroe pour mon accompte chez lui depuis un mois. Je crois donc que tout est arrivé avec la seule exception du journal contenant mes lettres de Vienne et de Venise. Ne voulant payer le port pour ces choses qui venaient la voie du Dresde, j'ai autorisé Hooker à Rome de refuser tous journaux de cette description et il l'a fait, je suppose. Les autres venaient à Florence et m'ont suivis à Paris. Tant que je sçais, je n'ai perdu rien. Sois tranquil!

Tu me donnes le conseil d'essayer un article pour la Revue,[2] sur la position générale d'Italie. Avant de faire réponse, je veux te remercier encore des soins que tu as eus, et la bonté que tu as montrée et que tu montres encore une fois par cette proposition, envers moi. Je le sçais bien, il-y-a bien peu de frères qui s'intéressent, comme toi, dans la succés et les efforts de leurs plus jeunes frères. Encore une fois; merci!

Mais je ne peux pas embrasser cette dernière idée. Voici mes raisons! ... C'est bien vrai, comme tu me dis, qu'un article tel que tu t'imagine pourrait me donner beaucoup d'avantages. Mais attends un peu! Tu sçais bien comment le travail est grand dans une essaye de cette sorte; particulièrement si elle est la première. Tu sçais combien d'études, de recherches il faut toujours faire sur des choses de ce genre. Tu sçais bien comme je serais faché de faire publier un premier effort sans des soins les plus exacts, sans une application la plus nerveuse. Eh bien! J'ai encore à Paris, en Europe, le space de deux mois; chaque jour j'essaie de donner dix heures aux études de la langue. C'est pour ça je suis venu ici! C'est pour ça que je reste encore en Europe! Comment donc écrire un article comme tu en veux; un article qui demande tant d'études, tant de soins, tant de temps! D'abord, il faut absolument dévouer tout mon temps à la langue; c'est un grand objèt pour ma vie; le nier, le négliger, ça serait oublier mon bout; échanger une avantage qui reste toujours, pour une avantage qui, en tout cas, doit venir un peu plus tard, si j'ai la force de la gagner à présent.

Voilà mes raisons! Enfin, c'est impossible. Deux mois ne sont pas assez, même pour cela. Mais, mon ami, puisque tu t'intéresses si vivement dans mes projets, je te parlerai d'un projêt que j'ai eu depuis longtemps, et pour lequel je me trouve plus bien adapté. C'est un article, ou deux peutêtre, du genre dont tu parles, mais qui se concernent avec les affaires d'Allemagne, non pas avec celles d'Italie. En Allemagne je suis plus chez moi. C'est un pays que j'aime beaucoup; que je respecte infiniment; et dont je connais assez bien les affaires, les peuples, et la litérature. De tout cela je sçais presque rien en Italie.

Mais toutes ces choses-ci restent jusqu'après mon retour. Je n'ai à présent qu'une occupation; celle d'apprendre la langue. J'écris; je lis, des heures en suite, tout haut; je vais tous les soirs dans les Théatres; je ne connais personne; et je fais de progrés; oui, sans doute, je fais de progrés; mais c'est lente et difficile. Eh bien; je puis déja lire et comprendre presque parfaitement; je puis l'entendre quand on parle, mais pas toujours; je puis l'écrire comme tu vois, avec une infinité d'erreurs, mais avec facilité, comme jécrirais en Anglais; mais je ne puis pas parler du tout. Il y a un mois que je l'essaie.

Voilà assez de mes affaires! Pourquoi ne me parles-tu des tiennes? Que fais-tu, donc? Jean s'engage et est amoureux; le père politise; la mère a ses vacances; mais toi, que fais tu? Estce-que tu es un avocat; mais, Mon Dieu, je n'écoute rien de tes clients. Et Horace Gray dont mamma parle dans sa dernière lettre; que fait-il à Quincy?[3] Estce que tu veux entrer dans une association avec lui?

Le discours de notre père à Fall River est bon. Pardieu, notre père s'avance. Ce n'est pas peu de choses quand on le place à coté de M. Everett dans l'estimation publique. Car M. Everett a une position inférieure a personne dans les Etats Unies et tout le monde l'écoute avec respect du moins. Mais il faut changer un peu le programme pour l'année prochaine. Tout en donnant à la question d'esclavage le plus haut rang, il faut que notre s'occupe avec les autres questions d'importance du jour. Ce n'est pas assez d'être un homme d'état sur cette question seulement. J'espère qu'il comprend la nécessité d'étendre sa reputation comme homme d'affaires; de s'identifier avec les intérêts publiques et de se faire respecter comme le représentatif des idées de New England généralement. Je serais bien content de le voir à la tête de quelque Département sous la prochaine Administration. Sa place dans le Congrés restera toujours à lui, s'il le désire.

En attendant mon retour je m'amuse assez bien ici. C'est vrai je connais personne. Théodore a beaucoup de connaissances ici et je le vois à peine. Je préfere rester tout seul et m'appliquer à mes études. Je vais tous les soirs au spectacle; c'est un grand moyen d'apprendre la langue. C'est aussi un grand plaisir, et tu comprends bien, quatre ou cinq heures chaque soir où on n'entend rien que Français, et où on s'amuse infiniment; c'est assez, ça seul, pour faire passer les jours sans ennui. Je ne comprends pas ce qu'est devenu de Crowninshield, Hollis, Shep et Bradlee. Personne n'a entendu rien; même le jeune frère et la tante de Hollis sçaient aussi peu comme moi. J'ai peur qu'un des quatre est tombé malade, et que les autres ne veulent pas écrire jusqu'à sa convalescence. La Marquise Lavalette est furieuse à la silence d'Hollis, et le Marquis aussi. Du moins, on le dit, et c'est bien raisonnable. Mes dernières lettres restent sans réponse, et je suis furieux aussi, moi! Ce n'est pas possible que tous les quatres se sont perdus en Norvège.

Kuhn est donc arrivé et reviendra certainement le Juillet prochain. Mon Dieu, il a tort. Ce n'est pas la peine de faire une si grande bruit pour six mois de plus. C'eut été mieux de ne pas rester du tout en Europe, ou d'y rester deux ans. Notre père a donné ses opinions sur ce sujet, à Kuhn, dans une lettre; il y a quelques mois. Cette lettre a été un peu forte; dans la manière de notre père, dont il n'y a pas de besoin de te rappeler. Tu la connais déja, et moi aussi. Eh bien, j'ai des raisons à croire que cette lettre a eue un effêt tres-considerable sur notre beau-frère, et qu'elle a ouverte ses yeux assez brusquement. Mais je ne sçais rien. Kuhn m'a jamais confés ses projets, exceptée une seule fois, le jour de mon arrivée à Florence, et depuis ce temps-là ses projets ont subis un changement et une amélioration. Je me suis tout-à-fait trompé, et sans doute, j'ai écrit des choses que je ne devrais écrire, et que je n'aurait pas écrits si j'avais connu la course des évenements.

Tu parles de Jean comme d'un homme perdu. Crois-tu en verité qu'il deviendra un George Howe. Tout est possible, et nous n'avons qu'attendre avec patience la fin de ces égarements d'esprit. Ça ne peut pas durer plus que deux ou trois ans après son mariage, et alors nous pouvons encore respirer. Pour toi, mon ami, il ne reste rien que de te marier. Fais comme tout le monde, mon pauvre garcon; je te pardonne. Et Tom Frothingham? Mets-le à la porte, le squatter! Avec ses enfants! Va-t-en! imbecile!

Mes amitiés à tous, Fanny ci-inclus si tu la vois.

Adieu   H.B.A.

MS: MHi

1. CFA's July 4 address at Fall River, Mass., declared it the duty of the federal government to settle the slavery question in the territories and keep hands off in the states; Everett's, at Boston, praised the Constitution. Everett was now vice-presidential candidate of the Constitutional Union party.

2. *The North American Review*, founded in Boston in 1815, modeled on the great British quarterlies.

3. Horace Gray (1828–1902) of Boston, Harvard '45, LL.B. '49, Supreme Court of Massachusetts 1864–1881 (chief justice 1873–1881) and of U.S. 1881–1902.

To Abigail Brooks Adams

Paris. August. 16. 1860.

Dearest Mamma

Since my last letter my affairs have taken a new change. Loo's letter took me down to Geneva all of a sudden and now I am living a sort of family life. I got the notification one Saturday; the next Tuesday evening I took the cars, travelled all night and at noon the next day was in Geneva. Loo had not arrived, so I took a bath and breakfast and wandered about the city. As I rambled along, the first acquaintances I tumbled on were uncle Sidney and Aunt Fanny who were perambulating the streets as naturally as could be. Uncle Sidney was badly used up by an attack of asthma which makes him look and feel pretty low. I dined with them that day and we managed to have a pretty jolly dinner in spite of sickness and all. If his party are strong in nothing else they certainly have a good hand in that. The same evening Loo arrived all right. I was hunting for her till ten o'clock at the steam-boat landing and at the depot, while she at eight had got to the hotel without my knowing it, and her maid summoned me down to her while I was undressing after having given up the search and come back.

The next day after doing all that was necessary at Geneva, we got off at two o'clock. This being my first effort at taking care of a female, I braced myself up to it, and struggled fiercely with the baggage and the parcels. Luckily Loo is a good traveller and knows how to look out for herself, so after about an hour of battle during which my mind was strained to it's highest pitch and the perspiration was called forth to an extent unknown for many months, I succeeded in forcing the passage, and we took possession of a coupé in company with ten bundles, a box of dominos, a package of sangwidges, a bottle of Burgundy, some books, and a fat old Swiss individual who sucked an unlighted cigar for a hundred miles. To this individual I owe my deepest gratitude, for with an infinity of patience he dug out the cork of the Burgundy with a pocket-knife, a thing which I never could have done myself. He left us towards evening so that we had our coupé all alone the rest of the way and it's appearance must have been quite edifying, for we quite made up our quarters there. An easier and pleasanter journey I never heard of. Loo slept all night; at least I believe she did, for I didn't, and I can testify to having watched her four hours without her opening her eyes or mouth. I found the Burgundy a great resource, and recommend it highly to all unprejudiced travellers. The next morning at seven we were in Paris, very dirty and pretty tired but on the whole very comfortable. We came straight to Loo's old house as I had arranged before starting, and in two hours, everything was as if we'd been in Paris a year.

Since then we've gone on quietly as can be, dining every day at some restaurant with Theodore, and wandering about the streets looking into the shop windows. Shep has been here and dined with us yesterday, and one of Loo's Florence acquaintances is now here too and enlivens our days. Every morning at about one o'clock these young men come in, Theodore plays the piano and we others talk and amuse ourselves. Lizzy Hooker is here on her way back to Italy. She looks ill, I think and thin, but she is good-natured as ever and hates to seem low-spirited. The Winthrops too are here but leave very soon. Shep went to-day over to England to meet Peter.[1] He made Loo a very pretty present of a Dresden porcellain painting; a piece of galantry which is quite striking for Shep and was certainly exceedingly well timed.

Louisa Adams Kuhn

Charles Kuhn

I acknowledge I find myself rather out of place in all this. Loo loves to have every one about her gay, brilliant and amusing, and dislikes stupid people as she calls them. Unluckily I am neither gay nor brilliant nor amusing, and am particularly fond of being stupid; that is, of sitting still and saying nothing. There never were two people more unlike than we are, and as I have no authority over her nor even the influence of age, I'm not over satisfied with my position. Not that she is disagreeable. On the contrary she is and always was particularly kind to me. But once for all, her world is not my world, and our ideas are as far apart as the two poles. We get along admirably together and the life is very pleasant. I never was made for this sort of thing. It makes me blue to feel that I can't be gay and fascinating, and that everyone should think me too old and mannered. It's true enough but precious unpleasant to have one's youth taken away so by force of arms. Still, it's no use trying to be what one isn't.

My passage is engaged for the 6th October. So you can expect me two months from today and as papa consents to my casting my lines at Washington, we sha'n't separate for some time to come after that. If Kuhn has not arrived by the 1st October, I shall leave Loo alone the few days till he comes, or under the care of any relation that turns up. A day or two doesn't matter. You will only have a letter or two more to write. That, I know, you won't be sorry for.

I take an immense interest in Fanny. If your account is right, she is young enough to become one of us and can grow into our style of things; a precious sight better than if she were to be all formed and strange. I hope she'll like me, for I'm sure I want her to and shall do the best I can to make her. I wrote to her again last week and sent her my photograph. Give her my love and the same to everyone. No letter this week to me.

Yrs ever   Henry.

MS: MHi
1. Peter Chardon Brooks (1831–1920), Harvard '52.

To Charles Francis Adams, Jr.

Paris le 23 Aout. 1860.

Mon aimable Garçon

Je viens de recevoir ta lettre du 7 Aout qui a été un peu en retard. Cette lettre sera bien probablement la dernière que je t'écrirai d'Europe et tu auras à peine le temps pour répondre puisque je compte quitter Paris le 15 Septembre et Liverpool le 6 Octobre. Si tu veux absolument écrire encore une fois, adresses ta lettre aux soins de Messrs Baring Bros. London.

Je me sens bien flatté par l'usage que tu as fait de mes remarques à propos de M. Seward. La fortune a été pleine de bonté envers moi en rapport de ces lettres Italiennes. Quand je partis de Dresde il y avait assez peu de probabilité que je trouverais Garibaldi en Sicile et sans cela mes lettres auraient été presque sans intêret. C'est vrai, elles n'ont pas été tout ce que je voudrais. A présent je voudrais bien en changer beaucoup et je me rappelle beaucoup de choses que je voudrais dire, surtout en rapport de Florence. Mais il faut attendre cela toujours, et je n'ai aucune raison de me plaindre de l'effêt des mes efforts. C'est vrai, personne ne m'en a parlé et je ne cours point de danger d'être gâté par des compliments, mais je trouve occasionellement des personnes qui les ont lus, et plus qu'ils sont étrangers, plus je me sens satisfait.

À present je mêne une vie assez tranquille et, il faut le dire, assez inutile et sans bout, et plus qu'assez expensive, à Paris, en attendant l'arrivée de Charles Kuhn. Je ne l'aime pas trop, cette vie, et je ne me trouve pas furieusement épris d'une existence de famille. Ma foi, si on peut juger de cette essai, on doit s'ennyer à mourir quand on est marié. C'est vrai, j'estime et j'aime plus notre soeur, mais je ne serais pas son mari si elle était la marquise de Carabbas, et j'attends le moment pour la donner dans les bras de son époux, avec une instance et un espoir vraiment touchant. Le temps aussi est une invention du diable. C'est d'une froideur d'enfer et on ne voit jamais un jour sans orages ni sans pluie.

Loo me semble de si rejouir d'une très-bonne santé, et depuis six ans je ne l'ai jamais vu quand elle s'est portée mieux. Elle est fraiche et a presque l'air d'une jeune fille. Les bons Parisiens qui nous regardent à grands yeux sur le boulevart, doivent se douter beaucoup de nos relations, et je me trouverais bien flatté si on croirait qu'elle est ma maitresse. Malheureusement je compromets la partie car on me reconnâit toujours pour un Anglais. Loo n'a point changé ses habitudes. Elle est souvent une véritable petite diable et me tourmente à me perdre la raison; mais alors elle se change tout-à-coup et me couvre de ses bienfaits et de ses caresses et regrette son injustice plus que je la regrette, moimême. Théodore est beaucoup chez nous et j'en suis bien content. Il l'amuse et j'espère qu'il aura plus de succès que moi pour la faire sentir la justice de nos idées. Mais c'est vrai, ce que tu dis; en rapport de la moralité, Florence et New York sont assez égales pour elle, et je me borne en ne voulant qu'une chose; c'est qu'elle ne pourrait faire aucune scandale. Cela nous concerne; le reste est tout-à-fait son affaire.

Pour moi je suis bien content de revenir en Amérique. Elle m'offre beaucoup plus que l'Europe et j'espere que je puis faire quelque chose digne d'un joli garcon comme moi.

Mais, mon excellent ami, Paris n'est pas tout-à-fait un desert. Il y a des choses ici que j'aime bien; d'abord, le vin et les diners. Ah, tudieu, commes ils sont bons, les diners! C'est quelque chose de nouveau et miraculeux, qu'un diner à Paris. Et le vin! Ah, mon pauvre garçon, je me gris tous les soirs et je me porte comme le bon Dieu. Alors les théatres! J'en ai déjà parlé beaucoup. Et alors les boutiques, qui me feront faire banqueroulte. Pour les femmes, je sçais assez peu de cette sorte de choses. Les lorettes[1] sont à peu près la même chose partout, en Amérique comme à Paris; c'est à dire, tant que je sache; et je n'ai jamais eu la bonne fortune de faire la connaissance d'une honnête femme, pas vertueuse. Je suis bien rangé, moi. Les lorettes sont une nécessité, pour moi comme pour tout le monde, mais jusqu'au temps quand j'en trouverai une bien différente de toutes celles que j'ai vues jusqu'ici, je n'aurai point de mâitresse.

Un soir, il y a environ huit jours, j'avais laissé Loo aux soins de Théodore pour l'apporter chez elle, puisque je voulais, moi, aller chercher quelque chose dans mon vieil appartement. J'avais bu ma bouteille de Macon à diner, et j'étais assez content de moi et du monde entier, mais ça m'ennuya, d'aller seul. Je voulais un compagnon, à tout prix, et m'appercevant d'une jeune femme; c'est à dire, d'un joli bonnet vis-a-vis de moi, je traversais la rue et lui souhaitais un bon soir. "Bon soir" a été la réponse. Avec beaucoup de bonhommie, j'ai commencé une conversation, mais imagine donc; elle m'a répondu à propos d'une question de sa demeure, par me demander si je donc adressais une femme sans la connâitre; d'un ton assez brusque. Mais, mon Dieu, est-ce-que-j'adresse les femmes que je connais! C'était ridicule. "Eh bien" ai-je dit "C'est à vous, non à moi, de continuer la connaissance," et étant venu à la porte de ma maison, j'ai ajouté, "Je demeure ici, moi." "Et moi aussi" a-t-elle repondu en entrant dans l'appartement de Madame, mon hôtesse.

Amusant, n'est-ce-pas? J'ai vu la personne souvent. Elle n'est pas jolie et je fus content de laisser tomber l'intrigue. Je cherchais ce que je voulûs, et en descendant l'escalier pour sortir, la porte de l'appartement de Madame s'est ouverte et mon amie a fait son apparence. Nous nous sommes passés; j'ai oté mon chapeau et dit "Bon soir"; elle a répondu quelque chose que je n'ai pas pu entendre, et a monté l'escalier que je venais de descendre. Je l'ai laissée aller. C'est une drôle d'aventure, n'est-ce-pas? Quel contretemps de tomber sur précisément la seule femme dans toute la ville qui pourrais me connaître; et comme c'eût été joli si cette femme eût été belle et aimable! Je suis faché maintenant que je ne l'ai pas essayée.

Tes reflexions à propos de notre belle-soeur sont d'une nuance bien plus fonceé que je crois nécessaire. Tu crois que F.C. doit exercer une influence dangereuse sur Jean, mais mon Dieu, c'est mieux, ça, qu'aucune influence, et je préfere, moi, d'avoir une soeur dont le caractere et les idées sont encore flexible, que d'en avoir une ou sans influence directe, ou avec un caractère déja formé. J'espere trouver dans F.C. une grande alliée, et je compte à assister dans la creation de son caractère. Mais d'abord il faut la faire une amie, et je ferai tout et je pardonnerai tout pour gagner cela. Je ne scais rien de la justice de tes remarques sur la pureté de la sang de cette famille. Mais cela de la famille de son pêre est pûre et bonne tant que je sache. Son frère est un modèle de santé et de vigueur. Ces tâches de sang ne sont pas éternelles. La sang s'en purifie avec le temps et des soins. Espérons-le, et souvenons-nous toujours que notre soeur s'appelle Crowninshield, non pas Sears.

Je suis tout-à-fait ruiné par Paris. Notre pere heureusement s'est corrigé.

Plus que je demande d'argent, le moins il me gronde. Sa réponse à ma lettre demandant $750, a été d'une très-belle humeur, et j'espère, quand je serais revenu avec encore quelques centaines de francs de dettes, il m'embrassera et me grondera parceque je n'ai pas été assez généreux.

Je ne connais personne à Paris et je n'ai pas cherché des connaissances. Shep, en retour de Norvege, nous a fait une visite, et nous a raconté ses aventures dans ce pays barbare et glaciale (pas mal, ça; à la Voltaire) mais son récit a été un peu monoton puisqu'il n'a rien vu, exceptés les nuages et la pluie. J'attends Kuhn le 29, et j'évacuerai cette chambre et je me transfererai dans un Hôtel avec une alacrité dont tu n'as pas la moindre idée. Le 15 du mois prochain je pars probablement pour Londres. Kuhn et Loo partiront probablement au même temps pour des pays inconnus. Son expédition en Egypte est douteuse et je crains qu'il faut la résigner à un second hiver à Florence. Mais peut-être la visite que Charles vient d'avoir fait en Amérique, aurait changé un peu ses vues.

Tu recevras cette lettre le 10 Septembre environ. Eh bien, le 16 Octobre nous pouvons causer ensemble de toutes ces choses; à présent je ne veux mieux que de me trouver fixé, n'importe où. Paris s'est changé depuis l'arriveé de Loo, et le temps m'ennuie à mourir. Il faut que cette lettre reste comme les photographies, sans retouche. Je n'ai pas le temps pour en corriger les erreurs.

Adieu   Henri.

MS: MHi

1. *Lorettes:* prostitutes (from the quarter of Notre Dame de Lorette, near Montmartre).

To Abigail Brooks Adams

Paris. 31 August. 1860.

Dearest Mamma

No letter to me this week but as Loo got one, I dont mind. I owe papa two letters which I hope to pay soon. This letter-writing though will soon be over as far as I am concerned. The answer to this is the last that you will be able to get to me and not even that unless it's written at once.

Things go on as usual. I expect to-day the news of the arrival of the Arago but as Kuhn does not know that Loo is here he may go to London to get his clothes so that I shall not be off duty so soon as I had expected.

Higginson has just come in with the news of the arrival of the Arago, so that Loo is content and expects news soon.

Our life is quiet as you please, though for me altogether too expensive; so much that I've decided to leave Paris the 15th instead of a week later. We dine every day with either Theodore or some one in some restaurant and are very jolly. As Loo gets used to me and my style of disposition, she adapts herself much better to me than at first, not scolding half so much nor bothering me to be like her. We get along admirably as I never interfere with her at all and she is very indulgent indeed to me.

We lead a pretty lazy useless sort of a life which is pleasant enough but rather bores me and I shall be glad when I'm fairly started for home. Now that I'm down at the very fag end of my European travels and there's nothing more to expect from them, all my ideas are beginning to run on what is to be done at home.

It's an independent little life that we lead though. No one knows us. We've called on no one and no one comes here except my friends and Theodore. The amiable Reader has departed, thank the Lord. He is as poor a lump of humanity as I know and a dreadful bore to Loo.[1] His appearance in the room has always been the sign of my having a pressing engagement on the other side of the city, and I never came back so long as I supposed he stayed. He departed yesterday and I took a most touching adieu of him, expressing the deepest regret and a warm hope that he might visit us some day in America. If he ever does I shall take refuge on the north pole and stay till he's gone.

If you could see me pegging along the boulevart with Loo on my arm, you would grin sympathisingly. She will look into every shop window and like a patient and a suffering lamb I wait and sigh for hours after her. As I'm the envy of all that see me however, I submit with immense patience. There are precious few women in Paris so pretty as she is and so chic-looking. We or rather she, attracts great admiration everywhere and as usual gets stared at to a degree quite beyond comfort. That's the penalty of being attractive. At Berlin two years ago it used to drive me into a fury but now I submit and take my revenge by staring at every one else.

She has had one head-ache, not very bad, since we came here, but as a general thing her health has been admirable and we are both of us so fat that we're afraid to wear our old clothes. She looks absolutely youthful and I am acquiring a double-chin worthy of a sexagenarian toper. I find my health perfectly tremendous and am a convert to good living. I never mean to try starving again or bad feed such as I used to exist on in Germany. I don't wonder that I was low-spirited and looked-badly.

Theodore looks well too. He was down yesterday with a sick head-ache, which is I suppose the result of too good living. I should have trouble too if I lived so very long but with my departure and sea-voyage so near I don't think it'll hurt me much.

Our principal amusement is to buy things; an amusement which is tolerably innocent and intolerably costly. False jewelry is the great attraction. I am an immense admirer of false jewelry and never cease regretting the extravagance that's led me once or twice to buy some real things. I can get you any amount of real false jewelry here that no one can distinguish from the real, at prices which are positively magnificent. For half a dollar the other day I became the happy proprietor of a resplendent gold scarf-pin set with pearls, which I wear on all great occasions and which is eminently good-taste. So you see, I can buy probably thirteen more at the same price that one real one would have cost. Imagine me displaying thirteen wonderful gold scarf-pins, all false. I think I shall bring home a cargo to give to my friends.

Loo eats like a pig and is a little drunkard. Really it does me good to see how well she is and how she seems to be enjoying it. I shall be glad to have Kuhn find her so. The weather which is beastly, suits her, I believe. It's heavy, sleepy, dark weather that doesn't excite her nerves and keeps her pretty equable.

I see that papa figured at Mr Seward's reception. I'm glad of it, partly for Seward to prevent Wilson and Burlingame's bolting him raw, and partly on papa's. I study the American papers hard and try to see what's what, but fail to discover whether Blair is elected for the short term and if not what people think of it. Everyone swears his candidate is as good as in, so that I'm almost induced myself to consider him at least sworn in.[2] Mr Preston, Spanish Minister just arrived here from home, says it's sure for Lincoln, so he ought to know.[3] At any rate naturalize me to vote for him. Sure as my name's H. I'll vote for both him and papa this fall.

Yrs ever. Henry.

MS: MHi

1. Reader is unidentified except by Louisa Adams Kuhn in a letter to ABA: "We dine . . . with young Mr. Reader, an Englishman whose sisters were very kind to me in Florence, at one or another café—and very merry & jolly these little dinners are" (Aug. 19).

2. Campaigning for Lincoln in New England, Seward stopped on Aug. 14 in Boston, where he was officially greeted by CFA and Sen. Henry Wilson. Anson Burlingame (1820–1870) of Massachusetts was representative 1855–1859 (American party) and 1859–1861 (Republican). Francis Preston Blair (1821–1875) of Missouri, Free-Soil representative 1857–1859, won his election to Congress as a Republican in 1860.

3. William Preston (1816–1887) of Kentucky, Whig representative 1852–1855, U.S. minister to Spain 1858–1861.

To Abigail Brooks Adams

Paris. September. 7. 1860.

Dearest Mamma

Your letter of August 21 got here a few days ago. It was immensely interesting and your account of Seward's visit is great. If some future historian of our good country ever gets hold of your letters to me, he'll howl with delight. It would give him stuff for a dozen volumes.

You seem to be unhappy at the prospect of returning to Washington. You know I always have thought that you gave yourself the unhappiness and I've said more than once that of all the women I know, you are that one who have least right to complain. I want to show you a case where I think unhappiness *is* justifiable, and perhaps you may feel that you're not so very hardly treated when your worst trouble is to have to be a lady, honored, envied and courted at Washington.

This last week Theodore and I have been called on, each in different ways, to act the good Samaritan. Theodore has devoted himself to trying to help a poor fellow, a Baltimorean, who has just lost a wife whom he adored and has been married to for six or eight years. The man was broken-hearted and clung to Theodore as if he were his only hope. Theodore who is as good-hearted a fellow as ever lived, gave himself up to help his friend.

My experience was rather different. You recollect that in my letters from Rome, I mentioned several times a family I knew there, and several young ladies whom I saw a good deal. It was a family of six women and no man. They were New Englanders and one of the most curious crowds I ever saw. The eldest was a Mrs Magee, a kind old lady of past sixty I fancy, very in-firm and invalid, but always pleasant and kind. Next to her was a Mrs Davis, a fine, handsome woman of fifty with hair almost white, but a health apparently splendid. Then came two girls of eighteen; one a Miss Baldwin, the other a Miss Cruthers. It was a curious story about these girls. When Mrs Davis was still unmarried, she and three of her nearest friends agreed that in case they should marry and should leave children at their death unprotected, the survivors, whichever they might be, should take these children and act as a mother toward them. It so happened that three of the four did die, leaving these children to Mrs Davis who has kept her word and educated them ever since they were babies.

Accordingly these two girls and a boy of eighteen, Leon Baldwin, have grown up to look at Mrs Davis in the light of something more than any or-dinary relation. She was more than their mother. They owed her every-thing and for eighteen months, ever since I was in Berlin with Mr Apthorp, I have always heard this family spoken of as the nearest approach to a per-fect unity of idea and thought, that ever was known. They and an Irish maid who had served Mrs Magee eighteen years, were in Dresden while I was there and I afterwards met them in Rome.

They were queer. The whole family were strong in their religious ideas and I believe I shocked them a good deal several times. They were very New England indeed and the very best type of New England; not rich nor very poor; not in society nor generally known but that sort of people that all the world speaks well of.

Another young lady, no relation; was with them in Rome, a Miss Forrest. She was much like the rest, not brilliant, but not ugly and rather attractive. I liked her though I thought her of no great count anyway.

I left them in Rome and had heard since that they were all well and were to stay in Italy. I never expected to see them again.

Last Monday morning I went as usual to John Munroe's to look for let-ters. As I came into the office a young lady jumped up and almost threw herself into my arms, crying out "Oh Mr Adams, how glad I am to see you." I hardly recognized her. It was Miss Forrest, but looking like death and the very devil; pale as a corpse; eyes swollen and black, blue, red and green. In short I saw that something had happened, and I asked at once what had brought her to Paris.

In half a dozen words she explained to me that Mrs Davis had died in Spezia where they were passing the summer. One afternoon she was playing chess at the Casino with the young Leon Baldwin, when she stopped an instant, rested her head on his shoulder, her heart stopped beating and she was dead without a motion or a word. After infinite troubles, without a protector, the rest of the party had now got to Paris on their way to England where friends expected them. In Paris they knew no one.

Of course I put myself at once at their disposal. Miss Forrest was sensible enough to make use of me as much as was possible. While we were driving about from one banker's to another and from the telegraph office to the Consul, she told me all the particulars and on the whole, I think I never was much more shocked in my life. These five women who were almost distracted and broken hearted at the death of their only friend, were made the prey of a system of rascality, and outrageous treatment in Spezia that must have been utterly horrible. Their only protectors were two Boston men, one named Rice, the naval commissioner at the port; the other no less than the great Timmins, who rose on their behalf to the size of a hero. It was ten days ago that all this had happened. So soon as they could, the body was put into a lead coffin and they came with it up here.

With a valet and Leon they got on as well as they could. They know how to take care of themselves and were educated to it. But that same morning Leon and the commissionaire had gone on to London with the body and the girls and Mrs Magee were all alone in a little Hotel in Paris, to get along as they best could.

Under Miss Forrest's orders I worked hard for them that Morning. In the afternoon I called to see the others, for as yet I'd only seen Miss Forrest and the maid. Miss Baldwin was the only one I saw and I talked with her about half an hour, trying to act as much like an unselfish being as I could, and to sympathise with her at least. You can imagine what this visit was. It's dreadfully trying to do these things and I could only say and repeat in different forms the trite remark of how sorry I was. She is a queer little decided person; that is, she was; but now she was so broken down by all that had happened that I shouldn't have known her. Yet to do her justice, there was very little crying and I got through the visit better than I had expected. After which I went to dinner and drowned my troubles and hers in Burgundy with Theodore who had his man on his hands and was bluer than a million devils.

Miss Forrest was to go to Orleans to stay with the Butterworths, my old Dresden friends who are now there. But they did not expect her yet. No answer came to a telegraph I sent. Accordingly I had offered to take Miss Forrest under my own care down to Orleans and the offer was accepted, the maid being tacked on for propriety. This was all arranged with Miss Baldwin.

To appreciate my conduct it's necessary to recollect that I do not usually arise from my slumbers at seven as I had to Tuesday morning, nor bolt my breakfast and cut my cigar and coffee with the morning paper. Still, my conduct was equal to the occasion. I was punctually at the Hôtel, took the two women and the baggage into my care and we drove past the Tuilleries and the church of Notre Dame that fine morning, the young woman and the Irish brogue still enlivening my spirits with all the choicest troubles at Spezia, and I trying to instil pleasanter ideas into their minds.

At noon we were in Orleans. If you had seen our entry into that deserted little city you would have died laughing. We had to get the address first at the Post, and then, capturing a carriage, I mounted beside the driver and talked to him in fluent French but unable to make out one single syllable in his much answering. We really got quite jolly over our ride out into the country and found our friends living in a pretty little house with a lawn and garden and everything homeish and pleasant.

I staid here till evening, talking and wandering about the grounds. At six o'clock I left them. The cathedral was utterly magnificent as I drove through the city at sunset, and it made quite an impression on me. At nine I was in Paris again, and leaving a card at the hotel for the young ladies to say that I should be there at six the next morning to see them off to England, I came to my room and went straight to bed.

At five the next morning I was up and kept the appointment at six. The four women appeared; I saw them into their omnibus without extra words wasted, and followed them in a carriage to the depot; got their tickets; registered their baggage; received their last commissions and their thanks and promised to see them at London. Then I telegraphed their departure on to London and with a relieved mind I returned to my room and slept two hours straight off. There was no conversation, nor effusion. I preferred to leave them undisturbed in their troubles and they had the good sense to take my small services as I gave them, without fearing that I should think them ungrateful.

Now, that is what I call an occasion for unhappiness. Such troubles as these leave all smaller things in the dark. That I call something to be miserable about.

I've received your and Mary's photographs and they're first rate. Hers is admirable and very satisfactory as far as looks go. How she's getting on intellectually I suppose I shall find out on my return and as far as I can assist in her education, I'll act as a perfect Solomon though I'm afraid three months is not enough to make me much of a French teacher. Charles will I suppose take this electioneering chance to write letters to some paper. At least I hope so for it will be a first rate chance and he can make quite a thing of it. The truth is, we can't help it. It must out. This taste for politics is a perfect mania in us.

I'm preparing my departure from Paris which comes now very soon and as the time goes pretty fast, my next letter will probably be the last from the continent. I suppose you wont be sorry now that there are to be no more weekly despatches for me. All goes well here. Charles Kuhn goes to England; or is gone already and Loo is again on my hands but as I have taken rooms again I can't move a fourth time to live with her.

I want you to remember me to Rebecca particularly. As I expect to be on the ocean a month from to-day, there's no need to send many messages. I'm utterly ruined pecuniarily, beyond hope, but that is a thing to be arranged at home. I shall have to work harder; that's all.

Yrs ever.   H.

MS: MHi

3.

The Great
Secession Winter
1860–1861

When Charles Francis Adams, newly reelected, returned to Washington for the short lame-duck session of the old Congress, Henry Adams gave up reading law in Boston and moved to Washington with his family. As the oldest son still in the household, he undertook—as his brother Charles had done before him—"the duties of secretary, of school-master, of reporter for the papers, and of society-man." Writing to Charles, who stayed in Boston to practice law, he reported his performance in all these roles. Beyond that, he gave a unique account of the political crisis, far more valuable than anything in his newspaper correspondence.

In his private letters, Henry Adams went behind the official explanations of Republican maneuvering. William Henry Seward in the Senate and his father in the House were trying to hold together a government until the new president was sworn into office. Their ostensible purposes were valid enough. Corruption and scandal were obviously bad in themselves, but the pursuit of corruption might also serve as a means of driving suspected disunionists from Buchanan's cabinet. Peace conventions and congressional compromises might conceivably succeed; but in any case they might delay secessionists in the Border States from following South Carolina's lead. Day-to-day political activities were directed to a consistent end.

Henry Adams learned statesmanship from the two principals. Seward, Lincoln's secretary of state designate, was the leading Republican in Washington. His friendliness to the young man touched a responsive chord, and Adams' analysis of Seward's masterfulness took on a tone of hero worship. Charles Francis Adams was naturally less flamboyant, and his son saw him more accurately as a leading power of the Committee of Thirty-Three, "doing his best to do nothing." Buying time was hard work.

As March approached, the Adams family convened in Washington for Lincoln's inauguration. In celebrating the presidential victory of their party, they also marked the congressional victory by attrition that had preserved a government for the new president to lead. Then, the legislative session over, they returned to Boston, and for the second time Henry began the study of law. With his father's appointment as minister to Great Britain, however, he almost immediately set Blackstone aside to become a private secretary again.

To Charles Francis Adams, Jr.

Sunday. Dec. 9. 1860.

Dear Charles

I propose to write you this winter a series of private letters to show how things look.[1] I fairly confess that I want to have a record of this winter on file, and though I have no ambition nor hope to become a Horace Walpole, I still would like to think that a century or two hence when everything else about us is forgotten, my letters might still be read and quoted as a memorial of manners and habits at the time of the great secession of 1860. At the same time you will be glad to hear all the gossip and to me it will supply the place of a Journal.

The first week is now over and I feel more at home though I've not made many acquaintances. It's a great life; just what I wanted; and as I always feel that I am of real use here and can take an active part in it all, it never tires. Politically there is a terrible panic. The weak brethren weep and tear their hair and imagine that life is to become a burden and the Capitol an owl-nest and fox-hole. The Massachusetts men and the Wisconsin men and scatterers in other states are the only ones who are really firm. Seward is great; a perfect giant in all this howling. Our father is firmer than Mt Ararat. I never saw a more precious old flint. As yet there has been no open defection, but the pressure is immense and you need not swear too much if something gives at last.

Of course your first question would be about Seward. He came up here last Tuesday evening and I heard him talk for the first time. Wednesday he came up to dinner and was absolutely grand. No one was there but the family, and he had all the talking to himself. I sat and watched the old fellow with his big nose and his wire hair and grizzly eyebrows and miserable dress, and listened to him rolling out his grand, broad ideas that would inspire a cow with statesmanship if she understood our language. There's no shake in him. He talks square up to the mark and something beyond it.

He invited us down to dine with him on Friday. His wife hasn't come here this winter, so he has persuaded Mr and Mrs Israel Washburne to put up with him till they go off.[2] We six had a dinner, at which the governor caused a superior champagne to be brought out; not his usual tap. Israel was as usual; ugly as the very devil, but good-humored and nervous and kindhearted as ever. The Governor was chipper as a lark and swore by yea and by nay that everything was going on admirably. The state of society here worries mamma very much and she was sorrowing over the bitterness of feeling and change of bearing in her acquaintances but the Governor was implacable. He swore he was glad of it and delighted to see 'em down. He'd been through all that and come out on the other side. They had been all graciousness to him as a Whig while they tabooed Hale and Sumner and Giddings.[3] They had tried to taboo him too, later, but then it was too late, and now he was glad they did feel cut up and meant they should.

He is the very most glorious original. It delights me out of my skin to see the wiry old scare-crow insinuate advice. He talks so slowly and watches one so hard under those grey eye-brows of his. After our dinner we went into the parlor and played whist. Gradually a whole crowd of visitors came in, mostly staunch men such as Potter and Cad. Washburne, Sedgewick and Alley and Eliot &c.[4] Among others who should turn up but the two R.I. senators, Antony and Simmons, both very fishy and weak-kneed.[5] Antony is the man whom mamma gave a tremendous hiding to, last Spring, for a remark he made more than usually treacherous, but he called on us the other evening notwithstanding. The whole company knew all about it however, and Seward knew they did. I was sitting somewhat back, just behind Antony and Seward and watched them both carefully. Antony remarked deprecatingly; Well, things look pretty bad, Governor; don't you think so?—No! growled Seward—I don't see why they look bad—Well! said Antony still more timidly;—these financial troubles coming so with the political ones—Why, answered Seward; You can't run a financial and a political panic together; the first will regulate itself—Poor Antony fairly broke down and acquiesced. The manner in which Seward spoke fairly bluffed him. But Seward was unmerciful. The first thing we knew he dragged mamma out; wanted to put her against some of these Carolinians; she was the person to take care of them; put 'em in a dark room and let 'em fight it out &c, &c; to all which mamma of course answered laughingly while everyone in the room was on the broad grin. I thought he'd never leave off this talk. He wouldn't stop, but rubbed it in and in till Antony looked blue. At the very first pause and change of topic, he got up and took leave. Of course it did not please mamma too well to be used as a sort of a false target in this way but the Governor only smiled grimly and neither apologised nor confessed his intentions.

Dec. 13.   This letter is still waiting to be finished and this week I've been regularly jammed up for time. What with the duties of secretary, of schoolmaster, of reporter for the papers, and of society-man, I have more than I can do well.

Frank Parker arrived here day before yesterday and will be with you nearly or quite as soon as this.[6] To me fell the duty of guiding his steps and I think he imbibed good republican doctrine and lots of it. All day yesterday we were up at the Senate talking in the cloak-room and to-day I left him in the House where he was well looked to. Last evening I took him down to Seward's, and to-day Seward and Mr & Mrs Israel W. came up to dine with us and him. By the way W.H.S. was urgent on me to tell you that he had lately received a letter from his wife in which she said that a letter dated last October I believe, and addressed "Auburn Mass." had arrived from you after going to its direction. With various complimentary remarks the Gov. said that as he was epistolarily exhausted, he wanted me to acknowledge the receipt of this letter &c &c &c. Mrs S. sent him on the letter I believe, saying that it was too good to be lost.

We had an interesting time to-day. As you of course see, all the mean material we've got is coming out now—Dixon of Con. flattened out, and so has Sherman; so will Antony, Foster, Collamer I believe, and a heap in the lower House.[7] The 33 committee is sitting now every day and all day, and they'll be reporting some damned nonsense or other soon.[8] Today we were all waiting for our good father before dinner, when in he popped in a state of considerable friction and reported that his committee had sprung a resolution on them yielding everything, which had passed in spite of him with only eight negatives; New England, New York and Wisconsin. Seward looked blue and little Washburne was disgusted. However, as it's not to be submitted to the House, but only intended for effect on South Carolina, there's no immediate danger, though it embroils things badly and will inevitably break the Republican line. So we went to dinner and Seward almost killed me by telling some stories and laughing over them. He goes home tomorrow to be gone a week and Mr & Mrs Blatchford who are coming to stay with him will be received by John and entertained by the Washburnes.[9] Why he goes home I don't know. *He* says it's not politics that drives him but W.H.S. is not to be sounded by ordinary lines.

I shall write for the Monday's Advertiser setting some things forth. You may be aware that our good papa bears up the opposition in the 33. I have therefore reserved my fire so far as he is concerned, but now he will have to be sustained. My communications will perhaps be on the crescendo principle and if the battle waxes hot and Charles Hale does not rise to it, you must thumb-screw him a little.[10] Send Dana and Horace Gray round. I shall write to Hildreth too, probably.[11] My theoretical letter of last Monday was good. Damned if it wasn't. I say it because I have my doubts. It takes forty-eight hours for a letter to go and be published so I didn't send one this evening as it would wait till Monday.[12]

We're chipper as can be here and I keep a general look-out over things. Our men are not afraid, but you must prepare for *any* compromise that the South chooses. Our only hope is that they'll kick us out and refuse everything. This is not improbable, but nothing is sure.

I am only making acquaintances so I can't give you much outside news. There is little or no society as yet and will be very little all winter unless the southerners accept the olive-branch. As I am very busy, I don't care much for there is so much life here as to allow one to dispense with balls. Sidney Everett I've seen twice but as yet not to make any treaty with him, so to speak, and I am the less anxious to do so, as he seems wholly taken up with his Carrolls and I see no hurry to get in with them.[13]

The man Bardolph informs me that he himself took the boxes to the steamer or boat or agent, receiving at the same time the bill of lading therefor; the which he is ready to swear to any amount of profanity, as well as the black gentleman who accompanied him. Does that suit you? If not, what would you more?

We are all well and happy. Our mother allows herself to be distressed somewhat by disunion, but in action she is straight and has a reputation such that the fishes are afraid of her. Parker will enlighten you verbatim as to matters here, as he has seen all our side and has gone deep into the state of affairs. I'm afraid however I only speak exact truth when I tell you to prepare yourself for a complete disorganization of our party. If the south show any liberal spirit, the reaction will sweep us out dreadfully and thin our ranks to a skeleton. Luckily we have our President and can hold on till the next flood tide. How many there will be faithful unto the end, I cannot say but I fear me much, not a third of the House. But the Governor will be great; *our* Governor I mean.

Hints of any sort are welcome.

H.B.A.

MS: MHi
1. HA returned to the U.S., voted for Abraham Lincoln, and began the study of law under Horace Gray. He left Boston for Washington to serve as CFA's private secretary for the new session of Congress.
2. Israel Washburn, Jr. (1813–1883) of Maine, Republican representative (earlier Whig) 1851–1861, and Mary Webster Washburn.
3. John Parker Hale (1806–1873) of New Hampshire, first antislavery candidate for the Senate, served 1847–1853, 1855–1865. Joshua Reed Giddings (1795–1864) of Ohio, antislavery Whig representative 1838–1842, resigned after censure by the House, was reelected to fill his own vacancy and served 1842–1859.
4. The five Republican representatives, four born in or north of Boston, were: John Fox Potter (1817–1899) of Wisconsin, served 1857–1863; Cadwallader Colden Washburn (1818–1882) of Wisconsin, brother of Israel Washburn, served 1855–1861; Charles Baldwin Sedgwick (1815–1883) of New York, served 1859–1863; John Bassett Alley (1817–1896) of Massachusetts, served 1859–1867; Thomas Dawes Eliot.
5. Henry Bowen Anthony (1815–1884), Republican senator 1859–1864; James Fowler Simmons (1795–1864), senator 1841–1847 as a Whig, 1857–1862 as a Republican.
6. Francis Edward Parker (1821–1886), lawyer, partner of Richard Henry Dana.
7. All were Republicans: James Dixon (1814–1873), senator 1857–1869; John Sherman (1823–1900) of Ohio, representative 1855–1861, senator 1861–1877, 1881–1897, secretary of the treasury 1877–1881; Lafayette Sabine Foster (1806–1880) of Connecticut, senator 1855–1867; Jacob Collamer (1791–1865) of Vermont, senator 1855–1865.
8. The Committee of Thirty-Three, one representative from each state, was established Dec. 4 to consider the secession crisis. CFA was the member for Massachusetts.
9. Richard Milford Blatchford (1798–1875) of New York, and his wife, Angelica Hamilton Blatchford.
10. Charles Hale (1831–1882), an editor and owner of the Boston *Daily Advertiser* 1850–1864, had published CFA2's letters from Washington earlier in the year. He published 17 unsigned letters by HA, designated as "our own correspondent," Dec. 7–Feb. 11, before coming to Washington to take over the correspondence himself.
11. Richard Hildreth (1807–1865) of Boston, historian and journalist; *History of the United States* (1849–1852).
12. Dated Dec. 7 and published on Dec. 10, the "last Monday" letter on the "republican theory of secession" concluded that "moderation and forbearance are the watchwords now." By Dec. 17 when HA wrote his next letter (published Dec. 20), his proposed defense of CFA proved unnecessary; he reported that the danger of "a violent contest in the House" splitting the North appeared to be over.
13. Henry Sidney Everett (1834–1898), Harvard '55, son of Edward and Charlotte Brooks Everett.

To Charles Francis Adams, Jr.

Tuesday. Dec. 18. 1860.

Dear Charles

I'm a confoundedly unenterprising beggar. It's an outrageous bore to make calls and as society is all at odds and ends here, I make no acquaintances except those of the family. Even political matters are slow. There are no fights. Everyone is good-natured except those who are naturally misanthropic and even those who are so frightened that they can't breathe in more than a whisper, still keep their temper.

This makes it almost slow work. Then we dine at five and after that I don't feel as if I wanted to run much, especially as there are no parties nor receptions. The President divides his time between crying and praying; the Cabinet has resigned or else is occupied in committing treason. Some of them have done both. The people of Washington are firmly convinced that there is to be an attack on Washington by the southerners or else a slave insurrection, and in either case or in any contingency they feel sure of being ruined and murdered. There is no money nor much prospect of any and all sources of income are dry, so that no one can entertain. You see from this that there's no great chance for any violent gaiety.

Every one takes to politics for an occupation, but do you know, to me this whole matter is beginning to get stale. It does not rise to the sublime at all. It is merely the last convulsion of the slave-power, and only makes me glad that the beast is so near his end. I have no fear for the result at all. It must come out right. But what a piece of meanness and rascality, of braggadocio and nonsense the whole affair is. What insolence in the South and what cowardice and vileness at the North. The other day in that precious Committee of Thirty Three where our good father is doing his best to do nothing, in stalked the secessionists with Reuben Davis of Miss. at their head,[1] and flung down a paper which was to be their ultimatum. That was to be taken up at once or the South would secede. The Committee declined to take it up till they had discussed the Fugitive Slave law. So out stalked the secessionists but not wholly away. They only seceded into the next room where they sat in dignity, smoking and watching the remaining members through the folding doors, while Davis returned to say that he did not wish to be misunderstood; they seceded only while the other proposition should be under discussion. Is that not a specimen of those men. Their whole game is a bare bluff.

The heroism of this struggle is over. That belonged to us when we were a minority; when Webster was pulled down and afterwards in the Kansas battle and the Sumner troubles.[2] But now these men are struggling for power and they kick so hard that our men hardly dare say they'll take the prize they've won. In Massachusetts all are sound except Rice, but we've some pretty tight screws on him and I think he'll hold. Thayer I count out. Of course he's gone.[3] But Pennsylvania is rotten to the core just as she was in the revolution when John Adams had such a battle with Dickinson. There is some sound principle in the western counties but Philadelphia is all about our ears. Ohio is not all she should be, and Indiana is all she should not be just as that mean state always was. Illinois is tolerably well in some respects and Wisconsin is a new Vermont, but there's too low a tone everywhere. They don't seem to see their way.

Dec. 20. Mr Appleton and Mr Amory have been on here the last four or five days engaged in saving the Union. Mr Appleton has buried himself among his southern friends so as not to encourage much any politeness on our side. After passing two whole days in the senate-chamber with Mason and his other attachments, he tapped Sumner on the shoulder and pretended to be very glad to see him. Sumner had not taken any notice of him of course till then, but on this notice, he turned round and they shook hands. The conversation however was not very brotherly, as Sumner in answer to some remark on the state of affairs, immediately began to haul the Boston Courier and Caleb Cushing over the coals as the great causes of the present misrepresentation, which Appleton of course couldn't quite agree in.[4] However, it was all friendly enough I believe. Appleton called here when he knew that our father must be at the House, without asking for mamma, and never has called on Sumner at all.

Mr Amory dined here to-day. Mr Etheridge was invited to meet him but didn't come.[5] Anthony of R.I. was also invited and did come. We had a very pleasant dinner. Mr Amory was amusing and told us his experiences in saving the country, which don't seem to have been very successful. He had talked with Douglas a long time and Douglas had been moral, demonstrating from the examples of Wellington and Peale, that a change of sentiments in cases of urgency was the duty of good citizens. Mr Amory seemed to think that Douglas was the very dirtiest beast he had yet met. He is, by the way, by his present course, destroying the power he has left. Pugh's speech to-day was disgusting.[6] Those men are trying to build the Democratic party up again.

That blessed committee is still at work all the time and tomorrow a vote will be taken on the territorial question. Our father's course will be such as not to need much active support since Winter Davis is assuming the decided course of breaking with the south and he will bear the brunt of the battle.[7] It seems likely that no minority report of any consequence will be needed. Tomorrow will decide and I have a letter all ready for next Monday's Advertiser in case the vote should go right. As to last Monday's letter which has not appeared, I am not sorry for it, as it was written when everything looked fishy. You can tell Hale this and mark what he says or looks, for I do much mistrust me that he suppressed that letter. One ought to have appeared this morning and I shall look with curiosity tomorrow to see.

I am not sorry that affairs have taken such a turn as to relieve our father. He will be strongly pushed for the Treasury and I don't care to have him expose himself now. Lincoln is all right. You can rely on that. He has exercised a strong influence through several sources on this committee and always right, but as yet there is no lisp of a Cabinet. Not even Seward had been consulted a week ago, though perhaps this visit of his to New York may have something to do with it.

As for my Advertiser letters, it will take a little time for me to make headway enough here to do much. But I do not wish to hurry matters. As yet there has been no great demand; that is, no active fighting, and I doubt if there will be. But these things will arrange themselves so soon as I begin to take a position here.

Johnson's speech yesterday was a great relief to us and it cut the secessionists dreadfully hard. Jeff. Davis was in a fever all through it and they all lost their temper.[8] Sumner dined here yesterday and was grand as usual, full of the diplomatic corps. He told Alley a little while ago that of course if he went into the Cabinet it could be only as Sec. of State, and Alley recommended him to give up all idea of it. I think he'd better.

H.B.A.

MS: MHi
   1. Reuben Davis (1813–1890), Democratic representative 1857–1861.
   2. HA dates the heroic struggle from the election of 1850 when reaction against the Fugitive Slave Law ended Whig control of Massachusetts and, in CFA's words, "the domination of Daniel Webster" (Diary, Nov. 12, 1850).
   3. Alexander Hamilton Rice (1818–1895), mayor of Boston 1856–1857, Republican representative 1859–1867; Eli Thayer (1819–1899), Republican representative 1859–1861.
   4. William Appleton (1786–1862) of Boston, Whig representative 1851–1855, 1861; William Amory (1804–1888) of Boston, Whig cotton manufacturer; James Murray Mason (1798–1871) of Virginia, Democratic senator 1847–1861; Caleb Cushing (1800–1879) of Newburyport, Mass., chairman of the Democratic conventions of 1860, joined the anti-Douglas, proslavery faction that left the Baltimore meeting and nominated John C. Breckinridge as its candidate for president.
   5. Emerson Etheridge (1819–1902) of Tennessee, Whig representative 1853–1857, 1859–1861.
   6. George Ellis Pugh (1822–1876) of Ohio, Democratic senator 1855–1861.
   7. Henry Winter Davis (1817–1865) of Maryland, representative 1855–1861, 1863–1865, first as American party, then twice as Republican, finally as Unconditional Union party.
   8. Andrew Johnson (1808–1875) of Tennessee, Democratic representative 1843–1853, governor 1853–1857, senator 1857–1862, became Lincoln's vice-president and successor; Jefferson Davis (1808–1889), Democratic senator 1847–1851,1857–1861, became president of the Confederacy.

To Charles Francis Adams, Jr.

Washington. Dec. 22. 1860.

My dear boy

I sent you off a letter last night, but begin another at once as events pass quick here. I sent off a letter this evening to Hale which is important: the most so of any yet, and perhaps a little indiscreet, but as I don't know how much the world knows, I can't judge exactly how much I ought to say. I hoped yesterday that our M.C. for the 3d would get through quietly, without rubbing, but it may not be so. They've been discussing the Territorial business in the Thirty, and Winter Davis has fairly cut himself loose and declared his intention to vote against the Mis. Comp. line as an amendment to the Constitution. He did this yesterday in a speech which followed one from C.F.A., and this speech of C.F.A.'s, may cause some kicking. Our men are now tolerably firm and face the music. Those who voted for the resolution a week ago, offering concession, "whether just cause of complaint existed or not" have been so dreadfully pulled over the coals for it by their constituents that they're now stiff. The President elect has signified too in more ways than one, what the Committee had better do and what leave undone. Now our good father in considering this ultimatum of the south, declared that rather than consent at this day, before the eyes of the whole civilized world, to see a constitution which did not countenance slavery and was made for freemen, turned into an instrument discountenancing freedom and protecting slavery, he would see the Union dissolved and endure the consequences whatever they might be.

Now if the Post or Courier get hold of this and misrepresent it, you must see that the case is rightly stated. Don't dodge the issue. Proclaim that sentiment as loud as you please. We shall stand by that. But recollect to state, in case of attack, that this sentiment was not an ultimatum of Mr A's. The ultimatum came from the other side, and it was an answer to a demand from the south. New England will mostly stand up to this mark, but it is not wished to force it on the Republicans, as a majority cannot be got up to it in Congress and there would infallibly be a disastrous split. However, it looks pretty well here now. After papa's speech, Winter Davis came out with his declaration, which had the effect of utterly discomfiting the southerners and of combining the North. So they did not take a vote, seeing that their ultimatum would be rejected by three or four majority, and today, finding that it was no use, they concluded to adjourn the committee over to next Thursday, so that we have a week's respite to draw breath and get ready for the next round.

The tone of the Republicans improves. Even Corwin is kept down and some of the fishy ones are wholly converted. Tappan of N.H. and Washburne of Wis. swear they wont move a hair nor concede a bad cent's-worth. Dunn of Ind. is all right and Kellogg of Ill. will keep.[1] You will see by my Adv. letter our ideas about compromise, and will understand that we would yield a good deal to avoid a split now which would be very bad. C.F.A. is decided to vote for Winter Davis' proposition, but this is private. It may never come up. Davis says that Maryland is all right; he has seen Gov. Hicks and is sure that there's no secession about her.

That cursed Senate will make trouble if it can. Douglas recants all his heresies; his past life is to be wiped out, and he inscribes the Slave power as his deity on the first page of the new book. I'll bet my head to his old whiskey bottle that this step will lay him out cold in Illinois.

The Pacific rail-road bill has been passed as a bribe to the Pacific states.

But it's not a good bill and at any other time our friends would all have voted against it.

There's nothing more to say. We are in a state of anarchy as far as the President goes, but I doubt the story of his allowing Fort Moultrie to be given up.[2] It can't be true even of him. Mr Amory told us the other day of a letter he had seen from a New York stock-merchant, which ran like this; "The market to-day much affected by political rumors of disturbing tendency. Towards the close of the day a report was circulated that Pres. Buchanan had gone insane, and stocks rose." Pretty commentary on the popular opinion of the President of these Disunited States. But Gen. Scott is reported as saying that Mr Lincoln is a man of power. Several letters have passed between them.[3]

Old Cass after having been kicked by all his colleagues for three years and ten months, has brilliantly invested the remaining two by resigning. He never made such good use of any other two months in his life.[4]

Weed is said to be coming here and if so, there will be trouble perhaps. He has behaved too badly. It may come to a struggle to get Seward to give him up. If he urges concession, C.F.A. will perhaps have to step in.[5]

Yrs ever   H.B.A.

MS: MHi
1. All were representatives: Thomas Corwin (1794–1865) of Ohio served as a Whig 1831–1840 (senator 1845–1850) and as a Republican 1859–1861; Mason Weare Tappan (1817–1886) served 1855–1861; William McKee Dunn (1814–1887) served 1859–1863; William Kellogg (1814–1872) served 1857–1863.
2. South Carolina formally seceded on Dec. 20; Fort Moultrie was the principal fort in Charleston Harbor.
3. General Winfield Scott (1786–1866), Mexican War hero and 1852 presidential candidate, urged strengthening federal forts and preparing defense of Washington. Ignored by Buchanan, he placed his expertise at the service of Lincoln.
4. Lewis Cass resigned as secretary of state Dec. 14.
5. Thurlow Weed (1797–1882), editor of the Albany *Evening Journal* and Republican party manager, was notoriously dictatorial and unsqueamish in handling elections and patronage.

To Charles Francis Adams, Jr.

Washington. 26 Dec. 1860.

My dear Charles

I received a letter from you last night, almost wholly occupied with criticisms on my Advertiser letters. What you say is perfectly true and I am and have been as sensible to it as you. Naturally it is hard at first for a beginner as I am, to strike the key note; still I think I can manage it in time; and meanwhile criticise away just as much as you please. I've had the deuce's own luck, though, for my last letter, intended for Monday's paper, seems to have missed too, and as my next was to have been a pendant to it, I wouldn't write it till I had seen the first in print. I wanted in them to explain the position that Winter Davis and papa are taking on a proposed measure of settlement to be offered by the Republicans on the Committee through papa. So I shall have to begin again and do it all over, I suppose. I can't imagine what has happened to the letter, for I'm sure Hale would have published it if he received it.

I have been rather busy this week in the recess in making calls and getting into a little society, though nothing has begun in that way yet. The only great political excitement has been about the defalcations which I'm not in a way of knowing much about.[1] Gov. Andrew has been on here and I had some talk with him which didn't lead to much.[2] But his visit here will have a good deal of effect on his course. He saw all the people and there is, I believe, no great difference of opinion among the leaders as to the course to be pursued. He told us of a curious conversation he had had with Senator Mason, who is one of that class of secessionists who want to use secession as a means of forcing the North ultimately into yielding everything. They have even a plan by which all the states except New England, New York and Wisconsin and perhaps Michigan should secede and reconstruct the Union without those states. Mason said that he knew of no possible compromise; that slavery and freedom were in conflict and must be; but that if all the Northern states would repeal all their laws prohibiting slavery, perhaps something might be done...But, says Andrew, Massachusetts never passed a law prohibiting slavery. Her courts held that slavery was abolished in Massachusetts by the adoption of the bill of Rights...Well, rejoins Mason, the bill of rights is of the nature of a law...Andrew repeated this conversation to us one morning when he came in to breakfast, and papa, who is posted up, immediately broke out...George Mason, this man's great grandfather was virtually the author of that Bill of Rights. John Adams merely adopted his idea......

So, you see, we are to be towed out to sea, up there in Massachusetts, and left to ourselves. Bon voyage!

Seward has come back but I've not yet seen him. The position of the Republicans is getting stronger every day, thanks to these defalcations and the treason of the Administration. I rather think they'll have to impeach Buchanan in the end. Tomorrow I expect to hear of this settlement measure of the Republicans on the Committee. It will be based on Winter Davis' proposition to admit New Mexico as a State, but I don't know the particulars.[3] Papa will be made to father the thing, being, as Corwin says, the Arch-bishop of antislavery. Davis will support it, I suppose. Andrew accepts it, but the Massachusetts men look very doubtful when they first hear it. With a few exceptions it will however have the support of all the Republicans, and the South will have to take the responsibility of it's rejection, which they will do.

Our good father stands in a position of great power. Crittenden says that he is the greatest block in the way of conciliation,[4] and some one else says that his speech on the territorial question in the Committee will prevent his confirmation as *Secretary of State,* which is rather a wild remark in more ways than one. Now he will have to bear the brunt of all attacks from the ultra men. But he can stand that well enough, and it may even do him good.

Cushing is said to be encouraged. On the one hand he labors under the delusion that there's a great popular re-action in Massachusetts. On the other, the feud between the Douglas and Breckinridge wings of the Democracy, is healed, and they hope that the southern states may be brought back, in which case we should be in a devil of a fix. Still, it is hardly probable that they should be such miserable idiots as to come back before the 4th of March, and once the Cabinet confirmed it's only a question of time anyway.

You see we feel much better here than usual. What may happen, God knows, but if we can drag on to the 4th March, it's all right. I've written a long letter to Hildreth and shall probably write tomorrow to the Advertiser, but nothing can appear till Monday.

I send you a bill of Rice's. "Let it be paid" as Webster said of his protested notes.

H.B.A.

MS: MHi
1. The press covered the case of Godard Bailey, a clerk in the Department of the Interior whose embezzlement came to light because of the secession panic. Less publicized were the major defalcations in the War Department, which prompted Buchanan privately to request Secretary John B. Floyd's resignation.
2. John Albion Andrew (1818–1867) was elected governor of Massachusetts in 1860. One of his first acts was to ready the state militia for war.
3. The proposal was to admit New Mexico without a prohibition of slavery. In testing Southern willingness to get out of the legislative impasse, CFA was confident that slavery could not survive there, for the Territory, organized by Congress with a slave code, had a total of 22 slaves.
4. John Jordan Crittenden (1787–1863) of Kentucky, Whig senator four times from 1817 to 1861, Unionist representative 1861–1863, proposed the Crittenden Compromise, a revival of the Missouri Compromise which would constitutionally guarantee slavery south of 36°30'. CFA was unequivocally opposed.

To Charles Francis Adams, Jr.

Washington 29 Dec. 1860.

My dear boy

I'm sorry to see that you've worried yourself so badly about the "backdown" but as I've written a long letter to Hale about it and as you can obtain from Andrew all the information you want, I can't undertake to discuss it. Just wait till the matter is aired, as it must soon be, for the Committees, after having consumed much time and leaving matters precisely as they stood at first, have adjourned in disgust, and must very soon report. In which case the speaking will begin.[1]

As you up North begin to get mad, we here are getting cool. Fizzle away. Perhaps when the North has been kicked enough, people will stop saving the union. When the northern democrats have had their noses sufficiently ground down by South Carolina, perhaps they'll get tired and resist. It's coming hot and heavy and in a month you'll be cool again as we are, and the Union-savers will be howling for war.

We had a funny dinner here yesterday which would have done you much good. Seward was here with Buffinton and the messenger with the electoral votes, I've forgotten his name.[2] As usual, Seward was great. He kept all the talking to himself and was as chipper as could be. He assents to the "back-down" as you see by the vote on a similar proposition in his committee. We talked away on all the matters of interest and he cussed and swore as usual. I said incidentally that if Major Anderson were disavowed and cashiered it would be a most unfortunate thing. Why so! says he... Why because it would make the north wild, said I, and provoke an outbreak of violence.... And what harm would that do? rejoined he in his gruff way. I hope they'll cashier Anderson and make Scott resign.[3] I *want* the north to be mad. So long as the democrats up there, and the great cities, stick to the south, they'll bully us. If they can only be kicked hard enough to make 'em hit out, there's some chance of settling this matter. Screw 'em up to the war pitch and the south will learn manners. But so long as New York city has it in its power to cut me off from New York state, we can't settle this matter.

The old file has taken a great shine to my cigars and we smoke our good papa perfectly dry after dinner. He submits like a Christian however, and the Governor always finishes two and pockets a third for the way home. He gave us last night a dissertation on dress which was magnificent considering his style of raiment.

After he left, old Pennington came in and sat a couple of hours. He delighted me to a degree inexpressible. I never had seen him before and had a precious tough piece of work to keep my countenance. He rambled ahead in his usual "bonhommy" style, gave his opinions on politics, told how his barn had been burned down at Newark with his horses and carriages; what a splendid run he had made in his District, nearly three thousand ahead of Lincoln and only two hundred behind his opponent, and how his defeat had all come about; what a piece of work he'd had in forming the Committee of 33, and how Eli Thayer expected to represent Massachusetts; how the southerners were over-rated and what a set they were, &c &c &c, till we all were tired to death. He seems to be a good-natured soul, with a great deal of shrewdness, and weak on the side of his self-esteem. He and Seward are two remarkable specimens of the men one meets here. Pennington is a big man and his legs sprawl out over the room and his boots are very prominent and he keeps his knife in his hand, opening and shutting it while he talks. Seward sprawls about too, and snorts and belches and does all sorts of outrageous things, but Pennington's talk is feeble and Seward's, though he says the same things, is brilliant from his manner of putting them. He is by far the roughest diamond I've ever seen, and the originality makes half of the attraction.

This evening mamma and I went down to the Bayards. We found Mrs Bayard and Mabel; your gurl wasn't there. Meb was very gracious and is in one respect, at least, particularly suited to my style; she talks for any number. They were both urgent in their inquiries after you and John and Arthur, and want you all to come on and have a lark before the marriages. Mebble insists that I shall devote myself to her, as both you and John neglected her for her sister. Florence is just now at Baltimore.[4] I shall go there again New Years day, when I've a heap of visits to make, and generally where I'm unknown. Hull and I shall paddle about together.[5] Sid Everett is too patronising by half. I'd rather go alone than go with him.

The Cabinet is in another row as the telegraph will tell you. Poor old Buchanan! I don't see but what he'll have to be impeached. The terror here among the inhabitants is something wonderful to witness. At least the half of them believe that Washington is to be destroyed by fire and sword. Some are providing for a retreat for their families.

MS: MHi

1. CFA's stand on New Mexico seemed a "back-down" because the House of Representatives had previously passed a bill (left pending in the Senate) revoking the slave code there.

2. James Buffinton (1817–1875) of Massachusetts, Republican representative 1855–1863, 1869–1875.

3. Maj. Robert Anderson (1805–1871), with written orders authorizing the decision, removed his Charleston garrison Dec. 26 from Fort Moultrie to the more defensible Fort Sumter. Neither the president nor the secretary of war knew of these orders until after the removal, so their first reactions lent credence to those who saw the withdrawal as military misconduct.

4. James Asheton Bayard, Jr. (1799–1880) of Delaware, Democratic senator 1851–1864, 1867–1869, whose father had served with JQA on the commission that negotiated the Treaty of Ghent. Mrs. Bayard was the former Ann Willing Francis of Philadelphia. Mabel Bayard (1838–1898), later Mrs. John K. Kane, and Florence Bayard (1842–1898), later Mrs. Benoni Lockwood, were their daughters. Arthur Dexter (1830–1897), a grandson of John Adams' secretary of war Samuel Dexter and an intimate friend of CFA2.

5. Isaac Hull Adams (1813–1900), a cousin (son of JQA's brother Thomas Boylston Adams and Ann Harrod Adams) living in Washington.

To Charles Francis Adams, Jr.

Washington. 2 Jan. 1861.

My dear Boy

Your letter dated 29th arrived this evening. I am now so hard worked that I have to subtract from the night in order to keep up my correspondence. First as to business. I am ready to pay you without inconvenience the whole of my debt. So if you want two hundred dollars just say so, and dont be afraid of pinching me. As to my letters, your remarks are very just.

I shall try to work on them. I see that the Times of this morning reprints one of my letters with copious italics. I don't like this. Can they suspect or have they been told whence they come?

Yesterday was quite jovial. Hull and I drove about making visits from noon till five o'clock, and I was introduced to more people than I ever saw before. Some were cordial; others doubtful. At the Bayard's was only Mabel who was jolly as usual, but I've not yet seen Florence. At Mrs John R. Thompson's I met the Carroll's with most brilliant complexions; really quite artistic. At the Pennington's I met Mrs Winter Davis who was indifferent gracious.[1] The Miss Lorings were fascinating as usual. Towards night I got over to Mrs Douglas where I sat a little while and told Mr Rust of Arkansas that I was very glad to see with how much moderation and forbearance gentlemen acted now, for that I thought if all bitterness of manner could be done away with, it would end three quarters of the trouble. Mr Rust is the only man in the committee who is rude and overbearing.[2]

People are in the dumps here; vide my Adv. letter on Friday or Saturday. But the battle is over, I believe, with Floyd's resignation.[3] Meanwhile our good father is becoming a very Jove in his committee. He has now pretty much the entire control of it, and has fairly driven the extremists out of the field, as vide my Adv. letter Saturday. He is making himself a great reputation here and on the whole he is sustained at home. He has an immense hold on Massachusetts.[4] No other men could have done what he has done, for he has changed the whole course of the State and is throwing her whole influence, and more than her due influence into the scale now. I consider that the unity of the Republicans is due in a very great measure to him, as well as the unity in the entire north, and I believe that his action alone may turn the scale in the border states.

Wilson was in here tonight and gave us some news about the Cabinet. He says that Seward will be Premier or rather that he is it already. This is good. Cameron's appointment to the Treasury is thought very bad. People fear jobbing. Bates is good; he will be Attorney General says Wilson. From New England we shall have Mr Gideon F. Welles, which is also good.[5] Of course our father remains where he is—to be Premier, I expect, in '64. He prefers his present position which is certainly one of great power, and I don't know that he's not right for the present. He's a growing man and will soon have a national fame and power inferior to no one unless it be Seward.

His position on the present difficulties will, I think, be sustained in the country, and if it is, as I hope, made the means of uniting the whole North and securing the border-states, our good father will be invincible in Massachusetts. His strong point is in not being a mere Massachusetts politician, nor confined to one idea. This is the second time he has kicked over the traces in Congress and I think it will be a great thing.

South Carolina has got to eat dirt; yea, repent in sack-cloth and ashes. I doubt if any other State goes so far, but all the cotton states may go and welcome if we can keep the border ones. You've no idea how deep the treason is. Joe Lane is said to be at the head of it; that is, when Washington is seized, he will be declared President.[6] Caleb Cushing knows about it too. Couldn't you hang him? I tell you, frater meus, we have just escaped a cursed dangerous plot, and if we have indeed wholly escaped it, it is by God's grace, not for want of traitors.

Seward is well and speaks of you. He's a precious foxy old man, and tells no one his secrets. I'm inclined to think that he has arranged or is arranging everything with Lincoln through Thurlow Weed.

It's one o'clock at night and I've been writing all day. So I must stop off. What did the New York merchant reply to the order of a Charleston house for flour? "Eat your cotton, God damn ye."

Yrs ever   H.B.A.

MS: MHi

1. Josephine Ward Thomson, second wife of Sen. John Renshaw Thomson of New Jersey. Nancy Morris Davis, second wife of Rep. Henry Winter Davis of Maryland.

2. Albert Rust (d. 1870) of Arkansas, Democratic representative 1855–1857, 1859–1861.

3. John Buchanan Floyd (1806–1863) of Arkansas resigned as secretary of war Dec. 29, not in disgrace because of defalcations, but on high principle because he opposed the defense of Charleston Harbor.

4. CFA's New Mexico maneuver had in fact cost him support among antislavery groups at home, but on Jan. 2 he balanced matters by opposing a move to perpetuate slavery in the District of Columbia and by speaking against further concessions.

5. Seward was designated secretary of state; Edward Bates (1793–1869) of Missouri, attorney general; Gideon Welles (1802–1878) of Connecticut, secretary of the navy. Simon Cameron was promised either the Treasury or the War Department (Dec. 30), then neither (Jan. 3), then finally War.

6. Joseph Lane (1801–1881), Democratic delegate to Congress from the Oregon territory 1851–1861, had run for vice-president on the Breckinridge (proslavery Democratic) ticket in 1860.

To Charles Francis Adams, Jr.

Washington. 8 Jan. 1861.[1]

My dear Boy

Your story temporarily bluffs me, but I'll see if I can't find something to go it better. The account shall be settled immediately. If you see Ben Crowninshield I wish you would ask him whether he has received a letter I wrote him in answer to one of his, and why he has not answered it.

I think we do not feel so confident here as usual. Seward is evidently very low-spirited, though that is owing partly to the labor of preparing his speech. But I have noticed a marked change in the tone of our excellent father, consequent on information which he has received but has not confided in me. Until now he has steadily believed that the border-states would not go, and his measures were intended to influence them. But now I think he gives it up. His theory is that all depends on Virginia and that Virginia is lost. If this turns out to be the case, it increases our difficulties very badly. It makes war inevitable; war before the 4th of March.[2]

God forbid that I should croak, or foresee what is not to come. You and I, friend, are young enough to be sanguine where others despair. For one, I intend to remain in this city. If there is war I intend to take such part in it as is necessary or useful. It would be a comfort if such times come, to know that the Massachusetts regiments are ready, and if one can be formed on the Cromwell type, I will enrol myself. Of course we can not doubt the result; but I must confess that I had hoped to avoid a real battle. If Virginia and Maryland secede, they will strike at this city, and we shall have to give them such an extermination that it were better we had not been borne. I do not want to fight them. Is thy servant a South Carolinian that he should do this thing.[3] They are mad, mere maniacs, and I want to lock them up till they become sane; not kill them. I want to educate, humanize and refine them, not send fire and sword among them. Let those that will, howl for war. I claim to be sufficiently philanthropic to dread it, and sufficiently Christian to wish to avoid it and to determine to avoid it, except in self-defence. Tell your warlike friends in Massachusetts that we want no blood-thirsty men here. If the time comes when men are wanted, it will be men who fight because there is no other way; not because they are angry; men who will come with their bibles as well as their rifles and who will pray God to forgive them for every life they take.

I am confident that if an actual conflict could be kept off for a few months, there could be none. The South are too weak to sustain such a delay. There would be a reaction among themselves from mere starvation and ruin. But if Virginia goes out, I do not see how it is to be avoided.

This is solemn, but I have enough self-respect to keep me from joining with any body of men who act from mere passion and the sense of wrong. Don't trust yourself to that set, for they will desert you when you need their support. They don't know what they're after. Support any honorable means of conciliation. Our position will be immensely strengthened by it. We cannot be too much in the right. It is time for us, who claim to lead this movement, to become cool and to do nothing without the fear of God before our eyes.

I passed this evening at the Bayards where I saw Florey for the first time. I like the Bayards well. They're ladies, which is more than I can say for most of the young women here. They send all sorts of regards to you and John and Arthur and hope you will come on. Tomorrow evening I shall take tea there with some of their friends.

Loo is here and is amiable as possible. Since New Years day, I have been laid up by a violent cold which completely upset me, but now it's over. I don't hear much that is very novel. Seward dined here yesterday and was for him quite subdued.

My letters have, I think, done some good in sustaining papa at home and it was a relief to see the Advertiser of yesterday declare itself at last.[4] I am convinced that his course is the only true and great one, and that it will ultimately meet the wishes of the whole North. You need not fear a compromise. The worst that is to be feared is, in my opinion a division in the party. No compromise would, I think, call back the South. We are beyond that stage where a compromise can prevent the struggle. Let them pass their measures if they can; the contest is on us and all the rotten twine that ever was spun, can't tie up this breach.

Yrs ever   H.B.A.

MS: MHi
   1. HA misdated this letter 1860.
   2. CFA, in a secret dispatch to Governor Andrew, Jan. 4, concluded "beyond a doubt" that "the revolutionists have determined to take forcible possession of the Government at Washington before the fourth of March" and advised raising money and troops.
   3. Echoing 2 Kings 8:13.
   4. The newspaper now supported the moderate position of Seward and CFA, who hoped to conciliate pro-Union Southerners and limit the spread of secession.

To Charles Francis Adams, Jr.

Washington. 11 Jan. 1861.

My dear Boy,

Edward Peirce's step in attacking papa in the Atlas & Bee surprises me.[1] I wish to God he would publish papa's letter to him in answer to one to papa; that would I think end him, not that it was severe, for it was not, as his own letter was very polite, but I think the State would prefer our lead. Du reste, what he says is easily demolished and amounts to a misrepresentation and gross ignorance of his subject. It is not that which troubles me. It is the fellow's treason. He thinks papa will go into the Cabinet and he wants his place, but in such a case I hope Claflin will get it.[2]

Apropos of the Cabinet, things are going all round the lot. Lincoln offered Cameron the Treasury without Seward's knowledge. Seward was utterly taken aback and would have preferred any other man. He sent Thurlow Weed on to Springfield to urge C.F.A. for the Treasury, but the New England man selected was Welles and Lincoln seems jealous of C.F.A., as too Sewardish. He wants some one to balance Seward's influence. Meanwhile Cameron's appointment has raised a tremendous storm round Lincoln. Every one is violent against it, and Cameron has actually been forced out. He told Alley lately that he was for C.F.A. for the Treasury, which is queer. He will probably keep the War Dept. for himself as he can job there too. The Massachusetts delegation were raving that Mass. was left out in the cold and all united in a memorial recommending C.F.A. as the N.E. member. Lincoln as yet has resisted all this influence and what will be the end, he knows. I do not. At all events it is not so sure that C.F.A. may not come in after all. He rather dreads the place as the hardest in the whole Government.

We had a very pleasant dinner of nineteen yesterday. Gen. Scott, Winter Davis and his wife, the two Conn. Senators and wives, with Pennington and his three women &c &c &c. Winter Davis wanted to be remembered to you. Scott was pompous as usual. He seemed to hint that the President was vacillating again, but we have him under the screws now so that I think he must go right. His Adj. Keyes wants Maj. Anderson to bombard Charleston in case they fire on his reinforcements. I am utterly delighted with the course of things down there, if only they've hurt some one on the Star of the West. It puts them so in the wrong that they never will recover from it.[3] Then it will raise the North to fever heat and perhaps secure Kentucky. My own wish is to keep cool. No man is fit to take hold now, who is not cool as death. I feel in a continual intoxication in this life. It is magnificent to feel strong and quiet in all this row, and see one's own path clear through all the chaos.

Many remonstrating and many impertinent letters come from the North about papa's propositions, but all either from Garrisonians or men without weight and generally both.[4] Meanwhile his name is kept before the country which is the great balance to any loss on that side. As a measure of statesmanship, I will stake my head on it. As a mere measure of low political policy I think it will help him too.

I sent you a check for $175.00. You can credit me for the balance of twelve dollars in case I have need to make any payments in Boston.

Yrs ever H.B.A.

MS: MHi

1. Edward Lillie Pierce (1829–1897) of Boston, confidant of Sumner and previously a supporter of CFA, attacked the New Mexico plan and other concessions Jan. 9.

2. William Claflin (1818–1905) of Newton, Mass., active in the Free-Soil party from 1848, state senator 1859–1861.

3. The *Star of the West,* an unarmed merchant vessel, carried reinforcements and supplies to Major Anderson at Fort Sumter. Fired upon by Confederate batteries Jan. 9, as it entered Charleston Harbor, it withdrew without casualties—and without Anderson's returning fire from Sumter. Lt. Col. Erasmus Darwin Keyes (1810–1895), military secretary to Gen. Winfield Scott 1860–1861, later commanded the IV Army Corps in the Peninsular campaign. His *Fifty Years of Observation of Men and Events* (1884) gives an intimate picture of Washington social and political life on the eve of the war.

4. The name of William Lloyd Garrison (1805–1879), editor of the *Liberator* and president of the American Anti-Slavery Society, was synonymous with abolitionism; HA notwithstanding, his cause had strong support from the Sumner wing of the Republican party.

To Charles Francis Adams, Jr.

Washington. 17 Jan. 1861.

My dear Boy

For the first time for a good while I have an evening to myself in consequence of not having got in at the Bayards by some chance or other. There is so much calling to do in this good city and it grows so on my hands all the time, that I am hard put to it, to do what I want to get done.

I tell you, my boy, we have been watching the political weathercock hard here for the last six weeks. Hard driven on this lea-shore, as we have been, and forced to sail so close on the wind that the sails keep a continual flapping, we have watched and prayed for a lull in the storm and some sign of a break in the sky. It is hard to say whether it has come now or not, but we think it has. Seward's speech has done great good.[1] As you must see, it sustains and relieves our father on one side, and cuts the ground right from under the feet of the agitators in the border-states as well as the northern Democrats and Whigs on the other. It is next to impossible now to get Maryland out of the Union before the 4th of March whatever may happen, and I think Kentucky and Tennesee are all right, so that we may sail through it all, yet.

As you might suppose, our people are a good deal divided. In Massachusetts, only Rice and perhaps Wilson will support Seward openly; the others have not the courage though several of them would be glad to. I was present at a funny little scene last Sunday, when Sumner and Preston King came up to dine here.[2] You know what sort of a man King is; the most amiable, fat old fanatic that ever existed. Sumner is always offensive to his opponents; he can't help it; but he can no more argue than a cat. He states his proposition and sticks to it, but the commonest special-pleader can knock him into splinters in five minutes. King is never offensive and is always so good-natured as to be pleasant, even when saying things that in Sumner's mouth would be unpardonable.

After dinner, when mamma & Loo and Mary had gone up, and King had got his cigar and decanter of wine, we got into conversation on the settlement measures of the Committee of Thirtythree and the New Mexican proposition and King attacked them in his genial way and Sumner sustained King in those round, oratorical periods that you know so well. I have noticed for some time past that our good father has been getting restive at Sumner. That speech last winter was against his advice, but then Sumner always acts with his eye on his personal figure before posterity and our father with his eye on the national future; which, as you see, are two different ends. This evening I foresaw fun, and sucked my cigar and kept still. Soon it began. After a little good-natured preliminary sparring, King hit out rather harder than usual with something about compromise, and papa parried the blow with some energy. Then Sumner struck in on the other side, with a re-assertion of our being right, and that the South must be made to bend. Egad, it would have done you good to see how papa faced round on him and hit in, one, two, three, quick as lightning. "Sumner, you don't know what you're talking about. Your's is the very kind of stiff-necked obstinacy that will break you down if you persevere," &c &c. All which Sumner took mildly as a lamb and hardly attempted an answer. Still he did make some remark about the unreasonableness of the southern troubles and the want of dignity in our descending to quiet them, whereupon I got out Lord Bacon and read him a few lines of the Essay on Seditions & Troubles which seemed to trouble him badly. The battle went on between King and papa after Sumner had been thus squenched and King maintained himself very well till they talked themselves out and agreed on the points where they should agree to differ. It amounted to this, that King thought that coercion was the only satisfactory end, and that papa declared coercion out of the question if the fifteen slave states go out together.

Sumner was up here again yesterday when papa rapped him again over the knuckles. Ultra as he is, he is the most frightened man round; not personally that I know of, but in believing and repeating all the reports and rumors round town.

Yesterday we had the funniest little party. Seward once invited us all down to dinner, but we insisted that not more than one of our younger set should go at a time with the parent birds. So, finding that he couldn't manage it any other way, he invited us four children to dine with him yesterday; Loo, Mary, Brooks and I. Loo had to leave her bed to do it, as she was just under one of her head-aches, but do it we did in grand style. The Governor was grand. No one but his secretary Mr Harrington was at table with us, but he had up some Moselle wine that Baron Gerold had sent him and we managed to be pretty jolly. He is now, as perhaps you do not know, virtual ruler of this country. Whether he is ever made President or not, he never will be in a more responsible position than he is in now, nor ever have more influence. Since the 8th of December he has been virtually Sec. of State and has been playing a game of chess with the southern men and beaten them too. Tonight he was full of the criticisms on his speech, and the Courier's delighted him. If the Courier said that, he knew he must have said exactly the right thing.

After dinner, the instant we got back into the parlor, out came the cards and he made Loo and Mary sit down and play whist in spite of all resistance on their part. He will have his own way and treats us all as his children. The other evening at our house, after taking off his boots to dry his feet, in the parlor, he patted mamma on the head like a little girl, and told her that she might come down after dinner and pass the evening with us, if she felt lonely without her children. From any other man this would make our dear mother furious, but he is so hopelessly lawless that she submits and feels rather flattered, I think. I have excited immense delight among some young ladies here by a very brilliant proposition which I made, to dye the old sinner's hair bright crimson, paint his face the most brilliant green and his nose yellow, and then to make an exhibition of him as the sage parrot; a bird he wonderfully resembles in manner and profile. If I had a knack at drawing, I would make some such sketch for Vanity Fair.[3]

Today my friend Mr Lars Anderson dined here; the Major's brother.[4] He has been in Charleston, has seen his brother and had all the talk with him he wants. The Gov. of South Carolina allowed him to do so. He says they are all crazy down there, but polite and chivalrous. Every one is a soldier, but no one holds any rank lower than that of Colonel, of whom there are five thousand. He says that his brother can hold out two or three months, though not with comfort, and yesterday when I called and had a talk with him about his brother, he had to wipe his eyes several times in speaking of him and the pride he took in his behavior. He has seen the President & Gen. Scott and had interviews with them, and the result will be one of two things. Either the rebels will allow the Major to have his letters and to get fresh provisions from day to day, or else supplies will be put in at any price and at all hazards. Mr Anderson did not say this, but I infer it. He is hopeful for the Union, and only asks time and line, to let the fit exhaust itself.

The truth is, my boy, a good deal depends for us on a little bit of a fight. Unless this had seemed inevitable, I doubt whether Seward would have made just that speech, or papa his propositions. If that does not happen, I'm afraid that the North may not fully appreciate the concessions of those two gentlemen. But the North ought to be worsted in the fight, in order to put the South in the wrong. If Major Anderson and his whole command were all murdered in cold blood, it would be an excellent thing for the country, much as I should regret it on the part of those individuals.

As for an elaborate paper on things in general here, it's no use. Papa will speak soon; Seward has spoken; I regard the critical point as passed and think that every day will strengthen those two gentlemen. Edward Peirce has dished himself, I believe, and what little temptation I once had to try to serve him up, has gone. The Atlas and Bee is a venemous little sheet and will do papa all the harm it can, which, thank God, is not much. I would like however to have the columns of the Springfield Republican open to me. It's the best paper in the State and carries most weight. Hale amuses me in his arrangement of my letters.

As to business, you wrote me that I owed you $176.25 and that you had $12.74 of mine in your hands. I sent you $175.00. Which according to my understanding leaves a balance of $11.49 in my favor in your hands. How the devil I've succeeded in paying you I hardly comprehend, but somehow or other so it is, and I've an ample margin to work on with till my return when my March dividends come in. If only my taxes don't swamp me.

I am easier about fighting. It is possible that there may be a war, but if I understand Seward, it's more likely to be a siege. We shall blockade and starve them out. They can be tired out in a year. I think, even if they all go; in two years certainly. The cotton states can be finished in nine months or I'm a beggar. It's a mere question of how much money they've got, and South Carolina has spent $1,400,000 in sixty days. That can't last long.

MS: MHi
1. In the Senate Jan. 12, Seward called for conciliation without acquiescence in secession.
2. Preston King (1806–1865) of New York, Democratic representative 1843–1847, 1849–1853, Republican senator 1857–1863.
3. *Vanity Fair* was a New York comic weekly 1859–1863, in imitation of *Punch*.
4. Larz Anderson (1803–1878) of Cincinnati, father of HA's classmate and friend Nicholas Longworth Anderson.

To Charles Francis Adams, Jr.

Washington. 24 Jan. 1861.

My dear Boy

I begin a letter to you though I've little to say, as no new developments have lately come out. We are waiting here. Our father is preparing his speech, the rough draft of which I have quietly read, and which I foresee will raise considerable hesitations in you Hotspurs of the North. I hardly know what to think of the condition of the North now. There are strong signs of a sweeping reaction there. You see our friend Washburne has lost his senatorial election in Wisconsin to a conservative man, and that in the face of his minority report of the Com. of Thirty-three.[1] Pennsylvania is all gone, headed by Cameron, it is hinted, in revenge for having been kicked out of the Cabinet. Lincoln's position is not known, but his course up to this time has shown his utter ignorance of the right way to act, so far as his appointments go. It is said, too, here, that he is not a strong man. I'm afraid they'll manage to compromise us, and for my own part, believing as I do that the game is ours anyway, unless we're forced into a war, I don't care much what they do, except that it splits the party.

Jan. 26.   It's a curious state of things here. I am trying hard to comprehend it, but as I only see one side and am so hard at work that I don't have much chance to see the other, it is rather hard to follow events with a proper appreciation. At all events I think disunion has run its length. With or without compromise it will end, and the states come back. All we have got to do is to see that the rebound doesn't knock us Republicans over.

The speaking has been good this week and the South Americans have come out bravely. Virginia will go, however, I rather think. Still, there's no knowing. I've seen no big men lately to speak of, except Seward who dined here yesterday. He puzzles me more and more. I can't see how he works at all. Now, I'm inclined to believe that all Weed's motions, compromises and all, have been feelers on Seward's part. He will not compromise, himself, but he'll let others believe he will, and anyway, this disunion matter must be stopped; is his theory. He is in communication with pretty much everybody; says he receives as many letters from Virginia as he ever did from New York. Scott and he rule the country and Scott's share in the rule is but small.

Jan. 28.   I am so crowded with work that I have no time to write much on my own account. I have been busy all day copying papa's speech for Hale to publish in advance of the ordinary course. I hope to get it done tomorrow and he will probably speak Thursday. You can judge of it when it appears. As I have not yet read it all in its last form, I can't express an opinion.

The last rumor is a resurrection of the old danger of an attack on Washington. Scott is said to have demanded ten thousand volunteers and Buchanan is unwilling to give them on account of a fear of irritating Virginia. These men are mad if they have such a plan, but mad-men are sometimes dangerous. Nous verrons.

I have written a letter to the Advertiser chaffing the five wise men of Boston, which Hale will not publish I suppose.[2] As he always cuts out the spicy parts of my letters, I don't expect it. Still I thought I would make the attempt.

You can tell Arthur that I've attended to his rooms or rather, room. The price will be a dollar a day for a place to sleep in. As I did not suppose he would want to entertain much, I only engaged, or rather got the refusal of a bed-room. Either Kuhn and Loo, or John and I, as it may be arranged, are to sleep in the same house and if you come on we'll have a mattrass there for you.

Mab'l wishes me to write to Arthur that she will thank him for his charades when he comes on, which she hopes he will do early as she and hers go home to Delaware at or before the 1st of March. They will not stay to the inauguration. Qu. Why? Bayard is a secessionist. Has he reasons for fearing a row, or is it merely hard on his feelings? I was there last evening and talked deep with Florry who thinks, I believe, that I'm something absurd—devil knows what.

There's no fun going on. I know plenty of girls and haven't seen one yet that has made me want to commit suicide, or otherwise. Parties are nowhere. Everyone is down in the mouth and the world is evidently coming to an end. Soit!

The ancient Everett is gadding about, making love to women, and breaking their hearts.[3] Qu. Is his engagement with Mrs Carson on again? The old villian broke it off once.

Adieu   H.

MS: MHi
 1. Washburn and Tappan opposed as unnecessary an amendment to protect slavery in the states where it existed, hating to introduce the word "slavery" into the Constitution. The victor, Timothy Otis Howe (1816–1883), Republican senator 1861–1879, had opposed Wisconsin resistance to the Fugitive Slave Law.
 2. No letter fitting this description appeared in the *Daily Advertiser*.
 3. Edward Everett was 65. He was in Washington as head of the Boston Union Saving Committee.

To Charles Francis Adams, Jr.

Washington. 31 Jan. '61.

My dear Boy

Papa has just spoken.[1] The House listened with a perfectly intense attention, and you could have heard them breathe, I believe, if you'd tried. They were evidently with him and every word told. The galleries which

Charles Francis Adams

Abigail Brooks Adams

were pretty full, applauded him several times. His hour out, an extension was granted which is rather rare now, and he finished, applauded at the close. As usual he held them with a regular grip, and when he ended, every one got up and a poor devil who wanted to speak got mad because no one would listen. I didn't see Sumner there, but old Winthrop and Everett were on the floor and seemed rather less well pleased than I should have thought they would have been. After it was over I saw nearly all the delegation come up to congratulate him very heartily, and a perfect host of others.

In my opinion it's a great speech and one that will tell effectively. It's the best stroke the old gentleman ever made yet. It's what the republicans have got to stand on, and you'll see that everyone will ultimately settle on it except the abolitionists and the disunionists.

Papa has been perfectly overwhelmed with congratulations, the delegation being delighted. Winthrop did not speak to him. Everett shook hands and said he agreed with *nearly* everything he said.

I've never seen papa more affected than by the reception he met. Buffinton got it in, inducing Corwin and Sherman to let him have the floor on the Pacific rail-road bill. This is a *very* rare thing.

The Herald man says he's going to telegraph the whole speech on to New York tonight. Fifteen or twenty thousand copies are already ordered for Maryland.

Loo and Mary called him out from the middle of a swarm of people, and hugged and kissed him in the passage before a heap of women who were all trying to congratulate him too.

On the whole, c'est une grande victoire. Voilà tout!

H.B.A.

MS: MHi
1. CFA spoke in support of the compromises offered by the Committee of Thirty-Three.

To Charles Francis Adams, Jr.

Washington. 5 Feb. 1861.

My dear Boy

Yours of the 17 duly arrived. You find fault with me for not writing more, but as I generally have to sit into the morning hours to write what I do, I can only say I am sorry. As for my Advertiser letters, Hale does not encourage brilliancy. Chaff seems to be his horror and he promptly expunges all that I write of an unfavorable personal character. The consequence is that I lose all interest in what I'm saying, as I'm never sure he will print it. So it is with all our Boston papers. Indeed the Journal has cut Poore's letters so that he pretty much stopped writing at one time I believe.[1] I never see the Journal so I can't say. That was the story here.

Thirty-odd letters arrived this morning full of the most enthusiastic praise of our speech. Personally I am more than satisfied with it and its reception but so far as it's influence on the South goes, I believe it might as well not have been spoken. I'm afraid the game is up and that we shall have to make a new Capital on the Mississipi, for a new Northern Union.

Virginia has decided our fate today. If she has gone, the trouble and violence will begin at once and I have little doubt there will be actual war before the 4th of March. Still, do not repeat this to anyone. It will be known soon enough before there will be any need of getting into a funk over it.

I have little that is new to tell you. Yesterday I went in to see Sumner and found that old beast Gurowski there.[2] I'm afraid Sumner is going to make a fool of himself. His vanity has been hurt and that is enough for him. The difficulty was a miserably small one and not worth the noise it has made. It seems he was consulted as to this appointment of Commissioners to come here.[3] He wrote a letter against it without consulting any of his friends, as any man, asked such a question, of no great importance, might do. The next day John P. Hale who had managed New Hampshire, wanting to be supported, came to C.F.A. and urged him to recommend the measure to Andrew. Accordingly C.F.A. wrote a short form which was signed by all the delegation until he came to Sumner, who then told him that he had written against it the night before. Sumner is said to be hurt with Hale's behavior which was certainly not open, for though Hale says he did not know that Sumner would oppose it, he probably believed he would, and ought at any rate to have consulted him. But meanwhile, Sumner was put in opposition to the delegation, and the Legislature in Massachusetts telegraphed forward and back, making a mountain out of a potato-hill, till it was almost a trial of strength between the two sides. When I saw Sumner, nothing was said, of course, and he told me he expected to dine with us, but he didn't come and I fear he means to make a personal matter of it. He thinks that C.F.A. has ruined himself, and no doubt the whole Garrison wing are doing their best to widen the breach.

Seward on the other hand received the speech with the most generous praise calling it what he had tried to say and had not said so well. A majority of the delegation are with us, I believe, and at all events I have no fear that they will hurt us. But Sumner is no great mind in these things. His vanity, or modesty, or what you will, is sensitive as a woman's.

I have seen no one lately except Col Keyes, Scott's Aid, who was here yesterday and full of war. He says that there is undoubtedly a plot against the Capital, and to put down every doubt and make us all right and as we should be, we need ten thousand men here. If Virginia goes we must have them instanter.

Of the Cabinet I know nothing. It is said that Fogg went to Springfield some time since with letters of introduction from various Senators, and told Lincoln that Cameron was not an honest man.[4] Cameron heard it and says he shall hold those Senators to account for it. God damn the whole thing. Cameron's a mean rascal and will do harm if he can.

You need not be surprised if a joint resolution is sprung on Congress and the votes counted and the election declared before the usual day. It is talked of, but I'm not sure that it can be done. I've not looked up the laws nor heard them discussed.

In spite of the troubles we are tolerably gay here and I am always going somewhere. As usual I passed last (Sunday) evening at the Bayard's where I found old Mason as usual also, and talked with Florence. Mab'l was ill. Complexion perhaps.

H.B.A.

MS: MHi
1. Benjamin Perley Poore (1820–1887), Washington correspondent of the Boston *Journal*.
2. Count Adam Gurowski (1805–1866), a free-lance journalist. A Polish refugee, he proved too dogmatic and mercurial for Boston and moved to Washington in 1860.
3. The "peace convention," called by the state of Virginia as "an earnest effort to adjust the present unhappy controversies," met in closed sessions Feb. 4–27 with 21 states represented. It accomplished little.
4. George Gilman Fogg (1813–1881) of New Hampshire, newspaper publisher and Republican campaign official in 1860, minister to Switzerland 1861–1865.

To Charles Francis Adams, Jr.

Washington. 8 Feb. 1861.

My dear Charles

On coming back from a little dinner with Kuhn and Loo and Mary at Gov. Seward's, I received your yesterday's letter. You counsel boldness at the very time when a bold step might close my mouth permanently. It was but this morning that C.F.A. cautioned me against writing too freely. The New York Times, which has always shown particular respect towards my letters, gave to one of them the other day an official character, reprinting it as a leader, with comments.[1] This makes it very necessary that I should be exceedingly cautious in what I say, unless I want to be closed up altogether. Besides, in the present state of the delegation, when there are but three or at most four who will follow our lead, I can't be very bold without bringing Pangborn on my back, and getting not only myself (which I would rather like) but Papa into hot water.

As for Sumner, the utmost that can be expected is to keep him silent. To bring him round is impossible. God Almighty couldn't do it. He has not made his appearance here for more than a week, though there is as yet, so far as I know, no further change in the position of matters between him and C.F.A. As usual I suppose he will stand on his damned dignity. Once Gov. Seward and he had a quarrel. The Gov. wanted him to vote for an Atlantic Steamship bill, and after exhausting all other arguments, tried to act on his feelings and urged him to vote for it as a personal favor in order to aid his re-election. Sumner replied that he wasn't sent to the Senate to get Mr Sewards re-election. On which the Governor, losing his philosophical self-command, said, "Sumner, you're a damned fool," and they didn't speak again for six months. I'm of Seward's opinion. Let Sumner get the idea that his dignity is hurt, and he *is* a damned fool. However, you can rely upon it, we shall do all we can to prevent his bolting, and I mean to flatter him all to pieces if I have a chance.

The Convention is in secret session. Like most meetings of this sort, I suppose they will potter ahead until no one feels any more interest in them, and then they may die. I have not yet seen any of our Massachusetts men.

This temporizing policy is hard work. I'm sick of it, but the 4th of March is coming and we shall soon be afloat again. These cursed Virginians are so in-grain conceited that it's a perfect nuisance to have anything to do with them. Let the 4th March pass and unless I'm much mistaken they will be allowed to send their secession ordinance to the people, and have it rejected too. Just now however there is nothing for it but to delay. Our measures will pass the House; and perhaps the Senate; at least I think so, but we shall see. Forty or fifty on our side will oppose them, but not violently.

We expect John and Fanny tomorrow night. When do you propose to come? John and I will have to live out of the house.

The ancient Seward is in high spirits and chuckles himself hoarse with his stories. He says it's all right. We shall keep the border states, and in three months or thereabouts, if we hold off, the Unionists and Disunionists will have their hands on each others throats in the cotton states. The storm is weathered.

Yrs ever   H.B.A.

MS: MHi

1. The *Times* (Feb. 6) cited HA's *Advertiser* letter of Feb. 2 expounding the Seward-Adams position and implicitly defending it against opponents who would guarantee slavery even where it did not yet exist (Crittenden) or, on the other side, who would yield no rights to slaveowners (abolitionist Republicans).

To Charles Francis Adams, Jr.

Washington. 13 Feb. 1861.

My dear Charles

The family have gone up to the Capitol to see the counting of the votes.[1] As I don't anticipate any show, and am no longer a reporter and wanted a little leisure to write to you, I've remained at home.

Charles Hale has come on and means to stay over the 4th. I have of course stopped writing for the Advertiser, and left it to him. He evidently had no objection, though complimentary in his remarks generally. On looking back over my letters this winter, I am on the whole tolerably well satisfied with them and their effect. They have had some good influence in shaping the course of opinion in Boston, and the Advertiser and the New

York Times have both profited by them. Now that I'm out of the traces I'm not sorry for it on some accounts. I'm no longer at home, and living out of the house destroys my evenings. Then our house is so full, and there are so many people here and so much society that it's next to impossible to do anything. And finally, the Convention has assumed the whole affair and I should have to take a world of trouble to find out what was going on, and probably couldn't do it at all. At any rate Charles Hale can do it better than I, and wants to, so I am willing.

I don't think much of the Convention. I don't see much ability in it, nor much life. I don't believe any great good can come from it, except to gain time. I think the battle is won. I'm beginning to lose my interest in it since the Tennessee election. In my belief everything is going to simmer down, and wise men will keep quiet. The next Administration will give us trouble enough, and I for one am going upon the business or the pleasure that shall suit me, for every man hath business or desire such as it is, and for my own poor part—look you—I will go write an Article for the Atlantic Monthly, intituled "The great Secession Winter of 1860–61."[2]

Mrs Douglas gave a crush ball last night. Her little beast of a husband was there as usual; God pardon me for abusing my host, whose bread and salt it is true I had no chance to touch, but a very little of whose Champagne I drank, diluted with water, the common property of the human race. Mamma and Fanny went first to the President's reception and afterwards to the ball, and I assure you, the young Crowninshield was some astonished with the sights she saw. It was without any exception the wildest collection of people I ever saw. Next to the President's receptions, the company was beyond all description, promiscuous. Mrs Douglas, who is said to be much depressed by the general condition of things, received and looked as usual—handsome—"Splendidly null"—Poor girl! what the deuce does she look forward to! Her husband is a brute—not to her that I know of—but gross, vulgar, demagogic; a drunkard; ruined as a politician; ruined as a private man; over head and ears—indeed drowned lower than soundings reach—in debt; with no mental or literary resources; without a future; with a past worse than none at all; on the whole I'd rather not be Mrs Douglas. Still, there she stood and shook hands with all her guests, and smiled—and smiled.[3]

A crowd of admiring devotees surrounded the ancient buffer Tyler;[4] another crowd surrounded that other ancient buffer Crittenden. Ye Gods, what are we, when mortals no bigger—no, damn it, not so big as—ourselves, are looked up to as though their thunder spoke from the real original Olympus. Here is an old Virginia politician, of whom by good rights, no one ought ever to have heard, reappearing in the ancient cerements of his forgotten grave—political and social—and men look up at him as they would at Solomon, if he could be made the subject of a resurrection. I nearly got into several fights with various men and women, in the attempt to get through the crowd. I tried a walze with my friend Miss Betty Blair and was obliged to drag her from the room in a suffocating condition, and administer ice to her. I couldn't find any one I wanted, and when I did find them, didn't care to see them again. I showed Fanny all that was to be seen and by twelve o'clock we were at home. Confound such parties as these.

I have little to tell you in politics. I am so taken up with work and play that I've no time to hunt secrets. Sumner still holds out and has not been near us, though he is very cordial when we meet. The trouble there was greater than I supposed. Our irascible papa got into a passion with him for attempting to call Alley to account in his (C.F.A's) presence. Perhaps Sumner might have forgiven this, but then Massachusetts has preferred C.F.A's lead, and that finished him. However, all quarrels and secessions must be healed soon. It's the order of the day.

I've not seen Seward very lately and don't know much about him. He is hard at work I suppose, and I don't like to go down and interrupt him. I can't get over my modesty about those things. The last time he was here he was very jolly indeed and sanguine as could be. Between Lincoln and the secessionists he must have a hard time.

You will be on here so soon that I can talk more at large than by letter, and indeed, you can see more than anyone can tell. Dana's step is a great thing.[5] It raps those confounded Rump Whigs who are doing their worst to hurt us. As it's ground is more than usually distinct and independent it will support us the more.

[*On a separate sheet:*] The votes have been counted peaceably and quietly. We are all right in these parts and waiting the President elect.[6] We shall have a confounded blow in a few days for the commissioners.

MS: MHi

1. The electoral votes were counted before a joint session of Congress.
2. HA wrote the article but did not publish it. It appeared in Massachusetts Historical Society *Proceedings* 43 (1909–1910), 660–687.
3. Adele Cutts (1835–1899), a Maryland belle, grandniece of Dolley Madison, married Stephen A. Douglas in 1856. Douglas suffered from severe rheumatism which he alleviated with heavy drinking. He died four months later at the age of 48. "Splendidly null"; Tennyson, *Maud* (1855), pt. I, canto II.
4. Former President John Tyler (1790–1862) presided over the Peace Convention.
5. Richard Henry Dana's speech at Cambridge, Feb. 11, declared that Lincoln's inauguration would be no menace to the slave states and that the Fugitive Slave Law, however odious, would be enforced. An antislavery Republican, he adopted the CFA policy of conciliating northern Whigs and southern Unionists.
6. The convergence of the Adams family in Washington for the winding up of Congress and for the inauguration, and then their return together to Boston, put an end to HA's letter writing for a while.

To Charles Sumner

Boston. 22 March. [1861]

Dear Sir[1]

We see the nomination of Mr Wilson by today's papers.[2] As I suppose this to be one of Mr Lincoln's selections, of course there is no use in commenting on it. Indeed my father seems rather pleased that the burden of deciding is taken off his shoulders.

Without troubling you further I will merely state that I write to express the hope that Mr Moran may be retained.[3] It is my father's wish also, though this is not an authorized assertion. You will see at once what a position the Embassy would be in if another fresh men were put in, especially if he were an incompetent Westerner though anyway it would be bad enough. Two competent men out of three is a large allowance in our politics. If Mr Moran remains we shall have every reason to be grateful.

Excuse this meddling, of which I know you have too much already. I should not do it except that I fear the appointments will much affect me myself if I am to be Private Secretary, and may throw a lot of work on me that I have no capacity for nor knowledge of.

The nominations seem to have given great satisfaction here. Bill Pennington however, I consider rather heavy.[4] Is it not so? Unavoidable however I suppose. Mr Burlingame will do us great honor.[5] I only wish he could have Mr Howe for second.

Yrs very respectly   Henry B. Adams.

MS: NRU

1. On March 19 CFA learned that Lincoln had nominated him to be minister to England. Sumner was bitterly disappointed at not getting the post himself. HA, whose relation to the old family friend had in Germany become more or less autonomous, kept up relations as his father could not, and so he became an unofficial go-between.

2. Charles Lush Wilson (1818–1878), editor of the Chicago *Daily Journal,* was appointed first secretary of the London legation.

3. Benjamin Moran (1820–1886), assistant secretary of the London legation. For Moran and his views of the Adamses and affairs of the legation, see *The Journal of Benjamin Moran, 1857–1865* (1948).

4. William S. Pennington (b. 1818), secretary of legation in Paris 1861–1865, was the son of William Pennington, speaker of the House.

5. Anson Burlingame was appointed minister to Austria.

To Charles Sumner

Boston. 1 April. 1861.

Dear Sir

Your letter or letters arrived this morning. So far as the papers are concerned only two have I believe made trouble. Much to our surprise the Transcript is unmanageable. Some old grudge against the Doctor.[1] As for the Atlas & Bee which is as usual blackguardly, the more that paper attacks you, the stronger your position will be. The Advertiser, Courier and Post have all been very polite. As for the Traveller and Journal, I suppose they will tail onto the stronger party as usual whichever it is. I have written a letter to the N.Y. Times on the Massachusetts nominations. I don't know that it will be published. If so, of course no one is to know who wrote it.

The Doctor dined here today and it would have done your heart good to see how much his new dignity has set him up. He spoke with great feeling of your action and of the trial you must have gone through for his sake. From many things I can imagine that the struggle must have been a hard one and if that scoundrel Pangborn had anything to do with it, I suppose of course he begged and bullied to the top of your bent. I congratulate you that it is over and trust that it will justify your course fully in the end.

My father got home this evening. He says that you are going off to the West and may not get back here in time to see us before we leave. In that case I have a favor to beg of you. As I may have occasion in England to make some little use of the press now and then, I want to know whether you can put me in the way, or can suggest a way, of getting an entrance into some of the English papers. As I shall be outside of the Legation and un-connected with it, I would like to act independently. Of course you will at once see the advantages of such a course. I make this application, supposing that you in your time must have done very much the same thing and can advise me better than anyone else. Still don't let me take up your time which must be, I imagine, of much value to you now. If you can assist me, it may be done just as well after we get to England, as before. If you cannot, it's no matter. I can manage it perhaps on the other side.

Wishing you a pleasant journey in the West

I remain   Very truly Yrs   Henry B. Adams.

MS: MH
1. Backed by Sumner, Dr. John Gorham Palfrey became postmaster of Boston 1861–1867.

4.

Trials of a
Confidential Secretary

1861–1862

War broke out with the firing on Fort Sumter on April 12, 1861. On May 13, the day the Adamses arrived in London, the British recognized the belligerent status of the South by issuing a Proclamation of Neutrality. Minister Adams' mission was evidently lost in advance. However, since the setback could not be ascribed to any failure on his part, his position was not compromised; he could with dignity keep trying to prevent full recognition. When that next step came, and he expected it soon, he would have to declare it a hostile act and take his official leave. In the meantime, he must act as if a diplomatic break could be prevented. For such a role, his great strength was the ability to seem unruffled. His secretary-son, though he could best ease the strain on his father by seeming unruffled too, practiced that skill at first with uneven success.

Henry Adams' ups and downs with every battle and diplomatic incident chart the fortunes of war. But he suffered his most acute distress from an incident brought on by his secretly doubling as a correspondent for American newspapers. One of his unsigned letters, in which he satirized London hospitality, was accidentally published with his name attached. In January 1862 he found himself ridiculed in the London *Times* and, he believed, "laughed at by all England." The lasting fear of a second such humiliation helped turn him toward the less exposed, more reflective pursuit of politics through historical and philosophical study.

A more mature Henry Adams responded to events by trying to understand them in the widest possible context and to trace their implications "for the next century." Socially as well as intellectually, his temperament became steadier. He endured the diplomatic regimen—as many as three or four receptions in an evening—with something like pleasure. This new self-possession served him well as he emerged from relative isolation and had his first taste of English country life and intellectual friendship.

To Charles Francis Adams, Jr.

London, May 16, 1861.

We are planted here in London, as no doubt other people's letters have told you, in a way that is to me anything but pleasant. Our hotel is poor, our quarters confined, our eating to my overeducated mind miserable. I feel in poor health myself and am easily tired and irritable. London is a great unpleasant body, and my freedom seems to me now of more worth than this sort of existence, where one has Earls' cards on one's table but can't stir a step for fear of violating etiquette. As yet I have no acquaintances. No one has asked me to dinner; nor have I found that my reputation has crossed the Atlantic before me. I pass my time in doing errands and am not sure that this will not be my duty and only duty always. I can assure you, my own share in matters in general will be very small. The Governor was presented today and the Queen was gracious, but made no remark further than to say she believed he had been in England before.[1] Mr. Dallas goes off tomorrow and leaves the Legation today in our hands.[2] Papa and Wilson have been informally introduced and now we have pretty much got going, except that we've not yet found a house. I've been to see several and there's one in Grosvenor Square that would do for six months, but the rent is five hundred dollars a month for three months and it's doubtful whether we could get it for six, even putting aside the rent question. As for taking one for the whole term, I am rather opposed to it now, until we've had time to look about.

The Governor is in the hands of all the usual crowd of old buffers and will begin his dinings out at once, I suppose. Mamma is in good hands and laboring hard with etiquette. Of course we have each day's lesson rehearsed four or five times for our benefit and that of visitors and friends, till there is no danger of any one's forgetting it. A hen with a brood of ducklings is a joke to it. Madam Bates and her daughter, Mrs. Van de Weyer, give us law, and their names are inscribed in high places in our household Gods.[3] Altogether I feel pretty sick and tired of the whole thing, though I am no more than a listener.[4]

Source: Ford I; no manuscript found.

1. Queen Victoria (1819–1901) reportedly appreciated CFA's adherence to court etiquette in his dress (satin breeches, silk stockings, gold braid), unlike his immediate predecessors, who wore ordinary black suits when presenting their credentials: "I am thankful we shall have no more American funerals" (Moran, *Journal*, II, 907).

2. George Mifflin Dallas (1792–1864) of Pennsylvania, minister to Great Britain 1856–1861.

3. Lucretia Sturgis Bates (1788–1863), wife of Joshua Bates of Boston, a banker in the London firm of Baring Brothers since 1828. Their daughter Elizabeth Anne (1820–1878) married Silvain Van de Weyer, Belgian minister to Great Britain.

4. Ford indicates that the rest of the letter was not printed.

To Charles Francis Adams, Jr.

London 10 June 1861.

My dear Charles

Your letters, to the family in general arrived this morning and gave great satisfaction in so far as they were letters, though they made the M. E. & Amb. Plen.[1] as glum as an English Viscount. At that date you had not received our first letters, and as I have not written since then, I feel as though I ought to answer yours at once. It is a relief to know that you are out of the fort and I hope to the Lord that no unhappy chance will carry you off to the wars, however much you may want to go yourself.[2] Not that I want you or anyone to shirk their duties, but simply because I can't see my way straight to where we shall be a year hence, and I don't like to see a man do his best pace on the first quarter. Talking of duties shirked, it has occurred to me that I am probably not innocent in that way myself, for I do not suppose that my property has been taxed. I am not of that mind which approves of neglecting these duties when most called for, and I therefore desire you to make a just estimate of my manifold possessions and hand it in to the authorities, paying said taxes out of such monies as may be received in the way of dividends or may be in your hands. The expenses in this city are enormous and if the Ambassador's private income fails, we must cut our establishment down to a very low figure, as one can do little here with less than forty thousand, and nothing with less than twenty five thousand dollars. People must occasionally live on less, but if so, they must have assistance from the public charities. The scale of living and the prices are curious examples of the beauties of a high civilization.

As for myself, I have only the same old story to sing which I have chanted many times, especially in my letters to you. I have done nothing whatever in the way of entering society, nor do I mean to take the plunge until after my presentation on the 19th. (Court suit = upwards of $200.00). Getting into society is a beastly repulsive piece of work here. Supposing you are invited to a ball. You arrive at eleven o'clock. A footman in powder asks your name and announces you. The lady or ladies of the house receive you and shake hands. You pass on and there you are. You know not a soul. No one offers to introduce you. No one even looks at you with curiosity. London society is so vast that the oldest habitués know only their own sets, and never trouble themselves even to look at anyone else. No one knows that you're a stranger. You see numbers of men and women just as silent and just as strange as yourself. You may go from house to house and from rout to rout and never see a face twice. You may labor for weeks at making acquaintances and yet go again and again to balls where you can't discover a face you ever saw before. And supposing you are in society, what does it amount to! The state dinners are dull, heavy, lifeless, affairs. The balls are solemn stupid crushes without a scintilla of the gaiety of our balls. No one enjoys them so far as I can hear. They are matters of necessity, of position. People have to entertain. They were born to it and it is one of the duties of life. My own wish is quietly to slide into the literary set and leave the heavy society, which without dancing is a frightful and irredeemable bore to me, all on one side.

After the 19th I must set to work to get a club and make acquaintances of my own age; no easy work with English. But I do not expect or wish to do a great deal in this way this season. There is time enough for all that.

You want to be posted up politically. If the Times has published my letters without mutilation, you will see what I think about it.[3] We arrived here just as the Queen's Proclamation was issued.[4] Of course the question arose what course to take. Papa's instructions and especially a later despatch, would have justified him in breaking off at once all diplomatic relations with this Government, and we felt no doubt that, as you say, the Americans would have upheld him. But I must confess such a policy appeared to me to be the extreme of shallowness and folly. In the first place it would have been a tremendous load for the country. In the second place it would have been a mere wanton, mad windmill-hitting, for the sympathies and the policy of England are undoubtedly with us as has been already shown. In the third place it would have been ruin in a merely private point of view. Two such wars would grind us all into rags in America. One is already enough to cut down incomes to a dreadful extent.

Papa took the course that seems to me to have been the correct one. He had an interview with Lord John[5] and told him, without bravado or bragg, how the matter was regarded in America, or was likely to be regarded, and announced plainly what course he should be compelled to take if the Government really entertained any idea of encouraging the insurgents, and demanded a categorical answer as to the course the Government meant to pursue. Lord John promised to send this answer by Lord Lyons,[6] protesting at the same time the unreasonableness of the American feeling, and the perfect good-faith of his Government. Since that time no opportunity has escaped the Government of proving their good-will towards us and unless you in America are run mad, and are determined to run your heads right against a stone wall there need be no more difficulty whatever.

Feeling as I did in the matter, of course I did my best in my letters to the Times to quiet rather than inflame. If you choose you can suggest to the Advertiser a leader developing the view which I take, and pointing out the good sense of our worthy Ambassador in maintaining the dignity of the country and yet avoiding a rupture, as contrasted with those noisy jackasses Clay and Burlingame who have done more harm here than their weak heads were worth a thousand times over.[7] I believe it to be essential to our interests now, that Europe should be held on our side. Our troubles have gone too far to be closed by foreign jealousies. The cotton-states would rather annex themselves to England or Spain than come back to us.

I have tried to get some influence over the press here but as yet have only succeeded in one case which has however been of some use. That is the Morning Herald, whose American editor, a young man named Edge, came to call on the Amb. He is going to America to correspond for his paper; at least he says so. If he brings you a letter, let him be asked out to dine and give him what assistance in the way of introductions he wants. He is withal of passing self-conceit and his large acquaintance is fudge, for he is no more than an adventurer in the press; but his manners are good, and so long as he asks nothing in return, it's better to have him an ally than an enemy.[8]

As to the Article on the last Winter which I left in the drawer of your table at the house, I left with it a note of directions. It was merely to the purport that I had not succeeded in making it fit for publication, and as it stood, it was not to be published, but if on reading it you thought you could make anything of it, you might have it for your pains.[9]

Our life here is not of the gayest, at least to my mind. Not that I care much so far as the outside of the house goes, but the Ambassador is more snappish and sulky than I have known him to be for a long time, and mamma has fits of homesickness that don't make us cheerful while Margaret thinks she's going insane with weeping—damn her, I wish she would,—and Bridget is little better, for Margaret infects her. Mary is of as little count in a house as anyone I ever saw and really is a problem to me, for she seems wholly different from all the rest of us. I'm afraid she won't improve with age. Poor Brooks I took off to boarding school this morning. He's a good boy as ever lived and I've become very fond of him though I treat him like a dog. He was very brave about it and indeed was rather glad to go, for our house is not over-cheerful especially for a boy of his age. His school seems pleasant and clean, and he'll learn to play cricket and be a man.[10]

Tuesday. 11th.   To return to politics, and this in absolute secrecy, for I let you know what I've no business to. A despatch arrived yesterday from Seward, so arrogant in tone and so extraordinary and unparalleled in its demands that it leaves no doubt in my mind that our Government wishes to force a war with all Europe.[11] That is the inevitable result of any attempt to carry out the spirit of the letter of these directions, and such a war is regarded in the despatch itself as the probable result. I have said already that I thought such a policy shallow madness, whether it comes from Seward or from any one else. It is not only a crime; it's a blunder. I have done my best to counteract it; I only wish I could really do anything. I urged papa this morning, as the only man who could by any chance stop the thing, to make an energetic effort and induce the British Government to put us so much in the wrong that we couldn't go further. I think he has made up his mind to some effort of the sort and I hope it will succeed with all my soul.

Does Seward count on the support of France? It is not likely, for this despatch applies as much to her as to England. But if he does he is just as much mistaken as he ever was in his life. Any one who knows Napoleon knows that he means to stick with England. I cannot tell you how I am shocked and horrified by supposing Seward, a man I've admired and respected beyond most men, guilty of what seems to me so wicked and criminal a course as this.

I do not think I exaggerate the danger. I believe that our Government means to have a war with England; I believe that England knows it and is preparing for it; and I believe it will come within two months—if at all. If you have any property liable to be affected by it, change the investment. Don't go into the army yet. Wait for a Canadian campaign and meanwhile live if you can on hay. Our incomes will soon have to go to pay our taxes. There's only one comfort that I see, in the whole matter and that is that within a year we shall all be utterly ruined and our Government broken down; in other words, the war on that scale must be short and we of the commercial interests shall be the first to go under. If I have any marine insurance stock, sell it and invest in Dick Fay's woollen manufacturing arrangement if you can;[12] if not, in anything reasonably safe; Massachusetts or Boston city stocks.

I'm in a panic you see.

H.B.A.

MS: MHi

1. Minister Extraordinary and Ambassador Plenipotentiary.

2. "A pleasanter or more useful five weeks in the educational way, I do not think I ever passed than those during which I played soldier at Fort Independence in April and May, 1861" (CFA2, *Autobiography*, 1915). His militia battalion was on garrison duty at the fort on Castle Island in Boston Harbor.

3. At Washington, HA had met Henry Jarvis Raymond (1820–1869), editor of the *New York Times* 1851–1869 and a Seward-Adams supporter, and secretly arranged to act as London correspondent. The *Times* printed 31 unsigned letters from him, June 7, 1861, to Jan. 21, 1862. His second letter, datelined June 8, was published June 21.

4. The Proclamation of Neutrality, May 13, accorded belligerent rights to the Confederate states but did not recognize their independence.

5. Lord John Russell (1792–1878), 1st Earl Russell after 1861, was foreign secretary 1859–1865.

6. Richard B. P. Lyons (1817–1887), 2nd Baron Lyons, minister to the U.S. 1858–1865.

7. Cassius Clay (1810–1903) of Kentucky, minister to Russia 1861–1862, 1863–1869, and Anson Burlingame were on their way to their posts, loudly denouncing Great Britain. Burlingame, who had befriended the 1848 Hungarian revolutionary Louis Kossuth, was not accepted by the Austrian government and was then sent to China instead.

8. Frederick Milnes Edge published *Slavery Doomed: The Contest Between Free and Slave Labour in the United States* (1860), in which he claimed to have been "behind the scenes" in the 1856 election and to be "personally acquainted with many of the leaders of opinion" in the U.S.

9. "The Great Secession Winter."

10. Margaret and Bridget were family servants. Brooks Adams, youngest of the Adams children, was 13.

11. Seward's Despatch No. 10 (May 21), asserting that the war was a rebellion and the South not entitled to belligerent status, originally instructed the ministers to England and France to demand cessation of intercourse with the Confederate commissioners to those countries. Lincoln modified the dispatch by giving his ministers discretion as to how much of its contents to convey.

12. Richard S. Fay (d. 1882), treasurer of the Middlesex Manufacturing Co. in Lowell, Mass.

To Horace Gray, Jr.

Horace Gray Jr Esq.
39 Court Street. Boston. Mass.

London. 17 June 1861.

Learned Doctor

It is pleasing at least, if not always beneficial to have a certain variety in life, and so far I have nothing to complain of against my destiny which has made of me within twelve months now a gentleman traveller in Europe, now a politician and correspondent of newspapers in Washington, now a student of three days under your fostering care, and finally a budding diplomat in this cheerful village. All four occupations have their pleasant sides and at least are capable of furnishing occupation. Whether the variety will be still further continued is somewhat doubtful, but I don't despair.

As for England, I confess to not being very fond of it. The people are too cold and formal. They never laugh and they amuse themselves with such gravity and earnestness of purpose as is appalling to a lazy person of a cheerful disposition. For my own part I believe that the learned Justice Blackstone is their greatest humorist and that his Commentaries are the best commentary on their character and disposition. I dont wonder that such shoals of them wander out to the uttermost parts of the earth after excitement and new sensations, for sensations seem to be prohibited here by act of Parliament to say nothing of Common Law, and society is as dull and stately as wealth and stupidity can make it. They are not many degrees removed from Chinese Mandarins, I imagine, and it seems to be their ambition to make the resemblance close as possible.

We arrived here some six weeks ago, and found things, politically speaking, in a deuce of a mess. It looked at first very doubtful whether we should not be with you again before you quite expected us. The accounts we got were so bad that we hardly knew what to believe, and people evidently knew so little about our affairs that one hardly knew where to begin. The southern Commissioners had been here for some time working like rats and doing their best to sink us, and had made a decided impression which that old imbecile of a Dallas had done nothing to counteract. Two days after our arrival the Queen's Proclamation appeared and of course compelled my father to make an immediate decision as to the course he was to take.

His instructions as you know were clear and unmistakeable and would have justified him and something more in at once refusing to hold any communications with the Government here. We knew too well enough that such a step would be fully upheld at home and if he had wanted to make a noise and make himself conspicuous, it was a first-rate opportunity. No doubt a good many of you at home fully expected it and would have cheered him on. But he decided otherwise and determined not to do anything violent. Cassius Clay and our friend Burlingame devoted themselves to that sort of diplomacy and a pretty mess they made of it, giving us and our party here a heavier load to carry than Cassius's own lazy, fat, conceited old carcass would have been. My father, though a good deal disappointed, went into the fight, bound to try it out, and not be knocked over by such a foul blow as the Proclamation. He had at once an interview with Lord John who was profoundly civil and disavowed all intention of doing us any harm or the southerners any good, and took amiably a pretty smart hint as to the consequences of pursuing his course, concluding the interview by asking my father in to lunch with him and Mrs R. and all the little Russells. This interview over successfully, my father's course was clear. Before long he was deep in society, invited everywhere and making acquaintances with all the Dukes and Marquesses and Earls in the Kingdom. The effect of these changes in our affairs here was soon very evident. The tone of the press began to change and would have done so much more if those devilish fools in Paris had held their blockhead tongues. In parliament our side at once came up, and Lord John and all the Ministry became wonderfully vigorous in extinguishing the unlucky orators who said anything against us. Finally, and what I consider the greatest victory of all, Lord John issued his orders closing the British ports to armed vessels on each side, and the House of Commons came down with a tremendous avalanche on poor Gregory which stopped his mouth permanently.[1] The southern commissioners fled in dismay to Paris and the field was fairly our own.

Now I don't know how you in America will regard all this, but I must say I feel some pride in our having weathered this very critical point without anything breaking. My father has had the option at any time these six weeks of forcing a war. His instructions would have sustained him and so would the country, but I consider our victory as infinitely more complete and satisfactory now than it could have been in any other way, and unless you at home still remain stuffy and pugnacious, I think it is permanent. My father and Lord John are on the best of terms socially and I see no reason why any more difficulties should arise for some time unless they come from your side of the ocean. Everyone here is polite and cordial as they know how, and though I half suspect I see now and then traces of our friend Sumner's hand not wholly favorable to Mr Seward (this is in deep secrecy, and you must never hint it to anyone) still it would be a very captious person who would not be satisfied with our reception everywhere.

My own part in all this has been small enough. Knowing how hard it is for a stranger to get into English society, I have not yet attempted it at all, but have staid at home reading Blackstone and the newspapers, until my mother has made headway enough for me to step in on her train. This I am going to set about at once and expect a labor duller than a treatise on feudal tenures, and which wont pay me half as well when finished. I have a long theory of action to work out. Literary acquaintances to make, legal and social institutions to examine, such as courts and model lodging-houses, the British Museum and the system of taxation, the daily press and the English Church, all which and much more are open to an enquiring even though a somewhat lazy mind. As usual I expect to be sent away from here just when I am getting into a way of obtaining a little practical knowledge and social position; but that is for the future.

I do not know that there is anything here in the way of gossip that would interest you. As yet I am unacquainted with the celebrities so that I have nothing to say about them. We are in the full blast of the London season which is said to be this year dull to what it usually is, in spite of a degree of solemn entertaining that alarms me of simple ideas. The process of working into our places has been nearly completed by my father and mother but not yet begun by me. On Wednesday we are all presented and make our first appearance at the Queen's drawing-room, which is to be in the deepest mourning for the Duchess of Kent.[2] My father and mother meanwhile are out every evening, generally to a dinner and a ball, or two balls, at which they complain grievously, and with reason, for their health suffers and my father looks and feels badly. But the season is nearly over.

This letter is *very* confidential, so don't quote me, for my good name as a diplomat & believe me

Very truly Yrs　　H. B. Adams.

MS: MH
1. William Henry Gregory (1817–1892) of Coole Park, Galway, whose motion in Parliament to recognize the Confederacy was indefinitely postponed.
2. Victoria Mary Louisa (1786–1861), duchess of Kent, mother of Queen Victoria, had died on March 16.

To Charles Francis Adams, Jr.

[London, 4 July 1861]

[*The first part of the letter is missing.*] . . . is trying them. I took one to-day in company with an ancient red-nosed man whose bodily structure was a curiosity. If I could draw, it would be a grand chance to make studies of the human form divine, for all the obese old port-swilling, gouty wretches, and all the very emaciated, scraggy devils in London frequent these haunts.

My letters in the Times will give you pretty much all I have to say about politics. They are very correctly printed; at least the three first which are all that have reached me. There is no doubt in my mind that all the trouble with England arose from a mere blunder of the Ministry resulting from the suddenness of the change in affairs with us. Here it seems to have been thought with reason that the dissolution of the Union would go as it were by default, without much resistance, and the Ministry and even our warmest friends thought that this would be best for us as well as for themselves. The English are really on our side; of that I have no doubt whatever. But they thought that as a dissolution seemed inevitable and as we seemed to have made up our minds to it, that their Proclamation was just the thing to keep them straight with both sides, and when it turned out otherwise they did their best to correct the mistake. America seems clean daft. She seems to want to quarrel with all the world and now that England has eaten her humble-pie for what was, I must say, a natural mistake from her point of view, I cannot imagine why we should keep on sarsing her. It certainly is not our interest and I have done and shall do all I can, to bring matters straight. As a counter-part to my letters in the Times, I am looking round here for some good paper to take you as its American correspondent. I don't know that I can get one, but certainly it will be a good while before a fair chance is likely to happen. When it does I will let you know.

Seward's tone has improved very much since that crazy despatch that frightened me so. If the Chef had obeyed it literally, he would have made a war in five minutes and annihilated our party here in no time at all. As it is we have worried through safely and are not likely to have much more trouble. There is nothing in the way of particulars to give you so far as I know, for there has been no great scene nor have I met with any remarkable event. Our presentation was only memorable to my mind from having caused a relapse for me, which frightened me nearly to death.

As to your going to the war, I will tell you plainly how the case seems to me to stand. The Chef is unwilling to do anything about it. His idea is that the war will be short and that you will only destroy all your habits of business without gaining anything. If you will take my advice you will say no more about it; only make arrangements so as not to be taken by surprise, and when the time comes, just write and notify him. He will consent to that as a "fait accompli" which he cannot take the responsibility of encouraging himself. As for mamma she drives us all crazy by worrying to let you go. When you are gone she will give us no rest worrying till you're killed. This is my advice, for I see that it is your only way.

As for business. You ask what I wish done with my income. As for that which comes from my property you may let it accumulate up to the sum of £50.0.0, ($250.00) —and then deposit it with Ward to my credit.[1] So often as you have that sum on hand, transmit it. As for my earnings from the Times, draw them every quarter and invest them in some safe way, or if you need it, you can use it yourself to meet your own notes, and credit it to me on your books. I wont charge you interest. It's not the interest that I care for so much as the satisfaction of being able to save something and live well within my income. I enjoy now an income of nearly $2500.00 a year and want to live on $2000.00.

We have at last engaged a house. Soon I hope to feel ready to pitch in again and do something, but just now I seem hardly worth my salt. Give Fanny my love and Remember me to the world in general. If you see Ben Crowninshield tell him to write to me. I have so much writing to do that I can't keep up all my correspondence. You can judge of our society when I tell you that tomorrow I dine at Sir Emerson Tennant's, of the Board of Trade, and go to a ball at Mrs Gladstone's in the evening, and Saturday to the Countess Derby's.[2]

Yrs truly   H.B.A.

Send us maps of the seat of war. The best ones.

MS: MHi

1. Samuel Gray Ward (1817–1907) of New York, American representative of Baring Brothers and longtime family friend.

2. Sir James Emerson Tennent (1804–1869), permanent secretary of the Board of Trade; Catherine Gladstone (1813–1900), wife of the chancellor of the exchequer; Emma Caroline Stanley (d. 1876), wife of the 14th earl of Derby, leader of the (Tory) opposition.

To Charles Francis Adams, Jr.

London 26 July 1861.

My dear Boy

I write again to tell you that I have not sent your pipes by the Crowninshields because I could not find the same ones that I got last Fall here. I shall make inquiries and send them to you as soon as I can get them.

There is nothing new here I believe except that mamma and Mary returned home again to-day from a little trip they have been taking with Uncle Edward.[1] They are full of what they have seen and seem to have had such a good time that I envy them. On Monday we go into our new house and I thank the Lord therefore. A more disagreeable den than our present one I never was in and hope I never shall be. The weather too is so damnable that it would make a crocodile swear. We are literally drowned in rain. Every day we catch it regularly and not enough sun to swear by. The season is over and London is empty; no more parties nor dinners. The Chief and I went to one ball this week at Countess Harrington's where we (of course) knew not one soul.[2] It was a young party with dancing, but very thin for London and many more women than men. The Countess was kind enough to ask if I danced, but as I am an enemy of violent exercise just now I was obliged to decline, so the Chief and I looked on for an hour and then retired. The girls were neither pretty nor attractive and the men dance badly. I did not care to be introduced even if I had known anyone to introduce me, for I should have been expected to dance. Parties amuse me a good deal, for there is a certain feeling of independence about marching into a room where you're an utter stranger; and the family portraits are usually interesting. The suppers are nothing at all. Indeed I never have touched anything anywhere except a little ice. So I stare at the people for a time and then retire as I came.

The tenor of our ways is remarkably even but I seem to effect nothing except a little desultory reading. I am struggling on with Blackstone but as I invariably go to sleep over him, my progress is not rapid. So far as politics go I have nothing to tell you for there is nothing going on. No one is in London nor seems likely to be. I rather fancy that we ourselves will begin travelling before long and see a little of England before the season of country visits begin, when Mary and I will be left in London to take care of ourselves. I tell you my affectionate brother, the prospect of next Fall and winter in London is not one on which my thoughts repose with silent confidence or patient rest. On the contrary I expect to have a pretty long and hard rub of it. It can't be worse than the last three months though.

You say that you wanted to go off with Gordon's Regiment. I tell you, sir, I would give my cocked hat and knee breeches to be with them at this moment. Egad I don't understand being sorry for them. I have no doubt that barring a few lives and legs and arms lost, they'll all like it and be the better for it. And as for the lives and legs, if they estimate theirs as low as I do mine, the loss won't amount to much. Pain is the only thing I should fear, but after all, one's health is just as likely to be benefitted as to be hurt by a campaign, bullets and all, so that this doesn't count. My own task however lies elsewhere and I should be after all hardly the material for a soldier; so that I do my own work and resign the hope of becoming a hero.

My good old Nick Anderson is a Lieut. Colonel, I see. How I'd like to see him. I suppose Rooney Lee has some command also, so it's as likely as not that he and Nick may come in contact.[3] There never was any friendship between them. Indeed they always hated each other, so that the collision would not be so painful to either of them as it might be. There are so many of our friends in the army now and under fire, that I watch with curiosity the lists of casualties. It won't be long before something happens, I suppose.

Give them all at home my love and if there are any young women still in existence, remember me to them. Though in fact the world is upside down just now and I don't expect to be remembered.

Yrs ever   H.B.A.

MS: MHi
1. Edward Brooks (1793–1878) of Boston, ABA's eldest brother, member of the Massachusetts legislature in the 1830s, philanthropist, residing in Europe.
2. Elizabeth Green Stanhope (d. 1898), wife of 5th earl of Harrington.
3. William Henry Fitzhugh Lee (1837–1891) of Virginia, like Anderson a classmate of HA, left Harvard in 1857 to join the army and was at this time a Confederate major of cavalry. He was the son of Gen. Robert E. Lee and was called "Rooney" to distinguish him from his cousin Fitzhugh Lee.

To Charles Francis Adams, Jr.

London 5 August 1861.

My dear Boy

We received yesterday the news of our defeat at Bull's Run,[1] and today your letter and John's with some papers have arrived. Though I do not see that this check necessarily involves all the serious consequences that you draw from it, I am still sufficiently impressed by it to decide me to take a step that I have for some time thought of. If you and John are detained from taking part in the war, the same rule does not apply to me. I am free to act as I please, and from the taste I have had of London life I see no reason for my sacrificing four years to it. Mamma is as well as can be and getting so fat that she puts to shame all her fretting and worry. She can get on perfectly well without my aid. Papa has no real need of me, and what assistance I can give him in the Times is not likely to be needed, as he will probably meet no opposition at home. Meanwhile in other respects my life here is and promises to be no more than that of an upper servant to take the children to walk and try to divert the family. I see no reason why I should remain here where I am of no use.

I wish you, then, on the receipt of this, to go to some one in authority and get a commission for me, if you can; no matter what; second, third Lieutenant or Ensign if you can do no better. They ought to be willing to let me have as much as that. If you can induce the Governor to promise this, see if you can find some fellow I know for a Captain. They say Horace Sargent is going home immediately to raise a regiment. I would serve under him and perhaps other Boston fellows could be mustered under him so as to make it pleasant.[2] If you decide ultimately to go in as Captain, I could serve under you. At any rate I wish to have a commission and if you succeed in arranging it, let me know at once, by telegraph if you can. I can be on the way home in three weeks from this time, almost. A day's notice is ample for me here, and as I know nothing of war or drill and don't care to learn a drill here that I might have to unlearn, it will be necessary for me to begin at once. I don't know that I shouldn't start tomorrow and march in on you with this letter, if it weren't that I don't like to be precipitate, and that I want to watch things here a while. I presume there will be restlessness here although I still believe that England will prove herself more our friend than we suppose.

I have said nothing to mamma about this step, and to papa I have only generally remarked that I should write home and offer my services. I don't care to create opposition which I don't mean to regard. But I wish you to understand that I am in earnest and that if you can get me the place and don't, I shall try to get it by other means. As for reasons for it, your own arguments apply with double force to me. Until now I have thought it my duty to do what I have done. But as the reasons why I should stay decrease, the reasons for going into the army increase, and this last battle turns the scale. It makes no difference whether you go or not. I am the youngest and the most independent of all others, and I claim the right to go as younger son if on no other grounds.

You need not apprehend difficulty on this side. Today is the 5th; this letter should reach you by the 20th and you ought to be able to send me an answer (by telegraph if necessary) by the steamer of the next Saturday to Southampton, or at furthest by that of the next Wednesday, so that I could receive it by this day month as near as may be. If it is favorable I shall leave here in the first steamer, and the first positive knowledge they will have of it here, will be simultaneous with my departure. Papa will not interfere. He never does, in cases where his sons choose to act on their own responsibility, whatever he may think. Mamma has been preaching the doctrine too long to complain if it hits her at last.

We are going on as usual here except that we have got into our new house which is a great improvement. I have two large rooms on the third story which I have been making comfortable. Braggiotti is here; dines with us tomorrow.

Yrs truly   H.B.A.

P.S. 6 August .... After studying over the accounts of the battle and reading Russell's letter to the Times, I hardly know whether to laugh or cry.[3] Of all the ridiculous battles there ever were fought, this seems to me the most so. To a foreigner or to any one not interested in it, the account must be laughable in the extreme. But the disgrace is frightful. The exposé of the condition of our army is not calculated to do us anything but the most unmixed harm here, though it may have the good effect at home of causing these evils to be corrected. If this happens again, farewell to our country for many a day. Bull's Run will be a by-word of ridicule for all time. Our honor will be utterly gone. But yesterday we might have stood against the world. Now none so base to do us reverence.[4] Let us stop our bragging now and hence-forward. Throw Bulls Run in the teeth of any man who dares to talk large. In spite of my mortification, I could not help howling with laughter over a part of Russell's letter. Such a battle of heels. Such a bloodless, ridiculous race for disgrace, history does not record. Unpursued, untouched, without once having even crossed bayonets with the enemy, we have run and saved our precious carcasses from a danger that did not exist. Our flag, what has become of it? Who will respect it? What can we ever say for it after this.

My determination to come home is only increased by this disgrace. I cannot stay here now to stand the taunts of everyone without being able to say a word in defence. Unless I hear from you at once, I shall write myself to Gov. Andrew and to Mr Dana and to everyone else I can think of, and raise Heaven and earth to get a commission. If we must be beaten, and it looks now as though that must ultimately be the case, I want to do all I can not to be included among those who ran away. Our accounts say nothing of the Massachusetts regiments. So far as we have learned, the Pennsylvania and foreign regiments are the only ones known to have disgraced themselves, and the Rhode Island ones stood well. Hurry up and send me my commission quick.

MS: MHi

1. On July 21, in the First Battle of Bull Run, or Manassas, 25 miles southwest of Washington, 60,000 men were engaged, with casualties on both sides totaling 4,700 men.

2. Horace Binney Sargent (1821–1908).

3. William Howard Russell (1821–1907), war correspondent of the London *Times*, reported the Union defeat at First Bull Run, July 22, 23, and the "disgraceful conduct of the Troops" (*Times*, Aug. 6).

4. *Julius Caesar*, III, ii.

To Charles Francis Adams, Jr.

London 7 September. 1861.

My dear Boy

I have to acknowledge several letters, papers, maps &c &c from you since my last. Your's in answer to mine written after the Bull's Run, arrived last night and I answer it at once. Whatever weight your arguments might have had on me in ordinary times, just now they are entirely superseded by the new turn things have taken since that letter was written. I could not go home now if I would, nor would I if I could. Work has increased to such an extent since our return from our excursion, that I am absolutely necessary here. Things have taken a turn which make it every day more probable that we must sooner or later come into collision with England, and of course with that prospect I can't leave the Chief and the family in the lurch. So you need not at present feel any alarm about my blundering home, as you call it, for I promise you fair warning so that you may be down at the wharf to receive me with the towns-people.

Warning you to preserve it a profound secret, I will disclose to you some of the horrors of the prison-house. Remember, your finger ever on your lip.

You may or may not be informed that among the first instructions to the Chef from the Department was one directing him to offer to the British Government the adhesion of the United States to the four articles of the Treaty of Paris. They related as you know to privateering, neutral goods, neutral flags and blockades. The Chef obeyed instructions and ever since we have been here this matter has dragged its slow length along through strange delays, misunderstandings, and discussions that in so simple a matter were very curious and inexplicable. At last the Chef acting under repeated instructions, broke through all objections and brought it to such a point that he and Mr Dayton were agreed to sign the Convention on the same day at Paris and London, with Earl Russell and with M. Thouvenel.[1] The day alone remained to be fixed.

Such was the condition of the negotiation when we went off on our excursion. Before we had returned a note was received from the Foreign Office suggesting a convenient day for signing, but transmitting also the draft of a declaration outside the treaty itself, which Earl Russell proposed to read before signing. It ran as follows;

"In affixing his signature to the Convention of this day between H.M. "the Queen of Great Britain and Ireland and the U.S. of A. the Earl "Russell declares by order of H.M. that H.M. does not intend thereby to "undertake any engagement which shall have any bearing direct or in-"direct on the internal differences now prevailing in the United States."

On receiving this Note the Chief sate down and wrote an elaborate reply. It was in his best style and was certainly an admirable paper. After tearing the whole thing up, and placing, as it seems to me, the British Government in a very awkward and untenable position, he ended by breaking off the negotiation until further instructions from home should command him to resume it. This Note Earl Russell has never replied to. A few days after he sent an answer which sounded to me rather like an apology than anything else, but in this Note he said that he should defer his answer to another time.

So that passed away, but only to give place to a greater excitement. Last Monday a special messenger arrived from Seward bringing the package taken on Mure, directed to Lord Russell. But besides this, which was legitimate, or might be, as coming from the British Consul at Charleston, a great quantity of letters were found on Mure, and among others one that very gravely compromised the British Government. It seems that the British and French Consuls at Charleston have acted *in concert* in making a treaty with Jeff. Davis, and that Treaty nothing less than this very Convention of Paris.[2]

Here was a pretty to-do. Whatever we might suspect, there was no direct proof against England or France nor was it our interest to make a quarrel. So the Chief sits down and writes a long despatch to Lord Russell complimenting very highly the perfect confidence to which the British Government were entitled, and returning to them the bag of despatches. In another short Note he quoted the letter I have mentioned, and demanded the Consul's recall.

To these Notes, no answer has yet been returned. No doubt the graveness of the matter will make a Cabinet meeting necessary, and just now every one is out of town. Lord John however was in Paris on Sunday. Was it to consult with the French Government? You see what a dreadfully tight place they're in and how inevitable the inference of bad faith of a very gross nature, is against them.

These are the signs of the times and will no doubt alarm you enough. I am myself more uneasy than I like to acknowledge in my public letters, but hope we shall worry through yet. They won't like the idea of our privateers here when it gets near them.

As for your recommendation to set up here as letter-writer to the Times, you know not what you say. In the first place, all that I know comes from my position and without it I were nothing. In the second place, there are few beings lower in the social scale in England than writers to newspapers. I should destroy myself beyond a hope of redemption.

No. I am very well as I am. I shall gradually make way and worry along. London does not satisfy all my longings, but *enfin* it is an exciting, hardworking life here, and the Chief and I are as merry as grigs, writing in this delightful old study all day long, opposite to each other. When I say delightful, I stretch a point, but it is not bad.

On the 1st of October I shall send you an order on Raymond for my pay. But bear in mind that if you are pressed for money you can make use of that as well as of my October dividends if you want to. I shall not buy my horse while times are so unsettled and I can easily get on till January with something to spare on my allowance though I mean to propose cutting it down after next quarter-day. The season—from April to August, is more expensive, but until then I can get along on my allowance.

I want you to hunt up the life of John Adams Smith.[3] Isn't there one in your bed-room in the Boston house? Send it to me in the bag. Give my best regards to every one, particularly to Fanny whom I hope to write to. But the pen is never out of my hand.

Yrs truly   H.B.A.

MS: MHi
1. William Lewis Dayton (1807–1864) of New Jersey, U.S. minister to France 1861–1864. Edouard Antoine Thouvenel (1818–1866), French minister of foreign affairs.
2. On August 16 Robert Mure was arrested in New York while en route to Liverpool as a courier for the British consul at Charleston. From a private letter he carried, it came out that the consul had negotiated with the Confederacy for acceptance of the Declaration of Paris and thus taken action which implied official diplomatic recognition.
3. John Adams Smith (1788–1854), son of William Steuben Smith and Abigail Adams Smith, secretary to his uncle JQA in the London legation 1815–1817.

To Charles Francis Adams, Jr.

London 14 September 1861

My dear Boy

Your last letter containing principally suggestions on the cotton matter, reached me this week. Also a bundle of newspapers. At present I am busy in another direction, so that I can't yet take up the subject you recommend, but when my immediate bubbles have burst, or have expanded brilliantly, I mean to see what I can do here. Yet I confess I do not promise myself much from the effort. The main principles which you aim at demonstrating; that the American monopoly of cotton is in fact a curse both to America and to Great Britain, and its destruction might be made the cause of infinite blessings to the whole range of countries under the torrid zone; this principle is and has always been an axiom here.[1] It needs no proof, for the cotton-merchants themselves are the most earnest in asserting it. The real difficulty with regard to cotton does not lie there. It is never the hope of a future good, however great, that actuates people, when they have immediate evils such as this want of cotton will produce, right before their eyes. Nor should I answer any real question by proving that in two years the world will be infinitely benefitted by our war, when what they alone ask is whether meanwhile England will not be ruined. My own belief is that she will be ruined. This next winter will, I fear, be a dreadful one in this country in any case, nor will it be bettered if they make war on us. It is not as if the cotton manufacture alone suffered, but the tariff and the war have between them cut off the whole American trade, export and import, and the consequence has been a very bad season, with a prospect of frightful pressure in the winter. Whole counties will have to be supported by subscription.

This is my idea of the real cotton-problem in this country. I have no doubt that the suffering interests will make a violent push to solve it by urging the Government to attack our blockade. But that is merely the last struggle of a drowning man. The Government will not do it, I think, and most Englishmen speak of the idea as preposterous. If they did, it would only complicate matters still more and I doubt whether even then they got their cotton. The winter over, the new era will dawn on us; that cursed monopoly will be broken and with it the whole power of the South; the slave-trade will then be ended and slavery with it, for the negro will be of no use; and we may expect sunnier days and renewed prosperity. This is the only view that I could advocate, and this, a generally acknowledged truth, is at best but small comfort to a starving people.

Meanwhile we are getting on in these parts. Lord Russell has just answered the Chef's Note, by *refusing* to dismiss Bunch; acknowledging that he acted under instructions;[2] justifying the step as one which implied nothing and in which even pirates might be admitted to join; (i.e. the neutral flag matter); accepting the responsibility for its acts and the consequences; but at the same time declaring that the Ministry has no present intention of recognizing the Southerners, or of leaving their old position.

Of course Seward will revoke Bunch's exequatur, but that need make no trouble. But it is by no means so clear what else may result from this. By a pure accident it was discovered that the British Government were *secretly* entering into connections with the insurgents, and they are now compelled to acknowledge that they have really been acting *behind our backs.* This is no pleasant acknowledgment to make, for evidently secrecy was their object, and the implication is direct against their good-faith. They feel that they have been *found out,* and this for an Englishman is anything but pleasant. The affair will hardly end here.

I have been lately hunting up the newspapers. The other day I called on the Editors of the Spectator and had a long talk with them. I mean to call on, or write to, Hughes, the Tom Brown man, who has vigorously taken our side. The Star too we are in with. Miss Martineau writes for the News and she is an invalid; not to be seen.[3] I may very likely myself turn up some of these days in the lists.

We go out to pass tomorrow at Sheen with old Bates of the Barings.[4] Brooks has gone back to school and I am preparing for London fogs and winter. Summer we have seen little enough of.

Yrs truly   H.

MS: MHi

1. CFA2 thought the British should be advised to break the Southern monopoly by growing cotton in Egypt, India, and other countries with the right climate and cheap labor.

2. Robert Bunch, British consul in Charleston.

3. Thomas Hughes (1822–1896), reformer-politician, educated at Rugby under Dr. Thomas Arnold, *Tom Brown's School Days* (1857); Harriet Martineau (1802–1876), reformer, author of books on her American travels, supporter of abolitionists.

4. Joshua Bates (1788–1864).

To Charles Francis Adams, Jr.

London 28 September. 1861.

My dear Charles

Time goes precious fast and yet seems to leave very little behind it. I have been very busy for the last three weeks but now am at leisure again, though I have some ideas of beginning on a new tack. Papa got back late last night from a visit to Lord Russell's in Scotland. I must say, I think Lord R. was rather hard in making him take all the journey, but as it couldn't well be helped, I am glad it has happened and especially so as it will have an excellent effect on the relations of the two countries. When I last wrote things looked threatening if I recollect right. Since then they have wonderfully cleared away. Lately, except for the Bunch affair and the Negotiation business, England has behaved very well. The Southerners were refused recognition and we are no longer uneasy about the blockade. Lord Russell has explained the Mexican business very satisfactorily and it appears that England is trying to check Spain, not to help her.[1] Lord Russell was very open and confidential towards the Chief and showed him confidential despatches proving the truth of the matter with regard to Spain, besides treating him in every way extremely kindly and confidentially. You know that these are state secrets which no one knows out of the immediate circle here, so you must be very careful not to let it out, even to write back here that you know about it, as it might shake confidence in me.

You may invest any money of mine that you may have, in Treasury Bills if you choose, unless you want it yourself. My own belief is however that the issue of these bills will drive gold out, and ultimately bring down all the stocks very low; say about Spring or the end of winter. In this case ready money will be wanted and good investments will be numerous. So I don't much care if you leave any moneys of mine you may have, quietly on deposite for the present. This loan business has got to be repeated more than once, and I see no hurry to move. Towards January I may want some money here, but just now I've about five hundred dollars which will last well through this year. Don't have any scruple about using any such moneys for yourself. If you must borrow, it would be better to borrow of me at a low rate (if you insist on paying interest) than of a bank at a high one, while the bank may refuse to continue just when you want it most. There ought to be over three hundred dollars of mine in your hands after the Times has paid me.

I have no news for you beyond what I've told. We are all right here, strong and confident. If you win us a victory on your side, the thing's finished. Rosencranz seems to be a good deal of a man, if I understand his double victory over Floyd and Lee.[2] The Lee business has not wholly reached us yet, but seems to be a first-rate thing, as he was one of their great guns.

I occasionally worry a newspaper writer, but advance slowly. Called on Tom Brown Hughes the other day but he was out of town and wont be back for some time. No one is in London, but in about a month I suppose the country visiting will begin and then one may make a few more acquaintances. I sent some little pipes to you by the Hammonds. Nowadays briarwood appears to be the thing, but I myself smoke nothing but clay and Latakia. Cigars are too expensive here, and our stay has been so very doubtful ever since we arrived, that I didn't care to order a quantity from Havana. From there I could get them without the duties.

We are settling down into the depths of a London Autumn. The fogs are beginning and the streets look as no streets in the world do look out of England. Berlin was never so gloomy as London. Every now and then, when things go wrong, I feel a good deal as though I would like to cut and run, but on the whole my position is much better than it was three months ago. I saw a little article of yours, (I suppose) in the Transcript a short time ago, and I hope that you will see in some of the London newspapers if not my writing, at least my hand. They need it, confound 'em.

I enclose an order on the Times. I didn't know precisely how to word it for I don't know how many of my letters he has published. Fourteen or parts of fourteen I know of, but there may be more. I wish you could manage to get the money from Raymond without letting the subordinates into the matter. I doubt if I can carry it on much longer without being known.

Yrs truly.   H.

MS: MHi
1. Benito Juarez, the new president of Mexico, suspended payment of external bonds in July. England and France severed relations and in September negotiated with Spain to send 6,000 troops to enforce payment.
2. In pro-Union western Virginia, Gen. William Starke Rosecrans (1819–1898) fought inconclusively against Gen. John Buchanan Floyd. Then, in the Battle of Cheat Mountain, Sept. 10–15, he decisively turned back the campaign of Gen. Robert E. Lee (1807–1870) to retake the region.

To Charles Francis Adams, Jr.

London. 5 October. 1861.

My dear Boy

Your letter and your articles in the Courier arrived last Monday. I sent one set of them down to Lucas, the Editor of the London Star, and received a complimentary note in return which I will enclose to you.[1] The other set I sent down to the editor of the Spectator, a weekly, and from him I have not heard. There was one article in the Star which was partly drawn from your's, without quoting it, but there has been no reprint. The Spectator never reprints, but if it notices you, I will send you the notice. Your Manchester paper I have made unavailing efforts to find, but London seems to despise anything provincial, and hang me if I can find the paper anywhere. London papers go to Manchester but Manchester ditto don't seem to return the compliment.

This week I have no news for you. Everything seems to be getting along well and the Government here behaves itself very fairly. I don't know whether my last letters will appear or not, but if they do you can form some judgment as to my inventive powers. The truth is that I've lately told so much in that way which was not generally known, that my position began to be too hot and I thought I'd try a little wrong scent. The facts are all invented therefore, but the idea is carried out as faithfully as I could, of quoting the state of English opinion.

We have been overrun by visitors this week. My friend Richardson goes in the Arabia to Boston, if he can, but I'm not sure that he wont have to make Halifax his terminus. He was in a horrible position. His family and property are in New Orleans and he has a brother in the Virginian army. He is himself a good Union man, I believe; at all events he talks so; but he does not want to do anything which will separate him from his family or make them his enemies. So he could not make up his mind to take the oath, and determined rather to run his risk without a passport. I believe he means to pass the winter in Boston. He told me all about his troubles and I strongly advised him not to think of ever living in New Orleans again; at least as an architect.[2]

Sohier and Charley Thorndike have been here this week.[3] Both leave for Paris this morning. Sohier was quite amusing, and dined with us twice. But the trouble about London is that no one ever stays here and I can't keep a companion. As for Englishmen I don't expect to know any of my own age for at least six months more, as this damned club business has got to be settled and the season to come round again first. We see no English people now, or very few, and the fogs are thick almost every morning. Hooroar! Can you find out (*not* through Sumner, who seems to have distorted even your ideas of Washington affairs) what ground Seward takes on the slave question.

Yrs truly   HBA.

I needn't say that the articles are devilish good and made me blue for a day, thinking of my own weak endeavors in the same way.

MS: MHi

1. Two editorials, "English Views," appeared Sept. 16, 17. Samuel Lucas (1811–1864), brother-in-law of John Bright, editor of the *Morning Star* 1860–1865.

2. Henry Hobson Richardson (1838–1886), Harvard '59, studied architecture at the Ecole des Beaux Arts, Paris, 1860–1865.

3. George Brimmer Sohier (1832–1877), Harvard '52, and Charles Thorndike (1834–1910), Harvard '54.

To Charles Francis Adams, Jr.

London 15 October 1861

My dear Charles

In your last letters I am not a little sorry to see that you are falling into the way that to us at this distance seems to be only the mark of weak men, of complaining and fault-finding over the course of events. In mere newspaper correspondents who are not expected to have common sense or judgment, this may be all natural, but you ought to know better, for you have the means for hitting the truth nearer. For my own part I tell you fairly that all the gossip and senseless stories that the generation can invent, shall not, if I can help it, shake for one single instant the firm confidence which I feel in those who are guiding our affairs. You are allowing your own better judgment and knowledge to be overruled by the combined talk of a swarm of people who have neither knowledge nor judgment at all; and what is to be the consequence, I would like to know, if you and men like you, who ought to lead and strengthen public opinion in the right path, now instead of exercising your rights and asserting your power for good, give way to a mere vulgar discouragement merely because the current runs for the moment in that direction. Call you that backing of your friends? A plague upon such backing. Every repetition that is given to these querulous ideas, tends to demoralize us worse than a defeat would, and certainly here abroad is sure to counteract every attempt to restore confidence either in our nation or her institutions.

Even if I believed in the truth of the sort of talk you quote, I would suspend the moral habeas-corpus for a time and deny it. But I don't believe it; and more than that, in all the instances which you quote about which I know anything at all, I know it to be false. You, like a set of people with whom you now for the first time agree, seem to have fallen foul of the President and Cabinet and in fact every one in authority, as the scape-goats for all the fault-finding of the day, simply because their positions prevent them from showing you the truth. Now, so far as military and naval affairs go, I know nothing at all, but one fact I have noticed and this is that our worst misfortunes have come from popular interference with them. Croaking is just as likely to bring another defeat, as that ridiculous bravado which sent our army to Bull Run. But your troubles don't end with the army and navy; if they did, I might perhaps think that your informants really knew something about a matter on which you and I know nothing. You go on to find fault with the President and the Secretary of State, or at least to quote others who find fault, as though there might be something in it. Here I am willing to make a direct issue with your authorities, and you may choose between us which you will believe and whose information you think best entitled to credit. They say that the Secretary of State's education and train of mind are not adapted for these times; that his influence is no longer such as it once was; that you can no longer discern under the surface of events that firm grasp and broad conception that we once admired and bent to, in the founder of the republican party; and finally you quote an old calumny, thirty years ago as common as it is to-day; a year ago as virulent as his prominence could make it; a calumny which you knew then from the testimony of your own eyes and ears to be utterly and outrageously false; and you seem now to suppose that mere repetition is going to shake my own knowledge of facts; my own certainty of conviction; and that too because men who are really ignorant attempt to make you believe that you are so.[1]

You say that Mr Seward's hand is not evident in the course of events. I disagree entirely to any such idea. I think it is very evident and so much so that, feeling perfect confidence in him, I have come to the conclusion that our ideas are wrong and that his are right, at least on one question. I am an abolitionist and so, I think, are you, and so, I think, is Mr Seward; but if he says the time has not yet come; that we must wait till the whole country has time to make the same advance that we have made within the last six months; till we can all move together with but one mind and one idea; then I say: let us wait. It will come. Let us have order and discipline and firm ranks among the soldiers of the Massachusetts school.

But apart from this, when you say that you do not see the hand of the Secretary of State in the course of events, I tell you plainly that you do not know that whereof you speak. I do assure you, and I do pretend to knowledge on this point, that his direction of the Foreign Affairs of the nation has been one of very remarkable ability and energy, and to it we are indebted now in no small degree; in a very large degree, rather; to the freedom from external interference which allows us to give our whole strength to this rebellion. Never before for many years have we been so creditably represented in Europe or has the foreign policy of our country commanded more respect. They will tell you so in Paris and they will tell you so here, if you don't go to such authorities as the Times for your information. The high tone and absolute honor of our country have been maintained with energy and lofty dignity, but are we not on good terms still with foreign nations? Have not the threatening clouds that were hanging over our relations with this country a few months since, been cleared away by an influence that no man of common experience would imagine to be accident? And what of Spain? And Mexico? Trust me, when you come to read the history of these days at some future time, you will no longer think that the hand of the Secretary of State has been paralysed or his broad mind lost its breadth, in a time of civil war.

Now let me read you a lesson in history. When the English nation in the year 1795 were struggling with revolutionary France, their armies were beaten, their allies conquered and forced to sue for peace; every military effort failed the instant it was put forth; famine was in the land; revolution raised its head boldly within the very hearing of Westminster Hall; ill-success of every kind, infinitely greater than our own, dogged their foot-steps at every move; and their credit sank under their enormous subsidies to Austria, and eternal draughts on the money market. But did the English people hesitate to give a firm and noble support to Pitt, their Prime Minister, in spite of his gross failures? Not a bit of it. His majority in Parliament and throughout the nation was firmer than ever, and when he threw open a loan at last to the people, even in such a dark hour as that after Bull Run was to us, noble and peasant, King and Commoner, snapped it up in a single week, at a rate at which the money-market would have nothing to do with it.[2] The English have the true bull-dogs grip, and that is what we must have if we expect to do anything either in victory or in defeat.

My dear Boy

If you think the above worth printing, send it to Charles Hale. If not, no matter.

Yrs truly   HBA.

MS: MHi
   1. When "founder" Seward led the New York Whigs into the year-old party in 1855, his speech announced the "Advent of the Republican Party." As to the baseless "calumny," CFA2 wrote (Sept. 29) that Seward's indecisiveness gave rise to a rumor of his being "befogged with liquor."
   2. William Pitt (1759–1806), second son of William Pitt, 1st earl of Chatham.

To John Gorham Palfrey

London 23 October 1861.

My dear Sir

You may remember that last Spring you suggested at our house one day, certain historic doubts as to Capt. John Smith and Pocahontas. They interested me at the time very much and I have ever since had it in my head to see if something could not be made of the hint, but till lately I have not tried to do anything about it. The other day however I devoted several hours to the matter at the British Museum, and now I want to put before you the conclusions I was forced to come to, so that, if you think there is still a case, I may go on with the search.

I don't think the objections to Smith will stand, at least so far as concerns Pocahontas. Your idea was, I think, that the episode was of London Grub-street manufacture, and the main reason for the doubt, was that Wingfield does not mention Pocahontas in his Diary, written at the time, on the spot.[1] On the other hand nothing is more sure than that Pocahontas existed. The saving of Smith's life he puts in 1607. His first published account of it was printed I believe in 1612, only five years afterwards.[2] Smith had many bitter enemies in Virginia and elsewhere, and if the story had been made up, it is hardly possible that it would not at once have been discredited, since five years are a mere nothing in such a case. But on the contrary it was received universally as true and created quite an excitement in London; naturally enough. In Virginia it seems also to have been known from the first, for we are told from other colonists that the same Pocahontas continued to have a great affection for Smith and the English, and not only saved them from starvation but brought them information at the risk of her life. What her motive was I cannot understand, for she was a mere child, only twelve years old, and could hardly have had a sentimental attachment to Smith; yet her services ceased when he left the province; and she went off to live with a relation on the Potomac. Perhaps it was some wild-Indian semi-lunacy that drove her to it, for I confess I am very sceptical about any pure philanthropy in an Indian child that would drive her through a forest in mid-winter many miles in order to betray her father. Such an act implies strong motives.

But this is not what gravelled me most in the search after doubts. You know that Pocahontas was captured by treachery, married Rolfe, and came to England in 1617. I find in Smith's book published at all events as early as 1625,[3] his letter introducing her to the Queen, and in this letter he re-states all the facts about Pocahontas and distinctly says that she saved his life by throwing herself over him just as the executioner was going to strike. Now could Smith have asserted this if Pocahantas herself, and through her of course her husband, had been able to brand it at once as a fiction? Smith details his own interview with her in England and to my mind it bears the strongest marks of truth. She seems to have been then at least nearly a stranger to him. She had not seen him for near ten years when she was still a child. Everyone who talked with her (and she talked English) must have mentioned this exploit of hers, and she could have had no motive to keep up the falsehood, if it was one. She was notorious enough without it, and seems to have been a sombre, silent, reflective, Indian sort of being, hardly up to such a deceit. Her father too still lived and long conversations of his with English people are extant. We do not hear that he ever denied Smith's story which must have been repeated to him, one would think. He was a remarkable man too. Some of his conversation is very touching, and strangely lifelike.

On the whole I give it up, but would like to know if you think a case is still possible. To my surprise Wingfield is not in the British Museum and I promised Mr Watts[4] to mention the fact to you to see if Mr Dean would not let them have a copy. It certainly ought to be there, and I left my father's at home so that I haven't it to consult. You are remembered still there, and I met Mr Somerby whom you know I presume, who seems also to be deep there.[5]

Your time is too precious for a long answer, so I shan't expect it. A mere line would satisfy me. Pray remember me to your family and believe me

Very respecty Yrs   Henry Brooks Adams.

MS: MH

1. Edward Martin Wingfield (fl. 1586–1613), *A Discourse of Virginia*, ed. Charles Deane (1860).

2. *A Map of Virginia: With a Description of the Countrey, the Commodities, People, Government and Religion,* by "Captaine Smith" (1612).

3. *The Generall Historie of Virginia, New-England and the Summer Isles* (1624).

4. Thomas Watts (1811–1869) of the British Museum library. Charles Deane (1813–1889), Boston merchant and leading collector and editor of early American documents.

5. Horatio Gates Somerby (1805–1872), American genealogist.

To Charles Francis Adams, Jr.

London 25 October 1861.

My dear Boy

Your last week's letter arrived duly. I am rather down in the mouth today so you need not expect a gay letter. The truth is I don't see where we are profiting by all our labors. Nothing seems to succeed. Incapacity seems to show itself wherever we are tried. I shall have patience till the end of the year, but then I shall be for peace, and if we are utterly without honor then, as we promise to be, I mean to come home and be a lawyer until I have money enough to go to Paris again and become an Epicurean hog, a Sardanapalus, by Jove, and drown our disgrace in absynthe and women. The North is a nation of shop-keepers. Look at that "Fanny" affair. By the eternal Jehovah, it's enough to drive one into idiocy.[1]

You complain of the manner in which England has been allowed to wheel round. I mean to write a letter to the Times on that matter some day. Do you know the reason why it is so? How do you suppose we can make a stand here when our own friends fail to support us? Look at the Southerners here. Every man is inspired by the idea of independence and liberty, while we are in a false position. They are active, you say. So they are, every man of them. There are no traitors among *them.* They have an object and they act together. *Their* merchants and friends in Liverpool have been warm and vigorous in their support from the beginning. *Ours* have been lukewarm, never uttering a hearty word on our side, and the best of them such as Peabody[2] and the house of Barings invariably playing directly into the hands of our opponents. They have allowed the game to go by default. Their talk has been desponding, hesitating, an infernal weight round our necks. How can you suppose that we should gain ground with such allies.

But we might nevertheless have carried the day if the news from home had been such as to encourage our party, which was once strong and willing. You know how much encouragement we have had from your side. Every post has taken away on one hand what it brought of good on the other. It has by regular steps sapped the foundations of all confidence in us, in our institutions, our rulers and our honor. How do you suppose we can overcome the effects of the New York press? How do you suppose we can conciliate men whom our tariff is ruining?[3] How do you suppose we can shut people's eyes to the incompetence of Lincoln or the disgusting behavior of many of our volunteers and officers?

I tell you we are in a false position and I am sick of it. My one hope is now on McClellan and if he fails us, then as I say, I give it up.[4] Here we are dying by inches. Every day our authority, prestige and influence sinks lower in this country, and we have the mournful task of trying to bolster up a failing cause. Do you suppose I can go among the newspapers here and maintain our cause with any face, with such backing? Can I pretend to a faith which I did once feel, but feel no longer? By Jove, I feel not seldom sorry in these days that I didn't follow my first impulse, and go into the army with the other fellows.[5] Our side wants spirit. It doesn't ring as it ought.

These little ups and downs; this guerilla war in Missouri and Kentucky, amount to nothing but vexation. Oh, for one spark of genius! I have hopes of McLellan for he doesn't *seem* to have made any great blunders, but I don't know.

We are all in a lull here. The English Government is perfectly passive and likely to remain so.

Will you get a copy of the History of the Ancient and Honorable Artillery Company and send it out in the bag.[6] Moran the Secretary of Legation, wants it.

I am preparing for a visit to Manchester to investigate cotton. Shall take letters from the bankers here, and shall write you a sketch of the result for you to print if you like.

Truly Yrs   H.

MS: MHi

1. The *Fanny* carried ammunition, cannon, and supplies for newly landed Union troops at Fort Hatteras. The unloading was so delayed that Confederate ships were able to capture it with cargo intact.

2. George Peabody (1795–1869) of Massachusetts, head of the London banking firm bearing his name.

3. The recently enacted Morrill Act imposed high protective tariffs, discouraging to British manufacturers and to British free-trade advocates who were Union sympathizers.

4. Gen. George Brinton McClellan (1826–1885) became commander of the Army of the Potomac in August.

5. More than 30 of HA's 90 Harvard classmates served in the Union army.

6. By Zacheriah G. Whitman (1820). This Massachusetts militia company dates back to 1637.

To Charles Francis Adams, Jr.

London 7 November 1861.

My dear Boy

We have just received the account of the disaster to the 20th, and, I tell you, I feel bad. That there was a blunder somewhere I have no doubt, and I am inclined to believe that it was Baker's and that he paid for it with his life. But to lose Lee and Paul Revere and to have your friends wounded and defeated is not atoned for by the fact of its being a blunder. Thank

God it was no worse and that no one was killed. You can imagine I trembled when I ran down the list of losses.[1]

The anxiety with which we are waiting now for the struggle that is coming, is not pleasant to bear. A general battle must come before the month is over, and on its result everything will turn. I shall wait to hear of it before I discuss anything about what is to follow.

Affairs here remain in the old position and promise to remain so until there is something decisive on your side. There is no danger of any movement from England, of that you may be sure, and I have done my best to induce the N.Y. Press to change its tone towards this country, but they *are* damned fools, and they will *remain* damned fools, I suppose, and make our difficulties as great as they possibly can be. The English Government are well disposed enough, at least so far as actions are concerned, and now we hate each other too much to care a brass farthing what our *opinions* may be, on either side. Last May was the time for the contest of opinions. Now it is the most wretched folly to waste a moment over what this or any other country *thinks.* We must induce them not to *act,* but as for their thoughts, I, for one, have been thoroughly satisfied that America can expect no sympathy or assistance in Europe from any Government. They all hate us and fear us, even the most liberal. We must depend wholly on ourselves, and so long as we are strong all will go on, but the instant we lose our strength, down we shall go. The New York press are playing into the hands of the party here which is organized on the basis of anti-blockade.

As for me, I am not wholly lazy. A few days ago I called again on Townsend, the Editor of the Spectator.[2] He says that the present Ministry will stand and that there will be no interference with us even in the case of another defeat. But he doubts about France. Then I called on "Tom Brown" Hughes and had a long talk with him, but not about politics entirely. He is a regular Englishman and evidently one who prides himself on having the English virtues. He is to ask me to dine with him next week.

But my great gun is the Manchester one. Tomorrow evening I start with a pocket-full of letters, for Manchester to investigate that good place. With such recommendations I ought to see everything that is to be seen and learn all that is to be learnt. I am invited to stay with a Mr Stell, an American there, and have accepted.[3] My present plan is to report with as much accuracy as possible all my conversations and all my observations, and to send them to you. Perhaps it might make a magazine article; except that it should be printed as soon as possible. If I find that I can make it effective in that form, I shall write it out and send it to you for the Atlantic. If not I shall contract it and send it to you for the Advertiser or Courier.

As for the matter of your becoming a correspondent of some paper here, I have had it always in my mind, but the difficulty is that every paper here has already one or more American correspondents. I intend to suggest it to Townsend, and should have done so earlier but that I do not think the Spectator cares for correspondents. As for papers against our side, of course I couldn't get you onto one of those, nor would I if I could. George Sumner is writing weekly vile letters in the Morning Post.[4] I wish you would put the screws on him to stop it. He does more harm than his head's worth. So does Charles, here and at home. They're both crazy, and George, at least, unprincipled. Charles, though I believe him to be honest, is actuated by selfish motives.

The Frothinghams leave Southampton for Lisbon to-day, and mamma and the Grand Mufti with our perfect aunt are down there to see them off. Mrs Emmons has arrived here on her way home.[5]

Yrs ever   H.

MS: MHi

1. On Oct. 21 at Ball's Bluff, near Leesburg, Va., Col. Edward Dickinson Baker (1811–1861), former U.S. senator and a friend of Lincoln, led his brigade into a Confederate ambush and was killed. Maj. Paul Joseph Revere (1832–1863) and Col. William Raymond Lee (1804?–1891), both in the 20th Mass. regiment, were taken prisoner. Total Union losses were 49 dead, 158 wounded, and 714 captured or missing. By "no one killed," HA presumably means among his friends.

2. Meredith White Townsend (1831–1911).

3. William Shorter Stell (1800–1863), Philadelphia-born merchant long resident in Manchester, was a friend of John Bright; he entertained many visiting Americans, including William H. Seward.

4. The letters from Boston in the London *Morning Post,* partisan to the South and regarded as Palmerston's newspaper, were attributed to Charles Sumner's brother George (1817–1863), a lecturer and journalist.

5. Nathaniel Langdon Frothingham (1793–1870), Unitarian clergyman, married Ann Gorham Brooks, HA's aunt. "Grand Mufti" is one of the fanciful epithets HA applied to his rich uncle Sidney Brooks. Mrs. Elizabeth Ware Wales Emmons was the mother of Samuel Franklin Emmons, HA's childhood friend and nearest neighbor in Quincy.

To Charles Francis Adams, Jr.

London 30 Nov. 1861.

My dear Boy

If I thought the state of things bad last week you may imagine what I think of them now. In fact I consider that we are dished, and that our position is hopeless. If the Administration ordered the capture of those men, I am satisfied that our present authorities are very unsuitable persons to conduct a war like this or to remain in the direction of our affairs.[1] It is our ruin. Do not deceive yourself about the position of England. We might have preserved our dignity in many ways without going to war with her, and our party in the Cabinet was always strong enough to maintain peace here and keep down the anti-blockaders. But now all the fat's in the fire, and I feel like going off and taking up my old German life again as a permanency. It is devilish disagreeable to act the part of Sisyphus especially when it is our own friends who are trying to crush us under the rock.

What part it is reserved to us to play in this very tragical comedy I am utterly unable to tell. The Government has left us in the most awkward and unfair position. They have given no warning that such an act was thought of, and seem almost to have purposely encouraged us to waste our strength in trying to maintain the relations which it was itself intending to destroy. I am half-mad with vexation and despair. If papa is ordered home I shall do as Fairfax did, and go into the war with 'peace' on my mind and lips.[2]

Our position here is of course very unpleasant just now. We were to have gone to Lord Hatherton's on Monday, but now our visit is put off, and I am not without expectations that a very few weeks may see us either on our way home or on the continent. I think that the New Year will see the end.

This nation means to make war. Do not doubt it. What Seward means is more than I can guess. But if he means war also, or to run as close as he can without touching, then I say that Mr Seward is the greatest criminal we've had yet.

We have friends here still, but very few. Bright dined with us last night, and is with us, but is evidently hopeless of seeing anything good.[3] Besides, his assistance at such a time as this is evidently a disadvantage to us, for he is now wholly out of power and influence. Our friends are all very much cast down and my friends of the Spectator sent up to me in a dreadful state and asked me to come down to see them, which I did, and they complained bitterly of the position we were now in. I had of course the pleasure of returning the complaint to any extent, but after all this is poor consolation.

Our good father is cool but evidently of the same mind as I am. He has seen Lord Russell but could give him no information, and my Lord did not volunteer any on his side. You will know very soon what you are to expect.

The house is not cheerful, and our good mother is in a state that does not tend to raise our spirits. Still we manage to worry along and I reserve my complaints for paper. Our minds have been so kept on the stretch for the last week that I feel a sort of permanent lowness and wretchedness which does not prevent laughing and gossiping though it does not give them much zest. Theodore writes me from Paris. No news of importance has yet reached my ears, but you will see my views as usual in the Times. We are preparing for a departure, though as yet we have taken no positive steps towards making future arrangements.

Beaufort was good.[4] It gave me one glorious day worth a large share of all the anxiety and trouble that preceded and have followed it. Our cry now must be emancipation and arming the slaves.

Ever Yrs   HB.A.

MS: MHi

1. On Nov. 8 Capt. Charles Wilkes of the U.S.S. *Jacinto,* acting without instructions, boarded the British mail steamer *Trent* on the high seas and removed the newly appointed Confederate envoys to England and France, James M. Mason and John Slidell.

2. Thomas Fairfax (1612–1671), 3rd Baron Fairfax, commander in chief 1645–1650 of the Parliamentary forces in the English civil war.

3. John Bright (1811–1889), M.P., Quaker industrialist and reformer, founder of the Anti-Corn Law League.

4. Port Royal Island, S.C., whose only town was Beaufort, was captured by Union forces Nov. 7.

To Charles Francis Adams, Jr.

London 13 December 1861

My dear Charles

Your letter to papa announcing your metamorphosis took us as you may suppose a good deal by surprise.[1] I endorsed it at once. As you say, one of us ought to go, and though of the three as a mere matter of accidental position I might have preferred that it should be John, still, as a question of greater or lesser evil perhaps it's best that it should be you. If we come home, perhaps I may try it myself a little, but if we stay abroad, or if I come home alone, I do not suppose I shall be compelled to do so. At the same time, as a personal matter, I'm sorry you're going, especially as I have, since this last shock, become satisfied that we must sooner or later yield the matter. As a mere question of independence I believe the thing to be settled. We cannot bring the South back. As a question of terms and as a means of thoroughly shaking the whole Southern system, I'm not sorry to see the pressure kept up.

Your good father was more overset by the information than any of us. He is, I regret to say, *tant soit peu* selfish on such points, and has a nervous dread of exposure. He even went so far as to talk pretty plainly with mamma about it, and almost drove her frantic by a bitter remark or two. So she moped about the house with red eyes for a day or two declaring that she never could forgive him, but I scolded and swore some and created a counter-irritant so far as I could, and between us Mary and I have managed to restore peace to the establishment. Luckily we have too many things to think of than to let us ponder long about any one. All I can say is: The scrape's a bad one; you were forced into it; and the sooner you are clear of it, the better.

You can imagine our existence here. Angry and hateful as I am of Great Britain, I still can't help laughing and cursing at the same time as I see the accounts of the talk of our people. What a bloody set of fools they are! How in the name of all that's conceivable could you suppose that England would sit quiet under such an insult. *We* should have jumped out of our boots at such a one. And there's Judge Bigelow parading bad law "at the cannon's mouth"[2] and Gov. Andrew all cock-a-hoop, and Dana so unaccustomed confident, and Mr Everett following that "Great authority" George Sumner into a ditch, "blind leader of the blind"! Good God, what's got into you all?[3] What in Hell do you mean by deserting now the great principles of our fathers;[4] by returning to the vomit of that dog Great Britain? What do you mean by asserting now principles against which every Adams yet has protested and resisted? You're mad, all of you. It's pitiable to see such idiocy in a nation. There's the New York Times which I warned only in my last letter against such an act, and its consequences; and now I find the passage erased, and editorial assurances that war was *impossible* on such grounds. Egad; who knew best, Raymond or I? War is not only possible but inevitable on that ground; and *we* shall be forced to declare it. England can compel us to appear to act as the aggressors in future as now.

Thurlow Weed is here and hard at work on public opinion. He is excessively anxious about the meeting of Congress and thinks we shall be talked into a war. I have had some talk with him and like him very much. He dined with us the other day in company with several people. His daughter is with him. Tonight he goes over again to Paris.

The Government has not yet condescended to send us one single word as to the present question. I wonder what Seward supposes a Minister can do or is put here for, if he isn't to know what to do or to say. It makes papa's position here very embarrassing, and if he were to see Lord Russell coming along the street, I believe he'd run as fast as he could down the nearest alley.

Why on earth didn't John or Fanny let mamma know that there was going to be a grandchild? Were they modest or lazy or what? We knew it through Loo and have waited patiently for official intelligence. I am glad of it, very. It relieves both of us from the necessity of marrying now and, (in case I want one) gives me an excuse for not marrying at all. You can go into the army with a calm conscience and I have a wide margin before me.

If you are still in Boston & have time I wish you'd go over to Charleston and ask Rebecca what she would like for a Christmas present. If you have no time, you or John can enclose her a five dollar bill on my account, and say that if there's anything I can get for her besides to make her comfortable, I'll get it at once.

Ever Yrs   H.

MS: MHi

1. CFA2 had applied for a commission as first lieutenant in the 1st Massachusetts Cavalry. He was officially accepted Dec. 19, and on Dec. 28 his regiment left Boston for Port Royal.

2. George Tyler Bigelow (1810–1878), justice of the Massachusetts supreme court 1850–1862, a Quincy neighbor of the Adamses; "Seeking the bubble reputation / Even in the cannon's mouth" (*As You Like It,* II, vii).

3. The seizure of Mason and Slidell was greeted in the North with jubilation. In Boston, Captain Wilkes was given a hero's welcome and a public dinner by Governor Andrew. George Sumner published in the Boston *Transcript* (Nov. 19) a widely reprinted letter citing historical precedents to justify the legality of the action. Edward Everett and others similarly found justification in international law.

4. The rights of neutral commerce.

To Charles Francis Adams, Jr.

London 28 December. 1861.

My dear Charles

I did not write to you last week as I was very busy and had little to say. Your last letter came duly to hand. I believe it needs no precise answer. Your disposal of the Michigan Central was wise and I don't doubt you are glad of it now. You say I've sounded the Alarm vigorously several times. So I have, but with reason. It was so about the Nashville and is so still more about the Trent.

The difficulty of our position here consists first in the fact that the South are in London a nation, and in Washington no nation; and second, that Seward will not submit to this fact as an evil of which the least said the better. No doubt you have read his state papers and see what I mean. They are admirable works; they show great ability; but they want tact. He shaves closer to the teeth of the lion than he ought. No one has a right to risk so much for a mere point of form.

It *is* a mere point of form. The Nashville business can have only one of two results; one, the recognition of the belligerent rights of the South by our Government; the other, a suspension of relations, either preceding or following measures of force, as threatened in the despatch I spoke of to you, now published.[1]

Again, about the Trent affair. Our lawyers have shown a strange want of close logic. The seizure of the commissioners can only be justified in one of two ways. If Seward sticks to his rebel theory, he must claim a right to do that which is most repugnant to our whole history and sense of right. He must defend a violation of the right of asylum.

If he claims them as contraband, setting aside other legal objections, he acknowledges the South as belligerents, by the act.

From every word he has written I am bound to believe that he will not do the latter. But if he adheres to his old view, I can see no means of preserving our relations with this Court in either the Nashville or the Trent difficulties.

For these reasons I think that our stay here is at an end. But I do not believe in war. I have written at some length on this in my letter to the Times this evening, and from that you can judge whether there will be war or no. Lord Lyons' departure will not make ours necessary unless Seward wishes it.

For my own part I am tired of this life. Every attempt I have made to be of use has failed more or less completely. I stand no stronger than the first day I arrived. I cannot find that I have effected a lodgment anywhere, in spite of many exertions. I am now at a loss again to what new point to turn, having been beaten back everywhere; and hope for an idea.

You are going into the army. I do not think it my duty to express any regrets at the act, or at the necessity for it. They are understood, and I do not mean to make the thing any harder for either you or myself, by mourning or maundering about it. About my own fortunes I am becoming more and more callous and indifferent; but about yours, I feel differently, and if it were not for the strange madness of the times, which has left no longer any chance of settled lives and Christian careers, I should be vehement against your throwing yourself away like this. As it is, I can only tell you to do what you think best, and I shall be always ready to stand by you with what aid I can give.

Inclosed is my quarterly draft on Raymond. With this and what money of mine you have now in your hands, there ought to be something more than two hundred dollars. I want you to use this on your outfit; to buy a horse; or equipments; or to fit out your company. It is my contribution to the war and to your start in pride, pomp and circumstance.

We are passing our time at the Sturgis's, about twenty miles from London.[2] I went out there with Mary on Monday, and came back Thursday evening, but go out again tonight. Mary and Brooks are there and we had a large child's party Christmas evening at which I made myself conspicuous. I had no intention of doing so, but I found it was going on very coldly and so I pitched in and laid myself out. It was hard work but I was as successful as I could have expected.

Thurlow Weed is still here, very active indeed. I have tried to be of what use to him I could, but without much result. He's a large man; a very tall man indeed; and a good-deal taller than I am. So I can only watch and admire at a distance.

Very truly Yrs H.B.A.

MS: MHi
1. The Confederate raider *Nashville* took refuge in an English port after burning the *Harvey Birch.* In his letter to the *New York Times* HA hoped that Americans "will not explode until it appears that we are wronged." England "will not refuse justice now, when it is clearly on our side" (Dec. 9).
2. Russell Sturgis (1805–1887), Massachusetts-born partner of Baring Brothers. His country house was Mount Felix, Walton-on-Thames.

To Charles Francis Adams, Jr.

London 10 January 1862.[1]

My dear Charles

Your two last letters arrived as usual, as well as the account. I believe I have nothing to say to the latter except that I see a small charge for a telegram or telegrams, which said article must be wandering somewhere about Greenland or Labrador I suppose, for nothing of the kind ever reached me. Let us hope that some one has derived benefit therefrom.

I have been staying with Mr Sturgis in the country for the last three weeks, only coming in every Thursday and Friday to do my work, so that I am not so well posted as usual and have little to say. The news of the surrender of the unhung arrived yesterday, and gave us much satisfaction.[2] It was particularly grateful to me because the ground taken is that which the Chief recommended in an early despatch to the Government in which he quoted Madison's words. The effect here is good and will help us, but I have little hope that we shall be able to maintain ourselves here much longer. I fear that the meeting of Parliament will be the signal for a grand battle, and March will see us *en route* for somewhere.

Still there is great activity among our friends here in preparing for the struggle and Thurlow Weed is organising our forces effectively. We shall die hard I think, and England will have little to be proud of. The blockade is the place where the shoe pinches, and the blockade is now very perfect, I should judge. We shall see what they mean to do.

They are a nasty set however in this country, and I have lost my respect for them entirely. Still there is some regard for appearances even among the people, and unless they have a tolerably clear case, as in the Trent business, they will not be at all unanimous.

Financially we are dished. There is but one resort, and that is severe direct taxation. It is in this way alone that the expenses of all modern wars in Europe have been born, and we must come to it at last, or repudiate. The latter is out of the question; but the Lord knows.

The Legation is tolerably quiet just now, with little doing. Government has behaved well in the Nashville business, and that vessel is now under our guns and without increased armament. Meanwhile the Sumter has turned up and is making trouble in Spain. I wish to God the Tuscarora could catch her and sink her.

Today I find myself in a scrape that is by no manner of means agreeable. The Courier in putting my name to my "Diary" has completely used me up. To my immense astonishment and dismay I found myself this morning sarsed through a whole column of the Times, and am laughed at by all England.[3] You can imagine my sensations. Unless something occurs to make me forgotten, my bed is not likely to be one of roses for some time to come. There is nothing to be done but to grin and bear it. But for the present I shall cease my other writings as I am in agonies for fear they should be exposed. I wish I could get at Raymond, as I don't want to write myself for fear my letter should get out. Couldn't you write to him and explain without mentioning names why his London correspondent has stopped for a time. My connection with him must on no account be known. The Chief as yet bears this vexation very good-naturedly but another would be my ruin for a long time. I don't want him ever to know about it. Our good mother, as usual, has been frightened and talks nonsense.

We all have our troubles, but just at the present moment I envy you in camp. Perhaps you won't be astonished at this, as you are not without experience in this kind of trial. Pity me and adoo.

Gibbeted Adams.

The sensation, as near as I can describe it, is much like what F.W.P's[4] must have been the morning after his famous drunk.

MS: MHi

1. HA misdated this letter 1861.

2. Mason and Slidell were released by the federal government.

3. On Dec. 16 the Boston *Daily Courier* published "A Visit to Manchester: Extracts from a Private Diary" and named HA as the author in order to compliment him: "This Diary shows that he has by no means degenerated from the hereditary ability of his

family." Expecting anonymity, HA had satirized the niggardly refreshments at London balls, "thimblefuls of ice cream and hard seed cakes." Reprinted *AHR* 25 (Oct. 1945), 74–89.
    4. Francis Winthrop Palfrey.

To Charles Francis Adams, Jr.

London 22 January 1862.

My dear Warrior

Your last would have surprised me, if I had not seen that it was written in a caserne.[1] You find so much fault with my regrets at the necessity of your departure that I really feel almost inclined to beg your pardon for them. I merely meant, however, that I was sorry that you should go off to be "exposed" (the word you object to) to all the annoyances and dangers of a campaign, when under ordinary circumstances you would pursue a career much more adapted to your tastes. But we are quite reconciled to your departure now, and I rather envy you than otherwise.

For life here is by no means what it is cracked up to be. The Trent business coming first destroyed all our country-visits, for people have given up inviting us, on the just supposition that we wouldn't care to go into society now. The small list of friends that we have are not always so American as one would like. So we generally dodge "exposure" as much as possible. But I am personally flabbergasted by the explosion of my Manchester bomb, or more properly, the return of the boomerang, which has made me too notorious to be pleasant. The Times gently skinned me and the Examiner scalped me with considerable savageness. For myself I care about as much for the Times or the Examiner as I do for the Pekin Gazette, but, unfortunately, the American Minister in London is at this time an object of considerable prominence; an eyesore to an influential and somewhat unscrupulous portion of the community. Accordingly I form a convenient head to punch when people feel vicious and pugnacious. I have, therefore, to change the metaphor, found it necessary to take in every spare inch of canvass and to run (on a lee-shore) under double-close-reefed mizzen to'gallant skysails, before a tremenduous gale. In other words I have made myself as little an object of attack as possible. This reduces my means of usefulness to almost nothing and I might just as well be anywhere as here, except that I can't leave the parent birds thus afloat on the raging tide.

We are somewhat anxious still and are likely to be more so. The truth is, we are now in a corner. There is but one way out of it and that is by a decisive victory. If there's not a great success, and a success *followed up*, within six weeks, we may better give up the game than blunder any more over it. These nations, France probably first, will raise the blockade.

Such is the fact of our position. I am ready for it anyway, but I do say now that McClellan must do something within six weeks or we are done. This war has lasted long enough, to my mind.

There is precious little to tell you about here. France has again renewed her proposal to raise the blockade and there has been a discussion, or a battle about it. Prince Albert was strongly for peace with us, and now that he is dead it is understood that the Queen continues to favor his policy.[2] Besides her, the King of Belgium has come over and is pressing earnestly for peace. His great object always is to counteract French influence when it points to war. We have a majority (probably) in the Cabinet of neutrality men, nor do I know whom to call the leader of the war-party in the Ministry. You must not misunderstand Palmerston.[3] He means disunion, but not war unless under special influences.

We gave a dinner last week to Bishop McIlvaine, and I went with mamma another day to breakfast with Mr Senior. Met there the chief man of the Times, Lowe. He never speaks to any of us, and I certainly shouldn't care to seem to make up to him.[4]

Hope deferred is a bad thing, but to my mind this being the shuttlecock of accident is worse. I shall go over to Paris towards March for a little run, and shall indulge in all the vices and follies possible. I doubt about Beaufort as a good place for a permanent army. With our foreign relations as they are, the danger is not small of some accident which would play the deuce there. Give my regards to all my friends.

H.B.A.

MS: MHi

1. CFA2 was writing from barracks (caserne) in New York, waiting to be sent to Port Royal.

2. Prince Albert died Dec. 14.

3. Henry John Temple (1784–1865), 3rd Viscount Palmerston, prime minister 1855–1865.

4. Charles Pettit McIlvaine (1799–1873), Episcopal bishop of Ohio, one of several unofficial emissaries in the campaign to influence British public opinion. Nassau William Senior (1790–1864), English political economist, commissioner of popular education. Robert Lowe (1811–1892), M.P., editorial writer for the London *Times.*

To Henry J. Raymond

(Private & confidential)

London 24 January. 1862.

My dear Sir

Circumstances make it advisable that I should, in the present state of affairs, cease to write or do anything that might be made public or that might by any accident bring me into public notice.[1] You will no doubt see how important this is, not only for myself, which I care little for, but for a variety of other reasons.

The position of affairs here is very critical, and yet very misty. Who it is who holds the true key to it, I do not know; but this much is certain. All England believes and asserts openly that France is urging the Ministry to attack our blockade, and all France asseverates no less earnestly that the pressure comes from England and that Napoleon means to remain neutral. There is evidently political trickery somewhere. Now, so far as France is concerned, there are pretty certain reasons for knowing that there is no hostile movement intended. It is equally certain that if such an intention exists in the present English Government, it can only be in a portion of it, and that the first overt act will be the signal for a conflict that will probably destroy the Cabinet and bring a tremendous struggle on the Parliament and people. It looks to me very much as though some contest were now going on here, though so far out of sight that it is only to be guessed at. The case lies thus. Government organs have distinctly made the proposal of intervention, and the Observer and the Morning Post, both Palmerstonian papers, have encouraged it. The Southern agents here have offered, or let themselves appear as offering, terms that amount to nothing less than utter ruin to the South, emancipation among them. This is announced by another well-posted paper, the Scotsman. King Leopold of Belgium is here, and if one is to believe the world, is warmly opposing intervention on any terms. The Times and the Globe, high authorities, have come out on the same side. This all seems to indicate some Ministerial division of opinion, and to those who know Lord Palmerston, it looks much as though he had been advancing the proposal in order to see what reception it would meet.

For the present there seems no doubt that this plot has failed, thanks to the brilliant ability of Mr Seward.[2] But Parliament is going to meet and the Southerners here are working with utter desperation to excite a popular movement. They are at their wit's end and can't stand up much longer. We don't know what success they may have, but everyone knows that agitation almost always gets its end in time, and though the middle classes are neutral in our fight, there is no great feeling in our behalf here that can be organised or made very active. One thing would save us and that is a decisive victory. Without that our fate here seems to me to be a mere question of time.

If we can't get the victory however, or if it's not decisive, we must prepare to stand a hot battle in Parliament, and the main thing for us to do is to strengthen our friends there. Mr Seward's late course has already done this very much. I certainly hope no effort will be spared in America not only to keep down the expressions of ill-will to this country, but to prevent subjects of controversy from rising, and to create points on which our friends here can rest. We have many and very able advocates, and, I believe, a majority of the Ministry. If no new quarrel rises and we suffer no military disasters, or no great ones, I think the Southerners can get little here. They have however the advantage over us in their organisation, and in the steady aid which the Times gives them. The Clubs too are hopelessly anti-American.

The main point of attack now is the Charleston harbor business, but this is to my mind a good sign as it shows how hard they are driven for a point which has any chance of being vulnerable, and as it relieves the efficiency of our blockade from attack and indeed from notice.[3] Still it would be something to take away even this cause of reproach and disavow any intention of permanent destruction.

There is talk of a popular movement against us among the poor of Lancashire and Yorkshire, and it is even said that all the wires are already laid to start it and it only waits for Mason's arrival and sanction. This, however, will be of little account, I think, if the Ministry remain firm.

This is the best summary I can give of our position here. As it is my last, I give it only in the hope that it may be of some little service to you. We are very anxious to hear of a success, but it really must be better followed up than our others if we are to be much strengthened by it here. I hope that what I have written may have been of use, and only regret that I have been unable to speak so openly as I could have wished.

Socially the position of Americans in England is not so pleasant as it might be. There is a cool ignorance and dogmatism about this people that is hard to bear, but I hope to see a spoke put in their wheel some day yet.

Very truly Yrs   H.B.A.

MS: NN

1. HA's last published letter to the *New York Times,* dated Jan. 4, appeared Jan. 21.

2. Lord Russell, satisfied with Seward's note of Dec. 26 agreeing to release Mason and Slidell, instructed Lord Lyons on Jan. 10 that Britain regarded the incident as closed.

3. To enforce the blockade that Lincoln had proclaimed at the outset of war, the Union navy on Dec. 20, 1861, sank 16 old whaling ships loaded with stones across the entrance of Charleston Harbor. The Liverpool Shipowners Association urged the British government to protest.

To Thurlow Weed

Friday night. [24 January? 1862]

My dear Sir

Will you do me the favor to read the enclosed? It seems to me to be advisable to give, if possible, an immediate direction to public opinion on the appearance of the documents. This letter is intended as a keynote, but of course I would not offer it for publication without your approval.[1] Nor am I at all disposed to press it. If you object to it *in toto* or *in parte* I would not on any account have it printed.

If printed, however, it must of course be done without the knowledge of my father, as that would commit him to it. As I do not wish, myself, to be known now as a writer for the press, I would prefer to have its origin kept secret.

Excuse my officiousness, I pray; and believe me

Very truly Yrs Henry Brooks Adams.

Thurlow Weed Esq.

MS: NRU

1. The enclosed letter, unfortunately lost, apparently referred to British-American discussions in 1861 on the Declaration of Paris; official publication of the diplomatic documents of that year was imminent. HA returned to the subject in "The Declaration of Paris. 1861," first published in *Historical Essays* (1891).

To Frederick William Seward

London 30 January 1862.

My dear Sir[1]

I hope you will excuse me for taking up your time, and not consider that this letter wants notice of any kind. I neither want an office, nor a contract, nor a pension, nor money, nor in fact any favor of any sort. My main object in writing is to express what I've long wanted to do, the extreme satisfaction we all feel here in your father's course, and personally the great admiration I have for his productions as Secretary of State. I have done my little best here to make people understand him, but till lately nothing would have any effect. Now the tide is turning, and if people here don't like him yet, they are at least beginning to fear him.

In order to encourage this gratifying frame of mind, I have suggested to Mr Weed the reprinting here of the diplomatic correspondence about the Declaration of Paris, and its circulation as a popular pamphlet. Mr Weed has assented and I hope we shall manage to get it all over Parliament. But as this is but a portion of the whole volume and as all is valuable, it seems to me that some good might be done if you could send over a dozen or so more copies of your Foreign Correspondence.

The truth is, we want light here. It is no business of mine to make suggestions or to offer advice, and I don't want to be so understood. But Parliament is soon to meet and the battle will be very savage. Our friends have got to be stuffed with statistics and crammed with facts. These facts will probably take a regular range. The point attacked most furiously will be, no doubt, the blockade. The Southerners will parade a great number of vessels which have run it. Our side must show an equal or greater number either captured, or chased, and must have at hand any evidence there may be from southern sources of the difficulties found in escaping our cruisers.

Also official statements if possible of prices ruling in the South, and of the articles most scarce &c &c &c. Another point will be on slavery. We shall be accused of indifference to it, and Mr Cameron's retreat will be dragged out as a proof.[2] Surely something may be done to give the lie to this. If some real emancipation step could be taken, it would be the next best thing to taking Richmond for us here. The plan of Mason will probably be to dodge his antecedents. Anything peculiarly damnatory about him would tell strongly here.

Mr Weed is working like a giant, and I don't know how we could get on without him. Bishop McIlvaine too is doing good, I believe, though he finds it tough work. I imagine that even England contains no tougher heads than those of the Episcopal dignataries and their subordinates. Wilson, however is rather too savage to be persuasive, and after one battle we had, when he and I almost scalped an individual at a tea-party, I retired from business and now never open my mouth to an Englishman on politics. This makes pretty much the whole force we have, and our success is not so complete as I could wish. If it weren't for Mr Weed we should be in a very bad way.

If you can get the time to see to it, a stock of reliable information on the points likely to be attacked, will be a most important assistance here. The more exclusive it is, the better.

I wish, if you remember it, you would tell your father that we cling to him as our sheet anchor here. In fact I believe he will before long take his right position among the English. He would have held it long since if it hadn't been for people on your side of the water.

My father has to be so cautious that it is next to impossible for him to effect much directly, and his greatest triumph will be to make no blunders. This seems also to be the policy of some of our Generals. The principle may be carried too far, but since Bull Run I feel a shudder at the idea of risking anything.

Waiting in fear and trembling for the next news, I remain

Very truly Yrs Henry B. Adams.

Hon. F. W. Seward &c &c &c

MS: NRU
 1. Frederick William Seward (1830–1915), son of William Henry Seward, associate editor of Thurlow Weed's Albany *Journal* 1851–1861, assistant secretary of state 1861–1869, 1877–1881.
 2. Because of corruption in the letting of War Department contracts, Lincoln was pressed to dismiss Sec. Simon Cameron, but because Cameron made himself a spokesman for emancipation, dismissal was politically difficult. Lincoln eased Cameron out of the cabinet in January 1862 by appointing him minister to Russia.

To Charles Sumner

London 30 January 1862.

My dear Sir

I have to thank you for the trouble you have taken to send me a copy of your late speech. I need not say how much we were pleased with it. The ground it takes is precisely that which we have preached here for two months past to unwilling ears, and is to my mind the only truly statesman-like position possible. It is an honor to the country to assume such ground at such a time, and some day justice may be done us for it even in England.

The excellence of any such effort is to be measured now in this country only by the amount of attack it calls out, and I was therefore much pleased to see that the *Times* lost its temper in criticising you. It is a significant fact that neither it nor any of its allies have ventured to reprint the speech. They confine themselves to a style of criticism that I should call blackguard against you, Mr Seward and Mr Everett, but they do not, I think, nor does Earl Russell himself, seem to comprehend at all where they are placing themselves, nor how completely [they][1] are now at our mercy. I suppose that you will at once come down upon them with a Convention, which will bother them badly. Not that I have any hope of seeing public opinion change in our favor here, for if all the angels in Heaven directed our Government and inspired our people, England would never see it. My belief is that they want to repeat the process that was so successful between 1790–1820, when the tendency to liberalism was checked and destroyed by the brute force of a national hatred. It has been done once and may be done again, but if it fails, we need not trouble ourselves to revenge our insults, for they will be likely to have another Commonwealth and another Cromwell. Your speech and the whole foreign policy of our Government is as likely to hurry such a result as anything.

As I avoid society and purposely keep myself as quiet as possible, I can tell you nothing of the effect the speech has had among your friends here. No doubt they will do that themselves. But the England of today is not the England that you knew. Your anti-slavery sentiments now are little more popular here among the Club oligarchy than your international law is, or than Mr Everett's semi-pro-slavery of two years since. We talk emancipation in vain now. England, or at least the upper classes of the English are getting an awful squint towards the "expediency" of the divine institution, and if they don't express it openly, its only from fear of their own record.

This is "rank calumny" of course, but none the less true in fact. I hear all the old arguments used here that we have heard so many years at home. There is a deal of rottenness in the state of England. We expect to have to stand a tremendous assault when Parliament meets, and I am not entirely sanguine of the result. Our position here is as painful a one as I care to be in. I've no doubt that many of your old friends will astonish you. Mr Parkes remains tolerably faithful and Mr Bright is grand. Mr Cobden has been, I am told, a little shakey on the blockade. The Duke of Argyll does not show his whole hand though I think he will turn up right. As for Lord Palmerston, he will be on the winning side, and that is all that can be said of him. Both parties are organising. I cannot learn how Lord Derby will lean, but perhaps the Queen will keep him straight.

Of course we do our best to avoid notice, and have to be very quiet for fear of giving some opening for personal attack, which up to this time my father has luckily escaped. No doubt it will come however at the first [chance.] Still a little more or less brutality will make small difference in the total.

I dare not say anything about home affairs or your position. With our own load to carry, it is useless to add to it the weight of yours. But I feel your difficulties with all my heart, and sincerely wish you some relief, I'm afraid to say what.

Very truly Yrs   Henry B. Adams.

P.S. It is very generally asserted here that certain letters from Boston in the Morning Post, are written by your brother, Mr George Sumner. As they are not altogether of a friendly tone and bear internal evidence of some other source than his, I have taken the liberty to deny the statement. It would however be useful both to him and to you, I think, if some authoritative denial were made or if I had the means of positively refuting it. As I haven't the pleasure of your brother's acquaintance, I make the suggestion to you.

MS: MH
1. Brackets here and below indicate damaged manuscript.

To Charles Francis Adams, Jr.

London 31 January 1862.

My dear boy

I have nothing to say this week, but as I suppose you will not be indisposed to receive a letter, and as no one seems to have written to you, I will see what I can do to fill one up. We are going ahead just as usual and our position has not varied.

The only fault I am disposed to find is the old and chronic one with our Chief, and for that matter, with me also, of not extending his relations enough. I want him to cultivate the diplomatic corps, which has been greatly neglected and from which many advantages may be drawn. About the English it does not so much matter. They are so extremely jealous of whatever looks like foreign influence that on the whole they are better left to themselves. We have now a tolerably good organisation in our branch of the press, and Weed is extending this rapidly. He can do everything that we cannot do, and a single blunder on our side that would bring the Legation into discredit, would much more than compensate for any advantage we are likely to get from bold action. Since my exposure in the papers here, I have wholly changed my system, and having given up all direct communication with the public, am engaged in stretching my private correspondence as far as possible. This I hope to do to some purpose, and with luck I may make as much headway so, as I could in any other way.

The two unhung arrived after all. Evidently they are born for the gallows, as the sea casts them out. Their detention of two months was a great stroke of luck for us in my opinion. Their party here had made all their preparations for a war, and stopped their old game almost wholly. Peace was a great blow to them, and has disconcerted all their plans. For two months they ceased to send supplies to the South; they kept the Nashville in port; and they worked on a whole line of manoeuvres which are now regularly knocked into a cocked hat. Slidell might have been dangerous in France, for the Emperor was very shakey, but Seward's course and Weed's dexterity just turned the corner and now Slidell's first reception is the announcement of Napoleon's continued neutrality.[1] Up to the last moment the beggars were confident that directly the opposite course would be taken. Then, in expectation of a war, the Nashville was kept in port. The Tuscarora arrived just in time; and now Mason is received here with the news that the Nashville can no longer remain in port but that both she and the Tuscarora must proceed to sea.

And now the great battle is coming and we shall see lively times. Parliament meets on the 6th. The reprobates are as usual very sanguine that there will be intervention, and that the Ministry will be compelled to recognize or resign. A battle there will be, no doubt, but unless we are defeated at home, I think we shall yet maintain ourselves here. The opposition to intervention of any sort will be bitter in the extreme. They are well organised, I understand, but they are too vulnerable to stand a long contest, and we shall not give up with a short one. Still, much is yet in the dark as to our relative strength. Lord Russell distinctly stated the other day, in private conversation with the Duc D'Aumale,[2] that he thought we should conquer the South in the end. If he thinks so he surely won't countenance interference. And if the Ministry are firm, we are safe.

Parliament will bring society, and this I dread. The son of the American Minister is likely to meet with precious little favorable criticism in London society in these days, and after all, I'm very little of a society man. I do not mean to press myself on this quarter, but rather to avoid notice and be all the more active where no one sees me. I can't do much, but I think I can make myself of some use.

I was surprised to hear that you were to go to Port Royal. I can't conceive of your being placed there except for service but I should guess that at least half your regiment would be more likely to break their own necks than to hurt an enemy in a battle. If you see the correspondent of the London Star there, a youth named Edge, pray make his acquaintance and tell him that Moran, Wilson and I are all particularly anxious to know whether *that* travelling suit is worn out yet, or the telescope used up. He is not a bad fellow, though rather long-winded, and his employers are warm allies of ours here with great influence. They like his letters, as we all do, but wish there were more of them and longer. At last accounts he was doing the fever, and toping on quinine. I hope you will forswear that luxury, not uncommon, it appears, in that neighborhood.

We are dreading the next news. I hardly dare think of a battle and we all are tacitly agreed not to talk about it. I am sorry to say that our advices are not quite so satisfactory as we would like. But the darkest hour before the dawn. Can't you invest in a cargo of cotton, or set your men to picking it and divide the prize money. Consign me a cargo if you can. Return stuffed with glory and cotton.[3]

H.B.A.

Charles F. Adams Jr.   Lieutenant &c &c &c

MS: MHi

1. John Slidell (1793–1871) of Louisiana, Democratic representative 1843–1845, senator 1853–1861, Confederate commissioner to France 1861–1865.

2. Henri Eugène, Duc D'Aumale (1822–1897), younger son of Louis Philippe, one of the several Orléanist refugees who took a leading place in London society after the Revolution of 1848.

3. Plantation owners in the South Carolina sea islands fled en masse when Union naval forces arrived in November, just as the cotton crop was maturing. Measures to pick the contraband cotton and ship it north were hastily improvised by U.S. Treasury agents.

To John Gorham Palfrey

London 12 February. 1862.

My dear Sir

Your letter of 19 Nov. which you were so kind as to write in answer to my small remarks on the mythical Pocahontas, has remained unacknowledged longer than I wished. But it reached me when we were on the verge of ship-wreck, and I had no heart nor time to think of any female of that age or any other. The storm has passed for a time, however, and I am so foolishly sanguine as to think that it was the crisis in our foreign dangers, and that now, if we must be ship-wrecked, we on this side the water shall have no voice nor hand in the disaster. Our work seems to me to be done, and I feel confident that Europe will now lie still until the home-crisis that seems to be inevitable, shall have come to some positive result. I have made use of the respite to run over again in a very superficial way, the question which we were discussing, and I think I may say, with a certain confidence, that I know considerably less about the matter than I thought I did before.

When I wrote last, I was under serious difficulty from having quite mistaken certain facts; an error which I perhaps shouldn't have made if the way of arriving at these same facts had been easier. I am obliged to Mr Deane for correcting me, and will try not to do so again.[1]

The British Museum, if properly searched, might perhaps give some light on this subject. But I have not yet succeeded in tapping any productive vein. You and Mr Deane are no doubt thoroughly familiar with all the sources of information yet opened. The best that I have arrived at in the way of enlightenment on the history of the romantic young woman, is a portrait purporting to represent her, decidedly hard-featured and wearing a stupendous sugar-loaf hat and garments in the height of the graceful stiffness of James the First's period. No doubt you are well-acquainted with this, as the book is hardly a rare one. In two letters of the day, she is mentioned as "the Virginia woman"; the ungrateful Chamberlain doesn't even give her the title of Princess.[2] But I think he was jealous that the King should have had her "well-placed at the masque." Not a word, however, of her connection with Smith, nor does the State Paper collection seem to mention her further. I can only find Hamer's book in a German translation published in Hanau in 1617.[3] Probably Mr Deane has the original, which is not in the British Museum, or, if it is, I can't find it. He, I notice, speaks of "Poca-huntas" as one "whose renown has spread even to England under the name *Non Parella*." This is at least more gallant than Chamberlain, but it puzzles me. If the epithet means anything, it must refer either to personal or to mental superiorities. Now, handsome was she not, if I can judge from her picture. Contemporary authority says only that she was not uglier than many English ladies, which, with deference, is barely a compliment to her. Have I not seen their descendents? But if her mental charms were *sans pareil,* what had she done at that time (before her capture by Capt. Argal[4]) to justify the title? Hamer however leaves this all in blank, and her goose of a husband, Rolfe, writes a long letter to justify his marriage, without ever descending to give such a terrestrial reason for it as a regard for his wife, or any merit in her that attracted him, except that she was a Pagan. I confess, this seems to me to show a degree of self-devotion on his part that does not tally with my idea of the character of the Virginia settlers. It belonged rather to the latitude of New England.

Smith's authority being ruled out, I must acknowledge that I have as yet succeeded in unearthing nothing that throws any light on Mrs Rolfe's antecedents. Unless some one else proves luckier than I, we must yield that the chances are in favor of Smith's turning out as powerful a liar as he was seaman. I fully expect that the ghost of John Randolf will haunt you and Mr Deane and me for this impiety,[5] but it wasn't my fault.

I presented Wingfield duly to the British Museum and received a letter of thanks from the Librarian of the Reading Room; and further it was said that the thanks of the Trustees would be offered to Mr Deane on their next meeting. Since then I have not seen nor heard from Mr Watts. I wish to thank Mr Deane also on my side for the trouble he has taken on my account.

We are all flourishing here, and living in firm hope of salvation. About six weeks ago the Boston Courier, by puffing an indifferent poor work of mine that should have remained anonymous, got me into a position that strongly resembled "Damien's bed of steel"; for I was roasted with pepper and salt by the English press.[6] Consequently, my small attempts to make progress here, have wholly ceased, and I live the life of a hermit, copying letters. I have, therefore, no news to tell, except that I think it a question whether you would find England as agreeable a residence now, as you once did. My own Anglicism is somewhat wilted.

With best respects to your family I remain

Very respy &c &c   H.B. Adams

Mr Parkes[7] wishes me to acknowledge a letter from you and Mr Dana. He has been quite ill for ten days and is not out of the house. But he has a letter on the stocks for you.

MS: MH

1. Palfrey sent HA's letter of Oct. 23 to Charles Deane, who replied on Nov. 17, enclosing a copy of his privately printed edition of Wingfield's *Discourse on Virginia* to forward to HA for the British Museum. "I perceive he is not yet possessed of all the facts," Deane wrote, noting that the earliest accounts of John Smith's captivity "are silent as to his rescue by the Indian girl." Deane urged HA to keep working on the matter in the British Museum.

2. John Chamberlain (1553–1627), whose letters date from 1598 to 1625.

3. Ralph Hamor (fl. 1610–1616), *True Discourse of the Present Estate of Virginia* (1615).

4. Capt. Samuel Argall (fl. 1585–1626), one of the first governors of Virginia.

5. John Randolph (1773–1833), a bitter opponent of JA and JQA, claimed descent from John Rolfe and Pocahontas.

6. Robert Damiens was tortured to death for attempting to assassinate Louis XV in 1757. HA quotes Oliver Goldsmith, *The Traveller* (1764), 1. 436: "The lifted axe, the agonizing wheel, / Luke's iron crown, and Damiens' bed of steel."

7. Joseph Parkes (1796–1865), Birmingham lawyer-politician, considered an intermediary between Benthamite radicals and parliamentary liberals.

To Charles Francis Adams, Jr.

London 14 Feb. 1862.

Good morrow, 'tis St Valentine's day
    All in the morning betime.
And I a maid at your window
    To be your Valentine.[1]

Hail noble lieutenant! I have received your letter written on board ship, and I am with you. Now that you are at work, if you see or do anything or hear something that will make a good letter to be published, send it to me and I think I can promise that it shall see the light. Thus you can do double work, and if you write well, perhaps you can get double pay. I shall exercise my discretion as to omissions.

About the money you refuse to accept, I have nothing to say. Take as much as you like; suit yourself and you'll suit me. I'm in no want of it, and not likely to be, for the older I get, the less I go about. My acquaintances are none under fifty years of age, and are not like your young seductive dogs who lead one into expenses. On the contrary they give me good dinners and many of them, and wine and cigars.

You find fault with my desponding tone of mind. So do I. But the evil is one that probably lies where I can't get at it. I've disappointed myself, and experience the curious sensation of discovering myself to be a humbug. How is this possible? Do you understand how, without a double personality, *I* can feel that *I* am a failure? One would think that the *I* which could feel that, must be a different *ego* from the *I* of which it is felt.

You are so fortunate as to be able to forget self-contemplation in action, I suppose; but with me, my most efficient channels of action are now cut off, and I am busy in creating new ones; which is a matter that demands much time and even then may not meet with success.

Politically there is no news here. We shall be allowed to fight our battle out, I think; at least for some time yet. Parliament has met and the speeches have been very favorable to neutrality. I think our work here is past its crisis. The insurgents will receive no aid from Europe, and so far are beaten. Our victory is won on this side the water. On your side I hope it will soon be so too.

Socially the season is just commencing, but we none of us want to go much into society. The tone of people here is insufferable to me. I lose my temper, or get sulky, and as for pleasure, don't know what it is. How is one to make friends when friends are only ball-room acquaintances. Such friends bore me. So I am going over to Paris on the 23d to pass ten days and see the carnival with Theodore. This will be my "season" and I don't mean to try to do anything in London society. When the great Exhibition commences we shall have enough to do to entertain Americans. John Bright is my favorite Englishman. He is very pleasant, cheerful and courageous and much more sanguine than I have usually been.

Is Ben Crowninshield with you at Beaufort? If so please suggest to him that he never has answered my last letter. Whether he thinks that conduct for a gentleman? I presume he has taken a negro concubine, down South. Inquire particularly of him on this point, as I feel curious as to him. Try to take Charleston by a coup-de-main and free Lee and Paul Revere.

We expect great news every day but it seems as though something *must* break soon. For three months the pressure has grown heavier and heavier until a crack will bring the whole thing down smash. It is intensely interesting to watch the coils tighten.

We are all right here. Mary and I try to be lively, and are so occasionally. But How long, Oh Lord,

How long!

MS: MHi
1. *Hamlet,* IV, v.

To Frederick William Seward

London. 14 Feb. 1862.

My dear Sir

The British Government have done ours the extraordinary favor of re-printing word for word all its diplomatic correspondence for 1861. This seems to relieve the Americans here from all necessity of further action in that matter, and every public man and newspaper is now, I suppose, pro-vided with everything needed in that way. I mention this as I took the lib-erty a short time ago, to ask you to send us out some more copies of the correspondence.

My desire to have the documents relating to the Declaration of Paris printed by themselves, is now, I presume, hopeless. Still, I cannot help wishing it could be done, especially since the British Blue Book has ap-peared, which throws great light on that negotiation. I have had a strong desire to write a history of this negotiation for the press here, but dare not appear as a writer, even anonymously, for fear of compromising my father.

Will you pardon me a bit of impertinence? If so I want to make a sug-gestion to you, that may be worthless but at least can't do harm. There is great difficulty felt here in supporting our Government on anti-slavery grounds. Even a small step would, I think, be of great use, especially if taken with sufficient noise and flourish of trumpets. I speak as an outsider, for I am little acquainted with the secrets of this Legation, to which I have little access. I believe, however, that immemorial custom has denied to ne-groes the right of citizenship abroad. What ground this denial rests on be-yond the mere dictum of successive Secretaries of State, I don't know. It is an evident injustice to many citizens whose votes went to elect Mr Lincoln, and while it remains, it is a reproach to our Government. My belief is that a formal instruction, reversing this rule and enunciating broadly the new policy of the United States as regards the black race, would create a good impression here. I beg your pardon for taking up your time with a sugges-tion which has no doubt long since had full consideration by your father; but the truth is, our side is hard pressed here for what is charged as want of boldness in grappling with this negro question, and any aid would be valu-able.

With most earnest good-wishes to your father, I am

&c &c &c   H. B. Adams

MS: NRU

To Charles Francis Adams, Jr.

London 15 March. 1862.

Leefteenant

Times have so decidedly changed since my last letter to you, which was, as I conceive, about three weeks or a month ago, that I hardly know what to write about. My main doubt is about your prospects. I see no reason why Davis and his whole army shouldn't be shut up and forced to capitulate in Virginia. If so you will be spared a summer campaign. But if he is allowed to escape, I shall be disgusted, and God only knows what work may be before you.

Meanwhile it worries me all the time to be leading this thoroughly useless life abroad while you are acting such grand parts at home. You would be astonished at the change of opinion which has taken place here already. Even the Times only this morning says: "The very idea of such a war is American, multitudinous, vast, and as much an appeal to the imagination as the actual brunt of arms." And again in speaking of the tone of the Southern papers, it says in a striking way; "Some of their expressions recall those in which the Roman historians of the later Empire spoke of the Northern tribes." The truth is, as our swarm of armies strike deeper and deeper into the South, the contest is beginning to take to Europeans proportions of grandeur and perfection like nothing of which they ever heard or read. They call us insane to attempt what, when achieved, they are almost afraid to appreciate. A few brilliant victories, a short campaign of ten days or a fortnight, rivalling in its vigor and results those of Napoleon, has positively startled this country into utter confusion. It reminds me of my old host in Dresden, who, when he heard of the battle of Magenta, rushed into my room, newspaper in hand, and began measuring on the map the distance from the Ticino to Vienna. The English on hearing of Fort Donnelson and the fall of Nashville, seem to think our dozen armies are already over the St Lawrence and at the gates of Quebec. They don't conceal their apprehensions and if we go on in this way, they will be as humiliated as the South itself. The talk of intervention, only two months ago so loud as to take a semi-official tone, is now out of the minds of everyone. I heard Gregory make his long-expected speech in the House of Commons, and it was listened to as you would listen to a funeral eulogy. His attacks on us, on Seward and on our blockade were cheered with just enough energy to show the animus that existed in a large proportion of the members, but his motion, a simple and harmless request for papers, was tossed aside without a division. I saw our friend Mason on the opposite side of the House to where I was sitting with Thurlow Weed. He is unlucky. One of the Bishops who happened to have come in and was seated near the door, heard a "Hear! Hear!" behind him, and looking round saw Mason. For a stranger to cheer is a breach of privilege, and the story went all over town creating quite a row. Mr Mason now denies it, I am told, and says it was some one else who cheered. He maintains now that the South always expected to lose the border States and that now that they are retiring to the cotton region the war has just begun. He coolly talks this stuff to the English people as if they hadn't always asserted that the border-states were a vital point with them. We on the other hand, no longer descend to argue such stories, or to answer the new class of lies; but smile blandly and compassionately on those who swallow them and remark that so far as advised, the nation whom we have the honor to represent, is satisfied with the progress thus far made, and sees no reason to doubt that the Union will be maintained in its fullest and most comprehensive meaning.

The blockade is now universally acknowledged to be unobjectionable. Recognition, intervention, is an old song. No one whispers it. But the navy that captured Port Royal, Roanoke and Fort Henry, and that is flying about with its big guns up all the rivers and creeks of the South, is talked of with respect. And the legion of armies that are winning victory after victory on every side, until we have begun to complain if a steamer arrives without announcing the defeat of some enemy, or the occupation of some city, or the capture of some stronghold, are a cause of study to the English such as they've not had since Napoleon entered Milan some seventy years ago. I feel like a King now. I assert my nationality with a quiet pugnacity that tells. No one treads on our coat tails any longer, and I do not expect ever to see again the old days of anxiety and humiliation.

Personally, however, I can't say that this suits me at all. My work is enough to occupy me every day so that I can do little or nothing for myself, or for any really permanent object. The last year has been one that I've no satisfaction in thinking of so far as I am myself concerned. My pen is given up. The risk in using it became too great and the consequences of a discovery would have been utterly destructive. Here I am, more dry-nurse than ever, dabbling a little, a very little in society; reading a little; copying a great deal; writing nothing, and not advancing an inch. I envy you who at least have an enemy before you. My enemy is only myself.

A fortnight or three weeks ago I made an excursion over to Paris and staid there ten days, but I didn't get much more satisfaction out of it than from London. Theodore was there, but sick, gloomy and used-up generally. Poor devil! He has lived Paris all through and now is trying to suck the cold corn-cob; not a grain of corn, butter or salt is there left. He complains of everything, especially of himself. One night I had gone to one of the great *bals masqués* at the Grand Opera, that you've heard so much about, and was boring myself dreadfully with some stupid domino that was dragging me round the foyer, when suddenly Theodore appeared looking so pale and mournful and inattentive to the crowd, marching straight ahead as though he were walking on a wager, that I seized him and laughed at him for looking more bored than even any one else there, though no one looked lively. So he and I rambled through the Theatre and tried to amuse ourselves with the swarms of flaming whores and the ridiculous masques, but it was no use; so we left the ball and retired to a beer-shop where he poured into my attentive ears a sort of song full of wailing and cursing against Paris and all that was in it.

Dick Parker was not much better. He was very kind to me indeed. I dined with him and breakfasted with him and walked with him. But he was full of fuss and complaints against persons and things, and I, having come for amusement, didn't quite appreciate it. Sohier was by far the most satisfactory companion of the crowd. His conversation was instructive and his spirits equable. Joe Bradlee was perched up in a garret on the fifth story of a house out of all human knowledge, but when one got at him, he was quite the old boy. I found him one evening at the ball with Leontine, his mistress, trying to keep her quiet, as she was inclined to raise the deuce. I thought he was rather jealous. But I believe he has had cause. At any rate he took her away early. I staid with Frank Emmons and a young Storrow, both of whom I did my best to debauch, but after all it wasn't very gay.

Charley Thorndike is engaged to a Miss Edgar. I met her at his house. She is pretty and nice, and Thorndike radiates with shining happiness.

Sidney Everett was there. Neither of us called on the other, but I met him at Munroe's and at the first bal masqué. He isn't well. His brother Willy is here in England.[1] He dined with us the last time he was in London and made such an owdacious speech about staying in our house when he came to town, that we were utterly aghast. He didn't get the invitation though, and I think it mortified even him.

I came back from Paris a week ago and in the middle of the exultation about our victories. London is as usual. The Queen is said to be all broken-down at her husband's death, and her most agreeable occupation is to send *cartes de visite* photographs of him, which the Princess Alice colors, to his former friends.

The Prince of Wales is in Egypt. He is said to have taken to women lately, and they point out at the Argyll Rooms the woman whom he came to London to see; a visit which made a great row with his father and mother. It is currently reported that on parting from this female he gave her a sovereign, saying that he would be happy to increase the sum but he must put it down as lost at cards or else his father would find him out.

Great news from our nephew, isn't it? I must say I am very much pleased at this continuation of the stock.[2] The more, the merrier. At the same time I'm not sorry to be three thousand miles away.

Success to your swords. Richardson who was here has ordered a stunner for Ben Crowninshield which he has left seven guineas with me to pay for. I shall forward it home as soon as it is received.

Ever Yrs   Jones.

MS: MHi
    1. William Everett (1839–1910), Harvard '59, a cousin of HA studying classics and mathematics at Trinity College, Cambridge.
    2. The first grandchild of CFA and ABA, John Quincy Adams III (1862–1876), born Feb. 23 to Frances and John Quincy Adams II.

To John Gorham Palfrey

London. 20 March. 1862.

My dear Sir

The enclosed letter has been sent to me from the British Museum, for Mr Deane. As I do not know his address I beg you will have the goodness to forward it.

I am "fou" of the Pocahontas matter. Lately I have had little to do, so have given myself up to it. The difficulty is that I have no books about me and have to do everything at the British Museum. It is no small matter to dig in this way through all those old gentlemen, but I have got enough out of Smith, Strachey, Hamor, Purchas, Wingfield &c, to make, in my opinion, a clear case, and as soon as I have completed my notes, I mean to see what I can make of it.[1] My present idea is to present the thing in as plain, businesslike, and purely critical way as I can, and leave all attempt at literary merit aside, to serve in case anyone should choose to take the battle up. But as yet I know nothing further than that I mean to try it.

I have discovered nothing in the way of M.S.S, but mean to make a more thorough search. There ought somewhere to be an M.S. of George Percy. Purchas gives the first part of it, which is very valuable from its simple plainness of statement and accuracy of date. But he breaks off just at *the* point, to take up with Smith. Purchas speaks also of an M.S. of Rolfe which he quotes in his Pilgrimage. As he also mentions Wingfield's, which has been found, I hope the others may turn up some day.

I doubt however if any M.S. will throw more light on the subject than we already have, for to my mind the chain of evidence is complete and needs only to be put together.

Perhaps you will be good enough to inform me who Mr Deane is.[2] If I decide to publish anything, his original claim must be acknowledged in a way that can leave no doubt about it.

I hardly know whether I ought not to be ashamed of myself for devoting myself to a literary toy like this, in these times, when I ought to be helping or trying to help the great cause. But my pen is forced to keep away from political matters, unless I want to bring the English press down on my head again, and in society I am a failure. So perhaps the thing is excusable, especially as it is in some sort a flank, or rather a rear attack, on the Virginia aristocracy, who will be utterly gravelled by it if it is successful. I can imagine to myself the shade of John Randolf turn green at that quaint picture which Strachey gives of Pocahontas "clothed in virgin purity" and "wanton" at that, turning somersets with all the little ragamuffins and "decayed serving-men's" sons of Jamestowne. Nevertheless, if it weren't for you and Mr Deane behind me, I hardly think I should dare to attack an article of American religious creed, so vital as this. Theodore Parker's heresies were a joke to it.

We are waiting with great anxiety for the course of events. Being used to this perpetual frying-process we mind it less than at first. But it's not pleasant. The President's emancipation message has delighted us and has given a violent cold-water-bath to our opponents here. They regularly gasp at it. But our position is now so firm here that nothing but a series of the most disastrous defeats could shake us, even without the anti-slavery sentiment.

My mother requests me to acknowledge a very interesting letter she has just received from you, which she means to answer at once.

Pray remember me most warmly to your family and believe me

Very truly Yrs   H. B. Adams.

MS: MH
1. William Strachey (fl. 1606–1618), *The Historie of Travaile into Virginia Britannia,* written c. 1612 (1849), and Samuel Purchas (1575?–1626), *Purchas His Pilgrimage* (1613 and later enlarged editions).
2. See HA to Palfrey, Oct. 23, 1861, note 4.

To Frederick William Seward

United States Legation.
4 April. 1862.

My dear Sir

My father, being pressed for time, requests me to forward to you the enclosed documents, as matters which are hardly official, and need only a word from your Office to be set straight.

I have to thank you for a letter, and a bundle of the State Dep. Documents, and was much gratified at the readiness with which you did me this kindness. I believe now there is absolutely nothing to ask, so far as influences to be brought to bear on this country are concerned. It isn't probably of much consequence to you to know what *I* think about it, but as I am writing, I may as well say that the manner in which your father has managed the Foreign Affairs has not only been extremely able, but completely successful. Even apart from our military successes I think you have managed to put England in a position from which she is absolutely unable to move. The whole tone here is now, however, so much changed, that it is hard precisely to find out the extent of our victory. I hope before long we may be able to begin a popular agitation to force this Government out of its belligerent ideas, with some shadow of success. As yet it would have no chance even among the people, far less among the ruling classes.

Mr Weed is a great loss to us.[1] I know you will be as much gratified as we all were at the very successful career he had here. Everyone speaks kindly of him, and he has become quite an aristocrat. Such a general favorite is very rare, and even the toughest of our opponents rather softened down under his mildness.

We are very quiet here, and hold our heads very high indeed. It is delightful to see how angry the English get at being accused of enmity to us. But they are not rapid in their motions and I don't expect to see any real change in their policy. Their very pride stops it.

Pray remember me to your father. If I can be of any service to you here, I shall be delighted.

Very truly Yrs   H. B. Adams.

F. W. Seward Esq.

MS: NRU
1. On March 12 Thurlow Weed went to Paris as part of his special European mission. In May he returned to London briefly before going back to the U.S.

To Charles Francis Adams, Jr.

London 11 April. 1862.

My dear boy

Your long silence has worried us here more than we like to acknowledge, and lately even I have begun to get a little uneasy. That our letters should fail to reach you is natural enough, but that you should not write to us is very strange. I had hoped by this time to have received a long letter from you for publication, as I suggested in one of my former letters, which, however, seems never to have reached you.

My last was written either a fortnight or three weeks ago, I forget which, and sent through John, as this will also be. We wag along here in a tolerably steady way. This last week I have been left alone here, as the rest of the family have gone over to Paris. I occupy myself in writing, reading and studying up history, as I propose soon to publish a book upon the history and products of the moon, or some other light subject of the kind. Society is very dull indeed. It will not fairly begin until after the first of May, and even then will be more labor than pleasure; though I am far from saying that there are not pleasant people here and even that at a pinch I might not be able to find young women who would almost come up to any small ideas on the subject that I've had in other lands. I don't say that I know any such at present, but perhaps I know where to find them.

Modest and unassuming as I am, you know, society is not the place for pleasure to me. Even at the Club I talk distantly with Counts and Barons and numberless untitled but high-placed characters, but have never arrived at intimacy with any of them.[1] I am a little sorry for this because there are several very nice fellows among them, and all are polite and seem sufficiently social. Then, too, my unfortunate notoriety, which I told you of, in a letter that I trust and pray may not be lost, some three months ago, tells against me, though it certainly has brought me into notice. I have no doubt that, if I were to stay here another year, I should become extremely fond of the place and the life. There is, too, a certain grim satisfaction in the idea that this people who have worn and irritated and exasperated us for months, and among whom we have lived nearly a year of what was, till lately, a slow torture, should now be innocently dancing and smiling on the volcano, utterly unconscious of the extent of hatred and the greediness for revenge that they've raised. When the storm does finally burst on them, they will have one of their panics and be as astonished as if they'd never heard of anything but brotherly affection between the two nations. Of course it would be out of the question for me to hint at the state of things to them. I have only to smile and tell gross lies, for which God forgive me, about my feelings towards this country, and the kindness I have received here, which, between ourselves, so far as the pure English go, has been brilliantly conspicuous for its almost total absence. Only a fortnight ago they discovered that their whole wooden navy was useless; rather a weakness than a strength.[2] Yesterday it was formally announced and acknowledged by Government, people and press, that the Warrior and their other new iron ships, are no better than wood, nor can any shot-proof sea-going vessel be made. In order to prove this, they've proved their Armstrong guns a failure, for he has given up the breech-loading system and been compelled to return to the old smooth-bore, muzzle-loader. So within three weeks, they find their wooden navy, their iron navy, and their costly guns, all utterly antiquated and useless.

To me, they seem to be bewildered by all this. I don't think as yet they have dared to look their position in the face. People begin to talk vaguely about the end of war, and eternal peace; just as though human nature was changed by the fact that Great Britain's sea-power is knocked in the head. But for my private part, I think I see a thing or two. And one of these things is that the military power of France is nearly doubled by having the seas free; and that our good country the United States is left to a career that is positively unlimited except by the powers of the imagination. And for England there is still greatness and safety, if she will draw her colonies round her, and turn her hegemony into a Confederation of British nations.

You may think all this nonsense, but I tell you these are great times. Man has mounted science, and is now run away with. I firmly believe that before many centuries more, science will be the master of man. The engines he will have invented will be beyond his strength to control. Some day science may have the existence of mankind in its power, and the human race commit suicide, by blowing up the world. Not only shall we be able to cruize in space, but I'll be hanged if I see any reason why some future generation shouldn't walk off like a beetle with the world on its back, or give it another rotary motion so that every zone should receive in turn its due portion of heat and light.

Such are my private reflections and I keep them to myself, waiting patiently for the moment when England will wake up, as she soon will. Her old sun is set. If a new one is to rise, she must look sharp.

We are putting on the diplomatic screws. A few more victories and it will be all straight. We understand that the Nashville has been taken or destroyed, and it is today telegraphed privately to us that the crew of the Sumter are to be paid off, and her Captain is coming to London. Bankrupt. The long purse, the big guns, and the men carry the day.

Our host has turned us out of our house, and we are soon to make a change.[3] But I never feel settled now. A month or two is all I've ever looked forward, since four years ago. Still we take the new house for three years and I hope long before that time is over, you will have come out here to relieve me, and let me return to do a little work. I tell you frankly, three more years of this, and I shall never pass my life in America, nor permanently anywhere else.

Tomorrow I take Brooks over to Paris and join the rest of the family. The Chief returned last night leaving them under the care of the good uncle and aunt. He seems much edified by Paris, and confesses to having had a good time. Mary writes that Paris is *splendid.* For weeks, and indeed for months, we've hardly seen the sun. Every day has been smokey, foggy and cloudy, in the peculiar grimy style of this city. But in Paris it is warm, sunny and blue as at home. Luckily I am tolerably well used to it, and perhaps if there were a sun here it would only make me miserable.

In the way of small gossip I have little to tell. Theodore has gone to Italy. I don't know whether any sudden change made him go, or what it was; but I don't wonder, for he was in a miserable way when I was there. The Chief saw and conversed with a number of French celebrities. They are surprisingly well-disposed towards us now that we are looking up in the world. Here in London we are as comfortable as possible. The newspapers are dumb except for an occasional sneer, or assertion, which is invariably acknowledged to be false the next day. I tell you it's not a bad thing to have seven hundred thousand fighting men behind one, to back one's words up. I am more and more convinced every day that we are very much feared. Indeed you can imagine what the change must be when we all here know on the very highest authority that in May last it was supposed that the revolution was complete, and the recognition was a matter of course. Men who have made such a political blunder as that, are apt to open their eyes wide when they find it out.

As for home affairs and your position, we are so ignorant that I shall not discourse on the subject. Of course we know all that the newspapers tell us and are waiting with a sort of feeling that is now chronic, for the flash and the thunder that is soon to come from the cloud over Richmond and New Orleans. I despise a mail that does not tell of a victory, and indeed for some time past we have been pampered. But every time that the telegram comes and its yellow envelope is torn open, I feel much like taking a little brandy to strengthen me up to it. There is a nervous tremor about it that is hard to master. The 24th did well at Newbern. I wish to God I had been with it, or were with the Richmond army now. I feel ashamed and humiliated at leading this miserable life here, and since having been blown up by my own petard in my first effort to do good, I haven't even the hope of being of more use here than I should be in the army. But I can't get away till you come over. I am like the damned cook we had the misfortune to inherit from our predecessor, who doesn't know anything about cooking, any more than a horse-mackerel, but whom I have tried in vain to drive from the house. She is or pretends to be honest, and has got round the head of the house, and in short we are stuck for four years with a table to which I am ashamed to invite any person who knows the A.B.C. of a cuisine. For myself I don't care a rap, but I would like to offer a good dinner to my friends, and could do a good deal in that way. So it is with my own position, fastened to a place where I am rapidly going to the devil and from which you alone can release me. I only wish my friend Mrs Hollidge would take a leaf out of my book and express a wish to leave. Sapristi! wouldn't I yank her out.

Our good mother has been left in Paris somewhat like a lost sheep. She is extremely penurious in her old age; indeed, between you and me, in perfect secrecy, her love for her children and fear of their being poor, seems to me to be exercising anything but a favorable influence on her. The Chief would do very well if I could only inspire her with correct ideas. But she is too timid for the position. *D'ailleurs,* I have inherited the quality, so ought not to complain.

I repeat my old proposal; write me a series of good letters and I will see that they are published and read.

Ever yours. Brown.

MS: MHi
 1. The St. James's Club, "to which the Minister's son could go only as an invited guest" (*Education,* p. 117), was founded in 1859 for diplomatic secretaries and attachés. It was located in St. James's Street.
 2. On April 5 Benjamin Moran noted: "The battle between the Monitor and the Merrimac is the one topic of conversation . . . John Bull is sorely frightened at the manifest weakness of his own navy" (*Journal,* II, 975).
 3. On April 25 the legation was moved to the London mansion of Russell Sturgis, an Adams family friend, at 5 Upper Portland Place. This was its fifth location since CFA arrived in London.

To Charles Francis Adams

Paris 15 April. 1862.

My dear Father

I dragged Mary to the Dentist's this morning. The result of the conference was a sort of Bull Run disaster. He declares absolutely that she must have an operation performed and her mouth overhauled thoroughly. As one of the fillings is for the front tooth, which will need separation with indiarubber, a matter of time, and as there are other delicate and troublesome things to be done, it seems likely that we shall have to come to some decision as to whether to lengthen our stay a few days, or do what can be done before Saturday and let the rest go.

Naturally this has been anything but a cheerful event. Mamma is thoroughly disgusted and in despair. Mary is also quite as disgusted and equally desperate, and I can't blame her. I am directed to write to you the state of affairs for your advice. This afternoon I hope that Dr. Gage will give us a tolerably close estimate of the time he needs, and then we shall be able to be more definite. I do not myself believe that he can get through comfortably before next Wednesday, but possibly he may find the work more easy than he thought it this morning, when he said that she ought to give eight or nine days to it. What we want is to know whether you think we should remain here for it, or come home on Saturday as well as we can. If there were any one here with whom Mary could stay, I might remain and let mamma who is tant-soit-peu homesick, return; but as yet we have discovered no arrangement of this kind. As I am not entirely enamored with my part in the position, any more than the rest are, I hope you'll answer *de suite.*

MS: MHi

To Charles Francis Adams, Jr.

[London, 27? April 1862]

[*The first part of the letter is missing.*] . . . detailing his injuries and making it a sort of national affront, besides trying to raise a jealousy between Stanton and McClellan. The Times, evidently exasperated at having its nose pulled in a way it never was put to before, has not made any violent complaints, but has become more bitter against us than ever.[1] We are delighted and my only wish now is that we may overwhelm the South straight-way, in order that we may have the satisfaction not only of kicking the gentlemen of the Times and their admirers till their tails are raw, but of pickling them till they grin. Such is my state of mind. But just at present we are rather losing ground here than gaining it.

As I only arrived from Paris last Monday night and as we have been extremely busy moving from our old house ever since, I have not done anything in the way of distraction here. This is Easter, and everyone is out of town for the holidays.[2] After this week the season will commence and I must set to work in earnest to get into society. Not that I care for it. To say the truth society has always been a trouble to me and an endless cause of annoyance and mortification, for, in my attempts to get along, I always disgust myself and end by a long fit of the blues and an oath to become a hermit. It is the usual fate of a person who would like to be a society man and hasn't the wit. Still, I must do it, and am steeling myself to stand all the labor and disappointment of a struggle to acquire a position in this great, dreary, scandal-mongering, censorious city. I would prefer a dozen times being a second-lieutenant in the first Massachusetts Cavalry.

For your trials and sufferings, I can only say I hope they are over. You've had bad luck but it may be followed by a run of good and if that's the case, it's all right. Remember me to all my friends. I expect soon to hear that you've been into action, and of course the expectation is rather too anxious to be pleasant. But if you're wounded, you can come out here and we'll exchange places, and perhaps you will be more successful here than I am or ever expect to be. I sent Ben, about a month ago, a big sabre, whose size and temper and wonderful qualities were all equally astounding,—as also its price, for it cost about fifty dollars. Richardson superintended its manufacture in person, and the brother of the Earl of Litchfield is responsible for its perfections. I hope Ben will spit a Carolinian on it and send him to me.

Adieu

MS: MHi
1. Edwin McMasters Stanton (1814–1869) of Ohio, secretary of war 1862–1868, refused permission to London *Times* correspondent William H. Russell to accompany McClellan on the Peninsular campaign. Russell, in a final dispatch before returning to England (publ. April 24), charged that Stanton acted from jealousy of McClellan "on political and personal grounds."
2. HA returned from Paris on Easter Monday, April 21; "This is Easter" refers to the season rather than the day.

To Charles Francis Adams, Jr.

London. 8 May. 1862.

My dear Boy

One always begins to doubt at the wrong time, and to hesitate when one should strike hardest. Knowing this my infirmity, I have made it my habit here abroad to frown it down with energy, and to persuade myself, when seeing most cause for anxiety, that the moment of suspense was nearest to its end. It needs to be here, among a people who read everything backwards that regards us, and surround us with a chaos of croaking worse than their own rookeries, to understand how hard it is always to retain one's confidence and faith. The late indecisive military events in America, are looked upon here as the sign of ultimate Southern success. I preach a very different doctrine and firmly believe that the war in its old phase is near its end. I do not see how anything but great awkwardness on our part can prevent the main southern army from being dispersed or captured in Virginia. But there is no doubt that the idea here is as strong as ever that we must ultimately fail, and unless a very few weeks show some great military result, we shall have our hands full again in this quarter. There is no fear of armed intervention, or even, I think, of immediate recognition; but a moral intervention is not impossible; or rather it is inevitable without our triumph before July. By moral intervention I mean some combined representation on the part of the European powers, in friendly language, urging our two parties to come to an understanding. If this catches us still in Virginia, it will play mischief. The worst of it is that the Governments here are forced to it. The suffering among the people in Lancashire and in France is already very great and is increasing enormously every day without any prospect of relief for months to come. This drives them into action, and has at least the one good side that if we do gain decisive advantages so as to make the Southern chances indefinitely small, we shall have Europe at our control and can dictate terms.

On the other hand, if it is right to suppose that we shall soon end the war, I am afraid we have got to face a political struggle that will be the very deuce and all. The emancipation question has got to be settled somehow, and our accounts say that at Washington the contest is getting very bitter. The men who lead the extreme Abolitionists are a rancorous set. They have done their worst this winter to over-ride the Administration rough-shod, and it has needed all Seward's skill to head them off. If we are completely victorious in the field, we shall see the slave-question come up again worse than ever, and Sumner and Chandler and Trumbull and the rest are just the men to force a new explosion.[1] Gradual measures don't suit them, and yet without their support it will be hard to carry gradual measures. I have immense confidence in Seward however, and there is said to be the most perfect confidence between him and the President, so that we shall go into the struggle with a good chance of carrying it through.

As for this country, the simple fact is that it is unanimously against us and becomes more firmly set every day. From hesitation and neutrality, people here are now fairly decided. It is acknowledged that our army is magnificent and that we have been successful and may be still more so, but the feeling is universal against us. If we succeed, it will still be the same. It is a sort of dogged, English prejudice, and there is no dealing with it.

Socially, however, we do not feel it to any unpleasant degree. People are very polite, and we seem to be in a good set and likely to get on well. The season has begun and we have engagements in plenty. I hope, with time, to get well into society, though just now I am only hovering on the outskirts of it. My greatest achievement in this career came off the other night when we were invited to the old Dowager Duchess of Somerset's who is decidedly original,[2] and to my unutterable horror, I found myself performing for the first time in my life, a double-shuffle in the shape of a Scotch reel, with the daughter of an unbelieving Turk for a partner. For twenty minutes I improvised a dance that would have done honor to Taglioni.[3] When I got through, in a state of helpless exhaustion and agony of mind, I was complimented by the company on my success.

Last night who should I meet at a little reception, but our friend Russell, the Special Correspondent of the London Times. Some one offered to introduce me to him and I consented with pleasure. He was a little embarrassed, I thought, but very good-natured. I said I was sorry he had returned, whereat he laughed and remarked that personally he was glad, but he regretted having lost the chance of showing his good-will to us by describing our successes. I only was with him a moment, and he closed the conversation by saying that if I thought it would be agreeable to my father, he would like to call upon him. I assented to this the more willingly because I am told that Russell declares on all sides that he is wholly a Northerner and always has been, and that between his private opinions and his opinions as suited to the doctrines of the Times, there is a decided difference.

I think it is about time for us now to begin to expect another breeze here in London and the usual panic and expectation of departure. If you were at home I should write particulars, but as I've never yet had one of my letters to you acknowledged or answered since you've been at Port Royal, and as I've written pretty regularly every fortnight, there's no great encouragement to trust secrets to paper. So much however, is pretty well known. Since we made our great step from Kentucky into Alabama, our Government has been pressing the European Governments energetically to withdraw themselves from their belligerent position. But anyone who knows English sentiment and politics now, knows that there is not the remotest chance of any such step. The sympathy of the Administration, of the Lords, of the Commons and of the people throughout the country, may be dormant perhaps; I hope it is, though I believe it's not; but beyond a doubt it is not with our Union. I have no fear that there will be any hostile acts on the part of this country, but before Parliament closes, which may be in June, you may be sure that the Ministry will do nothing that is likely to provoke attack; least of all anything so unpopular as the throwing over of the South would be. Meanwhile the contest between the two gentlemen here, is getting to be flavored with as copious dashes of vinegar as you would wish to see. About once a week the wary Chieftain sharpens a stick down to a very sharp point, and then digs it into the excellent Russell's ribs. The first two or three times the joke was born with well-bred politeness and calm indifference, but the truth is, the sticks became so devilish sharp that now things are being thrown round with considerable energy, and our friend Russell is not in entirely a good temper. The prospect at this moment is that the breeze will soon change into settled rough weather and perhaps we shall have a regular storm, for if we conquer in Virginia, I hope and trust that Seward will give this Government the option of eating their words, or having their rump kicked. And I don't know whether I should derive a keener satisfaction from seeing them forced to overthrow their whole political fabric as regards the South, at our demand, or from seeing our Minister here take his leave of the country until they are able at last to bring their stomachs down to that point without further prompting. In other words whether they will prefer to act the part of a well-bred dog, or suffer the kicking.

We are anxious to hear from you, and I expect soon something that will stand publication. There is no news except that we are a year older than when we saw you last. I wish I were wiser. At all events I am getting even more commonplace than ever.

Ever Yrs   W.E.[4]

MS: MHi
  1. Zachariah Chandler (1813–1879) of Wisconsin, Republican senator 1857–1875, 1879. Lyman Trumbull (1813–1896) of Illinois, Republican senator 1855–1873.
  2. Margaret Shaw-Stewart Seymour (d. 1880), widow of the 11th duke of Somerset and stepmother of the 12th duke, first lord of the admiralty 1859–1866.
  3. The ballet dancer Marie Taglioni (1804–1884).
  4. *W.E.*: a gibe at HA's pretentious and pedantic cousin William Everett.

To Charles Francis Adams, Jr.

London 16 May. 1862.

My dear Boy

My last letter to you was dated the 8th. Since then I have received a long one from you dated the 6th April with a postscript of the 11th. I was glad to get it for I had begun to think you had given up the pen for the sword with a vengeance.

Before this reaches you, I suppose you will be in motion, and I hope that the war will be at an end. It would be a mere piece of unjustifiable wantonness for the Southern generals to defend Charleston, if they are defeated in Virginia. So, although I would like to see you covered with glory, I would be extremely well satisfied to hear that you had ended the campaign and ridden into Charleston without firing a shot or drawing a sabre.

Last Sunday afternoon, the day after my letter to you had gone, telling how hard it was to sustain one's own convictions against the scepticism of a nation, I returned from taking a walk on Rotten Row with my very estimable friend Baron Brincken,[1] and on reaching home, I was considerably astounded at perceiving the Chief in an excited manner dance across the entry and ejaculate "We've got New Orleans." Philosopher as I am and constant in a just and tenacious virtue, I confess that even I was considerably interested for the moment. So leaving Sir Charles Lyell regarding my abrupt departure through one eye-glass with some apparent astonishment,[2] I took a cab and drove down to Mr Weed. Meeting him in the street near his hotel, I leaped out of the cab, and each of us simultaneously drew out a telegram, which we exchanged. His was Mr Peabody's private business-telegram; mine was an official one from Seward. We then proceeded together to the telegraph office and sent a despatch to Mr Dayton at Paris; and finally I went round to the Diplomatic Club and had the pleasure of enunciating my sentiments. Here my own agency ended; but Mr Weed drank his cup of victory to the dregs. He spread the news in every direction, and finally sat down to dinner at the Reform Club with two sceptical old English friends of our side, and had the pleasure of hearing the news-boys outside shout "Rumored capture of New Orleans" in an evening Extra, while the news was posted at Brookes's, and the whole town was in immense excitement as though it were an English defeat.[3]

Indeed the effect of the news here has been greater than anything yet. It has acted like a violent blow in the face on a drunken man. The next morning the Times came out and gave fairly in that it had been mistaken; it had believed Southern accounts and was deceived by them. This morning it has an article still more remarkable, and intimates for the first time that it sees little more chance for the South. This is, we think, a preparation for withdrawing their belligerent declaration and acknowledging again the authority of the Federal Government over all the national territory, to be absolute and undisputed. One more victory will bring us up to this, I am confident. That done, I shall consider, not only that the nation has come through a struggle such as no other nation ever heard of, but in a smaller and personal point of view, I shall feel much relieved and pleased at the successful career of the Chief.

You can judge of the probable effect of this last victory at New Orleans, from the fact that friend Russell of the Times (who has not called yet) gravely warned the English nation yesterday, of the magnificent army that had better be carefully watched by the English people, since it hated them like the devil and would want to have something to do. And last night, I met Mr John Bright at an evening reception, who seemed to feel somewhat in the same way. "Now," said he; "if you Americans succeed in getting over this affair, you mustn't go and get stuffy to England. Because if you do, I don't know what's to become of us who've stood up for you here." I didn't say we wouldn't, but I did tell him that *he* needn't be alarmed, for all he would have to do would be to come over to America and we would send him to Congress at once. He laughed and said he thought he had had about enough of that sort of thing in England. By the way, there is a story that he thinks of leaving Parliament.

This last week has been socially a quiet one and I have seen very little of the world, as I have no time to frequent the Club. I don't get ahead very fast in English society, because as yet I can't succeed in finding any one to introduce me among people my own age. It's the same way with all the foreigners here, and a young Englishman, with whom I talked on the subject, comforted me by acknowledging the fact and saying that as a general thing young Englishmen were seldom intimate with any one unless they had known him three or four years. He gave a practical illustration of the principle by never recognizing me since, although we sat next each other three hours at a dinner and talked all the time, besides drinking various bottles of claret. With the foreigners I do much better, but they are generally worse off than I am in society. Except for a sort of conscientious feeling, I should care little for not knowing people at balls, especially as all accounts, especially English, declare young society to be a frantic bore. But to come home without having a Lady Jane, or a Miss Cavendish, to spread about, would make me contemptible in the eyes of Boston; whereas, if I do spread them, I shall be called no end of a damn fool. For mere occupation, I have more than I can manage; for not only do I act the part of confidential secretary, but I have my dry-nurse functions to perform with as great regularity as possible, and then after the day is over and everyone in bed, I generally sit up till two o'clock amusing myself with literary toys; articles which I've had in hand in any quantity ever since I was a boy at Mrs Storey's in Harvard Street, and perpetrated "Holden Chapel."[4]

Of course I'm in love; I make a point of being that; and I know *of* a few eligible girls; but as to knowing them, a bow is the highest distinction I ever hope to receive.

Now as to your letter and its contents on the negro question. I've not published it for two reasons. The first is that the tendency here now is pro-slavery and the sympathy with the South is so great as to seek justification in everything. Your view of the case, however anti-slavery, is not encouraging nor does it tend to strengthen our case. If published, especially if by any accident known to be by you, it might be used to annoy us with effect.

My second reason, though this alone would not have decided me, is that it seems to me you are a little needlessly dark in your anticipations. One thing is certain; labor in America is dear and will remain so; American cotton will always command a premium over any other yet known; and can be most easily produced. Emancipation cannot be instantaneous. We must rather found free colonies in the south such as you are now engaged in building up at Port Royal; the nucleus of which must be military and naval stations garrisoned by *corps d'armée,* and grouped around them must be the *emeriti,* the old soldiers with their grants of land, their families, their schools, churches and Northern energy, forming common cause with the negroes in gradually sapping the strength of the slave-holders, and thus year after year carrying new industry and free institutions until their borders meet from the Atlantic, the Gulf, the Mississippi and the Tennesee in a common centre, and the old crime shall be expiated and the whole social system of the South reconstructed. Such was the system of the old Romans with their conquered countries and it was always successful. It is the only means by which we can insure our hold on the South, and plant colonies that are certain of success. It must be a military system of colonies, governed by the Executive and without any dependence upon or relation to the States in which they happen to be placed. With such a system I would allow fifty years for the South to become ten times as great and powerful and loyal as she ever was, besides being free.

Such are my ideas, and as the negroes would be extremely valuable and even necessary to the development of these colonies, or the Southern resources at all, I trust they will manage to have a career yet.

Ever Yrs   H.B.A.

MS: MHi
   1. Baron Egon von der Brinken (1834–1906), attaché of the Prussian legation.
   2. Sir Charles Lyell (1797–1875), geologist, a frequent visitor at the U.S. legation and staunch friend of the Union.
   3. The "Diplomatic Club" was the St. James's; the Reform in Pall Mall and Brooks's in St. James's Street were Liberal clubs, where good news for the Union might encounter skepticism but not hostility.
   4. HA's first contribution to the *Harvard Magazine* (1855).

To Charles Francis Adams, Jr.

London. 22 May 1862.

My dear Boy

We are still in great anxiety to know the results of the Yorktown business, having as yet arrived only as far as Williamsburg and West Point.[1] On McLellan's success in dispersing the Southern army and capturing all its means for carrying on a war, will depend more than I like to think of. If we can disperse them, too, we can immediately reduce our army one half, and all our expenses on the same scale. I dread the continuance of this war and its demoralizing effects, more than anything else, and happy would be the day when we could see the first sign of returning peace. It's likely to be hard enough work to keep our people educated and honest anyway, and the accounts that reach us of the whole-sale demoralization in the army of the West, from camp-life, and of their dirt, and whiskey and general repulsiveness, are not encouraging to one who wants to see them taught to give up that blackguard habit of drinking liquor in bar-rooms, to brush their teeth and hands and wear clean clothes and to believe that they have a duty in life besides that of getting ahead, and a responsibility for other people's acts as well as their own. The little weaknesses I speak of are faults of youth; but what will they become if America in its youth takes a permanent course towards every kind of idleness, vice and ignorance.

As for our position here, it is all that could be wished. Everyone congratulates us on the successes of our arms and there is no longer any hint at even a remonstrance, though there are questions between the Governments which in our bitter state of feeling may bring difficulty. I am very anxious to avoid anything of this sort. We must have peace for many years if we are to heal our wounds and put the country on the right track. We must bring back or create a respect for law and order and the Constitution and the civil and judicial authorities. The nation has been dragged by this infernal cotton that had better have been burning in Hell, far away from its true course, and its worst passions and tastes have been developed by a forced and bloated growth. It will depend on the generation to which you and I belong, whether the country is to be brought back to its true course and the

New England element is to carry the victory, or whether we are to be carried on from war to war and debt to debt and one military leader to another, till we lose all our landmarks and go ahead like France with a mere blind necessity to get on, without a reason or a principle. No more war's. Let's have peace for the love of God.

England will truckle to us low enough when we regain our power, and we can easily revenge ourselves on the classes of English who have been most venemous, without fighting them all. It is but to shut out their trade and encourage our own development. I am now a protectionist of the most rabid description. I want to see us developing our mines, manufactures and communications, with the most success possible. There is England's vulnerable point; but we shall have committed a blunder of the worst sort if we allow our personal prejudices to affect our national policy to the extent of a war.

By the way, I am inclined to think we shall have a great financial explosion in six months, more or less. A good deal of cotton exported might save us for a time, but it must ultimately come. I am writing to John my directions to look out for it.

This last week we have had that whited sepulchre General Cameron here, and as we were to have our first large dinner on Wednesday, he was invited to it. Then last night I took him to Monckton Milnes's[2] where he was the object of considerable interest as the man that swindled the United States Treasury. I can't say that I was proud of my charge, nor that I like his style. Thurlow Weed is quite as American, and un-English, but is very popular and altogether infinitely preferable. We all like Mr Weed very much, and are sorry that he is going home this week. As for Cameron I hope he will vanish into the steppes of Russia and wander there for eternity. He is of all my countrymen, one of the class that I most conspicuously and sincerely despise and detest.

I am getting slowly ahead here. My engagement book is well filled; one entry is as follows: Dinner at Sir William Martins'; Evening at the Duchess of Northumberland's; Countess Derby's and the Speaker of the House of Commons.[3] Don't quote this to my friends; they'll call me a damned fool. Most young men in London society have half a dozen engagements every evening, but I as yet am not a ball-goer. After all, I am as much bored by it as every one else seems to be, and a more ghastly stupid appearance than a London reception presents, damn me if I ever witnessed. It's country life that is pleasant and that I have now no chance to see, though I have a free swing of the Sturgis's place and should go down there if I had time. If I stay in England two years more, I expect to have to hunt. But another year will see me, I hope, or fear, at work on my great business in life, whatever that may be.

Mary will be a success. She does not come out this year, but will do so next. She wants depth and wit, and doesn't show so much quickness at catching and improving ideas, as I would like to have her; but she is pretty, sympathetic, and good-mannered; not highly accomplished, but tolerably well-informed. She was at dinner the other day and was much admired. By the time you get out here, you will find her ready to introduce you into society.

MS: MHi
1. McClellan's forces took Yorktown on May 4, but the month's siege allowed time for Richmond's defenses to be prepared.
2. Richard Monckton Milnes (1809–1885), created Baron Houghton in 1863, M.P., literary patron, "social power," and in his youth the author of "verses, which some readers thought poetry, and which were certainly not altogether prose" (*Education*, p. 124). His country house was Fryston, near Pontefract, Yorkshire.
3. Sir William Martin (1807–1880), scholar and jurist, chief justice of New Zealand 1841–1857; Eleanor Grosvenor Percy (d. 1911), wife of the 4th duke of Northumberland; Emma Stanley, wife of the leader of the Tory opposition, the earl of Derby; John Evelyn Denison (1800–1873), later Viscount Ossington, speaker of the House of Commons.

To Frederick William Seward

London 30 May 1862.

My dear Sir

x x x x x x x x x[1]

A few weeks ago a young man made his appearance in the office of the Legation when I happened to be there with the under Secretary, and asked for a passport, telling us that he had just arrived from Charleston in the British steamer Economist which ran the blockade about the 1st of April. He declares himself a Union Man: son of a Dutch merchant in New York. We cross examined him very closely, and he told a straight story. The particular part that I wanted to mention was that about their running the blockade. He had gone on board the Economist at night, for fear of being arrested, and they ran out at once. He says that they saw the blockading fleet all about them, the night not being dark, and that one of them, which he called (on what ground I can't say) the Wabash followed the Economist some distance at about a mile and a half off. So alarmed were they all on board, and so confused and out of trim with their start, that had the Wabash only fired a gun they would have surrendered, at least so our friend stated. But instead of this, after following them in a leisurely way for a few miles, the Wabash dropped off and left them to go on to Nassau. On board the Economist it was supposed that the Wabash had mistaken them for one of their own squadron.

I don't know that I should have troubled you with this story except that within a few days another man has been here with much the same tale, except that this time the vessel he was in was a small trading sloop or schooner. We have had dozens of such accounts, and though the political importance they once had, is now over, they are irritating to us and tend to lower our estimation among the English and all, as they say, for the want of a proper spirit of vigilance and dash among our seamen. They fight well, but they can't watch.

I hope that before this reaches you, Charleston will have followed Nashville, New Orleans, and Norfolk.

But it may be worth while that you should know the facts. x x x x x x x x x x x x x x x x x x x x x x x x x x x x x x x x x x x x x x x

I am &c &c &c   H B Adams.

F. W. Seward Esq.

Source: Copy of the extract sent by Gideon Welles, secretary of the navy, to Samuel F. DuPont, commander of the blockade squadron at Port Royal, S.C. The copy is at the Eleutherian Mills Historical Library, Greenville, Delaware. MS not found.

   1. The copyist's x's apparently indicate omissions.

To Charles Francis Adams, Jr.

London 6 June. 1862.

My dear Boy

I did not write to you last week, as I had nothing to say and no time to say it. It is very little better now, but still I shall drop you a line. This is now our season here, the Derby week, and I am run to death and ruined by cab-hire. You would enjoy it as a change more than I do as a business, though my danger is now by no means that of getting to dislike it too much. If I could only get a few intimates here, it would be very well indeed, but my time is too much occupied for that.

Yesterday I took Mary out to Eton to see what was once Eton Montem,[1] but now is only a sort of hybrid Class-day and Commencement. The Sturgis boys are there and Mr and Mrs Sturgis invited us out to their room. It rained like the deuce and Tuke Parker and I had the satisfaction of standing in the grass on the banks of the Thames and watching the antick spires, and the grand old castle of Windsor above us, through a gay rain and an evening fog, until near 9 o'clock P.M. We survived it however, and it only spoilt the boys' fun and my pantaloons.[2]

The day before was Derby Day. I didn't go; never have been; should go however if some one would invite me who would make it pleasant. Instead, Mary and I went to the Exhibition in the morning.[3] I suppose you in America have an idea that we drop in to the Exhibition every day or so. But as it's three miles off, and this is the season, the process is a difficult one. It's a splendid thing to see and I wish I could get there oftener.

The evening before the Derby, the Chief and I were down at the House of Commons from five o'clock P.M. till one A.M. listening to the great debate of the season. This is one of the sights that I enjoy most. With us debate has gone out, and set speeches and personalities have taken its place. But here, though they no longer speak as they used in the old days of Pitt and Fox, with rhetorical effort and energy, there is still admirable debating. That night we heard Palmerston, Disraeli, Horsman and Cobden.[4] Palmerston is a poor speaker, wants fluency and power, and talks the most miserable sophistry, but he does it so amusingly and plausibly and has such prestige that even Disraeli's keenness puts no quencher on him. Gladstone is the best speaker in the House, but next to him I should place Disraeli.[5] He looks precisely like the pictures in Punch, and speaks with a power of making hits that is infinitely amusing. He kept me in a roar three quarters of an hour, and the House cheered him steadily. Cobden was very good too. He damaged Horsman dreadfully. But the most striking part of the debate was that not a word as to America or interference was said in it. This was peculiar because the debate was on the subject of retrenchment, and retrenchment was necessary because of the American war. Six months ago such a debate would not have taken place, but in its place we should have had war-speeches with no end.

Our position here now, putting aside a few diplomatic questions, is much as it might be at home. The Speaker calls the Chief, "The Conqueror," and it is only now and then, when our armies stop a moment to take breath, and they think here that we are in trouble, that the opposition raises its head a little and barks. Indeed the position we have here is one of a great deal of weight, and of course so long as our armies march forward, so long our heads are elevated higher and higher until we bump the stars. I hear very little about our friend Mason. He is said to be very anxious and to fear a rebellion within the rebellion. He has little or no attention paid him except as a matter of curiosity, though occasionally we are told of his being at dinner somewhere or other. A Southern newspaper called the Index, lately started here, contains numbers of southern letters, all of which are so excruciantly "never conquer" in their tone, that one is forced to the belief that they think themselves very near that last ditch.

I've seen nothing from you for some time past, but I see it stated that Sargeant is now your Colonel. I've half expected to hear that you had applied for some command in the negro regiment that is being raised where you are. It wouldn't be pleasant work to be sure, but it offers perhaps a better field for usefulness than that you are now in. I hardly see what good you are doing now that you wouldn't be doing then, with much more besides; and though the labor may not promise much immediate result, it will give the blacks a certain kind of education and fit them for higher kinds. As for making them effective soldiers, I don't think it of much consequence whether you succeed or fail.

For me it is always *facilis descensus.*[6] I become bluer and bluer at the prospect. But then the country has been so turned upside down now, that all the world will be as little able to go back into a path as I am. We are in the full blast of society. Tonight we give a state dinner to Earl Russell. I don't know whether I ever mentioned to you that our intrigues against the cook were at last crowned with success, and now we have a good one who is a vixen and frightens our poor lady to death. I must now go out to leave some cards; so farewell. Ask Ben Crowninshield to answer my last letter.[7]

MS: MHi
1. An ancient Eton celebration usually held in May but abolished in 1847.
2. Henry Tuke Parker (1824–1890), a friend of Charles Sumner residing in London since 1854, assistant to Benjamin Moran. "Watching the antick spires": an allusion to Thomas Gray's "Ode on a Distant Prospect of Eton College" (1747).
3. The International Exhibition at Brompton opened May 1 in an immense new structure composed of two glass domes connected by a nave 800 feet long; it was two-thirds the size of the original Crystal Palace exhibition (1851).
4. Benjamin Disraeli (1804–1881), Conservative leader of the House of Commons, three times chancellor of the exchequer and twice prime minister; he was also a popular novelist whose political novels were favorites of HA. Edward Horsman (1807–1876), a Liberal M.P. unfriendly to the Union. Richard Cobden (1804–1865), Manchester textile manufacturer, founder of the Anti-Corn Law League, independent M.P., and strong defender of the Union.
5. William Ewart Gladstone (1809–1898), chancellor of the exchequer 1859–1866 and four times Liberal prime minister.
6. *Facilis descensus:* an easy descent [to hell]; Vergil's *Aeneid.*
7. Crowninshield was now a captain in CFA2's cavalry regiment.

To Charles Francis Adams, Jr.

London 4 July 1862

My dear Boy

It is sometime since I last wrote. I have hardly had the courage to do so in the face of what is now going on at home, and today we hear news of a battle near Charleston on the 16th which has done little to encourage me. Your last letter speaking of your illness and general position troubled our camp much. I had to pooh-pooh it more than I liked in order to stop the noise. Hard as your life is and threatens to become, I would like well to share it with you in order to escape in the consciousness of action a little of the struggle against fancied evils that we feel here.

The truth is we are suffering now under one of those periodical returns of anxiety and despondency that I have so often written of. The last was succeeded by that brilliant series of successes which gave us New Orleans, Yorktown, Norfolk and Memphis, and perhaps this may end as well, but meanwhile we are haunted by stories about McClellan and by the strange want of life that seems, justly or not, to characterize our military and naval motions. You at Charleston seem to be an exception to the rule of stagnation which leaves us everywhere on the defensive even when attacking. A little dash does so much to raise one's spirits, and now our poor men only sicken in marshes. I think of it all as little as I can.

Our own position here is now so uninteresting as to give us nothing to think of. After some pretty sharp fighting and curious experiences that I daren't trust to paper,[1] we are again quiet and undisturbed, waiting the event of the struggle at Richmond. Things are not over-inspiring with us, but I don't know that they look much brighter with the English or French. The suffering among the operatives in Lancashire is very great and is increasing in a scale that makes people very uncomfortable though as yet they keep quiet about it. Cotton is going up to extraordinary prices; in a few days only it advanced three cents a pound and is still rising. Prices for cotton goods are merely nominal and vary according to the opinions of the holders, so that the whole trade is now pure speculation. Mills are closing in every direction. Add to this that the season has been bad and a short crop is now considered a certainty, and you can comprehend how anxious people must be to know how they are to weather next winter. No doubt this state of things will soon produce fresh agitation for mediation or intervention before long if no progress is made by our armies, but as yet we enjoy quiet.

Meanwhile the London season has come and is nearly over, and after dragging ourselves from one house to another for nearly every evening in two months, we are beginning to look for a little quiet. I live wholly at home, very quietly, except for these evening battles which are sufficiently stupid to be a precious small attraction; especially as I stand on my dignity and never ask any favors, not even an introduction, and as it's not the fashion to introduce people here, I make slow progress in society. Certainly I personally have small cause for gratitude to the English people. Precious little attention have I received from them, young or old, except in a few very rare cases. I have no rudeness or slight to complain of, but I'm quite sure that if a young Englishman came to America and was received as I have been here, he would not be highly gratified. Perhaps it's my own fault. Indeed I know that by a little exertion I could force myself ahead; but it doesn't suit my ideas of the dignity of our calling to make advances to any one; far less to force myself anywhere.

Still I like it very well and know people enough to feel at home everywhere and sure of my position. If it were not for home matters it would be all well enough, but they have a good deal of influence here, which is felt rather than seen. We have entertained a good deal; evening receptions once a week for Americans, and several state dinners for English. Two are now coming off which will finish up all that work for some time to come and pay our debts. The Exhibition has brought a swarm of Americans to London who demand a good deal of attention, and all to very little purpose. I am tired of the work and hope to have you over here some day to relieve me and send me home, for as to profitable study, one's life is so unhinged in these days that steady mental application is beyond me. Mechanical work I do to any extent, but study is hopeless.

Bob Winthrop is now here; John Bancroft has just left for home. We have had the house crowded with family visitors, but are now quiet again and alone. There is no news to tell, not even gossip. The Queen's second daughter has just been married, but the Queen forbade any demonstration and attended during the ceremony in deep black crape. The couple were swung off in her dining room. Such behavior doesn't increase the gaiety here.[2] The season has been a gloomy one; many deaths and much mourning. When we shall see a bright sun and blue sky again I don't know, but after having fairly persuaded the Chief to take a country-house, the Chiefess has indicated a preference not to do so but for travelling; a process which means infinite annoyance to herself and to everyone else. I am planning for myself and the school-boy a foot excursion into Cornwall in August, but I have small idea that we shall ever carry it out.

Today there is an American Celebration at Sydenham Crystal Palace.[3] I have to go as no one else of the family will. But I should do it with an easier mind if I knew what was going to happen in America.

MS: MHi

1. On June 11 Palmerston wrote directly to CFA expressing outrage at General Butler's "infamous" order at New Orleans which directed that women who insulted Union soldiers were to be treated as prostitutes, that is, put in jail. Palmerston asserted that the order handed over "the female inhabitants of a conquered city to the unbridled license of an unrestrained soldiery." CFA responded indignantly and, after a week's exchanges, established that he declined to receive such a note (Moran, *Journal*, II, 1027–1029).

2. Seven months after Prince Albert's death, the queen was still in seclusion; the wedding of Princess Alice (1843–1878) to Louis IV (1837–1892), grand duke of Hesse-Darmstadt, was said to be more like a funeral.

3. A reconstruction at Sydenham, 6 miles south of London, of Sir Joseph Paxton's Great Exhibition Hall of 1851, remained a popular pleasure resort till the eve of World War I.

To Charles Francis Adams, Jr.

Saturday 19 July. 1862.

My dear Fellow

Knowing that you would probably be anxious to hear from us what effect the bad news of June 26–30 might have on our position here, I take the last moment to write in order to tell you what I think we are to expect.[1] Certainly it was a violent blow. We suffered several days of very great anxiety, knowing that the current here was rising every hour and running harder against us than at any time since the Trent affair. This reverse called out at once all the latent hostility here, and there was nothing to do but to give way. I shut myself up, went to no more parties and avoided contact with everyone except friends. I have given up trying to cultivate people. It's not my forte. Meanwhile mamma made day ghastly by her wails, and it was all Mary and I could do to keep any sort of cheerfulness up in the house. The only bright spot in the week was the reception of your letter. As we had all relied on your being safe in the hospital, or if not there, with your regiment which we knew was not engaged, your letter was quite welcome, as it told us first both of your going in and your coming out. I congratulate you, and apropos to that, I congratulate your General Hunter on his negro-army letter.[2] We *all* here sustain him and I assure you that the strongest means of holding Europe back is the sight of an effective black army.

Nevertheless our trouble here was extreme. As the week passed, it was not diminished. Nor is it now, I fear, permanently so. It arrived however at its culminating point last night. It so happened that last night was the occasion of an expected debate in the Commons on a motion in favor of mediation. We had been busy in preparing for it and had assurances that all was right. But lo and behold, at two o'clock yesterday afternoon, in rushes a member of the Commons, and half a dozen alarmists in his rear, with an evening paper whose telegraphic column was headed in big letters; "Capitulation of McLellan's Army. Flight of McLellan on a steamer. Later from America." This astounding news for a moment made me almost give way. But a single glance at dates showed us that it was an utter swindle, and that we had bulletins from McLellan of two days later than the day of the reported surrender. The next reflexion led us to see that it was intended for the debate of the same evening, and we, who know the seal, recognised the stamp of our old friends the Southern liars who juggled Georgia out of the Union by telegraph.[3] But the consternation among our friends was incredible and even when they knew it must be false, they still shook and shuddered with terror. Every Englishman believed it, or doubted in a tone that showed he wanted to believe it. As for me, I have come to consider it my whole duty here to keep up the spirits of the community and so did the best I could to laugh the lie off. Luckily its effect on the Commons was very good, for it disposed them to postpone action and tended to quiet them. Palmerston made a good speech, and the motion was not pressed to a division. This morning the Arabia's news has arrived, three days later, which relieves us again for a time of our anxiety, and induces us to believe that the enemy were as much crippled by their victory as we by our defeat.

Thus the pinch has again passed by for the moment and we breathe more freely. But I think I wrote to you some time ago that if July found us still in Virginia, we could no longer escape interference. I think now that it is inevitable. The only delay thus far has been caused by the difficulty in inducing the five great powers to unite, and Russia and Austria to act with England in any sense favorable to the South. That unity cannot much longer fail to be obtainable. England alone or with France will not move, but their idea is that if all the great powers were to unite in offering mediation, they could by their moral influence alone, force some result. If the North defied them, a simple recognition of the South by them, would, they think, secure her independence. And this belief is probably correct.

It must now be the effort of the North to cast upon the South the responsibility of standing against a settlement. Here will be three means of hampering European attempts; the slavery question, the boundary question, and the Mississipi; and it is the slavery question from which we can derive the greatest strength in this running battle. You see we are stripping and squaring off, to say nothing of sponging, for the next round. If our armies sustain us, we shall win. If not, we shall soon see the limit of our hopes.

All well and right. Give my best remembrances to all my friends.

MS: MHi

1. In the Seven Days' Battles (June 25–July 1) Lee set out to destroy McClellan's army advancing on Richmond. On June 27–28, McClellan withdrew toward the James River. He withstood Lee's attacks on Malvern Hill (July 1), and the next day Lee retreated to Richmond.

2. Gen. David Hunter (1802–1886) asked in an open letter for authorization to enlist all loyal persons, that is, to recruit blacks, to replace troops being withdrawn from his command, the Department of the South (S.C., Ga., Fla.), to reinforce McClellan.

3. In Dec. 1860, when congressional debate on compromise was at its hottest, Sen. Robert Toombs telegraphed his "fellow-citizens of Georgia" (through the Savannah News) that they could expect no guarantees from the Republicans and must recognize disunion as fact (Dec. 22). On Jan. 2 Georgia elected a no-compromise majority to its secession convention.

To Charles Francis Adams, Jr.

London. 5 September. 1862.

My dear Charles:

I have received two letters from you since I last wrote, which is now a month ago or more. Your's were dated July 27 and August 4, I think, or thereabouts. You complain of my not acknowledging your letters, but I rather think I've acknowledged all you've written which is not a large number of late.

Your appointment reached us some time ago and I was rejoiced at it, because I think such a place as this gives more room for expansion than that of a regimental officer.[1] I doubt whether the atmosphere of Lieutenants is healthy, or of Captains or Majors. I think you have grown rusty at Hilton Head and I want to hear more vigorous talk. As to your speculations about the end of the war and a peace, I won't say that I wouldn't consent to argue about it some day, but you know perfectly well that until we've driven the south into their cotton fields we have no chance even to offer those terms. Perhaps on the broad national question I look at the matter differently from you. Apart from other causes, I am here in Europe and of course am influenced by European opinion. Firmly convinced as I am that there can be no peace on our continent so long as the southern people exist, I don't much care whether they are destroyed by emancipation, or in other words a vigorous system of guerilla war carried on by negroes on our side, or by the slower and more doubtful measures of choaking them with their own cotton. Perhaps before long we shall have to use both weapons as vigorously as we now are using the last. But one thing is clear to my mind, which is that we must not let them as an independent state get the monopoly of cotton again, unless we want to find a powerful and a bitterly hostile nation on our border, supported by all the moral and social influence of Great Britain in peace; certain in war to drag us into all the European complications; sure to be in perpetual anarchy within, but always ready to disturb anything and everything without; to compel us to support a standing army no less large than if we conquer them and hold them so, and with infinite means of wounding and scattering dissension among us. We must ruin them before we let them go or it will all have to be done over again. And we must exterminate them in the end, be it long or be it short, for it is a battle between us and slavery.

I see that your regiment is ordered to Virginia which shows a gleam of reason in the war-department. What it was ever sent to Port Royal for, the Lord he knows. At any rate, however it has spared you some hard fighting, and with the prospect you have now before you, I think you needn't be sorry for that. For my own part I confess that I value human life at a pretty low price, and God knows I set no higher value on my own than on others. I always was a good deal of a sceptic and speculator in theories and think precious small potatoes of man in general and myself in particular. But I confess to feeling very badly when the news comes of our disasters and losses. Poor Stephen Perkins! Poor Hamilton Kuhn![2] What on earth was Union or the national future to Hamilton Kuhn! One would have booked him for a single care in life as he grew older; that of his own comfort. With Stephen it was different. I have a kind of an idea that Stephen thought much as I do about life. He always seemed to me to take rather a contemptuous view of the world in general, and I rather like to imagine him, after the shock and the pain was over, congratulating himself that at last he was through with all the misères of an existence that had bored him and that offered him little that he cared for; and now he could turn his mind to the exploring of a new life, with new duties and a new career, after having done all that man can do to discharge his debt to his God and his fellow-men in the old. There are men enough in Europe who hold these ideas with more or less variation, but Stephen and perhaps Arthur Dexter are the only ones among us whom I should call bitten with them. With Stephen, his eyes excused them. With Arthur, his digestion.

Our life here is quiet but very busy. No more is heard of intervention. Six hundred thousand men have put an end to that, and the English think besides that the South need no help. Of late the troubles in Italy have drawn peoples minds away from us and as their harvest is very poor, our grain is too necessary to joke about. I am hunting for a country house to take a month or so fresh air in, during the London fogs. Everyone has now left town. Frank Parker is here just now on his way home after a six weeks tour. We have ourselves been on a little journey in Devon, and I, as a relaxation in other duties, am trying to hunt old Henry Adams up.[3]

Ever Yrs.

MS: MHi

1. In August, when his regiment was ordered north to join the Army of the Potomac, CFA2 was assigned (through Seward's intervention) to the staff of Gen. John Pope. At the time of this letter HA did not know that on reaching Washington, CFA2 had decided to return to his regiment because it was "about to see active cavalry service" and Pope was said to be "a humbug and . . . sure to come to grief" (CFA2 to JQA2, Aug. 28).

2. Stephen George Perkins (1835–1862), killed at Cedar Mountain, Va., Aug. 9. James Hamilton Kuhn (1838–1862), the younger brother of Charles Kuhn, was killed at Richmond, June 30.

3. Henry Adams (c. 1583–1646) migrated with his family in 1638 to Mount Wollaston, which later became Braintree and then Quincy. JA identified the place of family origin as Devon; the actual location was finally established in 1927 by J. Gardner Bartlett, *Henry Adams of Somersetshire, England, and Braintree, Mass.*

To Charles Francis Adams

London. Saturday. P.M. [13 Sept. 1862]

Dear Sir:[1]

The enclosed despatches have arrived today. As you see they are not favorable, nor do I understand them. From the reference to a battle on Saturday I presume that the enemy must have resumed the battle of the 29th with the advantage on their side. Nothing more is heard from Pope and the whole thing is a muddle.

There are two days later yet to arrive which I will enclose also, if the telegram comes in time. Nothing else has come.

Very truly,   H.B.A.

MS: MHi

1. CFA was visiting Thomas Baring at Norman Court. These dispatches reversed the earlier news that the Second Battle of Bull Run (Aug. 29–30) had been a victory for Pope.

To Charles Francis Adams, Jr.

London. 10 October. 1862.

My dear Boy

I have received nothing from you since my last of some weeks back, and with such sharp fighting as is going on, I have a kind of dread of writing.[1] Still, as I suppose it's a pleasure to you to receive letters, I will try and hash up something. Only not about the war. A dozen times within the last two months I have been on the point of leaving this and joining you; and unless something *very* successful happens *very* soon in your profession, you may confidently expect to see me at home and enrolled early next year. Under present prospects here, short-handed as we already are, I must stay till the crash comes.

Our life is placid; our amusements not exciting, and our pleasures few. We drag on from day to day, writing, working and eating. I only wish some of you fellows could come over here and enliven yourselves with it, for it bores me, and yet I don't know what, as a matter of pleasure, I would rather do than stay here; certainly I shouldn't look for much pleasure in seeing people butchered without result, as you are doing. I hardly know how time passes, but it does go on, and as I am never wholly idle, I am well-enough pleased with it. There is almost always some-one passing through here. Some weeks ago it was Jim Higginson who cheered me up under the news of Pope's defeat; Ye Gods! how that cut us up here! You may tell Major Higginson, if you see him, that his brother looked well and was in very good spirits, doing his best to keep up mine. And I almost determined to go home with him, he wanted me to, so much. Then Hull and Lizzy came and just left us yesterday on their return home.[2] Hull was with me a good deal and I was quite jolly under the unaccustomed excitement. We went together to various places of amusement and haunts of vice such as Cremorne, which bored us dreadfully.[3] The poor old fellow's neck is still very bad, and he is not so vivacious as he used to be, but he was still dreadfully droll. I took him to the new Turkish bath here, a gorgeous establishment, fitted up with any quantity of eastern wrinkles, lined and paved with marble, where you lie on divans or carpets or the bare stone, in a dim dim religious light from a big brick dome, with a few holes in it for colored light. I am eastern in my tastes; a perfect satrap; and I affect the religious light, where you lie on marble, which, for marble, is perhaps not so very hard, and smoke your cigar and chibouc too, if you order it, and drink sherbet which is brought to you by grinning and perspiry Ethiop youths, especially imported from the east to minister to our effeminacy. While so reclining and dozing over my cigar in a temperature of $120°$, I usually lazily meditate upon you and reflect that this would do you good. Hull and I went together, and Hull began by stubbing his toes with the boot-jack which made him cross, and then flying into a passion with a small boy and cursing him loudly and indiscriminately till I howled over it. Finally we got stripped and he concluded reluctantly to try the public room, into which we were ushered; a sort of dusky Egyptian tomb, with dark figures lying about. When we were fairly reclined, he began to comment on the appearance of the parties present; especially one pot-bellied party, magnificently extended on his back on an elevated platform in the middle of the dome, then undergoing the champooing process, in a state of entire nudity. Hull's public observations kept me in a state of convulsion, and seemed to bewilder the gloomy Englishmen near us, who never smile in London and look with horror on anyone that laughs, damn 'em.

Geo. Howe and his wife are now here. No doubt, mamma will write you all about Alice who looks very ill, I think. George has not changed a single hair. He is as stately and magnificent as in his early days. I drove down to the city with him yesterday at his invitation, and we had a long talk. He and his wife dine with us today without company, as they go nowhere now.

I am buying a horse and we are meditating on a country-house for a few weeks; rather risky experiments with almost a certainty of ship-wreck within three months. However, I am tired of waiting for events; I have wholly drawn out of all society except American; I am occupied to my own satisfaction with other studies; and I am ready to go straight ahead until knocked down. It won't be long. If you really ever come to the conclusion that I had better come home (in case for example of our leaving here for the continent, as is not impossible, or to relieve John of the pressure on him to go to the war, by going in his place), a single word from you will bring me to the Potomac at once.

If you see Ben Crowninshield, tell him I shall answer his letter next week. I am immensely obliged to him for writing.

MS: MHi
1. CFA2 took part in the battle of Antietam, Sept. 14–17, in which McClellan turned back Lee's invasion north into Maryland.
2. Isaac Hull Adams and his sister Elizabeth Coombs Adams (1808–1903).
3. Cremorne Gardens, in Chelsea, a mid-Victorian site of fêtes, masquerades, illuminations, and balloon ascents.

To Frederick William Seward

London. 29 October. 1862.

My dear Sir:

The enclosed papers are rather amusing, but not necessarily official, so I inclose them to you in order to save my father the trouble of writing. Perhaps they will justify your father in placing the "Sailor's Home" on the black list of the Navy Department, and thus the "robed" Mr Luna may get his revenge. In that case the owners would pay dear for 2000 cigars.

I sent you in June last a note containing two important inclosures accidentally overlooked in making up the mail; but I am still a little doubtful whether you received them, especially as I am more than a little disgusted by the stories of southern origin here as to their success in learning our secrets; stories which unfortunately seem to contain a larger grain of truth than their origin would lead one to suppose. May I venture again to beg a single line to know whether you received that package, for if not I will at once send a duplicate.[1] As a general thing I hold myself apart from active politics, as my position here is just such a one as to get me into trouble if I mix in business. In that particular case, it was my father's direction, not my disposition that made me the copyist.

We have troubled you with our letters to my brother, not knowing how to get at him. I hope they have not put you to much inconvenience.

We are expecting Mr Weed continually. I hope he doesn't mean to disappoint us, for though the immediate danger of motion here seems to have again passed off, I am confident that we Londoners are going to have a stormy winter and he will be needed.[2] Luckily all Europe is in about as dangerous a state as we are, and if we must make war, it won't be long, I hope before we kindle a fire that will be curious to see. I see little of the world here, but my few diplomatic acquaintances shake their heads like Solomons when I ask how the Prussian question, the Danish question, the Eastern question, the Italian question, the Greek question or any of the other million questions, are coming on. As you see, the Greek one is now suddenly forced up.

Mr Blatchford passed through here last week, with his wife who is a great addition to your corps diplomatique.[3] With so many brilliant women as we have in America, I think the President might have given us one or two more to show in Europe. Mr & Mrs. B. were both extremely pleasant and gave us more information than we had received for months.

We are certainly not very contented here; much hostility and always-diminishing cordiality is the rule; but when I think of your father's position, ours becomes a Paradise.

With my best regards to him and all your family, I am &c &c

H. B. Adams.

F. W. Seward Esq. &c &c &c

Many applications from would-be emigrants come to us here, some of which are really valuable. Couldn't something be done for them?

MS: NRU
1. The enclosures were Palmerston's note of June 15 and CFA's reply of June 16, more or less ending the contretemps over Butler's New Orleans occupation policy.
2. On Nov. 7 Seward asked Weed to return to London, but withdrew the request at once because the administration needed Weed at home.
3. Seward's friend Richard M. Blatchford was minister to the Papal States 1862–1863.

To Charles Francis Adams, Jr.

London. 21 November. 1862.

My dear old boy:

It's some time since I last wrote, but as you never get my letters apparently, perhaps it doesn't much matter. Besides, I had nothing to say, nor have I now. Last week and the week before last we were out of town, and as I always tag after the family, I went with them to the sea-shore, the Chief and I relieving each other. The truth is, I stick my nose to the grindstone so

Charles Francis Adams, Jr., and fellow officers

my time may prove to have been wasted, and then
nothing left but a truncated life.

I should care the less for all this if I could see
your path any clearer, but while my time may prove
to have been wasted, I don't see but what yours must
prove so. At least God forbid that you should remain
an officer longer than is necessary. And what then?
The West is possible; indeed, I have thought of that
myself. But what we want, my dear boy, is a
school. We want a national set of young men
like ourselves or better, to start new influences not
only in politics, but in literature, in law, in society, and throughout the whole social organism
of the country. A national school of our own
generation. And that is what America has no
power to create. In England the Universities
centralize ability and London gives a field. So
in France, Paris encourages and combines
these influences. But with us, we should need at
least six perfect geniuses placed, or rather, spotted
over the country and all working together; whereas our generation as yet has not produced one
nor the promise of one. It's all random, insulated work, for special and temporary and personal purposes, and we have no means, power or
hope of combined action for any unselfish end.

Henry Adams to Charles Francis Adams, Jr.,
November 21, 1862

assiduously on purpose. If I were to let up here, and make friends of my own age and enjoy myself, I should destroy my purpose and had better go home. It's only on condition of being bored that I can conscientiously remain. Once too I had visions of an active agency in affairs here. This, even into its remotest branches, I have been forced to foreswear, and now begin by assuring everyone that I am connected in no way with official business, and am merely a visitor temporarily living with my father in England. Under cover of this character I can move much more freely than in any other, and the results of my unfortunate expedition to Lancashire a year ago thoroughly frightened me from every and any act that was likely to expose me even to the risk of a scorching of the same kind. Perhaps the lesson is a good one on the whole. My work is now limited to a careful observation of events here and assistance in the manual labor of the place, and to a study of history and politics which seem to me most necessary to our country for the next century. The future is a blank to me as I suppose it is also to you. I have no plans nor can have any, so long as my course is tied to that of the Chief. Should you at the end of the war, wish to take my place, in case the services of one of us were still required, I should return to Boston and Horace Gray, and I really do not know whether I should regret the change. The truth is, the experience of four years has done little towards giving me confidence in myself. The more I see, the more I am convinced that a man whose mind is balanced like mine, in such a way that what is evil never seems unmixed with good, and what is good always streaked with evil; an object never seems important enough to call out strong energies till they are exhausted, nor necessary enough not to allow of its failure being possible to retrieve; in short, a mind which is not strongly positive and absolute, cannot be steadily successful in action, which requires quickness and perseverance. I have steadily lost faith in myself ever since I left college, and my aim is now so indefinite that all my time may prove to have been wasted, and then nothing left but a truncated life.

I should care the less for all this if I could see your path any clearer, but while my time *may* prove to have been wasted, I don't see but what yours *must* prove so. At least God forbid that you should remain an officer longer than is necessary. And what then? The West is possible; indeed, I have thought of that myself. But what we want, my dear boy, is a *school*. We want a national set of young men like ourselves or better, to start new influences not only in politics, but in literature, in law, in society, and throughout the whole social organism of the country. A national school of our own generation. And that is what America has no power to create. In England the Universities centralize ability and London gives a field. So in France, Paris encourages and combines these influences. But with us, we should need at least six perfect geniuses placed, or rather, spotted over the country and all working together; whereas our generation as yet has not produced one nor the promise of one. It's all random, insulated work, for special and temporary and personal purposes, and we have no means, power or hope of combined action for any unselfish end.

One man who has real ability may do a great deal, but we ought to have a more concentrated power of influence than any that now exists.

For the present war, I have nothing to say. We received cheerful letters from you and John to-day, and now we have the news of McClellan's removal. As I do not believe in Burnside's genius,[1] I do not feel encouraged by this, especially as it shakes our whole structure to its centre. I have given up the war and only pray for its end. The South has vindicated its position and we cannot help it, so, as we can find no one to lead us and no one to hold us together, I don't see the use of our shedding more blood. Still, my boy, all this makes able men a necessity for the future, and if you're an able man, there's your career. I have projects enough and not unpromising ones for some day, but like most of my combinations, I suppose they'll all end in dust and ashes.

We are very comfortable here in London fog. Some sharp diplomatic practice, but, I hope, not very serious.[2] People don't overwhelm us with attentions, but that is excusable.

Ever Yrs

MS: MHi

1. Gen. Ambrose Burnside (1824–1881) was placed in command of the Army of the Potomac, Nov. 10.

2. The disastrous defeat of Pope at Second Bull Run (Manassas), Aug. 29–30, and Lee's progress northward had inspired secret moves in England and France toward mediation based on de facto recognition of the Confederacy. Although Lee was turned back at Antietam, the diplomatic offensive continued, especially after Gladstone's speech of Oct. 7 declaring that the South had made an army, was making a navy, and had made a nation. Only in mid-November did the cabinet decide not to join France in an official offer of mediation.

To John Gorham Palfrey

5. Upper Portland Place.   28 Nov. '62.

Dear Mr Palfrey:

I add a word to my father's letter before sealing it up, to ask you to remember me to Frank. We are anxious to hear further about his progress, and if there is anything in London that he wants, I am at his disposal. At present I believe I can do no more for him than that, which is certainly not much.[1]

Life here is very regular, very retired, tolerably industrious and not unpleasant. I have dished out our friend Capt. John to my satisfaction, and so he rests for the present.

With great respect, wishing to be remembered to all your family,

I am &c &c   H. B. Adams.

MS: MH

1. Francis Winthrop Palfrey had been wounded two months earlier in the battle of Antietam.

To Charles Francis Adams

Copenhagen. Monday. 15 Dec. '62.

My dear Sir:

After a disgusting journey I reached my goal (or gaol just now) on Saturday afternoon. The Channel was if possible worse than usual and at one time I distinctly felt my toes starting. Had the trip lasted another hour I should have turned inside out. This first experience was succeeded by a most uncomfortable ride to Cologne and then by another night on the rail, finishing with a passage of the Elbe at daybreak which capped the climax. The river was blocked with ice and we were an hour and a half in crossing to Hamburg, colder than the north pole.

I left Hamburg (stupid hole) the next evening (Friday) and travelled that night to Kiel and by boat to Corsör. Luckily it was calm and not unpleasant. But the Danes are a mighty people! Three inches of snow had blocked their railway for two days and our's was the first mail through, taking six hours instead of three.

I delivered the package at once and was hospitably received.[1] But Copenhagen is, to express myself with indubitable propriety and admirable exactitude, a hole. I would have started back today, but cannot, as Mr Wood has despatches,[2] and as I want to see the picture gallery tomorrow. I mean to make a day or two's delay at Berlin and shall be at home at the end of the week.

You may tell Mary that I have not seen the Princess. She was however yesterday at the English Chapel in mourning to celebrate the anniversary of her future husband's father's death. That's getting on the right side of her mother-in-law I do declare.[3] I did however see her sister, the young 'un, and should know her again anywhere. She's a rather good-natured looking young party who faced the stares of the theatre with immense composure. The gawky brother was also there. As there is no Court here, and good society cuts the Queen and King, I have no chance of parading myself.

Very truly   HB.A.

MS: MHi
1. An official present to Frederick VII (1808–1891), king of Denmark.
2. Bradford Ripley Wood (1800–1889) of Connecticut, minister to Denmark 1861–1865.
3. The bereaved Queen Victoria was prospective mother-in-law to the Princess Alexandra (1844–1925), daughter of Christian IX of Denmark.

To James H. Anderson

Hannover. 18 December. 1862.

Dear Sir:[1]

Travelling rapidly through Hamburg yesterday, I discovered on reaching Harburg in the evening that my purse was missing. As I hardly think it could have been stolen, I trust there is some sort of indefinite chance that it may be recoverable. The contents were ten English sovereigns and a watchkey; so that in addition to losing my money, I had the satisfaction of seeing my watch run down. As I had the purse last out in order to get some gold changed at a money-changers on the Jungfernstieg (the same entrance I think as the Hotel de Russie or one of the other hotels not far from the Bazaar) who only charged me 2½ per cent for the process, I think it not impossible that I may have left it by accident on the counter of that benevolent person. Or as I afterwards lunched at Utesch's Oyster-cellar on the corner of the Bergstrasse and the Alsterdamm, it may have fallen from my pocket there. If neither of these, I am afraid it was lost about the Harburg omnibus, on the top of which (a little one, supplementary to the main one) I crossed in the evening; and in that case, it's rather hopeless.

My object is to ask you to have the goodness to send some one to make inquiry at these places. If some astounding honesty should seize the finder, he might be willing to let me have some fragment of his plunder. Or if it be advertised by any gentleman, perhaps you may be kind enough to take up the matter. I've no objection to giving a couple of sovereigns reward, or if must be, to dividing equally. If the man won't do that, he's not likely to do anything.

Should you have the goodness to interest yourself in the matter, and succeed in doing anything about it, may I beg you to write to me, Care of C. F. Adams, Minister of the United States, London. The truth is, the fifty dollars are Government money, the loss of which I shall be under the disagreeable necessity of making up; so that I have the less hesitation in asking your assistance.

With many apologies for troubling you with this affair, I remain

Very truly   Henry B. Adams.

The Consul of the United States.   Hamburg.

MS: OHi
1. James H. Anderson (1833–1912) of Ohio, lawyer, U.S. consul at Hamburg 1861–1866.

To Charles Francis Adams, Jr.

London. 26 December. 1862.

My dear Charles:

I received your's accompanying Ben. Crowninshield's, and enclose you a response to him. The telegrams announce a battle on the 13th and from the scanty items I infer that it was another Antietam only worse.[1] In short I am prepared for a complete check and am screwing my courage up to face the lists of killed and wounded.

I have made a wintry trip to Copenhagen, of which I have given an account in Ben's letter. It was not pleasant in any way, but I always like to change about a little. It cleans the rust away. I only reached home last Monday evening and have been and am still worked to pieces. Yesterday (Christmas) all the family were out at the Sturgise's, and Moran and I worked all day here, till evening when I went out to Mount Felix and dined, returning with the Chief at nine this morning. We have our hands full and things are in a very lively state. The notes are becoming savage, but we have a clear case and are making headway.[2] I find myself, I think, of use, and am well content to be here. My former restlessness was caused by the Pope campaign which upset us all. On the whole I would infinitely prefer to be here to going into the army, and it is only when there really seems to be a superior call to the army, that I feel at all disposed to move.

Anxiety has become our normal condition and I find a fellow can dance in time on a tight rope as easily as on a floor. It is harder to keep one's temper, but even that I now contrive to do in very trying cases. A steady pressure tells better here than anything else, and if our people will be cool, I think we can set England straight.

There is nothing to tell you that you won't learn from the family letters. Mary sends you this week a box containing a set of campaign articles for the table, to spare your fingers. It goes to the State Department and there is a letter inside. By the way, you don't answer her question as to who Hodson is; a matter which has exercised us immensely, and is of importance as I propose to name a horse Hodson, should he turn out to be the great person you make him.[3]

Mary, by the way, has grown to be a very pretty girl and has already got a reputation for beauty. We have kept her very close, but if we remain here through the next season, and she comes out, our peaceful household will be revolutionised. The burden will I suppose fall on me to a great extent and it will drag me into society which I care less and less for, every year.

I have been staying several days at Monckton Milnes' place in Yorkshire where we had a very jolly little bachelor party. This was just before I left for the continent. In time (ten years say) I might make a set of acquaintances here that would be worth having.

Even the stoic steadiness of nerve that I am trying to cultivate, shakes under the apprehension of the next news.

Ever Yrs

MS: MHi
1. The battle of Fredericksburg on Dec. 13, a shattering defeat for Burnside.
2. CFA's first note claiming compensation for the "ravages of the British pirate" *290* (the *Alabama*) was summarily rejected by Russell, but the interchange concerning this and other Confederate privateers continued until the end of the war.
3. Maj. William S. R. Hodson (1821–1858), commander of "Hodson's Horse," a famous regiment in the Indian mutiny of 1857. Describing him as his "ideal, of a Christian, gentleman and soldier" (to ABA, Dec. 9), CFA2 had recommended that Mary read his *Twelve Years of a Soldier's Life in India* (1859).

To James H. Anderson

London. 28 Dec. 1862.

Dear Sir:

I have to thank you for your favor of the 24th instant, and the kind trouble you have taken on my account.

Not having had from the first any real expectation of recovering the money, the result does not surprise me.

To leave nothing untried, however, I may add that I sat half an hour that afternoon at Giovanoli's Conditorei on the Neuer Jungfernstieg, and it is possible that the loss may have occurred there.

I presume you have incurred some expense in this affair, which I shall be happy to refund in any way you point out.

With many thanks, I remain   Henry B. Adams.

James H. Anderson Esq.

MS: OHi

To Richard Monckton Milnes

London. 28 December. 1862.

My dear Mr. Milnes:

I think you will find the enclosed to be amusing reading, and I hope your library at Fryston contains all the authorities in case you are not so clear about the law as we are. It is a pretty little *thema* for Parliament.

When our copies of the blue-book come I presume you will receive a copy.[1]

Pray remember me to Mrs Milnes and your family, and if you see the maniac, pray call him to account for not sending me his poem.[2]

Very truly &c   H. B. Adams.

R. M. Milnes Esq.

MS: Trinity College, Cambridge

1. The legation was supplying a friendly M.P. with its own brief as well as State Department "blue-books" from which the Union cause could be argued.

2. The "maniac" was the "wildly eccentric, astonishingly gifted, and convulsingly droll" poet Algernon Charles Swinburne (1837–1909), who had just been a fellow guest with HA at Fryston (*Education,* ch. 9).

5.

The Slow Shift
of the Balance

1863

The Emancipation Proclamation, January 1, 1863, had an immediate effect on British opinion and thus on the morale of everyone in the American legation. Minister Adams, as he negotiated to prevent the escape to sea of Confederate ironclad warships, no longer felt obliged to sound less bellicose than his instructions. His son Charles's reports from Virginia battlefields were grim, but after Vicksburg and Gettysburg in July, victory seemed at hand.

Besides details of diplomacy and war, Henry Adams' letters convey a widening personal world. In 1863, with the choicest aristocratic backers, he joined a London club. On a visit to Cambridge in the spring, he met Charles Milnes Gaskell. American sympathizers whom he came to know through his father befriended him in his own right. Men like Richard Monckton Milnes, Thomas Hughes, and Sir Charles Lyell, political liberals and literary, social, and scientific leaders, confirmed him in thinking the American cause to be the cause of democracy and new ideas. His intensive reading of Tocqueville and Mill, Hobbes and Spinoza, pursued for its own sake, helped qualify him for their social world.

Commitment to high thinking, it must be added, in no way impaired young Adams' zest for high gossip and other lighter pleasures. A summer journey to Scotland and the Western Isles, an autumn retreat from foggy London to St. Leonards on the south coast, and a third Christmas with the Russell Sturgises at Mount Felix suggest that the Adams family, and certainly Henry Adams, were settling into a pattern of British life.

To Charles Francis Adams, Jr.

London. 9 January. 1863.

My dear Charles:

We have not heard from you directly since the 10th of December, but we learn that you were all right by the last letters from home; and so, though the thought of you and our other friends out on picket duty in the mud and ice and snow of Virginia does not tend to increase our satisfaction with the affairs of the world, still we think ourselves on the whole well off.

At present I am alone here; the other members of the family having gone on a lark to Ossington, where the Speaker lives. Mary no doubt will write to you about her adventures there; where she is to go to two county balls and to one meet of the hounds I believe; or at least I hope. Lord Tomnoddy and Capt. Fitzboots will undoubtedly be there.[1] Between you and me, I look forward with some dread to the possibility of our remaining our whole term in England, for whether Lord Tomnoddy were caught or whether he were not, I should be equally ill-pleased.

I am deep in international law and political economy; dodging from the one to the other; and as I see nothing of the world and am much happier when I see nothing of it, I have no news to tell you. In point of fact I am better satisfied with my position now than ever before, and think I am of use.

At this moment public affairs are becalmed, but Parliament is soon to meet and then we shall all be put on the gridiron again. Luckily one's skin gets callous in time. We are pretty strong, however, and *very* active; that is, our party here is; and I hope we can check any hostile plots on this side. Of course we expect to come in personally for a good share of abuse and social annoyance, but I suppose we can stand that. Some day et haec meminisse juvabit.[2] I'll make you laugh with our little passages at arms. As a general thing, however, we are simply avoided. By the way, if you can get Fred. Seward to send you down the volume of Dip. Doc. just published, I think it will amuse you. It has made a great sensation here, and our opponents have paraded it about as though it were a collection of choice blasphemy, or a compilation of bawdy stories. You would think that the unpardonable sin was in that volume. Unfortunately it is seriously open to ridicule, but apart from that there is really nothing to cry out at and much to praise and admire.

I congratulate you on your Captaincy if it be a cause of congratulation. You know I look on the service merely as a necessary duty, and my highest ambition would be reached by seeing you honorably and safely out of it. When that event arrives, I will resign you my place and retire to private life.

We are relieved by your explanation as to Hodson and the book has been procured and the horse is to be named. Mary goes about the country with her horse dancing on his fore legs and his nose. Gradually however she is learning to manage him and she already rides better than I.

Ever Yours.

MS: MHi
1. A Lord Tomnoddy (*Tom-noddy:* "a foolish or stupid person," *OED*) appears in Thackeray's *The Book of Snobs* (1848); Fitzboots (*boots:* a servant who cleans shoes) was probably suggested by Thackeray's "Fitz-Boodle."
2. *Et haec . . . juvabit:* and this will be pleasant to remember; Vergil, *Aeneid,* I, 203.

To Frederick William Seward

London. 9 January. 1863.

My dear Sir:

I have to thank you for your's, which I received some weeks ago in reply to a previous one of mine. I write now to say that as you were kind enough last year to send me some copies of the Diplomatic Documents, I would be extremely obliged if you would send me half a dozen of this year's volume.

I might add that John Bright (who has just been here, very curious about recent events at Washington, and who says that Mr Seward and he are the only true Americans in the world, meaning that that *par nobile fratrum*[1] alone keep up their confidence in the result) wants a copy. Mr W. E. Forster and Mr Monckton Milnes also deserve copies from your father.[2] In fact I have promised copies to all these gentlemen, and unless Government here re-publishes the volume as it did last year, there are many good friends of ours with whom a copy would be well invested.

I wish some day, when the 290 correspondence is closed, it could be published here as a political pamphlet with a legal introduction and notes by some jurist. I have set my heart on our gaining this case, as a matter of international law. I certainly trust your father won't abandon it, and I shall do all I can to urge my father to keep it well before the public here; a thing which with our means of working, is not very difficult. Of course there is no chance for the damages now; but a steady and firm pressure will do more with England than a thousand shocks. When Parliament meets, I think you will hear more about the 290. I need not say that my father is earnest about it.

You will hardly doubt on which side of the late struggle Senators vs. Secretaries, our sympathies lie.[3] Yet it is one more blow to our poor Constitution, and it comes from a quarter that ought to be the very last to introduce such destructive precedents. For your father's sake I am almost sorry that it failed. For our own, I feel that its success would have been to shake the Government to pieces much more rapidly than ever.

Pray present my warmest respects to your father. And if you can remember to remember me to Mr Weed whenever you see him, I would be obliged. I would like occasionally to write to Mr Weed, but am shy of giving him trouble. I repeat however that in cases where I write to you, I do not expect to be answered.

Very truly   H. B. Adams.

F. W. Seward Esq.

P.S. Will you do me a favor? In the Gales & Seaton edition of American State Papers, Vol. 1. p. 502, 14th line, is a passage in a letter dated 12 Nov. 1794, from Edm. Randolph to Jay, *objecting* to Lord Grenville's projet as demanding compensation for *more* vessels than Jefferson's letter of 5th Sept. 1793 contemplated.

Yet Lord Grenville's claim became part of the Treaty.

It has therefore occurred to me that Jay's objections to it must have been overruled by Grenville, and that Jay very likely, in some letter never published, explained his reasons for yielding this point. If such a letter exists, I suppose it may be in your Archives. At any rate it would be worth while to know *why* our Government consented to so great a concession.

Perhaps you could find a spare clerk to look over the unpublished archives of that period, if the British spared us any.

MS: NRU
    1. *Par nobile fratrum:* a fine pair of brothers; Horace, *Satires*, II, iii.
    2. William Edward Forster (1818–1886), of Quaker reform background, Liberal M.P., one of the "heavy-weights" among British champions of the Union (*Education*, p. 125).
    3. When the published dispatches disclosed a Seward comment attacking abolitionists, Sumner led a senatorial delegation to the White House and demanded Seward's resignation (which Lincoln refused to accept).

To Charles Francis Adams, Jr.

London. 23 January. 1863.

My dear Charles:

I have but a moment till it grows dark and the bag closes,[1] but I don't think I've much to say, so it don't matter. I've had a hard day's work too, as we generally do on Fridays, and am tired. We are in the dark as to movements at home since the 8th, no steamer being yet in owing I suppose to the awful gales.

We are as usual very quiet, having been dragged the rounds of the Christmas pantomimes and bored to death with them. I wish you or John were here to be funny and amuse people; you know I never could do it, and now I grow stupider and stupider every year as my hair grows thinner. I haven't even the wit left to talk to girls. I wish I were fifty years old at once, and then I should feel at home.

The Emancipation Proclamation has done more for us here than all our former victories and all our diplomacy. It is creating an almost convulsive reaction in our favor all over this country. The London Times is furious and scolds like a drunken drab. Certain it is, however, that public opinion is very deeply stirred here and finds expression in meetings; addresses to Pres. Lincoln; deputations to us; standing committees to agitate the subject and to affect opinion; and all the other symptoms of a great popular movement peculiarly unpleasant to the upper classes here because it rests altogether on the spontaneous action of the laboring classes and has a pestilent squint at sympathy with republicanism. But the Times is on its last legs and has lost its temper. They say it always does lose its temper when it finds such a feeling too strong for it, and its next step will be to come round and try to guide it. We are much encouraged and in high spirits. If only you at home don't have disasters, we will give such a checkmate to the foreign hopes of the rebels as they never yet have had.

We are all well and happy. I am at last on the point of buying a little mare and expect to have to hand her over to Mary, as her own horse is rather too much for her. Also having had my watch, hat and purse stolen at my celebrated Turkish baths, I have succeeded in obtaining a compensation of £15.0.0. with which I propose immediately to invest in a new watch. The exchange would be an inducement to invest at home, where I do not hear that my income has materially increased in spite of the superfluity of money. The mare costs £40.0.0 and will cost me at least £5.0.0 a month in keep.

Lebe wohl. Time is up and the Chief is a cussin and swearin like anythink for my letters.

Ever Yrs.

MS: MHi
 1. Diplomatic pouch.

To Charles Francis Adams, Jr.

London. 30 January. 1863.

My dear Boy:

We have received your's of the 2d of this month, and one from John of the 6th, telling about his visit to your camp. We all hope that you will succeed in changing your quarters. To be a Captain in a Cavalry regiment any way is a diminutive potato, but to be one whose routine of duty is abuse of his Colonel, however deserved, and disgust with inevitabilities, is what one is not called upon to endure if he can escape it. I hope you can, and think you ought. I am beginning to look forward to the day as not far distant when you will bid good-bye to the tented field and resume the toga. The war can hardly last six months more of active campaigning. You will then come over here and take my place. The Chief may ask leave of absence, and travel, and in such a case you will be wanted to travel with them. As for me, I have seen Europe, and shall be glad to yield the duty to you. What may happen to disturb our position here, of course I can't foretell, but unless some call to another position should take the Chief home, I don't think he's likely to go of his own accord; at least until he's seen Europe. So I feel a sort of hope that we shall receive you here sometime next August or September. Should there be an armistice, a call from your father to become his private Secretary, would be excuse enough for your leaving the service at once; and this, I take it, would be the more easy if you had only a staff appointment.

Since I wrote to you here last week not much has turned up. I look about occasionally for some book or so to send you, but I am no great reader of the literature of the day, myself, and hear of little that tempts me which you can't get more cheaply at Washington, so I haven't as yet troubled you with missives of the sort. Should you hear of anything that strikes your fancy and that's portable, I will get it and send it to you.

Politically things go on swimmingly here. The anti-slavery feeling of the country is coming out stronger than we ever expected, and all the English politicians have fairly been thrown over by their people. There was a meeting last night at Exeter Hall which is likely to create a revolution; or rather to carry on a complete revolution in public opinion, which was begun by the great Manchester Meeting on the 31st December. Last night's meeting was something tremendous, unheard of since the days of reform. The cry was "Emancipation and reunion," and the spirit of it was dangerously in sympathy with republicanism.[1] The Strand was blocked up in front of Exeter Hall by those who couldn't get in, and speeches were made in the street, as well as in another hall opened to accommodate a part of the surplus. As for enthusiasm, my friend Tom Brown of Rugby school-days who was one of the speakers, had to stop repeatedly and beg the people not to cheer so much. Every allusion to the South was followed by groaning, hisses and howls, and the enthusiasm for Lincoln and for everything connected with the North, was immense. The effect of such a display will be very great, and I think we may expect from Lancashire on the arrival of the George Griswold, a response that will make some noise.[2]

Next week Parliament will meet. Of course it will bring hot water, but the sentiment of the country will not tolerate any interference with us. I breathe more easily about this than ever. My main anxiety is about the Alabama case, which has been the subject of the sharpest kind of notes between the Chief and Lord Russell. As these notes will probably now be published, I can say that in my opinion my Lord has been dreadfully used up, and if you don't howl with delight when you read the Chief's note to him of 30th December, you won't do what I did. But our cue is still friendship, and we don't want to irritate. The strong outside pressure that is now aroused to act on this Government, will, I hope, help us to carry through all we want in time and with patience.

MS: MHi

1. Exeter Hall, which held 3,000 people, was used for evangelical and humanitarian meetings, like this one sponsored by the London Emancipation Society.

2. The *George Griswold,* a Union relief ship, arrived in Liverpool in February with food contributed by New York merchants for unemployed Lancashire mill workers.

To Charles Francis Adams, Jr.

London. 13 February. 1863.

My dear Charles:

I suppose this week's mail will bring a letter from you, but the steamer which was due last Saturday has only arrived today (Friday) so we shall not see our mail till this letter has gone. I can however imagine you in the snow and mud cursing at the Generals and the army, which indeed seems to me in a state of chaos. It seems precious hard that we should have to submit to this disintegration and grinding up of the nation, conscious of it all the time, and yet compelled to sit still and be crushed; but I suppose an end must come some day. Meanwhile, there's no great good in talking about it.

The last week here has been politically very quiet. I am surprised at it, for I thought that the meeting of Parliament would set the floods going. Lord Derby however, put his foot on any interference with us, on the first night of the session, and so we have obtained a temporary quiet. But the feeling among the upper classes is more bitter and angry than ever, and the strong popular feeling of sympathy with us, is gradually dividing the nation into aristocrats and democrats, and may produce pretty serious results for England.

Society is beginning. As it is almost certainly the last season I shall pass in London, I intend to see all I can. Society in London certainly has its pleasures, and I found an example of this, the other evening. We were asked to dinner at the Duke of Argyll's, who is a warm friend of ours, as well as the Duchess who is a daughter of the anti-slavery Duchess of Sutherland.[1] The party was evidently asked on purpose to meet us. There was Lord Clyde, who always has his hair on end and never seems to talk; Charles P. Villiers, a friendly member of the Cabinet; Charles Howard, a brother of Lord Carlisle; John Stuart Mill the logician and economist, a curious looking man with a sharp nose, a wen on his forehead and a black cravat, to whom I took particular pains to be introduced, as I think him about the ablest man in England; very retiring and embarrassed in his manner, and a mighty weapon of defence for our cause in this country. Then there was the famous physician, Dr Brown-Séquard; then Professor Owen, the famous naturalist, geologist, palaeontologist and so on, whom I have met before. Then came Lord Frederick Cavendish whom you know.[2] Frank Brooks[3] told us a very funny story about your astonishment at his appearance on meeting him at breakfast in Medford, where you addressed him as "Lord Edward" at first. As he has a brother Lord Edward, he must have thought you well posted in the peerage. These, with a sprinkling of others, formed the company, only two ladies besides the Duchess at table. I confess that I always feel a little self-satisfied in such society. I feel my self-respect increased by the fact of standing beside, and feeding with such men. For a distinguished company too, these men are not swells. You know your friend "Lord Fwedewick's" style of costume in America. It's not much better here. If a man chooses to neglect rules he can do it in London though not with impunity. As for example, our friend and cousin the phenomenon who has just graduated at the university with much lower honors than we had hoped for him.[4]

I have purchased my horse, a little dark brown mare, and I ride with Mary quite regularly. Today we have been over to Hyde Park to ride in Rotten Row. I can't say I like riding in Rotten Row. If I were splendidly mounted, I might not object; but as I don't care to do the fashionable unless I can rank high in it, Rotten Row is not so much to my taste as the country. Still, Mary likes it, and as she is now coming out, I submit to be led to all sorts of places where I ought to like to go, but in fact hate it more and more every day. Come and take my place. You have a physique, brass and a disposition for society. I suffer under a want of all these qualities, and perpetual and incessant mortification on that account. I want to be a Sybarite. The honors wait for you.

MS: MHi
1. George Douglas Campbell (1823–1900), duke of Argyll, lord privy seal, and his wife, Elizabeth Georgiana (1824–1878), daughter of Harriet Elizabeth Georgiana Leveson-Gower (1806–1868), dowager duchess of Sutherland. The dowager duchess, a philanthropist and antislavery organizer, was Mistress of the Queen's Wardrobe.
2. Field Marshal Colin Campbell (1792–1863), Baron Clyde, whose capture of Lucknow in 1858 ended the Indian mutiny. Charles Pelham Villiers (1802–1898), president of the Poor Law Board. Charles Howard (1814–1879), Liberal M.P.; George W. F. Howard (1802–1864), 7th earl of Carlisle, was lord lieutenant of Ireland. John Stuart Mill (1806–1873) published pro-Union articles in *Fraser's* and the *Westminster Review* in 1862. Charles Edward Brown-Séquard (1818–1894), neurophysiologist, Harvard professor 1864–1867. Richard Owen (1804–1892), anti-Darwinian paleontologist. Lord Frederick Cavendish (1836–1882), son of the duke of Devonshire and private secretary to the president of the privy council.
3. Francis Boott Brooks (1824–1891) of Boston, son of ABA's brother Edward and Elizabeth Boott Brooks.
4. William Everett.

To Charles Francis Adams, Jr.

London. 20 February. 1863.

My dear Boy:

We received this week your batch of letters, and I also got one from Ben Crowninshield through you, which I shall answer next week. I wish you were out of your "long siege in mud and rain" which is likely to be as unpleasantly famous as any in Flanders. Hilton Head, I should have thought, would have been Paradise compared with this.

Bad as your report is about the army of the Potomac, and bad as I fully expect the news to be of the attack on Charleston and Vicksburg, still I have derived a grain of comfort from what I think looks like a gleam of improvement in the political look of things at home. Of all results, a restoration of the Union on a proslavery basis would be most unfortunate. Yet I dread almost equally a conquest that would leave us with a new and aggravated Poland on our hands.[1] If we could only fight a peace that would give us Virginia, Tennessee and Mississipi river, then we might easily allow slavery to gather to a head in the cotton-states, and crush it out at our leisure on the first good opportunity; but such a vision is reserved for the just made perfect.

As to your avowal of belligerent intentions for life, if you expect me to quarrel with you on that account, you will be disappointed. As the Chief always says when his lady complains of my follies; "My dear; Henry is of age and can do what he likes." You are of age and even if you choose to become a Methodist minister, I don't propose to forbid the consecration. Perhaps I am prejudiced against your career from my observations on military men in Europe, where so far as I can judge, they are the greatest curse and nuisance in existence. The life of a soldier in time of peace seems here to have had a very bad effect indeed upon the mass of the officers. If I know it, our country has had about as much war as she wants for the present, and if we don't have peace and long peace, our game is up. You and I look at things from different points. My idea is that peace and small armaments will be our salvation as a united and solvent nation. You prefer to speculate on the chances of war or convulsions, and throw your net in troubled waters.

Though I don't propose to bother you with useless remonstrances, I must decline in toto to have anything to do with opening the subject in the family. My belief is that it had better not be mentioned till the time comes. Whenever the war does end and you then do become obliged to inform your relatives of your intention to cool your heels for life in some fortified swamp in Louisiana or Arkansas, I shall take a month's vacation and visit you till your said relatives come to the earth again. We can then discuss this and other matters over a pipe of peace, if you can provide mild tobacco. Otherwise I prefer a cigar. No whiskey, thank you! It makes my head ache.

We are beginning to be gay here. By the way, Monckton Milnes, who is the only man in England that ever did me a kindness, I believe, has had me invited to a literary club here, for a time, where I have a great chance to meet the curiosities of the place.[2] Tom Hughes has been of great use to me and has introduced me to numbers of very pleasant acquaintances; few young men there, however. The season is beginning again too and I am nerving myself to all the torture that invariably follows and accompanies all my attempts in this line. I have serious thoughts of quitting my old projects of a career, like you. My promised land of occupation however; my burial place of ambition and law, is geology and science. I wish I could send you Sir Charles Lyell's new book on the Antiquity of Man, but it wouldn't do very well for camp-reading.[3]

Ever Yours

MS: MHi
   1. An allusion to the Polish uprising against Russian rule that had begun in January.
   2. The Athenæum Club, founded in 1824 for eminent men of letters, artists, churchmen, and patrons of learning or the arts.
   3. *The Geological Evidences of the Antiquity of Man* (1863).

To Charles Francis Adams, Jr.

London. 6 March. 1863.

My bould Sojer-boy:

If you have such weather on the banks of the wide murmuring Potomac, as we enjoy on the shores of Regent's Park, I confess that I envy you and would like to try my hand at sojering myself for a limited period. If I could transfer myself for a few days, I would not object to the process. Summer has made a violent attempt at rape on Winter, and in my opinion has accomplished his nefarious purpose. The trees are sprouting and the hedges budding, and our rides into the country are as balmy as in that life before the deluge some indefinite age ago, when we used to ride at this season of the year, among the woods round Arlington, then *ignara mali.*[1] This week has reminded me continually of the week before inauguration day.

Such a bother and a fuss as all the world keeps up about this unhappy Prince of Wales, who would give his best pair of new breeches to be a very humble private individual for the next week.[2] He is quite popular here, for he is thoughtful of others and kind, and hates ceremony. So it seems as though a temporary bee had lodged in the bonnet of this good people, who have set to work with a sort of determined, ponderous and massive hilarity, to do him honor. I suppose you will get from first hand a correct account of the events of last Saturday at Court. Also you will receive a photograph of our sister as she appeared. She is now fairly launched.[3] Pretty, attractive, sympathetic and well-informed; but time and contact with the world will have to do much to develope her. To my mind London fashionable society, (routs, receptions, dances, I mean) is intolerably stupid. I've not the genius to find anything in it worthy of tasting, to one who has drunk the hot draughts of our flirtatious style of youthful amusement. If she can learn to prefer the heavy patronage of stupid elder sons, to a gayer style of thing, she will learn, no doubt, to have a good time.

But I am a fool in society. I acknowledge it, and beg that you won't ever mention me or my opinions in any of your letters. If it weren't that every man of sense I've met with sings the same song, I should give up my opinion and admire what I know devilish well is an artificial, wearisome, wretched state of things. As it is, I only depart after suffering as prescribed, to take refuge among the literary and freer crowd, and listen at a distance to Thackeray's talk which in my opinion is usually either stupid or vulgar or both.[4] I do not think highly of literary men in England, for I don't see any original genius among them, but they're the best one can find in the world, I suppose, next to the French in Paris who are, to me, more attractive still.

As to public affairs I have nothing to tell you, as we are going on excellently well. We have done our work in England, and if you military heroes would only give us a little encouragement, we should be the cocks of the walk in England. But diplomacy has certainly had no aid from the sword to help a solution of its difficulties. Couldn't some of you give us just one leetle sugar-plum? We are shocking dry.

Of course there is plenty to do. I am busy writing, recording, filing and collating letters and documents four or five hours every day, and my books and files for the last two years are beginning to assume a portentous size. Still it is very easy and mechanical work, and doesn't prevent me from another sort of application which is more on my own account. But it's precious hard to work on one's own account in these times, when the chances are indefinitely against one's ever succeeding in bringing his results into action.

Tomorrow is to be the entrance of the Princess Alexandra, and all the world is going to see it. Next Tuesday is the wedding and an illumination. Ye Gods! what an infernal row it is! Meanwhile many people, big, big, big people inquire after you and your whereabouts, so that when you come over here you will find yourself among old acquaintances.

MS: MHi

1. *Ignara mali:* ignorant of evil; *Aeneid,* I, 630.

2. On March 10 the Prince of Wales (1841–1910), later Edward VII, married Princess Alexandra of Denmark.

3. Mary Adams was presented at Court on Feb. 28 at a reception given by the Princess Royal.

4. William Makepeace Thackeray (1811–1863), whom HA disliked because of his Southern sympathies.

To Charles Francis Adams, Jr.

London. 13 March. 1863.

My dear Rank-hero:

Are letters of any consequence to you? If they are, well and good! Only letters from home used to worry me when I was abroad, about as much as home newspapers do now. I wished to the Lord I could fly the land and escape them. Perhaps you may indulge in the same irreligious sentiments, in which case I forgive you. As I take great care never to write anything that can possibly interest you, I consider that I have done my best to do well by you.

Your other correspondents will tell you about all the wonderful events that have happened this week including our involuntary pilgrimage on Tuesday night. Sybarite that I am, I condemn going rashly into crowds in language that partakes of the nature of strength. In fact, without making rules for other men's acts, I think that when I venture my own precious ribs and toes under the plebeian pressure of a London mob, I am not sensibly or in any degree removed from the quality of a damned fool. And it was not my fault that we wandered for seven hours the other night, like restless spirits, through the streets of this metropolis. Still, being done, it becomes, like most silly acts, a part of that experience which one would not wish undone.[1]

As usual, we haunt drawing-rooms and waste our lives in what an unhappy race calls society. My usual reflexion when I put on the war-paint of an evening, is that I were able to exchange places with some of you fellows for a few hours. A quiet pipe and talk over your camp-fires, and a little comparison of ideas and freshening of thoughts, would be a treat worth much. I know no young men here, and most young men who are worth much and are not corrupted by snobbishness and tuft-hunting,[2] do not seem to venture into the harness of balls. In consequence, my youngest associates are patriarchs of forty and gay in proportion. The results of such associations are not calculated to excite a *gaité folle,* as the Chinese say.

I'm sorry for my good friend the son of Higgins, who is a good enough fellow to be spared more trouble and care than necessary. Poor Nick Anderson writes to me from Cincinnati where he is laid up with his wound and is irate to the last degree with the copperheads, as he courteously calls them. I see too that Tom Stevenson has got into a row and that Gen. Hunter seems to be smashing things generally. If our Generals had done the enemy half the harm they've done us, the South would now be a wilderness.[3]

There is no great news so far as I know in the political world on this side of the water. All is quiet, and so far as we are concerned all must necessarily wait to see what way events will jump with us at home. At present nothing is heard of in this town, but the marriage of the Prince of Wales and the juggernaut festivities that have accompanied it. The literary society of

England is largely occupied in making smutty conundrums on the event and telling dirty stories. As for instance, it is announced that the Mayor of Newport, a little town in the isle of Wight, wrote an official letter to Lord Palmerston, setting forth that he was a magistrate—local dignitary—matter of importance to provincial interests—&c &c, and in short that he begged Lord Palmerston to consider favorably his claim to be present at the consummation of the marriage of the Prince of Wales. This letter was, I believe, the admiration of the House of Commons for several consecutive evenings. This however is mild. The English are a nasty set.

I understand that we have another nephew in prospect. The more, the better. Since you are going to adhere to arms and horses, I suppose marriage will not be much in your line, and as my own tastes don't lie in that direction, and the idea becomes more and more repulsive to me every year, it is well that John should do our duty for us. By the way, Brooks is waxing great and is nearly as tall as I. Unfortunately he doesn't show the genius of his two eldest brothers and is decidedly backward and slow, but a good fellow and excellent well disposed.

MS: MHi

1. The Adamses attended the royal wedding at Windsor. The holiday celebration in London that night left six people dead, trampled by the happy throngs, and the Adamses exhausted, their carriage caught in the swirl till 3 A.M.

2. Seeking to meet prominent persons. (The tuft is the gold tassel formerly worn by titled undergraduates at Oxford and Cambridge.)

3. Brig. Gen. Thomas Greely Stevenson (1836–1864) of Boston, assigned to Hunter's command in South Carolina, publicly refused to obey orders because he objected to serving alongside black troops. Hunter put him under arrest Feb. 16.

To Charles Francis Adams, Jr.

London. 20 March. 1863.

My dear Boy:

While you are resolving into the primitive wild Injun among the regions where Captain John Smith once roved to considerable effect, I am becoming every day more and more the man of rules and conventionalities. There's a pretty little set of verses by Clough on this sort of separation; the only pretty thing I ever have succeeded in discovering in his works.[1] So it is, however, and the part of a wise man is to make the best of his position. Sapientis est, optimum situs ejus facere.[2] You see how my Latin improves.

We are in a shocking bad way here. I don't know what we are ever going to do with this damned old country. Some day it will wake up and find itself at war with us, and then what a squealing there'll be. By the Lord, I would almost be willing to submit to our sufferings, just to have the pleasure of seeing our privateers make ducks and drakes of their commerce. But I'll tell you what I mean to do to pay off my personal debt. When I get home I mean to write a series of articles on England, and in them I mean to say with a patronising air of great good-humor just the things which I know will be as irritating to the English as a clean shirt to an American soldier; and then I mean to send copies of them to every damned Englander that I ever saw. They are nervously sensitive to all that is said of them and will kick like Jumping Jacks.

But meanwhile, as I say, we are in a worse mess here than we have known since the Trent affair, and the devil of it is that I am in despair of our getting any military success that would at all counterbalance our weight.[3] Where our armies try to do anything they are invariably beaten, and now they seem to be tired of trying. I'll bet a sovereign to a southern shin-plaster that we don't take Charleston; either that we don't try or are beaten. I'll bet five goulden pounds to a diminutive greenback that we don't clear the Mississipi, and that we don't hurt Richmond. My only consolation is that the Southerners are suffering dreadfully under the tension we keep them at, and as I prefer this to having fresh disasters of our own, I am in no hurry to see anyone move. But meanwhile we are in a tangle with England that can only be cleared with our excellent good navy-cannon. If I weren't so brutally sea-sick, I would go into the navy and have a lick at these fat English turkey-buzzards.

At the same time, individually I haven't at all the same dislike to the English. They are very like ourselves and are very pleasant people. And then they are quite as ready to black-guard themselves as anyone could wish, if they're only let alone. There are all the elements of a great, reforming, liberal party at work here, and a few years will lay in peace that old vindictive rogue who now rules England and weighs like an incubus on all advance. Then you will see the new generation, with which it is my only satisfaction here to have some acquaintance, take up the march again and press the country into shape. Thanks to Monckton Milnes, Tom Hughes and a few other good friends, I am tolerably well-known now in the literary and progressive set. I was amused the other day to hear that I was put up for a Club in St James's Street, by Mr Milnes, and seconded by Laurence Olifaunt, a thorough anti-American;[4] and better still, I am endorsed by your friend Frederick Cavendish, as he is commonly called here; the brother of Lord Hartington; the son of the Duke of Devonshire. Several other names are on the paper, I believe, but I don't know what they are. I'm thinking my character would not be raised in America if I were known to keep such malignant company. Certainly however, aristocracy is not my strong point. My most sought acquaintances are men like Hughes, and his associates, the cultivated radicals of England.

How long I shall remain in contact with this sort of thing, who can say? Verily, the future is black and the ocean looks as though it were yawning for us on our approaching passage.

MS: MHi
1. Arthur Hugh Clough (1819–1861), "Dipsychus" (published in part 1862; 1865), a dialogue on the conflict between moral idealism and worldly wisdom.
2. *Sapientis . . . facere*, a mock-translation of the preceding aphorism.

3. The depredations of the *Alabama* were increasing, more raiders were being built, and sentiment in Parliament was hostile.

4. Laurence Oliphant (1829–1888), novelist and adventurer, with books on Katmandu, Circassia, Minnesota and the Far West, and the American South.

To Frederick William Seward

(Private)   London. 20 March. 1863.

Dear Sir:

I am much indebted to you for the trouble you have taken to elucidate our Alabama precedent. My father desires me to thank you for the copy you obligingly sent him of Hammond's correspondence, and to say that he regrets to have caused so much labor. His wish was to get at Hammond's argument, which is contained principally in his note of 7th June, 1793, to which Jefferson's famous letter of September 5th is the reply.[1] The rest of the correspondence is of less importance and it is a pity that your clerks should have had so much of their time occupied by it.

I had supposed they would contest our claim by argument here. But it takes more than two years even of our sharp experience, to know the English. As yet they have not condescended to enter the lists, and on our side we have discouraged a Parliamentary debate on it, believing that it is better to give them time for reflection, and to prevent their committing themselves against the principle of compensation, as they certainly would do now. It's an uncommon large trout to land, and needs plenty of line and time. Diplomacy can at best only hook him; victorious armies and fleets can alone bring him ashore. There's a curious kind of sneaking conscience about these English, and they know when they've done wrong. The gingerly way in which they dodge this question of claims; ignore it or outface it, shows that they feel how hard it is to deal with. And the honest ones deplore it and pray to God we may soon catch the pirate.

The Cotton loan is a success. It is said that Erlanger took it at 60 and gets 90 for it.[2] If we were in better days we might go to war with England for these different performances, and I would give much to see the probable happy state of mind she would be in, if we applied to her a sudden and efficient system of reprisals and sequestration, after the style of her own Orders in Council; or a new edition of the rule of 1756.[3] Luckily we shall have the war cards to play at any time. The Alabama has furnished casus belli enough for twenty years to come. So I suppose you will continue to persevere as well as may be, in peace, and punish Europe with privateers. Certainly it is much to be hoped that not a pound of cotton will reach this shore.

You may suppose that our position is by no means pleasant, and that there is no little anxiety and distress at the way in which we are evidently drifting into a war. The danger is not quite yet seen on this side, and I doubt whether we can hope to improve things so long as the Premier lasts. Lord Palmerston is a bad man and detests everything American. I believe he wishes a rupture, provided that it shall seem to come from us, and he can draw France into it. Of course we don't want to play that game, and hence the Emancipation Proclamation was a God-send. It's effect has been very great in checking our enemies, and it is still working vigorously. If the present state of things lasts long, we shall soon raise a democracy in England that it will be hard for them to put to sleep again, for it is beginning to be felt how deeply the upper classes have been pledged to a cause hateful to the working men.

Pray remember us all warmly to your father. He is now the only means I can see, of doing what must be done if we are not to be ruined; either of bringing the people into harmony with the Government, or the Government into harmony with the people. More disasters would destroy any Government that ever existed, and ours is no more free from dangers than the rest.

I hear you have a new text-book of International Law in place of Wheaton. If so, and if you don't furnish Legations with copies, perhaps you could order a copy to be sent to me, and I will direct my brother to pay for it if they will send him the bill. I would not give you any trouble however, and beg you won't do anything about it unless you can do it without inconvenience. You know how often such works are needed in public places, and if I don't keep my father posted as to new books, he has too much to do to provide himself with them, and would go without. But I don't know anything about this new work, and therefore have no means of getting at it.

I am, very truly, H. B. Adams.

MS: NRU
1. Jefferson, secretary of state at that time, stated the policy that the U.S., as a neutral, would restore or pay for British vessels captured by the French and brought to American ports. George Hammond (1763–1853) was first British minister to the U.S. 1791–1795.
2. The Confederate government negotiated a $15,000,000 European loan, issuing bonds exchangeable for cotton. Erlanger was a French banking firm.
3. The Rule of the War of 1756 forbade neutrals to engage during time of war in trade from which they were excluded in peacetime.

To Charles Francis Adams, Jr.

London. 27 March.[1] 1863.

My dear Boy:

I have little to tell you this week, but at least nothing bad. I hope you will be able to say as much. A little society, an hour's horse-back ride, three or four hours work with the pen; and so on, make up my day, and one day galls the kibe[2] of another, time passes so fast. Spring has come again and the leaves are appearing for the third time and we are still here nor does there seem an immediate probability of our moving. In fact we are now one of the known and acknowledged units of the London and English world, and though politics still place more or less barriers in our path, the majority of people receive us much as they would Englishmen, and seem to consider us as such. I have been much struck by the way in which they affect to distinguish here between us and "foreigners"; that is, persons who don't speak English. The great difficulty is in the making acquaintances, for London acquaintances are nothing.

After a fort-night's violent pulling, pushing, threatening, shaking, cursing and coaxing, almost entirely done through private channels, we have at last succeeded in screwing this Government up to what promises to be a respectable position. How steady it will be, I don't know, nor how far they will declare themselves, do I know. But between our Government at home and our active and energetic allies here, we seem to have made progress. I went last night to a meeting of which I shall send you a report; a democratic and socialist meeting, my boy; most threatening and dangerous to the established state of things; and assuming a tone and proportions that are quite novel and alarming in this capital.[3] And they met to notify Government that "they would not tolerate" interference against us. I can assure you this sort of movement is as alarming here as a slave-insurrection would be in the South, and we have our hands on the springs that can raise or pacify such agitators; at least as regards our own affairs, they making common cause with us. I never quite appreciated the "moral influence" of American democracy, nor the cause that the privileged classes in Europe have to fear us, until I saw how directly it works. At this moment the American question is organising a vast mass of the lower orders in direct contact with the wealthy. They go our whole platform and are full of the "rights of man." The old revolutionary leaven is working steadily here in England. You can find millions of people who look up to our institutions as their model and who talk with utter contempt of their own system of Government. Within three months this movement has taken a developement that has placed all our enemies on the defensive; has driven Palmerston to sue for peace and Lord Russell to proclaim a limited sympathy. I will not undertake to say where it will stop, but were I an Englishman I should feel nervous. We have strength enough already to shake the very crown on the Queen's head if we are compelled to employ it all. You are not to suppose that we are intriguing to create trouble. I do not believe that all the intrigue in the world could create one of these great demonstrations of sympathy. But where we have friends, there we shall have support, and those who help us will do it of their own free will. There are few of the thickly populated districts of England where we have not the germs of an organisation that may easily become democratic as it is already anti-slavery. With such a curb on the upper classes, I think they will do little more harm to us.

The conduct of the affairs of that great republic which though wounded itself almost desperately, can yet threaten to tear down the rulers of the civilised world, by merely assuming her place at the head of the march of democracy, is something to look upon. I wonder whether we shall be forced to call upon the brothers of the great fraternity to come in all lands to the assistance and protection of its head. These are lively times, oh Hannibal.[4]

MS: MHi
1. HA misdated this letter January.
2. *Hamlet,* V, i.
3. For HA's official report of the meeting of March 26, see *New England Quarterly* 15 (Dec. 1942), 725–728.
4. HA enclosed on a separate sheet a copy in his hand of the last fourteen lines of Milton's *Samson Agonistes,* which CFA2 had tried to recall in his letter of Jan. 26.

To John Gorham Palfrey

London. 27 March. 1863.

My dear Mr Palfrey:

Pray make me aware of the objects of your desire in the State Paper Office, and it will gratify me much to have them obtained. For myself, my own antiquarian researches are laid aside, for after having finished with Capt. John Smith, I changed the field of my labors. On the whole I have concluded not to publish my elaborate argument on the old pirate, but shall be happy to send you the original should you think it worth sending for. It lies neglected in my cupboard and might as well lie at home as here.

We are making progress here. Before long we shall have made trouble enough for the "governing classes" under their own feet unless they look sharp. By slow degrees and ponderous exertions we are dragging this Government into a tolerable attitude. Diplomacy however has little to do with this, and I beg that you wont class me as a diplomate. I should consider myself as much lowered in dignity by accepting office. Heaven forbid that I should ever be called an Attaché, an article long and properly abolished in our service. I am an independent gentleman, the son of the American Minister, unconnected with official matters but supposed to enjoy the confidence of the Minister and occasionally to be employed by him in delicate affairs; I go into society as Mr Adams, and I look down with calmness from a prodigious height upon the herds of attachés and secretaries that haunt in a mournful manner the St James's Club. My own field is among English politicians and writers whose acquaintance I make desperate efforts to make. Politicians now-a-days work on public opinion and (we especially) hope little from aid of Court favor.

Pray remember me most particularly to your family, and consent to receive the renewed assurances of respect and consideration with which I am &c &c &c

H. B. Adams.

MS: MH

To Charles Francis Adams, Jr.

London. 16 April. 1863.

Sir Charles de Quincey

I wrote to you last week that I intended to take a few days vacation and
try a little sea-air. Things are looking politically so lame and limping that I
hardly cared to be away at a time which might be full of trouble. But as it
was to be only for three days, and as it was the only chance Brooks would
have, I concluded to go. So we went on board the Antwerp steamer on
Sunday at noon, and by eight o'clock that evening we were knocking about
in the German ocean. The next morning at five we passed Flushing and
were running up the Scheldt, the road I recollect so well from the time Ben
Crowninshield and I travelled it first, nearly five years ago. By ten o'clock
we were landed at Antwerp, and installed in my old hotel; and not many
minutes afterwards I was initiating my young pupil into the beauties and
curiosities of Antwerp churches, pictures and scenes. I delight in this old
city. It is a fascinating stupid place, and from the cathedral spire one sees a
hundred miles of flat country broken only by sluggish water courses and
Flemish hamlets, but for all that, quite as attractive as most things. The
spires of Bruges and Ghent, Mechlin and Breda are in sight. Even Delft,
Haarlem and Leyden are not far beyond; a country that has known civil
wars as bad as ours, my excellent young man, but which now doesn't seem
to think much of them. Antwerp itself is a sort of standing monument to
the power of conquest. And I suppose the Southerners will declare that
Antwerp had its Alva, and New Orleans its Butler. But nowadays the
Flemish cattle graze with damp feet upon the ground that the Spanish
tents covered, and for all that the world can see, Spain and Spaniard never
set foot or planted spear upon the Scheldt or the Zuyder Zee, nor was ever
a dyke cut or a city sacked. I wonder whether any of our ancestors were
with William of Orange, or whether any of our descendents will have the
fortune to moralize in peace and in a happy, free and prosperous South
over the obliterated traces of a civil war. It isn't likely to be you or I, mon
brave!

We had two charming spring days at Antwerp and it was a luxury to feel
once more a clean face and hands and a pure atmosphere. We saw all that
was to be seen, and even discovered an old building of the Inquisition with
its cells and towers and dungeons, which amused us greatly. The youthful
Brooks, a good and well-meaning boy withal, though not likely, I think, to
make much noise in the world, was much pleased with his experiences and
relucted warmly at the idea of returning to Chipperwick, as he once, in his
happy forgetfulness, called Twickenham. Still, two days are not eternal; so
after long studies on the Cathedral spire, and after various contemplation
of Rubens' pictures, and meditation over vespers in the splendid old Cathedral, and other such like amusements, we ascended the steamer on Wednes-

day noon and descended the Scheldt again, recrossed the Channel, re-ascended the Thames, and at ten this morning we reached home in time for breakfast.

Here I find myself again in the old atmosphere of smoke and fog, atmospheric, moral and political. The other side means mischief and we know it. But they will not open against us until we do something which will rouse national anger. Then you will see us struggle *in vasto*.[1] Oh, ye Gods! why not make a man of tanned leather as to his heart! The more I strive to be callous, the more I become only silent! Rage boils up my throat. My only consolation is the thought that as yet we have weathered the storm in spite of all the convictions of our foreign friends, and some day—God forgive me for the folly of wishing for what could do no good and must do harm to everyone—but some day I hope to see the time when America alone will take France and England both together on her hands, and be strong enough to knock their two skulls against each other till they crack. Fifty years more of peace would do it. A hundred years of union and peace would place Europe so low in the ranks as no longer to create jealousy. Look back to 1785 when old J.A. was here, and compare the situations.

MS: MHi
1. *In vasto:* savagely, devastatingly.

To Richard Cobden

5 Upper Portland Place.
Wednesday. 22 April. 1863.

My dear Mr Cobden:

As you are at present investigating the history of the Foreign Enlistment Act in America, perhaps you will excuse me for offering some little information as to its origin, which I fear you will not easily get from English sources.[1]

You know how that Act originated. The curious letters of M. Genet are famous enough, as well as Jefferson's answers; the best things he ever did, next to the Declaration of Independence. But one side of the affair has remained a good deal in the dark. Geo. Hammond was then your Minister at Washington, of whom Jefferson complained privately that he overwhelmed him with letters and remonstrances; yet few or none of these have ever been published, nor do they exist in the archives of this Legation, nor anywhere else so far as I know, except in the State Paper Office, the Washington Archives, and a copy which I have in my drawer.

This latter is of course at your service. The number of notes is large, and they do not all apply to the principle of armaments, though they do all bear on the origin of the Act. That is, they are not all directed against the fitting out of privateers, but in most cases to the restitution of prizes. They are not of so much importance as I had hoped, on reading the published correspondence, because Hammond seems to have done his most important discussions in conversation; but they are quite conclusive so far as anything we want.

In these letters, the principle of his claim of redress is laid down with great clearness; and certainly my father never stated it with more force. Perhaps the words may be of use to you. He says that he was persuaded "the Government of the United States would regard the act of fitting out "those privateers in its ports as an insult offered to its sovereignty, and any "prizes made by them as an unwarrantable aggression on the commerce "carried on between its citizens and the subjects of a friendly power, relying "on the protection of this Government, and unsuspecting that the means "of annoying them would be furnished within the harbors of the United "States, or would be sanctioned by any of their officers." 7 June. 1793.

You know the manner in which the United States responded to this claim; and the Enlistment Act was one of the measures then instituted. At this day I am afraid it cannot be got even to repeat the words; much less act on the principles urged in these letters. But if you would like to see them yourself, I shall be happy to put them in your hands.

I remain &c &c &c   H. B. Adams.

Richard Cobden Esq.

MS: The British Library, Richard Cobden Papers
 1. The act prohibited U.S. citizens from serving in foreign armies. Although England had a similar law, British sailors manned the *Alabama.*

To Charles Francis Adams, Jr.

London. 23 April. 1863.

My dear Boy:

Troubled times! troubled times! My own opinion is that our bed here is getting too hot for comfort and I dont much care how soon we are out of it.

The last storm really amounts to very little, but serves to show the temper of the people here, or rather, of the business men. I had not sent my last to you, when it burst, and you would have thought the devil was loose. Écoute, mon chéri!

The cursed blockade-runners got up a lovely scheme of trading to the Rio Grande, a few months ago, and to insure success they made a contract with J.D. at Richmond to furnish cotton at half price on the spot &c &c, and in accordance with the program, a steamer called the Peterhoff was sent out, which Admiral Wilkes very properly bagged, and deserves the thanks of the Government for doing so.[1] But the owners had covered the transaction under the appearance of a trade with Mexico and Matamoras, and finding their whole game spoiled and the officers refusing at any price to insure their ships or any ships to Matamoras, they set up a tremendous cackle, and the Times and the Telegraph and all the newspapers cackled, and deputations of blockade runners went to the Foreign Office and in short the whole blockade-breaking interest, the insurance Companies and underwriters, the ship-owners, and all and every their relations, friends and acquaintances, were exasperated and acrimonious.

Meanwhile two Americans named Howell and Zerman had been some time here engaged in purchasing articles on account of the Mexican Government, but mostly with British money. The capture of the Peterhof suddenly destroyed their chance of insurance. In great disgust they went to the Minister and asked him for a certificate of loyalty, on which they might act. The Minister saw his chance of hitting the Peterhoffers a hard blow, and at the same time of helping Mexico, and so wrote the letter which you have probably already seen in the newspapers.[2] Of course it was secret, for its publication would necessarily destroy the insurance, but it was intended for the gentlemen at Lloyd's. It had the intended effect. The policy was to have been executed the next day, when one of the very underwriters made public a copy of the letter which his clerk had surreptitiously taken in short-hand as he himself read it aloud to the other four underwriters; within an hour a deputation had gone up with it to Earl Russell; the Exchange was raving mad; the Times next day thundered at the Minister for his insolent attempt to license British trade; the Standard cried for his dismissal; the public cursed and threatened; even our friends were frightened, and all thought that at last salt had been deposited upon the caudal appendage of a very venerable ornithological specimen.

The Minister was grand. I studied his attitude with deep admiration. Not all the supplications of his friends could make him open his mouth either to put the public right on his letter or on the gross falsehoods told about the Peterhof. The time had not come. Of course he was cursed for his obstinacy, but he is used to that. We remained perfectly silent while the storm raged, and laughed at it. But you can't conceive how bitter they were in the city, and the matter was twice brought up in Parliament, though nothing was said there, nor shown, except a strong desire to get hold of the Minister. Luckily Lord Russell was firm and his course irritated the Peterhoffers so as to draw off a large portion of indignation upon him. Meanwhile the man who betrayed the letter in the hope of getting revenge for being called "dishonest and fraudulent," and of stirring up hostility to our Government, honorably refused to proceed with the insurance, and was blackguarded in his own office like a thief by Howell. To complete their discomfiture, a letter of the Minister to a London firm is published this morning, coolly putting it aright as to the licensing business, and referring British subjects to their own Government for protection. When the whole Peterhof story is told we shall reverse everything and overwhelm these liars, I hope, but meanwhile the storm seems to have blown itself out and we are still steady and going straight ahead. But England is not comfortable with such Irish rows.

24 April.   You may judge the state of feeling here by the debate in Parliament last night, where much bad temper was shown, but no case. You will observe that our friends kept silence and left the Government to manage the matter. As to Lord Russell's declaration about the Minister's course and the complaint at Washington, it is of course annoying and hurts us here, but I believe it to be only the result of the outside pressure, and I do not believe he expects really to affirm that the American Government has no right to protect its own citizens against its own fleets. One thing however is certain. There is great danger in this feeling of irritation on both sides and a rupture is highly probable. But then, if we can weather it and turn the current, as I hope we may do, if the Peterhof case is a strong one, we shall have plain sailing for another spell. Meanwhile we still bear up and steer right onward. Another debate comes on tonight and our friends will have their innings on the Alabama case. You will probably see this in our papers, but I shant be able to send it to you.

Henry Emmons turned up here yesterday in a deuce of a lot of trouble. He came over to see about two ships expected to arrive here, and finds that they have both been overhauled by the Alabama and compelled to give bonds, the cargoes being English. He is now trying to see whether he can bring the consignees to accept a pro rata share in the bonds. He dines here to-day.[3]

I sympathise with you in your blueness. Not that I am blue now. I like excitement at times and I enjoy all this row and confusion immensely, on my own account, as a spectacle and study, though of course in a national point of view it is a cause of anxiety to us all. But your position is by no means a pleasant one, and I don't wonder that you are down in the mouth. The camp as you now have it, must be a very unpleasant place. Perhaps however, your adorable preceptor may succeed in getting himself killed in the first skirmish, and it seems not unlikely from his renowned personal courage, and perhaps, if you're not killed too, you may be better off than ever. Accept my sincere wishes for so desirable a consummation.[4] In the meanwhile I can do nothing but sympathize, which I do from the bottom of my soul. The excellent Crowninshield still remains to you, I see. The good old Ben, who has a choice variety of excellent faults and weaknesses, but who is the only one of my college friends whom I have kept within speaking distance of me. How I wish you and he would come abroad! It is however, very highly probable that time will not be much older before I look in upon you myself. I shall expect to be received like the prodigal son, and to charge with you in some mighty battle, wearing a blue silk neck-tie and a shiny black tile.[5]

Where is Jim Higginson, of whom you do not speak? He promised to write, but confound him, he never even answers a letter until he's forced, and hang me if I'll write first this time. By the way, you speak of losing your Lieutenant Hayden. None of our Bostonians, I hope. I see that you and everyone speak of Fitzhugh Lee as commanding against you. Surely this cant be my friend Rooney.[6] It must be his brother, I suppose. I doubt whether Rooney would make a good cavalry colonel, though he might do well as a major or captain. I wonder what's become of Jim May and Ben Jones. I suppose that they too have been "gobbled" by this voracious cotton-demon. And Julius Alston![7] do you ever hear of him? If we can keep these foreign countries off some three months more, I rather think we shall hear of trouble down south. This long, steady pressure must be terrible to them; worse than fighting; and if their rail-roads are worn out and their food eaten up; riots in their cities; laziness or worse among their slaves; and strange corruption in all branches of their Richmond Government, it seems to me that their cause is, I do not say, desperate, but liable to be overturned at what would seem a small thing. Davis now alone unites them. Would Lee do so? or Johnson?[8] We hear of an attack on Charleston, but as you know, I have no faith in its success.

Ever Yrs

MS: MHi
1. J.D.: Jefferson Davis. Adm. Charles Wilkes (1798–1877).
2. Col. Bertram H. Howell and Gen. Jean Napoleon Zerman, U.S. citizens buying supplies for Juárez to use against the French, wanted an affidavit from CFA to convince Lloyd's underwriters that they were not running arms to the Confederates and so could be insured without risk of confiscation. Consequently, CFA gave them a safe-conduct letter addressed to Admiral Du Pont of the blockading fleet.
3. Nathaniel Henry Emmons (1796–1878), Quincy neighbor of the Adamses.
4. CFA2, tempted by a staff appointment, decided not to be driven from his company command by the detested Colonel Sargent.
5. A tall hat.
6. Both "Rooney" and his cousin Fitzhugh Lee were now Confederate generals, and CFA2 just missed direct engagement with Fitzhugh's cavalry brigade.
7. James May (1837–1876), Harvard '58; Benjamin Dewees Marshall Jones of Petersburg, Va., left Harvard in 1857 without taking a degree; John J. P. Alston (1837–1863), Harvard '57.
8. Gen. Joseph Eggleston Johnston (1807–1891), victor at Bull Run and commander of the Department of the West.

To Richard Cobden

5, Upper Portland Place.
Thursday eve. 23 April. [1863]

My dear Sir:

I hasten to answer your note, just received.

From all that I can discover, I decidedly believe that our Neutrality Act of 1794, was *not* passed in consequence of any direct pressure from England. With your permission I will try to show why no such pressure was exerted.

The illegal outfits in our ports commenced early in 1793. British vessels having been captured and brought into port, Mr Hammond brought the matter to the notice of Mr Jefferson, and in a note of the 8th May, he said, "he doubts not that the Executive Government of the United States will pursue such measures as to its wisdom may appear the best calculated for repressing such practices in future." In repeated notes he pressed for a decision upon his arguments and facts, but he adds; "the determination of the Executive Government of the United States relative to them is of a nature infinitely too delicate and important for him to venture giving an opinion on it."

Under this pressure, which was by no means relaxed, Mr Jefferson took repeated measures to check the abuses, but without success. Mr Hammond continued his remonstrances, till at last Mr Jefferson accepted the principle of pecuniary compensation. This was done at the end of August. And this was quite sufficient for Mr Hammond, as all the prizes seem to have been brought in to our ports, the privateers remaining near our coasts and apparently not being intended for distant voyages. He therefore had only to claim them, or compensation for them.

But of course, this compensation principle made the war practically one against America, and of course it became doubly necessary for Government to stop the French cruizers. The direct pressure rose however not from Mr Hammond, but from the effect of the principles which they had accepted at Mr Hammond's instance. The Neutrality Law, therefore, I take to have been a municipal regulation, adopted in order to protect the Government from what loss would result, if it were compelled to indemnify foreign Governments for the consequences of an infraction of its own sovereignty.

I am &c &c &c   H. B. Adams.

MS: The British Library, Richard Cobden Papers

To Charles Francis Adams, Jr.

London. 1 May. 1863.

Two years ago today, my boy, I last set eyes upon your beaming countenance. You remember perhaps the somewhat discouraging circumstances under which I began my adventures. I shall always recollect that day with a strong propensity to hilarious mirth. Most extraording how prostrated I was by sea-sickness on that voyage!

And so two years have passed over and gone, and still I am abroad and still you are a Captain of Cavalry. You meanwhile are near twenty-eight years old. I shall never on this earth see my twenty-fifth birthday again. Does not this fact suggest certain ideas to you? Can a man at your time of life be a Cavalry Captain and remain a briefless solicitor? Can a man of my general appearance pass five years in Europe and remain a candidate for the bar? In short, have we both wholly lost our reckonings and are we driven at random by fate, or have we still a course that we are steering though it is not quite the same as our old one? By the Apostle Paul I know not. Only one fact I feel sure of. We are both no longer able to protect ourselves with the convenient fiction of the law. Let us quit that now useless shelter, and steer if possible for whatever it may have been that once lay beyond it. Neither you nor I can ever do anything at the bar.

I should speculate with more ease on the matter, if I weren't deucedly anxious about you. There are rumors of movement and a report that Gen. Stoneman had entered Gordonsville. This I promptly concluded to be a lie. But as I presume you to be in his command, I am still not at ease. For he may be making some cursed raid or other and that may be preliminary to a rapid advance. What worries me the more is that from the general appearance of dissipation in Lee's army, of which a considerable portion must be operating against Foster and Keyes, I should judge that it was a fine chance for Hooker to attack.[1] So that between apprehension and desire, I remain in a silent state of tepid muddle.

Enough of that! If you have a fight I would like to go into it with you on certain conditions which I have explained in the enclosed note to regimental boot-black Higginson. You don't catch me entering the army now. Donner-r-r-wetter! it would be like entering college Freshman when all one's friends were Seniors. I have a trick worth twenty dozen of that. My friend Gen. Zerman who has been the means of kicking up such a row around us here, and who is an old Dugald Dalgetty; a midshipman under the French at Trafalgar; a *sous-officier* at Waterloo; a Captain at Navarino; a Russian Admiral; a Turkish Admiral; a Carbonaro; a companion of Silvio Pellico in the prisons of Spielberg; a South American officer by land and sea; and lately a General in the army of the United States; now a Major General in the Mexican service; and I've no doubt a damned old villain, though a perfectly jovial old sinner of seventy odd; this distinguished individual offers to take me on his staff with the rank of Major to Mexico.[2] By the Evangelist John, wouldn't I like to go! The chances are a thousand to one that my bones would bleach there, but for all that the chance is worth having for it would be a great step for a young man to secure for himself a control even to a small extent over our Mexican relations. But such magnificent dreams, worthy of the daring of those heroes Porthos, Athos, Aramis and D'Artagnan, are not for me. By the by, though, what a good Porthos, Ben Crowny. would make; you could do D'Artagnan;[3] I would put in for Aramis, and no doubt you could hunt up some one that might pass equally badly for Athos. Then we could all go to Mexico together.

No, my warlike brother! My hand could at best use a rapier. It is not made for a sabre. I should be like a bewildered rabbit in action, being only trained to counsel. My place is where I am, and I never was so necessary to it as now. All thoughts of escape even for a day, have vanished. We are covered with work, and our battles are fierce and obstinate. And this brings me back to my last letter, and the story the continuation of which you are no doubt curious to hear.

I left off by sending you the debate of last Friday night which contained

John Quincy Adams II

Charles Francis Adams, Jr.

Earl Russell's brilliant remarks on the celebrated letter of our Minister to Admiral Dupont.[4] In those remarks Earl Russell was indignant at the idea of his speaking to Mr Adams about it. No! No! He should go straight to Washington! But my Lord, having thus pledged himself in order to please the English copper-heads, to go straight to Washington, amused himself the next morning by sending straight to Mr Adams. Of course I know nothing of the conversation that followed. That is all a secret with Mr Seward. But I think it is not difficult to guess. It had suited Lord Russell to yield a little to the copper-head pressure on Thursday night; it suited him to allow Mr Adams to triumphantly purge himself of misdemeanor on Friday morning. It suited him to make the American Minister think that he (Lord R) thought him to be in the wrong—moderately. It also suited him to make the British public think that Mr Adams had confessed his error and contrition and had received pardon. English statesmanship consists in this sort of juggling and huckstering between interests.

Such was the position when I wrote to you, or rather, immediately after I wrote to you. Since then nothing has been heard of complaining at Washington. But now, oh! balmy youth, see the resources of a British Minister. Last Tuesday morning the *City Article,* what we call the money article, of the Times, in which most of the attack had been directed, contained the following paragraph:

"The public will be glad to learn that the difficulties occasioned by the recent issue by Mr Adams of the certificate or pass to Messrs. Howell and Zirman, are likely to be smoothed down. It is reported that Mr Adams is conscious of having acted in the matter upon imperfect representations and with undue haste, and that consequently he raises no pretensions such as would necessitate any absolute protest from one Government to the other on the subject. It is therefore believed that the relations between our Cabinet and the United States Legation in London will continue on a friendly footing—a result which in a personal sense will afford unmixed satisfaction, since the individual and historical claims of Mr Adams to respect and esteem have never been disputed in any quarter."

Now, is not this a remarkable State Paper? Did you ever see a case in which the butter was laid on so curiously over the interstices of the bread? The real fact is that you should read "Earl Russell" instead of "Mr Adams" in the 5th line. That would be the correct thing. But this statement has received universal currency and is accepted as a conclusion of the difficulty. It now remains for Lord Russell to make the explanation which no doubt Mr Adams must demand, at some time when the whole affair shall be forgotten, and then I hope this curious chapter will be closed.

Your long letter of the 5th April interested us much. I have no doubt that your decision as to the staff-position was correct, but I am sorry that you are so entangled with the regiment as not to be able to extricate yourself. Still I should be sorry to have you desert Curtis and the other fellows.[5] The future is not very clear, but whatever happens, we can only go on and meet it as honorably as we may.

Our own position here does not change. We lead a quiet and not unpleasant life, and I pass my intervals from official work, in studying De Tocqueville and John Stuart Mill, the two high priests of our faith.[6] So I jump from International Law to our foreign history, and am led by that to study the philosophic standing of our republic, which brings me to reflection over the advance of the democratic principle in European civilization, and so I go on till some new question of law starts me again on the circle. But I have learned to think De Tocqueville my model, and I study his life and works as the Gospel of my private religion. The great principle of democracy is still capable of rewarding a conscientious servant. And I doubt me much whether the advance of years will increase my toleration of its faults. Hence, my boy, I think I see in the distance a vague and unsteady light in the direction towards which I needs must gravitate, so soon as the present disturbing influences are removed.

We are surrounded by assistants. Mr Aspinwall, Mr J. M. Forbes, Mr Robert J. Walker and Mr Evarts are all here.[7]

MS: MHi

1. In the Chancellorsville campaign the cavalry corps under the command of Gen. George Stoneman (1822–1894) was sent in advance of the main army to raid Lee's lines of communication. From April 11 to May 4 two of Lee's divisions were engaged in an operation at Suffolk, Va., against Gen. Robert Sandford Foster (1834–1903) and Gen. Erasmus D. Keyes. Succeeding Burnside, Gen. Joseph Hooker (1814–1879) was commander of the Army of the Potomac.

2. Dugald Dalgetty was a soldier of fortune in Scott's *Legend of Montrose* (1819); Silvio Pellico (1789–1854), an Italian nationalist poet jailed as a Carbonaro by the Austrians.

3. The companions-in-arms in Alexandre Dumas, *The Three Musketeers* (1844).

4. Adm. Samuel Francis Du Pont (1803–1865), to whom Zerman's safe-conduct was addressed.

5. Lt. Col. Greely Curtis (1830–1897), the friend who persuaded CFA2 to stay with his regiment.

6. Alexis de Tocqueville (1805–1859), *Democracy in America* (1835–1840). His *Memoir, Letters and Remains* (1861), read by CFA when it came out, is among the HA books at MHi.

7. William Henry Aspinwall (1807–1875), Panama railroad and steamship entrepreneur, and John Murray Forbes (1813–1898), financier and Navy Department adviser, were on an unofficial mission to buy, if possible, Confederate cruisers being built in Britain. Robert John Walker (1801–1869), secretary of the treasury in Polk's cabinet, was in Europe selling federal bonds. William Maxwell Evarts (1818–1901), New York lawyer and Republican leader, was sent to try to stop the building and equipping of the Confederate ships.

To Charles Francis Adams, Jr.

London. 8 May. 1863.

My dear Boy:

My bulletin is calmer this week than has been usual of late. The little squall has passed and instead of pressing on the Minister, people here feel that Lord Russell was in the wrong in his attack that I sent you some weeks ago, and the Times has this week administered a second pacifyer in the shape of a flattering leader on Mr Adams' speech to the Trades Unions delegation. I send you a newspaper containing this speech. Notice also the Royal Academy Dinner and Lord Palmerston's remarks. They are not political, but are a noble specimen of lofty sentiment and brilliant rhetoric, worthy of the experienced statesman to whose power and wisdom this vast nation bows. And these men call Seward shallow and weak!

A much quieter feeling and a partial reaction against the blockade runners, has generally prevailed here for a week past. Our successes on the Mississipi, too, and the direct advices from the South are having a quieting effect here on the public, and the Polish question is becoming so grave that we are let up a little.[1] On the whole we have made progress this last week.

Meanwhile we have a complete Cabinet of Ministerial advisers and assistants. I wrote you their names in my last. Of them all, Mr Evarts is the only one whom I put very high. Dana too has written to call on my services for him. So I have done and shall do everything I can to make him comfortable and contented. Last Sunday I took him down to Westminster Abbey in the afternoon, where we listened awhile to the services, and then trotted off and took a steamboat up the river. We had a two hours' voyage up to Kew, where we arrived at half after five, and had just time to run over the gardens. Then we took a cab and drove up to Richmond Hill, where we ordered dinner at the Star and Garter, and then sat in the open air and watched the view and the sunset until our meal was ready. Much conversation had we, and that of a pretty confidential nature. We discussed affairs at home and philosophic statesmanship, the Government and the possibility of effectual reform. He is much like Dana in his views, but is evidently a good deal soured by his political ill-luck.[2]

Another evening I took him out to see London by night. We visited as spectators, various places of popular resort. He was much interested in them, and seemed to enjoy the experience as a novelty in his acquaintance with life. London is rather peculiar in these repects, and even an experienced traveller would find novelty in the study of character at the Argyll Rooms and at Evans's. At any rate, I consider that I have done my part there, and you may imagine that I do not much neglect opportunities to conciliate men like him, like Seward and like Weed. I would like to get further west, but the deuce of it is that there are so few distinguished western men.

With this exception I believe the last week has been quiet. I was rather astonished last Monday by one of Seward's jocose proceedings. The Minister had sent me down to the Trade's Unions meeting three weeks ago to make a report on it to him, for transmission to Washington. I did so and wrote a report which I had no time either to correct or alter, and which was sent the next day to Seward officially, appended to a Despatch. Now Seward writes back as grave as a Prime Minister a formal Despatch acknowledging the other, and thanking "Mr Henry B. Adams" in stately and wordy paragraphs for his report and "profound disquisition," &c &c. I propose to write a note to Fred Seward on his father's generosity.

Theodore Lyman and his wife made their appearance here today on their way home.[3] They are looking as well and comfortable as possible. Bob

Winthrop, to the utter astonishment of everyone, has gone back to Boston after three weeks absence. What may be in the wind, it is extremely difficult to say, but something. He called here on his passage.

Mary haunts balls, to which, praise be to the prophet Micaiah, I am generally not asked. So far there is not much gaiety.

————.[4]

MS: MHi
1. The question of British diplomatic intervention on behalf of Poland was being debated in Parliament.
2. Evarts had failed in 1861 to win election as senator from New York.
3. Theodore Lyman (1833–1897) of Boston, Harvard '55, B.S. '58, had been pursuing zoological research in Europe and collecting for the Harvard Museum of Comparative Zoology, of which he was a founding trustee. In 1856 he married Elizabeth Russell, of a Boston mercantile family.
4. HA uses a long dash here instead of his signature, a practice that henceforth will be reproduced but not noted.

To Frederick William Seward

London. 8 May. 1863.

My dear Sir:

I write a line to request you to say on some occasion, to the Secretary of State that "Mr Henry B. Adams" is pleased to hear that his "profound disquisition" is "highly appreciated." Pray add that he was somewhat alarmed at first at seeing his remarks placed on such a pedestal, but has since recovered and is doing nicely.

Mr Evarts is here, and we are trying to amuse him and show him the Britishers. I have no doubt he will prove socially a great success. As to his legal progress, that is a question that is to be argued chiefly by the learned advocates on your side; such as Halleck, Grant, Rosecranz, Banks and Hooker. Mr Evarts however is a great acquisition to our strength and is considered as a sort of guarantor of pacific dispositions. I rather think he will enjoy his visit. I have done what I could, myself, to show him London externally; and in a few days he will need no assistance in society.

If it is not an impertinence I would like to make a little interest for our Assistant Secretary Moran. He is an invaluable man, a tremendous worker, and worth any ten ordinary officers to Government, but here he has borne nine tenths of the labor of this Legation for seven years, and gets for it a miserable pittance of $1500 a year; about enough to support a respectable cab-driver, in this city. If any little means of assistance or even of public recognition of his services should come in your father's way, it really would be extremely well placed on him.[1]

I am &c &c &c   H. B. Adams.

F. W. Seward Esq.

MS: NRU
1. Moran for his part resented Seward's praise of the trades-union report (*Journal*, II, 1159) and repeatedly noted HA's encroachments on his duties and HA's favored social position.

To Charles Francis Adams, Jr.

London. 14 May. 1863.

My dear Boy:

The telegraph assures us that Hooker is over the Rappanock and your division regally indistinct "in the enemy's rear." I suppose the campaign is begun, then. Honestly, I'd rather be with you than here, for our state of mind during the next few weeks is not likely to be very easy.

But now that things are begun, I will leave them to your care. Just for your information, I inclose one of Mr Lawley's letters from Richmond to the London Times. It is curious. Mr Lawley's character here is under a cloud, as, strange to say, is not unusual with the employés of that seditious journal. For this and other reasons I don't put implicit trust in him, but one fact is remarkably distinct. His dread of the shedding of blood makes him wonderfully anxious for intervention. A prayer for intervention is all that the northern men read in this epistle, and Mr Lawley's humanity doesn't quite explain his earnestness.[1]

But if our letters from here have any real merit with you, it is because they give you a little change of atmosphere. So I will leave your affairs alone, in spite of your last letter which almost threw your dear mother into permanent dissolution because you said that under the bother of your difficulties you had one day taken to drinking and had struck one of your men. I think it will but slightly need a reminder to bring to your mind the lesson we should have given you, had you been here. "We certainly had thought that an Adams &c &c &c." All I can say is that I hope you stick it out with your regiment, for if you do work through, you will have had a good training not to let your passions trip up your heels. Yet I don't suppose it's an agreeable experience nor a cheerful prospect to look forward to. Don't you recollect that I wrote to you after the first Bull Run, announcing my intention of returning, and suggesting a new regiment then talked of, as my place, and your reply telling me by no means to put myself under that man for a Colonel.

This week has been quite a busy one with us here; socially at least, for politically there is a lull. I won't trouble you with an account of balls, at which I am usually a miserable attendant, looking and feeling like an exhibited horned owl. You already know my opinions about that species of society here, and no doubt you have been the confidant of the feminine portion of our humanity in regard to the silly manner in which I *will* behave. In short, I abhor it! but I go, in silence. Mary, too, drags me to the

Park and compels me to ride in Rotten Row, and I submit to that too, though I am not properly mounted for such show work, and it interrupts all my occupations. In fine, I feel more and more every day the want of life in others, and as I never had much of my own, I am slowly but certainly becoming a dead-head.

Once in a while, however, I get a little glimpse into a less offensive existence. If Mary writes to you this week, she will tell you, no doubt about a little dinner she and I were asked to, the other day, by some friends of ours. Our young lady, whom I suspect to be not a little vain, and whose vanity was not a little flattered, was much delighted with the attention she received from Sir Edward Lytton. It was a party of only eleven, and of these, Sir Edward was one, Robert Browning another, and a Mr Ward, a well-known artist and member of the royal Academy, was a third.[2] All were people of a stamp, you know; as different from the sky-blue, skim-milk of the ball-rooms, as good old burgundy is from syrup-lemonade. I had a royal evening; a feast of remarkable choiceness, for the meats were very excellent good, the wines were rare and plentiful, and the company was of earth's choicest.

Sir Edward is one of the ugliest men it has been my good luck to meet. He is tall and slouchy, careless in his habits, deaf as a ci-devant, mild in manner, and quiet and philosophic in talk. Browning is neat, lively, impetuous, full of animation, and very un-English in all his opinions and appearance. Here, in London society, famous as he is, half his entertainers actually take him to be an American. He told us some amusing stories about this, one evening when he dined here.

Just to amuse you, I will try to give you an idea of the conversation after dinner; the first time I have ever heard anything of the sort in England. Sir Edward is a great smoker, and although no crime can be greater in this country, our host produced cigars after the ladies had left, and we filled our claret-glasses, and drew up together.

Sir Edward seemed to be continuing a conversation with Mr Ward his neighbor. He went on, in his thoughtful, deliberative, way, addressing Browning.

"Do you think your success would be very much more valuable to you for knowing that centuries hence, you would still be remembered? Do you look to the future connection by a portion of mankind, of certain ideas with your name, as the great reward of all your labour?"

"Not in the least! I am perfectly indifferent whether my name is remembered or not. The reward would be that the ideas which were mine, should live and benefit the race!"

"I am glad to hear you say so" continued Sir Edward, thoughtfully, "because it has always seemed so to me, and your opinion supports mine. Life, I take to be a period of preparation. I should compare it to a preparatory school. Though it is true that in one respect the comparison is not just, since the time we pass at a preparatory school bears an infinitely greater proportion to a life, than a life does to eternity. Yet I think it may be compared to a boy's school; such a one as I used to go to, as a child, at old Mrs S's at Fulham. Now if one of my old school-mates there were to meet me some day and seem delighted to see me, and asked me whether I recollected going to old mother S's at Fulham, I should say, 'Well! yes! I did have some faint remembrance of it! yes! I could recollect about it.' And then supposing he were to tell me how I was still remembered there! How much they talked of what a fine fellow I'd been at that school."

"How Jones Minimus" broke in Browning; "said you were the most awfully good fellow, he ever saw."

"Precisely." Sir Edward went on beginning to warm to his idea; "Should I be very much delighted to hear that? Would it make me forget what I am doing now? For five minutes perhaps I should feel gratified, and pleased that I was still remembered, but that would be all. I should go back to my work without a second thought about it.

"Well, now Browning, suppose you, some time or other, were to meet Shakespeare, as perhaps some of us may. You would rush to him, and seize his hand, and cry out, "My dear Shakespeare, how delighted I am to see you. You can't imagine how much they think and talk about you on earth!" Do you suppose Shakespeare would be more carried away by such an announcement than I should be at hearing that I was still remembered by the boys at mother S's at Fulham? What possible advantage can it be to him to know that what he did on the earth is still remembered there?"

The same idea is in LXIII of Tennyson's In Memoriam, but not pointed the same way.[3] It was curious to see two men who, of all others, write for fame, or have done so, ridicule the idea of its real value to them. But Browning went on to get into a very unorthodox humor, and developed a theory of spiritual election that would shock the Pope, I fear. According to him, the minds or souls that really did develope themselves and educate themselves in life, could alone expect to enter a future career for which this life was a preparatory course. The rest were rejected, turned back, God knows what becomes of them; these myriads of savages and brutalized and degraded Christians. Only those that could pass the examination, were allowed to commence the new career. This is Calvin's theory, modified; and really it seems not unlikely to me. Thus this earth may serve as a sort of feeder to the next world, as the lower and middle classes here do to the aristocracy, here and there furnishing a member to fill the gaps. The corollaries of this proposition are amusing to work out.

So much for our dinner which has filled my letter and may serve to amuse you on some battle-field or in some temporary resting ground. Browning seemed much pleased to hear of your studies of him on your campaigns. He is at work on something new.

MS: MHi
1. Francis Lawley (1825–1901) became the *Times* correspondent in Richmond in the fall of 1862; his alleged investing on the basis of privileged information was under parliamentary investigation.

2. Edward Bulwer-Lytton (1803–1873), the popular novelist, and Edward Matthew Ward (1816–1879), whose historical frescoes were in the Houses of Parliament.
3. Alfred Tennyson (1809–1892), *In Memoriam* (1850).

To Charles Francis Adams, Jr.

London. 29 May. 1863.

Well! the great blow came! We had to give up our hopes, and I groaned for at least five minutes. But hope springs eternal. On the whole we usually give Hooker the credit of having done the most brilliant thing yet effected by the army of the Potomac under any of its various generals. I am satisfied that the South shook under it to its very centre and will find it hard to bear up against the destruction of its depots, the loss of its ablest general and the crippling of its best army.[1] L'audace! toujours l'audace![2] We want continual, feverish activity, and that is all. Worry them with cavalry raids! Give them all the plagues of Egypt! Let them have no rest, no hope! Revolutionize Louisiana. Lay waste Mississipi! By the time their harvests come, they will have no engines to draw it, no cars to carry it, no tracks to convey it on. And if at last they succeed in getting their independence, it will only be to lie down and die.

Still no letter from you. We suppose that we should have known of it if anything had happened to you, so we are not anxious. Still, I expect a long one by the next mail and of course want much to know what the army thinks about it all.

As for me, I have passed most of this week up at Cambridge with Mr Evarts. We went there to see the University and to visit Will Everett, and we chose the Whitsuntide holidays for that purpose. You have met Mr Evarts and you recollect, no doubt, that he wears his hat so that a plumb line dropped from its centre would fall about twelve inches behind his heels. His speech is Yankee and his whole aspect shouts American with stentorian lungs. Fortunately his conversation and mind makes up for his peculiarities of dress and appearance, so that I was always relieved when he took his hat off, and opened his mouth.

Will Everett never appeared so well as when acting the host. He is still dirty, ill-regulated in manners and at times piggish; but he was really extremely polite and obliging and did everything for us he could. He gave us an excellent dinner in his rooms, eight covers, and carried us about most perseveringly. He seems to be well thought of there, and he certainly has a very good set of friends, not very brilliant or noisy, but great scholars and pleasant fellows.

But the most humorous sight was when Mr Evarts and I went about dining in Hall with the Fellows of the different Colleges. When I found myself the honored guest, sitting among the College dignitaries, I could not help a sort of feeling that I was in somebody else's place and should soon be found out and expelled. However, it is astonishing what good fellows these gowned individuals may be, and how well they do live. If you could have seen Mr Evarts and me after dinner at one of the little colleges, conducting a jovial and noisy game of whist, with cigars and brandy and soda-water, and a Clergyman and a Fellow of an adjacent College known as Jesus, for our partners, you would have smiled among your sabres and pistols.

The truth is, we were deuced well treated at Cambridge and I enjoyed the visit immensely. We saw everything that was to be seen, and raked up all the dead celebrities, the shades of Milton and Cromwell, as well as the equally solemn shadows of present undergraduates. I wished to become a Fellow, but am afraid it can't be did. Seriously, I think I have learned enough in the world to be able to employ to much advantage a year or two of retirement.

You will hear of balls and so on from our feminine members of society. I hope they amuse you. Just now it is very hot here and the idea of summer disgusts me with town life. I have long since come to the conclusion that society doesn't pay, and that anything really remunerative is only to be found in chance holes and corners.

I have nothing to send you this week. We are so quiet here that there is nothing to read. It is about time however for another squall and I am looking about with curiosity for the quarter it is to come from.

Ever Yrs

MS: MHi
1. Hooker had been defeated at Chancellorsville, May 2–4, and his drive on Richmond stopped. However, Lee lost Stonewall Jackson, and his army sustained 20 percent casualties.
2. "Il nous faut de l'audace, encore de l'audace, toujours de l'audace" (Boldness! . . . always boldness!); George Danton before the French Assembly in 1792.

To John Gorham Palfrey

London. 29 May. 1863.

My dear Dr Palfrey:

Many thanks for your two kind letters, especially the last. There seems to be such a fog over the whole affair of that Mexican letter, and such complete bewilderment in America, that I should long ago have explained it in some of our newspapers, if it were not forbidden ground to me to appear in print on matter connected with the affairs of the Legation.

The truth is, the history of this affair is a series of illustrations of the weak points of the English system. It shows how commercial interests blind merchants to all moral relations; how sudden, direct, and unduly powerful a pressure the overgrown commercial interests of this kingdom can put upon their Government; how Parliament has encroached upon the governing rights of the Crown, and by means of that unfortunate system of making the Ministry their own equals, with seats in their own bodies, has left no real authority anywhere in England which does not bend to its dictum or even to its clamor; and how no English Minister in these days can be straightforward and retain office.

Two Americans came here and asked for a certificate that they were not blockade runners. Their object was to get insurance on some goods which were going to the Mexican Government. The capture of the Peterhoff had put an end to all insurance here on blockade-runners, and they were suspected of an intention to do so. They satisfied the Minister of their bonâ fide purpose, and he gave them the certificate, his ground being that a Minister is bound to protect his people so far as possible from injury from the acts of their own Government; or in other words, that a Government has the right to protect its own citizens from its own cruizers.

As to the cargo in question, it has nothing to do with the question. There is no blockade at Matamoras; the export of contraband of war is not a violation of neutrality; and neither France nor Mexico have ever made the request on foreign nations to remain neutral, even if the contrary were the case.

The underwriters had agreed to insure on the condition of having such a certificate. When it was produced, one of their number read it aloud to the others, three or four in all; it was not allowed to leave Mr Howell's sight, but their clerk took it down in short-hand, and made it public, presumably with their knowledge.

Then they refused to proceed with the insurance on any terms.

Eager to create a war in order to save their interest in the Peterhoff and their future hopes from six other similar vessels, all preparing to go, they rushed to Earl Russell and said that Mr Adams had assumed a power of licensing British trade.

Overpowered by popular clamor, Earl Russell without venturing to face the Minister, was glad to appease Parliament by declaring that Mr Adams had licensed a ship; that the act was unwarrantable; and that he should not dream of complaining to Mr Adams, but should go at once to his Government.

Having declared late one night that he should not go to Mr Adams, early the next morning he sent to ask Mr Adams to come to him.

The interview was curious, I presume. You are acquainted with the gentleman who represents our country at this Court. Well! He wasn't pleased.

The sum of the interview was that Mr Adams summarily denied having licensed a British ship, or any ship, and after explaining his real position, which had nothing to do with ships, he intimated that he thought Earl Russell might have taken the trouble to hear this before making his speech.

The result of this interview was a paragraph in the City Article of the Times two days later that Mr Adams was "conscious of having acted in the matter upon imperfect representations and with undue haste" and therefore would be allowed to remain at his post, "his individual and historical claims to respect and esteem never having been disputed." The dirty dogs!

Mr Adams let the matter rest for some weeks till the excitement was over. He then intimated to Earl Russell that his speech had not yet received any modification. Earl Russell replied that he had no objection to do so, *but might have to comment with some severity on the letter.* Mr Adams replied that an expression of opinion was free to him as to every man; that a statement of fact was another affair.

Accordingly Earl Russell did make what is really a retraction of his words. He acknowledged that he had been wrong in stating the fact, but his opinion was that the letter ought not to have been written.

Now, I know the predilections that you and Mr Dana have towards this country. It has been a fashion with the best class of our men to look up to the English system. All I can say is, that if our country ever descends to such contemptible equivocations and evasions and dishonest subterfuges as these I have related, then I hope it will be after my time. Certainly as yet the Republic never has so lowered its dignity in its treatment of foreign affairs.

Many thanks for your kind wishes in regard to my old friend Captain John, whose history I enclose herewith. It was written with the idea of publication in England, from which I was dissuaded by Mr Stephens,[1] and I'm very glad of it, on the principle that I never yet have had to regret the *not* doing a thing. After you have done with it, pray send it to my brother John who will put it away among my traps.

You must be rejoiced that one of your sons is out of danger, even at the price he has paid for escape. An arm is no joke, but it is at least as a *fait accompli* easy to bear compared with a continual dread of worse. Our anxiety about Charles is the worst part of our experience here. I hope you will remember me especially to Frank and to your family.

We are engulfed in the season, and my sister, who is just *out,* drags us to balls pitilessly. To tell the truth, I find them slow, but don't tell of me. Mr Evarts and I have been on a lark to Cambridge, stirring up the Dons who were very hospitable. My father sends his best regards and proposes soon to answer your last.

Very truly   H. B. Adams.

MS: MH
   1. Henry Stevens (1819–1886) of Vermont, in London since about 1845, expert on early colonial history, purchaser for the British Museum and many American libraries.

To Charles Francis Adams, Jr.

London. 5 June. 1863.

Most admirable Captain:

The weeks dance away as merrily as ever they did in that dimly distant period when we were boys and you used to box my ears because your kite wouldn't fly, and were the means of getting them boxed by disseminating at the tea-table truthless stories that I was painting myself a moustache with pear-juice. Incidents of an early youth which you no doubt have forgotten, as I was the injured party, but which have remained deeply rooted in my associations with an ancient green-room called the dining-room in a certain house on a hill. At the present day, life is a pretty dull affair, but it passes quick enough. Still, before I die I would like to have one more good time such as I knew in former aeras of the earth's history.

We were glad to get your letters, although they depicted a state of existence that I scarcely conceive to be Sybaritic. I beg however that you will confine your discussions as to the more especial advantages of your being immediately killed, as much as possible to any letters you may write to me. Your mother's nerves are not so steady as those of a confirmed egoist like myself. What with poor Howard Dwight's death, and your placid prognostications of furlough to a happier existence, she has been in a permanent condition of the most obstinate misery for a week.[1] The whilk is no easy addition to our usual burdens in the way of keeping firm face against the low ruffians of Britishers. The diseases and disasters of your horses and men too, usually cost her one night's rest a week. So perhaps if you reserve the harrowing parts of your experience so far as you may, to my ears, you will spare your mother a deal of misery. For God's sake, however, don't let it be known that I said this to you. Your mother's nerves are by no means stronger as she grows older, and although the accounts of your life make her miserable, she takes a sort of ascetic delight in torturing herself.

Your letters are too good however, to be abbreviated. Only, as I only read parts of mine aloud to the family, while the others are wholly read, I can reserve such tit-bits as seem suitable, for the more refined consideration of your father and myself.

I hope too that you don't keep our correspondence in camp. It had better be deposited at home. If you should be run off some night by a sudden attack, or if the papers were lost and in any way got into a rebel paper, it wouldn't be gay.

While you, like the Emperor Charles of Spain, are cursing the Rebels and the weather,[2] we are going on in the old track. I am tired of it and want to go home and take a commission in a negro regiment. We dawdle ahead here, going to dinners, races, balls; dropping a mild dew of remonstrances upon the British Government for allowing rebel armaments in their ports; riding in the parks; dining stray Americans and stately English; and in short, groaning under the fardel of an easy life. Such a thing it is to be pampered.

We are in short at vacation, politically speaking. I expect it to last a fortnight longer, and then I rather think we shall see the winds rise again. I fancy there will be a good storm by the middle of August. If we were let alone, the two nations would do admirably, but the rebels are doing their best to create a row, and I should not wonder if they succeeded. I believe we should have been at home by this time if the Alexandra hadn't been seized, and there are some iron-clads now preparing, whose departure would certainly pack us off. There's no telling what will happen, but I have no confidence in this Government.

Meanwhile we have a report from home that Gen. Grant has captured Haynes Bluff and was in a fair way to bag the rebel army.[3] Long trial and especially the late sharp experience, has made me slow to be moved by possibilities. I presume the next news will be that Grant has safely evacuated Haynes Bluff, and his army has returned to its old camp. But should any laughable and ridiculous accident cause his success to be real, I do not see but that according to the map, the rebels will have to yield the whole of Mississipi and retire behind the Tombigby. I see no other line of defence that would offer a chance. This would compel Bragg to retreat also, I suppose.[4] Should these absurdities follow, I am inclined to think that we might have a chance here of taking an effective tone.

Mary and I went out to Ascot yesterday, and did the races. But, oh father Ananias, is it a necessity that I should be a calf! What would I give to be able to say one good thing. Only one, by the high priest Jeremiah! Nowadays I feel the curse of sterility light upon my brain wherever I go. I would be only made blessed by a few of the crumbs that you and John used to throw about so loosely. But so it is. Stupidity is the lot of man in this country. If humor grows, it is only as an exotic, or else as a native weed, the one, too difficult of cultivation, the other too coarse for good society. As for me, a permanent blight has fallen upon my intellect, and I dread society because I know that I am as dull as the people I see about me.

Nevertheless we saw Ascot, and I attempted to be agreeable. It was but a weakly and gaunt attempt, and it failed so promptly that I don't think anyone perceived it. I retreated without loss and in perfect good order to my usual fortress of cold civility, and there I stick. God pardon me my follies and my weaknesses! Crimes I don't care for. But oh! fratello mio; Bruderchen mein; frater meus; this am a gay nation, and they look alarmingly brilliant and intellectual on the tops of drags getting boozy over luncheon.[5]

Who do you think was one of our party. None but the great Schlesinger whom you remember in the marble halls of Boston. He gave me gossip unlimited about that venerable hamlet, and I saw arise before me the manly forms of the men who still haunt Papanti's. I think we shall have to give them a title some day, such as Papanti's Heavies or something in that way. I'm glad to see that they are getting up a new Club in Boston, which I hope the returning officers will appropriate, and put a good solid brad-awl into those noble institutions the Temple and the Somerset.[6]

You will see perhaps that we've been having an election over in France, which has not been very favorable to our friend Napoleon. European affairs get worse than ever. They will have business enough to occupy them, and the Lord grant that Puebla may hold out.[7] If it can, or if it lasts only a few months or even weeks, and we are reasonably successful on the Mississipi, I think that Europe will turn with considerable disgust from our affairs and will not again burn its fingers with them in our time.

As there doesn't seem to be anything of interest in the periodical way to send you this week, I put into the envelope my little pocket Horace. It can't take much room and it may amuse you. You will find some few marks of mine in it, and certain odes where the leaf is turned down and pencil-marked, were the ones which Charles James Fox admired most.[8] They are certainly not the best known. If you find this considerable volume in your way, do not allow yourself by any idea of expense to be prevented from dropping it into the mud; for, if I recollect right, its cost was one shilling; and the value of the gift therefore not too extravagant. If it serves to distract occasionally your mind from running sores and sprung knees of horses, it may do good.

Aaron Charles Baldwin has turned up here. Not a line of his own handsome face is changed. Our cousin the phenomenon returns permanently to America by this steamer. In personal habits he remains stationary but in some general respects he is slightly improved. We are ourselves as usual all well, and tell Ben and the great J. J. Higgs's Son, that I expect to hear from them.

MS: MHi
1. Lt. Howard Dwight (1837–1863), Harvard '57, killed by guerrillas in Louisiana.
2. Charles V (1500–1558) led an expedition against Algiers in 1541, from which he was forced to turn back because of the sirocco.
3. Maj. Gen. Ulysses Simpson Grant (1822–1885), in his campaign to take Vicksburg and control the Mississippi, occupied Haynes Bluff (a few miles up the Yazoo) as a key point for cutting off supplies and reinforcements.
4. Confederate Gen. Braxton Bragg (1817–1876).
5. The seats on top of the private coaches called "drags" were used for picnicking, as shown in William Powell Frith's *Derby Day*.
6. Impatience with pro-Southern talk at the Somerset was a motive in the founding of the Union Club, dedicated to "unqualified loyalty to the Constitution and the Union."
7. The French army had already entered Puebla, Mexico, two months earlier, after a four-day bombardment.
8. Charles James Fox (1749–1806), parliamentary leader who supported the colonies during the American Revolution.

To Charles Francis Adams, Jr.

18 June. 1863.

Noble Captain:

Calm still prevails, praise be to God! But next week I expect a change. A victory would do us good here in preparation for the struggle which is coming, but then it has so happened that this season of the year has been twice remarkable for defeats and disasters. So that I rather expect them again. Mr Lawley has written from Richmond a poetical account of the Chancelorsville affair, from which I gather several results, which he perhaps does not intend to dwell upon.

1. Lee at that battle hadn't more than fifty thousand men.

2. He gave Jackson[1] almost all these, probably three fifths, to make his flank attack.

3. The question of supplies was of such enormous consequence to Lee that he was compelled to give up a whole division (Longstreet's) to hog-

catching at Suffolk, when he himself had not men enough to man the heights at Fredericsburg.

4. By Lawley's admission, his loss was ten thousand, and that is, as I take it, at least one fifth of his army, including his best general.

From all which I infer that Mr Hooker had a narrower escape from becoming the greatest man living, than even Gen. McLellan. If he had done anything on God's earth except retreat; if in fact he had done anything at all, instead of folding his hands after the first crossing the river, he must have been successful. There never were such chances and so many of them for a lucky man to play for, but the audacious gentleman wanted precisely what we all thought he had too much of; viz: audacity. And on the whole, much as I should be pleased with victory, it would have been dearly bought by inflicting us with Joseph for our model hero.

Meanwhile I hope that Lee's new movement will at least procure you relief from your old camp. Speculations are weak, but we do generally imagine here that Lee is compelled now by the same necessity that forced him to part with Longstreet's division at Fredericksburg. He must supply his army and is going to threaten Cincinnati and Ohio while he leaves you to break your teeth on the fortifications at Richmond. I guess that. But at any rate, all this looks jerky and spasmodic on his part, and my second guess is that friend Jefferson D. finds that the Confederacy has got into damnably shallow water.

The world here drags on after its usual style, a miserable, dangling, shuffling sort of existence that Englishmen call progress. Yesterday we had a pleasant dinner which the feminines will no doubt describe to you, at which Charles Dickens; John Forster, of "Goldsmith" and the "Statesmen"; Louis Blanc, and other distinguished individuals, were present; and a very jolly dinner it was.[2] Apropos, I have at last found an artist who can really paint. I have asked, or rather made interest to get him to take the Chief, but I doubt if he will consent, as he is a Parisian and is only here on a visit. If he does consent, however, I shall assess you and John for your shares of the cost, unless the Chief insists upon taking it upon himself. Frith too will have to introduce the Minister in his picture of the wedding and if his study is good, that might be worth buying.[3]

After two years delay, I have at last become a Club man, having been elected last week.[4] My particular backer seems to have been your old acquaintance Lord Frederick Cavendish and for the life of me, I can't conceive why. Lord Fwed seems to be a very excellent fellow, but I am no believer in unselfishness in this country. Nobody here has ever yet rushed into my arms and called me brother. Nor do I expect such a proceeding. Whether Frederick Cavendish, therefore, is impressed by the weight of debts of hospitality incurred in America, and is thus paying them off; or whether he feels his conscience touched by the vagaries of his brother Hartington; or whether he desires to show a general and delicate sympathy with our position; or whether Monckton Milnes has exerted an influence upon him; I don't know and can't guess. But the fact remains that he has been active in getting me in, and of course I am glad to have a Duke's son to back me. In other respects, it makes little difference to me whether I am in or out of a Club, ex- [*The rest of the letter is missing.*]

MS: MHi
    1. Thomas Jonathan ("Stonewall") Jackson (1824–1863).
    2. Charles Dickens (1812–1870); John Forster (1812–1876), journalist and historian, *Statesmen of the Commonwealth* (1836–1839), *Life and Times of Goldsmith* (1854), *Life of Dickens* (1872–1874); Louis Blanc (1811–1882), French historian and socialist leader in the Revolution of 1848.
    3. In the official painting of the Prince of Wales's wedding, William Powell Frith (1819–1909) carefully portrayed many of the public figures in attendance.
    4. St. James's Club.

To Charles Francis Adams, Jr.

25. June. 1863.

As I have regularly announced, my dear youth, the season of calm has again given way in this region, to the new period of squally weather. I have looked forward to this time so long that "impavidum ferient ruinae"; I am prepared in mind for everything.[1]

The prosecution, by means of which the two countries have been kept quiet so long, has come to an end. Not only has the decision gone against us, but the ruling of the venerable and obtuse Jamblichus who has slumbered upon the bench for many years and has not a conception of what has been vulgarly called the spirit of progressive civilization in jurisprudence; the ruling, as I was proceeding to observe, has triumphantly overset the little law that has ever been established on this matter and leaves us all at sea, with a cheerful view of an almighty rocky lea shore.[2] What will be the result of yesterday's work, I can't say, but I can guess. Our present position is this. There is no law in England which forbids hostile enterprises against friendly nations. The Government has no power to interfere with them. Any number of Alabama's may now be built, equipped, manned and despatched from British ports, openly for belligerent purposes, and provided they take their guns on board after they've left the harbor, and not while in dock, they are pursuing a legitimate errand.

Of course this is crowner's quest[3] law; crazy as the British Constitution; and would get England soon into war with every nation on the sea. The question now is whether the Government will mend it. Mr Cobden told me last night that he thought they would. I amuse myself by telling all the English people who speak to me on the subject, that considering that their maritime interests are the greatest in the world, they seem to me to have been peculiarly successful in creating a system of international law which will facilitate in the highest possible degree, their destruction, and reduce to a mathematical certainty their complete and rapid ruin. And I draw their attention to the unhappy, the lamentable, the much-to-be-deprecated, but inevitable result of yesterday's verdict, that you couldn't rake up on the American continent twelve citizens of the United States, who could be induced by any possible consideration, to condemn a vessel which they had the slightest hope of seeing turned into a pirate against British commerce. I think these arguments are far the most effective we can use. And I think the people here will soon be keenly alive to these results.

Meanwhile what is the effect of all this upon us! It brings stormy weather, certainly, but our position is in one respect rather strengthened by it. Public opinion abroad and here must gravitate strongly in our favor. This Government is placed in a position in which it will be very difficult for it to ignore its obligations. With the question between the English Government and its Courts, we have nothing to do. Our demands are on the Government alone and if the English laws are not adequate to enable her to maintain her international obligations, *tant pis pour elle.* She's bound to make new ones.

But there is another source of anxiety to us of late, though not so serious. A gentleman who is regarded by all parties here as rather more than three quarters mad, a Mr Roebuck, has undertaken the Confederate cause, and brought a motion in Parliament which is to be discussed in a few days.[4] Not finding his position here sufficiently strong, he has gone over to Paris and has seen the Emperor who, he says, told him that he was willing and earnest to press the question of mediation, if England would join him. So Mr Roebuck has come back, big with the fate of nations, and we shall see whatever there is to see.

The truth is, all depends on the progress of our armies. Evidently there is a crisis coming at home, and events here will follow, not lead, those at home. If we can take Vicksburg—so! If not, then—so!

We are dragging our wearied carcasses to balls and entertainments of every description. I had occasion to go last night to a reception over in Kensington, about three miles from us, and as it was a soft moonlight night, I walked part of the way. Accustomed as I am to London, and after seeing three seasons in it, I could not help feeling impressed by the extraordinary scene. I passed through Grosvenor Square and round Hyde Park to Apsley House, and the streets seemed alive with carriages in every direction. Gentlemen in white cravats were scuttling about, like myself; cabs were rushing furiously in all quarters; hundreds of carriages were waiting, or setting down or taking up their people before great houses, as I passed from street to square, and from square to street. There was a rush and roar all through the West End, that one can see only in London. Six weeks hence if I go through the same streets again at midnight, there will not be a soul there except a policeman. Acres and miles of houses will be as silent as a Virginia forest. And so they will remain until next April.

There is no doubt about it—every one, except children in their first season and a few peculiarly constituted people, feel all this riot to be a bore. Everyone looks intensely bored. Nobody enjoys it and nobody can enjoy it. These great routs are a sort of canonization of mediocrity. No one attempts to have a good time, and if they did, they would be voted vulgar. In the whole system I see nothing to admire, and sincerely believe that it hurts everyone who gets into it.

Lothrop Motley however, says it's the perfection of human society.[5] If his remark applied merely to a few dinners and a few visits to country houses with clever people, I shouldn't quarrel with it. But as for fashionable society here, I say clearly that in my opinion it is a vast social nuisance and evil.

You may believe then that in this respect I don't think that you are a loser on account of your residence in the midst of the refined society of Falmouth, and I am even more confident that I am no gainer by the liberty offered me of acting the part of one-thousandth guest at Miss Burdett Coutts' Ball,[6] or at Lady Derby's Assembly. I've no doubt that you or John could get much more amusement out of it than I can, but I'll be hanged if it would do you any good.

The question now rises, what are we to do this summer. To say the truth, I am not over anxious to travel. I would much more willingly take the chances of a raid with you, than the fuss and annoyance of a three weeks journey in the country with our family. What I would like is to take a house by the seaside from September to December, where we could have a mild climate, sea-air, and where I could keep a boat. But that dream, like most of my dreams, is likely to want realization. But if ever you and I escape from our manifold wandering, *multum terris jactati et alto*,[7] and return to pass a summer in Quincy, I trust that we shall know how to become sojourners on the mighty deep; a branch of pleasure more than usually innocent, healthy and beneficial, but too much neglected in our education. To catch a mackerel would be more than a delight to me. To broil and eat him myself would be the height of mental elevation. To shoot a duck would perhaps be more satisfaction than to murder a South Carolinian or an Englishman.

I believe we have nothing new to tell you of, except politically, as I have already commented on. It is intimated that the full bench will decide the points raised in Pollock's ruling (which I send you) and that a new law will be introduced should it be necessary. But as yet we wait the result of the exceptions taken.

On the whole, the one thing necessary is military success—and these are the anniversaries of McDowell's and M'Clellan's defeats![8] I hope nothing and expect nothing, but wait for motion. There will be a great emigration this year to us, and I hope we can get on without a conscription. But as yet it seems inevitable.

Ever Yrs

MS: MHi
1. *Impavidum ferient ruinae*, loosely translated by HA; Horace, *Odes*, III, iii.
2. Sir Jonathan Frederick Pollock (1783–1870), judge and chief baron of the exchequer, charged the jury that selling war vessels to a belligerent was lawful. The verdict went against the Union, and the Confederate raider *Alexandra* was released.

3. *Crowner's quest:* coroner's inquest.

4. John Arthur Roebuck (1801–1879), independent M.P. for Sheffield 1849–1868, 1874–1879.

5. The Boston historian John Lothrop Motley (1814–1877), minister to Austria 1861–1867, spent several sociable months in England 1859–1860 working on the sequel to his *Rise of the Dutch Republic* (1856).

6. Angela Georgina Burdett-Coutts (1814–1906), banking heiress and philanthropist, whose social activities made her, after the queen, the most publicized woman in British society.

7. *Multum . . . alto:* with much tossing from heaven to earth.

8. Brig. Gen. Irvin McDowell (1818–1885) was in command at First Bull Run, July 21, 1861; McClellan's Peninsular campaign against Richmond was effectively ended by the Seven Days' Battles, which began on June 25, 1862.

To Charles Francis Adams, Jr.

3 July. 1863.

We received this week the account of your fight at Aldie, which must have been a very gallant affair.[1] I hope Henry Higginson is not seriously injured. Of course we are very anxious, but think as little about it as we can. At any rate I hope the campaign will be over by the time this reaches America, and you will have come out all right, and be ready to hear of other things. So I won't even dilate upon the utter disgust, and contempt for myself that I feel in being here at such a time.

We too have had our excitements this week, as it was the time of the regular annual motion for recognition by the English copper-heads. There was a hot debate in Parliament, but the Southern spokesman succeeded in tripping himself up, and inflicting upon himself and his party a vigorous punishment that they will remember as long as they live. He has triumphantly seated himself as umpire over a dusky chaos in which Napoleon, the English Government, our own country and the rest of the world, are promiscuously calling each other to account for something somebody said or didn't say, or did, or didn't do. Mr Roebuck's decisions certainly do more embroil the fray. What is however of more consequence to us is that he has drawn public attention entirely from the question of intervention, and substituted a question of veracity between himself and the Emperor, a question of dignity between Parliament and the Emperor, a question of honor between the Ministry and the Emperor, and any quantity of other side questions, upon which public curiosity is greatly excited. But so far as our affair is concerned, Mr Roebuck has done us more good than all our friends.

We are likely therefore to have a few months more free from foreign interference, and so much room for our armies to work. The capture of Vicksburg would much simplify the question. I think we might then take our time about Richmond; but after all, we must do as the fates direct.

The rush and fuss of society is still going on and will last another week.

We have been here and there, knocking about at dinners, balls, breakfasts, from Rotten Row to Regent's Park, and entertaining at home in the intervals. We had a tremendous ball at a neighbor's on Tuesday and the dawn looked in on us while we were still at it. We watched the gathering light from the conservatories, and looked faded and pale. But the ball-room was the most magnificent I ever saw, and I really had a very tolerable time, for once, though only enough to remind me of the want of that happy absurdity which I feel in American society. Sleep in these times is scarce. One rides in the Park two hours in the morning, dines out in the evening, and goes to a ball; rises to a breakfast the next day; goes to a dance in the afternoon, and has a large dinner at home, from which he goes to another ball at half after eleven. Luckily this only comes by fits and starts, for two or three days together, and leaves the intervals tolerably clear. But if I chose to make any effort at all, I might have no end of engagements and running about.

I think unless the American news is highly disastrous, we shall again sink into placid rest here. The Alexandra is postponed till Autumn and will probably have to come before the House of Lords as final appeal next year. Parliament will adjourn by the end of this month, it is supposed. Everybody is to leave town on the 15th and we expect to get away as soon as Parliament does. Lord Palmerston is ill with gout, and, as I think, breaking up. I doubt if he'll have strength to stand another session. Everything promises unusual political quiet for the autumn, but the elements of confusion on the continent are so awkward that I rather expect trouble next year. If I could, I would cross the Atlantic and pass a month in camp, but these miserable domestic duties grind me down.

MS: MHi
1. CFA2 reported 32 casualties out of his company of 57: "My poor men were just slaughtered" (*Cycle*, II, 36).

To Charles Francis Adams, Jr.

10 July. 1863.

Our news brings us down to the 27th of June, and leaves us without the slightest conception of what is really going on. Of course we are extremely anxious, and though various and innumerable idiots about me are croaking hoarse notes and putting on that "I-told-you-so" expression of complacent misfortune which always irritates me beyond bearing, I find it needs an effort even on my part to sustain the appearance of placid confidence which we always make it a rule to bear, and which alone has any effect in shaming the sparrows. I wish people at home in respectable positions would at least hold their tongues, and not maunder over misfortunes before they come. There's our good uncle at Newport![1] By the great Panjandrum, I wish somebody would put on his heaviest cowhides, and kick him till his hair sprouted again. This the style of his letters to your mother. "Today we have accounts of a terrible cavalry battle at Aldie. I see the Massachusetts Cavalry were engaged and suffered severely. I trust that Charles has escaped. His name is not in the list of killed and wounded. But in the present miserable condition of things, I have no confidence in the good-fortune of our armies. I sincerely trust the fine fellow may have escaped. Should I hear anything about him, I will let you know in a post-script." And so on, miserably moaning about everything, when I suppose it's all his own liver, or ought to be, that's at fault. Our people would do well to recollect that ancient maxim of Frederick the Great or some one, that it's best to wash one's dirty linen at home. They have a way of putting it all out to wash, and the dirtier it is, the louder they call foreign nations to look at it.

The last fortnight has been a very rough one. You, no doubt, have supposed that it was the most worrying and anxious we have yet had. But it has not been so. On the contrary we have got through it wonderfully easily, and when I come to ask how this has happened, the only reason I can give why we should be less nervous now than at other times, is that we have had for several weeks past wonderfully fine, clear, hot weather and literally the sun has carried us through. It is astonishing what difference a blue sky and a brown one make in one's mind.

In these days I have very little work to do except in a domestic way, and of course I am becoming more and more uneasy and discontented. It hardly seems consistent with self-respect in a man to turn his back upon all his friends and all his ambitions, during such a crisis as this, only for the sake of conducting his mother and sister to the opera, and to ride in Rotten Row. I cannot tell you how much I am disgusted at this situation. If it were not for the Chief, I would not stay here a moment, but at least I hope my presence here is necessary for him, since I feel as though it were simple suicide for myself. My consolation is that we are approaching the end of our stay, and if things get worse we shall be recalled, while if they get better at home, the Chief will probably resign so soon as he can without appearing to shirk his duty.

The past week has been a very quiet one. In fact it has been so warm that quiet is a necessity almost. I have done very little besides riding in the Park near three hours a day with our juvenile Princess who has got the rage for the world, the flesh and the devil as bad as ever her sister Kuhn had it. Other hours I pass in sleepy struggle with philosophers and political economists, varied occasionally with a walk, which ends sometimes in eating straw-berries in Covent Garden, or reading French newspapers at the Club. We have occasionally a dinner, and sometimes we go to a dinner. I met your friend Sir Edward Cust at one, some time ago, who expressed great interest in you, and envied you your position, picket-duty being according to him, the liveliest and pleasantest part of a military life and a light mounted regiment being the pleasantest branch of the service.[2] He told me various stories of his adventures in Spain while engaged on similar duty, and I tried to learn from him what the best manual of cavalry tactics was that I could send you. On this subject he said he was not well posted. The German books were the best, and the Germans were better cavalry than the English. They took more care of their horses. If they were to march at five o'clock in the morning, they would up at three, groom their horses, and give them a feed, so that they would be all awake and fresh for the start. Whereas an English trooper would turn out and kick up his horse at the very last moment, and hurry him off without any sort of care. Sir Edward likes the German soldiers though they will steal, he says. They don't get drunk like the English, and they are careful and soldier-like.

Of your battle at Aldie we have three or four accounts, all of which are confused and each of which tells the story in a way that contradicts the other. I am anxious to know about it, but I suppose you will tell us so soon as you get time to write. We are so completely in the dark as to everything that is going on that I think it's best not to speculate.

I hope you get the newspapers I send you every week. They may serve to amuse your camp if they succeed in reaching it. While you are on the march I suppose nothing can reach you, but you have now been so long in the field that I imagine rest will soon become a necessity unless you are to serve as infantry. I trust that these newspapers will then find you out and give you a little variety from the disgusts of the campaign. I see that you have killed poor Frank Hampton and severely wounded W. H. F. Lee; is it my classmate?[3] Tell us about the Higginsons.

Ever

MS: MHi
  1. Sidney Brooks.
  2. Sir Edward Cust (1794–1878), a veteran of Wellington's Peninsular campaign, wrote military history admired by CFA2.
  3. Lt. Col. Frank Hampton (1829–1863) of Columbia, S.C., was killed at Brandy Station, Va., June 9. His wife, Sarah Baxter Hampton, was a friend of Louisa Adams Kuhn. W. H. F. Lee was HA's classmate "Rooney" Lee.

To Charles Francis Adams, Jr.

17 July. 1863.

We are in receipt of all your sanguinary letters, as well as of news down to the 4th, telling of Cyclopean battles, like the struggles of Saturn and Terra and Hyperion for their empire, lasting through sunrise after sunrise, in an agony such as heralds the extinction of systems.[1] It's a pity that we're civilized. What a grand thing Homer would have made of it; while in our day, men only conceive of a battle as of two lines of men shooting at each other till one or the other gives way. At this distance, though, even now it's very grand and inspiring. There's a magnificence about the pertinacity of the struggle, lasting so many days, and closing, so far as we know on the eve of our single national anniversary, with the whole nation bending over it, that makes even these English cubs silent. Dreadful I suppose it is, and God knows I feel anxious and miserable enough at times, but I doubt whether any of us will ever be able to live contented again in times of peace and laziness. Our generation has been stirred up from its lowest layers and there is that in its history which will stamp every member of it until we are all in our graves. We cannot be commonplace. The great burden that has fallen on us must inevitably stamp its character on us. I have hopes for us all, as we go on with the work.

And I, though I grumble at my position here and want to go home, feel at times that I don't know what I say, in making my complaints. I want to go into the army! to become a second lieutenant in an infantry regiment somewhere in the deserts of the South! I who for two years have lived a life of intellectual excitement, in the midst of the most concentrated society of the world, and who have become so accustomed to it that I should wither into nothing without it! Why, the thing's absurd! Even to retire to a provincial life in Boston would be an experiment that I dread to look forward to! But for me to go into the army is ridiculous!

The peculiar attraction of our position is one that is too subtle to put one's hand upon, and yet that we shall be sure to miss extremely when we leave it. The atmosphere is exciting. One does every day and without a second thought, what at another time would be the event of a year; perhaps of a life. For instance, the other day we were asked out to a little garden party by the old Duchess of Sutherland at Chiswick, one of the famous nobleman's places of England. Dukes and Duchesses, Lords and Ladies, Howards and Russells, Grosvenors and Gowers, Cavendish's, Stuarts, Douglases, Campbells, Montagus, half the best blood in England was there, and were cutting through country-dances and turning somersets and playing leap-frog in a way that knocked into a heap all my preconceived ideas of their manners. To be sure it was only a family party, with a few friends. You may be certain that I took no share in it. A stranger had better not assume to be one of the Gods.

Or again! I have just returned from breakfasting with Mr Evarts, and we had Cyrus Field,[2] Mr Blatchford and his wife, and Mr Cobden at table. The conversation was not remarkable to me; so little so that I should probably make only a bare note of it. But Cobden gave a vigorous and amusing account of Roebuck, whom he covered with epithets, and whose treatment of himself he described, going over some scenes in Parliament when Sir Robert Peel was alive. He sketched to us Gladstone's "uneasy conscience" which is always doubting and hesitating and trying to construct new theories. Cyrus Field rattled ahead about his telegraph and told again the story of his experiences. Mr Evarts talked about England and the policy of the country, for he goes home today, and indeed left us only to fire a parting shot into Gladstone. We discussed the war news, and Bancroft Davis came in, arguing that Lee's ammunition must be exhausted.[3] Cobden was very anxious about the battles, and varied his talk, by discussing a movement he proposes to make in Parliament before it rises. He rather regrets that they didn't force Roebuck's motion to a division, and wants to get in a few words before the close.

So we go on, you see, and how much of this sort of thing could one do at Boston! And the camp could only make up for it in times of action. Even the strangely hostile tone of society here has its peculiar advantage. It wakes us up and keeps our minds on a continual strain to meet and check the tendency. To appear confident in times of doubt, steady in times of disaster, cool and quiet at all times, and unshaken under any pressure, requires a continual wakefulness and actually has an effect to make a man that which he represents himself to be. Mr Evarts is grand in these trials, and from him and Mr Seward and the Chief, one learns to value properly the power of momentum.

All this to you seems, I suppose, curious talk, to one who has just got through with the disgusts of one campaign and is recruiting for another, as I suppose you are doing now. We are very anxious about you as you may suppose, but trust that your regiment is too much used up to fight much more without rest. Besides, in the confusion and excitement of the great struggle, we are glad to counteract anxiety by hope. And though our good friends down town do persist in regarding the news as favorable to the South, we on the whole are inclined to hope, and to feel a certain confidence that friend Lee has got his scoring. There is also the usual rumor of the fall of Vicksburg, as the *very* last telegram by the steamer, but we do not put much confidence in stories of that sort. Meade's despatch at eight o'clock on the evening of the 3d is all the news that I put any faith in. And with that I am patient.

As for us, the season is on its very last legs. Everyone is making a bolt for the country. It has been very hot for England, and is as dry as a Virginia road in summer. No rain for a month past. Politically we are trying to get everything in trim in order to have all clear during the next three months when England is without a Government and drifts. There is only one serious danger, and against that we are doing our best to guard. If you could win a few victories, it would be the best guaranty for good behavior, and I am free to say that England has remained quiet as long as we could reasonably expect, knowing her opinions, without solid guaranties of ultimate success on our part.

The week has been so busy, and every evening occupied with society that I have had little time to give to myself. Although not strictly a society man, and free to confess that I don't wish to be fashionable, I go about a good deal and am not so often now as formerly alone in a room. In fact we rather affect to have our own circle of friends, and to be socially as good as English people in society. They themselves seem to have adopted us, and of course it's more convenient to go into society as indigenous than as foreign. Mary has been a success as girls go here. She is being spoiled hopelessly, but I wash my hands of that, as I think she's old enough now to judge for herself and to carry her own washing-basket. I think myself that I see the old Johnson blood cropping out, and faint traces of Mrs John reappearing here and there, that might have been more distinct and may become so yet.[4]

Your shirt goes by this mail. I have got the best I could find for you. Your mamma selected them. This week I send you still another review and next week I shall send you your friend W. H. Russell's Gazette if he has as blackguard a notice of us in it as he usually does.[5]

Ever Yrs

MS: MHi
1. Of 150,000 men at Gettysburg, July 1-3, where Gen. George Meade defeated Lee, 54,000 were casualties. CFA2's company was there but not in action.
2. Cyrus West Field (1819-1892) proved the feasibility of an Atlantic cable with his short-lived success of 1858; he was in England raising new capital for his company among such business friends as Gladstone, Bright, and the Duke of Argyll.
3. John Chandler Bancroft Davis (1822-1907) of Worcester, Mass., legation secretary in London 1849-1852, London *Times* U.S. correspondent 1854-1861.
4. Louisa Catherine Johnson (1775-1852), JQA's wife, was born in London, daughter of an American merchant from Maryland and an English mother. After wartime residence in France 1778-1783, she seemed more French than English and, in HA's recollection of her charm and elegance, decidedly not a New England Puritan. Abigail Smith Adams (1744-1818), JA's wife, daughter of the minister of the First Church of Weymouth, Mass., and related on her mother's side to leading families of the Puritan theocracy; a great writer of letters, manager of JA's business and farm during his years of public service, she gave the impression of exercising authority over her family (see, for example, *Education*, p. 17).
5. On returning to England, William H. Russell had resumed the editing of the weekly *Army and Navy Gazette,* founded in 1860.

To Charles Francis Adams, Jr.

23 July. 1863.

I positively tremble to think of receiving any more news from America since the batch that we received last Sunday. Why can't we sink the steamers till some more good news comes? It is like an easterly storm after a glorious June day, this returning to the gloomy chronicle of varying successes and disasters, after exulting in the grand excitement of such triumphs as you sent us on the 4th. For once, there was *no* drawback, unless I except anxiety about you. I wanted to hug the army of the Potomac. I wanted to get the whole of the army of Vicksburg drunk at my own expense.[1] I wanted to fight some small man and lick him. Had I had a single friend in London capable of rising to the dignity of the occasion, I don't know what mightn't have happened. But mediocrity prevailed and I passed the day in base repose.

It was on Sunday morning as I came down to breakfast that I saw a telegram from the Department announcing the fall of Vicksburg. Now, to appreciate the value of this, you must know that the one thing upon which the London press and the English people have been so positive as not to tolerate contradiction, was the impossibility of capturing Vicksburg. Nothing could induce them to believe that Grant's army was not in extreme danger of having itself to capitulate. The Times of Saturday, down to the last moment, declared that the siege of Vicksburg grew more and more hopeless every day. Even now, it refuses, after receiving all the details, to admit the fact, and only says that Northern advices report it, but it is not yet confirmed. Nothing could exceed the energy with which everybody in England has reprobated the wicked waste of life that must be caused by the siege of this place during the sickly season, and ridiculed the idea of its capture. And now, the announcement was just as though a bucket of iced-water were thrown into their faces. They couldn't and wouldn't believe it. All their settled opinions were overthrown, and they were left dangling in the air. You never heard such a cackling as was kept up here on Sunday and Monday, and you can't imagine how spiteful and vicious they all were. Sunday evening I was asked round to Monckton Milnes's to meet a few people. Milnes himself is one of the warmest Americans in the world, and received me with a hug before the astonished company, crowing like a fighting cock. But the rest of the company were very cold. W. H. Russell was there, and I had a good deal of talk with him. He at least did not attempt to disguise the gravity of the occasion, nor to turn Lee's defeat into a victory. I went with Mr Milnes to the Cosmopolitan Club afterwards, where the people all looked at me as though I were objectionable. Of course I avoided the subject in conversation, but I saw very clearly how unpleasant the news was which I brought. So it has been everywhere. This is a sort of thing that can be neither denied, palliated, nor evaded; the disasters of the rebels are unredeemed by even any hope of success. Accordingly the emergency has produced here a mere access of spite; preparatory (if we suffer no reverse) to a revolution in tone.

It is now conceded at once that all idea of intervention is at an end. The war is to continue indefinitely, so far as Europe is concerned, and the only remaining chance of collision is in the case of the iron-clads. We are looking after them with considerable energy, and I think we shall settle them.

It is utterly impossible to describe to you the delight that we all felt here and that has not diminished even now. I can imagine the temporary insanity that must have prevailed over the North on the night of the 7th. Here our demonstrations were quiet, but ye Gods! how we felt! Whether to laugh or to cry, one hardly knew. Some men preferred the one, some the other. The Chief was the picture of placid delight. As for me, as my effort has always been here to suppress all expression of feeling, I preserved sobriety in public, but for four days I've been internally singing Hosannahs and running riot in exultation. The future being doubtful, we are all the more determined to drink this one cup of success out. Our friends at home, Dana, John, and so on, are always so devilish afraid that we may see things in too rosy colors. They think it necessary to be correspondingly sombre in their advices. This time, luckily, we had no one to be so cruel as to knock us down from behind, when we were having all we could do to fight our

English upas influences in front.[2] We sat on the top of the ladder and didn't care a copper who passed underneath. Your old friend Judge Goodrich was here on Monday, and you never saw a man in such a state.[3] Even for him it was wonderful. He lunched with us and kept us in a perfect riot all the time, telling stories without limit and laughing till he almost screamed.

I am sorry to say however that all this is not likely to make our position here any pleasanter socially. All our experience has shown that as our success was great, so rose equally the spirit of hatred on this side. Never before since the Trent affair has it shown itself so universal and spiteful as now. I am myself more surprised at it than I have any right to be, and philosopher though I aspire to be, I do feel strongly impressed with a desire to see the time come when our success will compel silence and our prosperity will complete the revolution. As for war, it would be folly in us to go to war with this country. We have the means of destroying her without hurting ourselves.

In other respects the week has been a very quiet one. The season is over. The streets are full of Pickford's vans carting furniture from the houses, and Belgravia and May Fair are the scene of dirt and littered straw, as you know them from the accounts of Pendennis.[4] One night we went to the opera, but otherwise we have enjoyed peace, and I have been engaged in looking up routes and sights in the guide book of Scotland. Thither, if nothing prevents and no bad news or rebel's plot interferes, we shall wend our way on the first of August. The rest of the family will probably make a visit or two, and I propose to make use of the opportunity to go on with Brooks and visit the Isle of Skye and the Hebrides, if we can. This is in imitation of Dr Johnson, and I've no doubt, if we had good weather, it would be very jolly.[5] But as for visiting people, the truth is I feel such a dislike for the whole nation, and so keen a sensitiveness to the least suspicion of being thought to pay court to any of them, and so abject a dread of ever giving anyone the chance to put a slight upon me, that I avoid them and neither wish them to be my friends nor wish to be theirs. I haven't the strength of character to retain resentments long, and some day in America I may astonish myself by defending these people for whom I entertain at present only a profound and lively contempt. But at present I am glad that my acquaintances are so few and I do not intend to increase the number.

You will no doubt be curious to know, if, as I say, I have no acquaintances, how the devil I pass my time. Certainly I do pass it, however, and never have an unoccupied moment. My candles are seldom out before two o'clock in the morning, and my table is piled with half-read books and unfinished writing. For weeks together I only leave the house to mount my horse and after my ride, come back as I went. If it were not for your position and my own uneasy conscience, I should be as happy as a Virginia oyster, and as it is, I believe I never was so well off physically, morally and intellectually as this last year.

I send you another shirt, and a copy of the Index, the southern organ, which I thought you would find more interesting this week than any other newspaper I can send. It seems to me to look to a cessation of *organised* armed resistance and an ultimate resort to the Polish fashion.[6] I think we shall not stand much in their way there, if they like to live in a den of thieves.

Ever

MS: MHi
1. Vicksburg, with its 30,000 defenders, surrendered to Grant on July 4.
2. *Upas:* a poisonous tree sap used on arrow tips.
3. Aaron Goodrich (1807–1887) of Minnesota, former federal judge, secretary of legation at Brussels 1861–1869. CFA2 met him while campaigning with Seward in Minnesota in 1860.
4. HA adds his own details to Thackeray's "The season was now come to a conclusion"; *Pendennis* (1850), ch. 46.
5. Samuel Johnson (1709–1784) made a journey recorded in James Boswell's *Journal of a Tour to the Hebrides* (1786).
6. That is, guerrilla warfare, as in the Polish uprising.

To Charles Francis Adams, Jr.

London. 30 July. 1863.

We've received your note of the 12th to John, dated at St James College.[1] I trust you will now have time to write up your journal. Allow me to add that you needn't be so damned careful not to be elated. On the contrary it would be extremely gratifying and extremely proper that the army of the Potomac *should* be elated. It's done a great thing and done it well, and it's just as well for it to say so, without an if or a but. Remember that the world nine times out of ten estimates people in proportion as they respect themselves. When a New Hampshire regiment arrived at Vicksburg to reinforce Grant's army, their steamer was hailed by a sucker[2] on shore, with; "Now move on; you needn't stop here; we propose to do this little job "ourselves, and don't want no Yanks to help us." I admire the sentiment, and I hope to see the day when the army of the Potomac besieging Richmond will be able to return the compliment to the regiments of Grant and Rosecranz.

As for our letters, there must be a large bag of them for you at Washington. You had better charter an army wagon and send it express. The newspapers alone that I've sent you, would keep you in reading for a month. But as it's not probable that I shall write again for several weeks, you'll have time to gorge yourself with stale epistles, and digest or reject them.

For I take it for granted that you will now rest, as Lee seems to have cut away so nimbly. Our next move ought in my humble judgment to be on one of the Carolinas, and before that the army ought to be reinforced. The enemy will hardly have strength to send another army north, and we ought to be wise enough to have learned to turn Richmond. Nevertheless, you know best, and if we are still to knock our heads against fortifications, so be it. We never yet have gained a success so, however.

On the 1st August we set out for Scotland. If I were alone, I should expect to have a high time, or with another fellow. But with such a caravan I fear that our progress will be a grave affair. We shall have to separate the party at times. I have a letter to Lochiel, the descendent of him who bewore of the day,[3] which I would gladly deliver did I succeed in getting an opportunity. In good time I shall write to you my adventures, and I hope they will amuse you.

This week I have passed mostly at Walton with the children. It was as good as cool molasses-and-water to get back again among the greenth. I lay in a hammock under the trees, and smoked and read and dozed beside the silvery Thames, and was content. Parliament has broken up; London is deserted; my friend Monckton Milnes has got a peerage and is now Lord Houghton; the Times has acknowledged the capture of Vicksburg; and generally, the world keeps moving. I hear from home various stories about the conscription, as for instance that Dick Parker and his two servants were drawn and his house taken for a fort on the same day. I rather expect to be drawn at Quincy but as yet have heard nothing of it, and I suppose I should quick enough, if it happened. If I only could, Oh! wouldn't I like to get appointed on somebody's staff and take a turn at it! That however is, I fear, not in store for me, though if Charleston were to fall, I think I should begin seriously to urge our leaving this place before winter for good. I have no wish to pass another winter here.

I send you one of Russell's sheets, he being less abusive than usual. As you don't get our letters, writing seems superfluous, but still, it may reach you some day. Next week and the next after, I sha'n't be able to write.

Ever

Is Jim Hig safe or not? Do tell about our friends and how it is that you are ever in command of the regiment.

MS: MHi

1. A boys' preparatory school at St. James, Md., closed during the Civil War.
2. One of Grant's Illinois soldiers. The state nickname, which dates from the 1830s, refers to a Mississippi River fish.
3. Donald Cameron of Lochiel (1835–1905), chief of the Cameron clan, was a British diplomat. HA alludes to the heroic ancestor in Thomas Campbell's poem, "Lochiel's Warning" (1802), which opens: "Lochiel, Lochiel! beware of the day."

To Charles Milnes Gaskell

Invergarry, Fort Augustus.[1] N.B.
Tuesday. 18 Aug. [1863]

My dear Gaskell[2]

I had supposed you were in Persia or Astrachan by this time, for your ancestral majestie whom I cross-questioned in Stratton Place (if that's right) was profoundly ignorant as to your whereabouts. As I left with a sigh of happiness all the delights of Rotten Row and Portland Place, a fortnight ago, I failed to get your letter till today. But having at last turned up in a Christian spot again, I take a spare moment to give you what little light I can. Consider that I have been, according to the pious writer, where I could read my title clear to mansions in the Skye, but as yet am far from bidding farewell to any tear or wiping my weeping eye[3] on that account. *Bref,* I've just passed five days on the isle of Skye, of which the rain descended and the floods came during three, with a vehemence that would have done justice to the tropics. I have fed on nothing but oat-meal porridge and hard-boiled eggs, and short allowance too, and my opinion of Skye, its inhabitants, climate, and "umliegende Ortschaften" (to use a phrase which I know you can't understand, for it's bad German) is one which I will have a regard for your feelings as an Englishman and a Britisher and not expatiate upon.

I have a letter from William which you may peruse, I suppose, taking care to forget the somewhat too characteristic allusions to his surroundings. I know nothing more of him than that. It is possible that he may try a little soldiering, as many do, but probably on some officer's staff, if anywhere.

Apropos to Octave Feuillet! You say you have read him through. Have you done so with his last work, Sybille?[4] I have read it since starting. As one can't quite think that everything depends on belief in the efficacy of prayer, I am sorry to say that Octave looks very like a dependent of the Faubourg, writing what he knows to be decayed matter (*vulgo,* rot.) for an earthly reward at its hands.

Very truly   H. B. Adams.

C. M. Gaskell Esq.

MS: MHi
    1. At the southern end of Loch Ness in Inverness-shire.
    2. Charles George Milnes Gaskell (1842–1919) and HA met in London, April 1863, but their lifelong friendship dates from HA's May visit to Cambridge, where Gaskell and HA's cousin William Everett were fellow students of classics about to take their degrees. He was the son of James Milnes Gaskell, Liberal M.P. for Wenlock, and Mary Williams-Wynn Gaskell. They were a Yorkshire family, whose houses were Thornes (near Wakefield) and Wenlock Abbey in Shropshire.
    3. HA's punning version of "When I can read my title clear," a hymn by Isaac Watts.
    4. Octave Feuillet (1821–1890), *Histoire de Sibylle* (1862).

To Charles Francis Adams, Jr.

Lowood Hotel. Windermere
Thursday. 3 Sept. 1863.

My dear Captain:

I have been indulging in a vacation, and hence my failure this month past to continue my regular series of letters to you. At this moment I am not likely to delight you much, for I am in the very situation which of all others is to me the most uncomfortable and harrassing. I am left in charge of your mother, your sister, your youngest brother, a lady's maid and a drunken foot-man; it rains like the foul fiend; our accommodations are pinched and unsatisfactory; our excursions for the day, put an end to; and I have the stern necessity of tomorrow resuming the dreary labor of posting, catching railway trains, making connections, and hunting hotels, before my eyes, until at last I can dump the whole caravan in London the day after tomorrow. Now all this is not new to me. I have done it much and often. But I don't deny that I like of all things to be independent, and of all things detest women's fuss and tongues. Trouble and labor I am willing to take, but only for objects worth such a price, and all your regiment of cavalry isn't half the bother to you that my squadron of female irregulars is to me. My dear boy! You who have been so long in camps as to forget or be gentle in your thoughts towards the soft spots in Courts! Listen to a person of more experience than yourself! Avoid this sort of thing! So help me Elisha, the Lord do so unto me, yea and more also, if I do not practice even according unto the precepts which I teach! Premising then, and as it were, indicating for an instant the condition in which I find myself, I will now commence a letter which shall be long in proportion to those which I have omitted.

Of our early wanderings in August, I will say nothing, since I suppose they have been described to you in the epistles of other members of our family. I joined them at York, having waited two days in London, for the mail. We went to Edinbro, Stirling, Loch Katrine, Loch Lomond, Glasgow, and so up the west coast to the Caledonian Canal. Here the party separated, our elders going to make some visits, and I myself with our youthful brother turning off to seek unbeaten tracks.

There was little in our journey that was marvellous, but it was not entirely unattractive, and perhaps an account of it may sound well in camp, where all variety is said to have its value. So you shall have my diary.

At six o'clock one showery Wednesday morning, I left my couch to see that the other branch of the party were safely shipped on a crazy old steam-bum that meanders up the Caledonian Canal. When I had seen them fairly under way, and trying to escape the shower that was coming down Ben Nevis, I returned from the lock to the hotel, feeling for the first time in many months my own master. Tudieu! what happiness! I breathed the mountain air as though I were monarch of the wilderness and chief of innumerable clans. Two hours I passed in various acts of the toilet, such as carefully washing my feet and bathing them in whiskey, as they were somewhat sore after a ten miles walk the day before. Then I waked the slumbering Brooks, and ordering breakfast and a dog-cart, indulged in most grateful broiled trout with a curious article much known as oatmeal porridge, while a tremendous rain-shower rendered our prospects cheerful. Rain in Scotland is however a matter of course. It stopped for us to make our start, and off we went, my proud white hat exciting the admiration of such scarce youths as were on the road. From Bannavie where we slept, our road lay for several miles along the head of Loch Eil. Then it rose among the mountains, wild and desolate scenery, where hardly even a miserable cabin is to be seen for miles together. At intervals it rained, and at times we caught a little sunshine, which had a wonderful effect in lighting up a scene so sad and dark without it that even our spirits could only counteract the impression by attempts to learn Gaelic phrases from our driver; a divertisement which kept us roaring for miles. At length, after some twelve miles of this work, we suddenly came upon a marshy plain at the head of a long loch, where a solitary stone column rose in a way that impressed me curiously with the dreary nature of the place. Of all things in the world a monument of that size seemed to be the thing one least expected there. I asked the driver what it was, and he told me it commemorated the spot where Prince Charles the Pretender was killed. I could not conceive what the blockhead meant, being aware that the Pretender had not gratified his enemies by getting himself put an end to. But as the dog-cart came to a halt for an hour to rest, a short distance further on, Brooks and I walked back, and after much wading and jumping and wetting, we reached the spot and found a long inscription in English, Latin and Gaelic, stating that it was here Prince Charlie raised his standard in 1745.[1] A more desolate, repelling spot I have seldom seen, and I appreciated for the first time the courage of that young fellow who could drag himself from Paris and sunlight, in order to lead a desperate venture of filthy barbarians and to plant his standard on a spot like this.

In long reaches of Scotch mist, diversified by gleams of gray sunshine, we climbed mountain after mountain, all barren as your saddle except for heath and water-falls, and all stamped with the same character of stern and melancholy savageness. The roads however are excellent and as there is never much snow or great cold, they keep in good order. We changed our horse some ten miles further on and then began descending towards the sea. As our miserable horse, urged on by steady and vigorous chastisement slowly worried forwards, the weather began to improve, and to my surprise, the country began to take on a civilised aspect. When at last we reached the sea-shore, we found a lovely landscape. Wide woods, and green pastures, cattle and even deer, a mild air and a pleasant sun, beaming upon us as though there never had been a Scotch mist (a phrase which means a damned heavy rain). This is the peninsula of Arisaig; a sort of Wood's Hole,[2] only much larger. A little hamlet lies on a pretty harbor, silent and deserted in the afternoon sun, and at an inn, the only one, we descended and dismissed our vehicle. Two cares oppressed my mind. The first was to order some dinner, for it was five o'clock. The second, to procure a boat to take us over to Skye. The first was soon eased. We had our dinner, if a dish of burnt steaks and potatoes deserves that honored title. The second was also relieved, but as it takes every Highlander two hours to do what should occupy fifteen minutes, and as our men had to be summoned from the plough and the anvil, it was seven o'clock before we were on board. Three men made our crew, and a boat like a man-of-war, and in this form, in consideration of the sum of five dollars, we were to be conveyed to the nearest public-house in Skye, a distance of ten or twelve miles.

The evening was calm, hardly a breath of air helping us, but it was fine. A gentle roll swelled against our quarter, and yielding to its influence, I lay down on the seat across the boat, and watched our course. This same gentle influence was felt also by Brooks who not only lay down, but confided his sorrows and his dinner to the ocean, with courageous heart and mirthful jest, the more praiseworthy as the trial lasted for hours. Luckily for me I felt no such discomfort, and enjoyed the passage greatly. The long, mountainous coast of Scotland, lighted by the sunset and twilight, looked very grand in the distance, and on our left were the mountains of Skye covered with heavy folds of mist. For three hours or more we went on in this manner, the men relieving each other at the oars, for they had to pull the whole way. I enjoyed immensely this evening sail on the Hebridean seas. Civil wars, disgust and egoism, social fuss and worry, responsibility and anxiety, were as far at last as the moon. They left me free on the Sound of Sleat. I felt as peaceful and as quiet as a giant, and saw the evening shades darken into night, and phosphoric waves of light swell in the air and under the boat, with a joyful sense of caring not a ha'penny when I had my breakfast.

Arrive we did at last, though Brooks thought we never should, but this part was rather embarrassing. The little hamlet near Armidale Castle boasts a landing place only at high tide, whereas the tide was now low. We had therefore to land on the rocks and paddle in the dark over the bogs to firm land. As we stepped along, our shoes, crushing the wet sea-weed, called out at every movement bright, flashing phosphoric flames, so that we seemed to be walking on liquid fire. Pretty thoroughly wet, we did at last reach a road and made our way to a wayside inn, from which much merriment and singing proceeded. The maid who appeared at our call, was innocent of the tongue of Shakespeare and Milton. She owned allegiance only to her native Gaelic. A man however was at length produced, who seemed mortified to have no better to offer us, but the nearest town was fifteen miles and more, and there were no vehicles. If there had been, we shouldn't have used them. There we were and there we meant to sleep, so we took possession of two rooms, which were new and therefore reasonably clean. Our sheets were clean but ragged, and the other bed-clothes! Well, they were rough! After nearly being assaulted by one of the band of minstrels, who were salmon fishers, drinking and howling a monotonous song, which they accompanied by stamping their feet, I got some supper, tea, toast, boiled eggs &c, and Brooks and I having sleepily supped, and waited long for the salmon-fishers' drunken dirge to cease, turned in towards midnight and so slept in peace.

The sun rose bright on our first morning in the Hebrides. I turned out at about nine o'clock, shuddered at the sight of my resting-place, and dressed with cheerfulness and a light heart. Poor Brooks however came into my room, looking very fishy, and complained of a sick head-ache. We had breakfast, and I swallowed much porridge, a dish that is in itself neither savory nor rich, but which is far superior to tough ham drowned in bowls of oil, or even to hard-boiled eggs. I then desired a conveyance to the next town, seventeen miles, but to my alarm (on Brooks's account) learned that no conveyance was to be had except one, which I proceeded to examine and which proved to be a heavy farm cart, which might have been drawn by oxen but which in fact was conducted by a horse. Que faire! Seventeen miles in an oxcart with a sick head-ache! Still, our baggage must go and my mind resigned itself. The sluggish cart was drawn before the door, and my pipe being lighted, I sounded boot and saddle. Before we departed however, the Gaelic damsel persuaded me through an interpreter to buy a pair of woollen socks knit by her fair hands, which I may send to you, and in case their proportions be too elephantine, you can make them over to some deserving foot.

I can't tell you how I enjoyed this morning. England boasts of few such days in her year. For ten miles I walked along the shore of the Sound, and a more splendid scene I couldn't put my finger on. The west coast of Scotland is rugged and wild, with deep scorings or indentations that form salt water lochs. Towards this shore I was looking, across a sound some five miles broad, which gradually was lost in the land towards the north. Mountains were all around, but they were so softened by the sun that again and again, I fancied myself in Italy. This corner of Skye is quite civilized too. There are trees, hedges and green pastures towards the sea-shore, and it was only as I advanced and at length turned away from the coast, that we reached a desolate region where heather and peat-bogs are the sole articles of production. I shall always remember my morning between Armidale and Broadford as a day comme il y en a peu.

Poor Brooks was far from enjoying it. Between the effort of walking and the jolting of the cart, he was put to it to make a choice, but after trying each, he subsided in moody silence into the cart. I was anxious about him, but could only press on, and one by one the slow milestones crept by. Resting myself at the tenth, having walked about two hours and three quarters, I too took a turn in the cart, and so at last we reached our aim, both coming in on foot. Here we again struck the sea, but this time on the northern coast of the island, and opposite to us was another part of the Scotch shore, while the ocean lay nearly open towards the north-west. As yet we had crossed no mountains, the land being only rolling and peaty.

At Broadford I wished to stay, but Brooks said no! So I ordered a dog-cart and dinner. The dinner even to my appetite, was barely touchable. Brooks cursed it and lay on a sofa. We were glad to be off again at four, leaving the small village and dirty inn behind.

If the morning's walk from Armidale was lovely and made me think of Italy, the afternoon's drive to Sligachan was enormous and belonged to no country on God's earth except Skye and Skye alone. Between smooth conical mountains, whose sides were tinged with a doubtful green where the gaunt skeleton did not break out, and the blue sea, our road drove on, round silent lochs and through a howling wilderness strewn with the debris of ancient glaciers, and offering not one blade of grass or grain, except on a narrow strip along the sea-shore. The mountains of Skye are peculiar, but more of that hereafter. Not only was our ride delightful on account of the beauty of the scenery, the exquisite evening and all that, but Brooks showed signs of returning peckishness, and from the rapid fire of questions which he, à la Charles Kuhn, began to open on the driver, I knew he felt better. Several miles of the distance we walked, and when we rounded the last headland and had but two miles more, I sent them ahead, and in solitude and deadly silence walked up the long loch at the head of which stands the solitary inn of Glen Sligachan, where I arrived just as the purple mountain tops were changing to a dark, cold, and solemn gray. It reminded me of my voyage with Ben Crowninshield up the Furca Pass in Switzerland. Solitude of utter barrenness on every side.

A supper of broiled salmon made up for our dinner, and Brooks had at last found his appetite. The inn was not a paradise, being, like all highland inns, of an ugly, mouldy and throat-cutting appearance. But you will have no great sympathy for me on this reckoning.

The next morning was cloudy, and I felt that a storm was brewing. As I have no fancy for early rising, and am quite ready to leave to you the benefits of that habit, I ordered breakfast at our usual hour of nine o'clock and ponies for ten. As Brooks and I were seating ourselves at breakfast, contemplating the broil with pleasure, in comes a new arrival, seats himself at the table and coolly asks me to help him to some of the salmon; *my* salmon by the Lord, and he poached it as coolly as though he were proprietor of fish in general. This man is a sucker thought I to myself, and we will avoid him. Consequently when we mounted our ponies and I saw that the person had also ordered a pony and joined himself to us and our guide, I was very short and sharp, and ignored him entirely, treating with silence his mild hints as to the route. So our caravan of three ponies and a guide, moved slowly off, up Glen Sligachan.

We were to see the one great sight in the island. About mid-way on the southern coast, a cluster of mountains called the Cuchullin or Coolin Hills, rises abruptly, and encloses a small lake called Loch Coruiskin. To reach it, one has to cross the island by a very rough bridle-path, and at last to climb a tough hill, from the top of which one looks down upon the lake and the sea. Glen Sligachan is itself a specimen of desolation. Along the whole seven miles there is no human habitation, no cultivation, not a tree or a shrub, and at best only a few Highland cattle and sheep try to support life on the heather and tufts of grass that partly cover the base of bleak mountain ridges. The path winds over the chaotic mounds of earth and loose rocks, that are called moraines, and that are the invariable indication of former glaciers. I walked much of the way, and climbed on foot the steep hill at its end. Beyond this there was no path at all. Our guide told us that we must walk down to the lake, and so we did, if scrambling down a precipitous mountain and over bogs can be called walking. It was only a mile to the shore of the lake, but it took us a long time and was precious tough work.

Quietly and between ourselves, I am no admirer of the Scotch mountain scenery. It is too uniform in its repulsive bareness. I like another sort of thing. Grand mountain peaks covered with glittering snow, whose base descends towards Italian plains and is green with olive trees and vineyards; that is my ideal of the sublime and beautiful. Yet certain it is that the scenery of Loch Coruiskin made an impression on me that few things can, and like all great master-pieces, the more I think of it, the more extraordinary it seems to be. Evidently it was formerly the bed of an enormous glacier. A vast volume of ice, creeping down year after year, to the sea, carried with it every trace of soil, and scored and polished the rocks over which it passed. When the glacier yielded to some unexplained change of temperature, it left behind it nothing but this lake among the rocks close to the sea, and in a semicircle around it, a series of sharp mountain peaks, jagged and excoriated, whose summits seem to have raised a barrier against the outside world. I might give you a good-sized volume of epithets without conveying the least idea of the really awful isolation and silence of this spot. There is as yet nothing human within miles of it, nor any trace of man's action. Even in Switzerland I recollect nothing like it, nor can there ever be, unless the ocean is brought to the foot of the Alps. Should you ever come to England, by all means go and see Coruiskin. I would like to have a chance to go with you, and even to pitch my tent there and pass a few days in examining this melancholy district.

For about an hour we lay on a point of rising ground above the lake, and looked about us. Then, feeling rather bothered by the idea of our return climb, we turned back, and dug our way with a tremendous amount of labor and some doubts as to our road, back to our ponies. It was just as well that we did not delay, for the rain began before we reached our inn at five o'clock, and a drenching storm set in that evening with tremendous force.

My original idea had been to go on to Portree and the extremity of the island, but as I found there was little or nothing to see there, and as the weather was so unpromising, I concluded to turn back and make my way to a civilised land. So the next morning we set out on our return. The salmon poacher asked to join us in a carriage, and we departed in an open wagon. Before we had gone five miles, the rain descended and the flood came.[3] Tremendous gusts of wind from the mountains drove down regular waves of water on us, and coats and umbrellas were wet through like sieves. The fifteen miles were long as the road to Heaven, and the scenery was, ah! quantum mutatus ab illo![4] When we arrived at Broadford I determined to go no further, and incontinently ordered a lunch of broiled herrings, which were indeed savory.

The storm which was furious, showed no signs of slackening that evening, and the next day, which was Sunday, it continued with the same violence. As the passage to the main-land was an unknown road to me, and as there are no inns near the ferry, I did not venture to leave my quarters. It was not gay. Brooks tried going to church, but having entered in the middle of service at about one o'clock, and listened some time to the Gaelic parson, he asked his neighbor how long it would last, and on hearing that it would be over at five, he precipitately fled. I made no such venture. The only satisfactory thing I did was to have a long talk with a man who had some reason to be acquainted with the island, as to the people. You must know that I have been greatly disgusted with the appearance of the brave highlanders. They strike me as stupid, dirty, ignorant and barbarous. Their mode of life is not different from that of African negroes. Their huts are floorless except for earth; they live all together in them like pigs; there are no chimneys; hardly a window; no conveniences of life of any sort. Dirty, ragged, starved and imbruted, they struggle to cultivate patches of rocky ground where nothing can mature, and in wretched superstition and preju- dice they are as deep sunk as their ancestors ever were. One of the best things in Scott's novel of the Pirate, which indeed apart from its absurd story, I rate higher than most men do, is a character of the people of Zet- land put into the mouth of Triptolemus Yellowley.[5] It would do tolerably well for the Hebrides as well. The character of such out-of-the-way people must always be narrow and ungenerous. Everything tends to crystallize and remain stationary. They are envious, jealous and prejudiced. Any pop- ulation is too much for such barren regions, and the numbers of the people always tend to undue increase, for they pup like rabbits. Hence a continual struggle for existence, and eternal misery and degradation.

Monday morning, it did not rain. We had some difficulty in getting away, and had to share a dog-cart with a lunatic-inspector as far as Kyle Rhea ferry. As the lunatic was slow we walked ahead, intending to be caught about five miles out. When we had gone the five miles, it began to rain again and as no lunatic made his appearance we trudged on, the whole eleven miles, to the wretched inn at the ferry. Here we waited and eat oat- meal porridge, Brooks amusing himself by feeding a small dog with it, till as he expressed it, he "burst"; that is, became very ill. At last the lunatic appeared and we got across the strait which is here hardly a mile wide, to Glenelg, where after much highland delay we had to take a carriage and went on, cold and wet, to Shiel Inn, where we got a dog-cart and pressed forward ten miles more to Cluny Inn. Imagination had painted here a lux- urious supper and snowy beds. Reality showid squalidity and starvation. Unable to stomach it, we took another dog-cart and drove on another ten miles across the mountains to Tomdown Inn. From its neat appearance we imagined wealth and plenty, as we came to it at ten o'clock at night, but our supper consisted of broiled ham and two eggs, all they had, which we eat ferociously.

The next day our family picked our baggage up as they passed from Mr Ellice's to Invergarry, and Brooks and I walked the eleven miles, and went to stay several days with Mr Peabody and Mr Lampson where I again re- sumed the miserable labor of taking charge of the party as the Chief had to return to London.[6]

I will not trouble you with any account of our stay at Invergarry, nor with my martyrdom in acting in command from here to Dunkeld. Brooks discovered the footman drunk in his bed-room; if the rascal weren't so good a servant I'd have settled his hash for him that time. Your mother, who has more confidence in a naked Hindoo, than she ever had or could persuade herself to have, in the capacities of any of her children, was difficult to please. The Children alone were amenable to control, and Brooks serves one glorious purpose, for by a system of badger he occupies your mother's attention, and as he is very good-natured and stands a deal of scolding, he helps one on.

At Dunkeld the Chief resumed command. We crossed to Glasgow and there our force again divided, the one squadron operating against the Argyll's at Inverary, and I disregarding the Duchess's invitation, set out with Brooks to explore the Cheviot Hills and the border.

Our start was not successful. We went as far as Edinburg, and as there was a violent storm, I wisely concluded to take shelter there for a day. The next morning we set off again and went to visit Rosslyn, a place about seven miles south of Edinburg. Here are the ruins of a fine ancient keep, and its chapel still perfect and a wonderfully pretty thing it is; a little jewel of a chapel. Unfortunately we had to walk rather more than a mile to it, and over a country that when dry is probably lovely, but in a drenching rain is damnable. Our return in this rain, which was indeed a peeler, was funny, but moist. We laughed till we were weak, but we were also wet. That evening we went on to Kelso where we passed the night.

The next morning was again fine, as our luck would have it, and we enjoyed a glorious day. First we went out and inspected the ruins of Kelso Abbey. Then we walked to the Meeting of the Waters, where the Teviot and the Tweed join. Continuing a mile further on, we reached the ruins of Roxburg Castle and an eminence just between the two streams. This was once a famous fortress. Now there is hardly a stone left. But the view is lovely. I was delighted with this lowland scenery, and we sat some time admiring it and enjoying the sun. Then we returned, and taking the train, went on to Jedburg where there is the ruin of an old Abbey, in which I smoked a pipe and was content. Lunching here, we took a dog-cart and drove up the valley of the Teviot to Hawick, a pretty drive, which brought us at five o'clock on a lovely evening to one of the most prettily situated towns I have seen. I immediately seized Brooks and dragged him out about two miles to visit a curious specimen of a border keep, one of the few perfect examples existing. We discovered it on a rising ground above the river; a square tower with thick walls of rough stone. These places were in fact only houses built to resist attack. It is now a sort of barn and lumber house. We coolly entered it and explored every cranny without troubling ourselves to ask permission. There is little to see except a stone stair-case and the traces of what seemed to have been the kitchen, on the second story. There is, however, a good deal of satisfaction in this kind of independent exploration, and especially where the object is not a regular traveller's sight. So we occupied an hour over it, and then lay down on the grass outside and en-

joyed the sunset and the view. Just opposite here is the old castle which is
the principal scene of the Lay of the Last Minstrel.[7] The country is hilly
and fertile, and well cultivated, and a pleasanter sight than the valleys were
this evening, seldom meets one's eye. It was not till our dinner hour approached that we turned our backs on Goldielands and made our way
along the banks of the noisy Teviot to our inn.

The next day was Sunday. The Scotch are furiously strict in their observance of this day, which they reserve exclusively to get drunk on. As I had
no time to lose, I went on as usual. It was a fine morning, and we left
Hawick in the train before nine o'clock. Our ride was not very long, but the
railway rises just on the border, over the Cheviots, and at a solitary station
at the highest point, we got out, leaving our baggage to go on. We found
ourselves in a wild, bare country, among brown hills covered with marshy
grass. As there was no road convenient, we struck over the hills, and a precious moist bit of work it was. At one spot, according to Brooks's account I
was seen to pitch forward onto my shoulder and to make violent and repeated efforts to stick my white hat into the ground. In fact I had stumbled
and fallen into a sort of ditch from which I could with difficulty recover my
balance. After an exhausting climb through the rank grass that seems
everywhere to cover these hills, we reached the summit and began to descend into a wide valley, some miles broad, in which, on the bank of a little
stream, we saw from afar off the large and solitary gray castle that we
sought; the remains of Hermitage Castle. If you remember, there was once
a knight, Sir Somebody Ramsay, who like the Duke of Rothsay, was stuck
in a dungeon and starved to death. The poor devil died hard, as a little
grain fell through a crevice in the roof of his cell and kept him alive near a
month. This was the scene of that piece of work, and the cell is still there.[8]
Down the hill-side, across a stream, scaring the sheep on the meadows,
Brooks and I laid a straight course, arriving in due time at a farmhouse
where we had some delay in order to send a ragged brat for the key. Then
under the guidance of a young fellow whose English was of the most unin-
telligible, we explored the old ruin. A strange old place it is. Externally, except for the roof, it is still perfect; a large, square granite pile, with a great
Gothic arch at two ends, as though the builder had once seen a Cathedral,
and had tried to make a castle with ecclesiastical reminiscences. Inside it is
hollow except for a few foundation and partition walls. By the aid of lad-
ders which we dragged about, we mounted to the niches and windows, descended into vaults and ransacked every corner. We found poor Ramsay's
cell, a hole like a coal-cellar which is entered by a sort of trap-door from
above, and has no light. We risked our necks in clambering up the old walls
and ruined stairs. We speculated hopelessly as to the arrangement and
purposes of rooms; and finally we came out and lay down on what was once
the wall of the moat, and watched the old pile which looked almost attractive in the sunshine. These border fortresses do not seem to have been
placed in cheerful spots, for except on so bright a day as this, the place must

be dreary to a degree. Among these bleak hills there is little beauty of vegetation; few trees and scanty crops. They rise in broad slopes all around, brown as leaves in winter. On one of them there is an old Druid's circle, and there, once upon a time the people of the neighborhood, having got possession of an unpopular lord of this fortress, did boil him. This, I believe, is true.[9] The caldron is said to have hung between two of the stones, and the happy man was cooked in melted lead. This was the hill on which I had my fall.

Having indulged our curiosity sufficiently, we resumed our march, and went on down the valley till we entered Liddesdale. I had just been reading Guy Mannering, so had my mind full of Dandie Dinmont and his native valley, but my experience is that the days of adventure are passed.[10] During five years of foreign life, I have been in many queer places, but never had an adventure. Nothing interrupted for our benefit the Sunday quiet of the valley, though we sat down on the bank of the river and bathed our sore feet in its water. I smoked my pipe there in peace, and soon afterwards we reached the village of New Castleton, and got our dinner. Our walk was little more than eight miles in length, but we had been more than five hours in motion, and were tolerably tired. That night we went on to Carlisle.

This practically ended our excursion. On Monday we went on in a drenching rain to Keswick where our family met us on Tuesday. My letter has spun out to such a fearful length that I will only add that it is now the 10th of September and we have long been safe at home. The Lake District was very charming and we saw a magnificent old Abbey ruin there. On reaching London I found politics in a very bad way, but that will serve for next week's letter. As this has been a pure vacation epistle, I will merely observe that I have received yours of July 18th and August, 2d enclosing Major Higginson's, to whom I write by this mail.[11] This letter is too stupid for any place except camp, but as you are there, it is good enough for you.

Ever yours.

MS: MHi
1. Charles Edward Stuart (1720–1788), the Young Pretender, unfurled his standard at Loch Shiel, Aug. 19, 1745.
2. Then a small fishing village on Cape Cod, Mass.
3. Matthew 7:25, 27.
4. *Quantum . . . illo:* How very much changed from that; *Aeneid*, II, 274–275.
5. Triptolemus Yellowley is an innovating farmer from the Scottish mainland scornful of the backward people of the Shetland (Zetland) islands, the setting of *The Pirate* (1821), by Sir Walter Scott (1771–1832).
6. Edward Ellice (1781–1863), M.P., deputy governor of Hudson's Bay Company, was equally hospitable to Confederate (Mason) and Union (CFA) friends. Curtis Miranda Lampson (1806–1885), deputy governor of Hudson's Bay Company and director of the Atlantic Cable Company, was, like Peabody, an expatriate American.
7. Narrative poem (1805) by Scott. The castle is Branksome Tower near Hawick, Roxburghshire.
8. The Duke of Rothsay, David Stewart (c. 1378–1401), was seized by his uncle Albany and imprisoned at Falkland, where he starved to death. Sir Alexander Ramsay (d. 1342), Scottish patriot, was imprisoned in Hermitage Castle by his rival William

Douglas. Rothsay is a character in Scott's *Fair Maid of Perth* (1828), which also mentions Ramsay by reason of his similar death.

9. The punishment is said to have been ordered by Robert Bruce for Sir William Soulis (c. 1321).

10. Novel (1815) by Scott.

11. Henry Lee Higginson was wounded at Aldie, June 17, and invalided home.

To Henry Lee Higginson

London. 10 Sept. 1863.

My dear Major:

Your letter, after slumbering in my brother's pocket for an indefinite period, did at last manage to cross the Atlantic and not finding me in London, had to take another long journey and follow me to Scotland. There at last I received it, and as I was at that time on my vacation travels, and not able to attend to labors, I had to put off all action till my return a few days ago. It was then so long since your directions as to the garments that I had some doubt whether I ought not to refer it back to you for confirmation and new directions, but concluded on reflection that military men are well known to be ferocious, and that as they like to be implicitly obeyed, if I were to fail to carry out orders I might get my ears cut off with such a ferocious sabre as I forwarded to Ben. Crowninshield. Accordingly I hurried straightway to Poole's and the articles are now in process of making and will be sent on in due course. May they be pleasing to your eyes and soften your wrath against your slave.

I remain in no little trouble about Jim. As yet I have had no account of how he was taken or when he is likely to escape. So soon as he does get again into the land of the free, I hope he will write me a letter, especially as I wrote the last to him. Give him my energetic sympathy, whenever you can, and tell him that I exult in the punishment of Rooney Lee (not his hanging, however) as a make-weight on our side of the account.[1]

You are more fortunate than I. After your work you will enjoy your fun, and when you do again come abroad what a good time you will have. Whereas I, who now for so long have been living as a Sybarite, am no longer able to enjoy America or Europe. I want to come home badly, and when I do come, I shall expect an invitation to reside with your regiment as a volunteer, until I have had some experience in military life and duties, and can make interest to get an appointment on some cuss's staff. As for the army as a profession, video meliora, proboque;[2] but can you expect a vile diplomat who has a profound contempt for Courts and a still profounder disbelief in the virtues of camps, to follow so illustrious an example. I fear that the experience of an amateur will be all that I can swallow, long custom having given me tastes which are decidedly inconsistent with dirt, routine, and salt pork, but who knows! Perhaps we shall have a war with France or England, and in that case we may all hope for honor.

News have I none, not even of Berlin, Vienna or Paris. It is now more than a year since I was at the latter spot, but I trust to run over there again soon. Joe Bradlee has gone home, and no one except Fez Richardson is left at Paris, and he is politically on the fence. New friends I have none, and the old ones don't seem to turn up. Why doesn't John Bancroft come back! I hope he doesn't mean to become soldier. Floods of people are perpetually passing and repassing, but as we have to dine them all, and as I don't meet any pretty girls among them, our acquaintance stops there. We feel tollable well just now, and talk up pretty plain to the Britishers, only I hope you will manage to give the rebs another gentle suasion before the year's out, as a quiet hint to hurry. A good dose once in three months, keeps the Britishers quiet.

The particulars as to your garments shall be sent hereafter. How to get them over I know not now, but they shall come.

Ever Yrs H. B. Adams.

I have omitted to offer my sympathies for your wounds, especially because I am brilliantly in the dark as to their nature and extent. Hoping they were only enough to get you a pleasant vacation, I trust you'll be spared any more.

MS: MH

1. James Higginson, Henry's brother and a lieutenant with the 1st Massachusetts Cavalry, was captured at Aldie and confined nine months in Libby Prison, Richmond. Rooney Lee, recovering from his recent wounds, was seized by Union raiders at his wife's family home in Hanover Co., Va.

2. *Video meliora, proboque:* I see and approve better things (but I do worse); Ovid, *Metamorphoses*, VII, 20.

To Charles Francis Adams, Jr.

London. 16 Sept. 1863.

My dear Boy:

When I came to the end of my long volume of travels, I intimated to you that I had found things here in a very bad way on my return. We were in fact in the middle of the crisis which I have so often warned you would be the dangerous and decisive one; and now it was going against us.

You have heard much of the two iron-clads now building at Liverpool; formidable vessels which would give us troubles. Ever since their keels were laid, now some eighteen months since, we have been watching them with great anxiety. Luckily they were not at first pressed forward very rapidly, and the delay has given us just the time we needed. But we have never attempted to disguise to the people here, what would be the inevitable result of their being allowed to go, and both Mr Evarts and all our other supernumerary diplomats have urged with the greatest energy some measure of effective interference. This had been so far successful that we had felt tolerably secure under what appeared to be decisive assurances. As the summer wore on, the vessels were launched and began to fit for sea. Our people, as in the case of the Alabama and Alexandra, were busy in getting up a case, and sent bundles of depositions and letters in to the Foreign Office. This was the position of affairs when I left London, and although I am violating the rules by telling you about it, I suppose the facts are so public and so well understood that there would be no great harm if anyone knew it. But what has since passed is as yet known to but few and not understood even by them, in which number I include myself.

The law officers of the Crown were funky, as the boys say here. They were not willing to advise the seizure of the vessels under the Neutrality Act. In this respect, I think they were right, for although there was perhaps a case strong enough to justify the arrest of the vessels, it was certainly not strong enough to condemn them, and it would have been too absurd to have had another such ludicrous sham as the trial of the Alexandra, where Mr Evarts acted as drill-sergeant, and the prosecution was carried just so far, and no farther than was necessary to show him that everything was on the square. The result, as declared by Chief Baron Pollock was the most amusing example of the admired English system, that has yet taken place, and if my ancient Anglomania which swallowed Blackstone, and bowed before the Judges' wigs, had not yielded to a radical disbelief in the efficacy of England already, I believe this solemn and ridiculous parade of the majesty and imperturbability of English justice, would have given such a shock to my old notions as they never would have recovered from.

The law-officers were right therefore, in my opinion, in wishing to escape this disgrace, for unless the work was to be done in a very different spirit from the last job, it would be a disgrace, and they knew it. In fact this was no longer a case for the Courts. Any Government which really assumes to be a Govern-ment, and not a Governed-ment, would long ago have taken the matter into its own hands and made the South understand that this sort of thing was to be stopped. But this form of Government is the snake with many heads. It may be accidentally successful, and so exist from mere habit and momentum; but it is as a system, clumsy, unmanageable, and short-lived. You will laugh at my word *short-lived*, and think of William the Conqueror. You might as well think of Justinian. This Government, as it stands today, is just thirty years old, and between a reformed Government under the Reform Bill and an aristocratic Government and nomination boroughs, there is as much difference as between the France of Louis Philippe and the France of Louis Quinze.

At any rate, the English having in their hatred of absolute Government, rendered all systematic Government impossible, now inflict upon us the legitimate fruits of their wisdom. On a question which is so evident that no other Government ever hesitated to acknowledge its duties; not even

England herself in former days; it now comes to a deadlock. The springs refuse to work. The cog-wheels fly round wildly in vain. And Lord Russell after repeated attempts to grind something out of his poor mill, at last is compelled to inform us that he is very sorry but it wont work, and as for the vessels, Government can't stop them, and wont try.

It was just after the receipt of this information that I reached London. You may imagine our condition, and the little disposition we felt to shirk the issue, when the same day brought us the story of Gilmore's big guns and Sumter's walls.[1] In point of fact, disastrous as a rupture would be, we have seen times so much blacker that we were not disposed to bend any longer even if it had been possible. The immediate response to this declaration was a counter-declaration, short but energetic, announcing what was likely to happen. Lord Russell is in Scotland and this produced some confusion in the correspondence, but it was rapid and to me very incomprehensible. My suspicion is that they meant to play us, like a salmon, and that the Note of which I speak, fell so hard as to break the little game. At all events, within three days came a short announcement that the vessels should not leave.

Undoubtedly to us this is a second Vicksburg. It is our diplomatic triumph, if we manage to carry it through.[2] You will at once understand how very deeply our interests depend on it, and under the circumstances, how great an achievement our success will be. It would in fact be the crowning stroke of our diplomacy. After it, we might say our own minds to the world and do our own will. A public life seldom affords to a man the opportunity to perform more than one or two brilliant rôles of this description, and no more is needed in order to set his mark on history. Whether we shall succeed? I am not yet certain. The vessels are only detained temporarily. But the signs are that the gale that has blown so long is beginning to veer about. If our armies march on; if Charleston is taken and North Carolina freed; above all if emancipation is made effective; Europe will blow gentle gales upon us and will again bow to our dollars. Every step we make, England makes one backward. But if we have disaster to face, then indeed I can't say. Yet I am willing to do England the justice to say that while enjoying equally with all nations the baseness which is inevitable to politics carried on as they must be, she still has a conscience, though it is weak, ineffective and foggy. Usually after she has got herself into some stupid scrape, her first act is to find out she is wrong and retract when too late. I think the discussion which is now taking place, has pretty much convinced most people that this war-vessel matter is one that ought to be stopped. And if so, the mere fact that they have managed to take the first step, is to me reasonable ground for confidence that they will take the others as the emergencies rise. There will be hoisting and straining, groaning and kicking, but the thing will in some stupid and bungling way be got done.

Meanwhile volumes are written. To read them is bad enough, but to write them! I believe this to be really of little effect, and think I see the causes of movement in signs entirely disconnected with mere argument.

The less said, the shorter work. Give us no disasters, and we have a clear and convincing position before the British public, for we come with victories on our standards and the most powerful military and naval engines that ever the earth saw. Unceasing military progress. The rebels are crying to high Heaven on this side, for some one to recognise them. A few months more and it will be too late, if it's not already.

MS: MHi
1. Gen. Quincy Adams Gillmore (1825–1888) destroyed the Confederate artillery at Fort Sumter with heavy bombardment from Morris Island; however, failure of the Union attempt to take the fort Sept. 8 led to abandonment of the Charleston campaign.
2. As his culminating protest, on Sept. 5 CFA sent Russell the famous warning: "It would be superfluous in me to point out to your lordship that this is war." Russell had on Sept. 2 ordered the ships detained but, uneasy about the legal liability of his government, delayed notifying CFA until after the note of Sept. 5 had been dispatched.

To Charles Francis Adams, Jr.

London. 25 Sept. 1863.

My dear Lieut-Col-Major-Captain:[1]

I do not think that the steady current of good news which we have had since the first of July, has turned our heads here, for as each successive steamer has piled it up, my dread has gone on constantly rising, for fear a change should again blast all our hopes. At this moment indeed I can see no place likely to furnish news at all. We have realized all our stakes except Charleston, which it is rather a pleasure to polish off by bits. From the tone of Mr Lawley's letter of 29 August and 7 Sept. from Richmond, I infer that Lee cannot move again into Maryland, and will not move against Washington direct. What the deuce they can do now that Johnstone's retreat from Chattanooga has exposed such a wretched state of things in the West, I confess I am utterly puzzled to know. It appears that their leaders still keep up their tone and brag as loudly as ever of what is to be done in November, but I do much suspect that we have put a little spoke in that wheel; or perhaps I should say, we have taken one out. I suspect the English iron-clads constituted a main feature in any plan they may have invented, and the blow which we have inflicted upon them by our diplomacy may save another Gettysburg and Antietam. At any rate, the rats are moving more rapidly than ever, and some pretty large rats who hold offices, are putting out feelers that puzzle me.

The news that will please you more than even a medium victory, will be that which must have reached America a few days before this letter, of the formal rupture between the Southern Government and the British, and the departure of Mr Mason from England. I hardly know what more striking proof could be given of our individual triumph. There is something highly humorous to my mind in the recollection of Mr Mason's career on this side of the water, and of the two years English campaign that his forces have had with ours. With varying success we have battled and marched, but the battle of the iron-clads was our Gettysburg, and Mr Mason has sullenly retreated before the frowning batteries of the Governor. We have routed him, horse, foot and creeters! We have pitched him into the Channel and have wrung the arrogant withers of the poor, old, ruined, broken-down, drunken slave-driver, until he must curse the day that ever he saw the inside of a British war-steamer. Better to rot at Fort Warren![2]

Yet, between ourselves, I am at a loss to understand why this step has been taken. Certainly I know none of the reasons which may have had a secret influence on Mr Davis, but as I look at it, this movement of his is a blunder. Mr Mason's mere presence at this place has been a source of annoyance both to us and to the British Government. His departure will tend greatly to allay the dangers of our foreign affairs. Either England or France must take the brunt of our ill-will. Why should Mr Davis aid our diplomacy by himself directing all our causes of alarm towards France, a nation whose power we have no real cause to fear, and away from England, with whom we are or have been on the very verge of war? For myself, I look forward to a possible war with France as by no means a cause of alarm to us. So sure as Napoleon proves so false to France as to take up the cudgels for monarchy against democracy, just so sure he will lose his throne. You at home have not known what is so terrible to all the Kings and Nobles here as "the Revolution." You have a curious anomaly of a rebellion where people are trying to turn themselves backward into the Middle Ages. Here the Revolution is always trying to jump into the next century. And whatever France has been since 1789; republic, Empire, Kingdom or anarchy, she is always revolutionary to the core. She leads Europe whenever she moves. She is the head of civilisation, and the great agent in the process of social progress. Whatever ruler she has, he must be true to the Revolution, "les principes de '89," if he is to keep his throne, and it is because every successive ruler has been false to those principles, that he has fallen. But if Napoleon dares to attack us, he attacks the great embodiment of the Revolution, and we shall know how to shake a few of these crazy thrones for him, if he drives us to it.

Meanwhile our lives here are still placid and regular. The only visitor I have had this week to speak of, has been Geo. Bangs.[3] He looked, as I thought, very well, but was evidently in low spirits, and said he was almost in despair of ever regaining his health. He wants to get home to get married, and laments that he wasn't shot in preference to dragging on existence under a burden of ill-health such as he has to carry now. I rather think he'll pick up in the course of a few months.

We had heard the details of your promotion question, some time since. I am glad of your decision; I cannot doubt of its wisdom, and I applaud your magnanimity.[4] Very true is it that promotion is not progress, and you and I have worked out that problem for ourselves at just about the same time, though by rather different paths. My ideas on such subjects have changed in two years more than I could have guessed, and I fancy, if we ever manage to get back to Quincy, we shall find that this scattering of our family has left curious marks on us. For my part I can only promise to be liberal and tolerant towards other people's ideas; let them leave me equally to mine.

Tell Major Higginson, if he is with the regiment, that his clothes will go by next week's steamer to our brother John, as I had no address. The cost is £7. I dont know yet whether they will pay duty. He had better have a deposit to that extent made with S. G. Ward to my credit, and he will notify the Barings in regular course. I hope they will please him.

How is it about newspapers? Shall I continue to send them, or have you any choice?

MS: MHi

1. With his superior officers sick, wounded, or on leave, CFA2, along with a few other captains, was in charge of the regiment—hence the string of titles.

2. Mason and Slidell were held at Fort Warren in Boston Harbor after being taken from the *Trent*.

3. On March 29 George P. Bangs resigned his captaincy because of ill health.

4. CFA2 had declined to be promoted over the head of Capt. L. M. Sargent, despite his dislike for the man. Captain Sargent and his brother Col. Horace Sargent were the only superiors CFA2 could not get along with or satisfy during his military career (*Autobiography*, pp. 146–147).

To Charles Francis Adams, Jr.

London, 2 October. 1863.

My dear Centaur:

The Scotia's telegram has just arrived, and for an hour or two past, I have been reflecting on the news it brings of what I conceive to be a very severe defeat of Rosecranz.[1] At this distance and with our mere scraps of doubtful intelligence, I am painfully impressed with the conviction that our Government has been again proved incompetent, and has neglected to take those measures of security which it ought to have done, expecting as we all did, just this movement, or the corresponding one on Washington. I imagine that this mischance ensures us another year of war, unless the army of the Potomac shows more energy than usual and more success than ever yet. The truth is, everything in this universe has its regular waves and tides. Electricity, sound, the wind, and I believe every part of organic nature will be brought some day within this law. But my philosophy teaches me, and I firmly believe it, that the laws which govern animated beings will be ultimately found to be at bottom the same with those which rule inanimate nature, and, as I entertain a profound conviction of the littleness of our kind, and of the curious enormity of creation, I am quite ready to receive with pleasure any basis for a systematic conception of it all. Thus (to explain this rather alarming digression) as a sort of experimentalist, I look for regular tides in the affairs of man, and of course, in our own affairs. In every progression, somehow or other, the nations move by the same process which has never been explained but is evident in the ocean and the air. On this theory I should expect at about this time, a turn which would carry us backward. The devil of it is, supposing there comes a time when the rebs suddenly cave in, how am I to explain that!

This little example of my unpractical experimento-philosophico-historico-progressiveness, will be enough. It suffices to say that I am seeking to console my trouble by chewing the dry husks of that philosophy, which, whether it calls itself submission to the will of God, or to the laws of nature, rests in bottom simply and solely upon an acknowledgment of our own impotence and ignorance. In this amusement, I find, if not consolation at least some sort of mental titillation. Besides, I am becoming superstitious. I believe Nick Anderson's killed, though I've not yet seen his ghost. Write me that he's not yet gone under, and I will say defiance to the vague breath of similar chimaeras.

My last week has been wholly occupied in acting as a detective policeman. Our butler has imitated some persons of a better class, and after a long system of undiscovered thefts, at length seceded from the establishment. I have had to seize and arrange his papers, and to investigate his course of villainy. So far we find that he has stolen about £40,0,0.; forged to the extent of £40 more; drunk or disposed of about fifteen dozen of sherry, madeira, port, whiskey, brandy &c &c; besides neglecting his duty, intercepting our correspondence for fear of his affairs being discovered, and destroying our character in the neighborhood. Now here is a case that has completely puzzled all my preconceived ideas. I knew the man to be a coward, and I supposed his cowardice would guarantee us from crime. I knew that he was a liar, and dishonest, but believed that this was the result of education and that his disposition was good. When we discovered his true character, I at once supposed him to be a thorough villain, and took it for granted that he had fled the country. After an absence of three days, he came back, penitent, and wanting to be forgiven and taken back. He confessed the forgeries, and also to the cask of sherry, which he said he "expected" he'd drunk. He lied like a sculpin on every matter where lying was possible, to the last. Yet for months, six months now since the first forgery, he has been struggling to keep his head above water, and while trusted with large sums of money, has generally devoted it to paying bills. The man is a dastardly, rotten-hearted scoundrel, but his character is such a mixture of every meanness and weakness that can make human nature contemptible, all covered with a plausible air of candid, gushing honesty and fidelity, that I would like to have had Balzac or Thackeray analyse and dissect this carrion. The Chief bore it like an angel.

Tomorrow I take the females to Hastings to abide a period.[2] For myself, I am ridiculously attached to London, but still like an occasional sun-beam and sniff of the sea. I come to town occasionally henceforward.

———

MS: MHi
1. Rosecrans, defeated in the battle of Chickamauga, Sept. 19–20, fell back to Chattanooga.
2. Hastings, once a major port on the southeast coast, was a seaside resort.

To Charles Francis Adams, Jr.

9 October. 1863.

My dear Charles:

I have no time to write a letter today, as I am engaged in superintending the removal of our household down to St Leonard's where we are setting up a rival establishment.[1] The duties of a diplomate are indeed varied. As you ride at the head of your squadron, pray fancy me, heading a cohort of cooks and maids, and followed by a cartload of sauce-pans and table-cloths. As your mamma has been dexterously inveigled down there in advance, and left in a helpless condition at a hotel, your papa and I make short work of the business of moving. Imagine the horror of a London household, on receiving a brief order to be ready to move in twenty four hours. What a row there would have been in former times. But just now our servants are not in a frame of mind which would lead them to tempt the wrath of his Excellency.

St Leonard's is seventy miles, or about two hours and a half from here by rail, and both the Chief and I have to be up at least once a week. I don't greatly object to this, as I have so little chance of freedom in London, that an occasional night at my own disposal is not an unpleasant thing. Just now, however, I am a Committee of one on Butlers, and I have the onerous duty of receiving applicants and as it were filtering them. So I inspect about half a dozen every day and as yet am almost as far from a conclusion as ever. Between this and the direction of the moving, I am not so comfortably situated as I could wish. Another week however, will, I hope, see us running the machine again with regularity.

Otherwise our affairs move on without trouble. The political position of England is now fixed with a sufficient degree of firmness to relieve us of any immediate anxiety, and all our care centres upon things at home. The Chickamanga affair remains a mystery. The published report of that battle which appears to have been furnished to the associated press, seems to me to be so extraordinary a document that I give no faith to it until further confirmation. The defeat I care comparatively little for. But the confidence I have had in Rosecranz, founded on a military career of such successes as those at Corinth, Murfreesboro and Shelbyville, is not to be shaken by a newspaper writer from Cincinnati. Especially when his statements are in such contradiction with those of Rosecranz himself. I suppose we shall soon know whether it is the Ohio copperheads who are trying to add dishonor to the defeat, or whether we have in fact got to give up our old confidence in the General.

I doubt whether you will succeed in getting a fight out of Lee. Ah! if our good Government would now but throw Meade's whole army upon North Carolina and cut off that little game of shifting corps from one army to another, I think we might with a little energy, settle the affair. As for Washington, if the destruction of that city were simultaneous with the end of the rebellion, I don't know that such a result might not be very willingly risked. Meanwhile I feel fresh anxiety for you at every advance, as I suppose the Cavalry must be very hard worked just now. Of course we do not discuss the subject, as I've no fancy for raising trouble in feminine buzzims. The mystery in which the army of the Potomac is wrapped just now, adds to my doubt, and the next telegram is by no means likely to be opened with less sinking of the stomach than usual.

Ever Yrs

MS: MHi
1. St. Leonard's, adjacent to Hastings, was the newest and most fashionable part of the resort area.

To Charles Francis Adams

Sunday. 11 Oct. 1863.

My dear Sir:

Mr Wood has just been here. He had not received your letter, and called only at the suggestion of Ensor. According to his account, the man is all that is perfect. As a butler, he says he is thoroughly capable, both of doing the entertaining and of controlling the household. He is perfectly temperate. He writes well and is intelligent; more than usually so; hence there is reason to suppose (Mr W. thinks) that he will be quite equal to any accounts. He is a hard-worker; rather too willing, for his own health. He has been in a large household before coming to Mr W's, where much entertaining was done. He is thoroughly acquainted with London.

Per contra. ——

Mr Wood fears that much going up and down stairs will be bad for his health, and I expressed my opinion that he would be called on to do a good deal of it. He thought the man hardly capable of standing this. But he thought at least you might try him, and settle this point by experience.

Ensor is a friend of Harvey's, Mrs Sturgis's man. Perhaps you could learn something about him there.

Mr Wood's language could not have been stronger and his recommendation was positive and unrestricted.

Mamma says that she is disposed to take him on the word of Mr Wood, and let him do his work up stairs if necessary.

I want to come up tomorrow or Tuesday, if you can make it convenient to come down to conclude your negotiation with Ensor. There are some other matters of small domestic importance that might be best settled by you.

Ever yrs affly   H.B.A.

Hon. C. F. Adams.

MS: MHi

To Charles Francis Adams, Jr.

London. 16 October. 1863.

Caro Capitano:

My letter of last week informed you of my campaign to St Leonard's. It was completely successful so far as my share was concerned. I superintended the removal of the servants and their impedimenta, and after installing the family in the house, came up again on Monday to relieve the Chief, and have remained here with Bridget in magnificent state. The family are charmingly situated down there, with the ocean rolling under their windows; and the more I look at it, the more I feel how far the ocean is superior in grandeur to every other object in nature. To have it always under one's eyes is certainly the most easy way of obtaining the grandest amusement in the way of spectacle, that the world affords. The climate on that coast is mild and the atmosphere clear and free from smoke. Your poor mamma was very homesick at first, but I think she will soon learn to like it, and the Chief expands under its influence.

As for me, I am getting to be of Dr. Johnson's opinion that nothing is equal to Fleet Street. Not that I take so much pleasure in looking at it as I do at the magnificent changes of the ocean at St Leonard's, but the fact is, I feel the want of London more when I leave it, than I appreciate it when here. Still, I am very contented to be here alone, although I am still allowed little freedom of hours. My drunken footman is the only man besides myself in the house, and I have to set a good example. So there's no being out late of nights, nor dallying with the charms of harlots in the morning twilight, as some of my friends in the regiment would be apt to suspect. I am ruining my constitution by studying far into the small hours, and yet I think the profit balances the wear and tear. Silvyer and gold have I none,[1] nor do I ever expect to realise my labors in that shape, but Oh my friend and mentor! I have learned that there are objects of ambition which may be held separate from the opinions of men or the applause of listening Senates.

The ancient Sir Henry Holland summoned me to breakfast the other morning to tell me that he had seen you three weeks ago and that you were well and prosperous.[2] He seemed to have less acquaintance with your situation than I should have supposed he would have tried to get, on our account. He did however declare himself pleased with your appearance, and Ted Lyman had apparently been sounding your praises largely. It is well to have friends at head-quarters.[3]

Harrison Ritchie and his wife are here. He is on some agency for the State, I suppose.[4] He is in a state of great admiration of the regulation saddle used in the service here, and proposes to take one back with him. It has occurred to us that perhaps you might like to have one. It is pretty large, and weighs without the trappings about fourteen or fifteen pounds. It might be got to Boston or New York easily enough, but I don't know how so large a box could be made to reach you. Nevertheless, if you feel a disposition to indulge in a pig-skin that is certainly a fine piece of work and probably very easy to the horse and perfect in its bearings, we will do our best to gratify you.

Public matters are very quiet and I trust will remain so for some time. We watch with interest the military position at home, and I am on sharp pins to know what will be the next act of the play in Tennesee. If the rebs can drive us out of there, they will save themselves for the time, but I feel confident that they would have to pay a price for it, of which Chickamanga is a first and limited instalment.

London is now utterly deserted, and if anyone were here I shouldn't know it. There are no dinners and no routs. It is as if there were several square miles of Beacon Street in August. I have to rack my brain for somebody or something to look for when I go out to walk. At best my acquaintance is not large and in these days I am totally alone except for the Secretaries with whom I have little or nothing to do. But when one's own insides, you know, are illuminated by that cheerful and perpetual sunlight which is a characteristic of my own, there needs no external assistance to render the course of time a blissful delight. Do you ever have fits of the blues as a cavalryman? I am curious to know whether that existence permits the vagueness of feeling which is so miserably unpractical in low-spirits. I find that my residence here has greatly freed me from such amusements, and the want of any excitement and especially of clever women's society, has spared me pain as well as lost me pleasure.

So Major Higginson is engaged! Well! I wish to God you would get leave, and pass a few weeks north. I want you to marry. Did you send my letter to the Major?

MS: MHi

1. Acts 3:6.

2. Sir Henry Holland (1788–1873), the queen's physician, frequent contributor to the quarterlies, and a social lion. Friend of American ministers and American presidents, he visited Lincoln and toured army headquarters in September.

3. Lyman joined the army in Aug. 1863 as a lieutenant colonel and aide-de-camp to Gen. George Meade, the new commander of the Army of the Potomac.

4. Lt. Col. Harrison Ritchie (1825–1894) of Boston was on a mission to buy ordnance.

To Charles Francis Adams, Jr.

London. 23 October. 1863.

My dear Captain:

Here I am still, alone in this cheerful city since Monday, but this evening I return to St Leonard's. My stay in London this week has not been so pleasant as usual. I am pestered and prodded about by cursed domestic thorns that make one curse the very name of man. I have a profound contempt for human nature in almost every shape, for even the highest and the purest have flaws somewhere, or else our own minds become fatigued in trying to comprehend them, but there is no species of human nature for which I entertain such a vile despicion as for the tribe of London servants. Do you recollect a passage to the same effect in Alton Locke![1] The pure London servant is radically, totally corrupt, with no conception of moral duties, and no aspirations for a life of a *man*. The whole atmosphere is one net-work of all the cardinal, yes and the ordinal vices. I have been forced to see the system and to try to grapple with it, but Lord bless you, I might as well struggle with the laws of nature, and after six weeks of perpetual irritation, I only ask to escape from contact with corruption that sickens and humiliates me. If I could only give you the regiment of servants I have had to deal with! To have them all killed would do the world no harm, and might do them some good.

In other respects my existence has been calm as the philosophic mind within me will allow. I write and read; read and write. Two years ago I began on history; our own time. I labored at financial theories, and branched out upon Political Economy and J. S. Mill. Mr Mill's works, thoroughly studied, led me to the examination of philosophy and the great French thinkers of our own time; they in their turn passed me over to others whose very names are now known only as terms of reproach by the vulgar; the monarchist Hobbes; the atheist Spinoza and so on. Where I shall end, *das weiss der liebe Gott!* Probably my career will be brought up at the treadmill of the bar some day, for which, believe me, philosophy is as little adapted as war. Who will lead us back to the pleasant pastures and show us again the rich grain of the lawyer's office! Verily I say unto you, the time cometh and even now is when neither in these mountains nor in Jerusalem ye shall worship the idols of your childhood!

Did you ever read Arthur Clough's Poems? the man that wrote that pastoral with the unpronounceable name; the Bothie of Toper-na-Vuolich. If you have not, I would like to send them to you.[2] Young England, young Europe, of which I am by tastes and education a part; the young world, I believe, in every live country, are reflected in Clough's poems very clearly. Strange to say, even Oxford, that most Catholic of conservative places, has become strongly tinged with the ideas of the new school. John Stuart Mill ranks even there rather higher than the authorities of the place itself, with which he is waging internecine war. Whether this gentle simmering will ever boil anything, who can say?

Meanwhile we wait still for the result of your military evolutions. I cannot imagine that Lee means to attack you, and yet I am equally unable to comprehend how he can maintain himself. I don't think his report on the Gettysburg campaign has raised his reputation here. There is such a thing as too candid confession of defeat, and he certainly doesn't conceal his blunders.

We've received your letter of the 29th September to John, with its indications of lively work. I have a dreadful and a trembling longing to be in a battle. Coward as I am, I would like once to see in practice that great monstrosity of human nature; men committing suicide by profession. If I come back in time I shall certainly try it, and if I get killed in the lark, then erect me a statue in the family chapel.

Politics on this side are quiet. The nations are busy among their own sewers, and don't care to stir our muck. What a gay generation is ours!

Ever Yrs

MS: MHi
1. Novel (1850) by Charles Kingsley.
2. Arthur Hugh Clough, *Poems* (1862).

To Charles Francis Adams, Jr.

London. 30 Oct. 1863.

My dear Captain:

If it weren't for our anxiety about you, I think we should get on swimmingly in these times. The war has taken a chronic shape, and it seems pretty clear that it must burn itself out, or perhaps I should say, burn the rebels out. After having passed through all the intermediate phases of belief, I have come out a full-blown fatalist, and what has greatly aided this result has been the observation of the steady movement of affairs at home.

The world grows, my friend, just like a cabbage; or if the simile is vulgar, we'll say, like an oak. The result will come when the time is ripe, and the only thing that disgusts me much is the consciousness that we are unable to govern it, and the conviction that a man of sense can only prove his possession of a soul, by remaining in mind a serene and indifferent spectator of the very events to which all his acts most eagerly contribute. This has been in one form or another the result of every philosophical system since men became conscious of the inexplicable contradiction of their existence, and though it may seem damned nonsense to you with bullets flying round, it does very well for a theory of existence so long as it has no occasion to regulate the relation between one man and another. But there I confess, it rubs, and naturally enough. So I can contemplate with some philosophy the battles and the defeats, which are indeed only of the same sort of interest as the story of Marathon or Naseby, a degree intensified, but not so with your hasards.[1] The race will go on all right or wrong; either way it's the result of causes existing but not within our reach; but unfortunately if you were to get into trouble, you might not go on at all, which from my point of view would be disagreeable to us all, yourself inclusive, and would not admit of the application of your old though fallacious maxim that life is a system of compensations, a maxim probably just, if we speak of the race as a unit.

Such are, or have been, my reflections during the past week on hearing of Lee's advance and of the severe skirmishing that has been going on. Your letter from Hartwood Church has somewhat quieted my mind—it has just arrived—but of course we are not at ease.

News as usual is scarce. St Leonard's is a quiet retreat where your excellent father and myself did and do still if possible indulge daily in a bath on the sea-shore—ye holy saints, how cool! Mary and I ride over the hills and among the valleys, in the cool October days, and I have frequently had occasion to study the battle-field where the admirable Harold got so durable a thrashing. Battle Abbey is a landmark for the district and a charming place. Suggestive also, from a point of view like ours.[2]

But the sea-side is only an exchange for the City. I came up on Wednesday (my letters are always written on Friday) and do my week's work. It is very quiet here, except old Ruggles who made his appearance yesterday and put me to shame by finding me not yet down.[3] It was not betimes. Do you like scandal? Probably not, for I have reason to believe that on such matters the army while in camp is virtuous. Still it may interest you to know that the Clubs for want of better news have of late been circulating a bit of charming scan. mag. The chief performer in the scene is no other than our friend Lord Palmerston, a lively youth only in his eightieth year, and with all the vigor of eighteen. For some days it was widely asserted in St James's Street that the Premier had had an intrigue, and was to be sued in the Courts by the husband. The lady, so it was asserted, was Mrs Du Cane, formerly Miss Copley, a daughter of Lord Lyndhurst, and cousin of your beloved Boston Amorys. This story was rendered more probable by certain old scandals not yet forgotten, more's the pity. The Copley scutcheon however was soon all gules again, for the story has now taken another shape, and it is declared as final that the lady is a Mrs O'Kane, wife of an Irish clergyman, whose husband has refused six thousand pounds hush-money and swears he'll prosecute unless Lord Palmerston makes him a Bishop. So the case is to go before the Courts. Of course it won't, and how much of the story is true, you may guess for yourself. But the ancient Palmerston is a strange bird, and the conduct of many of these English noblemen is anything but delicate. The funny stories told of Lord Brougham are innumerable.[4]

Ritchie says your "General" is to be transferred to Louisiana. Your regiment seems to be going to pieces in the officer line and I should think the officers were about all that were left of it. Salve, frater!

MS: MHi
1. Remote battles, but decisive: Marathon (490 B.C.), where the Greeks turned back the Persian invaders; Naseby (1645), where parliamentary forces defeated the army of Charles I.
2. William the Conqueror built the abbey to commemorate the Battle of Hastings.
3. Samuel Bulkley Ruggles (1800–1881) of New York, en route as delegate to the International Statistical Congress in Berlin.
4. Henry Brougham (1778–1868), 1st Baron Brougham and Vaux, reform and antislavery leader, was a notorious eccentric frequently caricatured in *Punch*.

To Charles Francis Adams, Jr.

London. 6 Nov. 1863.

My dear Captain:

"How flash the weeks along!" Here I am again inditing another epistle to you, on pure faith, for I have a shaking terror that you may be by this time in the Libby. Our last accounts left Lee performing most curious antics inexplicable to me except on the ground that he means either to retreat or fight, and of the two I infer the latter. If so, he will do his worst and Gettysburg will be a trifle. Naturally, with this expectation, I am not a little anxious.

I can't tell you how I felt the removal of Rosecranz; our best general, and steadiest support, broken in our hands. And now three months at least before we can resume the aggressive, I suppose. But for all that, I do not see that the South have any sort of chance since the elections.

I suppose your St Leonard's letters will tell you what very small gossip is to be collected down there. Holy whistle! how it has blown there for ten days past. A fellow couldn't go onto the doorstep without having his clothes blown into the sea, nor open his mouth without his teeth being blown down his throat. This becomes somewhat tedious in time, and ten days of it are very rough. But your mamma's improvement in health and spirits is or was when I came away last Wednesday, very encouraging. She was quite her old self again and her nerves seemed steadier and her mind calmer than I have known it since we left home. This is a great thing, and needs one to have had a long experience to appreciate it.

In town for the last two days nothing has been heard of but the Palmerstonian scandal that I wrote you last week. It has created a most unearthly uproar and rumor has had many hundred tongues. I could fill a book with an account of it. But it seems to be ascertained that much of the former story was embroidered, though the facts remain that there is a bill filed in the divorce Court, charging Lord Palmerston as the co-respondent with having had criminal connection with the lady on three separate occasions in June last, at Cambridge House in Piccadilly (his town house). Further, the case is not to be compromised but will come up for trial. Palmerston is going to meet it with a high hand and sue the suer for conspiracy, it is said on high authority, or bring him before the police Courts as the only means of reaching a speedy result. I believe myself that it's a made-up thing, and have no doubt that the old fellow will in the end make political capital out of it. But if he should fail to clear himself, it will be his destruction; for the Queen is a dragon of virtue, and the nation is as rigid in profession as it is lax in practice.

This week's joke however is yet to come. As if it were not enough for this pure and moral community to have the virtue of its Premier drawn before a divorce Court, it now appears that Layard, the Under Secretary for Foreign Affairs, is to figure in the same place as co-respondent in a similar suit.[1] It appears that while he was making excavations in Babylonian ruins, he was also engaged in some little interesting amusements with the wife of one of his companions, a rather aesthetic lady well known in London society. All the world supposed that the husband had long since condoned the offence, but no one seems to doubt the facts. So that poor Layard will probably catch the devil.

Such are the questions with regard to whose progress the Clubs receive hourly bulletins. The press has already begun on Palmerston's affair, the opposition paper containing a bitter article about the "centenarian." Well regulated people all express (in private) the opinion that if the charge is true, Palmerston ought of right to receive a medal. But people's public talk is amusingly in contrast with their secret expressions. Such is the test of civilisation.

I have no other news. Your mamma sends you some garment or other which I hope it may suit you

Ever.

MS: MHi
1. Austen Henry Layard (1817–1894).

To Charles Francis Adams, Jr.

London. 13 Nov. 1863.

My dear Captain:

As the Lord liveth, I have not one word to say to you this week. Positively there has nothing happened under the light of the sun and moon that I can tell you about, except it be our friend Napoleon's Congress and speech to the Chambers; but I suppose the Cuisinier will give you the benefit of his solemn judgment on that affair.[1] I came up to town the day before yesterday as usual, and have been busied with a heap of things, none of which are epistolary. It is astonishing even to me, how long I may remain in a place without growing to it. Friends! I have none, and my temper is now too bad ever to make another. Society! I know it not. Laziness, stupidity and self-distrust have shut its doors to me. It is wonderful—stupendous to consider, how a man who in his own mind is cool, witty, unaffected and high-toned, will disgust and mortify himself by every word he utters or act he does, when he steps out of his skin defences. Thus it has happened that now after five years of uninterrupted travel and mixing with the world, and after a steady residence of half that time in this place, surrounded by the thickest of the rush of society and fashion, I now find myself in London alone, without a house I care to go to, or a face I would ask to see. Melancholy, is it not! And yet I never was so contented since the last time I was in love and fancied like an idiot that man was a social animal.

Apropos to the Congress, you may perhaps be pleased to know that I am as ignorant on the matter as an Irishman. Of course my Club is a turmoil of excitement on the subject and there I should learn the daily news—war or peace—Congress or none—and so on. But although I believe I did once know an attaché, such is not the case now. My circle of acquaintance does not include any of the sources of information, and is restricted to a few English fellows, the farthest removed from political connection that I can find. You, my dear Brother Imperator, will probably sneer a bitter sneer at me for this neglect of opportunities. To skulk away like this, when I might make myself so necessary—so useful and so well-known! Truly, most noble Captain, such were also my ideas two years ago, and a damned little fool I was, as indeed I am still. But my present course is not entirely without system and justification. Your military experience has probably cured you of much of that letchery for publicity which always marks our young men. Here, of all places in the world, a man must guard himself from exposure, and must mind his own business. Moreover, the European powers are all socially connected and there is a bond of union among their representatives. We on the other hand are democrats, and you may be sure that in Europe a democrat is never and never can be really received into the circle of monarchists. In purposely keeping aloof therefore, and forestalling the people I meet, in maintaining a mysterious reserve on public affairs, I believe I can best maintain our own dignity and alone retain any good position.

We occasionally receive a letter from you but not very often. As Lee seems to have fairly gone off, I suppose my late fears of a battle were groundless, and yet how he can expect to make a Tennesee campaign at this season, I can't guess. But I do trust there will be no more advances in Virginia on our part. Any where else you please, but God forbid that we should swell the lists of Chickahominies, Bull Runs, Chancelorville's, Fredericksburgs and so on, by any new entries. Let us attack Virginia from the South and not go on filling that damned great grave-yard with northern bodies. Yet our latest news intimates a new advance by Meade. By the way, what does Rosecranz's removal and Meade's threatened removal mean![2] We are utterly in the skies about all this removing. Who does it? Wherefore? Why this mystery? What are we to think or desire? Stranger than all, no word of explanation has come to us as yet about Rosecranz, which is contrary to custom. I suspect greatly, and I have no confidence in Washington strategy.

MS: MHi

1. On Nov. 4 Napoleon III had proposed that a congress of European powers be held in Paris to discuss questions threatening their peaceful relations; CFA believed he was motivated by the instability of his own position in France. *Cuisinier:* CFA, called by HA the "Chief," or in French, the "Chef."

2. Rosecrans was removed after his defeat at Chickamauga. Gen. George Gordon Meade (1815–1872) was almost removed because he had not pursued Lee after Gettysburg and then had been outmaneuvered by him in the Bristoe campaign.

To Charles Francis Adams, Jr.

London. 20 Nov. 1863.

My dear Captain:

A late telegram has given us just a bare announcement of a sudden dash by Meade which seems to have had the effect of "gobbling" a brigade or so of Lee's army. Of course we are again very anxious to hear of your safety— of course the first thing we think of—and next, whether Lee will fight.[1] I fancy he would feel the want of Jackson now, for it must be somewhat the situation before Chancelorsville over again. But I don't believe he will fight. He could gain nothing even by defeating us, and if himself defeated, would spoil all his pudding.

We do not hear from you directly though John seems to have something later than our last. Perhaps your regiment has now reached that degree of tenuity that it's not perceptible. I amuse myself by fancying you executing a brilliant cavalry charge with your servant looking on from a neighboring eminence, and the two constituting between you the 1st Mass. Cav. Your company returns ought not to occupy a great deal of time.

Really one more great success would I think do for my interest in the war, external to that belonging to your affairs. It is now localised. One more step would reduce it to a struggle of reasonable dimensions. After that it must at best change to a slow social revolution which will outlast our lives. We shall never see the south thoroughly pacified. When this stage is reached, I think the war will become secondary to the social question, and to hunt robbers through cane-breaks will be your agreeable duty.

Of our life at St Leonard's I have very little to say. If the weather were anyway decent, it would be very enjoyable, but English weather at this season is simply infernal. Mary and I ride every day, as I suppose she writes in her epistles to you. To say the truth my life here is of little practical benefit to anyone except to her, and as she is something of a domestic tyrant in her way, I resign myself without a struggle to this state of things. Should I do myself or the family any more honor or advantage in another capacity? Que nenni![2]

At all events one thing is clear, and that is that the health of your mamma is amazingly improved by her quiet. So I am only too glad to remain down there although my trips up and down every week cost me near half my income. Fortunately my anti-social habits are favorable to economy; an advantage which alone would prejudice me in favor of a hermitage. Debt is of all things my horror, although I like as little as any man to have to count shillings.

Ritchie is back here again from Paris, full of his big guns. Much to his disgust, he has been chosen to the General Court. Old Ruggles also returns home with this letter. His son James has been quite ill for some weeks past.

Of all things here abroad nothing has caused us more gentle slumbers since the seizure of the iron-clads than the delicious state of tangle Europe has now arrived at. Nothing but panic in every direction and the strangest combination of cross-purposes you can conceive. The King of Denmark has just died with a clearly perverse purpose of increasing the confusion, and any day may see a Danish war.[3] Russia expects war and France acts as though it were unavoidable. Meanwhile England hulks about and makes faces at all the other nations. Our affairs are quite in the background, thank the Lord.

I am much pressed for time today. So have had to hurry. You say nothing in your letters about wanting newspapers sent you, or books, so I have sent none. In fact most of the books I would like to send are so large as to make it difficult. I receive no letters from the army now. People will all write in a crowd, I suppose.

Ever

MS: MHi

1. According to a telegraphic dispatch in the London *Times* on Nov. 18, Meade in an attack on Nov. 7 at Kelly's Ford, Va., took 800 prisoners and forced a Confederate retreat towards Culpeper. His advance was checked by Lee at Mine Run early in December.

2. *Que nenni!* Oh, no!

3. Because the late king, Frederick VII, was also duke of Schleswig-Holstein, Denmark claimed the duchy. England supported the new king, Christian IX (Alexandra's father), but was not prepared to intervene against Prussian force.

To Frederick William Seward

London. 20 Nov. 1863.

My dear Sir:

I write a line to ask you, if you have the time to remember us at the meeting of Congress, to favor us with as liberal a number of the Secretary of State's documents as may be convenient to you. By "us," I of course don't mean to speak for the Legation, though no doubt your publications will properly go to it. In the course of time, however, one picks up private acquaintances who are apt to make interest for this volume, and naturally I fear that the few copies I am tempted to steal on my own or my father's private account, may be rather too much missed.

To one who has worried through the autumns of the two last years in this country, the freedom from anxiety which has blessed us since the seizure of the iron rams is a sensation so new as to be very agreeable. And now that matters look so black on the continent, one breathes with a freedom that has not been felt for three years, and an American may flatter himself that the time will soon come when his importance in Euope will be guaranteed. This may seem very little to you at home who have been backed up by public opinion, but it is everything to those who have known what England can do in the way of abuse.

Pray remember me to your family very warmly. We are anxious to hear of the recovery of your brother, whose health has been reported upon by Sir Henry Holland to us. The old gentleman has himself been very much shaken lately by an attack of fever, though I've not been able to learn how he has passed the last week as I have been out of town. I doubt however whether even the combined skill of your father, Mr Weed and Mr Everett,[1] has been quite successful in clearing the nonsense out of his head on our American question.

If you should see Mr Weed and should remember to give him my respects, I would be gratified. We hear very little of him. We had hoped to see Mr Evarts again as the Alexandra case came on, but perhaps he is too much disgusted with what he saw of Sir William Atherton and Chief Baron Pollock last summer.[2] He would find a great improvement in tone now.

We are looking at last to the day of return as not far off. Hoping to see you some day or other, none the worse for your trials in the State Department, I am

Very truly Yrs   H. B. Adams.

F. W. Seward Esq.

1. Everett was minister to England 1841–1845; long acquaintance thus made him useful as a semiofficial spokesman when Holland visited the U.S.

2. Sir William Atherton (1806–1864) participated as attorney general in the *Alexandra* case, over which Pollock had presided.

To Charles Francis Adams, Jr.

London. 27 Nov. 1863.

My dear Captain:

We received this week your two letters of 29th October and 5th Nov. for which we were very grateful. Your trials have my earnest sympathy, but I hope they are now drawing to a close. Mr Lawley's last letter to the London Times from the rebel army at Chickamauga, is chaotic. He says it took him forty hours to go by rail the hundred and thirty miles from Atlanta to Chattanooga, in the filthiest, meanest cars he ever saw. They are wearing out, down there. Do you observe how they have concentrated. They meet us only at points now, and our cavalry cut into their sides and meet no resistance. A few plunges more! Some desperate kicking that will yet disturb our nerves, and I trust the end will come. They are looking for it here, and the worthy British people are turning their eyes away from the gashed and mangled giant whom their aristocracy wished so much to see successful.

Meanwhile you cannot conceive how differently we feel here in these days. There is no longer any perpetual bickering and sharp prodding necessary to exasperate this Government into doing its duty. All is oil and spikenard; attar-of-rose and eau-sucré. I haven't succeeded in getting my eyes shut yet at the astounding energy with which they are making war here on the rebel outfits of vessels. Every day I am bewildered by new instances of the radical change of policy. Certainly the rebs put their foot very far into it, when they assumed such a high tone here against the Government, and if their policy is sound, then I'm sorry that their case is so hard. Ah! but to us it is the pleasure of the Gods to put off our heavy burden, and lie beside our nectar, looking down oer wasted lands, blight and famine, plague and earthquake, roaring deeps and fiery sands, clanging fights and flaming towns, and sinking ships and praying hands. Oh! we smile; we find a music centred in the doleful song.[1]

Meanwhile, the cloud that seems at length to be breaking away and letting sunlight over us, is settling down darker and darker over Europe. England has refused to join the Congress; so that chance is over. I am no Solomon, but such as I am, I read the English reply as the elegy over the entente cordiale. Napoleon must have allies. If England won't, then who will! Germany won't; that we all know! Italy alone is not enough. Evidently the Emperor has no choice! He *must* draw up to Russia, and if he and Russia once declare that the Polish question and the Eastern question go hand in hand, and that free Poland means Russian Turkey; then there'll be the devil to pay in Europe, and you'll see a row in which the democracy is sure to come up in the end! That is the problem of the day; and I consider that Europe has practically already declared that our rebels must expect no aid or countenance from here, with such emergencies staring kings and aristocracies in the face.

We had here yesterday a Thanksgiving dinner in obedience to the President's Proclamation.[2] The Minister made a speech; as usual a very clever one. I will try to send you a copy. I suppose the report of the whole affair will be printed in a pamphlet, which I will some day send you. I believe the overseers would have had the brass to call me out; but I am rayther too bald an old bird to be made a fool of by such clumsy bait; I came away early. With regard to private affairs, all moves on as usual. Mary and I scour the coast of Sussex and have races on the turf of the cliffs. I ought to go down there this evening but shall remain up here in order to dine with one of my English aristocrats. On such occasions, I always wish that you or John were in my place. I am such a stick in society.

Is it fight or not? I hope not. No more battles in Virginia! I congratulate you however on the clever way in which you managed to boot Mr Lee across the Rappahanock.

Ever

MS: MHi
    1. Tennyson, "The Lotos-Eaters" (1832).
    2. President Lincoln's proclamation of Oct. 3 established Thanksgiving as a national holiday. The dinner at St. James's Hall was attended by 150 Americans; the opening prayer was said by Sella Martin, a former slave.

To Charles Francis Adams, Jr.

St Leonard's on Sea.
Thursday. 3 Dec. 1863.

My dear Captain:

As I don't go up to town till tomorrow, I shall this week indite my epistle to you from here, where a regular hurricane is raging and I have nothing to do but to read Hallam.[1] Next week we shall return to our duties, and bid farewell to the quiet of the sea-shore. On my own account I shall be well satisfied to return to town, but I would not be sorry to keep the family down here all winter. You've no conception how much easier it makes existence. Just now, however, as your other letters probably have told you, there is much excitement in the family on account of a visit from you which is strongly hoped for in January. This has served to give interest to the prospect for the winter and I much hope you will find the plan feasible. As you are the best judge of what is for your own advantage and pleasure, I don't undertake to supply you with arguments from that point of view, but merely urge the fact that by coming over you will be of considerable assistance and benefit to us, collectively and individually. However, they have all so set their minds upon it, that if you refuse the chance, there will be a row that I dread to contemplate. In fact we all need you, and you must not let any small difficulties stand in your way.

Things are going on politically here from complication to confusion. Not that our own affairs are essentially changed, though this last week has been more lively than usual, owing to the rebs having bought a Government war-steamer and sent her out of a Government dock-yard to cruise against us.[2] This was cleverly done but I doubt whether it was good policy, any more than the other measures they've adopted of late towards England, which are calculated to throw the Ministry a good deal onto our side. I fancy this performance will only strengthen Lord Russel's hands, should he come before Parliament with his new neutrality bill.

But meanwhile the devil only knows what will happen on the Continent. Certain it is that there is already a violent pressure in the money market, which approaches a panic, and I should not be surprised if something were to blow up before long. People are uneasy enough, and with reason. If you come over you will probably see a curious state of things.

London, having nothing else to do, rings with the Palmerstonian scandal. Ballad-singers howl a dismal song under the windows of the noble Lord. A copy of it was read with infinite delight at a dinner I was at the other evening, and I shall take care that it is properly known on our side, in return for the many scandals sent over from Washington by the young Englishmen who reside there, like your friend Brodie, who, by-the-bye, bears no good character here and is now at Rio Janeiro.

London. 4 Dec. I have nothing very new to add this morning except that the financial crisis is going on and pressing people hard. It looks to me as though there would be plenty for Europe to think of for some time to come without troubling us.

By next Friday we shall all be again domesticated in town. I suppose we shall pass our Christmas at Walton as usual, and it is proposed to make a visit to Paris in January. Should you come over, it will be just the thing for you to go over to Tweelerie Street with the caravan. At least, I suppose you would like to see Paris, and you needn't expect that you will be allowed to escape the affectionate attentions of your beloved parients and sister and brother; so you must either go about with them or not at all. I have strong reasons for believing that Bridgets expects to bring you a glass of wine-whey every night at half after nine o'clock when she comes in to tuck you up.

Ever

MS: MHi
   1. Henry Hallam (1777–1859), *The Constitutional History of England* (1827).

2. With the connivance of the master rigger at Sheerness, H.M.S. *Victor* was fitted and manned for the Confederates and put to sea as the *Rappahannock*.

To Charles Francis Adams, Jr.

London. 11 Dec. 1863.

My dear Captain:

Our souls were raised up to mirth and rejoicing beyond our wont by the news of what I take to be practically the raising the siege of Chattanooga. The results of that success cannot, as I take it, by any means as yet be fixed, beyond this point, that the siege is raised. Should the reports of the rout of Bragg's army be true, which we hear, but to which I give as yet only such limited credence as the result may hereafter justify, I suppose Davis will be forced again to contract his lines and give up either Georgia or Virginia. Meanwhile we wait with some natural anxiety to hear of the result of your advance; not that I believe Lee will fight now. If you couldn't get a fight out of him before, certainly nothing but the clearest necessity will make him fight now. But I suppose there must be some sharp marching, plenty of skirmishing, and a change of base. At all events, if you don't pass January with us, I hope you will be picketting some line far to the south of the Rapidan.

The success at Chattanooga has had a very considerable effect here, and the English papers acknowledge it to be an important advantage in a military point of view, though of course it only makes the ultimate independence of the South more certain than ever.[1] A better test is the state of the Confederate loan, which under the pressure of the news and the tightness of the money market, has fallen to 35–40. It is only some eight months ago that it was brought out at 92. So that we may at length conclude that the opinion among capitalists is fairly become that the chances are against the independence of the rebels. Meanwhile the financial pressure that I mentioned last week has been checked. I don't see much reason to suppose that this is more than a lull, and I'm quite sure that if our armies could suddenly release and send over here a million bales of cotton or so, half England would be ruined. Of course our own position here is now as comfortable as could be wished, and a victory or so more, will set us in a position to put the grand finishing stroke to our work. I hope that before next September the English Government will have seen fit to recall its belligerent proclamation, and all our ports will be open again, or occupied. When this point is reached, I think our return to peaceful and private pursuits would be graceful and opportune.

Here we are, all of us, again in London. The sea-side is already a dream, though only twenty four hours old. For my own part, I am devilish glad of it, as the weekly trips to town were deuced expensive, and the trips to St

Leonard's broke one's work all to pieces. But don't whisper this to anyone, or I shall catch a week's row.

As we only came up yesterday, I have seen no one and have heard no news that would interest you. Things as yet have taken no decisive turn on the continent. We shall soon see, I fancy, which way Napoleon means to strike. My own belief is that we shall have a jolly blow-up, and shall be all the better for it.

George Bangs came to see me the other day. He is now on his way home in better health, he says; and hopes to be married. Col. Curtis, I see, is married. Bangs either constitutionally or through the influence of his weak condition, is, like most Potomac-army officers that ever I saw or heard from, disposed to look on his own affairs and those of the world in general, through rather brown media; and that is an amusement that I generally prefer to reserve to myself, because I can do it on a more universal and radical scale than anyone else. I cheered him up with the first instalment of news from Chattanooga. The eminently respectable Sol Lincoln has also lately paid me a visit; did I mention the fact? George Lyman too is here, on his way home.[2] I don't much fancy his appearance, but India isn't a nice place for a man. By the way, I'm very much puzzled not to hear from Henry Higginson. Did he ever get that letter I sent to him through you? His last to me seemed to think that I was offended at being asked to do a commission for him, so that I infer you never told him how many months you kept that document in your pocket.

Ever.

MS: MHi

1. Grant defeated Bragg, Nov. 24. The London *Times,* quoting an American newspaper, stated that as the South was "a step nearer subjugation, it is a step further from reunion" (Dec. 9).

2. Solomon Lincoln (1838–1907) of Hingham, Mass., law student and tutor in Harvard College. George Theodore Lyman (1822–1908) of a Boston textile family engaged in eastern trade.

To Frederick William Seward

London. 11 Dec. 1863.

My dear Sir:

The young gentlemen of the English Legation at Washington didn't spare us here any of the little bits of gossip that they used to pick up in regard to the White House formerly, and send over for the benefit of the London Clubs. I don't know why we should be any more charitable than they, and perhaps the inclosed poetic effusion may amuse the Washingtonians.[1] It was given to me by an English lady of pretty high rank, with whom I was dining, on the understanding that it should go to America, after it had been sung with tremendous applause by her husband. So that its respectability is guaranteed. As nothing else has been talked of in society for a couple of months, the poem has had a prodigious run, and is sung about the streets and under Lord Palmerston's windows. I know of one case in which it was produced at his table; naturally without his knowledge. To you it may probably appear horrible doggerel; but to an Englishman who knows the parties, it is immensely ludicrous; and the definition of the Premier as having "one foot in the grave and the other not far out" is as true to nature as the description of poor Lady P. is laughable.[2]

As to the merits of the case itself, whatever they are we may be sure that my Lord will have the better of them. Nothing will come of it. But the Conservatives maintain stoutly that the charge itself is true, and that the proofs are to be had. This would be by no means the first time the same gentleman has been known to have been in a similar position except the publicity, so that from a moral point of view there is little defense to be made.

Personally I believe of course that the whole thing is a vile slander and a wicked conspiracy. But pray don't mention that I placed this curious document in your possession.

The good Sir Henry tells me he has received a letter from your father praising highly the conduct of Lord Russell. Your father may be very sure that his words will reach all Sir H's numerous circle of acquaintance, inclusive of Earl Russell himself.

Very truly Yrs   H. B. Adams.

F. W. Seward Esq.

MS: NRU
   1. The enclosure was a broadside ballad on the latest Palmerston scandal.
   2. Lady Palmerston is described as once "A tender bit of lamb / But now she's getting old and tough."

To Charles Francis Adams, Jr.

London. 18 Dec. 1863.

My dear Captain:

Nothing, I imagine, could be emptier than the ordinary run of letters you receive from here in these days. What indeed is there to tell you? We do nothing. Life is merely a habit, so far as we are concerned, and it is the toughest of all work to describe or enliven a habit. I don't want to talk about the war, yet what else is there to mention. The Chief, I know is at this instant describing to you at his table over there, the Westminster play that we went to last night together, where he and the Archbishop of Canterbury were seated side by side in the front row, the dignitaries of the occasion. I was amused with the performance and came to the conclusion that the

Greeks and Romans knew precious little about play-writing, however clever they were in other matters. In many respects however the piece shows a state of society quite ahead of our own. I could wish that we could return to the excellence of their primitive views respecting the relations between the sexes for instance. But our age is hopelessly lost.[1]

The letter of Mr Lawley which I inclose to you, will probably have been published in the American papers before you receive this. The truth is, it tells us more than I had ever hoped. Mr Lawley is demoralised. On the question of Meade's fighting, he is as you perceive, of our opinion, and I was therefore the more pleased to see that the General had saved us from another Fredericsburg. I suppose Meade will be removed. Nothing indeed can surprise me since the removal of Rosecranz, and I fully expect that our eastern army will in the end be utterly disorganised by this repeated interference of the War Department. In the end Stanton must be turned out, but he has been probably as bad a Secretary of War as circumstances allowed him to be, and if he can deprive us of success, he will. Lawley says distinctly that it takes weeks to transfer a single corps to the West, and that cooperation does not exist between the armies. This being the case I had hoped to hear that we had brought half Grant's army to Virginia to cut between Lee and Richmond while Meade held him on the flank. But I fear the opportunity is gone. From Lawley's intimations, I have no doubt that we could put two armies into Virginia, each nearly double Lee's force, before he could get a division from the South.

Pazienza! Nur ruhig zu! Meade, whether removed or not, has my sympathies, and I believe him to have done us more good by avoiding a great battle than if he had done as Burnside did and fought against his judgment.[2] We see that your regiment suffered severely. So little must be left of it now that I am really in hopes you'll be able to come over as we wish in January.

Life flows on here in such an equable, peaceful way that I really believe we shall go ahead till we wake up some morning and find ourselves quietly dead in a green old age. We are rooted here thoroughly. Your mamma has found a new set of friends who insist upon kissing her just as the women used to do in Boston, and the Chief, if he has no set of intimates like the immortal trio of Boston, is still contented and placable.[3] As for me, my old tendencies grow on me more and more. If we lived a thousand years ago instead of now, I should have become a monk and would have got hold as Abbot of one of those lovely little monasteries which I used to admire so much among the hills in Italy. Those who choose to play the Luther may try it for all me. They had better let it alone in my opinion, for the universe is rather too big to be so precisely guaged by their yard-stick. I prefer the character of Luther's friend, Melancthon wasn't it, for my own part, and the difficulties that can't be conquered by plain reason had better be left to that weapon till they can.[4]

All which is written to fill up a page in want of anything else to say, as well as because, you being a man purely of action are bound to call it all damned nonsense.

MS: MHi
1. The boys at Westminster School performed Terence's *Adelphi*.
2. At Fredericksburg, Nov.–Dec. 1862.
3. The trio were Richard Henry Dana, John Gorham Palfrey, and Charles Sumner.
4. Philipp Melanchthon (1497–1560), scholarly collaborator of the militant Martin Luther.

To Henry Lee Higginson

London. 18 Dec. 1863.

My dear Major:

You wrote to me last May asking me to order some clothes. My brother Charles kept your letter three months in his pocket and it reached me in August when I was in Scotland. So soon as I came back to town I ordered the garments and at the same time wrote a letter to you on the 11th of September explaining the delay. But before either the clothes or the letter could have reached you, I received a second epistle from you, from which I infer that you think I feel my dignity damaged by being asked to do a commission. *Keineswegs,* mein Feld Mareschal! But as I hoped you would in the interim receive my letter of Sept. 11th (sent also through Charles), I delayed answering yours of September in the hope of again hearing from you.

Not having had that pleasure, I resume my letter-paper. And first of all, let me say one word as to your announcement to me. As a general principle and in the most offensive sense of the word, I consider him who marries to be an unmitigated and immitigable ignoramus and ruffian. In your particular case, however, I incline to the opinion that there are palliating circumstances. I have not the honor of knowing Miss Agassiz, though I have an indistinct recollection of once seeing her somewhere.[1] But I have heard a great deal about her, from an early youth, and this has induced me to believe that she is a person whom weakminded men like you and me, instantaneously, profoundly and irredeemably adore. Probably I shall have some occasion to tell her so, some day, if ever a misguided Providence permits me to go home. Meanwhile I only hope that your life won't be such an eternal swindle as most life is, and that having succeeded in getting a wife so much above the common run, you will succeed in leading an existence worth having. If I knew your fiancée, I should congratulate her upon getting for a husband one of the curiously small number of men whom I have ever seen, for whom I have morally a certain degree of respect. This perhaps wouldn't be quite so enthusiastic praise as one might give, but it's more than I ever said of anyone else. The truth is, a good many of my acquaintances have been getting engaged lately, and I believe your's is the only case that has made me really, sincerely glad to hear about.

Under these circumstances I have a favor to beg of you—or of her, if necessary. It is that you will give me photographs of you both. I do not know what latitude is now allowed in America to photograph-giving, but if you choose, the likenesses shall go into my sister's book and be called hers. They will do us honor and shall be pointed out to Dukes and democrats. I shall be greatly pleased and flattered if you will do me this kindness.

Col. Ritchie gave me the first real information I had about your wound, for Charles's letters are few and short in campaigning, and as for Boston correspondents, I doubt whether in the whole city a single person ever takes the trouble to remember the existence of a five-year absentee. To this day I never have heard what has become of Jim since his capture at Aldie, nor have I the least idea whether he has yet been exchanged or not. Now, my long residence in England has not increased the very small number of friends I ever had, and it would be gratifying to hear occasionally what has become of the old ones. I see no reason why you shouldn't be heard from unless your wound is still too bad. Do try and send me a little good news.

Your first informed me that your home was in future to be with the regiment and that you hoped after the war to run over here again for a visit. Your last announced your engagement and countermanded the clothes you had ordered. Am I to understand that you have changed your mind as to a military life? As the clothes had already gone, I couldn't countermand them and can only hope they arrived all right.

The war progresses. I'm glad Meade didn't fight. Let's have no more battles north of the James. We stand here with our noses pretty high in the air now.

Ever Yrs   Henry B. Adams.

MS: MH
    1. On Dec. 3 Higginson married Ida Agassiz (1837–1935), who was the daughter of the Swiss-born Harvard naturalist Louis Agassiz, teacher and friend of HA, Theodore Lyman, and William James.

To John Bright

5, Upper Portland Place.
19 Dec. 1863.

My dear Mr Bright:

I suppose you have had or will have copies of your famous speech printed for distribution, in some form or other. In such a case, may I beg for one, as I have lost the Times which contained it.[1]

You made there some statements as to population; the number of paupers; the rental of the houses of the lower classes, and the like. I am curious

Mary Adams

Brooks Adams

to know whether these were founded on your own knowledge, or on any publication that combines a tolerably good view of such matters. Poor law returns and census estimates leave me no wiser than before.

I don't suppose you care much what Mr Delane says about you, either in or out of the Times.[2] Still I believe I may venture to congratulate you on the very severe scoring Mr Cobden has given him. Of course "society" is shocked at Mr C's asperity, and does its best to shield Delane; but his position is too absurd to protect him long, I imagine.

Very sincerely Yrs   Henry B. Adams

John Bright Esq.

MS: The British Library, John Bright Papers
1. At Rochdale, Nov. 24, Bright advocated manhood suffrage, free public education, and wider distribution of land and argued that American institutions derived their strength from such policies.
2. John Thadeus Delane (1817–1879), editor of the London *Times* 1841–1877.

To Charles Francis Adams, Jr.

London. 24 Dec. 1863.

My dear Captain:

All this week we have been worried half to death by the coming of Christmas. The mental friction required to select a quantity of Christmas presents, is no joke. Mary wanted a ring with her monogram stamped on it, or rather cut upon it, and there has been more consultation, discussion and exploration on account of this tremendous article than the most important week's work we ever did in the office, ever came to. Finally it is done to her satisfaction and I suppose she will give you the benefit of an impression. Then your brother Brooks has come home for the holidays. The young miscreant is taller now than I am, and eruptive in countenance as you and I were. He's a clumsy, good-natured, nice-looking boy so far as expression goes, and to my profound astonishment and his father's very considerable satisfaction, he has of late taken quite an industrious turn, and developed a taste for Mathematics and Milton's Paradise Lost. I think that with good luck and copious licking, something may be made of him yet, though boys of that age are such shapeless cubs that you can't tell how they'll turn out. The improvement is great however; but you would die laughing to see how English he is. He has all the accent and turn of phrase; and indeed we have all of us caught this a good deal. I always hesitate and stammer like a Lord, in talking, and talk about an "awful swell" and "such a funk" as calmly as though I were native to the language. I expect to excite the derision of the natives when we return to Beacon Street, and can hear already the lovely young women imitate what they will be pleased to call my snobbishness. The poor Brooks will be martyred at Cambridge. Home he has come, however, with a pile of prize books, and discourses to me largely and sufficiently sensibly on general topics. I have a sort of an idea that he comes to me as to a sort of exercise, and sharpens his polemics on my mind, in order to get the ideas which he is to use at school. At any rate my wisdom seems to fructify and take root in his mind, for I detect my language cropping out occasionally. Occasionally I am put into rather a tight position, for he attacks subjects upon which my mind is certainly sufficiently made up, but unhappily does not by any means tally with what all good boys must believe. So, as I don't undertake to express my opinions, and on the same basis require other people to leave them alone, I can neither give the youth information or advice, nor yet refuse to give it.

All the family go out to Walton this afternoon, and I follow them to eat my Christmas dinner there tomorrow. Mrs Sturgis, you know, is one of my favorites. She takes the place of what Mrs Bigelow used to be. And as she has been gracious enough to be very kind to me, (God knows why, for I neither amuse nor ornament her drawing-room) I shut my eyes and hold my tongue as to her faults and foibles. She is a charming woman as women go; fond of luxury, eating, drinking, and display; and so am I, sarpedieu! Why not? Only I can't afford it. She is hospitable as her house is large and tolerant and goodnatured as few people are in the world. I am happier in her house than anywhere else. I have repeatedly taken refuge there when disagreeable things were making London a smokey hell, and I never failed to get back my courage and spirits there, and forget the storm for a day or two, just when the need of rest was greatest. You may however justly conclude from my account of the mistress, that your pa and ma are not exactly the people to admire the pattern, even though their minds have developed considerably within three years. Accordingly we differ in our tastes quietly; not that we have many words about it. If I were to maintain in argument the points of difference between myself and the elders, my residence with them would be brief. But we differ. And accordingly this Christmas period is about the only time when they are induced to go to Walton. To be sure the Chief has other good reasons for not going much there, but perhaps they might be conquered if it were not for private uneasy rubbings. You know however how far he is from happiness when he is torn from his own hearth.

We have no letter from you for several weeks. I hope we shall soon hear that you're on your way to us.

Ever

MS: MHi

6.

"Silent and Expectant"

1864–1865

In February 1864, when their young cavalry captain, on recuperative leave, joined the Adams family in London, the war seemed almost over. But Charles returned to active duty with the Army of the Potomac, and by May he was taking part in the bitterly fought Wilderness campaign. In London, although at times the end of the war was foreseeable, uncertainty was the usual fare. Minister Adams expected an early recall—perhaps because the victory would come, perhaps because McClellan would be turning the Lincoln administration out of office.

Still, American affairs were no longer at the center of the London stage, and the pace did ease. Besides copying documents, Henry Adams had time to study political economy, to analyze Grant's campaign in Virginia and Sherman's in Georgia, and to sample the pleasures of country life. At the end of September the Adamses moved to Hanger Hill, the country house near Ealing where they took refuge from the smoky fog of the London autumn. Henry Adams was thus able to exchange visits with his friend Gaskell, going for the first time to Wenlock Abbey, the Gaskells' recently acquired place in Shropshire.

In February 1865 the private secretary became a "hybrid courier-nurse" in charge of his family's travels on the Continent. He punctiliously reported to his father the health complaints of his mother, sister, and younger brother and the day-to-day expenses. To his brother Charles, he reported humorously on his Italian "campaign" and exultantly on receiving news of the long-awaited fall of Richmond. He also learned, when a telegram from London brought word of Lincoln's assassination, what it meant to be shocked beyond expression.

The darker news subdued his spirits only briefly. If an epoch was over, then it was time to look ahead. In England, in the summer of 1865 the influence of democratic and thus, in young Adams' mind, American ideals seemed assured as John Stuart Mill and Thomas Hughes, two of the men he most admired, won seats in Parliament. For himself, he was aware that he regarded the future with more zest than his father and that intellectually they were becoming less close. He seemed on the point of breaking away from the legation and beginning an independent career.

To Charles Francis Adams, Jr.

London. 1 January. 1864.

My dear Captain:

So there goes the "3" with a "4" written over it. I've just returned this morning from Walton where for the third time we saw the old year out and the New Year in, last night. It makes me feel devilish blue. We wait in the billiard-room, boys and girls and men and women, rather more than a dozen this time, chattering, chaffing, flirting, billiard-playing and smoking, while the bells all over the country are ringing, until the clock strikes, and we gather to the open windows and listen in silence till the last stroke; and then begins universal handshaking, kissing, and "Happy New Year Henry"; "Happy New Year, Mrs Sturgis"; "Happy New Year Julian, Harry, Mary," and so on.[1] Bright and gay; kind and affectionate; healthy and happy; by the eternal symbol of the prophet, I always suck my whiskey-and-water with a gulp after this ceremony, and curse me if I don't feel very like crying. Each time there's less chance of it's happening again. We are dancing in the air always, and God knows where any breath may blow us. It isn't that I care so much to repeat the same experience, as it is the satisfaction at looking back, and the vague dread and helplessness of the future, that makes me feel such a shiver over the instant that tides us beyond a new sounding. I don't find that age has impressed me with much sense of power. I feel more the creature of the present than I used, and care little to think of the chances for the coming time.

There is another ceremony at Walton which is always formally carried out. At dinner every one is made to fill up his glass, and we drink solemnly to the health of "Absent Friends." This is also particularly a holiday custom and it is pretty hard for any one to go through it without some sense of its meaning.

Well, my boy; I've had another pleasant Christmas, and here I am back again at the old shop. You will draw the contrast quickly enough between my Christmas and your own. You may be sure we have felt it too, and hope next year will see a more satisfactory state of things. Meanwhile I hope long before then, we shall have met again.

Meanwhile, I suppose if you still retain your old literary tastes, the news which the last steamer carried out of poor Thackeray's death will trouble you.[2] I did not fancy him alive, but the difficulty was natural enough. I set him too high as a man and wasn't willing to allow for the failings that are human. It is so hard to distinguish between the ideal and the concrete, and to help badgering a poor devil like ourselves for faults that we should never have noticed unless he had written a book. Besides we all of us have a perfect right to our faults, and for my own part I claim at least the right to have my business let alone by other people if they will be so good. Poor Thackeray had more friends than most of his enemies ever will have.

Our last news from you is through John, who appears to be in a regular bog about his own affairs, and writes in addition that you have been run out of your camp and lost everything. We wait for particulars. I am afraid you must have had a hard time of it, and am rather anxious to hear that it's all right again. I suppose you must have lost your papers too, and I rather anticipate seeing some of my letters published in extenso in a southern newspaper. They would have some pretty stupid reading if they were.

I suppose your mother and Mary will write you all about the way we passed our time out at our Christmas residence, and who was there with us. Col. Ritchie and his wife were there several days, and the Major of the Massachusetts 53d (was it?) being over here on a visit with his children, gave us the benefit of his society. I grew a boy again, and dropped ten years of my life in order to play battle dore and shuttlecock, and race across country with the young 'uns. We all, that is, the Major and seven of us boys and girls, went off on the drag one day to see grey-hounds course hares in the Home Park at Hampton Court. Another day we went to a meet of the harriers and didn't see the run. We had a Christmas party of children, and kissing under the mistletoe, where Mrs Sturgis, as she declares, kissed me, and the Major responded upon your mamma and Mr S. kissed everybody, as he always does. And so we go; and Ah! such dinners! You must eat one!

MS: MHi
1. The children of Russell Sturgis and his third wife, Julia Boit Sturgis, were Julian Russell (1848–1904), Henry Parkman (b. 1847), Mary Greene (b. 1851), and Howard Overing (1855–1920).
2. William Makepeace Thackeray died Dec. 23, aged 52.

To Charles Francis Adams, Jr.

London. 15 January. 1864.

My dear Captain:

We have sent away our females to Paris this week where they now are, and I am to follow them next Tuesday. I trust that this experience will terminate all our wanderings, and leave us to begin work again with the Spring. I shouldn't wonder if another year found me at home again with life to begin at twenty-seven! So that what remains to us here is reasonably short.

This week has been rather a busy one, what with one duty and another, as well as a steady atmosphere of yellow coal-smoke which however does not always prevent one's seeing as far as the opposite side of the street. But the most amusing experience I have had, was at a dinner with one of the City Companies, the old Guilds you know, at their Hall down in the heart of London. One of my acquaintances in society asked me to dine there with him, he being a member; and I accepted with pleasure, as I was curious to see the style. So down we went one evening, three of us, and made our appearance in a party of about a hundred and fifty individuals including the Lord Mayor. It was a curious place; a fine old hall, wainscoted and hung about with pictures and decorations. I was immensely delighted with discovering our ancient acquaintance Dick Whittington there, a shining light; without his cat; but dignified as a dozen Lord Mayors.[1] The dinner was *ausgezeichnet* as the Dutchmen used to say; deuced good; and so were the wines and lots of them. In fact, the style of the good Corporation of Mercers so far as their feed went, was unexceptionable; and I eat two plates of real turtle soup, with serene satisfaction, calipash and all. Our third friend however, took too much wine, and so did a curious and simple snob opposite to us. All of a sudden, to my profound astonishment, a violent altercation sprang up across the table, and each party began to vituperate the other like a Shoreditch cabman. Both parties declared that they were grossly insulted, and the gentleman in the retail haberdashery business opposite, my curious snob, who was very drunk and a Mercer, insisted upon dilating in a loud voice on the personal attractions of our man, thus driving him into the most insane rage. He also happily touched off my character, apparently noticing that I was observing him with pleased curiosity. Having rather failed in an attempt to stare me out of countenance, he burst into a loud laugh, and remarked that I was "a good fellow but damned ugly." Ye Gods! what a delicious specimen of the City Snob it was!

We sat through the dinner, glaring over the table, but rose early and retired. Our opposite neighbors rose with us, and met us in the ante-room. Of course there was a fight, you will think! No such matter, my boy! As I was acquitted by them of any share in the matter, I stood on one side and looked on. The others went in, and for half an hour raised an infernal row, scandalising all the old gentlemen who said that nothing of the sort had ever occurred before, since Whittington was drunk there in the year two thousand and fifty five before Christ. Our man reviled the Mercerian snob with every species of contumely. He told him that he was a damned shopkeeping snob; that he might send in his bill at Christmas; and finally he descended to the lowest cloaca of abuse and called him by an epithet applied only to the descendents of the destroyed cities of the plain.[2] This seemed to settle it. I had supposed that nothing short of a fight could wash out so diabolical an insult. But instead of a blow, our red-whiskered Mercer at once shook hands all round, and became as friendly as possible. He was perfectly satisfied with the explanations which were refused. He was delighted with the apology that he couldn't get. And as for the epithets, he had returned them!

I was keenly gratified with all this, and tried in vain to decide whether my man or the Mercer were the more wonderful specimen of Snobisma Anglicanum. I am still meditating this point. It was an experience which was far too good to be lost, for studying the character of our charming cousins.

We wait expectantly to hear of your start.[3]

Ever.

MS: MHi
1. Sir Richard Whittington (1359–1423), Lord Mayor of London.
2. Sodom and Gomorrah, Genesis 19.
3. CFA2 was given a 70-day leave, partly because his was the one company in the regiment to reenlist; he was also recuperating from "enteric troubles" which had finally incapacitated him. He arrived in England, Feb. 16, went to Paris, March 5, for a week with HA and William M. Evarts, and returned to the U.S., April 6.

To John Gorham Palfrey

London. 15 January. 1864.

My dear Mr Palfrey:

Your very kind letter of August 8th, has been on my table ever since, and has been unanswered only because I had nothing on earth to say. Since the seizure of the iron-clads our repose has been so little disturbed by the old worry of anxious times, that we are beginning to think it very dull, and I am in hopes of seeing my father begin to meditate a final retreat from this wilderness of coal-smoke. Not that I dislike the life, or that he does. But merely to vindicate to a pacifying degree our consciousness of free will.

Nothing could be more quiet than our existence here. I see no reason why we mightn't do in Boston all that is done here, and much better. There is to be sure a certain amount of official business, but there is no diplomatic society; no close relations with anyone, and only a quiet kind of occupied existence, just as would be the case at home or in Rome or Paris.

I am however all the more willing to look forward to our departure, because it seems to me that the time is coming when our relations with this country will be rather difficult to maintain. The points of collision between them are thick as possible; claims, remonstrances, complaints; all kept under only by the deadly fear each party entertains of the other. But the gradual restoration of the Union, which seems to be tolerably probable, will not only be the signal for a rise in our tone, but will, I think, be simultaneous with a general republican movement in Europe. Things move slowly, indeed, and what seems to me likely to take shape within eighteen months, may swallow as many years; but since '48 the Reds have never been so active and confident, while the late elections in France and Prussia have startled Europe by proving that the democratic feeling is stronger than ever. I don't do our English aristocratic friends the wrong to suppose them conscious of this, but they are conscious of the uneasy feeling it causes, and hence their passion for peace. A war could not benefit any but the Reds. Now, should such a state of things rise, with our renewed strength and innumerable sources of quarrel with England, the position of Minister here would be intolerable.

People bother themselves here about war in Denmark, as they did about war in Poland, and try to stop it. It seems to me pure nonsense. Everyone knows that those are merely external symptoms. There is no one who will not confess that these troubles are caused by the great liberal action which is overflowing Europe, and which breaks out at those points because they're the open spots. But if bandaged up there, it will break out elsewhere more dangerously. And yet, instead of meeting the real question which is one of simple political reform, they go distracted about this, that and the other pimple or sore.

You will laugh at my political philosophy, as I'm ready to do myself if it will do any good. But you know my opinion of the English mind. England fulfils a very important function in the world. She is the stomach which takes all that the brain procures for it, and makes a prodigious fuss; declares the food is bad, and the brain crazy; and ends by digesting and existing on it. By the brain of England, I mean France. This will appear to you, I fear, little better than rank infidelity.

We are full of hopes of seeing Captain Charles very soon. For six months I have had the honor of meeting no one. Lord Houghton remains at Frystone. I've tried to read his poems. Lord Wensleydale is very gouty.[1] My people have been staying with him. Mr Jo. Parkes is as hard to talk with, as he usually is, but was much troubled by the death of Edward Ellice who was his patron. Mr Froude continues his history, which I haven't read;[2] and poor Mr Thackeray is dead too.

Pray remember me to all your family and believe me &c &c &c

H. B. Adams.

Many thanks for your kind notice of Captain Jo. Smith. I have done with the old pirate, I believe, but should hesitate a long time before attacking so respected a gentleman, as a coup d'essai in print.

MS: MH
1. James Parke (1782–1868), Baron Wensleydale, a judge of the court of exchequer 1834–1855.
2. James Anthony Froude (1818–1894), *History of England*, 12 vols. (1856–1870).

To Charles Francis Adams, Jr.

[London, 15? April 1864]

[*The first part of the letter is missing.*] While this has formed the great and pervading amusement of the week, our other divergations have been yet occasional. My Sunday at Walton was very calm. We drank your health (even I too) and were peaceful and verdant. On returning to town I found all mankind gone mad about Garibaldi, whose arrival was the signal for a tremendous demonstration of the sans-culottes. Wednesday night the Duchess of Sutherland, who has acted as chief bear-ward, had a rout at Stafford House in Garry's honor, and we went. I discovered poor Garry in a blue military poncho with a red lining, in the middle of a big room, with the stunning-handsome Duchess gloating on him as it were, in front, while

the ponderous figure of the Duchess Dowager with corpulent and condescending smiles, hovered heavily, like a bloated and benevolent harpy, on
his shoulder, and your friend the Duchess of Argyll blandly protected his
rear. The Duke of Sutherland with his hands in his pockets capered about
the central group, while the lofty and dignified noise and hair of the Duke
of Argyll appeared in proximity to his wife. I will not dilate upon the lesser
lights of the Gower tribe. You know the style. The Duke has got a pretty
place at Stafford House and certainly the sight was worth seeing, but entre
nous, our friends the Sutherlands are rather a bore, though the young Duke
seems to be an original and the young Duchess is superb.[1]

The season meanwhile commences, and I groan in spirit and in body.
But I hope it may be the last. Politically we are silent and expectant. The
idea is universal here that our armies are depleted and our last hour coming, while the tone of the sympathisers is more defiant than ever. I am willing to wait and I expect a terrific crash when it does come. No more news
about our negotiation. In fact all this is a period of placid quiet just before
everything breaks loose again. I expect about a fortnight more of it before
the tussle begins that is to do for us one way or the other. Meanwhile existence floats along and time passes, thank God!

MS: MHi
1. George Granville William Leveson-Gower (1828–1892), 3rd duke of Sutherland,
and his wife, Anne Hay Mackenzie (1829–1888), countess of Cromartie. The dowager
duchess also entertained Garibaldi at her house in Chiswick.

To John Gorham Palfrey

London. 15 April. 1864.

My dear Dr Palfrey:

I believe I left your's of the 22d February unanswered, during the busy
time of the Captain's presence with us, and since then, as I supposed you
would see and talk with him on his return, I thought a letter would be mere
superfluity. I gave your message to the good Parkes, who, by the way, has
had a very unpleasant time of late with scarlet fever in the house; and now
poor Mrs Ellice's death, following that of her father-in-law so soon, troubles
him greatly, as the Ellices were his patrons and great admiration. If his letters however are as rambling and futile as his conversation is apt to be, your
loss in not receiving any, might be reparable. He is a curiosity; a creature of
clubs and aristocratic sunlight; and though no one ever could dislike him
perhaps, one can't help laughing occasionally at the pertinacity of his
strange delusions about foreign affairs. I gave up long ago trying to argue
with him, but even to this day he aggravates my mother's combativeness to
a red heat.

Time rattles along so fast that this letter will scarcely reach you before the third anniversary of our departure. We are settled here now nearly as much at home as though we were in Boston, so far as familiarity with our surroundings go, and yet London never seems to me to allow any homelike feelings. I never quit it even for an afternoon at Richmond or a Sunday at Walton, without feeling a sort of shudder at returning, to be struck as freshly as ever with the solemnity, the gloom, the squalor and the horrible misery and degradation that seem to me to brood over the place. The magnificence I know and can appreciate. It has done its best to make me a socialist and has nearly succeeded. The society I think dull, and the art and literature poor. So that you see I am well suited to return to Boston unspoiled by my travels, a sadder and a wiser man.

Our great event just now is the arrival of Garibaldi, and his reception. Of all curious events, this is the most extraordinary. You know what Garibaldi is; the companion of Mazzini;[1] the representative of the "cosmopolitan revolution"; a regular "child of nature," unintellectual, uncultivated; but enthusiastic and a genius. Every Government in Europe dreads him, or rather his party, and he is the enemy of them all and of none more, whether he will or no, than of England. Suddenly he drops down here, and the people, the real "dangerous classes" go out to meet him with such a reception as never was known before. It was a regular uprising of democracy. But then to our delight, the young Duke and Duchess of Sutherland get hold of him, and at once compromise the whole English aristocracy, and give a hoist to the *rouges* and the democracy throughout Europe, by bringing him to Stafford House and making themselves co-conspirators with every refugee in England, to murder Napoleon, destroy Victor Emmanuel, and proclaim equality and division of property. I don't think I exaggerate the moral effect of this affair on the minds of the democrats. I am a real Garibaldian, and ready to accept, if necessary, his views, at the same time that I think hero-worship, as such, is a precious dangerous thing to meddle with. But here is the whole Clan Sutherland, with the young Duke dancing about at its head, forcing Garibaldi down the throats of the English nobility, who daren't openly say no, and who make the worst faces at the process, you can conceive. A few nights since, Stafford House was thrown open for a reception in honor of the General. By the way, what a glorious palace it is. I would like to have such a one at Quincy. We went; the only diplomats there except the Turk. Garibaldi was there; quantum mutatus ab illo Garibaldio that I saw four years ago, surrounded by a yelling mob in Palermo, with a few hundred guerilla troops, and not a nobleman among them! The beautiful young Duchess had him by the arm; she glittering with *the* diamonds; he in a military, loose poncho, or cape. The Duke pirouetted before, behind and on either side. The Duchess Dowager sailed majestically alongside, battling fiercely for the honor of being chief-keeper, but kept silent by her splendid daughter-in-law. In a tangled and promiscuous medley followed the Argylls, Tauntons, Howards, Blantyres, and every Leveson-Gower that draws breath. They paraded through the appartments, as well as Garibaldi could limp along, and we poor lookers-on drew aside and formed a passage for the procession triumphant to pass through. It was superb! And yet almost the last great occasion that Stafford House was open, was to allow this perfect nobility to do honor to Mrs Beecher Stowe, and both then and now the whole thing too strongly resembles a desperate humbug for me to be much impressed by it.[2] Sentimental liberalism is pretty, but it won't hold. Garibaldi is pretty safe to suffer the fate of Mrs Stowe, and American anti-slavery, whenever he stands in need of aristocratic aid. Meanwhile he sits at the feet of the beautiful Duchess (and there he is indeed to be envied) and smokes his cigars in her boudoir, and goes to bed immediately after dinner, and smokes in bed; and has two shirts (the famous red flannel) and a light blue cape lined with red (*rouge*, you see, always), which constitute his entire wardrobe. And in short, I rather doubt whether the good hero yet quite knows where he is, or has any clear idea of how it happens that he who has declared war to the knife against aristocracy and privilege everywhere, has become himself an aristocrat so suddenly. Meanwhile the non-Sutherland aristocracy growl fiercely, but are regularly over-slaughed by the popular wave, and we outsiders think it all as good a practical joke as ever was got up.

When shall we come home? After this season is over, we shall become very restless and if the war is over, as we strongly hope, we must leave here. I wonder whether Sumner wouldn't take the place. I suppose he might get it if he wanted it, on our departure. Then Gov. Andrew could replace him in the Senate, which would be an improvement. I hope to find you and your's, including Frank, well and prosperous at my return; and for my own part am ready to leave the society of Courts to those that are courtiers, and rest awhile at the law-school in Cambridge or elsewhere. My family send their best regards, and I am as ever Yrs

Henry B. Adams.

MS: MH

1. Giuseppe Mazzini (1805?–1872), Italian republican, took part in the unification of Italy but refused to support the monarchy established under Victor Emmanuel in 1861.

2. When Harriet Beecher Stowe (1811–1896) visited England in triumph after the publication of *Uncle Tom's Cabin* (1852), crowds greeted her arrival; at the great Stafford House reception the duchess of Sutherland (since 1861 the dowager duchess) bestowed on her a gold bracelet made to resemble a slave's chain.

To Charles Francis Adams, Jr.

No. 6.[1]   London. 13 May. 1864.

My dear Captain:

If this weren't one of the loveliest summer days imaginable, and if I hadn't just returned from my usual morning ride in the Park, I should sit down to write to you this week in poorer spirits than at any time since last July. It has needed all the virtue of fine weather and good health to keep me up to the mark. I hope that dwelling upon our evils, will not make me lose my start of them.

I am anxious and nervous. First, I am in a panic terror about our Virginian campaign. I am told that Grant has not pleased our eastern people and that confidence in him has not increased. Ignorant as I am of his arrangements, I can't judge of what he means to do, but if, as seems understood, he intends to move in three columns at once, it does seem to me that the chance of failure is increased.[2] To be defeated again would be horrible. The expectation of that telegram headed, "Defeat of the Federal Army," makes me sick and weak.

Our second trouble, and perhaps the more serious, or immediate one, is poor Loo's condition. We have received a letter from her which has frightened us all to death, and from the silence about her in your letters and John's, we rather infer that she must have been very seriously ill. We are excessively anxious about her, as you may suppose, and I so dread our letters that I almost wish no more vessels would ever cross the Atlantic, and we might remain in blissful ignorance of misfortune and trouble.

These forebodings, read by you in the light of knowledge, may seem very absurd or they may seem very just. But at any rate I do not see but that they are well grounded in the data that we have. As for politics, there has been scarcely any time when our hopes stood so low in the opinion of persons in this country. The current is dead against us, and the atmosphere so uncongenial that the idea of the possibility of our success is not admitted. I am not sorry for this state of feeling. If we are defeated, it will be only what is already considered certain. If we conquer, the moral triumph here will be double.

MS: MHi
1. After CFA2's return to the U.S., HA began to number his letters to him; we publish all those that survive.
2. In March, Grant was placed in supreme command of all the federal armies; he made his headquarters with the Army of the Potomac.

To Charles Francis Adams, Jr.

No. 7.   London. 20 May. 1864.

My dear Captain:

In a heat of the tropics, with the social duties of the season, and a heterogeneous mass of other duties which drive me into a perpetual St Vitus's Dance, I hear this morning that you have crossed the Rapidan, and that our fate is again trying conclusions. You may imagine that we are anxious, though not so much as when you were in the line.[1] The violence of the excitement will I suppose come next week, and I am glad to postpone it till then. Meanwhile we are now all veterans. It is not that one feels less, but that one learns to bear it, and faces the music from habit. I hope we shall hear good news, but I suppose we shall be able to support existence under bad, and anyway, old boy, point de regrets!

I will not speculate on your movements of which we know literally nothing except that you had taken position near Hooker's old battle-field. I am rather surprised to learn that you have gained this position without a fight, since it seems to place Lee in the position of attacking you, and leaving his connections open to Grant who may push Burnside towards Hanover Court House. But long experience has taught me to give not the slightest weight to my reasons for military movements.

Such weather! Your mamma who used to like the heat so much, is now nervous and worried to the last degree, by it, although the nights are cool and the days nothing excessive. I delight in it. There is nothing so depressing to me as a cloudy sky, and most of the evils of life are lighter for a bright sun. Mary and I ride almost every day, sometimes in the evening before dinner, and when the Park is choked up by a mass of carriages and people that look for all the world just as your army might look on the march to the Rapidan. This riding takes up all my time, which I haven't in large quantities to spare, but it does me such excellent service, and keeps my tail so blistered that I should be sorry to give it up. [*The rest of the letter is missing.*]

MS: MHi
1. CFA2 had joined Grant's headquarters as cavalry escort just before the Wilderness battle (May 5–7), the opening of which HA refers to here.

To Charles Francis Adams, Jr.

No. 8.   London. 26[1] May. 1864.

My dear Captain:

It will not be hard for you to imagine our situation here, and our varying faces, as the news of your experiences in Virginia reach us, one day all up, and the next all down. Just at this moment the Scotia is in, and after we have been exulting all the morning over the last news with the announcement of Lee's retreat, we are now brought up standing, at a minutes notice, by the announcement that Lee has not retreated, and that various events have happened which are of a character far from pleasant.[2] So long as the doubt of our fortune remained, I refused to think about it, and invested in French novels, to amuse my mind. When at last, our success seemed assured, I indulged in foolish and exulting thoughts. Celeres quatit pennas![3] I shall at once return to my novels. Meanwhile a letter from you would give us more real knowledge of what our true situation is, than any twaddle we are likely to pick up in the newspapers.

It is not worth while to dwell upon the campaign. You will, I hope, tell us about it. And it's pure waste of time to describe feelings which have been so common for three years past as to have become commonplace.

Meanwhile we go on here without a sign of change. The season is quieter than usual, so far as we are concerned, and as for me, I am the same placid hermit as ever, and except for my daily ride with Mary, seldom or never show my nose out of doors. Work is light, and the world is endurable.

We have people to dine, and a good many of them, from time to time. Yesterday was the Derby Day, and all the world was wild about it, but although it was the fourth Derby I've passed in England, I never have been to one and am not likely to go. Instead of that, I stayed at home, ran a match with Mary in Rotten Row and read novels all day. All regular work is broken up for the present, and the only object I propose to gain by study, is a little mental titillation and amusement.

European politics that were so threatening three weeks ago, are now quiet again with a pretty strong tendency towards peace. England has backed down from every position she has taken, and this being the case, there seems to be no more reason for a fight. The Danish question is likely to be settled at the cost of Denmark, which is satisfactory to all parties except the Danes, and it was the very object of the war to squench these. I see no reason now for supposing that there will be any further trouble in Europe this year. Meanwhile, our iron-clad rams at Liverpool have been offered by their owners to the British Government, and M. Bravay was even so generous as to lower his original price, that Government might take them.[4] Accordingly the Government has taken them and they are now a part of Her Majesty's Navy. Sic pereant![5]—I wish things were in as prosperous a way on your side as they are here.

Time is flying away terribly fast and actually the London season is pretty nearly half over. The next time I date a letter to you, will be in June, and it is not long from June to August when we shall, I hope, bid good-bye to the last experience we shall have of society in this part of the world. To get away seems to be the accompaniment of an end to our difficulties, and I am more and more restless to have some point of certainty appear.

It is now three weeks, I think, since we have heard anything about Loo, and I am more than anxious about her. I am already beginning to consider her recovery scarcely possible. If she was so low three weeks ago as she described to us, and has not gained strength enough to write another letter, I am violently afraid that she will scarcely be able ever to do so. It seems entirely incomprehensible that some body does not write to tell us how she is.

I hope you will send us better news some day, but meanwhile take your own time.

MS: MHi

1. HA misdated this letter 20 May.

2. As reported in the London *Times* on May 26, General Hancock's attack (May 12) in the Battle of Spotsylvania had cost Lee 25 cannon and 3,000 prisoners. However, the *Scotia* brought word that the battle was indecisive.

3. *Celeres quatit pennas:* If Fortune flits away, I can give back all she gave me; Horace, *Odes,* III, xxix.

4. The Confederate ironclads purportedly belonged to Messrs. Bravay and Co. of Paris, agents for the Pasha of Egypt.

5. *Sic pereant:* so let them sink.

To Charles Francis Adams, Jr.

No. 9.   London. 3 June. 1864.

My dear Captain:

As we are now in fact no wiser than we were last week, as to our home affairs, I don't see that I can say much about them. We have news to the 21st but the telegrams are utterly deceptive, and we can't trust to them at all. The Scotia's telegram sounded so badly that my last letter was blue in consequence, but the details were almost all of a cheerful kind. Meanwhile the suspense has become chronic and we are hardening to it as you harden to the sight of blood and death. My difficulty is now to comprehend how the rebs can get on without driving us away, so that I shall be tolerably well pleased provided we can maintain our present positions. But of course the army alone knows what it can do, and we are in utter darkness as to the morale of Grant's forces.

Our position here has not been nearly so much affected by all that has taken place, as it was last year or the year before. One cause of this is the fact that our whole question is now old and familiar to every one, so as to have become actually a bore and a nuisance. The enthusiasm for the slave holders has passed away like that for the Poles and other such people, enthusiasm being a sentiment which is a precious poor lot to last. Whether it will return or not I can't say. Perhaps it would if the rebs were to capture Washington, Philadelphia, and New York. Meanwhile the rebel cause is rather low in estimation just now.

Another reason for our comparative ease this year is the continued troubles in Europe. England has consented to betray Denmark, and Denmark, having found it out, has declared its intention not to be betrayed. It will go under, if necessary; but no influence shall induce it to seal its own condemnation and declare itself to have been in the wrong. This was the result reached yesterday by the Conference, and although I do not doubt that Denmark is right in her protest, I doubt just as little that England will throw the Danes over, remorselessly, and add insult, as the Times does this morning, to the most flagrant treason.

Still England has a conscience or a part of one, which is uneasy. It is not strong enough to beat loud and firm, but it dodges about and excuses itself and frets. So that it gives us a happy respite from attention.

If any of the women-kind write to you, they will probably discourse much about the Comte de Paris' wedding this last week, and the Duc de Chartres' ball.[1] This latter, I also attended, being asked. It was in fact a very jolly affair, and went off with great spirit. Chartres himself was in brilliant force, dancing like a maniac and treading on every individuals corns. He attempted with partial success to nobble the Minister, who was very nearly knocked down, deprived of his wind, and saved himself only by a rapid and demoralised retreat.[2] There was a crop of royalty so scattered about as to make it difficult to move, and for once royalty seemed to have a good time and to be willing to damn the expense. Stupified as I am getting to be by the deadness of English society, this glimpse into another atmosphere seemed for a moment to arouse me to a consciousness of my degradation. But as my whole effort for three years past has been to arrive at perfect stupidity, I promptly repressed the rising emotion.

In point of fact the occasion was very sad to a philosopher—et j'en suis un, s'il en fut jamais. The old friends of a fallen dynasty, three times proved unequal to the wants of the age, raked together with a painful observance of royal forms, to do honor to the marriage of the heir to the Crown! But even the few adherents to Orleanism are falling away every day, and there hardly remains a corporal's guard to support it.

Society is rather busy now. There are more or less affairs going on every evening, and what with riding every morning, and calls on a shoal of wandering Americans, time is taken up and the world glides on. We had another howling dinner last night, for which may the Lord pardon us.

Mr S.R. is discussing Mr Y. at this moment.[3] But as yet nothing seems to be possible to put things in train again.

MS: MHi
1. Louis Philippe d'Orléans (1838–1894), count of Paris, was claimant to the throne from which his grandfather had been deposed in 1848. He married his cousin Princess Maria Isabella on May 30. He and his brother Robert (1840–1910), duke of Chartres, served on the staff of General McClellan in 1861.

2. *Nobble:* British slang, to stun or knock out.

3. CFA2 was privy to secret diplomacy, having carried a key message from CFA to Seward in April. John Scott Russell (1808–1882), London naval architect and shipbuilder, came to CFA with what he claimed were Confederate terms for an armistice. Although skeptical, Seward and CFA approved as unofficial liaison James Erwin Yeatman (1818–1901) of St. Louis, head of the Western Sanitary Commission (forerunner of the Red Cross). The effort collapsed in May because of Yeatman's ineptitude and unreliability.

To Charles Francis Adams, Jr.

No. 10.   London. 10 June. 1864.

My dear Captain:

As I sat last Sunday at our Club window (by the by, we've built out a bow and made it the best in the street) reading the weekly papers, a brute of a man came running along outside, shouting "Great Federal Defeat, Sir," and brandishing his vile Observers. My face, Sir, was of iron! Quite so! But my stomach collapsed and stopped working. I rose presently with a frown, and lounged with an indifferent air out of the door and round the corner, at which point I pursued with vindictive animosity the wretch, who began now to cry "Great Federal Victory." When caught, he sold me a paper, from which I learned that Lee had retired to the No. Anna. Naturally, the revulsion in my mind was not a little pleasing. At the same time there is no danger of my becoming very sanguine. In fact so far as I can see, our turning Spottsylvania is only a proof that we have failed to defeat Lee there, which I presume was Grant's purpose. Nevertheless, to go forward is an immense gain and as the war seems now destined to assume more than ever its peculiar pulverising character, I can only hope that each step gained is something added to us and lost to them. Only I do trust that Grant will not assault Lee's present position. My plan of campaign is for Grant now to destroy the Virginia Central utterly, as well as Gordonsville, Charlottesville and the road to Lynchburg; then moving down the left bank of the North Anna, cross the Pamaunkey at Hanover Court House or still lower. If Lee now chose to attack, well and good. Grant's aim however, whether before or after a battle, would, I should think, be the James, and he ought to be able to throw the army across the Petersburg and Richmond Railroad if Butler or Smith have a little spirit, before Lee could stop him. At worst however, even if he failed to cut this road, it would be far easier to "fight them rough" from the James than on the North Anna, and whenever we can get the control of the southern approaches of Richmond, we win.

Such are my ideas. I wait therefore with anxiety for the next news. Grant is such an awful fighter that I fear another battle which, so away from our base, must be a more than usually severe one for the wounded and the army.

Your letter of the 19th was highly appreciated. We found also a notice of your squadron as clearing the bridge over the Ny on the 21st from which we infer that head-quarters were hard up for cavalry.

It is almost absurd to talk about London during such amusements at home. Nevertheless the world does move on without even thinking of what happens upon it, and so here we are going along in the old style, so that I become more and more doubtful every day as to what life is made for, and whether this mechanical existence which is led by almost every one I ever heard of, is of so much consequence as our self-conceit affirms. The dullness of mankind in this country is simply appalling. Quite so!

Miss Dayton is staying with us for a few days but our style of existence is not especially changed thereby. This week has in fact been a very quiet one to me; hardly any evening engagements at all and not any agreeable ones at that. I find it a quiet season and I am praying for good news from your army in order to feel free to run out to Mt Felix for a day or two and take a bit of fresh air which we are all beginning to want. Politically I have nothing to tell you from this side, all European affairs being still in a state of simmer. The Conference is still at work, and I lean to the idea that she will hatch something finally, but as yet she only cackles.[1] Some people are not so sanguine. A few feeble barks have been raised against us, but without much effect, so far as I can see, and of course the only probable effect would be to prick up our hostility to these people here. For my own part I've long seen what so many Americans will not see, that our system and the English system are mortal enemies. I mean to write a book about it one day—not for publication however; as I consider stupidity a necessary condition of a good book, and the public read only amusing works. It shall be written for you, my dear boy; for you! to read—if you can!

MS: MHi
1. England tried to mediate the Danish boundary question and end the war at a general conference in London. The conference failed, and Prussia imposed the Treaty of Vienna on Denmark (Aug. 1), forcing the cession of Schleswig-Holstein.

To Charles Francis Adams, Jr.

No. 11.   London. 17 June. 1864.

My dear Captain:

I congratulate you on your arrival before Richmond. As my last letter implied, I was rejoiced at Grant's movement across the Pamunkey, although the rebs here are much disgusted that you refused to storm the works at Sexton's Junction. Lee was never so cautious before, and I infer from this his relative weakness. I allow him eighty thousand men. Is that fair? I see no reason why you should not take time now, until Sherman finishes Georgia and can spare you forty thousand men.[1] Our cavalry seems to me the arm of the service which is most deadly to the rebs and I'm rather surprised that it's not more used to the South of Richmond. I should think the whole country from Weldon and Dalton to Petersburg and Lynchburg might be kept clean by our cavalry. But Grant appears to me now to have the game in his hands. So enormous a force as he can collect north and south of Richmond, must crush it by sheer weight. So, as he has thus far obtained my unbought commendation, I wont at present deprive him of his command.

I feel in fact more confident than ever before, and quite disposed to take things calmly. But my confidence is a very recent birth and the result of a prodigious scare, the other night. I went through one of the old-fashioned, double-barreled nights of misery, such as recall such associations only as M'Clellan's retreat and the second Bull Run. It happened in this wise. Last Tuesday evening I was campaigning in society. I began by a musical party at Countess Bernstorff's, where I remained five minutes. I then drove up to Berkeley Square where I looked in at Lady Colchester's, and passing rapidly through the rooms, walked off to Devonshire House which is not far off, as you know. Having said How do? to the Duke and passed through the rooms, I descended the marble stair-case, and resumed my journey in a cab up to Princes Gate where Mrs Schenley had a ball. I know this female's balls and they *are* rude. Of course I only put in an appearance here, and made off as rapidly as decency permitted.[2] It was then between twelve and one, and so I took another cab and returned down Piccadilly to Miss Burdett Coutts's, where there was another ball, a regular chaos, consisting of all London and its suburbans, with most of foreign nations. Here I met my people, but I couldn't stand the ball room. The Turkish Bath was a joke to it, so I retired to the supper room and waited for my women who under Mary's mild but persevering control, sweltered in a beefy and suety crowd till near two o'clock.

Lord Houghton came in while I was amusing myself with a mild salad and a modest beaker of claret, and he in his usual gouty but sociable way, chaffed a little, and then introduced me to Lady Galway who was standing near, and to Lord Galway.[3] They inquired about you with much earnestness. Lord Houghton ran Lord G. hard about his speech to you at table, and the latter was evidently sore about it and changed the subject at once, saying that he had mounted you and taken you to the hounds, and also had taken you to see Bracebridge Hall, although at the time he didn't know it to be Bracebridge Hall.[4] He then fell back upon the war, but cautiously, and said there was a story that Grant had attacked Lee's right and been repulsed. I treated it as a matter of little consequence whether it was so or not, and we soon parted.

When my people came down and we were driving home, I learned that they had heard people exulting in the repulse of Grant and the defeat of Sherman with severe loss. There were no means of verifying the report, so I did what I have done many times before in similar cases, I sat at my window and watched the cold gray light spread over the Park and Hampstead, while I smoked my bitter pipe, and contemplated the failure of our campaign.

The next morning, a glance at the telegram relieved my anxieties, and I then cast up in my own mind the balance between us and the rebels. On the whole it seemed, as I have said, so much in our favor, as to warrant me in assuming a tranquility which has not often been my good luck.

This week has been rather a gay and busy one. Miss Dayton is still here, and I have been delighted with her visit. It is difficult to calculate how much good a visitor sometimes does by merely keeping a certain tone up in a house. Mary has enjoyed it very much, and naturally, for it isn't often she sees a young person except in ball-rooms. I have been on my good behavior, and have officiated as guide and matron on various occasions. Our riding has suffered but this is rather lucky for me, as I've had a new boil on my seat, which has been worse than usual and very annoying. These things are not our American boils, but some cutaneous affair very common in England, and both Brooks and I suffer under it severely.

The season is well along, but all our plans are loose, till we know the result of the campaign, and until Loo arrives. This month will perhaps mark important events for us, but I am calm and wait for them stoically.

MS: MHi
1. Gen. William Tecumseh Sherman (1820–1891).
2. Count Albrecht Bernstorff (1800–1873) was the Prussian minister. Elizabeth Law Abbot (1799–1883), Lady Colchester; her husband the 2nd Baron Colchester was in the Conservative cabinet 1858–1859. William Cavendish (1808–1891), duke of Devonshire, was also the owner of Chatsworth and of one of the major art collections in England. Mary Croghan Schenley (d. 1903), a Pittsburgh heiress, wife of Capt. E. W. H. Schenley, who had fought on the British side in the War of 1812.
3. Lord Houghton's sister, Henrietta Eliza Monckton-Arundell (1814–1891), Lady Galway, and George Edward Arundell (1805–1876), 6th Viscount Galway, an Irish peer and Conservative M.P.
4. Aston Hall, near Birmingham, was the model for Washington Irving's ideal country house, in *Bracebridge Hall* (1822).

To Charles Francis Adams, Jr.

No. 12.   London. 24 June. 1864.

My dear Captain:

The news this week is not so satisfactory as I could have wished. I did not expect any rapid success against Richmond, being firmly convinced that we must get to the south of Richmond before we can force its abandonment. But I did trust that Sherman would not have much difficulty in dealing with Johnston. Yet, to judge from our latest advices, Johnston has stopped Sherman at Dallas and forced him to look sharp about him. I consider everything to depend on the fall of Atlanta in this campaign, and believe it would make the fall of Richmond inevitable. Hence I feel very sensitive to every bit of news from that quarter.[1]

Meanwhile, on we go here! The season is still hard at work, and works us hard. Last night we were at a ball at your friend Lady Waldegrave's at Strawberry Hill, ten or twelve miles out of town.[2] It was a handsome ball, very, and Strawberry Hill is a nice place; quite so! Your friend Lefevre was there. So were all the fashionable people of London. I was bored as I always am. I'm afraid my vicious habits in this particular are too well formed to permit a hope of change. Meeting Lawrence Oliphaunt however, who is an old soldier in every species of existence, both London balls, Central American filibusters and Japanese assassinations, I found that he also was bored, and we discussed the situation. Finally he raised a couple of cigarettes in a friend's overcoat, and we retired by stealth to the grounds which were illuminated. It was by no means a warm evening nor dry, the weather being very like April, but we discovered a pleasing summer house into which we retired and enjoyed the weed. This you know is as good as high treason in England. The majestic tonnage of Lady Fife, caught us here and glared in upon us, and Lady Constance Grosvenor passed by and tried hard to distinguish our faces in the gloom.[3] But no one else troubled us and we were much refreshed by the relaxation. I supped on a vile chicken, on returning, and then drove in the dawn back to town. It was four o'clock this morning when I got to bed. Tonight is another great ball at Devonshire House. I trust that this breaks the back of the season.

And so we have sunk the Alabama. That at least was well done and has I think no drawback to unmixed pleasure. But the spitefulness which the English have shown has revived all my irritability. Semmes sought the fight, knowing all about the Kearsage and expecting to whip her. He was so cut up as to be compelled to strike his colors, and actually cut the cross out of his flag, and ran it up again as a white flag. He sent a boat to the Kearsarge and surrendered the ship. And then was pulled out of the water, shouting for help; was stowed away at his own entreaty under a tarpaulin, deserting his own men, and running away by violation of every honorable demand through the treachery of a neutral flag kept near him for the purpose. And they're trying to make a sea-lion of this arrant humbug. I expect the matter to give us more diplomatic bother.[4]

Fortunately for us in these rough times the attention of people here is pretty thoroughly absorbed in their own affairs. The Conference seems at last to have come to an end, and the prospect is very blue. The crisis will come on Monday unless some last resort is dragged into play tomorrow at the formal close of the Conference. The curious part of the whole matter is that everybody is equally anxious to avoid war, and both rulers and people are running into every rat-hole to keep out of it. I send you herewith a copy of our newspaper of the season, the "Owl," so that you may get an idea of the way things are going. The Owl is probably edited by Lawrence Oliphaunt, with assistance from half the young men about town. We consider the wit pretty fair for London and at any rate much better than the letterpress of Punch.[5] Meanwhile it is said that Gladstone will leave the Ministry next week, in which case he will probably be followed by Gibson, Villiers, and perhaps Argyll; our friends.[6] But another account says Russell is to go out. Palmerston and he have been in favor of a strong policy, but were outvoted in the Cabinet, five to four. I should not wonder if there were a complete reconstruction of the Government. No one seems to suggest it, but I see no reason why the Tories or the moderate half of them should not come in under Palmerston, and Derby retain a reversionary interest. Will war be the result of a change? C'est ce que je ne crois pas. At all events it busies them, and as I am now satisfied that Prussia must mean war, or at least means to obtain its ends at any risk of war, I do not quite see how Europe can long be quiet. There may be many more calms and squalls before that though.

I see no books published that will interest you, but I send you a military catalogue and should you see anything you want, let me know. Everything is reprinted so soon in America as to make it useless to send an old book.

Ever Yrs

MS: MHi

1. Moving from Chattanooga on May 7, Sherman took the offensive against Gen. J. E. Johnston's army. Forced back to a position near Dallas, about 30 miles from Atlanta, Johnston outmaneuvered Sherman in an action there May 25–27.

2. Frances Braham (1821–1879), titled Countess Waldegrave from her second husband, was now married to Chichester Parkinson-Fortescue, undersecretary for the colonies; she restored Strawberry Hill, Horace Walpole's pseudo-Gothic villa at Twickenham.

3. Agnes Lady Fife (1829–1869), wife of the 5th Earl Fife, formerly a Liberal M.P. Constance Lady Grosvenor (1834–1880), daughter of the duke of Sutherland; her husband, Earl Grosvenor, later duke of Westminster, was a Liberal M.P.

4. The *Alabama* was sunk off Cherbourg, June 19, by the Union ship *Kearsarge*. Capt. Raphael Semmes (1809–1877) was rescued by an English yacht.

5. *The Owl: A Wednesday Journal of Politics and Society* published ten numbers, April 27 to July 13. There is a bound set in the HA library, MHi.

6. Thomas Milner Gibson (1806–1884), president of the board of trade 1859–1866.

To Charles Francis Adams, Jr.

No. 13.   London. 1 July. 1864.

My dear Captain:

We have had nothing but excitement this week. Naturally we were delighted to hear that you had succeeded in crossing the James undisturbed, and it relieved our minds of great anxiety. But it came to us coupled with the story that Petersburg was captured, and that of course raised our hopes extremely. This morning they are very much cooled down by the announcement of the battles of 17th and 18th, so that the reaction may give my epistle today a shade of blueness not warranted perhaps by the facts. It is a remarkable proof of human folly, and a strong encouragement of the philosopher, to see how really weak our minds naturally are, and how little the severest training can keep them from making damned idiots of themselves by trusting their hopes and wishes. As the balance shifts slowly between Federal and Confederate, and the anxiety of the wise man is merely to learn which scale falls, we wretched creatures on each side are always looking for some sudden change that will reverse the whole order of creation. The ups and downs are rough on such poor things as nerves, but the strain is wearing rather from its long continuance than from its immediate pressure. Through them all, some party is continually getting ahead slowly, and some day or other I suppose the infinite region of barren lies will be passed, as you have left the Wilderness behind you, and we shall come out upon some firm and evident truth. Meanwhile:

> Non meum est, si mugiat Africis
> Malus procellis, miseras ad preces
> Decurrere, et votis pacisci
>   Ne Tyriae Cypriaeve merces
>   Addant avaro divitias mari![1]

The crisis has also passed here. The Ministry have announced that war would be inconvenient; that America is too formidable a power to have in the rear; that Germany is a bully, and Denmark a little fool; that the blame all belongs to France, and is owing to the hatred of Russia to England; that when the war is over and Denmark destroyed, Palmerston will call Parliament to know whether to send the channel fleet to the Baltic; that in short everything is in a muddle and no one knows how to get out of it except by frankly backing out and refusing to act at all. We have been immensely delighted with this utter confusion of England. There is about it so simple and undisguised confession of impotence that it almost excites pity, and would do so wholly if it weren't that they are so ill-natured and currish in their expression of their disappointment. But it is not a little grateful to see the utter contempt felt for this country all over Europe now. The newspapers are filled with elegant extracts from French and German sources, all expressing in varied terms the opinion that the English are cowards. For my own part, the case does not seem to me to be so bad. The English are not cowards, but they have the misfortune to be damned fools, and to have the same class of men for their rulers. Once in this mire, they are cross, but make the best of it, and all the contempt of Europe will be swallowed without shaking the firm conviction of the "true English gentleman" as Kingsley calls him, that somehow or other he is right and all mankind is wrong. They will not even turn out the Ministry, it is said, and I can well believe it. But the European complication is not ended yet, and England will have to swallow more dirt before the end. What the end will be, I don't know. But I look for a great movement towards liberalism some day.

The labor of society still keeps us hard down to the mill. We have also sent out cards for a grand American reception on the 4th, Monday; and such a curious list of names and addresses, you seldom have heard of. All the strange and outlandish beings in the kingdom will be here, excepting only the English, of whom we ask not one.

But the season will soon be over now, thank God! Mary and I are plotting to make sure that this be our last season, but all depends on the news, and the news is exactly like a fever; now a chill, and now a boil. I think of going home myself at any rate next winter. I am getting old, and must be at work. The Chef can do without me, if he only tries, and Brooks had better go home with me. We will both settle in Cambridge. All this however is as yet unknown to the heads of the family, and much depends on Loo.

I received your letter of the 10th and am rejoiced at your lift to Jim Higginson. He's a man to be trusted. You'll have a conscientious sub if there's work to do.[2]

Meanwhile I send in a parcel, two dozen glove buttons (2 sizes); one pair buckskin gloves (I want to know whether they fit.); three pair cotton stockings, and the first volume of the new Life of Sir W. Napier.[3] Another invoice will come next week.

MS: MHi

1. The passage from Horace's *Odes,* III, xxix, follows the one quoted on May 26. "If the mast groans in the storm wind from Africa, I'll not [*non meum est*] resort to piteous

prayers or bargain with holy offerings, to keep my goods from Tyre and Cyprus from adding to the hoard of the greedy sea."

2. Higginson, returned from Libby by prisoner exchange, was promoted to first lieutenant.

3. Henry Austin Bruce, ed., *Life of General Sir William Napier* (1864).

To Charles Francis Adams, Jr.

No. 14.   London. 8 July. 1864.

My dear Captain:

What do you say to the news you've been sending us for a week back? Grant repulsed. Sherman repulsed. Hunter repulsed and in retreat. Gold, 250. A devilish pretty list, portending, as I presume, the failure of the campaign.[1] To read it has cost me much in the way of mental consumption, which you can figure to yourself if you like. And now, what is to be the end? "Contemplate all this work of time."[2] We have failed, let us suppose! The financial difficulty, a Presidential election, and a disastrous campaign are three facts to be met. Not for us to meet, but for the nation, our own share being very limited. *Ebbene!* Dana's idea a year ago of throwing off New England, is I suppose, no longer practicable. But what is practicable seems to be a summary ejection of us gentlemen from our places next November, and the arrival of the Democratic party in power, pledged to peace at any price.[3] This is my interpretation of the news which now lies before us.

Shall you be sorry? not for the failure of course, for our feelings on that subject are well enough known to us. But for the loss of our power. For my own part, I don't know. I am not sure. It is becoming clear that we must have peace. All the talk of our orators of the impossibility of disunion is damned nonsense, between you and me. If we fail to get Richmond, as I imagine we have failed, there will be a popular majority for disunion in the North, and the question of terms ought not to stand long against the pressure for peace North and South. But this work is not for us to do, and I don't envy the men that are to do it. Therefore I am not sure that we shall not be lucky to escape the task of accomplishing the humiliation of the country.

But the struggle to die is painful. The next nine months will be slow to pass, and I wish either that one could put one's nerves into one's pocket, bottled stoutly up; or that one could run away from the future. I would like much to go to bed, and sleep peacefully till next March. I want to escape the alternations of hope and dread; the hectic phenomena of our decline; and bid farewell to my strangely disastrous experience as a politician.

Lucky is it for us that all Europe is now full of its own affairs. The fate of this Ministry seems to be pretty nearly decided, so far as Parliament can decide it, without an appeal to the people. The division takes place tonight, and the excitement in society is tremendous. Everyone who has an office, or whose family has an office, is in a state of funk at the idea of losing it, and every one who expects an office is brandishing the tomahawk with frightful yells over his trembling victim. As for the degree of principle involved, I have not yet succeeded in seeing it. The nation understands it in the same way, as a struggle by one set of incapable men to keep office, and by another set of ditto to gain it.

Society is almost silent among the hostile warriors. I breakfasted with Lord Houghton last Wednesday, and what do you think was the subject of conversation? Bokhara and the inhabitants of central Asia. Some twenty prominent people discussed nothing but Bokhara, while all Europe and America are on the high road to the devil. And a delightful breakfast it was to me who am weary with long mental and concealed struggles for hope. I reveled in Tartaric steppes, and took a vivid interest in farthest Samarcand. Except for a drum at Lady Belper's the other evening, I believe we have done scarcely anything this week. Miss Strutt has nearly been put an end to by her horse in Rotten Row, and performed gymnastics on her head that only didn't take it off. As she was not killed, however, she has got well, and was receiving company with her ma.[4] Mary and I ride nearly every day, but now more often just before dinner, when the row is less crowded, and also, as I suspect, because there are more men and fewer women at that hour. But our existence is going to receive a great change. Loo and Kuhn have arrived in the Scotia, and will be here, I expect, tomorrow. I am heartily rejoiced at it, because, *entre nous,* our people are becoming by mere inertia, much too English and old fogy.

I send you this week a flannel shirt and a pair of drawers. Next week I will forward the second volume of Napier. These English books are so bulky that they hardly go into anything short of a cotton-bale.

MS: MHi

1. Grant at Cold Harbor, Va., Sherman at Kennesaw Mountain, Ga., and Hunter at Lynchburg, Va., provided the bad news.

2. Tennyson, *In Memoriam,* canto 118.

3. In June the Republicans renominated Lincoln, and the Democrats nominated McClellan.

4. Amelia Otter Strutt (d. 1890) was the wife of Edward Strutt, 1st Baron Belper (1801–1880), friend of Bentham and Mill, Liberal spokesman on free trade, president of University College, London, 1871. "Miss Strutt" probably refers to Sophia, eldest of their four daughters.

To William H. Seward

Rhyl. North Wales. Thursday. 25 August. 1864.

Dear Sir:

My father has put into my hands the letter in which you have authorised him to offer to me the situation made vacant by the promotion of Mr Moran.[1] I feel particularly grateful to you for this kindness since neither my father nor myself had solicited it.

At the same time I have not hesitated to decline it without delay. My reason for doing so is that although I wish nothing better than to be useful either directly or indirectly to the country in its difficulties, yet all that I have seen here in the course of the past three years has only strengthened my earlier belief that I should not be acting in the best interests either of the service or of the Minister, or of myself, in accepting any official position in the Legation.

I have therefore notified the Minister of my decision, and it only remains for me to thank you personally for your very kind proposal.

I have the honor to be

Yr obedient Servant   Henry B. Adams.

Hon. William H. Seward

MS: DNA (Diplomatic Branch, Record Group 59)
1. Moran succeeded Wilson as first secretary Aug. 17.

To Lord Houghton

London. 5 September. 1864.

My dear Lord:

I have a note of your's of the 24th which arrived while I was away in Wales, and my mother has received her autographs which will no doubt do her good. I have been something puzzled by your request about some Government Report of which I have no acquaintance. Mr Fessenden, or whoever has the charge of it,[1] has not favored us with a copy, nor have I ever seen it, nor do I know anyone who has. If I can get it for you, I have no objection to your reading it to the Social Sciencers or to your noble and most reverend colleagues in the House of Lords, if you like, but I question whether the document is to be found outside of the town where it originated.

I hope that you and Lady Houghton[2] are doing well. You are going to Bath, I suppose. The Minister talks of accepting an invitation, but finds the hotel full, which appears to bother him. We have just come from North Wales, where we had as pleasant a journey as one could ask; and now we are meditating a removal to the country. As there now remain only six months more residence for us, under the shade of the aristocracy, you can imagine that we are becoming restless.

Very truly Yrs   H. B. Adams

Lord Houghton. Fryston.

MS: Trinity College, Cambridge
1. William Pitt Fessenden (1806–1869) of Maine, senator 1854–1864 and 1865–1869, secretary of the treasury 1864–1865.
2. Annabella Crewe Milnes (d. 1874), sister of the 3rd Baron Crewe.

To Charles Francis Adams, Jr.

No. 19.   London. 16 Septem. 1864.

My dear Colonel:[1]

I had scarcely sent my last letter despairing of the success of our armies in time to save the election, when news came of the fall of Atlanta. I heard it on Sunday afternoon, and Kuhn and I got into a Hansom and cut down to the Observer Office with a rapidity commendable for our time of life. After all we only got the announcement that Slocum had entered the place, and Sherman had fought a battle at East Point said to be successful. To this minute we know no more. Of course even this is doubted by the Times, and disbelieved in the City. But fancy our anxiety to hear more. If Sherman's battle was as successful as he meant it to be, Hood's army must be put out of humor to stop his marching straight to Macon, and resuming his campaign against Augusta, with Montgomery and Mobile for a second base.[2] Georgia and Alabama would be wholly ours, and in future we should have but one army to fight, and that cut in two, so long as Grant holds the Weldon road. Such are my hopes from a success. But disappointment has usually been our fate in like circumstances, and the future may be of a different color.

Under these circumstances I do not care to speculate about elections or battles or sieges. If last Sundays news is substantiated, it is the best probably that we ever had, and the most encouraging. In that case my dismal apprehensions would be only thin air. But if not, you may easily conceive the double darkness of the pit we plunge into.

Mary has been steadily recovering during the last week, and is now apparently quite well, except for a loose cough and a tendency to snuffle, the remains of her attack, and a proof of the still delicate condition of the mucous membrane, say the Doctors. We wish to get her strong and thoroughly well again, before taking her away. As yet it is not settled where we shall go. The Doctors give a very confused sound in reply to our inquiries, but I do not expect it will be very far. We must decide next week and be out of town by the 1st of October.

Loo has been ailing and I am very much afraid she always will be ailing. Her illness last winter, and the mercury she took, have shaken her, and I don't believe they will ever let her forget them. She is evidently very much bored by our life, and very properly; and she would like to go on to the Continent, [*The rest of the letter is missing.*]

MS: MHi
    1. CFA2 was promoted to lieutenant colonel July 15.
    2. Gen. Henry Warner Slocum (1827–1894), corps commander under Sherman; Confederate Gen. John Bell Hood (1831–1879), forced to abandon Atlanta, Sept. 1.

To John Gorham Palfrey

London. 16 September. 1864.

My dear Dr Palfrey:

I received from you a note while I was traveling with my family in North Wales, which contained some further directions about the documents, which however had already been sent, and to which I could not have attended till my return. On my return however, I have received yours acknowledging the reception of my package, and from that I judge that the papers answer your purpose, and are what you wished. I have never been able to discover any trace of the earlier memorandum, and have not the slightest recollection of any such paper. I see I led you astray by sending you the bill without explanation. I had already paid it, so that it was not necessary to pay Tuke again. I shall however get it out of him, and you need not give yourself any further trouble about it.

Summer has come and gone, and the days have grown long and are growing short, without any sign of that change which my sanguine mind had hoped would have given us freedom from diplomatic ties by this time. I have dreaded another winter in England more than anything except absolute suffering. But here we still are, making our plans for the winter as though the war had just begun and a Presidential term before us. You know my sister Mrs Kuhn and her husband are with us, and we have all been making a trip through North Wales together. I have visited the vale of Llangollen, and stood at the grave of Llewellyn's hound, and ascended Snowdon, and devoted considerable research to ascertain from what point the Bard could possibly have plunged into Conway's roaring flood.[1] We have seen ruined castles till they have become a mere every-day song. And now here we are back in London, at the old treadmill again.

Of course, if things were going well at home, we could resign ourselves easily even to London in September. But all our correspondents except our Lieut. Colonel are in the depths of despondency, and announce certain discomfiture at the elections. Till very lately they have also predicted military disaster, but this last mail seems to indicate that Farragut and Sherman and Grant are beginning to exercise a good influence on the public morale.[2] We have an announcement of the fall of Atlanta, but no particulars, and our English cousins discredit it vehemently. The steamer due today will tell us how it is, and you can imagine how anxious we are, when we think how much depends upon half a dozen words in the next telegram.

Should we go out next March, as I am told we shall, and should I once more be useless to anyone, I hope to return for a time to Cambridge to follow my studies, especially as I have a young brother whose college career I want to inaugurate. I have now studies immediately on hand, that will certainly require a hundred years of incessant activity, to complete, so that it is high time to begin. I look forward not without pleasure to a return to my College life at an advanced age.

I am very sorry to hear that Mrs Palfrey is unwell. We can sympathise with her, for we have two invalids ourselves to take care of. Mrs Kuhn is still recovering from her severe attack of last winter, and my sister Mary has taken it into her head to have two sharp attacks of congestive asthma, or rather one attack of pure congestion which returned as asthma, and frightened us out of our wits until we found out what it was. England is perhaps the worst place yet discovered, for both these patients, but for all that they seem likely to winter it out.

You know the extent of gaiety which characterises London in September. To a person who wishes to work, there is no more agreeable place. But to us it is far from cheering. We meditate taking a house in the country till winter or the new year, and meanwhile we have only to wait what news you will send us, and hug ourselves in the thought that six months more will bring us home.

My father and mother wish to be remembered warmly to Mrs Palfrey. I am glad to see what a success your Engineer's campaign has been.[3]

Very truly Yrs   H. B. Adams.

MS: MH
1. Thomas Gray, "The Bard" (1758).
2. Adm. David Glasgow Farragut (1801–1870) won the battle of Mobile Bay, Aug. 5.
3. Capt. John Carver Palfrey (1833–1906), U.S. Military Academy '57, specialist in siege operations in the Mobile campaign.

To Charles Francis Adams, Jr.

No. 21.   London. 30 Sept. 1864.

My dear Colonel:

At last we are fairly in the country. We moved out yesterday with considerable difficulty, and took up our quarters at a place called Hanger Hill, at Ealing, about six miles from our London house, with the railway running at, or under, our very door here. We have a Park and ancient cedars and a fine view towards Richmond on the south and Harrow on the north, and if you wait till next week I have no doubt you will get all other particulars from your female correspondents. I rode out with Mary yesterday afternoon, the first time she has been on horseback since her illness. It has been lovely weather and the country is perfection. If it only continues! And if the place is healthy and Mary is well! In that case I should not be surprised if we remained there all winter! Kuhn and Loo are domiciled with us and promise to remain till December. Poor Loo will bore herself to death, I fully expect, but I don't know that she can rightly blame us for it. Poor girl! she is too clever to occupy herself permanently, and also too clever not to be martyred by want of occupation.

I passed the night out there and came back this morning with the Chief to get the mail off. I shall sleep here tonight, and tomorrow I am going a hundred or two miles down into Shropshire to pay the youth Gaskell a visit for a few days. On returning from his place, I expect to go off with the papa and the mamma to Lord Belper's, your acquaintance. If Mary consents to go, I shall stay at home, but as yet she is not thereto inclined. This however will not be till next Saturday, and I shall be back here next Friday certainly. Meanwhile Kuhn and Loo and Mary will be left alone at Ealing. I have some doubt how this will work, but as a rule I prefer not to run ahead of annoyances.

The victory of Sheridan in the Shenandoah has reached our ears with a gratifying sound.[1] I should imagine that it must be a pretty serious thing to Lee, who seems now to be living on expedients. But as we do not yet know whether Lee had weakened Early after Grant's success on the Weldon road, I am still in the dark about the prospects. Will Lee attack us? If he means to do so, why is he building this new railroad of which we hear much? And if he means to do so, mustn't he be in a hurry, in order to get through in time to stop Sheridan? My own impression begins to be that Lee is determined to stick to the defensive as much as possible, and save his troops. If so this defeat of Early must bother him badly. May it not even compel him to contract his lines, even at the expense of abandoning Petersburg?

When I study Sherman's campaign, I shudder to think what a close thing it was, and how nearly desperate that superb final march was, in the sense of its being a last expedient. As you know, I had frequently despaired. How could I reckon on the mere personal genius of one man? Now that it is over, I feel almost incredulous, and do not wonder at all at the persistent conviction of the southern press that we should be defeated. If they were unable to hold that place, I cannot see where they look for the place they will hold; and if they could not in the whole Confederacy raise more than ten thousand men to reinforce Hood at the most excruciating pinch, where can they get men to meet our new levies. The courage of the rebs has been marvellous; but human nature has its limits and unless the sun shines a little, the devil himself would lose heart in such a case.

Meanwhile quiet still reigns supreme on this side. We hear nothing of any consequence. Your friend Mr Y. has gone back to Richmond and Mr S.R. says he suspects his hand to be in various articles in Richmond papers looking peaceward.[2] There is a great financial crisis down in the City, all due to our war and the fall in cotton consequent on the peace panic. The rebel cotton-loan has fallen twenty per cent from its high estate, and brought down with it a flock of lame ducks on the stock-exchange. Old Mr Bates meanwhile, is dead and buried.[3] You remember the gloomy magnificence of our call there, and how the poor old man sat in that sombre vastness, and waited for death. I have seen few sights more rich in comments on human vanities than the picture of the good old gentleman dying; for of all England, and in spite of all the years he had lived here, and fed and entertained all the world, not an Englishman except his partners seems to have cared whether he lived or died. After all, his mourners are Americans, although he has probably founded an English family.

I intended to have sent you some book, but have been awfully busy. Perhaps I may find one in time.

MS: MHi
1. Gen. Philip Henry Sheridan (1831–1888) defeated Gen. Jubal Anderson Early (1816–1894) at Winchester, Va., Sept. 19.
2. Yeatman and Scott Russell (see letter of June 3).
3. Joshua Bates, whose wife and daughter had instructed ABA in London diplomatic protocol in 1861.

To Samuel Bulkley Ruggles

London. 30 Sept. 1864.

My dear Sir:

I have received your letter, as well as the documents brought by Mr Curtin, and have sent one of the latter to the Editor of the Daily News according to your direction, with a note. I shall be proud to place one in my father's collection of pamphlets. But I am sorry to say, in regard to the third, that poor Mr Bates had just died as the Address reached me. For months he has been on the point of death, and recovery was known to be quite out of the question. His whole system seems to have decayed, and he dropped out of existence with the most perfect ease, and apparently unconscious of the nearness of the event. I do not see that our friends the English people seem to trouble themselves about him, and I'm afraid the kind old gentleman would have had more friends if he had lived in America, than he ever gained here. I suppose he has succeeded however in his wish of founding a family, and the Van de Weyers will rank as members of the purest aristocracy in the world, by the right of pure blood.

We are indulging in hopes of political success in November, from the tone of our American news. I hope it may be the means of relieving us soon from our occupations here. Another Minister has now a right to the place, and we shall not, I think, dispute it. I hope the choice will be a good one.

Pray remember me to your son, and believe me

Very truly Yrs   H. B. Adams.

Hon. S. B. Ruggles.

MS: PHi

To Charles Francis Adams, Jr.

No. 22.   London. 7 October. 1864.

My dear Colonel:

We receive this morning the news of Sheridan's second victory in the valley.[1] The Ealing breakfast-table resounded with shouts of applause over it. To me, although I am still in doubt whether the two divisions of Longstreet's corps were or were not there, it seems to demonstrate that Lee must prepare to quit Richmond. This hurrying small bodies of troops this way and the other, to shut stable doors from which plunder has already been taken, appears to me likely to be now as before, the precursor of a Waterloo. Evidently Lee must send a corps at least towards the valley. If so, he will have to contract his lines at Richmond, will he not? The Richmond papers hint at this, while threatening Grant with new dangers, before they had yet heard of Early's defeat. Am I rash in saying that I think it possible Lee may abandon Petersburg and throw his right well back towards Burkesville, to avoid being caught in a trap by Grant on a line hopelessly long? At any rate I cannot help thinking that Petersburg is to be the reward of Sheridan's victory.

I told you last week that I was going down to Shropshire to visit my friend Gaskell. I only returned last night at eight o'clock, and am off again tomorrow to Derbyshire. My visit to Wenlock was very enjoyable. God only knows how old the Abbot's House is, in which they are as it were picnic-ing before going to their Yorkshire place for the winter. Such a curious edifice I never saw, and the winds of Heaven permeated freely the roof, not to speak of the leaden windows. We three, Mrs Gaskell,[2] Gask and I, dined in a room where the Abbot or the Prior used to feast his guests; a hall on whose timber roof, and great oak rafters, the wood fire threw a red shadow forty feet above our heads. I slept in a room whose walls were all stone, three feet thick, with barred, square Gothic windows and diamond panes; and at my head a small oak door opened upon a winding staircase in the wall, long since closed up at the bottom, and whose purpose is lost. The daws in the early morning, woke me up by their infernal chattering around the ruins, and in the evening we sat in the dusk in the Abbot's own room of state, and there I held forth in grand after-dinner eloquence, all my social, religious and philosophical theories, even in the very holy-of-holies of what was once the heart of a religious community.

Wherever we stepped out of the house, we were at once among the ruins of the Abbey. We dug in the cloisters and we hammered in the cellars. We excavated tiles bearing coats of arms five hundred years old, and we laid bare the passages and floors that had been three centuries under ground. Then we rambled over the Shropshire hills, looking in on farmers in their old kitchens, with flitches of bacon hanging from the roof, and seats in the chimney corners, and clean brick floors, and an ancient blunderbuss by the fire-place. And we drove through the most fascinating parks and long ancient avenues, with the sun shining on the deer and the pheasants, and the "rabbit fondling his own harmless face."[3] And we picnicked at the old Roman city of Uriconium, in the ruins of what was once the baths; and eat partridge and drank Chateau Léoville, where once a great city flourished, of which not one line of record remains, but with which a civilisation perished in this country. Then we dined with a neighboring M.P. whose wife was excentric in her aspirates and asked me if I didn't like that style.

In short my visit to Shropshire was a species of quiet success, so curiously different from the usual stiffness of English society, that I shall always feel a regard for the old barn, though it was as cold a place as one wants to be near. Mr Gaskell was urgent upon me to come up and see them in Yorkshire, and if it is repeated in December, I shall go. Mr Gaskell père, who is a very agreeable man, evidently prefers comfort to antiquity.[4] They are relatives of your friend Lord Houghton, and if anything, a little in his rather sensual and intellectual style.

I have not had time to get you Russell's critique on Sherman, nor have I seen one. Russell's comments on our war have been poor, so far as I have observed, and give me no information. Meanwhile I enclose you a little sketch of Thackeray. You may have seen it, or you may not. I have not read your last letter, so I am not au fait in your affairs, but I understand you are doing well. Pray God we get a few more successes, and our hopes will take a turn homewards.

Ever

MS: MHi
1. Sheridan pursued Early and defeated him again at Fishers Hill, Sept. 22.
2. Mary Williams-Wynn Gaskell (d. 1869).
3. Tennyson, "Aylmer's Field" (1864).
4. James Milnes Gaskell (1810–1873), Conservative M. P. for Wenlock 1832–1868.

To Charles Francis Adams, Jr.

No. 24.   London. 21 October. 1864.

My dear Colonel:

Our news this week stops with unusual abruptness what promised to be a very remarkable episode. Grant moves like the iron wall in Poe's story.[1] You expect something tremendous, and its only a step after all. Of course the process is all the more sure from its methodical slowness, but it alters the nature of the drama. Here am I puzzling myself to understand why it is that Petersburg does not fall, and when Grant means to take it. For it seems to me that he might now compel its abandonment in several ways. And yet Lee prefers to see us creep nearer and nearer our point, and does not accept what to an outsider seems the necessity of his position. Jeff. Davis's speech at Macon gives more light on the question than anything else. Of course there may be some inaccuracy in reporting, but his explanations are very reasonable, and his statement about Early's campaign shows how much he expected from it. That failing to draw Grant away, there seems nothing left but to draw out their resistance to the last moment. But how Lee can cover Meade on three sides, and protect Richmond and the connecting railway too, I can't quite see.

We have news to the 8th; two days before the elections. Of course they now form the main subject of curiosity. You have already long known the result. We shall be able to guess at it in two days. I hope for the best.

We go on at Ealing in our usual quiet way. I am still not quite up from my little trouble, and have to be cautious and quiet. But my organs appear to have very nearly regained the natural size, and I hope soon to be all right. Mary seems well, and Loo is fatter than a porpoise, and in spite of your admonitions, curses England from morning till night. She bores me extremely with her perseverance of vituperation, for although I'm no great lover of England, I have led here a not unhappy life, and indeed should not have the energy to hate any country or person as she does. Besides, human nature is, I fancy, human nature in America as well as England, and in France as well as in Spain. I regret to say that ignorance, stupidity, vice and pigheaded pride are not peculiar to this fat land.

Stanley has returned and yesterday made his appearance at Ealing where he passed the better part of the day, and dined. He has seen everyone that ever lived, and will, of course, I guess, write a book.[2] I think I know [*The rest of the letter is missing.*]

MS: MHi
1. "The Pit and the Pendulum."
2. Edward Lyulph Stanley (1839–1925), later 4th Baron Stanley of Alderley, had been visiting the United States. No book of his on this subject was published.

To Charles Francis Adams, Jr.

No. 25. London. 28 October. 1864.

My dear Colonel:

The results of the October elections are just beginning to make themselves clear to us. They indicate precisely what I have always most dreaded, namely a closely contested Presidential vote. I only judge by the Pennsylvania election, where the Democrats seem to have carried everything. How it may be in Ohio and Indiana I do not know, but I fear a similar result. They gain just enough to place Lincoln in a very weak position if he is elected. These ups and downs have been so frequent for the last four years that I am not disposed to put too much weight on them. At the same time I cannot help remembering that a down turn just at this moment is a permanent thing. It gives us our direction for a long time. But I must see our papers before I can fairly understand what is to happen. Meanwhile there appears to be a hitch in army affairs and some mysterious trouble there. This is also rather blue.

I have scarcely anything to write you on our own account. We are at Ealing most of the time and lead most temperate and quiet lives there, especially since the weather has changed to damp which keeps us more in the house. I have to all appearance pretty nearly quite recovered from my difficulty, although as usual in this complaint, the tenderness, or rather the tendency towards a return of the inflammation, remains and requires caution for a good while after the attack. But I go about as usual, and am to all appearance well. Mary continues apparently well and strong. I wish to God, however, that we had carried Pennsylvania and could look forward with a confident hope to getting away from here this year or early in 1865. I think she is just in the condition when a change would be very valuable.

Kuhn has gone over to Paris and will, I suppose, remain there from ten days to a month. Loo has at last taken to horse-back riding and she and Mary explore the county. We have visitors continually out there, young and old, and it is a far more agreeable existence than what we have usually led in London. Of course your mamma is continually making plans to return to London, as though she delighted in that charming residence, but for my own part I mean to oppose the most effective resistance in my power to any further abode in London at all; and if fate decides that we are to remain here through the winter, I shall try to postpone a return to London till the latest moment. After our last experience here, I shan't of my own accord be caught repeating the experiment.

In fact, we are now under any circumstances within four or five months of our departure from this country. I am looking about with a sort of vague curiosity for the current which is to direct my course after I am thrown aside by this one. If McClellan were elected, I do not know what the deuce I should do. Certainly I should not then go into the army. Anyway I'm not fit for it, and to come in when the anti-slavery principle of the war is abandoned, and a peace party in power, would be out of my cards. I think in such a case I should retire to Cambridge, and study law and other matters which interest me. Once a lawyer, I have certain plans of my own. I do not however believe that McClellan's election can much change the political results of things, and although it may exercise a great influence on us personally, I believe a little waiting will set matters right again. So a withdrawal to the shades of private life for a year or two, will perhaps do us all good. If that distinguished officer would only beat us all to pieces! But if Lincoln is elected by a mere majority of electors voting, not by a majority of the whole electoral college; if Grant fails to drive Lee out of Richmond; if the Chief is called to Washington to enter a Cabinet with a species of anarchy in the North and no probability of an end of the war—then indeed I shall think the devil himself has got hold of us, and shall resign my soul to the inevitable. This letter will reach you just on the election. My present impression is that we are in considerable danger of all going to Hell together. You can tell me if I am right.

MS: MHi

To Charles Francis Adams, Jr.

No. 26.   London. 4 Nov. 1864.

My dear Colonel:

Seldom even among the many rapid changes that my letters have recorded during the last few years, has there been one so great as that which has occurred in my feelings since my last letter. That was written under the effects produced by Reuter's telegram that "the Democrats had carried Pennsylvania by a large majority which the soldiers' vote could not overcome"; and that "Maryland had rejected the anti-slavery constitution." Of Indiana and Ohio nothing was said. The few returns from Pennsylvania we had received were not calculated to refute this statement, and as a necessary consequence the prospect looked more alarming than I even described it in my letter. You of course, the danger passed, and breathing an atmosphere of sympathy, may consider my alarm to have been unnecessary and absurd. As for me, I look back upon the crisis as I would on a hair-breadth escape from a horrible accident, or from sudden ruin. It seemed then so close if not inevitable, that the sense of relief is enormous.

Once breathing freely again after this tremendous strain, and seeming now to see our way pretty surely to firm land, I think we may shake hands all round, and thank God for a prospect of peace at last. The rebels are beginning to hit wild, it appears to me. Hood's movement, if he really means to enter Tennesee, looks to me like the commencement of that irregular warfare which they have always threatened us with, in the event of their country being over-run. Longstreet's blow at Sheridan, cleverly executed as it was, is at best only a return to Lee's thread-bare plan of threatening Washington, which has thoroughly failed this year, all along. There is no new resource developed by Lee that I can see, and he has hitherto been excessively cautious towards Grant. On the whole, I cannot help thinking that the end is near. I suppose Lee will get a few thousand, perhaps fifteen or twenty thousand ill-disposed recruits by the new measure of calling in the details, but I do not see how they can do more than die like their predecessors.

But the great thing is that we have now gained time. The result at any rate is now clear. From certain articles in the rebel papers I infer that Lee's army, especially Early's command, is no longer what it was, and does not fight as it used. I do not quite understand Sheridan's success on any other ground. In fact the wonder is that demoralisation has not long ago set in over the whole South. Some day or other it must come, or human nature change.

Meanwhile I have still only a peaceful rustic life to record. Kuhn is still away in Paris. Loo is quite unable to accustom herself to our stupid existence, and is unhappy in consequence. I was so myself the first year of our residence. But Loo will never be happy anywhere any more. Mary continues well, but today is quite cold, a sharp frost, and I am curious to see how she will stand it. My own health is quite restored and I am trying to get fat on cod-liver oil, Guinness' Stout, and just as high living as may be. Come over here again and we'll have that other bottle of Burgundy.

Your photographic productions arrived in safety and have excited much interest. Also I received with them a letter from you written the 16th I suppose, but dated the 15th. So far as we can judge, you appear now to be balder than ever. I could observe no other difference. All the other figures were strangers to us except by name in one or two cases. On the whole I thought the picture was rather an attractive one, representing a not unpleasing phase of existence. The Morter picture is remarkably curious. It will be a great gun to show the English who visit us. But how many of them will ever see it, I can't guess, for now another fortnight will prepare us for a new change. I hope that the Chief will retire, or at least offer to retire at once after the election. I shall do my best to get him away. Pray Heaven we may not immediately exchange the London frying-pan for the Washington fire.

I send you Salem Chapel. It is a clever picture of one sort, or two sorts, of English life.[1] I don't know the author, nor whether you've ever read it.

MS: MHi
1. The unsigned novel (1863) by Margaret Oliphant (1828–1897) depicts a Nonconformist minister and his congregation of tradesmen; a lurid subplot involves aristocrats.

To Charles Francis Adams, Jr.

No. 27.   London. 11 Nov. 1864.

My dear Colonel:

Your papa, your mamma and your sister Mary have just this moment gone off to visit his Grace the Juke of Devonshire at Chatsworth, in almost the thickest London fog I ever saw. I have already intimated to you that our mother, for some reason only referable, I think, to the curious instability of feminine character, has been doing what she could to induce us to return to town, and has met a vigorous opposition on the part of all of us, in the course of which there have arisen one or two lively debates. When I arrived in town therefore by the train this morning, it was not without a certain satisfaction that I saw this pall of night overspreading the city, into which the carriage with the ladies, plunged headlong when about half way from Ealing. You can easily imagine the immediate practice Mary made with this weapon so happily offered to her hand. She did not draw attention to the atmosphere, for in fact there was no possibility of attending to anything else; but she kept up a continuous and effective fire of remarks, and arrowy words, and allowed no doubt to remain in regard to her probable fate if once planted in such an air. I was greatly amused when, as she followed her parents down stairs, discharging her artillery in this style, she looked up to me who was lighting them from above, and remarked *sotto voce* and with a highly pleased expression of countenance, "Couldn't be better"; and so departed.

Meanwhile Kuhn has returned from Paris and he with Loo and I are left alone at Ealing. Loo as usual is ever in some state of emotion. I am more and more astonished that any frame is capable of enduring the tortures of so restless a spirit. Kuhn is also a devil at nagging when his stomach is a little out of order. I think Paris has put it a little out of order this time, and I do not anticipate a calm during the next few days. I have asked my friend Gaskell out to pass them with us, but do not know whether he will come.

Meanwhile my hopes of our escaping from England soon, are not so buoyant as they, perhaps unreasonably, once were. I feel a feeling that your papa may fail us at the pinch. Should he be pressed to stay, I fear he will do so, and I am almost convinced that he will either remain here or go into the Cabinet. This is the only alternative I can see, and I dread either almost equally. Nevertheless I wait what may turn up, to adapt my plan of operations accordingly.

The decision must soon be made. We shall next week know the result of the election. We drank to Abraham's success at dinner last Tuesday. If all goes well, another month will see us settled here for another year, I suppose, or preparing to break up between December and April. This is however a critical time. Although we have news down to the 2d, I would be glad to know that our corner was safely turned, and do not therefore venture to build much on the future. There are some ugly diplomatic questions also, that have chosen just this time to come up, and I dread their influence on us.[1]

We are as usual void of news except from the war. I do not comprehend Grant's moves. They do not seem to be made in earnest. He has the air of playing with Lee, and Lee seems to think so, to judge from Mr Lawley's last epistle to the Times. I have been expecting for a long time a movement of the combined army across the Appomatox from City Point, on the rear of Petersburg and onto Lee's flank or rear, as it may be. What is the use of Lee's extended lines, if we always attack the same points? Nevertheless, the election once over, I am willing to wait patiently if necessary; for the cautious game is probably now our sure play.

I have no literature for you this week. In fact I read less now myself than at almost any time for years.

MS: MHi

1. Questions about Confederate activities in Canada and the transfer of ownership of a British vessel to Captain Semmes.

To John Gorham Palfrey

London. 16 November. 1864.

My dear Dr Palfrey:

Your's of the 16th ulto. with its inclosure to Lyulph Stanley came to hand safely and I forwarded your letter, to which I now enclose his response. Stanley has the merit of being "plus royaliste que le roi"; at least when he has his aristocratic friends here to argue with. On indifferent occasions his love of argument would, I believe, lead him to question the existence of the sun; but his tendencies are certainly very strong towards democracy, or human equality, as he would rather call it; and he upholds our cause hotly on this side, even in his own family where he meets an energetic opposition. I dare not always say Yes to his doctrines myself.

Everything is of course now waiting the result of the election, about which, as yet, we know nothing. I have been living in hopes that among its results might be our immediate release from this happy existence of ours in England; for I saw no reason why Mr Lincoln should keep us here this winter if we are to obtain our discharge at any rate next spring. But it is so hopeless to look forward or to make plans, that I do not venture even to guess when we shall be permitted again to see Boston. I have no wish to act longer as appendage to this Legation, yet I scarcely know what to look to after leaving it. So the best plan is the easiest, namely to follow the current so long as it runs, and not try to control the paths of Princes.

I think I have nothing to tell you that is even an apology for news. We are still indulging in our ease at our country-place at Ealing, whence we come to town every few days, my father and I, to do our work. This is, as you know, a sufficiently gloomy period of the year, and the country, unattractive as it is, appears a region of happiness as compared with the town. My father and mother and Mary have just returned from a visit to Chatsworth, while Mr & Mrs Kuhn and I stayed at home and kept house. Your friend the Duchess of Argyll has another baby, her twelfth. To my mind this is a very strong dose of domestic luxury, considering the Duke's very moderate means of supporting them; and seven portionless daughters to marry is a horrible idea! I have discovered however, an antidote to this evil; or rather a point wherein the British Constitution is susceptible of developement. To complete the system of primogeniture it is absolutely required that each elder son or heir should have several wives to counterbalance the cadet bachelors. No one who knows society here can doubt that this just and necessary reform, if once sanctioned by the bench of Bishops, would be highly popular among the British females, in whose interest it would indeed be made.

I am delighted to hear that your new volume is so near launching and I hope some day to tell you in person how I enjoy it. Pray commend me to Frank, who I am glad to hear, intends to get married. Many of my friends have married and, I suppose, grown old; but when I return I beg to have it understood that I recommence where I left off, at twenty-one.

Ever sincerely Yrs Henry B. Adams.

MS: MH

To Charles Francis Adams, Jr.

No. 29.   London. 25 Nov. 1864.

My dear Colonel:

Our last advices announce your arrival at home. I hope you will not return to camp until you have got wholly rid of your dysentery.

The election is over then, and after all that excitement, worry and danger, behold all goes on as before! It was one of those cases in which life and death seemed to hang on the issue, and the result is so decisive as to answer all our wishes and hopes. It is a curious commentary upon theoretical reasoning as to forms of Government, that this election which ought by all rights to be a defect in the system, and which is universally considered by the admirers of "strong Governments" to be a proof of the advantage of their own model, should yet turn out in practice a great and positive gain and a fruitful source of national strength. After all, systems of Government are secondary matters, if you've only got your people behind them. I never yet have felt so proud as now of the great qualities of our race, or so confident of the capacity of men to develop their faculties in the mass. I believe that a new era of the movement of the world will date from that day, which will drag nations up still another step, and carry us out of a quantity of old fogs. Europe has a long way to go yet to catch us up.

Anything that produces a great effect in our favor on this side, usually produces a sort of general silence as the first proof of its force. So this election has been met on this side by a species of blindness. People remark the fact with wonder and anger, but they have only just such a vague idea of what are to be its consequences, as shuts their mouths without changing their opinions. Only the most clear-headed see indistinctly what bearing it is likely to have on English politics, and I expect that it will be years yet before its full action gets into play. Meanwhile the Government is now stronger than ever and our only weak point is the financial one. May our name not have to stand guard on that!

You can imagine with what enthusiasm we received the news, and drank to the success of the new Administration. For the time, all interest has centered in the election, and even the incomprehensible state of things in Georgia has been overlooked.[1] How many more campaigns we shall have to make, seems very doubtful, but thus far our rate of progression has been regular, and if continued, ought to bring us to Augusta at the next round. We can afford to be patient however, now, for all we have to fear is pecuniary ruin, and that is tolerably certain.

I don't know that I've anything to tell you that's new or original on this side. Loo Brooks came through this week on her way home after five weeks of most harrassing contact with her mamma-in-law, who appears to have been superbly herself. Poor Loo was happy to escape, and we cheered her and little Fanny amazingly by a few hours at Ealing. I sent by her a cargo of books to the young 'uns, our nephews which ought to keep them in literature till they're old men. By the way, should you go to Washington, try and have a talk with Seward about our affairs. The Chief, by this steamer, sends *privately* a request to be relieved. You can intimate to S. that if compelled to stay, he means at any rate to send his family home and break up the establishment, remaining himself as a temporary occupant till a successor is appointed. He even talks of doing so at once, and sending the women to Italy in January preparatory to their going home in June. Seward must see that a change, if necessary at all, had best be made quickly for the public good. Don't quote me however. On no account let what I say, come back. You will probably get at first hand all the information you want. Best say nothing at all, yet, of the idea of retirement except to S. if you see him. Let me know what he says.

You see we are in a "transition state." But I do not see a chance of release before March—unless for worse chains.

MS: MHi
1. Sherman had started from Atlanta, Nov. 15, on his March to the Sea.

To Lord Houghton

London. 28 Nov. 1864.

My dear Lord Houghton:

I send you by the post the report which you wrote to ask me for, some time since. I am told that there never was any difficulty in Chicago, as was supposed. The scandal occurred in the Treasury Department at Washington, and the confusion must have arisen from the fact that a very bitter Copperhead journal at Chicago was prominent in making a disturbance about it. I've not examined it carefully enough to see what the rights and wrongs of the case are, but I don't believe there was more in it than will sometimes happen in the best of our lecherous human societies.[1]

I've not had the pleasure of hearing anything of your health and whereabouts for a long time, whence I am led to suppose that you are well and quiet. Pray give my best regards to Lady Houghton.

The Presidential election being over, I am led to hope that our term of service at your Court is over also, or nearly so. Of course I don't mean to imply that we dislike it. But the best of friends to England may without disrespect, wish to see his own home again after four such years. I scarcely think we shall pass another season in London. If I should not see you again, I hope you will remember me as being one of your warmest friends.

Very truly Yrs   H. B. Adams.

Lord Houghton.

MS: Trinity College, Cambridge
1. The London *Times,* which garbled an old story, evidently prompted the question. A banknote printing company tried to corrupt a treasury official, but congressional investigation found no fraud.

To Charles Francis Adams, Jr.

No. 31.   London. 9 Decem. 1864.

My dear Colonel:

The devil seems to have a happy knack of tumbling upon people in a lump. Here is Mary who by some perverse quality which is thoroughly feminine, persists in refusing to get well, and alarms us by visions of sudden collapse and constitutional break-down. She has this simple wound on the head, which by all ordinary rules of health ought to heal of its own accord in twenty four hours, but which has now a second time reopened and shows no sign of closing. Evidently there is something very wrong about her system and the best encouragement I can imagine is only that the wound may prove a relief to the system by drawing the danger from a more serious part. This is however only good in the case it goes no farther, but the doctors evidently fear it will go farther, and are nervous about erisypelas. Meanwhile we can only wait and take such precautions as may be.

Then comes your illness which is a source of no little anxiety to us. I still hope that rather than return to camp with it hanging over you, the supreme necessity of health will bring you over here even at the expence of your commission. I understand that the Chief wrote to you last week in the same sense. We are in a devilish coil too, about this Italian visit, which seems determined upon, but which strains our forces to accomplish.

Kuhn and Loo go off tomorrow to the continent. Since this decision she has regained her spirits very much, and seems comparatively well. We three went over to Walton to pass Tuesday with the Sturgises, and as usual, I found all the old pleasure in basking in the light of that luxurious household. I met there the father of your old friend at Harvard, Johnny Lerman;

a notorious secesh, but an agreeable and gentlemanly sort of person. We got along very well, politics of course not being mentioned.

If I had been in the humor of being gay, I might this autumn have passed very near all my time running about to make country visits. As it is, I have, with one or two exceptions, kept pretty much at home, and reserved myself for Christmas at the Sturgis's. Yesterday afternoon I ran down to Eton to see Harry Sturgis who is ill with a very painful attack of sciatica. He was in bed and suffering very much. As I walked through the town and out on the Slough Road, I was forcibly reminded of our visit last spring, and of the nearness of that period of the year again. I don't know that anything has happened since then, to surprise us very much, or that on the whole we have not had as much good fortune as anyone could reasonably ask. But there is always a little sense of pain in going back over the footprints of the morning track, especially in the damp and foggy twilight of a December evening. I stumped along to Slough courageously enough, but rather inclined to curse things generally. There has been a pervading sense of worry about our existence for some time past, and it does not seem likely to diminish much for the present. The anxiety that worried us two years ago about the national prospects, was on the whole perhaps harder to bear, but this comes nearer home.

Of course Sherman's march is creating great excitement here. The newspapers, one after another, and about every other day, prove conclusively that he must lose his army and fall a victim to "clouds of confederate cavalry on his front, flank and rear"; to "swarms of patriotic guerillas behind every bush"; to failure of supplies which are all to be destroyed as he moves; to the obstruction of roads, and finally to the army in his front. I will say however that the latest advices of the alarm existing in the rebel kingdom, have made their friends here far less confident than they were. My consolation is that by this time the result must have been arrived at, one way or the other; and as I have as much faith in Sherman as I have in any individual of ancient or modern history or mythology, I keep a very stiff courage up and wait confidently the result.

Ever

MS: MHi

To Charles Francis Adams, Jr.

No. 32. London. 16 Decem. 1864.

My dear Colonel:

Your letter of the 29th November, as well as a package of maps which came by post, reached me this week. The maps, especially that of Sherman's campaign, are very valuable. Government has supplied us with all but that, and we have been cussing a good deal at wanting it. By the way, you forgot about ordering us the Army and Navy Journal, which would be very useful just now when the war news is becoming so prominent. Popular opinion here declares louder than ever that Sherman is lost. People are quite angry at his presumption in attempting such a wild project. The interest felt in his march is enormous, however, and if he arrives as successfully as I expect, at the sea, you may rely upon it that the moral effect of his demonstration on Europe will be greater than that of any other event of the war. It will finish the rebs on this side for a long time, if not as I believe, for ever.

Meanwhile I can't say that I am surprised at your continued illness. You may depend upon it that three year's campaigning is as much as is good for a man and that the diarhoea is a hint that he'd better mind his eye. You have had my opinions upon it in my last letters, however, and so I will leave them this time for another occasion. There is one principle however that to me seems tolerably safe; whatever the value of life may be, great or small, as people happen to think, life without health is worth just nothing. Therefore mind your constitution.

Loo and Kuhn have left us; gone off into space, chattering and fighting and scolding according to their wont; just like two sparrows kicking up an eternal little row around their busy selves. Loo has missed her mark in life; in fact I dont know whether her nature ever would have allowed her to hit it; and she is destined to be an unhappy little woman. If her health lasts, she'll carry her weight well enough. But if not, I shouldn't wonder at anything she did or didn't do.

MS: MHi

To James Clarke Davis

London. 22 Dec. 1864.

My dear Davis:[1]

I have just received your letter of the 6th instant, and the Triennial for this year. Charley Allen would, I think, have been more diffuse in the latter, than Dexter has been, and I should not have been sorry for a little garrulousness. But then so far as it goes, there is no fault to find, and I am happy to acknowledge that the highly objectionable destiny announced for myself in the first report, has been properly corrected in the present. My threats, therefore, of personal violence to the Reverend Chowles will not be put in execution. That middle-aged hypocrite may congratulate himself.[2]

I have read the report over with great interest. You know I've not had the pleasure of being at home more than a few weeks since we graduated, and the recollection of our class, or of such a part of it as I ever knew well, has remained tolerably fresh. I was sorry that Lee and Ben Jones should have been dropped out of the list, for I would like to know how all our old acquaintances live and die.[3]

As for the object of your letter, I enclose herewith a draft for $25.00 on my brother, which will be honored, I suppose, on the spot. If not, you can let me know.[4]

Hoping that the law proves a good trade, and is productive of much mun, and a high degree of virtue,

I remain

Very sincerely Yrs   H. B. Adams.

MS: MH, Archives

1. James Clarke Davis (1838–1905) began to practice law in Boston in 1862.
2. The *Second Triennial Report* of the Harvard class of 1858 had a short preface by George Dexter, who succeeded Charles Adams Allen as secretary. (Allen finished his theological studies in 1864 and was ordained a Unitarian minister in Montpelier, Vt.) The 1861 occupational summary listed under "Various": "Adams, diplomacy." The 1864 entry stated: "Continues in London as private secretary to his father. Writes that he is to be called a student of law."
3. Rooney Lee and Benjamin D. M. Jones, who had left Harvard in 1857 without degrees, were restored in the 1868 report.
4. The class had voted to ask each member to give "at least five dollars yearly for the Class Fund" until $1,000 was reached.

To Charles Francis Adams, Jr.

No. 34.   London. 30 Decem. 1864.

My dear Colonel:

Back again in London with the usual graceful accompaniment of fog and smoke. A gay old place is this, but as I do not anticipate a much longer residence here, I will not abuse it. We do not as yet know what the Washington oracle says, but anyway we shall not see much more of London.

We quitted Hanger Hill, at least I did, with a certain degree of regret, which might have been greater, had we not been immediately on our way to Mt Felix to pass our Christmas. Mary and Brooks and I are of an adamantine firmness in our allegiance to Mt Felix. It has been an oasis in the English desert to us. Balm flows into my soul on crossing that luxurious threshold. The spirit of the lotus pervades my nerves when I lounge in those halls. My glass of bitters before dinner is flavored with distilled waters of perpetual youth, and Sturgis's port and Madeira go deep into my soul, even to the fountain of tears, especially when I take a good deal of them, as I genewally do. As for Mary, who is not apt to feel very strong attachments, it is quite out of the question to check her bent towards Walton. Her papa and mamma, after trying to do so for three years, seem at last to have given up the effort, and indeed are glad enough to find a place where they can leave her to be happy and amused in these rather anxious days.

As for Mrs Sturgis, who shall say harm? I know of a woman who has been kind to me with no possible motive—who always has a warm and genial welcome for me—who always listens to me, and shows an interest in what I am doing—who has put her house and her household at my service as much as if I were her son—who bears with my follies, humors my weaknesses, and sympathises in my troubles if I have any. And all the harm that I know of her is that she likes the flavor of dinner and a good glass of wine; a taste which I cannot deny to exist in myself. If Mrs Sturgis eats too much, I've not got to digest it. If she drinks more than I can, my head has not got to stand it. And the wine is not mine.

What irritates me is that people don't know a good thing when they see it. They haven't the common sense to know what *is* good even under the most brilliant circumstances. I see a wilderness of stupidities about me here, each of whom appears to have a surrounding of its own, quite irrespective of its merits. And when I try to get hold of something that strikes me as particularly good, I am sure to find it to be thought by the public rather exceptionally poor. That is the nature of this population.

Poor Harry Sturgis is surrounded all the time by all the guests, trying to amuse and interest him, but he has a long road before him and a very painful and fatiguing illness to bear. Mary too does not get well, although she looks well, and weighs nearly as much as ever. In fact I have not been so anxious about this business in her head, as about her throat, which is really a serious affair. Still, I'm not disposed to worry even about that.

Mrs Sturgis proposed your health at Christmas and it was drunk in good wine. I hope some day you may enjoy it as I have done.

Sturgis came out one evening quite exuberant, and "What will you give for the news?" says he. It was that of Sherman's arrival at the coast, and Hood's defeat at Nashville. You may judge of our exultation. It seems at last that this war is going to come to its end. This last campaign will, I suppose, narrow the field of the war to the Atlantic States, and when that is done, the result is inevitable and must come soon. What a fellow Sherman is! and how well Grant is managing! The combinations of this war are getting so tremendous that there will be nothing left for us in a foreign war except to make the moon a basis, and to march our armies overland to conquer Europe. The result has thrown great consternation into the minds of the English, and with reason. This Canadian business is suddenly found to be serious, and the prospect of Sherman marching down the St Lawrence, and Farragut sailing up it, doesn't seem just agreeable. They are annoyed at Dix's Order. If they are not sharp they will find annoyance a totally inadequate expression for it.[1]

MS: MHi

1. A conspiracy to release Confederate prisoners from Union prisons began with a raid from Canada on a St. Albans, Vt., bank, in which one person was killed. Gen. John Adams Dix (1798–1879), commanding the Department of the East, ordered the pursuit of Confederate marauders into Canada.

To Charles Francis Adams, Jr.

No. 35. London. 6 Jan. 1865.[1]

My dear Colonel:

After another week passed in running about, I come back to town to get off the mail, and then again disappear myself for another week. Most of my time has been passed at Mt Felix, which is however not so agreeable a residence now as it was, and to which nothing but my regard for Mrs Sturgis carries me. Poor Harry's condition is grave, and although his main difficulty seems to be no worse, and perhaps better, there are symptoms that his system is reduced and that complications may rise at any day, which are the more dangerous because unforeseen. Mr and Mrs Sturgis make a brave fight, and sustain their courage stoutly, but it is dreadfully hard work, and the strain is beginning to tell. It is a punishment to me to see all this. Poor Sturgis gradually has stopped his jokes and his laugh has ceased to come easily, while Mrs Sturgis who has to be with Harry all the time, fairly broke down yesterday on the appearance of a new and serious trouble, and lost her steadiness wholly, for a time. I was not there, and when I returned at night, all was going on as usual, only every one was a shade more gloomy than before, and I had to drink like a fish at dinner in order to be gay and funny. Poor Mary who still remains there, was in very low spirits about it. She has herself had a cold which alarmed me a good deal for a time, but which seems to be passing off, although I don't feel too confident yet.

On Tuesday I went down to pass a few days at Tom Baring's place in Hampshire, Norman Court.[2] Thomas, as you may recollect, has a certain reputation for hospitality and his country-place is noted for a certain sort of luxury which is rather peculiar to himself. I found there a large party, among whom was Lord Houghton who inquired particularly about you, and who grows more sensual, and sleepy every day. There were a bevy of Bridgman Simpsons, and Wodehouse Currys, and Bingham Mildmays; and there was Sir Charles Wyke, and Mr Bankhead, to do the diplomatic; and a couple of stray Barings who filled up.[3] Altogether it was a pleasant party, in which I was tolerably at home, although I never yet much enjoyed a first visit to any house. All the rest of the family, including Kuhn and Loo, have been there before, but I was never asked and did not expect to be. As it was, I could only stay two days, and had to come up on Thursday to be here today, sleeping at Walton *en route.*

I suppose this place of Baring's is as near the true idea of aristocratic perfection as is permitted to imperfect mortality. Some people say that one's ear is offended by the rustle of bank-notes. It is a calumny, if said invidiously, for there could not be more luxury with less show. But if this sound does offend one's ear, it is the only sound which does so. Thomas is a bachelor, and his house is perfect order. It radiates with luxury at so many points as positively to embarras a mean republican.

In one sense, society is much more agreeable now than it used to be. I no longer feel any dread of conversation about our affairs. The name of Sherman has of late placed us who are abroad, in a very commanding position, and our military reputation is at the head of the nations. You can imagine that this relieves us of our greatest discomfort, and in fact we now receive compliments where we used to hear nothing but sneers. Even the Times is converted, and gives us a long leader full of praise of Sherman. The fall of Savannah is needed to complete the opinion of the world here, and I suppose Savannah will fall of its own weight very soon. Then the final struggle will begin, and these good foreigners will learn a new page in history.

We do not yet know what we are to do. We leave England on the 15th or 16th, and I am to take charge of the party. I do not consider it a joke; but anything to be amused! (Other people would say, any thing so long as I'm useful. Hypocrites!)

MS: MHi
1. HA misdated this letter 1864.
2. Thomas Baring (1799–1873), M.P., managing partner of Baring Brothers and grandson of the founder.
3. Henry and Frances-Emily Baring Bridgeman-Simpson; Philip Wodehouse Currie (1834–1906), diplomat; Henry Bingham Mildmay (1828–1905), partner in Baring Brothers; Sir Charles Wyke (1815–1897), minister to Mexico 1860–1861; Charles Bankhead (d. 1870), minister to Mexico 1843–1851.

To Charles Francis Adams, Jr.

No. 38.   London. 27 January. 1865.

My dear Colonel:

Once more I write to you and once more our departure is postponed. The cold and cough that, I told you, were bothering your mamma last week, have stuck to her desperately and almost blown her to pieces. She will no doubt describe her suffering with her own graphic pen, so there's no necessity for my doing so. The upshot is that here we still are, with Mary still at Walton, and I devoting all my leisure time to the study of Italian. Yet it is only right to say that I have no very absolute certainty in my own mind, that I shall even see Italy. Our plans are so indefinite and so liable to be knocked in the head by news from your side of the water, that I feel myself about equally balanced between the probabilities of going to Italy and remaining there till summer and then bringing the family home, or of not going there at all, but staying here to pack up our duds and take them home in advance of the rest of the party. Mr Mackay, the intelligent and gentlemanly New York correspondent of the London Times,[1] has written to that journal, I am told, that Mr Seward is to return to the Senate and our present Minister at the Court of St James is to take the Secretary's place. I suppose this tale is only an appendage to that which transfers Senator Morgan to the Treasury,[2] for I see no other means of giving Seward a vacancy. Thank the Lord, it can't be true, or else Mackay wouldn't write it, but it's an annoying idea to have on one's mind, and I am not sorry that our departure is postponed if it enables us to settle our projects before going, and eliminate these disturbing quantities from our equation.

Meanwhile life has flowed away with calm, since my last, but with weather of an heroically disgusting nature. Nothing but fogs, east winds, rain and snow varies the charms of heaven's blue sky. This morning it snows! I thought I was in Boston when I woke. And as it snows, it partially melts, and slosh predominates.

According to the quiet of the season, I am deprived of all interesting subjects of talk. We had a little dinner yesterday, to eat some venison that our ex-Secretary Wilson sent over, and absolutely there was no gossip to be extracted from the usually prattling young men. Palmer was quite dumb.[3] Gaskell's highest strain was that Lord Palmerston had the scarlet fever, and the Duke of St Albans was up in a divorce case as co-respondent. The Duke is the brother of Lady Di Beauclerck, and a very fashionable young man. By the way, I would have given much to have been able to send you the report of the Chetwynd divorce case that came off last month and created great excitement in society. It was s-o-o-perb and calculated to enlighten society even more than Kalloch and Coburn, although its particulars had none of the racy humor of a crim.-con. suit.[4] The lady, who sued for divorce, and *got* it, was a clergyman's daughter; was seven months gone with child when Chetwynd married her, he not knowing who the father was; she was a great hunting woman and fond of smoking a pipe in the stable, besides being given to general attachments to gentlemen which were certainly not at all philosophic, though probably not criminal. You may imagine what the husband was; a Squire Western, exaggerated.[5] It was amusing to see how society deprecated the publication of all this case, on the ground that it showed so shocking a state of things existing in the upper classes, that *it would set a bad example to the lower orders.* They are very praiseworthy in their laudable attempts to benefit the lower orders.

Your photographs have not yet come home. If you are at work on finances, you had best take Taxation too. I will send you McCulloch's work on that subject if you want it. Mill is best on Currency, and indeed on all other subjects, but large and expensive. You had best get him from Washington. Meanwhile I have got Fawcett's adaptation of his work, which is much more useful to study up on.[6] This I suppose the Minn will send you.

MS: MHi

1. Charles Mackay (1814–1889), journalist and popular songwriter, succeeded Bancroft Davis as New York correspondent of the *Times* 1862–1865.

2. Edwin Denison Morgan (1811–1883), Republican senator from New York 1863–1869, was offered the Department of the Treasury in 1865.

3. Ralph Charlton Palmer (1839–1923), a barrister whom HA had met in 1863, became a lifelong friend.

4. In 1857 R. H. Dana, Jr., successfully defended Isaac C. Kalloch in a criminal conversation suit that generated much publicity.

5. The coarse country squire in *Tom Jones* (1749).

6. John Ramsey McCulloch, *A Treatise on the Principles and Practical Influence of Taxation* (1845). Mill, *Principles of Political Economy* (1848). Henry Fawcett, *Manual of Political Economy* (1863).

To Charles Francis Adams

Hotel Wagram. Paris.
Saturday. 4 Feb. 1865.

My dear father:

Before beginning the second stage of our journey, I suppose you will not be sorry to receive from me an account of the first. Mary has kept you well posted as to our experiences, I believe, down to our arrival here. They were remarkably free from unpleasant accidents and far more agreeable than I had any reason to expect. Mamma got happily across the channel, thanks to her camphor I think, and Mary did not suffer from the exposure. We came on to Paris the next day without adventure, and found everything ready for us. Our stay here has been tolerably dissipated, considering that we are invalids, and I have been on pins for fear of Mary. But we start again tomorrow for Dijon, and perhaps we may escape the colds I have dreaded. Luckily the weather is mild. Hitherto mamma has amazed me by her gaiety and freedom from nervousness. I think the reaction after London has set her up, for I've not seen her so full of spirits and so equable for months. She herself proposed our dining at the Palais Royal, and we went there last evening with George Sohier and had a nice little dinner very agreeably. She will tell you herself of what she thinks of aunt Eliza.[1]

In respect to expenses, I cannot console you with the idea that travelling is a cheap amusement. No invention has yet been discovered here for that purpose. You know from our English journeys about the rate of disbursement that is necessary in a family-party. I estimate it, when on the move, at not less than £10. a day. I have thought it best to draw here for enough to carry us to Nice, and then I shall be able to estimate more exactly our probable outlay. General Butler (as our courier is commonly called) is thus far efficient and steady. I don't think he can cheat us much.

I have seen Mr Bigelow several times, and he has just been up to call, but I was alone at home. He is exercised about a ram which they are trying to get out, and which the Government is not so favorable to us in stopping, as he would like. I think he is well pleased with his new dignity, as is not Pennington who had already issued cards as Chargé.[2]

I congratulate you on the end of the Wilmington matter and the general tenor of the news by the China.[3] The talk about Seward's succeeding you seems to be gathering strength, and rather annoys me though I do not credit it. Perhaps the China will tell you something. If you are anxious to let us know it, or to stop our advance, you can telegraph to us at Dijon (Hotel de la Cloche) or at Lyons (Hotel de Lyons (Grand). I mean to reach

Nice Thursday, if nothing happens to delay us. At Avignon we go to the Hotel de l'Europe. As yet we have received no letter from you.

Sunday. 5th. We start for Dijon in half an hour. Last evening we dined at the Trois Frères with Uncle Edward and General Barlow.[4] About the dinner, mamma will have a story to tell you, which has been the occasion of a good deal of worry to her, and of disgust to me, and which is in fact a very laughable, but rather expensive joke.

When Barlow comes to London he will report to you, and I hope you will do for him all that lies in your way. Perhaps he would like to go to Court if there is a drawing-room or levée.

We have received nothing from you. Possibly mamma may like to break our journey at Avignon, and take a day to visit the sights there. If so, and the weather is good, I shall encourage the idea. We have done so well thus far that I am very anxious to keep it up so.

I can't decipher the banker's name at Nice, so if you please you can direct to poste-restante, or ask R. Sturgis.

H.B.A.

MS: MHi
   1. Elizabeth Boott Brooks (1799–1865), wife of ABA's brother Edward.
   2. Minister Dayton died Dec. 1. John Bigelow (1817–1911), formerly editor of the New York *Evening Post*, consul at Paris 1861–1865, became chargé d'affaires and then minister 1865–1866. Pennington, who had hoped to be chargé, was secretary of the legation.
   3. The forts protecting Wilmington, N.C., had been blown up and the port sealed against blockade runners. The China: S.S. *China*.
   4. Maj. Gen. Francis Channing Barlow (1834–1896), who was wounded at Gettysburg and led a division at Spotsylvania, was in Europe on sick leave.

To Charles Francis Adams

Avignon. 8 February. 1865.

My dear Father:

Behold us at Avignon, taking a day's rest, not before it was needed. I expected to receive here a letter from you, but nothing has appeared since we left home. I don't much care, myself, but mamma frets a good deal at not hearing. You know she has not yet learned to think that no news is good news.

Mary wrote to you from Lyons. Our stay there was short and nasty. We left it on a cold and cloudy morning, and in hopes of reaching some less hideous climate, if there was any such. As we crept slowly down the banks of the Rhone, the clouds broke away and the sun came out brightly for the first time in our journey. The scenery is lovely even in winter, and made us forget for a time even the wretchedness of a slow and crowded train. But soon another evil made its appearance. With the sun came the mistral which followed us down the valley, always increasing in force, till it blew a perfect tempest and colder than the arctic region. What with this, and our slow progress, and the late hour, we had an unpleasant and fatiguing journey, with the usual accompaniments of such incidents in the shape of general crossness. We reached Avignon at seven, in an icy hurricane, but here was balm! The hotel is admirable, and rest before us. Mary indeed seems none the worse for the exposure, but mamma is evidently rather used up, and wants quiet.

Today has been really warm and fine. I got mamma and Mary out this morning and walked them about. The view was extremely fine, and the sky clear, with a sun such as we none of us have seen for years. I believe mamma really did enjoy this, and acknowledged that it was a pleasant change. We sat in the sun looking at the Rhone and the hills covered with snow. The mistral gradually died away and tonight it is cloudy again.

We may leave here tomorrow or not till Friday. I never can decide till the moment, because I can't foresee at all mamma's wishes. If we travel, she is fatigued and complains of her head. Today she is homesick, and let down, after the excitement of movement. Under ordinary circumstances I should think she would prefer to make one day from here to Nice, but as we can't hear from there about rooms in time to go through tomorrow, we must either stay here over tomorrow, or go on to Marseilles or Toulon. The latter was our original plan, but our slow trains and the fatigue and exposure of our frequent stoppages, have so annoyed us that we had decided to change it.

Our expenses seem to average about the sum I mentioned in my last. The courier continues very efficient.

This finishes, I believe, all that I have to say. From it you will judge as to our progress, and our condition. We have done in fact quite as well as I expected, but I shall be well-pleased to resign my command whenever you may see fit to relieve me. You would have enjoyed our researches today, extremely.

Mamma would write, if I did not.

Ever your son   Henry B. Adams.

MS: MHi

To Charles Francis Adams

Nice. 12 February. 1865.

My dear Father:

We arrived here at seven o'clock Friday (10th) evening, and yesterday morning received your letters with enclosures.

My last letter was from Avignon. I would have much liked to have staid there, for it is, beyond all comparison the most attractive specimen of antiquity I have seen in France. When you come through, by all means break your journey there, and see it. You will find few more curious places in Europe.

But when Friday morning, or rather Thursday morning came, with it came the mistral again, blowing a hurricane, with a sky so brilliant and a sun so bright that travelling seemed the only way of enjoying ourselves. We heard too from Nice that our rooms were taken for Friday night, and as mamma did not discover that she liked Avignon till it was decided to leave it, there seemed no reason to keep us there. So we came on to Marseilles, with the mistral following us and blowing two or three gales across the plains. In the train we did not feel it, and of course kept under cover at Marseilles. But it was very cold that night and the next morning ice stood everywhere all day. We had now arrived at the fact that the fallacy of a warm climate had been exploded beyond a doubt by the only sure test—experience. We therefore hoped that by turning again to the northward we might regain a little of our lost ground. In that hope we came to Nice. I doubt whether we have gained much. It freezes as hard here as elsewhere, and if the wind is not so violent, it is quite as sharp. Without being a hot climate, it is near enough to it to deceive one with the idea and to encourage dissipation in the open air. In other respects it reminds one of other sea-side places. There are sixty four American families here, of whom we stand in deadly fear, and if we stay long, they will surely catch us. As for the English their name is a corps d'armée. But we know few or none of them.

Mamma has sustained a new shock and is grievously troubled in her mind. On retiring to bed last night, she tumbled over a large black trunk. If it had been a ghost, or a spectral illusion, she could not have suffered a greater blow, for this was the very trunk which she had fondly imagined was on its way by sea to Naples. I had seen the trunk every day, but knowing nothing about it, had never noticed its presence except in the charges for baggage, and had not thought it best to say anything about these, knowing how mamma worries herself, and how much trouble had been taken to reduce the amount. It appears that Harris told the maid that this trunk was to go to Paris and thence by sea to Naples. So, no orders having been given, it has followed us all our march.

As to our plans, I am at this moment a good deal bothered. I don't want to go by sea to Genoa, for a multitude of reasons. I do want to pass a few days at Mentoni, in the hope of finding more genial air and a touch of spring. But vetture are scarce; all the world is going south; and at Mentoni one is left as it were between Heaven and earth, unless one has secured one's line of march. Still, unless I am decidedly stuck, I mean to go by land not only to Genoa but to Spezzia also. Mamma and Mary are rabid against the sea, and I scarcely dare breathe the word.

Meanwhile you had best write to us at Genoa, care of Grants Balfour & Co, so far as I can make out their name. Probably we shall leave here Tuesday, the day after tomorrow. If we like Mentoni, we may stay there a few days. At Genoa we shall certainly stay a day or two. At Spezzia we may also delay a little if it suits us. But beyond Pisa, I can't see clear. Shall we go to Florence or to Leghorn and Rome? It will depend upon what we hear from Naples. Meanwhile your letters can go to Genoa till we decide.

If Seward won't relieve you, he might give you a leave. But he *must* be quick.

Is there *any* hope of selling those horses?

Ever your son   Henry.

MS: MHi

To Charles Francis Adams

Nice. 13 February. 1865.

My dear Father:

The general came to me this morning and told me that a vettura had come in yesterday; that he had seen the vetturino and had got the refusal of his carriage; that the price was twenty Napoleons to Genoa; and that the man would come to see me in a few minutes. This information was well enough, all but the price. I saw the man; went to look at his carriage; and then passed several hours in running about to make inquiries unknown to the General. These inquiries quite satisfied me on one point; to me a very important one. The price was legitimate, and I could do no better on this road.

This established, I came back and consulted mamma. The amount of assistance I got there was limited. In fact I was left to decide for myself, with the right of criticism reserved. I accept this as a part of the duty put on me, but in deciding I want to have it understood that I choose only what I think the safe part. My reasons are too many to give, but are conclusive to my mind against the steamers wherever we can avoid them, at this season. It was also an argument that you incline towards delay, and this will take us nearly a week if we stop a day or two at Mentoni. The expense is only 100 francs a travelling day; considerably less than the railway travelling has averaged.

Nice is a failure. It is not warm and is far too fashionable to suit any of us. We hope to start tomorrow.

The General says that the fever is confined to Naples, but does not touch the high shores of the opposite side of the bay. I don't see, moreover, that delay will help us in any case, unless we drop Naples altogether, and then what are we to do?

Until next Sunday we shall be cut off from the world. I hope to get letters at Genoa, if we get none tomorrow.

Ever Your Son   Henry.

Tuesday. 14th.   Your's of the 11th has just hit us. We start in an hour for Mentoni; a superb day, warm and quiet. You will hear from us and about our adventures from there where, we propose to stay two days. Mamma says if you've any more oranges, send Mrs Parkes a few.

MS: MHi

To Charles Francis Adams

Mentoni. 16 Feb. 1865.

My dear Father:

I add a line to mamma's letter to say that our progress thus far has been satisfactory. We had a superb day for our drive from Nice, and the scenery was equal to everything I ever have heard of it. This place pleases me very much. It would have done, I think, for a long stay, so far as climate is concerned; but disease is prominent. Tonight it rains and I am in fear for our journey tomorrow. If the weather is bad, I shall try to wait over. If we have a pleasant trip, I shall have to decide as to continuing the vettura to Spezzia. I find it is two if not three days from Genoa to Spezzia and the expense would be about fourteen Napoleons.

We are all well. Mamma complains of neuralgia, and discourses considerably on her hatred of travel, but to all external appearance she is in better health and spirits and more amused and happy than I have seen her for months. Mary and Brooks have had slight bilious troubles but seem all right now. The weather is warmer, but cloudy for two days.

Mamma wishes to have the enclosed letter mailed to Charles.

Ever Your son   Henry.

17th. 11 A.M. Heavy rain all night. We postponed our departure this morning, but it now promises to clear and mamma is anxious to go, so I have ordered the vettura to get ready and we shall go on to San Remo tonight. It is cool and damp, but I fancy there has been a heavy storm elsewhere.

MS: MHi

To Charles Francis Adams

Genoa. Sunday 19 Feb. [1865] 9 P.M.

My dear Father:

We arrived here at seven this evening after a very successful journey. Mamma will give you the details of it, so I will only say that we reached San Remo the first day, and slept there. On Saturday (yesterday) we started early, and came on to Finale, arriving at about six. The day was absolutely delicious, and the scenery exquisite. It was summer idealised. We slept at a queer old Italian inn, after a delightful dinner, and started again this morning at 9.30. We came through to this city, after a pleasant but rather fatiguing day, reaching our hotel (Grande Bretagne) soon after six.

In short, and, as you may imagine, vastly to my relief, our journey has proved a "succés éclatant." But I am not disposed to take the responsibility of continuing it. Unless your letters or mamma's wishes back me up decidedly in this matter, I shall go on from here by sea. At the same time, I doubt very much indeed whether that course is wise, and does not risk the loss of much ground already gained. Only two reasons drive me to it. One is mamma's restless anxiety to get to some point of rest, where she will remain quiet. The other is the expense, which I cannot take on myself without decisive reasons.

You will receive more full letters by tomorrow's mail. Then we shall have got our own letters from home.

Ever your son   Henry.

MS: MHi

To Charles Francis Adams

Genoa. 21 Feb. 1865.

My dear Father:

We are again on the point of moving, and as the weather here is miserably cold and windy, we shall not be sorry to start. Genoa is a fine city. I have carried mamma and Mary to see some of the palaces which seemed to amuse them, and I have myself explored the city pretty thoroughly in these two days. There seems no cause for further delay.

When I last wrote, I was inclined to take the steamer here for Civita Vecchia; two nights. On talking with the courier however, we found that we should reach Rome in the very middle of the Carnaval, when accommodations could scarcely be found. I have decided therefore not to go to Rome, but to reach Naples at once. Boats go direct from Leghorn in twenty two hours. But with the certainty of this trial before us, I would not add to it another night by sea from here to Leghorn. So we shall continue our Vettura to Spezia, and go on to Naples on Saturday or Sunday from Leghorn. We sleep at Sestri tomorrow night; at Spezia Thursday; at Pisa Friday; and (I hope) at Naples on Monday at latest, if the weather permits. I am very far from liking this voyage, which in this weather must be disastrous, but we can't escape the night at sea and we must reach Naples before the people rush down from Rome.

I drew today for £50 more, to carry me through the month. This makes no less than £200 for February. Besides this, you gave Giorge £15 and me £10: = £225.0.0 in all. I have advanced £5.0.0 to mamma on your account. This leaves £220 for 28 days travelling, including some few purchases. Not quite £8 per diem. This is about my first estimate to you. The next month will, I trust, not much exceed the half of this average. By the way, am I to pay Giorge; and how much?

Your's of the 15th–16th reached me promptly. I hope you will ask for a leave if there is more delay. I expect your arrival at Naples very early in April.

Ever your Son   Henry.

MS: MHi

To Charles Francis Adams

Spezia. Thursday. 22 February. 1865.

My dear Father:

In pursuance of our plan, as I explained it to you in my last from Genoa, we left that place yesterday morning at nine o'clock. The weather has been clear, but by no means warm, and a sharp north wind, which blew quite a gale in Genoa the two days of our stay there, made us glad to get away. We had two superb days, cool on the mountains where the ice stood all day in quantity; but warm in the sun and under cover of the hills. The scenery was if possible, more superb than ever, and to-day the road went inland and carried us high among the Appenines, in a cooler region than we expected. We arrived here this evening before five o'clock, and go on to Pisa tomorrow at ten. Either Saturday or Sunday, if the weather suits us, we shall go to sea. Thus far we have got on very fairly, considering all things. I fervently hope to report soon the completion of our journey, when I shall begin to look for new orders from you. I certainly have not hurried our movements thus far, not having understood you to wish it; and as we shall have been a whole month on our way, I think we have done our best to obey your wishes in that respect.

I have had no great difficulty with any of my flock. Brooks is very obedient and admirably good-tempered. Mary seems very well. Mamma is in excellent condition, although she finds herself frequently homesick and tired.

Ever Yr Son   Henry.

MS: MHi

To Charles Francis Adams

Naples. Sunday. 26 Feb. [1865] 1.30 P.M.

My dear Father:

Here we are at last! If you were as much relieved as I am at seeing the termination of our wanderings, you would astonish the Legation by a triumphal war-dance.

If you have received the letter from Mary, to which I added a few words in pencil, and mailed yesterday at Leghorn, you know pretty much all that there is to tell of our adventures to that point. We started at noon. The wind was off shore and there was as little motion as there well can be at this season. We had a good boat and the best cabins. In fact, if a voyage was to be made, I don't think any better opportunity could have been found.

Mary was not absolutely sick. She passed the night in the cabin, on her sofa, without taking off her clothes, or even her hat. I suppose she had no great courage to move. Brooks was ill, though slightly. Mamma however suffered excessively, and, of course, became very nervous and shaken. She declares she never passed so bad a night even on the Atlantic. We got her on shore at noon, however, when we arrived, and she is considerably better since getting into harbor. She will describe her sufferings tomorrow when she can write. The General proved to be an excellent nurse and they praise him very much.

On the whole, our night was just what I expected, only rather better. I would not try another.

Naples is very full. I shall probably send Giorge to Sorrento tomorrow to arrange for us. Splendid weather. Our letters will reach us tomorrow.

Ever Your Son Henry.

MS: MHi

To Charles Francis Adams, Jr.

No. 39.   Sorrento. 2 March. 1865.

My dear Colonel:

Your's of February 4th reached me at Naples three days ago. As you are now not in active service, and as I am in the middle of a fatiguing, not to say harrassing campaign, my letters necessarily and properly have become fewer. If they average once a month instead of once a week, it is much.

You have probably heard of our departure from London, our little so-journ at Paris, and then of our slow and stately march across Europe down even to this point. Of the pleasures of the journey I might say a good deal at a pinch. The whole distance from Paris to Leghorn, including especially Avignon, Nice, the Cornice road, Genoa, Spezia and Pisa, was new to me, and very neatly complemented, and dove-tailed itself into my two previous visits to Italy. Our vettura traveling was unexpectedly pleasant. The weather was perfect. We had no mishaps, and in short, I found my duty far easier than I had expected.

But it is easier to grumble, and still more satisfactory to laugh. Luckily for me, and unluckily for my parent in London, I have a lazy and indolent temper. The duty of acting as scavenger to society by wrangling about bills, is one which I am weak in performing. Accordingly my soul is disturbed by visions of the unhappy Minister, groaning over my draughts. He has behaved hitherto like an angel. Not a reproach has yet passed his lips. But just four weeks heavy traveling have cost him at the rate of £8.0.0 a day. You can make that calculation if you like, and see what the total amounts to.

But this is a light evil. The greatest is of a different sort. You know from former letters how I abominate this family work. As for its being a pleasure, I simply laugh at the idea. To be sure, on this journey, I will do my people the justice to say that they have behaved better than I had any idea of. They have not worried my liver and lights out more than once a day. They have not fought more than half the time, nor made my existence intolerable without exceptions. If you could see our sainted mother traveling, you would laugh (unless you swore) even to wildness. Mary rises into humor in describing her, after a lovely day's journey, and an excellent dinner, eaten with excellent appetite, in a most comfortable hotel, sitting before a crackling wood fire, with her feet on the fender, entertaining us thus before going to her warmed and neat bed. "Well, for my part I confess I do not understand at my time of life the pleasures of traveling. I have seen nothing yet on this journey that any one could call pleasure, and if it weren't for Mary's sake, I never would have left home. Mary's health was our single reason for taking this journey and I do think that Mary is the most perverse and obstinate girl I ever saw in all my life. She will not take care of herself. She will sit with draughts blowing right on her, and there! she's sneezing! yes! she's caught cold! I told her she would in that carriage today. And considering that we have been at all this trouble and expense solely for her sake, she might try to take a little more care of herself, I do think. Henry, I'm homesick! I do wish I were in my own room in Upper Portland Place. It does make me utterly miserable, this never staying two nights in one place; there! it does! and I can't help it. I do want rest so! I get so fatigued with this continual motion. Couldn't we have gone quicker by sea? Why didn't we then? And this is so much more expensive! And you knew I wanted so much to get to Sorrento and it was so necessary for Mary's health! Dear me, what a draught there is! Mary, you are crazy not to wear your jacket! Oh Henry, how you do look with that beard! I really think it is wicked in you to go so, when you know how it pains me and disgusts me to have you seen so! There! now I'm going to bed. Now, do be punctual tomorrow to breakfast. You know you never are, and we start early. Oh dear! there, I am *too* homesick!''

God forgive me for thus ridiculing one of the most devoted of mothers! But I grow old and cynical, and I have learned to be silent, but in return, I must have my laugh. The example I have given is a favorable one. It is far from exaggerated and every word is true. This perpetual feeble worry; this unvarying practice of dwelling on the dark points of a picture, and bearing hardest on me at the most difficult moments, make me contemplate a journey with alarm and complete it with relief. The children are obedient, good-natured and willing, with me. But the battle is perpetual between them and their mother. And if there is one thing that I flinch under, it is the sound of perpetual dispute.

Such are my little amusements, from which I escape as I best can, flying in a cowardly way at the sign of a storm, or maintaining a vigorous silence. In return, consolation and balm sometimes flow into my soul when I climb among the olive-groves, and cool myself in their delicate shade, or ramble through the orange-groves, and smoke my cigar beneath thousands of oranges and lemons which look as poetic as the heart of man could ask. Just now the Tramontana, or north wind, is blowing a tremendous gale across the bay of Naples, and the weather therefore is not altogether agreeable. Your angel mother, who has done nothing but urge me forward all the way, and pray for rest and the repose of Sorrento, is already showing signs of restlessness and an intention to move somewhere else. Meanwhile I have performed my duty. I have brought the party safely here. And I wait new orders from London, whether to return or to stay. You know I am but a subordinate, and obey orders with military precision and silence.

You find fault with my silence about the war, but it seems to me that the silence shows the state of things clearly enough. The rebel cause is in Europe all in the dirt. What may yet happen, or what has already happened since the 13th Feb. I don't know, but unless we are very unlucky, England has taken her final stand, acknowledges our success, and gives up the case.

I saw Barlow in Paris. Uncle Edward gave him a dinner which perhaps some of your letters have told you about. I know I paid four sixths of the dinner, and our uncle one third, and he ordered it. Barlow was very pleasant and amusing. I hope he did well in London.

What you say about family jars is very true. Kuhn and Loo have already managed to make a pretty wide separation between them and us, which will certainly become a break in time. Loo is near insane, and will kill herself ultimately, I think.

You say nothing about your own plans and I can have nothing to say on that subject myself, as I have no data to go on. You already know my opinion of the necessity of health. As to my plans which you inquire about, I know no more than you. The Minister says I am too useful here to be spared; therefore I am here; not absolutely in Capua, but precious near it.[1] I solace myself in performing this duty of guarding the women and children during the battle, by studying Italian which I shall learn to read at least, and by yielding to the influences of the places we visit. For the time, I am counted out. I was twenty seven the day before we entered Italy. I have been nearly seven years abroad. And I run visibly to seed.

Mary and Brooks and I have this afternoon been rambling up high on the hill-sides. Sorrento was lovelier than you can guess; the air purer and softer than mere intellect can conceive; all the plains below us were dotted and yellow with oranges and lemons; and we sat under the olives with the sunlight filtering down on us; and looked across the Piano del Sorrento, and the bay of Naples, to where Vesuvius was smoking, and beyond Vesuvius the landscape ended in the long line of snow-covered Appenines. It was pretty, oh Fratello mio! quite so! I trust you may come to see it. Come in April or May.

Talk not to me of wars. I have had no letters since one dated the 21st at London. I see no newspapers. We are out of the world, and for all that I know the war in America may be over and peace declared. What I should say would read to you like comments upon Roman history.

We are all pretty well. Mary has got an appetite of the best, and can climb mountains with stout legs. Mamma is given to colds, but otherwise all right.

Ever Yrs.

MS: MHi
    1. Literally, about 35 miles from the proverbial city of leisure and luxury ("Capua corrupted Hannibal"); metaphorically, as close as he cared to be.

To Charles Francis Adams

Sorrento. 3 March. 1865.

My dear Father:

I send a letter for Charles, and at the same time add these few words to say that we are at last settled here, very comfortably so far as our quarters go, but quite out of the world. The weather as yet, even with the Tramontana, is soft and warm in the open air, but the Spring is opening and so makes it changeable. I doubt whether we are likely to remain here so long as we expected, unless the weather becomes very warm and fine. We young ones are contented enough, but I think I see symptoms of restlessness on mamma's part, especially since the Ellice's have talked to her about Amalfi.[1] As I consider myself now to have performed the duty I was sent to do, I shall not interfere any further in the direction of our movements, until it is decided that we *are* to move. Should the weather be cold, I am not sure that Amalfi would not be better than Sorrento, and the change would be a small affair.

We have been unlucky about our letters and have as yet received none since yours of the 21st. Today or tomorrow I expect to get later ones, and then I shall write to you at more length. Meanwhile you may rest tolerably at ease about the health of your delicate and fading daughter, who yesterday climbed for a couple of hours up and down the roughest of mountains, on a very tolerably stout pair of legs, and then eat as handsome a dinner as most young ladies in robust health could have managed to tuck away.

Brooks is working faithfully at his French, but I am afraid there is no hope of finding him a teacher here. As yet I cannot even get an Italian master for myself. The natives all speak it with the bad Neapolitan accent.

We have not even been able to see a newspaper with the American news of the 16th.

Ever Your son   Henry.

Mamma wishes you to address the enclosed to Aunt Fanny. Uncle Sidney's address is in the paper box on the table in her dressing room.

MS: MHi

1. The younger Edward Ellice (1810–1880), M.P., and Eliza Speirs Ellice.

To Charles Milnes Gaskell

Sorrento. 3 March. 1865.

My dear Gask:

Since I last saw you, I have made a ponderous march across Europe. It took precisely four weeks to reach this place, never sleeping more than three nights in the same house. I took a vettura at Nice and we did the Cornice, coming down to Spezia in that way. Our whole journey was a success, but that part of it was a triumph, and I consider myself to have earned the laurels of high Generalship in my skilful direction of this arduous campaign in midwinter. We had weather fit for Gods to travel in, and not a mishap nor a difficulty.

At present behold me installed at the Tasso, surrounded by my amiable and interesting family, over whom I exercise a mild and paternal sway. My prime minister is my Italian courier, and my form of Government is constitutional, not absolute. Like other kings I reign but do not govern, and my premier though gentle and protecting, is my master. As I do not travel for my own amusement, this state of affairs is not burdensome.

Sorrento is empty or nearly so, except for a stray American or two whom we do not know. I don't think it a good winter place. Amalfi would be better, with equally good hotels. But the air is soft and the orange and lemon groves full of fruit. I can contrive to drag on a burdensome existence, even though it does rain today; especially as the cuisine is good. I could wish that the weather was a little steadier and that there was some medium between a rainy Sirocco and a howling Tramontana, but if one must be a victim to weather, one suffers as little at Sorrento as at most places. I can still smoke my Italian cabbages under the oranges, and cultivate philosophy in the shade of the olives, with one eye on Naples and the other on Vesuvius. My courier could do it better than myself, for he squints like a colossus.

At Pisa I saw Sir Robert Cunliffe's name on the board, as occupying a room in our hotel, and I took the occasion of sending you a message, to make his acquaintance.[1] As he said he should write to you, he probably has, or will inform you that he came in to make us an evening visit, and to make himself very agreeable. The next morning we went on to Leghorn to suffer miserably on the sea, and he went on to Florence, so that I saw him no more.

I asked him to inform you that our plans forced us to leave Rome aside, so that your letter and commission would be a trifle stale if it waited my arrival at the holy city. It is to be hoped that you contemplated this possibility in writing it. Otherwise you can write a new one, once a month; codicils, so to speak; and I will deliver them all, with proper directions for reading. I say 'once a month,' for I have not the most distant idea when I shall turn my face northwards, or when it will please my father to order me to some new occupation. If I am to remain here abroad to enact the honorable and active part of sheep-dog, I shall certainly do my best to keep the sheep quiet, and to keep them here, as I do not delight in moving my flock when it has found good pasturage.

We have met one or two acquaintances at different places. The last was Edward Ellice, who was here when we arrived. I have no wish to meet any more. My sheep are always made more or less restless by them, especially since the middle-aged traveller is always a confirmed grumbler. All the plagues of Egypt are loose in the land, according to the way-side rambler, who has nothing to do but to find them out. We are innocent and we are happy. It is the true doctrine of the true Church.

I trust that as I have nothing whatever to tell you, the equilibrium of correspondence may be kept up by your sending me a quantity of news. I understand that Her Majesty has at last invited me to Court, and that I have respectfully regretted being a thousand miles away, more or less. As it has taken four years for my existence to be recognised by authority, I'm in hopes it will be kept in mind should I return. But I can't say that I mean to come back this time, for the pleasure of again showing H.M. my legs in pink silk stockings.

Remember me to your father and mother and write soon to me (Rogers Brothers &Co. Naples.)

Ever truly Yrs   Henry Brooks Adams.

I sent Ralph Palmer a major general. If you see R.P. apologise to him on my behalf for the liberty; say that from an American point of view no entertaining is required in such a case; and that I did it because he knows and can show London better than most people. I hope he saw the Maj: Gen:[2] who was a remarkable specimen of a very live Yankee.

MS: MHi
    1. Sir Robert Alfred Cunliffe (1839–1905), 5th baronet, of Acton Park, Wrexham, in north Wales; with Gaskell he became the closest of HA's English ties.
    2. Maj. Gen. Francis C. Barlow.

To Charles Francis Adams

Sorrento. 6 March. 1865.

My dear Father:

Your's of the 28th to mamma and Mary arrived today. As they seem to show less and less probability of any present change in our situation, and as they contain no sign of your intentions in regard to us, I must open the matter myself, for time is rapidly passing. By the time you receive this, you will know the new Cabinet, and will be able to decide as to your chance of escape. If Government releases or recalls you, my questions will need no reply. If you are to remain, I must have new orders.

So far as I personally am concerned, although it is not by any means the thing in such times for a man to be acting as a sort of hybrid courier-nurse to a party of females, you are quite free to dispose of me as you can make me most effective. I am contented enough, and am working hard on Italian which I shall probably learn. My time therefore is not lost to myself. The difficulty is not there, but in the want of certainty what is to be done in case you keep me here.

Our way just now is clear enough until the 1st of April. I have settled the party here. The place seems to agree with them. They will not need to be moved; and our expenses are less extravagant, averaging about £4.0.0 a day. Should you not be able to come here by the 1st of April, however, and should you still keep me here, what am I to do? Mary and mamma seem to expect to go to Rome then. Is that your wish? Because, if they are to go, we must order rooms early. If we do go on to Rome, what is to be the next step? And can you not give me some idea of the general course you wish us to take, either until you join us or we join you. In fact, I came away calculating on six weeks absence. That time is nearly over and to all appearance my absence has just begun.

Your letter to mamma seems to hint for the first time at the possibility of your remaining at London. In such a case, shall you make it a condition to have three months leave allowed? It is annoying that the London season should come just at the time when you would want to travel, but if you really decide to stick to your post another year, I suppose the least expensive and troublesome way would be for me to settle the family somehow quietly on the continent, at Florence, or in Switzerland, until you could join them. I could probably manage to return to you in that case. Kuhn and Loo are coming over sooner or later, and though I am decidedly of the belief that another three months together would probably widen the distance between Loo and us into a regular breach, it may be necessary to risk it.

These of course are all mere speculations and I don't expect you to be able to say that you will certainly do one thing or another. But I can get no answer to this within a fortnight, and by that time I must act. All I want to know is what you propose to do in the contingency of your not joining us at once. Never mind me personally. But pray let me have directions.

Our weather here divides itself about equally into good and bad. First we have a violent Tramontana which clears the sky; then we get one beautiful day; then the Sirocco springs up, and blows clouds and rain from the South; then it shifts to the north again and another gale gives us the sun. Thus we box the compass about once a week.

In writing to us, I wish you would mention the principal items of news from home. We never see even the meagre telegrams published in the Naples papers.

We have made one acquaintance here, a family of Martin of New York. I trust it may amuse mamma, who is not much better fitted for a hermitage than Loo is. She finds it rather dull here, I'm afraid, and as she does not take kindly to donkeys, it is rather difficult to amuse her even in fine weather.

I have at last discovered a person who will do after a fashion for an Italian teacher. I hope he may answer my purpose, and at all events I can hardly fail to learn something. But no sign of a French teacher is to be found.

Ever Yr Son   Henry.

MS: MHi

To Charles Francis Adams

Sorrento. 27 March. 1865.

My dear Father:

I received today your letter of the 20th instant. I have only waited for it, to write to you again to announce our plan of campaign.

We leave this place tomorrow (Tuesday) for Salerno. Wednesday is set apart for Paestum, and the same night I expect to get round to Amalfi. Saturday (1st) we propose to leave Amalfi and go up to Naples. The following Saturday we expect to go on to Rome, where I think the family will do well to stay till the 1st of May.

All this is subject to possibilities. It supposes good weather in the first place, whereas our weather varies between howling north-winds with snow, and hurricanes from the south with rain. We have averaged of late two good days a week. In the second place, the arrangement supposes our getting rooms at Rome, which, non-obstante Giorgi, I cannot but think doubtful.

My small regiment, which is as you know sufficiently difficult to govern and particularly apt to disagree in its views, seems tolerably clear in assenting to this programme. It will be well, therefore to consider it settled, and in future to direct to Maquay, Packenham & Hooker till further orders.

So much for this part of our affairs. As to your own position, I have read carefully what you say, but I don't quite follow your conclusions. At this distance, one can't properly judge about the matter. It looks to me, however, as though Seward had considered his answer to your request for recall, as final. If so, unless you absolutely resigned, the only proposal he would be likely to entertain, would be that for a leave for a definite time. Whether you have made this, I do not quite understand. But I cannot see why, supposing you to get such a leave from the 1st May, you might not still join the family in Italy and travel with them. There is no time when Italy is more attractive, and if you are to stay on in London, it seems to me to be a matter of indifference when you come onto the continent.

You do not say whether you adhere to the plan of sending the family home in the summer. But any of the summer months are equally good for the sea passage. Unless the economical reasons over-rule the situation, I do not see why this should prevent your coming.

Apart from the wish that you should see Europe, I have selfish reasons for hoping that you will not give up the plan of joining the party. One of them is that the prospect of your arrival smooths our path very much. Mamma becomes very restive under the idea of your not joining us, and I'm afraid it will make her quite unmanageable under my slender authority. She already threatens to return to London in such a case, and although I don't put any great weight on that sort of talk, I dread extremely whatever tends to encourage nervousness and discontent in her mind. It more than doubles my difficulties. And what is of much more consequence than any convenience of mine, it tends to destroy the very purposes of the journey. Therefore I earnestly hope that you will reconsider your conclusion.

Mamma and Mary have no doubt kept you informed as to the course of our quiet existence here. We have got along not badly. Kuhn's visit came in very nicely and we have found or made acquaintances enough to keep us alive. The only drawback has been the weather, and that seems to have been equally bad everywhere.

We have great difficulty in getting home news. Charles's engagement was a God-send to us.[1] You seem rather hurried to marry me off also, but I don't find it convenient at present. Having two sons settled, you may find it convenient to keep one *en disponibilité.*

You don't mention poor Andrew Johnson's horrible exposure, which I read today in Galignani.[2] It is a bad look-out for the next four years. Perhaps however it may shock the country enough to shame Washington into a reform. The President's character is now a greater source of strength to the Administration than ever. From M'Cullogh's beginning I infer that he at least has a policy, which is consoling.[3] Meanwhile the rebels seem scarcely to preserve an appearance of hope.

Ever your son   Henry.

MS: MHi
1. CFA2 was engaged to Mary Hone Ogden (1843–1935), daughter of Edward and Caroline Callender Ogden of New York City.
2. Andrew Johnson, at his swearing in as vice-president, gave an extemporaneous speech that was considerably extended by reason of his being drunk.
3. Hugh McCulloch (1808–1895), Indiana banker, comptroller of the currency 1863–1865, secretary of the treasury 1865–1869. He began converting the vast array of notes and short-term obligations of the government into a bonded indebtedness, and he urged Congress to return the currency to the gold standard, both conservative policies long supported by the Adamses.

To Charles Francis Adams, Jr.

No. 41.   Rome. 9 April. 1865.

My dear Colonel:

The eccentric course of the world has managed to juggle me back into this city again, five years older than when I was in it last; and with this single exception I rather doubt whether either the city or I have got far ahead of where we then were. It seems as natural as London would; or indeed, as any place except Boston, would seem, and on the whole, I can drag out existence here, if the Minister absolutely will not call me back to more manly duties. As we have not heard from you since your supposed return to camp, and our letters in answer to your engagement must only now be reaching America, I shall write you a long epistle about our proceedings here.

My last was from Sorrento, where we remained nearly through the month. What the weather could do to spoil our residence there, it faithfully did, and if it weren't that Sorrento is one of those few places in this christian world, whose beauty takes hold of the heart of the weary pilgrim, and makes him happy in a peace that passes understanding, I should have learned to dislike it with an energy to which I am not given. Good or bad, however, the time passed over us with no greater excitement than that brought by your letters, and at the beginning of the fifth week we moved round to Amalfi, where the weather was, if possible, still worse, and over-flowed rivers barred our road to Paestum.

With our arrival at Naples the skies cleared and the sun brought us summer in a moment. We remained there from the first to the eighth April, just a week, all of which was divided between buying coral and visiting the Museum, with the episode of one day passed at Baja.[1] You, my envied brother, whose acquaintance with women in domestic relations, has yet to begin, and that too, under a form exceptionally agreeable, know little of the meaning of a week's shopping. But when that shopping is for jewelry, and when that jewelry is coral, at Naples, all ordinary shopping becomes an amusement and a jest. Coral is as you are aware, no doubt, a marine product, made for some reason inscrutable to the eyes of purchasers, in different shades of color. These shades vary from absolute white to deep red, but the white is not valuable, neither is the red, nor yet is the light pink esteemed, since it has an imperceptible shadow of yellow. But a certain translucent rose, "rivaling" as Mr Everett says, "the first blush of youthful love", or more precisely I think, "the living carnation" of ditto, is the perfect ideal, the aspiration of young women, and my own nightmare. In search of this, I went through every shop in Naples, and I may say that there is little coral in that city which has not been seen and priced by me. Mary invested a heap of money in it, and kept me for a week in training as a shop-boy. My own purchases were small, but choice, and cost me much anxious reflection and mental toil, but I happily survived it all, and even paid the bills.

The shops however were slightly varied by the Museum, and what time I did not pass in one, I managed to spend in the other, which, if you don't already know it, is one of the most interesting collections in the world. As I recollected it of old, I was not required to *do* it like a tourist, and had a chance to look for what pleased my own taste, and admire that. As the simple savage seems to be about to return to social life, I suppose it won't hurt him to hear that there are some new antiques lately dug out from Pompei, which please me much and which rank high among the gems of art. Two bronzes, both discovered within the last year, both small and both graceful enough to drive our artists frantic, struck me with more satisfaction than I have felt over a work of art for a long time. One of these is a tipsy Silenus, reeling just so much as still to leave his balance straight, and with a drunken flavor oozing out, not only in the face and the limbs, but in the unsteady poise of the figure and the slight forward stagger which seems just enough to show the artist's skill, without becoming coarseness. One hand is raised above his head and on the palm he balances a round vessel, on which a glass vase for wine or flowers once stood. The other hand, stretched down as one does in balancing oneself, held a glass goblet. The bronze is not more than three feet high. For delicacy and freedom of workmanship combined, I have seen few things to beat it.

But though the Bacchus is good, the Narcissus is better. This is a bronze figure about three feet high, clothed carefully in elaborate sandals, and nothing else, except a fillet with light clusters of grapes in his hair, and a goat-skin on, rather than over one shoulder. He stands a little inclined forward, his head bent forward and on one side, one hand resting on his hip, the other with the index finger out, held up as when one listens intently. The face, which is exquisite, has a half smile on it. He is listening—

the very poetry of attention. Can you tell me what he is hearing? Is it an echo from some Grecian mountain, or a faintly-heard chorus of nymphs in some legendary forest or stream, or is it the call of the naiad that he is in love with? Am I right in my misty recollection of Narcissus as a youth whom Venus admired in vain, but Luna used to visit on the top of a mountain, and was killed by a wild boar for looking at Diana in a bath? Why the dickins should Narcissus listen, is a question that has bothered me to wildness, and is still unsettled in my mind;[2] but be that as it may, the statue is a touch of perfect grace and delicacy, and so much was I charmed with it that I almost bought a copy, intending it as a wedding present for you and Minnie. But I thought better of it, doubting that the S.S.[3] had not preserved the tastes that would make him happy in the contemplation of bronzes, and doubting still more whether Minnie would be pleased with so classic a gift. I will get her a something pretty here in Rome, and you shall write to me what it is to be. Or rather, you should, if there were time, but I should not get your answer for an age. But now, I think, if my fancy for Narcissus still lasts until my departure from here, I shall buy him for other purposes, since I am not rich enough to sport bronzes of my own. The beautiful face of the divine youth, listening with his raised hand and bent head, to the far-off song of the nymphs, would always remind me of something pleasant, for it all carries with it an odor of summer and song and Greek beauty. But such property does not suit a young man of a wandering turn of mind and debauched habits like myself. I will give him away. I will carry him off to England and leave him there.

Naples was lovely. Not so lovely as it was five years ago next June, when I saw it in its full summer dress, but still there are few places that even make a pretence to beauty beside it. I was sorry to leave it, though I expected to see some of the party catch the fever, and am not even yet at all sure that we have escaped. But we did come on to Rome yesterday, and are already flying about and mixed up in the whole riot of the Holy Week. The Dexters are here and Arthur and his mother are beaming, while Hooker and our Minister's family look after all our sight-seeing.[4] I hope now for a little freedom. Ah, fratello mio; freedom is still sweet, even though I do not deny that a bondage more pleasing than mine, may be still sweeter. The Minister writes as though he expected me to marry at once, but I have tried it at the wrong end, and having once learned what the duties are, without the pleasures, I shall have to wait long before trying either duties or pleasures again, if I've got to take them together.

Still Rome is pleasant even to the head of a family, and the weather has been superb. Your mamma, suddenly become friskey as a young kid, does nothing but run about and see—and see—and see! Mary has required a little nursing. She has had a little bilious trouble, and the deuce take me if I know how she is ever to get rid of them, nor what new form these attacks may at any moment take. This time however it has not seemed to amount to much more than a trifle.

I have seen little or nothing that is new, unless I except a visit yesterday

(13th) with Arthur and his mother to Storey's studio, where we interrupted the great sculptor in the act of giving a sitting to no less a person than General McClellan, who is now his guest. And by the way, I will say that a more common, carrotty, vulgar-looking hero than he of Antietam, I have not frequently seen. I exchanged a few words with him and admired his simple want of expression. But it was not of him that I wished to speak, so much as of Storey, who is to my mind, head and shoulders beyond any other sculptor of the day. You know what a success his Cleopatra and Sybil were at London in the Exhibition.[5] Since then he has produced two great works more. One is a Saul; a superb, massive figure, seated, with his right hand and fingers twisted in his beard, like the Moses of Michael Angelo. The face is great. The Spirit of the Lord, as the Bible says, is on it, and though I have only seen it in plaster and in Arthur's photographs, I think it an advance even on the Cleopatra. The other statue is a Medea meditating the death of her children. This is, I firmly believe, the best thing he has yet done. Every line of it is so bold and vigorous that it cuts into one's memory like a knife. It is a standing figure, quite in repose, and draped simply, so as to show the curves of the figure as clearly as possible. The left arm is folded across her, and on the left hand she is resting her right elbow, so that her right hand comes up to her chin. Her head is bent over a little and so rests on the hand. If you understand the attitude, and put anyone into it, you will see in a moment how expressive it is, and how exact it is to suit the instant of determination, or just before the completion of a decisive plan. But the face is something to remember in one's dreams. Such a concentration of idea can't often be worked out of marble. As for describing it—*pas si bête!* Imagine any woman with a face as beautiful and as hard as Greek marble, about to commit a murder under the circumstances mentioned, the idea of elaborating the most ingenious revenge conceivable, predominating in a mind as hard as her face. How Storey can make such statues I cannot understand.[6] He is not a great man. He is vain, flippant, and trifling, and what is worse he has a wife who is a snob! Tudieu, what a snob! And he is under her influence habitually. Until the Cleopatra he had never created anything more than pretty. But the artist actually grows under all this weight of vanity, weakness, folly and flattery, and goes on excelling himself until he promises to reach a height unknown in art for centuries. Understand this who can. To me it is one of the mysteries of human nature.

I have now dosed you sufficiently with art. You may not care for it, but what of that! How can I write of other matters, when I have to get all my accounts of them from so far? All that I can say of ourselves is that your papa is down in the blue dogs at not getting his release; that I am by no means pleased at having to continue as patriarch; that your mamma is delighted with Rome and too much occupied to be thoughtful of other things; that Mary seems well enough, though I have not the least idea whether she is really well or no.

(Saturday. 15th) We have received your letters with Minnie's photograph. There is only one danger now about your position, and that is that the accounts we receive of her from our correspondents, written with more than a lover's enthusiasm, may lead your family to look for more than mortal imperfection can ever supply. The photograph is not calculated to lower these expectations. When you discover any faults in her, let us know. I don't refer to your own epistles, which have been comparatively silent, but to those of aunts, sisters & sich.

(Monday. 17th). We have received the news of the fall of Richmond! What think you, I had best do about it? I waked Arthur up to tell him, and he said he forgave me, but had it been anything else, he wouldn't. General McClellan last night doubted it! Arthur and I exulted over it over Storey's table. Shall I drink up Tiber, eat an obelisk? The Pope illuminated St Peter's last night, of course in honor of the news. The temptation is vehement to do something, but what can I do? With the news, I got your letter of March 26th, which makes me anxious to hear of your safety. If you are all right, I suppose your path is now clear, and you can resign and marry and come out here as soon as you like. Never mind the Minn. Your engagement and this news are the only bits of comfort he has had since we left home, and so you can tell Minnie, if she won't believe what I wrote her myself.

A chaotic letter! But *que veux-tu?*

Ever

MS: MHi
1. Baja: ancient Baiae, on the bay of the same name, visited for its view and Roman ruins.
2. HA mixes myths of Narcissus, Echo, Adonis, and Actaeon, all in Ovid's *Metamorphoses*. The *Drunken Satyr* and the *Narcissus* (now identified as *Dionysus*) are in the National Museum of Naples.
3. Possibly Second Son.
4. Gen. Rufus King (1814–1876), editor, Union general, minister to the Papal States 1863–1867, and Susan Eliot King (1821–1892).
5. Story's *Cleopatra* and *Libyan Sibyl* captivated the public and the critics alike at the London Exhibition of 1862, bringing Story fame as a sculptor.
6. The *Cleopatra* and *Medea* are in the Metropolitan Museum of Art, New York.

To Charles Francis Adams

Rome. 20 April. 1865.

My dear Father:

I have received your's of the 12th, which, if not answering my hopes as to your joining us, was more encouraging in its reflection of our good state of affairs politically. Since then, Sheridan and Grant seem to have placed us at last beyond the chance of more danger. The news of today, mutilated as it comes to us, seems to put Lee in a position where recovery is no longer possible, and I have no doubt that Sherman will by this time have completed whatever Sheridan may have left over. My exultation in this news is only sobered by anxiety for Charles, which I feel more than ever now that the cavalry has had so much of the heavy work to do.

Meanwhile my campaign here in Italy is in a state of repose which I acknowledge myself not in a hurry to disturb. Mamma seems to like Rome, and there is society enough here to amuse her and to prevent her mind from dwelling so much as usual on herself. We are in full summer and in fact find the weather too warm for comfort. Thus far Rome seems to agree with us as well as any place, and certainly amuses us more than anything yet.

I do not intend therefore to discuss our start until your further directions come. You will have to write to me whether you wish us to stay here until your plans are decided, or to leave punctually on the first of May for Florence, and receive your final orders there. There are several routes to Florence, but the longest is the best, not only in scenery but in accommodations, and I incline towards chartering a vettura and going on by way of Perugia, which will give us five days to Florence. I would like to know what you have to say on this point.

In the next place, Mary seems very much set upon seeing Venice. I would like to know whether you assent to this, in case our journey is allowed to go on regularly.

As I am now carrying on our affairs by drawing checks on Hooker, for which I shall give him a single draft on leaving, I cannot tell you much about expenses. On the whole, there have been several unusual calls for money. One extra expense is for a carriage, which was indispensable, as you can imagine, and which I took till the first of May. Then I have advanced eighty dollars to pay for a bracelet which we bought and sent off yesterday to Miss Ogden, by Mr Dale of Boston. Finally, I have paid Mina, the maid, her three months wages, £6.0.0. I have paid every month £5.0.0 to mamma. If I did not notify you of it, perhaps it was because I may have thought it unnecessary, as it was a regular item.

I suppose some bills are coming in for me in London. Newmans, I believe, is the only important one. If you will pay it, you can charge it against me, or I can pay you on returning.

The telegram this evening announces an accident to Seward, which, to a man of his frame, I should think might prove serious.[1] I hope it mayn't still further delay the settlement of your affairs.

I suppose mamma keeps you posted as to our amusements. Rome is certainly just as attractive as ever; quite as full of strangers, and of feuds; and almost as dirty. The Storeys have had us there, and I almost thought myself in Belgrave Square again. It made me ill, and I fled. I do not find that after a respite, a new trial of English society makes me like it at all better.

Saturday. I have waited in hope of receiving more letters, but none have yet reached us. As I do not see Charles's regiment yet named among the casualties I hope he was with Weitzel or in garrison.[2] But I am still very anxious about him. You will of course let us know at once if you hear from him.

MS: MHi
1. On April 5 Seward had a carriage accident, falling heavily to the street as he tried to catch the reins of bolting horses; he was in fact seriously injured.
2. Gen. Godfrey Weitzel (1835–1884), in command of the troops occupying Richmond, April 3.

To Charles Milnes Gaskell

Rome. 23 April. 1865.

Caro amico mio:

Your letter reached me duly at Naples, for which receive my thanks. Meanwhile I have transferred the family quarters to Rome, coming up here on the 8th for the functions of Holy Week, and meditating a contingent remainder till May. Thus far my expedition has not met any mishaps, but I am still in the dark as to our future movements.

Your letter and book have been duly delivered and cards duly exchanged. But I am told that the Marchesa has been very ill this winter, and not able to go into society nor entertain as usual. Before I go away I shall make an effort to see her, and to take any return message she may have to confide to me. Meanwhile my society relations are quite limited and the care of a family as exigeante as mine takes up all my time. But happening to be at a reception of Mrs Story's the other evening, and looking about me in that distrait manner acquired from long practice in London drawing-rooms, I saw quite a pretty blonde in blue enter the Barberini halls, and I at once inquired her name, supposing her a fellow citizen of the Republic one and indivisible. "Miss Macallister" was the response. Vague recollections of her name as associated with you, entered my mind. Not remembering however, what you had said about her, I thought it would be easiest to ask herself, what it probably had been, and I accordingly requested Mrs Story to introduce me, which she at once did. No sooner was I in her august presence than I suggested your existence as a fact possibly productive of topics of conversation. Not having ever had the pleasure of meeting the gentle female before, I can't say whether she was embarrassed or blushed, or was natural as usual, but I am quite confident that her powers of conversation appeared remarkably limited, and though she certainly did acknowledge the general fact of your existence as possible, and perhaps even probable, it was all she seemed prepared to grant. I was therefore rapidly driven from the field and was soon glad to escape from the monosyllabic Hebe, much discomfited. This is all I can tell you of your Roman friends.

Rome, however, in spite of the cantankerous men and women in it, is as enjoyable as ever. That is to say, whatever power is still left for enjoyment

in a miserable and worn-out ruin like myself, is as available here as elsewhere. I am in no hurry to leave it, for the summer has come, and the
Borghese is not a bad place to lie at the feet of damsels in blue, and to
smoke cigars at one scudo e mezzo the hundred.

(Florence. 10 May.)   I should begin a new letter, but the above is a sort
of guaranty that my intentions were better than my performance. In fact I
delayed finishing this epistle at Rome for two reasons. The first was that I
might get from Story two M.S.S. which were from the unpublished correspondence of my cousin William, and which were said to be most extraordinary productions of his pen. Story had lost them, so that I was deprived
of the amusement of reading them, and you also must go without it. If you
see or write to Will do not ask for them nor mention them. He made a very
unpleasant, not to say offensive impression.

My second reason for waiting was to see your friend the Marchesa, who
was ill of bronchitis and whose husband was in Naples. I did succeed in my
object, but except to tell you that she has been very ill and is now, I suppose, on her way to England, I have little to say. She told me that I might
tell you that the serene Anglo-Roman society had been extremely quarrel-
some apropos to the races, which everyone had wished to manage in his
own way. I might say the same of the Americans who are slandering each
other like angels.

I remained in Rome until the 3d of May. It was full summer, hot, green
and fascinating, but the charge of a family has made me prematurely grey
and bald, and Heaven forgive me if I was glad to make a new step towards
London. I was absolutely glad when we rolled under the Porta del Popolo
with our faces northwards. I dragged my party round by Terni and Perugia, and came down to Siena, before reaching Florence, where we arrived
on the evening of the 8th. We stay here till the 17th or so; then go through
Bologna to Venice, Milan, and (if I can manage it) into Switzerland by
June 1st, but not stay there. If alive, I mean to be in London before the 1st
July. I am rabid to get back there. You can imagine my reasons in public
matters without baptising me with any new-born adoration for that city.

Lady Frances Gordon desired me to get her some stones of turquoise-
blue.[1] Did she say for a necklace or a bracelet? I have racked my brains to
recollect which, but without success, and finally I got a half dozen stones
which she can do what she likes with. Between you and me, in your secret
ear, *she* said *lava* of turquoise blue. I find that the thing does not exist. What
she had is a composition made in Rome and moulded, not cut. Altogether
it gave me more trouble than Lady F. is ever likely to deserve at my hands.
But if you mention it, you will surely perish.

We have been very nearly broiled to death on our way from Rome. We
have not had a drop of rain since April 1st. This city is going into fits over
the Dante festival, which I wish was in Dante's Inferno. Such is my news.

I received today a letter from Ralph Palmer all about the President's
assassination.[2] He seems (forgive the equivoque) rather proud that

Englishmen are disgusted by it. To us the assassination of the President is a matter of personal feeling, the result of his qualities as a man. If other people don't feel as we do about it, we might be disgusted, but that they should is so much a matter of course that I should never have doubted it. But as for the nation, pity is wasted. I am much too strong an American to have thought for a moment that we are going to be shaken by a murder. I shall answer Ralph's letter soon.

If you know Miss Montgomery (the blonde) tell her that she looks like the Venus of Medici. I am coming back to write a new work on art, which is to smash the Greeks. You shall get the Westminster to publish my introduction. If you answer this, send it to the Legation.

Ever Yrs   H. B. Adams.

My best regards to your papa and mamma.

MS: MHi
1. Isabella Grant Gordon (Lady Francis Gordon), a frequent guest at Bretton Park, a great house near the Gaskells' in Yorkshire.
2. This installment of May 10 was written after the April 27 letter on Lincoln's assassination printed below.

To Charles Francis Adams

Rome. 27 April. 1865.

My dear Father:

Before breakfast this morning General and Mrs King came round with your telegram which had arrived at midnight.[1] Of course nothing else but this news has been thought of all day. There is no need of telling you how it has shocked everyone. There is something so unheard-of about it, that no ordinary form of phrase seems at all suited to the case. As yet, people don't seem fairly to conceive it.

I had already decided, on the receipt of your last letter, to leave this place on Wednesday, the 3d, and to go on by way of Perugia to Florence. We should in that case reach Florence on the 8th, and your letters had best be addressed to the care of Maquay and Packenham at Florence.

But it may be that you will want to stop us, or give us orders before quitting Rome, in which case you had best telegraph to us at the Hotel de l'Europe here, or after Wednesday, to General King who can send it after us. Everyone here is assuming as a matter of course, that your recall is for the purpose of putting you in Seward's place. Knowing the circumstances, I don't expect this, but of course want to be prepared, if it should turn out so. Otherwise, in case your successor has not been appointed, your remaining at London seems now necessary.

Loo threatens to join us in Florence and travel with us. I am less now than ever in the humor for such an addition to my ranks. Were you to re-call us to London, I think none of us would much regret it.

I have never felt so much as to-day how out-of-place I am, and how little I have to do here. Roman history, even, doesn't console me. But of course in such cases, passive obedience is more necessary than ever, and as I can't aid you, in London, I sha'n't increase your difficulties from here. If necessary we can reach London in eight or ten days, I think.

Mamma would write but is not up to it.

Ever your son   Henry.

MS: MHi

1. Minister King brought news of Lincoln's assassination, as well as word, pertinent to CFA's prospects, that Seward had been attacked and his life was despaired of.

To Charles Francis Adams, Jr.

No. 42. Florence. 10 May. 1865.

My dear Colonel:

I can't help a feeling of amusement at looking back on my letters and thinking how curiously inapt they have been to the state of things about you. Victories and assassinations, joys, triumphs, sorrows and gloom; all at fever point, with you; while I prate about art and draw out letters from the sunniest and most placid of subjects. I have already buried Mr Lincoln under the ruins of the Capitol, along with Caesar, and this I don't mean merely as a phrase. We must have our wars, it appears, and our crimes, as well as other countries. I think Abraham Lincoln is rather to be envied in his death, as in his life somewhat; and if he wasn't as great as Caesar, he shares the same sort of tomb. History repeats itself, and if we are to imitate the atrocities of Rome, I find a certain amusement in conducting my pri-vate funeral service over the victims, on the ground that is most suitable for such associations, of any in the world.

But the King being dead, what then? Are we to cry Live the King again? To me this great change looks like a step downward to our generation. New men have come. Will the old set hold their ground, or is Seward and the long-lived race about him, to make way for a young America which we do not know. You may guess how I have smiled sweetly on the chains that held me here at such a time, and swore polyglott oaths at Italy and everything else that keeps me here. I have looked towards London as earnestly as What's-her-name looked from Bluebeard's tower, for the signs of the com-ing era,[1] but no sign is given. The Minister is waiting also apparently. I have written to him that *of course* now he must remain where he is, but whether he agrees to the of course or not, I can't say. It is clear to me that if Seward lives, he must stay; and if Seward retires, he should leave upon the new Secretary the responsibility of making a change. To throw up his office would be unpatriotic; it would also be a blunder. Do you assent to my doctrine? To be away from my place at such a time is enough to enrage a tadpole. And I can't be back before the end of June.

Are you curious to know about my adventures on the journey from Rome? It was but a repetition of the pleasures I described to you in another letter, with the addition of a violent heat. We drove five days among the Appenines. My hair is thinner in consequence. I have seen some cities that I hadn't seen, and some bad inns that I didn't want to see. One summer evening, returning with Mary and Brooks to our inn after a little excursion to see the falls of Terni, I found Minnie's letters in reply to ours, and smoked a cigar over them on a balcony over a crowd of screaming Italians in the noisy little market-place. Before writing again I wait to hear of your retreat from the army, which I suppose is now on the cards.

The truth is, in regard to traveling, this three months experience has made me old. I grow horribly solemn. I haven't had a good time for an age, nor laughed for a year. They call me Mausoleum, do the children. And well they may, for temper and nerve have been worn to a point that leaves little hope for me except in a tomb. However, I hope to see you before long, and till then—basta! We will have a quiet talk somewhere some day.

What a good time one can have in Italy, though, if one goes the right way about it. This traveling in one's own carriage is luxury itself. One starts in the early morning, and climbs mountains or crosses valleys with historical names and exquisite views; the walls of old Roman or Etruscan cities stare from the tops of hills; great convents rise in the valleys; the vines and flowers of Italy line the road, and if by noon it weren't hotter and dustier than Dante's Purgatorio, one might go on agreeably all day. Towards noon one stops and rests two or three hours, and then jogs on again till he winds up some hill at sunset, on which a very dirty, mediaeval and picturesque town perches itself, and where one looks with a species of distrust of one's own senses, on five centuries ago. But the old peculiarities are fast yielding now, and little remains of them except those which are still protected by the aid of religion, which in this country is the prop and shield of everything degrading, stupid, and bad. Arthur Dexter says that the only good and valuable men in Rome are the atheists. If you are not in a hurry you will miss the old order of things, for in another year railways will run in every direction about Italy, and whatever it may become, the antidiluvian character of the place will be lost. Whether the Papacy will stay or not, who knows? Like many Americans who have lived long in Europe, I have become much more radical in my convictions than is usual in America, where you exist in amusing ignorance of the fact that you are rapidly being caught up with and will soon be left behind by Europe. Of course you may answer this by the usual platitudes about the great republic. It's true enough that you and I never shall see the day when America will stand second, but the fact remains that since 1788 we have with difficulty sustained our position, while Europe has made enormous strides forward. At present there are two great influences holding Europe back. One is the English aristocracy, the other the Roman Church. Both of these will go down as sure as fate. I can't tell you when or how the change will take place, but whether it's ten or whether it's a hundred years, it will come, and when all the world stands on the American principle, where will be our old boasts unless we do something more.

I won't trouble you longer with my ideas on these matters, for they are dull. Perhaps I will write something on the matter some day, and bury it in the depths of the Atlantic—Monthly. At all events I am in theory a violent radical, inclined towards every "ism" in the faint hope of detecting within it some key to the everlasting enigma of progress. How the devil does one add two and two, and what is the answer? Such is philosophy; ditto politics.

At any rate here we are in Florence, which is a live city; an Italian Paris. The place was never a very great favorite of mine, for I never could see why people are so fond of it. We shall stay here till about the 18th; we shall then go to Venice, Milan, and perhaps across Switzerland and down the Rhine, and arrive in Paris on the 20th June. By the 1st July at latest I expect to be at London.

There I shall expect to see you some time towards October, for I do not suppose you will care to punish Minnie by a winter passage for any sins she may have to answer for. Nor will you be wise to trust the equinox. Either the first of September or the first of October is your best time, unless you can make it earlier still.

As to your being married in our absence, I think both your papa and mamma expect it and are waiting to welcome you here. It is so impossible to say in such times what is to happen to us that they have given up every idea of really getting to America. At least they talk so, though what they may do at the last, the Lord knows. You can foresee better from the current of events in America what will be our course, than we can judge it here. Undoubtedly, should Seward go down, there will be a struggle between the factions, more personal than political, for the control of the new Administration. I do not know where to discover in the whole political horizon, a single star whose influence would be favorable to us. Except Seward we have not one friend. Possibly this might be our strength. But on the other hand a vehement push will be made from other directions in favor of the advanced wing of the old Republican party. What their distinctive cry would be, I do not understand, unless it were the reversal of the Shakesperian text "Mercy should temper Justice."[2] But besides the battle between these two, which we won with so much difficulty in 1861, there is the Western element which may cut in between the others, or decide the success of either. For ourselves, we stand merely as cards for other men to play. Of course the Minister does not mix in the fight. But Thurlow Weed has written to London; a very unusual thing, which sets me to thinking, as the movements of that complicated statesman generally do. Does he turn his head that way indeed? If so, he must be hard pressed, for I cannot believe that he has any real taste for our advancement. On the other hand there are but two men with the proper knowledge for the State Department; Sumner and our Minister at London.

Do not imagine that I am anxious for the promotion to Washington. But I do feel that the new emergency opens all the old difficulties, and is of no little importance. Once decided, I shall care little, for then our course will be fixed. In the meanwhile our state of doubt is very embarrassing, and who can say when it will end.

We have received your letters describing your entrance into Richmond. It was just the right ending for your martial life.[3] Now for another kind of experience!

Ever

MS: MHi
1. In the fairy tale Sister Anne watched for the help that would rescue Fatima.
2. HA is paraphrasing *The Merchant of Venice*, IV, i.
3. CFA was moved by the "singular circumstance that you, in the fourth generation of our family, under the Union and the constitution, should have been the first to put your foot in the capital of the Ancient Dominion" (CFA to CFA2, April 28).

To Charles Francis Adams, Jr.

No. 44.   London. 14 July. 1865.

My dear Charles:

I have been so buried up to my ears in work ever since reaching Paris a month ago, that I have laid aside all letters and visits and personal occupations, in order to finish up the enormous mass of copying which has accumulated on my hands. But the world has run ahead of me so fast that I can't now catch it up. Bad as your illness is, I felt a relief when I heard of it. In the first place it cut the knot of your connection with the army, which I began to think would never be untied. And in the second place it saved you from Texas, which I was dreadfully afraid would have utterly finished you.[1] As it is you will have a few weeks or a few months of prostration and despondence, to be followed by a few years perhaps of shaken health. But with care and prudence, you will come out all right, and health once regained, all is right again. I don't admit, you know, that the struggle for a living is any cause for trouble, as long as health lasts. Of course you will croak damnably. All men in your condition do so. It it their only amusement. But that does no harm. Only for God's sake this next time, take care not to overdo yourself again.

As you have probably heard, we had a very successful week in Paris, killing and burying Aunt Eliza, and taking care of uncle Edward in such a way as to win the applause of the world.[2] That satisfactorily performed, we came over here, and I cursed my fate when I once more stood on the beach at Folkestone and saw the watery, grimy, despondent sky and coast of

England. Luckily for me, I had no time to think, and had to go to work again so hard that my low spirits passed away in state papers. We reached London only at the very end of the season, but I had time to find it changed since I went away. America is a subject dropped out of sight now, except by those who have been our friends. Society avoids it as a disagreeable topic. They feel that they went too far, and they feel that we know their feelings. The only question now upon which they venture to be aggressive, is the fate of Davis. They take the keenest interest in him, and talk very impertinently about our executing him. I am convinced that we must do it, if only to vindicate our right, but even our best friends here are very earnest in begging to have him spared.

We are in the middle of a general election the only feature in which is the return of John Stuart Mill; a creditable thing to do. Tom Hughes also comes in. In fact our friends everywhere show very strong, and so far as America is concerned we have nothing to do but to restore peace and arrange our finances, and our influence on England will be strong enough to carry a new reform through within ten years. Circumstances might hurry it, but naturally and peacefully it will come in about ten years, I think. Then there will be another long step forward here. Piece by piece the only feudal and middle-age harness will drop off, that still remains. I look to see in Europe during the next quarter of a century, the public acknowledgment of a heap of changes that are now simmering quietly in the minds of society without much expression. You have no idea how thoughtful society is in Europe; even more so in some respects than in America, because there are practical hooks to hang thought on, like the Church, education, poverty and the suffrage, which are points all forgotten with us, but very much alive here, and lead men far, when they once begin.

I find the Chief rather harder, less a creature of our time, than ever. It pains me absolutely (and I am not given to suffering for other people) to see him so separate from the human race. I crave for what is new. I hanker after a new idea, in hopes that it may solve some old difficulty. He cares nothing for it, and a new discovery in physics or in chemistry, or a new developement in geology never seems to touch any chord in him, any more than if the sciences were in as subordinate a position now as they were when the Puritans landed at Plymouth. He bases his world upon moral laws. I rank moral laws with all other laws, as matter for study, developement and perhaps of change. I am continually puzzled to know how we get along together.

Politics seem queerly confused in America. Sumner, Dana and the rest are in an amusing provincial hurry to get into opposition. Why so fast? We have done with slavery. Free opinion, education and law have now entrance into the south. Why assume that they are powerless, and precipitate hopeless confusion? Let us give time; it doesn't matter much how long. I doubt about black states. I fancy white is better breeding stock.

Ever Yrs.

P.M.   A package goes next week by Eliza Gardner for you and Minnie.

MS: MHi
1. Orders were issued for a cavalry expedition to Texas, where Gen. Kirby Smith's army refused to surrender. But CFA2 was invalided home with malaria June 1. He was discharged Aug. 1 as brevet brigadier general.
2. An allusion to the death of HA's aunt Elizabeth Brooks.

To Charles Francis Adams, Jr.

No. 48.   London. 20 October. 1865.

My dear Charles:

Your two letters in reply to my two pugnacious epistles, were very satisfactory indeed. I had become seriously afraid that your illness was going to affect your character and temper, and I looked to your reply to my "eye-opener," as the test of your condition. Nothing could be more conclusive in this respect. Indeed the skilful manner in which you turn my flank and rout me with an attack of flattery on my weakest points, satisfies me that you will yet keep a week or two, if carefully put away in the ice-chest.

Enough of that subject, which I did not willingly begin, and am glad to be done with. As this is the last letter I can send to you, there is a great deal to be said in it, without blowing at dead coals.

The last two weeks have been very busy, and there seems to be no great prospect of any relief. The whole force of the Legation is overworked, and the shoals of Americans that are always passing through town, give us a leisure afternoon and evening very seldom. I don't know that we were ever so little rested in the quiet season.

Before this letter reaches you, the American papers will have republished our passage-at-arms with Earl Russell.[1] These notes made here a very deep sensation, and have created a very uneasy feeling. The newspapers have treated our portion of the documents with great respect, for them, and hammer away, day after day, with long leaders, trying to overthrow our positions. All this is of course a great personal triumph, and I think that your papa's reputation as a public man is scarcely inferior now in England, to that of any of their own men. In point of fact these notes of his are in my humble opinion, not surpassed. I do not know whether America will notice them. Others as good have lain and will lie buried forever in Seward's hopeless volumes of Pub: Docs: It is possible however that so unusual an English endorsement may persuade the Americans that some good writing may come out of their own country, and induce them to honor us with their notice. At present your papa's English reputation is greater than his American. I flatter myself that the dictum of this Legation now is listened to with a respect, and reflected upon with an earnestness not usual in the English mind, nor ever before felt in such a degree. We hold at this moment the whole foreign policy of England in our hands. She can't express even an opinion. If she tells Count Bismarck that he'd better mind his eye, the Count winks at us, and puts on his heaviest cowhides, and administers to her a kicking that excoriates her figure.[2] She can't resent it, because our Legation, while she meditates revenge, comes forward with profound bows and presents a few more items of our little bill. This process has already lasted two years, and Lord Russell is aware of it even to a degree of lively sensibility. We have already checkmated them against Russia and Prussia, and if I could suggest an idea secretly to the Emperor of Russia, it would be to strike now for Turkey. We wield a prodigious influence on European politics now, and the time is coming when the world will see it with a painful clearness. At the same time we have never touched an intrigue and have not even a single secret source of information or a single channel of communication other than those that are regular and legitimate, with any Court or party in Europe.

A system more directly opposite than this to the old practice of European diplomacy, could not be invented. Lord Palmerston and Lord Russell have belonged both to the old school of secret and intriguing diplomacy, though the former was much deeper in it than the latter. We have got the better of both of them. How much the better, time will show. Lord Palmerston was a man without any fixed opinions. If a clear and decided majority of the people, had by some perverseness decided to turn back upon its track and re-enact all the abuses that flourished under Lord Castlereagh, Palmerston would have undone the work he had helped to accomplish, with perfect good-nature, and maintained that he merely went with his time; forward or backward, it mattered little.[3] But for all this, our friend who is dead, had one really active antipathy, and that antipathy was America. He would have worked with her, or flattered or conciliated her, if necessary, for he was as callous as a rhinocerous, and to get a useful instrument would swallow his strongest attachment or his strongest dislike with an equally cheerful face. But he would much have preferred to do her a harm, and he did what he could for that purpose. We not only survived his attempts, but we have survived him, though he lived long enough to see us resume our offensive, and throw England on her back. What is to be the result of his disappearance? I think it will weaken England and strengthen us. Lord Russell is no match for us, as has been long evident, and Lord Clarendon would certainly not be an advance on Lord Russell.[4] Palmerston gave the Government great internal strength. A new Ministry must inevitably devote itself to internal affairs and face serious questions at home. Our attitude therefore will become more than ever embarrassing to them, and our action or abstenance from action may in future preserve or ruin Ministries.

Under these circumstances I must confess that I doubt whether Mr Seward will care to change our representation abroad or would be wise to do so. I have much doubt whether we shall be released next spring, as your papa still pretends to expect. Seward as yet has given us not even the ghost of a sign, although the resignation has been for three months in his hands, and Mr Evarts, to whom I wrote on the subject, after seeing Mr Seward, could not give me any reason to suppose that a change was practicable. If the change of Ministry, coming as it will on the published correspondence on our claims, does not give Mr Seward a good reason for compelling us to remain here, if he really wants us to do so, I am much mistaken. For my own part, I should not object. I am doing as much for myself here as I should be likely to do anywhere.

This letter will reach you on the very verge of your marriage, I expect, and just in advance of your start. I don't suppose you are altogether inclined to look upon your new start as a joke, but I don't mean to moralise upon it, nor to condole with you as though you were going to be hanged. I've no doubt you'll find the pleasures and pains of life pretty fairly balanced, and at any rate it's no use worrying, if they're not. As for the ceremony of being wedded, I have always had my own opinions about it, but I won't trouble you with them. I have thought at times lately that my own objections to marriage were not radical, though deep, and a certain temporary weakness has come over me at seeing the process through which my friends seem to renew the faculty of enjoyment that generally is confined to children. But it doesn't last. Only a great passion could finish me now, and though I can imagine a great passion, I do not think I could ever feel it. When I marry, too, I want a woman who will take care of me, and keep me out of mischief, a good, masculine female, to make me work, and be blind to Burgundy and French cooking.

Give all my love to Minnie, and tell her that I shall be on the gay and sunny Mersey, to see her arrival.[5]

Ever   H.

MS: MHi

1. CFA had sent Russell a long note on U.S. grievances and claims for damages. Russell contested the claims, but suggested appointment of a joint commission; on Oct. 10 he published the exchange of notes in the *London Gazette*. Russell subsequently explained that he wanted such a commission to review, not the *Alabama* claims, but British claims against the U.S.

2. Otto Leopold (1815–1898), Count Bismarck, prime minister of Prussia.

3. Palmerston died Oct. 18. He had supported the Reform Bill of 1832 as a member of the cabinet. Lord Castlereagh (Robert Stewart, 1769–1822) was a leading Tory opponent of reform.

4. Russell became prime minister in the new government and George Villiers (1800–1870), Lord Clarendon, succeeded him as foreign secretary.

5. With the honeymoon couple leaving for London after the wedding Nov. 8, correspondence between the brothers ceased until CFA2 returned home in September 1866.

To Lord Houghton

Brighton. 17 November. 1865.

My dear Lord:

Some weeks ago my father gave me a message from you, intimating that your invitation to me to Fryston was still open. I was extremely obliged to you for remembering me. It was a kindness that few people except yourself would have thought of. But it was then, and it still is impossible for me to get away, though I have waited till now in order to be sure that I had no chance.

Next week I am going down to Liverpool to meet my brother, whom you know, who has married a pretty wife, and comes to visit us. I look forward to his taking my place long enough for me to go down to Yorkshire about the 1st of January, and pass a few days at Thornes with Charles Gaskell. I don't know whether you will still be in Yorkshire at that time, but if you are, I will take the liberty of writing to beg a night's lodging of you before I come back to town. There is no saying when I may leave England, and I should be sorry to go without at least one chance of talking with you.

The new Ministry has not begun its career very successfully as regards us. I'm afraid the Shenandoah business will have a very irritating effect in America.[1] This is by no means pleasant to us who have already as heavy a load to carry as we can manage.

Pray give my best regards to Lady Houghton and believe me

Most sincerely Yrs Henry B. Adams.

Lord Houghton.

MS: Trinity College, Cambridge
 1. The summer after the war's end the Confederate cruiser *Shenandoah* captured or destroyed 38 Union vessels, mostly whalers in the North Pacific. Upon receiving word of Appomattox on Aug. 2, Capt. James I. Waddell sailed all the way to Liverpool in order to surrender her to British authorities, thus avoiding being tried for piracy in an American court. Although British courts cleared everyone charged with violation of neutrality, the American minister pressed claims for damage done by the British-built ship.

To Lord Houghton

Brighton. 6 Dec. '65.

My dear Lord:

I am dreadfully disappointed at not being able to get to Fryston, but there's no hope of my being free before the new year. I have promised to go down to Yorkshire then at any rate, after which I shall accompany my brother and his wife to Paris, so that my present attention to work has got to atone for a month's vacation afterwards. I hope you will be in town so that we can show you my new sister who is charming.

As you say, we Americans can't brag much of our management of the nigger now. I hope we shall improve however by the example. I think we may now venture to hang Jeff. Davis with the applause of the Times.

Ever most truly Yrs Henry B. Adams.

MS: Trinity College, Cambridge

7.

A Man of
the World
1866–1868

For Henry Adams, staying on in London after the war could have been, in his term, a vice. He had lighter and lighter duties at the legation, and the labor of escorting his family on their travels hardly justified his not going home to attend law school and begin a career. Yet he stayed on without a murmur. Leaving politics to his brother John and business to Charles, he settled into the role of man of the world. He moved in society with easy assurance, cultivated friendship with candid affection. The man of affairs in him relished discussing investments. The emergent connoisseur began to buy drawings—and to comment knowledgeably on high cuisine. The student analyzed American politics at long distance and continued to read science and philosophy. The last touch of worldliness, however, was that he managed to work extremely hard without calling attention to the fact.

The object of Henry Adams' labor was to make himself a writer. He resumed research for his article on Captain John Smith, but put his major effort into "British Finance in 1816" and "The Bank of England Restriction, 1797–1821," major studies of British experience with war economy and its aftermath. He also undertook to review the newly published tenth edition of Lyell's *Principles of Geology*. In writing heavy unsigned articles, he sought to attain intellectual authority rather than to "fill a large or small place in the popular eye as such." Most of all, he committed himself to a craft: "A life is not such a tremendous time to learn to express your ideas."

When his father's mission finally ended, Henry Adams had not yet finished his essay on Lyell and the changes in geology since 1830. Besides this unfinished work, he brought home a conception of the writer as a public man, like Tocqueville or Mill, whose function was to raise the level of political and intellectual discourse. Although he did not explicitly state that purpose, he had clearly framed it when he wrote about his returning home: "I have made my plans and am ready to begin the march."

To Blanche Smith Clough

5, Upper Portland Place
Tuesday, 13 March 1866.

Dear Madam:[1]

I have many thanks to offer you for the prompt kindness with which you answered the request I ventured to make through Mr Palgrave, for a copy of the work which I had the happiness to receive yesterday morning. As the published volume of your husband's poems has been a favorite study of mine for a long time, and as it has been my fortune to be thrown more or less on both sides of the Atlantic, I think I may venture to say that I shall value this volume enough to justify the liberty I take in asking for it.[2]

          I am   Very truly Yrs   Henry B. Adams.

Mrs A. H. Clough

MS: Oxford, Bodleian Library, MS.Eng.lett.e.76,fol. 20.
   1. Blanche Smith Clough, widow of Arthur Hugh Clough and editor of his literary remains.
   2. Mrs. Clough had privately printed her husband's *Letters and Remains* (1865). The copy she sent HA is at MHi. Francis Turner Palgrave (1824–1897), poet, anthologist, and art critic, had written the introduction to the London edition (1862) of Clough's *Poems,* to which HA refers. Clough had lived in Charleston, S.C., as a boy and in Boston (1852–1853), where Ralph Waldo Emerson and Charles Eliot Norton were among his closest friends.

To Charles Francis Adams

Shanklin. Sunday. 8th. April. [1866]

Cher Papa

You may expect us on Tuesday. We tear ourselves from Shanklin at half after ten, and we arrive at Waterloo at quarter after three.[1] I'm sorry for you, as I foresee that your quiet and sunny progress will be considerably disturbed by our arrival, and that your labors will be proportionably severe. But I certainly hope that nothing will interfere with our return on the day named. Nothing can reconcile me to the position of head of a family. In the last five years I've had experience enough in that way at least until I shall have had a long repose, and grown self confident or presumptuous again. Our two fine days have saved us this time from homesickness, and gave me a chance to tramp over the hills, than which excursion, with the return by the cliff, I have seen nothing finer in England.

Perhaps it would be as well for you to enclose me a couple of £5 notes tomorrow. I don't know that I shall need them, but I don't like to run too close, and I might have to borrow money of Mrs Durant, which would not much amuse me.

Mary has a cold, but I see no reason to fear its becoming serious.

Ever Yrs   H.

MS: MHi
1. Shanklin is a resort town on the Isle of Wight.

To Charles Milnes Gaskell

54, Portland Place. [2 May 1866]

Dear Carlo:

Many blessings light upon the wig![1] I too once hoped to reach the proud distinction you have gained, but now that this hope has been permanently crushed, I hereby make over to you to have and to hold in fee simple or by any other tenure you prefer, all my right and title in any glory, gain, or emolument whatsoever, which might have become mine in the pursuit of a legal career.

You are either so early or so late that your note found me still in bed this morning. I studied it for ten minutes before comprehending its meaning. Five minutes before, my mind had been crossing the Isthmus of Panama, and was greatly exercised at having left its boots at Aspinwall in the hurry of departure.[2] On returning to 54 P.P., it was still hazy in its vision. I sent a verbal 'Yes' at last in reply, and tomorrow evening will appear in my war-paint and feathers at ¼ to 8.

Where think you that I go tonight? To swell the noble Houghton's train! I dine for the Literary Fund and if you were the man I took you for, you would go there too.[3] But the world grows dull and duller. Lady Cranborne has not asked me.[4] But Mrs Gladstone remains.

Ever   H.

Wednesday 2 May.

MS: MHi
1. Gaskell, after reading law at the Inner Temple, was called to the bar April 30.
2. HA's dream was evidently suggested by news of the explosion April 3 of a ship in the harbor of Aspinwall (now Colón) on the Isthmus of Panama; the *European*, carrying nitroglycerin for the California goldfields, was totally destroyed, 50 were killed, and much of the port was leveled.
3. The annual dinner of the Royal Literary Fund (to benefit indigent writers).
4. Lady Cranborne was Georgina Caroline Anderson Cecil (d. 1899), wife of Robert Cecil, Viscount Cranborne, later Lord Salisbury and Tory prime minister.

To John Gorham Palfrey

54, Portland Place.   London. 4 May. 1866.

My dear Dr Palfrey:

I am very happy to be able to do anything for you, and send the Dod by the first mail.[1] As for the cost, I don't know what it is, and care not for the filthy dross until you increase it by some commission which costs gold. Then I will send you in my bill for all. Stanley has received his package and will no doubt acknowledge it, unless his perturbed mind goes wholly mad in the reform crisis.

We have returned here to a bucolic age, with nought to trouble us or annoy. My mind has run back to my old friend Smith of Virginia, whose reputation needs smashing. I have sent to John for the M.S. which I propose to re-examine and perhaps re-write, with an idea of publication. But what do you think a proper form of print? The thing is too long for a review. I've a mind to print it separately and call it a Monograph. What do you say to this?

Charles and his wife are so happy in Italy that I could envy them if it were not that "something ere the end," that undiscovered country from whose bourne, no bachelor returns makes me rather "accept the ills I have, than" the rest. Hamlet's logic is good for more cases than suicide.

Pray give my regards to your family or to such as still remember me, and believe me very sincerely

Yrs   Henry Brooks Adams.

MS: MH
1. Probably *Dod's Peerage,* by Roger Phipps Dod.

To Oliver Wendell Holmes, Jr.

54, Portland Place.   Saturday. 2 June. [1866]

My dear Holmes:[1]

Mrs Gladstone has sent you a verbal invitation through my mother to breakfast there next Thursday at ten o'clock. Send your note in reply direct to Mrs G.

If you would like to go to Lady Waldegrave's, I will take you with me this evening if you will come here at 10.30.

If not, perhaps you may like to dine here tomorrow.

Very truly Yrs   Henry B. Adams.

O. W. Holmes.

MS: MH-L
1. Oliver Wendell Holmes, Jr. (1841–1935), son of the famous physician, poet, and essayist, veteran of three years with the Union army, had just finished his legal training and was making his first trip to Europe. He arrived in London on May 9 and saw HA—and Mary Adams—on several occasions.

To Lord Houghton

54, Portland Place.   4 July. [1866]

My dear Lord:

We expect the Me-and-the-rest-of-him in the Thames shortly. You shall certainly know when to go down, but if the Prince goes, I suppose he will take one day for himself.[1]

Poor Austria will scarcely get to Berlin this campaign. Still she has one more chance to keep the Prussians out of Prague. You and I may hope she will fail, but as usual, we are in a minority here so small that silence is the only alternative to ostracism.[2]

Ever Yrs   H. B. Adams.

MS: Trinity College, Cambridge
1. The American monitor *Miantonomoh* was coming from Spithead for the convenience of those in London who wished to visit her. The Prince of Wales inspected her at Sheerness on July 15.
2. War between Austria and Prussia broke out in June, and on July 3 the Austrian army was defeated at Sadowa.

To John Gorham Palfrey

54, Portland Place.   July 5. 1866.

My dear Dr Palfrey:

Since receiving your note I have been waiting in some doubt what to do about the ancient liar Smith. This doubt has been increased by the arrival of Mr Deane who was so kind as to send me his edition of Smith's first book.

Mr Deane has left nothing for me to do, so far as I can see. I may certainly review his book and make, I am almost sure, an interesting magazine article out of it. But I can do nothing in the way of original speculation or statement. Do you think it worth the while to take the trouble for so little object? I am inclined to think it is, for I don't know that there is anyone else likely to do it at all, and it should be done.

If you agree to this, and see no reason for my keeping quiet, can you find for me a means of getting hold of whatever periodical is worth most for the purpose? I am absolutely ignorant who edits, and what is edited. If, however, you know any of those wonderful beings who read M.S.S. and can get him to promise me room for any particular number of his honored but heavy publication, I will be sure to be ready. The thing would want about thirty five pages of the North American. If not, I will publish here, and be hanged to him. Only in the latter case I shall pepper it a shade higher, and not pay much regard to anybody, except yourself and Mr Deane, nor to anything in the form of popular prejudices.

Of course I must rewrite it all. It will be a great bore but I shall wait till I fairly know whether it is to be served up hot in a Boston Magazine.

We are all now pretty well, hoping soon to get out of London.

Very truly Yrs H. B. Adams.

MS: MH

To John Gorham Palfrey

54, Portland Place. 13 July. 1866.

My dear Dr Palfrey:

May I ask you a favor. I cannot find in London any copy of the last edition of Bancroft's History. In the earlier editions he has a curiously absurd little note to his account of Pocahontas and Smith. "The full account," he says, "is found in the black-letter pamphlet, called the True Relation &c." When Deane published Wingfield, Bancroft changed this note, and I want a copy of the text as it now stands.[1] If you send me this, which amounts, I suppose, to only a few lines, you will assist me to point a sharp moral, and adorn Mr Bancroft's tale.

Very truly Yrs Henry B. Adams.

Dr. J. G. Palfrey.

MS: MH
1. George Bancroft (1800–1891) in *History of the United States* (1834–1875) expanded the little note (I, 132) with a noncommittal "Compare Deane's note on Wingfield."

To John Gorham Palfrey

54, Portland Place. London. 23 August. 1866.

My dear Dr Palfrey:

I hope you will not entirely renounce my acquaintance when you find that instead of one article for Norton, I herewith send him two.[1] Indeed I am by no means proud of my literary powers. Had I possessed any real confidence in myself I should not have almost reached thirty without an effort to win my spurs. But this I do know. There is more study and laborious application in the enclosed portfolio than in any number of the North American that I usually see.

I would be greatly obliged by your reading the second Essay, (I care little about the Smith) and if you really conclude that its publication would on the whole not do me credit, I beg that you will at once suppress it (as well as my letter to Mr Norton which I leave open for you to read) and transfer it under cover to my brother John. Pray don't allow yourself to be influenced by any idea of sensitiveness on my part. I have suppressed so many articles on my own judgment that it is a relief to have some one else decide on a matter which costs me no end of disgust and doubt.

Mr Dana and Frank Parker have been here, and are going back to America on the 15th of September in the same boat with my brother Charles. One by one we have had almost all our old friends out here except you. But I expect that another year will bring us back to Boston before you have a chance to come out.

I am sorry to see what a political coil things are again in. Both Dana and Parker had long discussions about it at our table, which I would have liked to have had you listen to. The long and the short of it seems to be that my father is again in a miserable minority in Massachusetts, without a friend to work with. Yet he considers the cause so great, and the ultimate result in its effect upon free and representative institutions, so surpassing in pressing importance, that I do not think even the tolerant and magnanimous threat of the Daily Advertiser to close his political career, will change his views. At this distance I am very open to deception, but it does seem to me as though everything in America had turned a back somersault. I find the pure northern Congress, just such a one as we prayed for twenty years ago, violating the rights of minorities more persistently than the worst pro-slavery Congress ever could do. I cannot but think that it has violated the Constitution habitually, to say nothing of having botched every single measure demanded for the public good from finance down to Fenianism.[2] I find all our old friends in Massachusetts, those who suffered so bitterly as a minority, utterly savage, intolerant and intolerable towards minorities now that they have themselves become a majority. I find even the Respectable Daily actually ostracising a man like my father, not so much as for expressing an opinion; but for allowing his son to do as he thought right.[3] It is time that this stopped. The tyranny of majorities in our country must be tempered by resistance, and I believe it would be good policy to support the most profligate political opposition rather than to allow one party to rule unchecked. If the Republicans get a thorough good thrashing this autumn, it will all do well. We shall all come back to the party and keep the Government. If not, I foresee that my family has got to go through another period of political banishment in Massachusetts, as has happened to it pretty regularly at intervals of about twenty years throughout the century.

I don't in the least write this with any idea of complaining, for I confess I rather like fighting for the weaker side. But John, who is all alone, or whose companions are worse than none, excites my compassion and my interest. The pressure of a united public opinion against one man, is an awful thing.

I don't do you or Mr Dana the injustice to put you in the same class with Messrs Sumner, Wilson, and their tail of Congress-men. Dana had a tremendous battle with my father about it, though. The argument was so keen and spirited for two hours after dinner, that I would have given a heap of money to have taken it down as a campaign document. I thought that Dana did not quite do himself justice except on the minor point of the war power which he pushed as well as it could be done. On the Constitutional question he was apparently undecided and weak. But I've written enough.

Ever faithfully Yrs   H.B.A.

MS: MH

1. Charles Eliot Norton (1827–1908), editor of the *North American Review* 1863–1868, had tentatively accepted HA's essay on Smith. HA's second article was "British Finance in 1816."

2. The Fenian Brotherhood (Sinn Fein) was founded in New York in 1858 as the "government" of an independent Ireland. In June, after a Fenian raid into Canada, 700 raiders were arrested and President Johnson promptly ordered the army to prevent future expeditions. Radical Republicans in Congress countered by introducing legislation that would emasculate U.S. neutrality laws and permit Fenian operations on U.S. territory.

3. JQA2 was a delegate to the National Union convention at Philadelphia, Aug. 14, called to support the conciliatory policies of President Johnson. The Boston *Daily Advertiser* and the Radical Republicans regarded his attendance as an official act of the Adams family.

To Charles Eliot Norton

London. 24 August. 1866.

Sir:

I send you in the accompanying portfolio the review of Mr Deane's late publications which Dr Palfrey has been so kind as to take under his protection. I hope it may interest you, as the investigation, four years ago, did me.

In the same portfolio however, I have placed another manuscript on a subject which I consider of much more interest. My absence from America has been so long that I know scarcely how or where to turn to get a public hearing on any large and rather difficult subject, else I should not try your patience by sending you two manuscripts at one time. If I were not still more ashamed to continue the process, I should express a wish to be allowed next year to offer you a third Essay, on the Suspension of Specie Payments in England from 1797 to 1819. If however you have the patience to wade through the two heavy Articles which I now send you, and to accept one of them, it is all that I can reasonably wish.[1]

I remain

Very truly Yrs   Henry Brooks Adams.

Charles Norton Esq.

MS: MH

1. Norton published both articles: "Captain John Smith," *NAR* 104 (Jan. 1867), 1–30; "British Finance in 1816," *NAR* 104 (April 1867), 354–386.

To Charles Francis Adams, Jr.

Berlin.[1] 10 November. 1866.

My dear Charles:

Yours of the 20th and 24th of October reached me at the same time this week. I communicated to the Minister your remarks, and I left to him the disposition of your 5.20s. He wants to sell his own also, but hankers after 70. They are now 68–69. I think he will sell on his return to London ten days hence.

In regard to your other question or commission, damn you, you are treading on my toes. You are mistaken in supposing that the North American has an article of mine on the return to specie payments. I am going to go to work on that article immediately on my return to London, and it may appear in the July North American. But, as yet, though I've read up a good deal on it, I've not written a letter. So that although the legal tender business will appear in it at some length, I am not thoroughly able to answer your question. The state of things in England was this. From 1797 to 1803 or thereabouts, there was no depreciation. In 1803, or somewhere round there, depreciation began. Lord King took it into his head to insist that his tenants should pay rent in gold, and issued a circular to that effect. It created a tremendous excitement, and it was found that no legal right existed, by virtue of which he could be prevented from doing so. In fact down to this time the Bank paper had been received at par only by common consent, and although the Bank itself had suspended specie payment, the country banks were still obliged to redeem their issues with gold, or its equivalent, Bank paper. So Lord King's manifesto created a revolution.[2] Parliament discussed the matter voluminously, but as I've not read the debates, I can't say what is in them. The end was that a law was passed making the Bank paper a legal tender.

This is all I recollect of the matter and I am happy to add that my information ends just where you want me to begin. I know not that any question ever was raised as to the legal meaning of coin, but if you find any case in point on record, I should be obliged to you if you would supply me with all the knowledge you can obtain on the subject. I can make good use of it, though my field is wider and more historic than yours. If I turn up anything about it after I resume work, I will tell you. But as I am just now a good bit away from books and references, I can't help you much.

Just as you left Queenstown the news came of the President's Cleveland speech, and soon afterwards the Maine election. I laughed to think what a wholly new state of things you would find in America, and I shut up shop *subito*. We are all back again as Republicans, our conspiracy having failed.[3] Let us now wait and see the new issue.

I have an idea. Qu'en dis-tu? Sooner or later there must be a smash financially in America. One year, five years, ten years; enfin, sometime. A man who has ready money can then make something. Furthermore, the political state of affairs makes American values particularly dangerous. Why put all one's cargo in a single ship, and that leaky?

My idea is to get rid of about half my property, or in other words send one thousand pounds over to England where I think I can with my means of information, invest it so as to produce four or five per cent with a good chance of a rise in value. In case of a collapse in America, sell out here, and reinvest on the other side. In case of political troubles, a nest egg elsewhere is always a resource. What sayest?

Mamma seems all right again. I think London doctors ailed her as much as anything, but the journey no doubt has done her good. The Min. Plen. has been as happy as a boy of ten. I myself have learned something on our journey, but not much, as I knew pretty near everything before. I want to get to London again and be at work, but can't do it much before the middle of January, owing to visits &c. We shall return to England before the 1st of December.

I suppose John has lost his election and some day I mean to write to him about it.[4] In the mean time I suppose you have told him all that was worth his knowing, about our "moral support." Who could have foreseen A.J. Esq. at Cleveland! Give my love to M. Ogden. I expect that you and she don't feel as though life had been a burden in Europe.

Ever Yrs.

MS: MHi
1. The Adamses were vacationing in Germany.
2. Peter King (1776–1833), *Thoughts on the Restriction of Payments of Specie at the Banks of England and Ireland* (1803).
3. The "conspiracy" was an effort by some Republicans to join Northern Democrats in opposing Radical Reconstruction. Thus, JQA2 joined the Democratic party. Johnson, to slow the party shift, undertook a campaign against the Radicals and for a Republican policy of reconciliation with the South. At Cleveland, Sept. 3, he exchanged bitter words with Radical hecklers: "What about Louisiana?" "You let the negroes vote in Ohio before you talk about negroes voting in Louisiana." In the Maine election, Sept. 10, and in other state elections, Johnson's supporters were overwhelmingly defeated.
4. JQA2 in fact won election to the Massachusetts legislature.

To John Gorham Palfrey

54, Portland Place.   London. 30 Nov. 1866.

My dear Dr Palfrey:

About the 24th October, when I was wandering with my family in the wilds of Germany, I received a note from you dated Sept. 10th, and written in haste to catch the Washington bag. I assumed that "September" was a misdate, and October the true reading, until I received a letter from Norton, dated October 3d and obviously subsequent to your's. The clerks of the State Department, I suppose, found your few lines so difficult of comprehension that they pocketed your letter for a month, in order to study it. If so, they did me a great wrong, for your letter was one of the very few I ever received which gave me full and complete satisfaction, and which established a principle to regulate my course upon. Had your judgment been unfavorable, I should have accepted it as law, and turned round to work for another five years in silence, till I was ready for a new trial. As your approval is decided, I accept it equally as law, and consider myself as authorised to go on. Norton wrote me a very handsome letter afterwards; so handsome that I suspected you to have prompted it. Had it been only phrases I should have mistrusted it, but I could say nothing in doubt of the perfect good-faith of a man who accepts on the spot two long Articles and asks for more. Still I have not thought it worth while to answer the letter, for reasons of my own. If you see Norton, perhaps you could remember to tell him that I thank him for it.

I am extremely sorry to hear that your barn had such a piece of ill-luck. But I hope that we are coming now into quieter times, and that you will for the present have no more barns to burn, nor mischief-making newspapers to worry you. In looking at the state of things in America from this side, I shall continue to rejoice that my family reposes in peace here. There is mighty little that I can see in America now which is pleasant to look at. I hope with all my heart that you enjoy all there is that is enjoyable.

We have just returned from a two months absence on the continent, during which my father has for the first time had an opportunity of seeing something not Anglo-Saxon in the world. I am sure it has done him good, and he enjoyed it as much as he would going home, almost. At least there were no drawbacks to it, in the shape of political contests and financial difficulties. My mother, who had been very unwell for several months, has returned quite recovered, I hope, and we have settled down to our sixth winter in London, as though we had not fully depended on already being at home.

Your package for Mr Dixon is attended to.[1] I have a note from Frank which shall also be quickly attended to. With best regards to all Yrs

I am   Henry B. Adams.

MS: MH

1. William Hepworth Dixon (1821–1879), historian and editor of the *Athenaeum.*

To Charles Deane

London. 30 November. 1866.

My dear Sir:

I am not aware that our friend John Smith's will has been *discovered,* in the sense that it ever had been lost. Some years ago when I was looking up the evidence, I had his will searched for, and copied. This copy I enclose to you, and you are welcome to make such use of it as you like. If I want another, I am conveniently situated to get it at any time.

I told you that I should review you, and it appears that Mr Norton will put us into the January number of the North American. I hope you will think I have presented the case properly, and that it is toned down enough to convince even Mr Bancroft, in spite of the *notes,* which I have felt it my duty to quote. I should have asked Mr Norton to put the article in your hands before publication if it had not been that there is so much question of yourself in course of it, as to make it better that it should be independent. It is not likely that our case can be established without a long battle, especially if there are any hot-headed literary Southerners left, to put on the war-paint and feathers and scalp us for our treatment of their hero. Therefore I prefer in a cowardly manner to hide myself under your name.

With many good wishes for the success of your further inquiries

I am very truly   H. B. Adams.

Charles Deane Esq.

P.S. I enclose another original document also, which you already know, with a fac-simile of Jo. S's signature.

MS: MHi

To Charles Francis Adams, Jr.

London. 21 December. 1866.

My dear Charles:

Two voluminous letters from you have reached me lately; one of 24th Nov., and the other dated the 27th. I will proceed to answer them with that force and skill which is so conspicuous in all my utterances.

Your first letter was very dismal, terminating in thoughts of suicide which were a natural consequence of the frame of mind you were in. As for the suicide, I quite agree with you, having long ago made up my mind that when life becomes a burden to me I shall end it, and I have even decided the process. The only difficulty is that every year I live, I feel on the whole less of this despondency than formerly, and the worst time of all was the earliest; when a boy at school. As a rule I have found this melancholy disposition a consequence of a slightly disordered stomach, or too low system, which was best corrected at this season by a pill and a week or two of cod-liver-oil. This however is only the result of my loose theory of morals, as the Governor rightly calls my ethical opinions. (He gave me a tremendous rasper in connection with this, the other day. Bless his dear old puritanical incorruptible soul! I didn't mind, and he apologised afterwards.) I only suggest the stomach from a materialistic point of view, and having done so, will move up higher.

You may not be aware that Goethe was a great practical genius as well as a great poet. Now this Goethe said one day to his friend Eckerman, who was, as might be said, in your situation: "There must always be a sequence in life."[1] He hit it as true as you live. Life ought to be the demonstration of a mathematical problem; the triangulation of so much time, and your last triangle must, to be correct, have one or more of its sides in common with the preceding one. Now, how stands your case. You can't use your military triangle as the base of your new one. You then go back a step to your legal base. But you can make nothing out of that. What remains but to recommence your operations from a wholly new point, and to slowly and carefully measure your new distances and calculate your new altitudes, calculating to work your old measurements in again so far as possible, as you go along, in order that your old labor may not be wholly thrown away. I don't suppose the process is pleasant, and to be effectual it must and ought to be slow, no doubt. But I dont see that you have any reason to be afraid of the result, except in one alternative. Whatever line you are now drawn into, you must stick to it, for the chances are enormous that a third change would be fatal.

As for me, you mistake the point. I have never varied my course at all. From my birth to this moment it has been straight as an arrow. Such as I am, I am complete. All the accidents of life have fallen in with the bent of my disposition and the previous course of my training. I repeat it, such as I am, the product is unique and positive. I shall get along; and if I am in the end what you in your sublimity call a failure, I shall still have enjoyed what I, in a spirit of more philosophical and milder tendency, consider a rounded and completed existence. Our ideas on this matter are radically at variance, but I think you can understand what I mean if I hammer at you long enough.

For instance, by the time this reaches you I suppose I shall be out in the North American, and perhaps one or two more articles of mine will appear there. But I don't want to repeat my old mishap of five years ago. I don't want to be affiché as the writer of this or that clever or dull or obnoxious or blundering Essay. I would rather my name were wholly unmentioned. Some year or two hence it will all be the same. The estimate the world has of a man, filters ultimately through the masses better in darkness than in the heat of the sun. If five years hence I published a book I would prefer to have the non-reader have a vague idea that I was a clever and rising man, than myself receive a host of newspaper criticisms and society compliments. I don't want to rise by leaps to high position. I don't care for your short cut to eminence. I don't aspire to fill a large or small place in the popular eye as such. I have no fear about what is to happen after my return home. I mean to develope the life I have lived, and to do that I need no external support. I work on the hard pan, if necessary.

So much for our different views of life, which resolve themselves at last merely into a difference of temperament; you, bold, energetic, even arrogant in your demands upon your fellow creatures and on life; I, cautious, timid, and so much inclined to doubt my own mind that I might let the greatest good go by untouched, rather than expose myself to what I should consider an evil. But at any rate, I am patient, and I despise the world and myself so honestly and reflectingly, that whatever fate comes, will probably find me ready to bow to it with a good grace.

This brings me direct to the second point of interest in your letters. I hope that in taking my affairs out of John's hands you did not let him suppose that I wished it. John has taken good care of my affairs during a busy time, and I should be sorry to have him think that I am ungrateful for it. I've no doubt that he is very willing to hand the work over to you, but still I dont want him to suppose that I think your management preferable to his.

I wish that the first work you perform in this connection, would be to send me (unless John has already done it) an exact account of all receipts, disbursements, investments &c. since July, 1865. If not too much trouble I would like for the future a semi-annual account in July and Jan. I shall expect you however, in return, to charge me a per-centage for management as you would anyone else. In that case I can feel at my ease, and find fault with you if I like.

I approve the sale of the factory stock, though I hope you bagged the dividends. Yet I don't understand how the Merrimack can be doing a poor business with a 15 per cent dividend. And if her stock falls much at any time, apart from special reasons of bad-management &c, I wish you would buy in heavily. It has divided 22½ per cent this year, and 23 per cent last year, and John bought at par; the best thing he ever did for me. I go in on factories in the long run.

But I cant see how Michigan Central Bonds at 106 wont shrivel as you say. I should think Chicago City 7.s. at par were cheaper. But I know little of the matter. I wish I were quite as sure of no internal political trouble as you. I wouldn't sell the Phil. Wil. & Baltimore stock though. There's not much and its a great line. The great pressure will, I suppose, fall on the banks and it is well to be clear of them. U.S. Bonds have stood well and are likely to do so. As a rule, I have gone on the principle of scattering my investments, but your movement now is one of concentration and its object is to obtain steady and easily convertible securities. Such are U.S. Bonds, and Massachusetts and Boston Stock. But on the other hand, if Congress expands again, as I fear, I shall be left high and dry for a long time.

The Governor sold your Bonds very well, I believe. He took the '64 bond himself at the home price.

The article you mention in the Edinburgh must have been about two years ago. It was about the Bank rate at 7 per cent, or something of the kind. You can easily find it.

Thanks for your legal notes. I think you are wrong. Gold demonetised is a commodity to be stated not by coin but by weight. So many ounces of gold should be the legal term. Nevertheless your argument will be worth making and I shall be glad to read it.

MS: MHi
1. Johann Peter Eckermann (1792–1854) was, like CFA2, in his early thirties and unsettled in life when he became unofficial secretary and companion of Johann Wolfgang Goethe (1749–1832); *Conversations with Goethe* (1836–1848).

To Charles Francis Adams, Jr.

London. 1 February. 1867.

My dear Charles

An attack of illness which laid me up for a week, prevented my attending sooner to your directions. On getting about again, I turned my thoughts to your silver. On trying to discover something to send with it, however, I was unsuccessful. Both the Minister and your mamma denied indignantly that there was anything they wished to send home, and I myself after long reflection, failed to convict them of a falsehood. I have myself only John's cigars to send, and I imagine that this is not the kind of padding you wanted.

So I must send the silver alone, and it will go as soon as I can have it safely packed. I have got the kettle for you; the smallest size, because though it is "pure nickel silver plated," I thought the price exorbitant. I shall have the whole thing insured for safety. It will probably start next week.

I wish you to look over your account with Baring, and see whether, or when, you were credited with some sum from me, on account of those cigars. Send me a memorandum of the event. I cannot recollect how that matter was arranged though I do recollect telling Sturgis to make the transfer and giving him a check for the sum. Nor do I understand an entry of Feb. 1866 in John's accounts for $80, for "return cash cigars."

Further. I wish you to send me a list of the securities belonging to me, which John handed over to you; and the par values of each security noted. This in addition to the long account since July 1st *1865,* which I have already asked you for.

Finally. Your sales were excellent and just in time. I see no occasion to hurry about reinvestment. Fort Wayne I see has already fallen to 97, and I do not doubt that everything will go on falling throughout this year. Just look at it.

Europe can at any time bankrupt us. The only question is; will she?

You know about the Atlantic and Great Western Railway and James McHenry. It broke down Peto, Overend Gurney &Co, the Bank of London, and in fact caused last year's crisis. About £6,000,000 are said to be held in it here. This year it has got to blow up, and is now engaged in doing it.[1] It will turn out a gigantic swindle and will cast all American railways here into discredit.

The President will be impeached. You must see that the radicals have no other course; to stop is ruin to them, if to go on is ruin to the country. They will go on, and our credit will go down as they go on. The tide will turn against all American securities, and you will be swamped with them. I wish you would convert any 5.20 or 7.30 bonds I have into some security less liable to fluctuate.

If you see any signs in business or politics that make you more hopeful than I am, act on them of course. But for my own part I see troubled waters ahead, and hope to fish in them. To do so I wish to keep a good supply of bait on hand. There is no hurry about reinvestments. Hell is about to break loose.

I haven't heard anything from the North American about *pay*. They don't suppose I work for nothing, do they?

There seems to be no particular news here. We are waiting for Parliament to meet. Seward makes a hitch, it appears, in rê Alâ. et al.[2] You had best not mention it however; but I don't think so well as I did of our prospect of settling it all up. Another damned ropes-end let loose to trip us up.

MS: MHi

1. The Atlantic and Great Western Railway, of which the British entrepreneur James McHenry (1817–1891) was the largest stockholder, suffered heavy losses in the London financial crisis of 1866 and in April 1867 went into receivership.

2. The *Alabama* claims.

To Charles Francis Adams, Jr.

London. 16 February. 1867.

My dear Charles

I must again try your patience about the silver. I had it already to go by the Asia today, when I was told by Edward Baring that there was a drawback of 18 pence an ounce which I could obtain on it at the Liverpool custom house.[1] As this would have put £20 into your pocket, I thought that I was justified in stopping the expedition till I could ascertain the facts and give the necessary orders, even though it would at any rate delay the de-

parture of the box another fortnight. On inquiry I learned that the drawback was only on new silver, and that it was necessary to make an affidavit
that it had never been used. As this would have slightly clashed with another affidavit to the exactly opposite effect, which I had just made to the
Consul here, I thought it would be rather tall swearing, especially as the
age of the silver is rather apparent.

So you must wait another fortnight. Next Saturday I will send you the
key of the box, and the affidavit required, with a list of the articles. There is
no invoice proper. If there were an invoice, you would have to pay duty. As
it is, you need not. Everything will be done through the Barings, who will
insure for £150. and to whose agent you will look for instructions.

I have received your letter of the 26th January which my own letter of
about the same date (2 Feb.?) has already answered to all intents and purposes. After going over again all the arguments in the case, I see nothing to
change my opinion that the President must be impeached and that the
conservative strength of the republicans is powerless to resist the pressure
that will be brought on it. We shall soon see which of us is right. At all
events the chances are nine in ten that in the present critical state of the
country, politically and financially, one side or the other will do some act
which will throw everything into confusion. In my opinion the new tariff is
alone enough to ruin the country. It has made me feel more bitter against
Congress than all its other mad or imbecile acts together. I care little in this
respect whether it become law or not. Their part in it is equally great and
blameable.[2]

On the whole I hope not only that you have sold all my U.S. securities,
but that you have not invested, unless in Boston or Mass. gold bearing
stocks, and will not invest until we can see more clearly. The sale of our
bonds in Frankfort has been already checked, by several causes. My own
belief is that the high-water mark of radicalism is at impeachment, and
that no ebb can be expected till financial ruin has brought us up sharp. I
think that the month of March or April ought to settle the question, and I
look for a struggle for gold combined with a panic and struggle for credit, a
crash in prices, a crash in banks, a Congressional attempt to expand the
currency, and a howl of agony from the whole country, as the natural effect
of what is passing and has passed. As for politics I care not a damn whether
the South rules us or not. In the worst of times they never ruled us so badly
as Congress rules us now.

I notice that Seward or some other old mole is at work trying to upset the
radicals by offering a new plan of reconstruction. If this really affects the
party, I should expect it to stimulate to the last degree the movement for
impeachment, for it will alarm the extreme wing intensely by the fear of
losing power. The conservative strength of the party under the most favorable form, seems to be about 40 to 85 or there abouts, and not likely to be
increased in the new Congress. A difference of ten votes may decide as to an
impeachment, but that Stephens and Butler will force it to the vote I can't

doubt.[3] I have yet to see any proof that the conservatives dare break from party lead on a party question.

Our ideas meanwhile as to investment seem to agree. The world is out of joint, and Hamlet was a damned fool for trying to set it right instead of trying to make money on it. I should say that by the middle of April, perhaps by the end of March, we might be able to drink our little draught out of the hell-broth brewing now, and if you can find a Mephistoph or a witch to help you pray don't stick at the date of redemption they fix for our souls.

MS: MHi

1. Edward Charles Baring (1828–1897), Thomas Baring's cousin and partner, had served in the firm's Liverpool branch.

2. The protectionist bill which passed the House was being amended in the Senate; in the event, no tariff was enacted.

3. Thaddeus Stevens (1792–1868) of Pennsylvania, representative 1849–1853 and 1859–1868, and Gen. Benjamin Franklin Butler (1818–1893) of Massachusetts, representative 1867–1875 and 1877–1879, were the Radical Republican leaders of the House.

To Charles Francis Adams, Jr.

London. 23 February. 1867.

My dear Charles

I send you herewith the affidavit required for the passage of the chest.

Also the key of the chest, with the small silver key of the tea-caddy attached to it. Next week I will send a duplicate key.

The chest will go next Saturday by the Africa (I believe). You will receive notice direct from Liverpool, and will be able to get your goods immediately. There ought to be no difficulty or charge. I shall be anxious to hear that they have arrived safely in your possession, but as I shall have them insured for £150. there is little danger of absolute loss except from possible trouble with the custom-house.

So much for the silver, which I am sorry to have delayed so long.

There is not much for me to write about this week. I was very much surprised last Monday by finding that the Pall Mall Gazette gave no less than two columns to a review of my Smith, and paraded me by name as its author.[1] I cannot conceive who wrote this elaborate notice, the least bad which I have yet seen among about a dozen. I shall try to find out. Meanwhile such an advertisement in the Pall Mall naturally woke up all my acquaintances. It is currently believed by the public that I have written a book, attacking Bancroft and everyone else, and playing the devil with the world at large. I do not deny the story, and, when asked, regret that no copies of my book are to be had in England; which is a lie, as Trübner knows.[2] As it seems to be my fate to be advertised, there is nothing to be done but to submit. The very last line I printed, five years ago, cost me a leader in the Times;[3] and my next effort gives me two columns in the Pall

Mall. Any way, I shall have made my mark on London as Sam Weller said when Mr Pickwick threw the inkstand at the wall.[4]

Nevertheless I become nervous as I think of my second article, which I hope to God will not get to England. If you send a copy, which you need not do, as I can get them at Trübner's; send it to me, and not to the Governor. You see, my step in this better known part of history is not so firm, and my reliance on other people's ignorance not so confident, as with Smith. Besides, there *must* be serious mistakes, for it is a subject never yet written about, and very complicated.

My reviewer says that I have "fleshed my maiden sword" on Smith. Now I think it a damned disgusting thing to speak of "fleshing a maiden" anything, but it seems amusing to have it said of me, on whose effeminate hide the Times fleshed its extremely prostitute sword five years since.

Another week has passed, while we have watched with immense interest the course of events at home. All seems still to go whirly-whirly. I can't yet see where the grand Walpurgis-night dance is to stop. But expansion or not; impeachment or not; reconstruction or not; the country is in a devilish bad way, and is liable at any moment to collapse. Under these circumstances I recommend extreme caution in investments. Nor do I consider United States securities a safe investment.

MS: MHi
1. The reviewer regretted that HA had attacked Smith "with considerable effect. Our purpose is to call attention to the danger which impends over the fame of one who is as much an English as an American hero." Like most articles in *NAR*, HA's was unsigned.
2. Nikolaus Trübner (1817–1884), London publisher, agent for American authors.
3. HA to CFA2, Jan. 10, 1862.
4. Charles Dickens, *The Pickwick Papers*, ch. 10.

To Charles Eliot Norton

54, Portland Place. London, 28 Feb. 1867.

Dear Sir

Sometime about the 1st November I had the pleasure of receiving a very obliging letter from you in reply to mine of an earlier date; but as it did not seem to require an immediate acknowledgment, I preferred to wait before writing until I should be obliged to occupy a moment more of your time.

Since then the January number of the North American has been received. I notice a number of newspaper comments on, or rather abstracts of, my article, both in America and here, but as yet no attempt at criticism or controversy. Should any serious attack be made on my argument or conclusions, I trust that you will allow me to claim your assistance again.

I do not know whether you still propose to publish my "British Finances" in April. If so, I would like to have you correct a small error I have somewhere made in speaking of "Mr Frederick Robinson, Lord Goderich or Lord De Grey and Ripon, by whichever name one may choose to call him"; or words to that effect, if my memory serves me. I find that Lord Goderich became the Earl of Ripon, and that his son only after his death inherited from an uncle the second Earldom; so that the passage should read "Lord Goderich or Earl of Ripon" &c. It is a trifling matter, but Boston is supposed to be rather learned and sharp in the English Peerage, and there are certain to be errors enough in the articles without inserting this.

I presume that if this article does go into the April number, you will consider that the North American has had quite enough of me for the present. Still as I have an elaborate and unexpectedly difficult essay on the Bank Restriction: 1797–1820, in hand, which may, when finished, be worth your consideration, or may not, I would be obliged by your sending me word at what time you would like to receive it. In other words as I could now write it all in a few days, if necessary, I shall merely go on reading and making notes until you are ready to listen to it, and as the questions of currency are not matters which easily exhaust themselves, however easily they exhaust us, I can without trouble go on reading and annotating till the day of Judgment, if you wish to postpone the matter so long. The American people may instruct themselves in the interim, but this seems highly improbable.

I am so unlucky as to be in a position that subjects me to the annoyance of being pilloried in print on the slightest excuse; in other words my name is a trifle too heavy for me. It is thought, on good or bad grounds, that persons connected with diplomacy should be cautious about seeking publicity. There are special reasons for observing this rule in my case. I suggest this with the idea that perhaps it would be as well not to *print* my name to the article now in your hands. I have suffered so much from publicity that I prefer over-caution.

Very truly Yrs   Henry B. Adams.

MS: MH

To Charles Francis Adams, Jr.

London. 1 March. 1867.

My dear Charles

I am greatly obliged for the promptness with which you sent the account. I now comprehend the situation for the first time, and see where the £3000 that I missed for eighteen months, went to. In a few particulars which I will mention, there are still some things a trifle misty to me.

No. 1. Your estimate of my property contains an error. I do not own ten shares in the State Bank, but only seven. This deducts $336.

No. 2. U.S. 6% Bond. 1882. Bought 1 Sept. '64. and sold 1st Nov. '65. I should have supposed that at least two and perhaps three coupons would have accrued, but I cannot find that I was ever credited with any.

No. 3. Wilmington Railway. 11 shares. Dividend paid 1st October, '65; and 1st July '66. I thought the Wilmington had paid its five per cent semi-annually with great exactness. Yet I got but one dividend in '66.

By the way, if you think proper, you can buy me nine more shares of Wilmington in case you ever don't know how to invest a loose balance. I dislike small fractions like $550.

No. 4. Lawrence Gas. 7 Shares. Bought May 1st 1866, for $550; that is: @ 78½. Yet you value them at 115. Queer rise?

No. 5. Why the devil should my tax be doubled, when my income in 1866 was $200 less than in 1865, and never more than $1300? And why have I to pay a State & County tax at all? Damn it! I'll emigrate.

I believe that's all. Now mind! I don't want any anwer to any of these comments unless there is some actual change necessary in the account made out. As I have no doubt that Nos. 2, 3, 4 & 5 are all merely due to some accidental change in the system of accounts, and as No. 1, I know, is a natural error, as I really did hold ten shares before the conversion; there is nothing in the whole list which I suppose to really indicate a mistake. Hence, I do not care to bother you with useless explanations, unless they are to lead to some correction of my account-book.

In other respects I am abundantly satisfied. The Ludlow business surprised me, I confess. John had forgotten to notify me of it, and until your letter, I still thought it impossible, as your own letters were quite silent about it when speaking of my factory stock. As I do own it, I shall hang on to it, unless there is very strong reason for not doing so. I always meant to go into Mills, and why not that as well as another. It is a gambling business anyhow, and all depends on management.

You have quite met my views in another case. Your previous letters led me to suppose that you had bought 5.20s for me. I see that you credit me only with Boston 5% Bonds. This is excellent.

I see nothing in the whole list now that is not very firm, except the Mills, which, as I say, are meant as a speculation. There is the $4000 City of Boston, and nearly the same amount of Bank Stock, which you ought to be able to raise money upon at any time. Upon that security it is hard if you can't borrow $5000.

I have communicated your account to Bridget. She was less curious than I, or at any rate, asked no questions.

I will see about the Buckle.[1]

Your silver should have reached you before this letter. I sent you the sworn list last week, with the key. I enclose a duplicate key this week. By the way! I forgot to tell you that the most effective way of extracting the false bottom, is to tip the chest upside down.

Do you know, things look awfully black to me at home. I begin seriously to doubt whether the country can ever get out of it. The whole South must be soon like Greece and Asia Minor; a society dissolved, and brigandage universal. Eliot's and Stevens' Bills ought to produce that effect, if any; and though it is now law that the negro is better than the white man, I doubt whether even the negro can restore order to the South.[2] The issue presented to the President in answer to his advance, is sharp. He has no alternative but to meet it, for these bills are monstrous. The impeachment therefore seems to my mind to have come a long stride nearer. I watch the price and course of 5.20s every day with an interest gradually becoming peaked.

Bridget requests me to thank you for the account, and is pleased to say that it meets with her approval.

I do not know that I have any other news to tell you. I am not yet well, being in Erichson's hands for a promising stricture, the cause of all my woes.[3]

MS: MHi

1. Henry Thomas Buckle (1821–1862), *History of Civilisation in England* (1857–1861).
2. Thomas Dawes Eliot (1808–1870) of Massachusetts, Republican representative 1859–1869, proposed for Louisiana Reconstruction a test oath to exclude from office any former supporter of the Confederacy, thus creating a black government. Thaddeus Stevens, in another Radical bill, called for temporary military rule in the South to guarantee black voting rights and exclusion of former Confederate leaders.
3. Sir John Eric Erichsen (1818–1896), surgeon and professor of surgery at University College Hospital.

To John Quincy Adams

London. 2 March. 1867.

My dear John

Your letter of the 29th Dec. has remained in my drawer unanswered longer than I ought to have allowed, but as our correspondence at the best has never been rapid, and now threatens to come to a miserable end, there seemed to be no reason for the display of an unseemly haste in closing it. I shall now proceed to do it with proper solemnity.

First, I have to acknowledge your account of my affairs for 1866. You have looked out for my interests for five years, and in your hands my colossal estate appears to have increased by about one half, measuring not in your dirty currency, but in probable value. The income of it is now large enough to make me at a pinch, quite independent, which was the principal object of my vows. This is the only tangible result I have got for five years of life when most men lay the foundation and build the lower stories of their future fortunes; and for this I am largely indebted to you. I am not aware that you have ever lost me a dollar, or made a bad investment, or done, or left undone, anything that I could find fault with; and knowing that you would do far better for me than I could possibly do for myself, I have been glad to throw the whole responsibility upon your shoulders.

And now, turning from the agreeable contemplation of gradually accumulating wealth, to the other subject-matter of your letter, let us balance our account there.

From your letter and from a paragraph in the same spirit read to me by his Excellency in an epistle he had received from you, I am led to the conclusion not only that you reject my idea of your political activity, but that you considered yourself as more or less personally aggrieved by my supposition that your course would or could have been influenced by a knowledge of the ultimate results brought about by the mistakes of your *ex officio* chief.

Now no man respects more than I do the intellectual courage which forces any one to follow a train of argument and to accept its conclusion, though it shakes high heaven. If I value less that more animal energy which obliges some men to invariably express the opinions they have reached and to appeal to the public for endorsement, it is perhaps because I am little formed by nature to act the part of a combatant. If I were to express even in private all the opinions I hold, I should sacrifice my influence, the little I have, and perhaps my character, without stirring other people's opinions a hair's breadth. If I am ever obliged to attempt influencing other people's opinions, I shall regulate my standpoint by theirs, and shall argue towards the result I aim at, but shall argue from the place they occupy. If I know in advance that my attempt is likely to fail through outside influences, and that my struggle may result only in alarming or embittering people, it certainly will be a question with me how I can best modify my course.

I understand you to reject this view. You propose that the world shall swallow J.Q.A. without regard to the state of its stomach. You are indignant at the suggestion that your course could have been influenced by a previous knowledge of the President's. You not only mean to live from yourself outwards, which I think admirable; but a part of your plan is that everyone else should live from you inwards to themselves; reversing your individual process. Self developement I understand and adopt if you will, in the sense that by attending strictly to our own developement we are doing the greatest possible good to mankind as a unit; but your project implies a living to oneself that embraces others as well, and imposes on them a limitation of their right to their own self-developement.

Remember that what I have here written is a defence, not an attack. I admired your course and actually read your speeches, which struck me as the sort of thing I should like to do if I could. But *on est homme d'état, ou on ne l'est pas.* You *are.*

MS:MHi

To Charles Milnes Gaskell

London. 26 March. [1867]

My dear Barrister

I am nearly at the point of death from pure curiosity to hear your travels. Reflect however, that if you publish, you will at once be known, and therefore moderate the personalities. I think you might entitle your work: "Journey &c: By various hands"; and include a chapter by H.E.L.J—m; and another by Lord P—n. I am going to ask Sir C. Lyell whether there are any investigations *now going on* near Liege; if not, there's no chance of our seeing anything. If there are, I shall be able to get the proper directions. It is easy enough to write on the subject without any acquaintance with it, but a dash of truth would add a certain base to the dish.[1] Could you not hammer out a few couplets in the style of Heine or some other fellow, on the Bos primigenius? Or any other subject? There is nothing like an experiment. Catch an idea, and then hammer out the rhymes. Or omit the rhymes and do it in classic style; Horace, Catullus, Tibullus, Propertius, or some other blessed antique. You send me one verse and I will try to cap it.

Palgrave, by the way, is scoring my North American wildly. I've not read his comments yet, but I saw the thing at his house, and the marginal notes made it look like a variorum edition of Plato. He has instigated me into going to an auction sale and giving £12.0. for a Cuyp. He swears it's dirt cheap at the price. You shall see it when you come up. I've sent it to be framed and shall hang it in my room.[2] I fully expect to be ruined by him ultimately, for drawings are my mortal point and I can't resist.

I was at Lady Margaret's on Saturday but found it crowded and dull;[3] Lady S. was there, and found it particularly pleasant. You see we pull apart. Lady S. is making a desperate fight, but how foolish to have a baby in the middle of it. I am still looking for an object, and have achieved an idea. I smell future dinners in Berkeley Square. More when we meet, as the subject is one of grave importance.

I saw your mother on Sunday. She had been exacerbated by a certain Mrs or Miss Murray, and was being calmed down by Mrs Butler-Johnstone.

I have literally nothing on hand but Belpertia. You may imagine that I find it a trifle dull. To amuse myself I study currency.

Bye-bye! Let me know how the travels come on, and *do* hunt up one or two good Latin quotations, with a sting in their tail, out of some imaginary middle-age poet.

Ever Yr   H. B. Rampho.[4]

MS: MHi

1. Gaskell had written a preface and six chapters of a satiric travel account roughly following the itinerary of the trip he and HA were planning to take in early April. He asked HA for ideas and to write something of his own on fossils. In the published ver-

Charles Milnes Gaskell

Robert Cunliffe, at Acton

Charles Milnes Gaskell, Robert Boyle, and
Henry Adams, before the Chapter House at
Wenlock Abbey

Ralph Palmer

sion, "The Easter Trip of Two Ochlophobists," *Blackwood's* 102 (July, Aug. 1867), 42–59, 188–207, he took up HA's suggestion, dedicating the first chapter to "H. E. L. J—m" and another to "Viscount P—n" (Lord Palmerston and presumably Hubert Edward Henry Jerningham [1842–1914], whose *Life in a French Chateau* was tepidly reviewed in the *Athenaeum* as a specimen of "genteel authorship" [Feb. 16, 1867]). In his preface, "Henry Stuart" (Gaskell) jokingly ascribed most of the account to his companion "Granville" (HA).

2. *A View of Rhenen,* a wash drawing by the Dutch landscape painter Albert Cuyp (1605–1691), is now at the Fogg Art Museum, Harvard.

3. Lady Margaret Anne de Burgh Beaumont (1832–1888), granddaughter of George Canning; her husband was Wentworth Blackett Beaumont, M.P., son of a founder of the *Westminster Review.*

4. Gaskell addressed HA as "Dear Rhamphorynchus," a genus of pterosaurs, adding an etymology: ῥάμφος, "the crooked beaks of birds, esp. birds of prey, generally a beakbill."; ῥύγχος, "short muzzle, strictly of swine—*generally a face! Crétin. Incest!"* (undated note, 1867). Gaskell in his *Blackwood's* article described seeing a live rhamphorynchus in Liège and concocted an imaginary interview with it (pp. 198–199).

To Charles Francis Adams, Jr.

London. 3 April. 1867.

My dear Charles

I received two letters from you by the last mail, one of the 16th; the other of the 19th March. The latter announced the arrival of your silver, and was a considerable relief to my mind. By the way, if we are to remain here another year, I expect that John's cigars will not improve by it. Yet I don't know what to do with them.

Your Buckle, which I sent as you requested, cost £1.0. The expenses connected with your silver, including insurance, will not exceed £2. or £2.10. I will let you know so soon as I settle the charges.

I wish no better investment than Pacific Mail, and I scarcely think it will fall much lower, although I doubt it's rising much for a year or two. The Western Roads I feel less confidence in. They may pay 10% and they may pay nothing. Fort Wayne is good at 93, but would be better at 80; and I suspect you will do well to hold on for the chance. Sooner or later prices must go lower, low as they may now be. Yet I leave it to you, for I really can't judge at this distance, and don't want to. All I see with clearness is that what with Bank stock, manufacturing stock and the like, my income this year will be gracefully slender. Luckily I am independent of it.

It is curious how rapidly the tides shift at home. You recollect last autumn how quickly it rose between your leaving England and reaching America. Only a month or six weeks has passed since my last letter, and the change has been equally decided.

In February I overestimated the radical strength. I tested it by the passage of Eliot's Louisiana Bill in the House, and by the known energy and determination of Stevens and his associates. I knew that the impeachment alone would give them success, and I thought their party could see at least that to stop was ruin. But the event has proved that the party was little better than a mob of political gamblers, and timid time-servers. They funked the whole issue. They saw a turn of public opinion in the air, and they knuckled down on the spot.[1]

The crisis is over, with the month of March, and I breathe free again. The New Hampshire election satisfied me, and that in Connecticut I felt too sure of, to doubt.[2]

It is while I am good-natured and softened by these sudden turns of fortune, that your letters reach me, and I read what you say about your father and myself. You may be right. He and I may have been too long away to keep up with your rapid marches. But recollect how fast you used to march in Virginia and how short a distance you commonly advanced. You consider our constitutional doctrines to be a species of fossil protozoon; a primary petrifaction of an intellectual creation nearest the vegetable nature. I believe, on the other hand, that you are merely bewildered by the chaos about you; that you have lost your head in the tumult, and will come right by and by, with everyone else except the permanently insane like Sumner and Boutwell.

You are quite wrong, I believe, in thinking that the American people are disposed to abrogate or alter the Constitution, or that they can do so. The last month proves it to me. The truth, to my mind, is that the duty of guarding the Constitution was put by the people in the hands of the Republican party; that party has betrayed its trust, and the Democratic party has succeeded to it, since the people had no other choice. And now your friend Dana, and Andrew, and Palfrey and the rest, see the false position they are in when the Democrats turn upon them and ask what they have done with the Constitution. John alone has acted the part of a man. I care mighty little who gets the offices or the popular applause, but I admire John all the more for what he has done, in proportion as I feel how in his place I should have fallen.

I tell you frankly that when I think of the legislation since last year, my blood boils and I feel my lazy temper ready to break out in any sort of expression that could signify direct and personal hatred of every man in that Congress. Depend upon it that what affects me so violently will affect the average man at last. The Connecticut election is a sign. As for the President, he may be an object of supreme contempt, and he may do all the harm he can; but for all that it may not be impossible that the Democrats should renominate him next year and elect him too. Popular fluctuations are queer things. Remember Lincoln's case. It is sacrilege now to name the two together: but four years ago!—

There! take that for your "practical people," and reflect on it!

MS: MHi
1. Even without impeachment, the Radicals did not lose. The Reconstruction Acts of March 2 and 23, passed over Johnson's veto by an alliance of Radicals and moderate

Republicans, imposed military rule on the Southern states. The Command of the Army Act and the Tenure of Office Act, also passed on March 2, deprived the president of control of the army and of the right to remove civil officials, including members of his cabinet.

2. The Democrats, opposed to military Reconstruction, cut the Republican majority in New Hampshire and elected a governor in Connecticut.

To Charles Milnes Gaskell

54, Portland Place.   London. 4 April. 1867.

My dear Carlo

Since receiving your note I have seen your mother, who leans to the idea that we shall start on Wednesday morning by the early mail. For my own part, I assent to this arrangement. I find that I have a ball on Tuesday evening at Mrs Ewing Curwen's, and that house is very convenient to the Victoria Station. Though why we should go by Victoria I can't see. Charing Cross is nearer and nicer.

Let me have your opinion on this point. If you decidedly prefer it, I am willing to go down to Dover on Tuesday night, and if its calm, to cross and sleep at Calais. If stormy, take the chance of better weather by the morning boat.

I dined out twice in succession this week, which always does for my stomach. In consequence I have been seedy. The truth is, we eat too many sweet things, and drink too many wines—not too *much,* you understand. That I should deny.

I have a suggestion to make to you. Will you tell me the most disagreeable thing you ever heard said of me? Without giving its author of course— I will in return set the conversation with all my acquaintances running upon you, and when anything sufficiently ill-natured has been said, you shall have it hot.

Lord have mercy upon us, miserable sinners! I would do anything to experience new sensations, even disagreeable ones, and a good, spiteful, vicious attack is such a tonic!

I met Lady William and the two Sweet Williams,[1] at Mrs Baillie's, as well as Miss Wortley, and a number of other young women who looked all manner of dislike at me for not dancing. It was a nice ball, I should think, although I am not very learned in such matters. I stayed till half after one, and talked incessantly—gabbled, in fact.

Since your departure I have got me Owen's Palaeontology, which has a list of all the Greek names at the end, and their meanings. I am trying to look over the book, but one idea in ten pages is the best I can collect.[2] Geology is low comedy in comparison.

If this devilish wind continues to blow, we shall have a mauvais quart
d'heure on the channel.

Ever Yrs   H.

C.J.K.L.M.G. Esq.

MS: MHi
1. Wilhelmina Hervey (d. 1885) and her sister Augusta, daughters of Lady William
Hervey (d. 1871), were the "Sweet Williams" in a number of HA's letters. The late
Lord William Hervey was a younger son of the 1st marquess of Bristol.
2. Richard Owen, *Palaeontology, or a Systematic Summary of Extinct Animals and Their Geological Relations* (1861).

To Charles Francis Adams, Jr.

London. 30 April. 1867.

My dear Charles

Yours of April 13th reached me two days ago.

The North American improves. Really $80.00 though no pay at all for
such work as ours, is deuced high for the trash that stock-writers wind out
of their tape-wormy entrails. I shall have one more article in the October
number, on the Bank of England Restriction, 1797–1821. Then I shall stop.

I've read your article. In style I don't think it better than mine, and mine
I frankly assure you is damned bad.[1] Yours too is flabby in places and
wants squeezing to take the fat out. Mine, I regret to say, is also a little too
greasy. Never mind. I shall do better, and so will you, I've no doubt. I've
not read any of the other articles, but I've no idea that they have any mus-
cular tissue at all. Lowell is our best writer, and Parton is very clever.[2] But
the rest are pure fat. I am now going through a course of training, with the
idea of sweating off my superfluous words.

I wish you would subscribe for me to the New York weekly; the Nation,
isn't it? There seems to be merit about it.[3] I wish also that you would send
out to me anything that appears to you worth noticing in American literature; anything new, I mean, which seems to you to be capable of standing
criticism. If I write here, I shall write what I think, and not be soft on people's corns. And as I shall write merely for practice and not for reputation,
it matters little what I say. Therefore if you hear of anything that owns a
voice and not an echo; that talks itself, and not Dante or Tennyson, send it
me, and add your own comments on the margin.

My opinion about raising the $3000. is this:

Boston City Bonds	$1000.
State Bank Stock	700.
Merchants Bank (10 shares)	1100.
Total	$2800.

There should be June dividends enough to cover the rest, but if not you can raise the extra $200 as you like. That infernal certified check system must cost me some hundreds of dollars any way, and I might as well pocket the loss at once. If I hold on, the loss may be doubled, and must anyway be at least $140. By selling now, I am $170 out of pocket, with a chance of losing a lot more if the Merchant's has to pay. If not, I lose nothing more. If I hold on, and the State has to pay, I escape with a loss of about $140. The case then stands thus. If I sell, I must lose $170, and may lose $570. If I hold, I must lose $140, and may lose $600. The difference is trifling either way. This is my judgment. You can exercise yours however you like. Meanwhile I think the other $3000. Boston City may lie quiet, as my reserve. The "two handed engine at the door"[4] has given us a precious sharp hug this spring, and stands ready to hug us some more. I am a good deal on the high pressure now; $4000. in Manufacturing; $3000. in Pacific Mail; $2000. in Banking, perhaps the worst of all. I do not think that $3000 is too much to keep by me in case of sudden wants. The Spring flurry seems over now, and perhaps we may sail along briskly for a while. But the times are mighty queer. By the way, that 10% Fort Wayne stock doesn't seem to me more than a fair 8% stock in reality. And further, if Jerome or any of his peers gets into a concern I am in, just sell out whenever the stock rises.[5]

Since my last letter I have been to Luxemburg, Treves, down the Moselle, up the Rhine, round by Saarbrück, Saarlouis, Saarburg &c and back by way of Spa. You see it was a military and strategic excursion. I come back inclining to France. We all hate cant I suppose. I hate, for instance, your cant of submitting to all that is because it is; as much as you hate mine of objecting to it for the same reason. Among other cant, I detest the German rot about nationality. Luxemburg is really French more than Prussian, and as to its military value to Prussia except as a menace to France, it's utter fallacy. Luckily both nations are now so equal in strength that they hesitate before fighting. Otherwise we should have had a war long ago. But sooner or later they *will* fight, and it is just as well to remember that fact. If you speculate, remember that well-informed people here expect war.

The truth is, as you justly observe, the world is in a transitional state and no fellow can tell the result. But my studies of Aug. Comte and his allies lead me to doubt very much whether your charming fatalistico-optimistico-scientifico-philosophy is either in his spirit, or logically defensible.[6]

MS: MHi

1. CFA2, "The Railroad System," *NAR* 104 (April 1867), 476–511.

2. James Parton (1822–1891), prolific popular writer, biographer of Horace Greeley, Aaron Burr, Andrew Jackson, Benjamin Franklin, and others.

3. The *Nation,* edited by E. L. Godkin, first appeared July 6, 1865.

4. The instrument of God's justice in Milton's "Lycidas" (1638).

5. Leonard Walter Jerome (1817–1891) of New York City was an active financial backer of the Union, a promoter of horse racing, and father of the famous sisters Clarita, Jennie, and Leonie. He was known as a daring speculator.

6. Auguste Comte (1798–1857), founder of positivism, *Cours de Philosophie Positive* (1830–1842).

To Charles Francis Adams, Jr.

London. 8 May. 1867.

My dear Charles

Since my last I have received your letter of the 19th April, and an enclosure of newspapers. Permit me to call your attention to the address of the latter which struck me as curious, though no doubt I am wrong to have considered it so.

Your letter begins by asking an account for the silver &c. I find that I am charged £2.4.6 on that account. The Buckle, as I wrote, is £1. Total £3.4.6.

The next item of your letter informs me that you have invested $1700. for me in bonds and shares of the Boston, Hartford & Erie Road.

Although I should myself perhaps have been inclined to hold off longer, in the belief that speculations on a falling market generally take the chances against them, and that I was already pretty well coaled for the cruise, yet as the case is an exceptional one and the sum not large, I readily approve the investment.

At the same time I consider the money in this case, as a stake on a roulette table. It is a pure gambling operation. I have carefully read the statements you sent to me, and they are very reasonable and fair. But there is one fact which to me seems the most important, and which I have not got at. Who manages the undertaking? If well managed, it will succeed. If badly managed it will fail (as an investment, I mean) and all the prospectuses under the sun will not help it. Such an undertaking depends on too many side influences and accidents to allow of a man's calculating with any certainty upon it. Besides, the stock is sure to become the "Erie" of the Boston Stock Exchange.

Thirdly, as to the means of meeting this draft of $4700. Since my last I see that those damned banks have kept on falling till it is: State, 90: Merchants, 108. While this sort of thing lasts, its no use to express an opinion. I *must* lose my whole proportion of the whole loss, if I sell at such rates. I'm not sure that it's not better to hold on to both. Exercise your own judgment. I incline at any rate to meeting the mass of the debt with the City Scrip. In the meanwhile let's stop here. I can't afford to lose more than half my princely fortune.

At the remainder of your letter I was greatly pleased. Keep your temper, my boy. Above all, forget that you are a national eagle. The admirable Mr Disraeli in his philosophical novel called Tancred, remarks: "The disciples of Progress have never been able exactly to match this example of Damascus; but it is said they have great faith in the future of Birkenhead."[1]

At the bottom we all practically agree—with a difference. As I understand it, the case stands thus.

We write to you in great alarm: "If the country doesn't stop, it's going to Hell."

The country does stop. You are nearest and see it first, and write back telling us we are fools to be frightened.

I write back acknowledging my mistake, but attacking you and the other silent patriots of the North for allowing us to fall into the error.

You write back furious: "Damned little cuss," "damndest collection of panic-stricken howls," "*you* lecture *me*," "Here's richness." And so on, ending by exulting over our terror and offering to prove it by my letters as though I had denied it.

What really made you so irascible I take to be some sore point in yourself, though I know not. I said, and I say it again that your theory of "fighting it out within the party" is a piece of self-delusion which you use to cover your own intellect from seeing and confessing what is really fear of public opinion. I said that Dana and all his friends and the whole Conservative Liberalism of New England had been whipped and kicked like a mangy spaniel by Sumner and his party, and had cowered under the flogging without a growl or even a whine. *Did* they ever try to "fight it out within the party"? Was ever a voice raised within the party? If so it didn't reach us. Dana is a sucking M.C. and at nurse. He couldn't risk popularity. Andrew was better, but he too had too much to lose by open rebellion. John alone said that his soul was his own.[2]

Again I say that your constitutional ideas seem to be muddled. You seem to think that a mere breath of popular will is enough to settle the law for ever. I think that the result must be to return to the type.

Practically however we are tolerably agreed. The epithet "monstrous" which seems to have weighed on your mind, was applied by me to Eliot & the other man's Louisiana Bill and the tariff bill, not to Sherman's measure,[3] which I then supposed to be a general application of Eliot's. We all consider, I suppose, that the Southern states had better try to do something with the existing law. As to the Constitutional question, it will in such a case merely lie in abeyance. I don't believe you will find it very easily settled, however.

As for the Republican party, the future will have to decide what our relations to it are to be. Next year I expect that party lines will be pretty much rubbed out, unless the Republicans try to nominate some other candidate than Grant. After that we shall have a new division of parties, I hope. You and John and I are likely to be found together in such a case, and, I suspect, not in Republican ranks. But we shall have first to wait and see what the issues are to be.

Dana meanwhile writes an elaborate letter which it would amuse you to read, I am sure. Dana seems to have become as thorough a politician as Sumner, and to have lost far more than he the faculty of looking at things from an "objective point" of view, if you will forgive my using the term. He is or seems to be tormented by the fear that our chief is going over to the Democrats. His fear of Democracy is very like an English Bishop's hatred of dissent.

You can quiet his mind on that point. I believe nothing is further from the mind of the party in question. The time for such a change, when it could have done good, is passed for the present, and no occasion whatever now exists for changing the position hitherto occupied.

This brings me to the last part of my reflexions. I think another effort will be made to get out of our present situation and I think that the close of this year will see us free. In that case our return would not take place, however, till August 1868. Many reasons combine to make me think it desirable that this arrangement should be carried out. What say you? Do not write to the family as though the idea came to you from me.

MS: MHi
1. A near quotation from Disraeli's novel (1847), bk. 4, ch. 5. Birkenhead, where the *Alabama* was built, was a new shipbuilding port.
2. HA analyzed a problem that was to recur for him in many forms: Dana, a first-term state legislator hoping to run for Congress the next year, was too innocent to scramble for public support either within the party or, changing parties, among the electorate as a whole. Governor Andrew advocated moderate Reconstruction despite the prevailing Radical temper, but he did so only in his farewell message of Jan. 1866.
3. John Sherman (1823–1900) of Ohio, brother of Gen. W. T. Sherman, Republican senator 1861–1877. He was a Radical Republican but less extreme than Stevens, as indicated by his substitute proposal for military Reconstruction of the South, enacted by Congress on March 2.

To Charles Milnes Gaskell

54, Portland Place. Saturday. 11 May. '67

Dear Karl

Your departure was a surprise to me. Hervey, Lady William, and the Sweet Williams, were all expecting you at Lady Waldegrave's ball; and when I called the next day in Stratford Place to see what had become of you, behold you were gone. For your sake I was glad. You know I have always preached change of air and no medicine. Turn over a new leaf. Scour the Edge and dig Nummulites or some other fellah out of the limestone. Grow fat. But don't take drugs. I live on pepsine and cod-liver-oil, but then I don't call those drugs.

Of course you want to know about Lady W's blow-out on Wednesday evening. By the way, I went to Lady Goldsmid's first, and I assure you I have never seen so superb a display as her rooms made, in any private house. It was actually royal. But I had to escape through the conservatory in order to go down to Lord Stanley's; and thence to Lady W's.[1]

The best thing I did at Lady W's was to march up and talk to the Comte de Paris, who didn't know me in the least. I had to patronise him a good deal before he remembered me.

I have made such violent love to Lady William that the consequences will be disastrous to me, as the young ladies will consider me a bore. The whole Hervey clan was on parade at Lady W's, jewels and all.

On the whole I enjoyed the ball. I admired John Hervey who danced like a sylphide.[2] There was a very swell tribe of people, whom I did not admire so much. Two or three dozen Duchesses who looked awful. By the way I did the Argyll girl, and rather liked her. She has a pretty complexion; not very nasty features; and is very fresh and unaffected; at least, so I thought, after 90 seconds conversation.

Console yourself on your absence. I have on my engagement book just three names—three and no more—and what do you think they are. No. 1, the best, is a dinner at my friend Forster's. No. 2. Mrs Darby Griffith!! No. 3. The Lady Mayoress!!!

What have I done to suffer humiliation like this. And what are we to do, if it goes on.

I've not seen your mother since her return, in spite of my efforts, but I shall try again tomorrow.

I am regularly done by those brutes of tailors. I ordered my spring clothes on the 23d and have not been able even to try them on yet. What to do!

H.

P.S. My termination, as above, would satisfy Hubert.[3]

MS: MHi
  1. Lady W is Lady Waldegrave. Louisa Sophia Goldsmid (1819–1908) was the wife of Sir Francis Henry Goldsmid (1808–1878), 2nd baronet, M.P., first Jewish barrister, and advocate of removal of religious disabilities. Edward Henry Stanley (1826–1893), Viscount Stanley, had been one of the Cambridge Apostles, along with Hallam, Monckton Milnes, and Tennyson; he was now foreign secretary in the ministry of his father, Lord Derby.
  2. John William Hervey (1841–1902), third son of the late marquess of Bristol.
  3. Hubert Jerningham.

To Charles Francis Adams, Jr.

London. 18 May. 1867.

My dear Charles:

Your's of the 4th has just come to hand.

The "Thompson's Hotel" is explained. I did you injustice, for I supposed that you had done it inadvertently, apropos to some one else's being or having been there. What misled you was merely a pencil memorandum of the Gov.'s of a call to make; and in want of paper more suitable, he seems to have written the Mem: on the back of an envelope, which I afterwards used to save me the trouble of getting another.

I have already written to you about the B.H. & E.R.R. and have nothing more to say. I notice that the bonds have risen from 48 to 60; but the stock is as yet stationary. I suppose people argue about it as you do.

You sneer at my prognostications of collapse in March and April. Upon my word I came as near the mark as I could have expected. The collapse of prices and credit was quite severe enough for the time, and I thank God you sold out part of my Bank stock then, and wish you had sold the whole. I *lost* 15% on $3000, and 23% on $700, in consequence of my prophecied collapse which as you say didn't take place. If you merely mean that it didn't take place in the precise *way* I predicted, you are welcome to your triumph, if it is one. I am satisfied with the general justice of our reasoning.

As for the reason you give for our coming down easy because credit is not extended, I suppose you are right. But I don't see how that will protect the Banks. They will depend on their individual management, and I should think were a good deal exposed.

Apropos to the Mont Cenis I advise you to consult several articles in the Revue des Deux Mondes, during the last few years. But I will try and see what I can do.[1]

I will send Arthur his Shakespeare.

Bridget is in trouble about her house. She doesn't know what has become of it. So far as I can understand her, John has the title-deeds, I believe, and William Gregory has charge of the house. But no reports have been made to her by Gregory, and she now wants to sell the house. What do you think about it?

Have you sufficient discretion and delicacy of touch to effect an object for me, unknown to *anyone* else. I want to know why Fanny has left mamma's letters unanswered since last November, and whether John or Fanny or both have any grievance. Don't blunder about it, for God's sake.

Love to Minnie

MS: MHi
1. Built 1857–1871, the Mont Cenis railway tunnel through the Alps required engineering and economic organizing on an unprecedented scale.

To Charles Francis Adams, Jr.

London. 22 June. 1867.

My dear Charles

Since I last wrote, I have received your's of May 18th, an intermediate one, the date of which I cannot remember, and today a note of June 11th. As I have been excessively busy and in beastly health, I have let them go unanswered. A few words will do for them all.

There is no amusement in our abusing each other. You know my low opinion of you. I shall not repeat it. A sow's ear is silk to your's. But I never said, as you quote me, that my article was better than your's. I never thought so. Your remarks on my criticism demonstrate idiocy. I did say that your *style* was no better than mine, and mine was damned bad—which is true. My critique was limited to style, if I recollect it, and I cannot understand why a man may not be poetic and concise, amusing and condensed, at the same time. Nor why he should not observe the ordinary rules of composition and grammar, though I confess that I sin in that way more than you.

The subject of your second letter was, as you expected, very like an earthquake to me.[1] For twenty four hours I wanted to cry, to swear, to beat some one. Now that a week has passed, I can't for the life of me help laughing whenever I think of it. That I, whose pride it is never to quarrel; I, who am willing to bear anything rather than stir up strife; I, who thought myself so happy in being a million miles out of the way of any possible complication; that I should have been a head and front of offending,[2] and plunged over head-and-ears in about the most contemptible damned little viperous snakes-nest that ever a small provincial town bred,—By the everlasting Jehovah, it is too good a joke on me. I have nothing to say. I burned your letter within an hour after receiving it. I have not breathed a whisper of its contents to any one, and shall not do so. In mamma's present state, the consequences of telling her might be serious. As to the rest of us, it seems to me a clear case of ignorance being bliss. Since I wrote to you, a letter has arrived from the party in question, so that the subject is for the time forgotten. But it is very sad, and as you say, I mean to get out of the way when the inevitable explosion comes. Yet I fear more for the next generation than for ours. Meanwhile the great point is for all the men to keep their temper.

I made enquiries and gave orders about the Mont Cenis tunnel, but have been unable to obtain anything about it. As to your other railway authorities, I will look them up. I had already noticed the curious behavior of Hartford & Erie, but this is a stock from which we must expect curious behavior. On the other hand I see that Pacific Mail is at its old tricks; run up 15 per cent in ten days. The Merrimack has declared a dividend, I notice, but Frank Crowninshield never deigns to tell us what it is. As for Ludlow, as usual, all the air a solemn stillness holds.[3] I only trust it is not actually losing money. What is to happen now? In *spite* of your scornful and contemptuous treatment, I venture to think that there has been this spring a more severe and a more general fall in prices and destruction of credit than has happened since 1861, and that our prognostications were essentially correct. Are we at last at the bottom? Or is there to be a tremendous fall in grain, which may for a time send us lower? I can't reason it out. But I should hope for a recovery by next Spring at latest.

I shall forward to your care next week an article much longer than your's in the Law Magazine, and nearly as dull, which you can send to Norton any time before August 1st.[4] You needn't read it. In fact, you can't. No one but George Lefevre could, or some such blue-book.[5] But you might run your eye over it, and when you come to the law of Lord Stanhope's Gold

Bill, see if I've made any mistakes. The study has taught me a great deal, but my article is ghastly to be sure.

I congratulate you on your success at the State House. Coin it into mun.[6] Love to M.

P.S. If I were you, I would take, or read regularly, the London Economist.

MS: MHi

1. The mission to his brother and sister-in-law that HA had entrusted to CFA2 in the preceding letter had apparently backfired. CFA2 was not noted for "discretion" or "delicacy of touch."

2. *Othello,* I, iii.

3. Thomas Gray, "Elegy Written in a Country Churchyard" (1750).

4. CFA2, "Legislative Control over Railway Charters," *American Law Review* 1 (April 1867), 451–476. HA's article was "The Bank of England Restriction," *NAR* 105 (Oct. 1867), 393–434.

5. With a career brought into being by the Reform Act of 1832, which required settling new electoral divisions, Sir John George Shaw-Lefevre (1797–1879) worked on fact-finding commissions for major social legislation and produced numerous bluebooks (parliamentary reports, so named from their blue covers).

6. CFA2's article was referred to in legislative debate over railroad regulation.

To Charles Eliot Norton

London. 28 June. 1867.

Dear Mr Norton

According to the directions in your letter of March 19th, I have this week sent my M.S. to America. It has gone to my brother Charles, who will hand it over to you.

The essay has two great faults; its length and its dulness. There are plenty of others, but these two are the crime of all crimes for a review. In regard to the dulness, there is no excuse to be made. You must not publish the thing at all, if it is not readable. In regard to its length however, it seems to me that the subject and not myself is to blame. I have skinned and scraped my first sketch until little is left besides the skeleton, and I have crowded books into sentences and years into lines. How to compress further, with any regard to the unity of the argument and story, I confess I do not know. But I am happy to pass the scissors over to you, and have no doubt that if anyone can do it successfully, you can. Such omissions as you have heretofore made in my articles, so far as I noticed them, have been decided improvements.[1]

This will in all probability be the last time I shall trouble you with my manuscripts. I have not yet said quite all I have to say, but a few years silence will ripen the rest, and the world will get along pretty well, I suppose, even if these valuable utterances never come to print at all. We lead so hap-hasard a life here that I never can pursue any study vigorously, and after writing laborious reams of paper in the scarce intervals of leisure that one can find in a London season I now look forward to a long, if not a permanent separation from all my means of study. In retiring, therefore, I have only to thank you personally for the readiness you have shown to print my very prosy remarks, and the politeness with which you received them. If you treat all your new contributors equally well, they certainly cannot complain of wanting encouragement.

I must however repeat the request that my name may not be printed on your usual list of authors. It is not in the least that I fear any harm from publicity, but I dislike newspaper personalities whether favorable or adverse. I have already been immortalized in a Times leader. I have this very season undergone two whole columns in the Pall Mall. In so concentrated a society as that of London, and in so exposed a position as I am occupying here, this process is annoying. But my objection applies merely to newspaper notoriety, and I am very far from objecting to any private avowal of authorship. You are at liberty to do whatever you like, so long as I escape the affliction of newspaper gibbeting.[2]

Pray remember me to Professor Lowell and remind him that I am one of his scholars. Why doesn't he come over here? In four weeks, say in the month of July, he could roar, the loudest lion of them all, through May Fair and Belgravia, for between ourselves poetry is here dreadfully out at elbows, and poor Browning has to officiate as the permanent social representative of his class. Nothing would have given me greater pleasure than to have danced attendance on Mr Lowell through every drawing-room in London, and smoked indefinite cigars with him in all the out-of-the-way holes where men of genius stuff themselves. But I'm afraid that it's now too late; my reign here draws to a close.

My father and mother wish to be remembered to you. Believe me

Very truly Yrs   Henry B. Adams.

MS: MH

1. For instance, Norton had excised from "Captain John Smith" a paragraph in which HA, denying "any ill-natured disposition towards the memory of either Smith or Pocahontas," associated himself with "the one great literary triumph of our century . . . its bold and brilliant application of the laws of criticism to historical composition" (MS: MH).

2. HA improved the story. The two columns in the *Pall Mall Gazette* (Feb. 18) consisted mainly of conscientious summary of the Smith article. The only condescending note, about his fleshing "his maiden sword," he had fastened on for riposte in his letter of Feb. 23 to CFA2.

To John Gorham Palfrey

London. 28 June. 1867.

My dear Dr Palfrey

I am glad that the books arrived safely. As regards Hepworth Dixon, he bears here the reputation of great deficiency in exactness (diplomatically expressed, I flatter myself!). I have not read the book nor do I know the man, nor care to. But he amuses, and that is his justification. We don't exact truth from Alexandre Dumas, and yet his *Corricolo* is the cleverest book of travel ever I read.[1]

As for Lorne, whom I do know, he flies on a very different level. The future M.P. and budding Duke has only to avoid mistakes, and he then ipso facto achieves success. I think in this sense that the boy's book is very creditable.[2] He will fill a place, a stall, at the Government crib, as well as his father. This is not enthusiastic praise, especially as we are *liés* with the Argylls; but though I am fully posted up as to the value of the political friendship, I confess that my political and my personal alliances are at desperate variance. I am only too often found in the enemy's camp. The truth is, the Argylls and the old Duchess are the best of people, although the Duke's red head bears somewhat too conspicuously the ducal coronet, yet it is an undeniable fact that they are excruciatingly dull; and not only they, but all their connection is dull to the last degree; the women are stupid, and the men are walking blue-books. You may take it where you like; Charles Howard and his son George; the Argylls; the Blantyres and the Miss Stuarts; the Cavendish young men; the Leveson-Gowers (except the present eccentric head of that house); Lady Taunton and the Labouchere girls; I defy you or anyone to pick out a really agreeable person from the lot.

You have delayed your visit to us, I fear, beyond the limit. You should have come *Consule Carolo*,[3] and who knows what Teuton barbarian may rule here in our place before another season passes. We are ready to abdicate. I am longing, like a worn-out consumptive, for a winter in warmer and brighter air, and who knows whether a break-up, once effected, may not be final?

You are very kind about my "Bank Restriction." I certainly did not intend to include you among the "groundlings," although I hold it as one of the curiosities of the times that persons like yourself, and on a lower scale myself, should be plunging into the well of financial theories. My article is very long, very dull, and worse written than either of its predecessors, though I never knew how they sinned till I saw them in print. Not knowing the present stage of public knowledge in America, I was forced to aim at a guess in order to hit my object. Hence my opinions may seem absurdly revolutionary or absurdly antique, as it happens. But as the study has taught me a vast deal that I never had suspected, I have got my reward, and care little what is thought of this dry digest of facts and arguments. I have sent it to Charles, who has directions to hand it to Norton. If you really care to read it, I have no doubt that either Charles or Norton will give it you. It is the last such effort I shall attempt.

My bookseller's bill places your items as follows:

Dixon's New America	£1. 5.0
Lorne's Trip to the Tropics	12.6
Total	£1.17.6

Charles is now my agent and you can settle all business affairs with him.

We are very near driven to death just now. The bother and annoyance of July in London are enough to make standing on one's head a relief. But another fortnight will, we hope, carry us over the rocks and give us rest somewhere.

Ever Yrs   Henry B. Adams.

MS: MH
1. Dixon's *New America* (1867), on his travels in the United States in 1866; *Le Corricolo* (1843) by Alexandre Dumas (1802–1870), on his carriage travels in Italy.
2. John Douglas Sutherland Campbell (1845–1914), marquess of Lorne and later 9th duke of Argyll, *A Trip to the Tropics and Home Through America* (1867).
3. Mock-Roman dating: in the consulship of Charles, that is, while CFA was still minister.

To Charles Francis Adams, Jr.

London. 30 July. 1867.

My dear Charles

I take the first minute of leisure I am likely to have, in order to polish off your article.[1] As we leave England next week, I must either do the work quickly or not at all, and to leave it undone would annoy me, for this kind of criticism very often does more good to the critic than to the critiqué.

Imprimis, I don't hesitate to say that the worm is a good worm. I would publish by all means. Your idea is more than good; it is one of those which seem likely to act as hinges for future statesmanship. Of course it is not original with you, but if you can ride it, practically it is your horse. I say therefore—publish.

But when you ask of me a criticism that shall be only rigid and hostile, I am bound to stop short here with my compliments expressed or implied, and to balance my conclusion—which comes first—by pitching into your whole production with a single purpose of showing that it is too bad for any self-respecting man to own. I know what this means, for I invited Frank Palgrave to treat my Captain John Smith in the same way, and his success was so decided that to this day I can never read that essay without a sense of shame.

My criticism must relate to two separate points, and I have got to begin by drawing the line between the matter and the form of your article—between its argument and its style. As the matter is more important than the form, I will begin with the harder task, after which I promise myself and you much light enjoyment from a right appreciation of your merits as a writer of your native tongue.

I take it that your whole point—that is, in its more limited bearing—rests in the general and notorious fact that the wealth of Boston and its influence are relatively decreasing. The first part of your essay shows or attempts to show why they are decreasing, and the last part is intended to suggest a remedy for the evil. Now let us see how you go to work to prove the causes of your acknowledged fact.

Your argument, if it is an argument, and not an illustration or a contrast, consists of an elaborate comparison between Boston and Chicago. I have no right to parade my personal tastes, or I should express at once my utter fatigue at the strain which Chicago has put upon my intellect. Decidedly Chicago bores me. That western hub is a greater nuisance than ever Boston State House was. Is it absolutely necessary for you to glean the stubble of Parton's harvest?[2] Can't you discover a new case in point? Read the article on the Suez Canal in the Revue des deux Mondes which I am going to send you, and take a hint from Port el Said.

This is only a point of taste, however, and I don't urge it, but I have a much more decisive objection behind and this I do urge. Do your facts justify your argument? Why does Boston not grow like New York and Chicago? You reply: because she does not like New York and Chicago, extend her lines of communication? And why then has she failed to extend her lines of communication? It may do, for your purpose, to throw the blame upon bad legislation, though how bad legislation in Massachusetts could have prevented the Boston, Hartford & Erie from being built in Connecticut, under a Connecticut charter as the road is, I do not comprehend. But though you may make—though you have in fact abundant materials to make a very effective attack upon the legislation, beware of pressing it too far. The truth is, Chicago rose as a colony of New England. She is herself the proof of New England's energy. If you find fault with Boston for backwardness, you must admit that she is weak because she has given her strength to her rival. The question is one of common-sense. If Boston capitalists think that by building railways for Chicago, or sinking copper-mines in Wisconsin, they can double their money, it is unlikely that they will invest it on the Hartford & Erie or any other eastern enterprise which only promises 50 per cent.; and as both are purely and solely questions of investment, the fact is itself the proof; they do not build railways in New England—therefore they must think the other investments better.

I doubt therefore the value of your elaborate argument from the example of Chicago, and I believe that the decline of Boston has been simply due to the fact that other parts of the country were thought to offer, and in fact did offer, quicker and larger returns on expenditure of wealth or of labor than New England could afford to do. So Boston has pitched millions of money into the gutter; she has gambled almost as recklessly—nay, far more recklessly—in gold and copper and petroleum stocks, than ever England did in Grand Trunk, Erie, or Atlantic & Great Western Railway securities. The same feeling has carried her young energy away to New York, Chicago and San Francisco. The stakes were heavier, the gains larger, and the losses identical, since ruin can only ruin, whether in Boston or the west. To say therefore that this process of depletion was caused by want of enterprise and bad legislation, seems to me to be equivalent to saying that a thing can cause itself, or that what is subsequent in time can be precedent in condition.

If I had my way therefore, I would soften this part of your argument. You don't require it and it gives a tone of injustice and unfaithfulness to your picture. The fact is all you want. New England is depleted. Her wealth and life are drawn irresistibly towards more promising markets. Her capitalists lose millions in wild copper speculations, and refuse money for the Hartford & Erie. They build railways through solitary wildernesses in the west, where wild turkeys and prairie chickens are their only probable passengers, and they despise a line of steamers to Charleston or Europe. Legislation has done its best to create and continue the situation. The representative system in its first stage has broken down, since the legislature has shown itself incompetent to originate a new policy or even to reform its old one. Your statement on this point is full of force and might be developed further with good effect, at the expense of your introduction. I will not try to improve it.

Having thus considered the evil, you now proceed to inquire whether there is any remedy. I agree that you lead up to your point very well, but I think you encourage a little too implicit a confidence in one particular panacea.

The central idea should of course be that as you cannot stop the drain of resources, it is absolutely necessary to husband carefully and to employ economically all the force that is left. In your place I should be strongly tempted here to go more carefully into the whole field of activity; to draw the railways a little back, and to push the adjuncts which you only indicate slightly, a little forward. And finally you can bring out your railway commission as the best available remedy for the most pressing evil, not treating it, however, as a certain success, but as a necessary supplement to the acknowledged deficiencies of our political system. Between ourselves, commissions are a useful, but an unfortunate make-shift. The main-spring of life has got to lie in the people; the capitalists and the thinkers. If capital and thought will run away, commissions will not stop them; and our real hope must be in a reaction from the speculative fever of the last twenty years. All we can do in the interval is to economise our forces, and a railway commission, if it consists of really good men, may do something in that way. What is however of more importance to us is that such commissions open a door to men of our ability. This argument, however, is unfortunately not admissible and must be kept well out of sight.

After this running commentary it is needless for me to say that I think the last seven pages considerably better than the first twelve, and that the whole would be certainly improved by cutting the first twelve down to six, while a considerable addition and developement might be given to the last six, in my opinion, to a corresponding extent. I object to your sketch of Boston thirty years ago. It has a false air of archaeology; one is tempted to ask where are the mediaeval remains. But this is rather a question of style than of substance, and after all, though I got through my Holden Chapel period in College, I have no right to blame others for being deceived by its flimsiness.[3] My main objection is that the argument of your first half is weak and had better be left out. If you confine yourself to drawing a simple contrast between the two cities, which is all you want, half the space is ample. Besides, the lower your key is pitched at the beginning, the more effective will your climax be, and if you are bound to wake Boston, you had best do it in the most dramatic way.

And now I will turn, since your challenge or invitation requires it, to the style of your production, about which I assure you I have much more complaint to make than I had about the substance of it. You are, no doubt, a live American, and like the ancient barbarian kings, you are super grammaticam. Our noble countrymen enjoy as the privilege of their free birth, the right to be proud of ignorance and vulgarity. My criticism therefore will be of no use, but you ask it, and, by the Prophets, you shall have it.

In regard to style in general, I will begin by enouncing an axiom. That is best which is truest. If you wish to write a sentence, how ought you to begin it? I say, like the belier in Hamilton's fairy story: commençons par le commencement.[4] Begin with your subject. You say: No, I prefer to begin by transposing the middle of the sentence, or indeed the end, to its head. I will put my predicate first, or a wholly irrelevant adverb, or needless paraphrase first, in order to give life to my style. And so you mask, or break up and enfeeble the strong lines of honest composition, by an attempt to deceive the eye. If you cannot succeed in lending diversity, elegance or force to your style without sacrificing the solid basis of your sentences, it is better by far that you should abandon the idea of possessing a style at all, and content yourself with writing good grammar.

I maintain the same principle about the whole as about the parts. I execrate—I abhor from my deepest soul every attempt to make a thing what it is not; to write for men as though they were children; to varnish a plain story with a shining and slippery polish; to make use of traps in which the reader's attention may be caught, and the idiot may be waxed into ideas. Let those do such work who like it. No man who knows what a true style is, will condescend to use such upholsterer's art.

Nor have I much more patience with works which offend from excess of knowledge, than with those for which mere ignorance and vulgarity are responsible, or mere harmless affectation. Our oratory is a falsehood which degrades the nation. Our Everetts and our Sumners remind me of the Treasury Building at Washington. A plain flat wall and a set of business offices are by this style disguised like a Greek temple, and our barbarism is made more evident than ever by the shameless audacity of our theft.

Depend upon it, there is but one good style, and that is the simplest and the truest. Such a style may want elegance, but it can't be bad.

Your own writing seems to me to be just this, except in those parts where you attempt more, and there you are dreadfully bad; so bad, that unless I knew how I sin myself, I should be ashamed of you. You wrote better than this at College. Your affectations are intolerable. You flounder like an ill-trained actor in your efforts to amuse and to be vivacious. Nervousness thrusts itself out in your sentences as in your ideas. One seeks in vain for that repose and steadiness of manner, on which alone an easy and elegant style can rest.

But my great objection is to your profuse expenditure of words. This trick, which I am myself painfully conscious of sharing, was, I suspect, an inheritance from Charles Dickens and Frank Palfrey, which principally shows itself in affectations of expression and contortions of thought. This is its worst form. Then comes the habit of saying in two words what can be said in one.

Yet I scarcely know whether on reflection I blame this more than I do the brutal inelegancies and vulgarity of expression which you take no pains to correct or avoid. Why on earth the live American glories in vulgarity, I do not know, but I do know that the Greek, dead or alive, never did so, and that the most active Frenchman takes pride in his language and taste. Let us leave to Parton and the school of which he is far too good a chief, the exclusive possession of these arts by which the people are to be flattered. If you and I have one reason for existence in America, it is that we may do battle with just this national tendency.

I have already mentioned an article in the Revue des deux Mondes, and I come back to it and to that Review generally as my justification in this criticism. You will find in it many styles, but you will seldom find one that is florid employed upon a practical subject, nor one that is imaginative upon a narration of facts. Far seldomer, perhaps never, will you see its severe correctness of language sink into vulgarity. Whenever you and I can write our language as these Frenchmen write theirs, we may hope to accomplish something in our country, for people are vulgar in the mass only because they are ignorant, and they enjoy good-taste the instant they become familiar with it. They will listen to us when we know how to speak.

You will find the first page of your M.S. crammed with as many notes as I could get upon it, and a careful examination of these will illustrate what I have tried in this letter to express more at large. To continue this style of treatment throughout would have been too hard work, and was not needed. You can judge for yourself from the specimen. Nevertheless I have dotted a few other notes here and there, while on page 12, I have tried to show you what I meant once by calling your style too fat.

I send you this week a bundle of Parliamentary Papers which Tuke Parker got for me from a Mr Dodson to whom I sent your law article. As Mr Dodson is an M.P. and an authority, you might perhaps write to thank him and so found a correspondence.[5] I do not know how else I could have found the papers. You had better thank Parker too. He may be useful to you.

Brooks arrived last night, well and stout. We leave London on the 10th August.

MS: MHi
 1. The manuscript of CFA2, "Boston," part 1, *NAR* 106 (Jan. 1868), 1–25.
 2. James Parton, "Chicago," *Atlantic Monthly* 19 (March 1867), 325–345.
 3. "Holden Chapel," *Harvard Magazine* 1 (May 1855), 210–215, was the first of HA's eleven published undergraduate writings.
 4. Anthony Hamilton (1646?–1720), author of *Mémoires du Comte de Gramont* (1713) and of literary fairy tales, including "Le Bélier."
 5. John George Dodson (1825–1897), deputy speaker of the House of Commons.

To Charles Francis Adams

Baden. Thursday. 22 Aug. [1867]

Cher Papa

We have just arrived here after a quiet journey. I found that we could not come through direct from Chalons, as the trains did not connect, so we stopped at Strasburg and passed an uncomfortable night. Yesterday was a good days work, however, and I think it would have been best to stop at Strasburg under any circumstances.

I can say very little of Baden yet as we have not been here an hour. Our rooms do not suit us and we expect to change to another hotel, but the town is excessively full and as yet I don't know what we can get. Luckily the weather is beautiful and the place charming. Everything has gone tolerably easily and I think we shall find no trouble in remaining quiet for some time to come.

Ever Yrs   H.B.A.

MS: MHi

To Charles Milnes Gaskell

Baden-Baden. 25 Aug. '67.

My dear Karl

Life has been a burden to me for the last fortnight so that I have not been able to put pen to paper since I left England. We crossed to Paris on the 10th and in that infernal city we remained till the 20th, waiting for ladies' dresses and the milliners' bills. You should run over to Paris by all means. Otherwise you will be deprived of the precious privilege of abusing it; a privilege which I value so highly that I have done little else but exercise it since I arrived there. I do not hesitate to say that at present it is a God-forsaken hole, and my party unanimously agreed that their greatest pleasure since arriving, was in quitting it; and as we are all more or less familiar with the town, our opinion is entitled to weight. I never imagined the city so throughly used up, and given over to hordes of low Germans, English, Italians, Spaniards and Americans, who stare and gawk and smell, and crowd every shop and street. I did not detect a single refined-looking being among them, but there may have been one or two who like ourselves had drifted there by accident or necessity, and were lost in the ocean of humanity that stagnates there in spite of its restlessness. As for the Exhibition, I advise you to go to see it, but go at eight o'clock in the morning and come away at ten, and don't go too often.[1] Plaster temples of Karnac, and canvas Mexican structures, and eastern palaces in slightly worn-out stucco may be seen once. The pictures are worth a good deal of study to fully appreciate that they are not worth it. For the rest, I recollect a chaos confounded. The devil only knows what is in it. I did not go there as a sensible being ought, in the reserved hours from eight to ten, and the consequence was that I was disgusted. I went five times, and hate it in consequence.

You will be delighted to hear that I got into a row which came very near being serious to us. We went to Versailles on the 15th, the *fete Napoleon.* Coming back, our train was overfilled and at a station about half way a great crowd of ouvriers in blouses could not get seats. About twenty were at our door trying to get in, so I stood up in the door-way to stop them till the guard came. A big devil tried to force his way in, so I put my shoulder against him and pitched him out into his friends' arms. Upon this the crowd flared up into a regular French passion. We pulled the door to; the foremost of them tried to force it open, or struck in through the window at my brother and me; my big friend I saw howling in the middle of the mob, shaking his fist at me and shrieking at *cet homme-là; je veux me venger de cet homme là;* while I, expecting to be dragged out by the legs, was preparing to hurt as much as I could the first fellow that got in, sure of getting no mercy from the rest. Luckily the crowd got in each other's way, so that although the door was several times partly opened, no one could enter. It must have been nearly a minute before the guard came and just then the train started. One blouse did then come in, but the rest, my vengeur among them, were left on the platform howling.

In short our ten days in Paris were horribly expensive—hotel bill, frs. 2,500—and far from agreeable. We threw up our hats on reaching this place, not that there is not a shocking crowd here too, but at least we have fresh air and some one decent—or indecent—to look at. Everyone who is usually at Paris, seems to have taken refuge here. Such a swarm of our country-people! The twang of my native land is echoed in every direction by the British burr. The two nations glare contempt at each other in the correct fashion. I have found no English acquaintances here, but we are already in three days over-run with American, and knowing well the national jealousies I am quite willing not to have to combine the two. It is hopeless to try the management of a double team.

Morally Baden is delicious. The females one sees, are enough to make one's hair stand out in all directions. The men are mostly vulgar, but whether Germans, French, English or Americans are most vulgar, is a serious question about which I am led to reflect much. The styles are different, but the result reached is identical. Play runs high. A brother of the Viceroy of Egypt, after losing £6000 at Homburg, has come here where he plays day and night, but whether he has won or lost I do not know, though I saw him lose nineteen thousand francs in half an hour. Modern version of the Egyptian Sphinx. A beast he is to look at, but very like his brother. I occasionally try a five franc piece at roulette but as yet have lost nothing.

We stay here a fortnight or so longer. If you write, address care of F. S. Meyer, Banker. Remember me to your father and mother. I hope you keep on writing but after all, writing is only one half the art; the other being erasure. No one can make real progress that doesn't practise the latter as vigorously as the first. I have done it so effectually as to have expunged all my last thing.

Addio   H.B.A.

MS: MHi
1. The International Exposition of 1867.

To Charles Francis Adams

Baden. 3 September. 1867.

My dear Father

I have drawn once upon my letter: 23 August. £80. F. S. Meyer. I suppose you have directed that these drafts of mine should go to your account. Our expenses here are naturally about £40. per week. Purchases and traveling may run it higher.

Brooks will leave us on Sunday, I suppose, and perhaps I may go with him as far as Cologne. He wants to stop at one or two points on his way. He should be in London by Thursday morning at latest.

I think the waters have done mamma no harm, and I have hopes they will give her strength. She is contented here and amused. It is true that she complains a good deal of having to get up so early, and becomes exhausted before breakfast, but it does not seem to hurt her. I am much in favor of her going on with the experiment, as her doctor says that a three weeks course will be enough, and she has already had nearly half of it. Besides, I want the heat to pass before we recommence traveling, as I believe it to be positively dangerous for her to exert herself in hot weather.

In case you are of the same opinion about her carrying on the treatment, I suppose you will write to her to that effect, and appoint some day about the 20th for rejoining us in Switzerland. We want you to cross the Simplon to the Italian lakes, returning by the St Gothard. If you care to try it, you might go straight to Ouchy or Vevay and pick us up there. If not, you can suggest some place you prefer.

Parker went off this morning.

Very affectly Yrs   H.

MS: MHi

To Charles Francis Adams, Jr.

Baden. 4 September. 1867.

My dear Charles

I have your letter of the 10th August, all about business and politics. Just now I have dropped these two lines of activity, and am willing to accept on trust all you say. Let us hope that Ludlow will prosper and the President do right.

I am at it again, as you will have heard, trying hard to drive my team of women. But as Brooks will soon follow this letter to America, I don't think it worth while to write what he will certainly tell you better by word of mouth. So I refer you for family details to him. On the whole I have not had more trouble than I expected.

You will give my love to Minnie. I was relieved to hear that she had got so well through her trial. I read some rubbish you wrote on the subject shortly after her confinement, but as my last letter contained criticism enough for a time, I will refer you to that by way of comment. In a year or two I shall return home and find you training your daughter[1] to theory, I suppose. If I have a chance I'll spoil her as sure as my name is Henry Brooks.

As you know, we passed ten days in Paris while on our way here, and there I saw Hunt's picture of the Minister which he completed while we were there.[2] As you and John no doubt feel an interest in it, I want to say a few words about it.

The picture is not a full-length; it comes only to the knees. The ground on which the figure is painted, is perfectly simple; a warm, foxy color, which age will darken to black. There is no background other than this. The figure itself stands out boldly; the face slightly turned to the left; the black frock coat buttoned up, a scarf covering the shirt, and only the collar showing any bit of white. There is no color anywhere. One hand is thrust into the coat front; the other hangs down with a roll of paper. The expression of the face is marked but not excessively so, and I think you and I have seen him rise to speak in public, when he had almost precisely the same air and manner.

You can understand from the description that Hunt has dealt with his subject in the most honest and straight-forward way. There are no tricks nor devices in the picture. It is in the severest and truest style, so severe that most people will think it commonplace. I imagine that you and everyone else except a few professional men, will look at it with a sense of disappointment, and feel that something is wanting; a bolder or freer touch; a more expressive attitude; more animated features; a less subdued background, or a dash of color in the dress. There is nothing for the eye to fasten upon and to drag away from the whole effect. In your language, as applied to literature, it is dull.

You know by this time my canons of art pretty well, and you know that what pleases the crowd would have a poor chance of pleasing me. Whoever is right, the majority must be wrong. I consider Hunt's picture to be just what a portrait of our papa should be; quiet, sober, refined, dignified; a picture so unassuming that thousands of people will overlook it; but so faithful and honest that *we* shall never look at it without feeling it rise higher in our estimation. I need to see it among other portraits in order to get at its relative merit, but at any rate I don't hesitate to say that I think we have a first-rate likeness of the Governor. I expect it to be in the next Royal Academy Exhibition, and I shall then be able to fix its merits as compared with other paintings. Until then we will let it rest.

Frank Parker has been with us two days and has gone on this morning to Switzerland. We had our usual annual talk, and some pleasant walks in the hills. He was much amused with our life here and scandalised us by suddenly leaving our party to wait for him while he rushed off after Cora Pearl.[3] The distinguished Cora is only one among many women of the same style here, who this week certainly rule Baden, respectability going hopelessly under. But to see Parker drawn in the train of the most shameless and probably the least pretty of the class, was delicious. I swore we would split on him to Dana. Finally he had the bad grace to come back and abuse poor Cora for the very qualities he and all of us run after her to see.

Mamma is hard at work taking the Griesbach waters here. I do not know yet whether she is better for them, but I certainly do not think she is worse, and she seems contented here. As I am more than ever convinced that it is necessary to do something energetic to prevent the progress of her difficulty, I encourage her staying here. Next week the fashionable season will be over, and I hope we shall have a quiet week more for carrying on the experiment. I doubt whether we start for Switzerland for a fortnight.

If I were here alone with a few thousand pounds to throw away, I should dive into the hell of iniquity we have round us, and try what pleasure there is in a regular blow-out. But alas, I am poor, I am well-known, and I have three shrinking women to protect.[4]

MS: MHi
1. Mary Ogden Adams (1867–1933) was born at Quincy, July 27.
2. The Boston artist William Morris Hunt (1824–1879), on an extended visit to Europe, had begun CFA's portrait in London early in the year. It is at Adams House, Harvard University.
3. Cora Pearl (assumed name of the Englishwoman Emma Elizabeth Crouch, 1836?–1886) was a leading courtesan of the Second Empire; mistress of Prince Napoleon 1866–1874.
4. His mother and his sisters, Louisa and Mary.

To Charles Francis Adams

Baden. 13 September. 1867.

My dear father

Yours of the 6th arrived safely.

On the 7th September I drew again for £80.0.0.

In regard to our plans I am decidedly in favor of remaining here until you leave London, and then joining you at Basle. We are so near it that you will only have to telegraph from London when you start and we shall arrive there before you.

I am now satisfied that mamma's stay here is doing her much good. She looks better and seems to feel heat and fatigue much less than for some time past. She is contented and does not complain of anything. I think it would be a mistake to begin traveling again before it is necessary.

If you are pressed in London and can't get away conveniently, I think we could wait here even as late as the 1st of October without difficulty. Mamma can continue her baths; I am going through a course of the waters; Loo will be glad to diminish the time she will have to wait for her husband after we separate; and Mary will be glad to postpone the return to London. I merely suggest this in case you can't come on the 20th. The physician here does not seem to think it very important to what part of Switzerland mamma goes, and Baden is as high and the air is as good as one could find anywhere except on a mountain.

I observe what you say about your situation politically.[1] Unfortunately I have heard a similar story with regularity every year since we have been in England, and have long ceased to regard it. If however anything should turn up, I have no doubt you will have ample time to get back to London or anywhere else without affecting your position.

If you decide to start on the 20th I shall leave here the same day and stop for the night at Freiburg, reaching Basle on the 21st.

Affectionately Yrs   Henry B. Adams

MS: MHi
1. "I very much fear that the present Cabinet is about to break up. This may have the effect of precipitating my decision about holding any office at all. At any rate it leaves me in suspense" (CFA to HA, Sept. 6).

To Charles Milnes Gaskell

Baden. 22 Sept. 1867.

Caro Carlissimo

What the deuce is Frank Doyle's rank, regiment and address?[1] I am afraid I've got it wrong and so I send it to you to correct. If you will forward it, I will pay you the postage by cheque or otherwise as you prefer. The youth must have his letter after I've taken the trouble to write it.

To my astonishment who turned up here the other day but Pollington mit Gattin und Bedienung;[2] also mit papa-in-law and other sister. I went at once to see him and we chatted a while. He swore you were a humbug for not writing to him, so I read him your letter to me. Since then I've not heard of him, whence I infer that he is still swallowed up in the arms of the Gattin. He has not gone however, for I saw him in the distance last night, hedged in by Erringtons. As I am occupied all the time by my woman-kind, I infer that he is ditto (to use his own elegant style.) She was very chatty however, the moment I saw her.

The Houghtons also appeared on the same day, and went on to Berne. They said they were in better health and to winter at Nice or elsewhere.

As you can imagine from seeing us still here, we find Baden too pleasant to care for leaving it. We pass almost the whole day in the woods, among the hills, and trouble ourselves very little about the world. Fashionable people have gone away. Lord Houghton arrived too late to give another breakfast to Cora Pearl. I suppose we shall have to move our quarters also this week, but whether up or down the Rhine I can't say; probably towards Switzerland, and then some of these days back to London, but when or wherefore I know not, inasmuch as everything is a muddle and mankind a humbug.

One thing however seems certain. I shall not get up to the latitude of Yorkshire this year—perhaps not even the next; so I want you to give all sorts of the prettiest messages to your mother and say that the weight of several nations on my shoulders all at once could alone prevent my coming up to see her. I had meditated a letter to her, but on the whole thought she would be more bored than pleased by it, so abandoned the idea.

I was shocked at one passage in your's. You say that the hero in Gerald Estcourt entreats the heroine to distinguish between "l'infidélité du corps et l'infidélité du cœur," and that this is new. Now, it is many years since I read Tom Jones, but if you will turn to Chapter something of that work, I am sure you will find this very speech;[3] and Sophy's reply is that she never will marry a man to whom the infidelity is not in each case the same. At which Thomas, the town bull, as one of my literary friends called him, was disgusted.

I have amused myself here for the last fortnight by drinking a bottle of water every morning and walking about five hours every day, so that I am now in good condition. Moreover I had a rapid run (not on foot) down to

Cologne, and was sorry not to be able to take Trèves on my way as you would wish to have the last news from the Rothes Haus and Doctor Staub.[4] As it is I shall scarcely be able to bring you any at all.

A sigh of regret passed through my soul when I read of your party at Wenlock, but when fate takes me by the coat-tails I am only too well contented to be dragged to as pleasant a place as this. The gallant Baronet and my noble friend, I am sure did no harm to the partridges.[5]

Ever Yrs   H.B.A.

MS: MHi
1. Francis Grenville Doyle (1848–1882), eldest son of Sir Francis Hastings Doyle, was with his regiment in India.
2. With wife and servants. John Horace Savile (1843–1916), Viscount Pollington, later 5th earl of Mexborough, was with Gaskell at Eton and Trinity College, Cambridge. He married Venetia Errington, daughter of Sir Rowland, April 24. *Half Round the World* (1867) recounted his tour to Russia 1865–1866.
3. The nicety, "infidelity of the body and infidelity of the heart," is from *The Confessions of Gerald Estcourt* (1867), by Florence Marryat. Compare Henry Fielding, *Tom Jones*, bk. 18, ch. 12.
4. The Rothes Haus (Red Inn), where HA and Gaskell stayed, is mentioned in Gaskell's *Blackwood's* article, where Dr. Staub appears as "Dr. Rausch."
5. Cunliffe and John Hervey.

To Charles Milnes Gaskell

54, Portland Place.   Friday. 18[1] Oct. [1867]

Brute

Your offer is most liberal, but I should think you might put yourself down for something and not leave it all for your guests. I appreciate deeply Miss Alderson's generosity.[2] As for the Baronet, it is only what I expected.

I am at my desk nine hours a day, doing up awful arrears of work. Dogs, or red hot tweezers applied to the toe-nails might draw me away. Nothing less; not even Thornes.

This devotion to duty is all on the supposition that we are going to Rome and I must then get leave of absence; it will come easier if I am laborious now; but I am beginning to fear that things look bad for Rome; there's the deuce to pay there, and a grand continental war and day-of-judgment on the cards. If there is a war, I suppose Rome will be hard to get to and uncomfortable when reached. Nevertheless, *justum et tenacem* &c; I stand firm though the skies fall.[3]

Though in person I am compelled to absent myself, yet remind your interesting guests that in spirit I am with you even when agitated Fenians require most letters.[4] That long-promised sight of Wentworth will never come off; but it's not of the least consequence, as poor Mr Toot's used to say;[5] I've no doubt it's a humbug; everything is;—except you and your family, and the Barnet and Lady Alderson and the Misses Alderson (2) and

Thornes and Wenlock. Shall I also except Palgrave? He and his wife dine with us tonight along with the Froude's and Browning.[6]

I saw the sweet-williams last Sunday; mamma and daughter. They were cordial, with the usual dash of satire; what do they say of us within their happy domestic circle? I suspect we catch it, but we can bear much, and after all we have faults; few and slight, it is true, but *enfin* we are not perfect.

Oblige me by not consuming more of the *old* port than is absolutely required. In regard to the rest of the wine I will not restrict the company.

Remember me to your mother. If I did not know what a pleasant party she had, I should come merely to be of use to her; as it is, there are no stupid young ladies for me to talk to; besides, the Barnet is there.

Bye-bye. Fenians call

MS: MHi

1. HA misdated this letter 19 Oct.

2. Florence Alderson, youngest daughter of Lady Georgina Drewe Alderson and the late Sir Edward.

3. In September, Garibaldi had embarked on an expedition to capture Rome for Italy. Papal troops and the French force sent by Napoleon in late October defeated him at Mentana, Nov. 3. *Justum et tenacem:* Neither the people's rage nor that of a tyrant can shake the settled purpose of a "just and resolute man"; Horace, *Odes,* III, iii.

4. Two former Union officers were among the defendants charged with murder of a guard during the Sept. 18 rescue of two Fenian leaders from Manchester prison. One was reprieved after CFA's intervention; the other was executed, having once before used U.S. citizenship to escape British jurisdiction.

5. Wentworth, seat of the Fitzwilliams about 15 miles from Thornes, had an extensive art collection. "Not of the least consequence" is the refrain of the ever-disappointed Mr. Toots in Dickens' *Dombey and Son* (1848).

6. Cecil Gaskell Palgrave (d. 1890), Gaskell's sister.

To Charles Francis Adams, Jr.

London. 22 October. 1867.

My dear Charles

I have received from you at various times letters dated the 10th August, the 24th August, the 6th Sept. and the 5th October. According to your wishes I have sent to you Mr Crawford's Speech on Railway Legislation (N.B. there are no such things as rail-*roads* in this country), and the scientific treatises on railways, the two volumes in one. I have also read your article in the Law Magazine and forwarded it through H. T. Parker to Mr Dodson.

For two or three reasons I preferred to let our argument on the best form of writing drop for a while. In the first place, I was travelling and hated writing at all; after our return I was too busy; but the best reason was that in my own mind I was satisfied that I was right and you were wrong, and that this fact was sure to impress itself little by little on your mind whether you would or no, so as to save me the trouble of wasting Government paper. Now as I take up again your letter of August 24th I feel no doubt that your intelligence must have reached the point where, while still holding fast to all you then said, you will try your hardest to do just the opposite. Your whole argument was too bad for you to defend a month after you had made it. It rested on the supposition that you had not cleverness enough to interest readers unless you made yourself vulgar. You may be right. At any rate you have even here the advantage of me, for whether I am refined or vulgar I begin to despair of ever interesting anyone. But right or wrong you have no business to say it without first trying the better way—and the trial ought to last your life. A life is not such a tremendous time to learn to express your ideas. I don't suppose that Swift when he wrote the Drapier's letters or Cobbett when he edited his Review "fired over the heads of his audience" as you seem to think a man must do who says what he has got to say, and says it in the one-single-sole-unique-possible way.[1] There is but one good way of writing; in the first place, catch your ideas. And now you tell me practically that you've no ideas and have got to take clap-trap. What rubbish! Your ideas are excellent. All that they want is that you should work them up properly. I can tell you I know as well as most men what a labor this is; day after day and week after week I go back to it myself with the feelings, as I should imagine them, of a well-bred dog returning to his vomit. But then I should think myself a mighty ornary cuss if I knocked off this work which is hateful to me as brandy-and-water, calmly remarking, as I sent a crude, half-finished essay to the press: Ah, the public likes it so! The public prefers clap-trap!

You be damned! Yes just that! Give the public a chance. So it is vulgar! So it will drag you down if you let it! But just try once or twice the effect of a clever, pointed article, with all the big words and all the useless words knocked out, written as Heine or Thackeray would write, and then you see which the public will enjoy most. The vulgar experiment may last a day. The other will put you with one jump at the head of American authors. The public is a pretty contemptible thing; that I confess. I've no very high opinion of it myself; but men who propose to influence the public have got to be really great men; otherwise they find themselves talking a deal of stuff in a vulgar jargon, which after all is only an echo of public talk. If I am to drive, I want to sit above my horses. If you are to address an audience you will do well to stand on a platform, morally, intellectually and every other way. So in future stop talking rubbish to me, your dearest brother, and don't deceive yourself with the fancy that your laziness is the same thing with public bad-taste. Just read a page of Macaulay or Balzac or who you please, and then take up a sheet of your or my stuff, and you'll see quickly enough why we still want an audience.

So our friend Stack thought me a humbug![2] His critical acumen is wonderful, and I only wish it had the additional merit of being correct. If I only could manage to endure the drudgery of copying and recopying every word I write, there would be a good chance for me yet to leave half a dozen agreeable volumes in the family library; more than all the rest of the family has ever produced altogether. But unfortunately Stack is in error. I have never copied but one letter since I was a boy, and that one was in answer to Mr Seward's offer of the Assistant Secretary's place here. Stackpole ought to know, and you too ought to know, that when a man has been worried by a subject and thought it over till he does what few people ever will do— that is, knows something about it, his words and sentences flow easily enough, even into "antitheses and rhetorical finish." But I am not going to protect myself under the miserable subterfuge of your combined blunder, bad as it is. I maintain that in calling me a humbug for having (grant I did it) written a familiar letter like an essay, or rather an essay like a familiar letter (take your choice of the charges), you and he said just the thing which is most discreditable to your critical taste. Attack me if you choose for employing art badly, and for not knowing how to write my own wretched style, but don't be so intolerably barbarous as to fancy that art itself is bad. "Copied in cold blood" is your charge, and I wish to God it were true. What of it? If Goethe at eighty could say that he had devoted his whole life to learning to write German, it isn't either you nor friend Stack-pole that is big enough to look down upon his labor—no, not by several inches. Clean that idea promptly out of your combined intellects. I am sensitive on points of art. Personally I am willing to acknowledge anything you choose in regard to my own success in employing it, but I consider the meanest bungler who sets to work patiently and with a comprehension of his ignorance on the task of mastering his art, to be worth more than a half dozen clever charlatans who plunge into the most difficult of careers be-lieving that education is a humbug. I have seen Story in Rome work for hours over a lock of hair on a statue, and days on the fold of a bit of cloth. I hope to reach the point when I shall be able by working hours over a sen-tence, to make it perfect. But whether I do or not is of mighty little conse-quence. I would rather fail in trying to be a gentleman than succeed in being a turned-up-nose snob. If it weren't for the pleasure of following something above me, I believe I would drop the whole infernal affair.

Bye-Bye Snob*s*.

MS: MHi
1. Jonathan Swift (1667–1745), *The Drapier's Letters* (1724). William Cobbett (1762–1835) published *Cobbett's Political Register* (London, 1802–1835); in an American phase, he published *Porcupine's Gazette* (Philadelphia, 1797–1799).
2. Joseph Lewis Stackpole (1838–1904), CFA2's classmate at Harvard, was a Boston lawyer.

To Charles Francis Adams, Jr.

London. 16 November. 1867.

My dear Charles

I received this week your letter of Oct. 26th. As regards business and the fall in stocks, I have only to say that I dont know anything about it and do not mean to interfere. I wish my property could get big enough to give me

$2000 a year clear when I come home; I suppose the Governor would allow me another $1000, and then I could be bravely independent. But as this is too much to ask of it, I don't care a cuss. Only if you can buy Ind. & Cin. at 34, the price I see quoted, I should say do so. Otherwise do as you please.

We have received this morning the election returns.[1] Curious! It takes, as you see, only one year for a nation to follow the lead of its most sagacious men; a fact which in my opinion is worth noting. It is almost equivalent to a vessel's turning on its own length; at least, it does obey its rudder. As for our brother John, I kotoo before him. Tell him that I should write a letter of wisdom to him, if I weren't afraid of being suspected of worshipping a rising son and brother. The only aspect in which I derive the keenest satisfaction from his brilliant début, apart from the fact that he is a S. & B. as above, arises from the confident belief that Messrs Sumner and Wilson have received a distinct and dignified reprimand for the insult they thought proper to put upon us last summer in respect to the custom-house. I confess that rankled. I have not forgotten it, nor shall I.[2] There is too a certain genial pleasure in thinking that after all, our family and our name command sympathy and some support at home. We grow in a dry and rocky soil, but we grow. We are a power, if not a very strong one. The 65,000 have my thanks. We don't care for the damned old Governorship, but we are pleased by 65,000 compliments to our youngest. You will say so, please—from me.

The death of Gov. Andrew troubled me principally on your account, for my own relations with him were, as you know, limited to having seen him. But my second thought was one of deeper regret. I had hoped that he would run Sumner out of the Senate next year. In his absence who can our conservative friends concentrate upon? Our Governor Senior? And if so, are we to fight the Senatorship *and* the Governorship next year? Isn't this cutting it a trifle too fat? Supposing we run *you* for Gov. and John for Congress. Then I think we should try for as many offices as we can conveniently hold.

Charles Norton's wit improves, in fact, its value has nearly doubled since last January. But the triumph of earning $240 in paper in one year does not satisfy my ambition. John is a political genius; let him follow the family bent. You are a lawyer, and with a few years patience will be the richest and the most respectable of us all. I claim my right to part company with you both. I never will make a speech, never run for an office, never belong to a party. I am going to plunge under the stream. For years you will hear nothing of any publication of mine—perhaps never, who knows. I do not mean to tie myself to anything, but I do mean to make it impossible for myself to follow the family go-cart. One thing only or at most two, can change my mind; ill-health, or marriage for love. With these exceptions to destroy my wind, I shall probably remain under water a long time. If you see me come up, it will be with an oyster and a pearl inside. If not, why—so!

I am glad to hear that your article on Boston has gone to the publisher.

He will print it, of course. At least if he doesn't, he's a hatter. Even as I saw it, it was worth a number and a half of his Atlantic rubbish as it goes. I shall be curious to see it and rejoice that you have worked upon it. Depend upon it, nothing but work will do. It breaks one's spirit and crushes one's hope to keep one's eyes fixed on an unattainable standard; but it's the only way for a man who is not a dunce or an ass. The miserable part of it all is that so many men with the same desire, have yet broken down and failed.

MS: MHi

1. For governor of Massachusetts, Alexander Bullock (Rep.), 98,306; JQA2 (Dem.), 70,860.

2. The senate rejection on March 12 of the appointment of JQA2 to the Boston Custom House was presumably engineered by the Massachusetts senators Sumner and Wilson in reprisal for the Adamses' opposition to Radical Reconstruction.

To Charles Milnes Gaskell

London. 26 November. 1867.

My dear Carlo

I have waited for something decisive from Ireland until I am ashamed to wait any longer. Nothing comes, at least down to this moment nothing has come to me, which makes me at all wiser than I was last Saturday. So I think it best to write at once and proceed on the supposition that you are coming along tant bien que mal but still hopefully. A letter is all I can offer you and it may keep up your spirits a little which Cork alone would depress sufficiently, and which must be completely used up between Cork on one side and your brother's illness on the other.[1] I can't write about unpleasant things, for that wretch Palgrave, who on Friday promised solemnly to keep me informed, has never sent me a sign, and I only know what I can learn at your door.

Your sudden departure was a thunderbolt in our various camps. Within an hour after getting your letter, I received a note from Lady Alderson asking me to fill your place at dinner on Saturday, which I naturally promised to do. You will be curious to have a report of the dinner; I will satisfy your wishes. There were about a dozen people there; I took the lovely one to dinner and we were, I am obliged to confess, somewhat gay.[2] You can measure it by the fact that we became sentimental and poetical before we rose from table. I gave a short discursive sketch in about fifteen minutes, of the nature and objects of love. She blushed and listened. Of course I spoke only as your representative. The elder sister flirted abominably with that old Hindu idol, that cross-legged Buddha, Brahma, Vishnu, Siva, and the rest of them—I mean the Saturday Review.[3] Remembering the wrongs of humanity, I avoided this Juggernaut. I glared at him across the table. He told stories after dinner, and I went to sleep in his face; I was in my right, for the stories were stupid. That was all I had to do with him. Not having received from you authority to act, I could not make him disgorge the brains he has swallowed. He did not show a proper appreciation of me, by requesting articles for his wretched newspaper. My dinner—I beg pardon! *your* dinner—amused me and I hope I acted your part with feeling and propriety.

Sunday afternoon I sat one hour and twenty minutes in Cadogan Place; a feat which shows that I make progress even as I approach thirty. We passed the time in abusing you. I told them I should repeat all that was said, but unfortunately I have forgotten it, all except my concluding touch, which was to invite the eldest girl[4] to go down to Thornes with me on the 1st of January; a carriage to be reserved for us at Euston Square or King's Cross—wherever it is—and I to be allowed to smoke. This arrangement delighted me. There was a calm impudence about it in the touch of my asking her to your house, which is equal to our best. She accepted the invitation. We are also all going together to Rome, with your mother to matronise.

Sunday I dined with Mrs Russell Sturgis. Yesterday I dined at a new house, out in Bayswater, an American girl who married an Englishman. I admired her as a girl; she was fast but handsome and lively. I had a dinner there last night which carried me off my legs. I talked all the time, eat all the time, drank all the time. In short, I was en train. I drank a great deal too much and fell desperately in love with my hostess and told her so. There are oases in the desert of life. Such a one was Inverness Terrace last night. My only regret was that you were probably not finding such an oasis at Cork.

Tonight I dine at the United University with Ralph Palmer and young Malcolm. My family is rejoicing at Rendcomb, where the party remains till Thursday. I have a note from my father giving me good advice and a list of guests; the Heads; old Mrs Mildmay; Admiral and Mrs Stopford (?); Mrs Goldsmid, and "three or four young men" making eighteen at table. Which do you think preferable, Cork or country-houses? I don't know myself. After Cork one would certainly relish the country-houses, but after the country houses one might relish Cork.

Work comes forward very slowly. My progress is not only far from rapid but very unsatisfactory. I pass most of my time every day in erasing what I had written the day before. I have read your Chapters I.II.III. They are not so good as I have read of your work; all the religion will have to come out, as you remarked, I think; but vigorous compression is all it wants. I've no doubt they will do, with a little filing, and come out like new-laid eggs, warm and fresh.[5]

Of course all this is for your eye exclusively. I wish I could have seen your poor mother before all her trouble came. It seems now so long since I came near her, that I feel a stranger. I shall go to Lady Doyle's funeral if allowed.[6] If Palgrave doesn't appear soon, I must hunt him up for instructions.

Ever Yrs   H.B.A.

MS: MHi

   1. Gerald Milnes Gaskell (1844–1897) was in the Royal Irish Fusiliers.

   2. The "lovely one" was Lady Mary Hervey (c. 1845–1928), daughter of the 2nd marquess of Bristol.

   3. John Douglas Cook (1808?–1868), founder and editor of the *Saturday Review* 1855–1868, had lived in India.

   4. Wilhelmina Hervey.

   5. The manuscript has not been identified.

   6. Mrs. Gaskell's sister Sidney Doyle, wife of Sir Francis Hastings Doyle, died Nov. 23.

To Charles Deane

London, 21 December, '67

My dear Mr Deane

Many thanks for your letter of the 21st ulto: It was very interesting to me, especially the enclosure which only proves how differently men can argue from the same facts. If I had seen this article from the Literary Messenger beforehand, I should not have changed a line in my own, though I might perhaps have added a paragraph.[1]

I hope the Maryland Historical Society will take up the case as its President promises. But for its own sake it is to be hoped that this may not be done in any wretched spirit of compromise or sentimentality. Your charge is true or it is untrue. If true it ought to be sustained, and so far as I am concerned I promise you that if the Society dodges the evidence or tries to put vinegar and brown-paper on Smith's damaged reputation, I shall do my little best to show up Smith and the Society too. If there is to be a battle over Smith's carcase your first step will be, I suppose, to enlarge its field. Smith's later works are filled with lies; his earlier ones with misrepresentations. I think a choice selection of these, illustrated by such evidence as can be found, will do more to break Smith down, and his supporters with him, than if you continued the battle on the narrow ground of the Pocahontas story. If I had time I would go over Smith's books with care for this purpose, but unluckily I am just setting out for Italy, and next summer I shall probably come home to America, so that I can do no steady work for a long time. I think, however, that we shall have a very pretty quarrel, in which I am certainly enlisted on your side, and if anything is to be done I hope you will keep me informed of it.

The subject is attracting attention here too owing to Dr Woods, who is deep in the British Museum and wants me to review his future publications also.[2] Unfortunately I have not made a study of his subject, but I tell him if he wants a humbug exploded, I am ready to command the torpedo-boat.

Very truly Yrs   Henry Brooks Adams.

MS: Knapp
1. "Smith's Rescue by Pocahontas," *Southern Literary Messenger* 36 (Nov.–Dec. 1862), 626–632, severely criticized Deane's editing of Wingfield's *A Discourse of Virginia.*
2. Leonard Woods (1807–1878), former president of Bowdoin College, was doing research on the early history of Maine.

To Charles Francis Adams, Jr.

London. 24 December. 1867.

My dear Charles

I received last night your letter of the 5th December, and answer it immediately.

As you have no doubt learned, the dice have at length come down. Our departure from this abode of good spirits is fixed for next summer. I am glad for many reasons; sorry for none. As to the future, I know that the prospect is misty, but I have made my plans and am ready to begin the march; for march it will have to be, since Boston is not big enough for four Adamses, and I claim my right to remain, what I have been for ten years, an independent cuss. But before starting my new campaign I am going to have a grand, final, drunken blow-out on this side. About ten days hence I leave for the continent in company with two English friends, trusted pals of mine. Where we shall go I know not. What we may do I cannot foretell. Our intention is to enjoy ourselves along the shores of the Mediterranean and I hope that three weeks hence I shall be lying under olive and orange groves, with the Alps behind me and Corsica hull-down on the horizon. Genoa, Spezia, Pisa, Florence, Rome, loom in the distance. The fact is, my name it is Columbus and I'se born to be a butcher-boy by Jesus or die. I am going to spend just what money I damn please, and postpone paying the bill till I get back, which will be in two months. Let no one bother me sooner than March next. If Pacific Mail and Indianapolis R.R. and Ludlow Man. all blow up together, they are not to disturb my pleasure before sixty days. Good-health and good-weather is all we want to be monarchs of this vile world.

Hence I write to you at once, that the duty may not remain on my mind. About business I have very little to say. I see the Ludlow has its meeting on the 17th. If it declares a dividend it is I that will be surprised. You will not have time to send me my January statement before I go away, so that I can't tell where the devil you got the money to buy 25 more shares of Ind. & Cin. nor what else you have been about. Luckily I don't much care.

Do whatever you like. I shall be at home in six months, and after that there will not be much income left to invest, at least if it's true (as mamma tells me that John writes) that the Governor is too poor to allow himself the expence of a visit to Italy next Spring!!!!!!!!!!! I have not ventured respectfully to suggest that there must be some misapprehension. Hunt's picture broke the Gov's back. It cost £300, or rather less than the best artists charge here for nothing like so good portraits. So I expect to have my allowance cut down, or rather my pay stopped; for my allowance is, I believe, what it used to be; whizz: $250 per annum. As I am bound to make up the $3000 in one way or another, my pen will have to work. The whole thing is no great matter to me; either way I can get on very well. But you will have to become counsel to some one, if they turn you out of doors. Put money in thy purse.[1] By the beard of Moses, when I think of our coming home, and the extraordinary kettle of fish we shall find, I laugh grimly. I shall scuttle out of it rapidly, my boy! I smell battles afar off. I shall get in a distant place, and look on.

Who edits the Atlantic? tell him he's a hass! eave a brick at im! *local* indeed, with that damned pinch-beck Parton and his cursed twaddle in the very last number! how many electrotype spoons does Parton get for such jobs![2] I have almost taken an oath that I will never write in another periodical, but as for some things it is the best vehicle, I shall not give it up yet. I have a few more articles in view for future use, but I mean to change their purpose a little. Vedremo! We will have a leetle gun-powder plot! we will have an Adams Club and turn out something new. There are still heads to hit in the world.

Your Dubosq I have never been able to get, but I will try again. The Revues have been all sent. I wonder whether John ever received a box of cigars (his own) through Dr Lothrop. If he did, was there any duty paid? He is too great a man now to think of acknowledging things, so perhaps you will find out for me. His New Hampshire speech I liked; it was just vulgar enough to spoil it for my taste, but to make it palatable to the public. I accept and admire it as I would admire Milton writing farces. The great point in speaking is, I suppose, to interest one's audience; therefore pimp to them. Observe I say "in speaking"; in writing we are agreed that taste rules absolutely, or in other words, if we mean to write at all it is time thrown away to be vulgar or common. Yet after all it is the public which controls us and in the long run we must all obey that beast.

Bridget again wants to know whether you can find out what the devil has become of her house.

Give Brooks $15 as a N.Y. pres. on my account.

MS: MHi
    1. *Othello*, I, iii.
    2. James T. Fields (1817–1881), who turned down CFA2's "Boston" as too "local" despite its being cast as a sequel to Parton's "Chicago" (March 1867), found room in the current issue for Parton's "Among the Workers in Silver," an effusive account of the Gorham silver company in Providence.

To Charles Milnes Gaskell

54, Portland Place.   Monday. 30 Dec. 1867.

My dear Karl

Your note arrived this morning. Many thanks for the historical information it contains. I have no immediate use to make of it, but will put it aside and make it come into something one of these days.[1]

I am led to infer that your hopes were disappointed. My poor boy, this world is a disappointment altogether. Let us quit it punctually next Sunday.

My impression on the whole is one of relief at not having shared your adventures. Now that a new sun is beginning to shine upon me from beyond the Atlantic, I am beginning—yes, decidedly I have begun to be tired of having stupid people with titles sit upon me habitually. William the Conqueror was good once, as our view of Punch was; but in the long run he is a bore. You and I have done our best to resist the attempt to subdue us. We have carried the war at times into the enemies' country and harried their young women. But we are but two, and dullness is omnipotent, omnipresent, eternal. I am going to run away from it, and you had better give up resistance at once. Sooner or later you will be its victim and why prolong the struggle? "Ancient associations and a prejudice in favor of" the Athanasian creed[2] will get the better of your immortal longings[3] ultimately. Mammas and brothers and William Rufus put together are irresistible—when they're not one's own. On the whole, if you are driven to accept the English creed and swear that you believe in one Duke the master &c, and one mother-in-law who corresponds to the Roman idea of the Sainte Vierge, I hope you will get your own mother to make the selection. I've no faith in any of those that we have chosen.

If I were to go to a big place now, so strong is the spirit of the devil in me since your departure, I know I should do something shocking. Rebellion is good! I like to rebel against everything. Poor Lady William! if she knew my feelings she would think you certainly lost and destroyed in such company.

I have seen no one—not a living being. I mean to make no calls. Certain rheumatic twinges, or some unpleasant pains, warn me that we had better start at once. If the Barnet arrives on Thursday, when shall you come? He suggests starting on Saturday.

In hopes of a certain remeeting

Ever Yrs   H.

P.S. Your letter is not burnt. Nor do I understand whether Lady M says she's not a negative or is a positive, or is not positively negative; or whether it is that she has not a better appetite after the Athan: Cr:, or finally whether it is that she has not grown. Grown or not she is too tall for you![4] beware.

MS: MHi
1. Gaskell, staying at Ickworth, country house in Suffolk of the Marquess of Bristol, Lady Mary Hervey's brother, passed on the "information" given in a county history that "William the Conqueror's real name was 'Harvey'" and that his son Rufus had "built the present house" (Dec. 27).
2. Gaskell, who was Broad Church, reported that Lady Mary "read in a firm & audible voice alternately with the clergyman the Athanasian responses on Xmas day" (Gaskell to HA, Dec. 27).
3. *Antony and Cleopatra,* V, ii.
4. "Lady Mary has grown, & certainly could not get out of her rabbit-hole in her present condition . . . Some of the *Harveys* are capital negatives & only require warmth or sunshine to make excellent proofs. This is an aphorism! *Friday evening.* Lady Mary denies this in toto & in fact is under the impression that she is much shorter. *Burn* this" (Dec. 27). HA evidently thought that Gaskell had been disappointed in his hopes of marrying Lady Mary. Gaskell replied Dec. 31: "I can quite believe in your not quite understanding my letter as it was written at odd moments, & commented on at intervals by the 2 young women" (Lady Mary and Wilhelmina Hervey).

To Charles Milnes Gaskell

54, Portland Place. Wednesday. 1 Jan. 1868.[1]

Dear Karl

What the deuce do you mean by talking about being lame and going to Suffolk again? I rather think you had better be here by Saturday at latest. If not, ——! Never mind! I shall go, even if you and Cunliffe both fail and the eternal skies tumble. Next Sunday *I* mean to be on my way to France. If I am in my bed I can't go, but if destiny hasn't got some better way of balking a fellow than by the exercise of mere brute force, destiny may go hang. If allowed a fair field I mean to leave London next Sunday at latest. Come!—or beware!

The Palgraves called here this morning! I told a lie to your sister. She asked where you had been since Christmas and I said you had told me you were going to Cambridge. Let that sit heavy on thy soul tomorrow! I don't see but that you must keep the thing secret now on my account if not on your own.

I have no news, having seen no one. London is beastly. The weather brutal. I hope we shall be at Vaucluse this day week, out of the reach of snow and ice. I don't want to be caught by the impending storm on this side Lyons.

Nothing more from the Barnet from which I augur well. He should report at headquarters tomorrow evening.

Letters from my brother-in-law and sister at Florence expect our arrival. They are very gay—*tant soit peu* fast I suspect, but agreeable.

Hoo Hoo! mauvais soldat! according to the Grande Duchesse. I recognise the Bretton party.[2] I hope you gave an eloquent message on my part to Lady Comet; you can't pitch it too strong now that I am going away. Intimate a long but hopeless and suppressed passion, and that my nervousness won't allow me to meet her again. How is it that Lyvedy isn't there? I suppose he is, by this time. Ah well! another Christmas I shall not have the pleasure of losing the charms of Bretton. You will be there, and I hope you will be caught like poor mute inglorious Milton,[3] and yoked to a Beaumont or a Lascelles or some such cattle. Then indeed you will have earned your reward like dear Wayland.

I intend to write to your mother before our departure. May I mention the engagement? As things look now I shall not be in London or in England much more than two months after we return; three at the outside; perhaps only a few weeks. So in real truth, this departure is my break-up. I only return to pack and toddle.

Alas for Blacky! Never mind! We will cook up something for him among us and you shall put it on paper. If he fails to print that, he's a Dutchman.[4]

By the way, I read nearly all the second volume of Piebald.[5] It certainly does read itself. It is natural, simple, easy; there is a vein of sentiment in it which seems to me quite "tender" as F.T.P. would say.[6] I am not criticising Balzac or Walter Scott or Thackeray, but *enfin* Boyle. And I was agreeably disappointed.

Sunday. 1.40 P.M. Through.

MS: MHi
1. HA misdated this letter 1867.
2. The soldier-hero of Jacques Offenbach's comic opera *La Grande Duchesse de Gerolstein* (1867) was accused of being a disgrace to the service. By going to Ickworth, Gaskell missed (HA thought he evaded) the Wentworth Beaumonts' Christmas party at Bretton Park.
3. Thomas Gray, "Elegy Written in a Country Churchyard."
4. John Blackwood (1818–1879), publisher and editor of *Blackwood's Magazine.* As a result of former rivalry between England and the Netherlands, "Dutchman," as used in expressions such as "If not, I'm a Dutchman," was a derogatory term.
5. *Piebald, a Novel* (1867) by Robert Frederick Boyle (d. 1883), a friend of Gaskell.
6. Francis Turner Palgrave.

To Charles Milnes Gaskell

Florence. Thursday. 5 March [1868]

My dear Carl

I ought to have written yesterday and did not—*pour cause.* I ought also to have started for London today, but did not—also *pour cause.* My reason for not going as I intended was that my sister made a point of my staying to a little dance of hers on Friday night, so that I shall have to start Saturday morning and travel through without stopping even in Paris. After all, I shall reach London Monday evening, and that is soon enough.

My second reason is a corallary from the first (a devilish word—the 4th letter is *o*—d'ailleurs it is spelt right or I'm a Dutchman). You will easily infer that I preferred to wait if I could, till I had something to say; which I have accordingly done it.

Hence (let us be logical—otherwise why read J.S.M,[1] not to mention Aristotle whom, as in fact you know, I never did read) hence, I say, you may rashly infer again that I have now something to say. Under all ordinary rules this apparently legitimate deduction would be incorrect. I never have anything to say when I write. In this exact case, you happen however to be exceptionally right. I have something to communicate.

For two days I hunted hotels in vain. This morning I began at the Ponte Vecchio and went down the street knocking at every door, and at the last house before the Cascine (I mean the Hotel de la Paix) I discovered the names I sought. Disregarding the mendacious assertions of the porter that they were sortiti, I grasped the trembling caitiff of a courier and sent him up with my card. Need I say that I was at once admitted?

My lady was very gracious and told her tale.[2] They had remained three days in Genoa which they left yesterday morning coming through by our route in one day. Her Ladyship was astonished at my having found them so quickly. I explained that I had come to the hotel intending to call on an acquaintance, and very much by accident seeing their names, thought &c &c &c. Her Ladyship goes to Rome on Monday and has secured rooms at the Europe.

I was the recipient of various inquiries about you, which I answered according to my instructions. Finally with a pleasing air of embarrassment her Ladyship asked whether you had ever received a letter from her. Cynic that I am, I thought to myself that I had heard people ask that question before, and I looked stolid.—No, I thought you could have received no letter. At least you might have done so, but you had not told me of it. In fact, perhaps you had, but in short I knew nothing about it.

I was then informed that such a letter had been written late in January, requesting you to look out for rooms, and with mixed sensations of alarm and horror they had in vain awaited an answer. On inquiry I ascertained that it had been addressed to the poste-restante at Rome. Hasten there, my friend, and obtain the valuable autograph.

Other conversation I had, but it was of a general nature. I will only add that I saw my Lady Mary also, and as she had her visor down, ready to go out walking, I could not tell how she was looking. I sat fifteen or twenty minutes and then took my leave for an indefinite future, though she says she will be in London late in April.

Such, oh my Geliebter, is my story. Further I have nought to tell. I go to a dance tonight and dance again tomorrow night; what awful riot! Saturday, Sunday and Monday I travel. Rest! oh rest!

I have found no books to buy, except an Aldus Dante of 1502;[3] forty francs; very pretty, but how about the price!

Addio, caro mio! Remember me in your days of amusement

Henry Brooks Adams

Charles G. Milnes Gaskell Esq.

MS: MHi

1. John Stuart Mill.

2. Lady Bristol (Geraldine Georgiana Anson, d. 1927), wife of the 3rd marquess, was Lady Mary Hervey's sister-in-law.

3. Dante's *Divine Comedy* published by Aldus Manutius (1450–1515), founder of the Aldine Press of Venice.

To Charles Francis Adams, Jr.

London. 28 March. 1868.

My dear Charles

Since writing two weeks ago I have two letters from you.

Bridget has executed the power of attorney and I enclose it to you.

I also enclose a note from Robert Winthrop. You can judge for yourself as to the propriety of purchasing.

As to the matter of electing a residence. I have always sworn a good deal at the way they tax me in Quincy and never could understand what right they have to make me pay a State tax at all, nor how they could oblige me to do it, if I chose to refuse. I've no property in Quincy, nor do I reside there, nor do I mean to reside there. I did once cast a vote there, the only vote I ever did cast,[1] and possibly the only vote I ever shall cast. I am very willing to pay the income-tax, but it grinds me to pay a local and infernally heavy tax for the benefit of a place I never mean to live in. I doubt the propriety of changing to Boston however. When I come home I will decide as to my residence, and might as well make one business of it then. Still, if you are very anxious to snub Underwood you may transfer me anywhere—to Walrussia if you choose, and as the only advantage or disadvantage of one place over another seems to be in the possession of $\frac{1}{6,000,000\text{th}}$ part of the national voice on election day, I shall be contented however you put it.

I am delighted to think I shall get $300, or even $5, out of the Ludlow. I shall believe it when I receive it. A dividend of ten per cent (to view it in that way) is very fair for one year; and instead of being damaged by the loss of $3000, I shall have some $20 a year more income than before. John is a ass to feel poor.[2] He will really be richer.

I doubt whether the Revue is any cheaper, taken on this side and sent over by post. But it can be done if you wish it.

All your Punch (i.e. the whole as far as reprinted, 1860–1865,) was got before your letter arrived.

MS: MHi

1. HA had voted for Lincoln on Nov. 6, 1860.

2. An allusion to Mr. Bumble, "If the law supposes that, . . . the law is a ass, a idiot"; Charles Dickens, *Oliver Twist* (1838), ch. 51.

To Charles Milnes Gaskell

London. 30 March. 1868.

Dear Carl

Got your note—your peripatetic note—this morning, after so long a silence that I was almost persuaded to believe Miss Hervey who declares we have quarreled. Glad you are coming, and hope you will like London better than I do. I have been regularly to Cadogan Place for the last three Sundays to learn news of you—to very little effect; but was smiled upon. The Sheriff has come to town but is rusty; his dignity has turned his head.[1] When he can spare time from his aristocratic acquaintance he means to come here to dinner—though we no longer give dinners. It's so kind of him! He has promised to come on Wednesday (my Governor is out that night) and if you come by way of Calais you will have time to come in too—and there we shall be, the three heroes! I don't go anywhere now, being already forgotten by London, not having left cards; but I expect to go somewhere—the Lord knows where—out of England, after Easter. I pass my days in packing-cases like big baths and have almost finished with them. Books, drawings, bronzes and all, will soon be hermetically sealed. Dined last night with the Goldsmids, and a good dinner with true feeling in the Boudins Richelieu which were not like Roman ones;[2] and a divine discovery in the cheese way. You should have been there; the others were incapable of taste. Tonight I do Tom Baring! I shall be a rude critic, and Thomas may well quail before my eye. No other good dinners, only political ones. Had an invitation for you the other night to go to Mrs Benzon's to hear Clara Schumann and Joachim play.[3] Frank Palgrave has given me three of his drawings, to my great delight. Called yesterday at the A—ns' and sat an hour alone with Flo![4] Nothing came of it. Sir Ivor Guest is engaged to Lady C. Churchill! What do I care? The opposition is to have 23 majority on the Irish Church; if you doubt it, wait till Friday.[5] Gladstone's Latin makes me shiver—what is exantlatis[6]—I've no Lexicon and never saw the word. Byebye! Oh yet remember me!

Ever.   H.B.A.

MS: MHi
1. Robert Cunliffe had recently become High Sheriff of Denbighshire, in Wales.
2. *Boudins Richelieu,* made of finely minced chicken, are not at all like *boudins,* blood sausages or blood pudding.
3. Elizabeth Lehmann Benzon (d. 1878) and her husband, Ernest Leopold Benzon (1819–1873), a German-American financier, were friends of Robert Browning and William Wetmore Story. Clara Schumann (1819–1896), German pianist-composer and widow of Robert Schumann, and Joseph Joachim (1831–1907), Hungarian violinist, regularly played in England.
4. Florence Alderson.
5. Gladstone, as leader of the opposition, moved to disestablish the Church of Ireland; a procedural vote on April 3 showed an opposition majority of 56. The bill eventually passed in the House of Commons (it was defeated in the Lords), and after a general election Gladstone succeeded Disraeli as prime minister.
6. Archaic Latin for *drawing* water, *enduring* labors; more accurately *exanclatis.*

To Charles Eliot Norton

London, 10 April.[1] 1868.

My dear Sir

You were kind enough in your last letter to express a wish to receive other articles from me. If you are still of that mind, I would like to ask your—and the public's—patience to the extent of some thirty pages in the North American, for a review of Sir Charles Lyell's "Principles of Geology. Tenth Edition."

If you see no objection, I would like further to have my hearing in the October No. I expect myself to return to Boston in July, and will have the M.S. ready by that time, if the confusion I shall live in during the next three months will allow of it.

I ought perhaps to add that I shall try to express more valuable opinions than my own, though I don't wish to be controversial. As it is long since I have had the pleasure of talking with Mr Lowell, and neither your opinions nor his are very well known to me, I would rather run no risk of offering to you anything which might seem not conservative enough for your united tastes. Therefore if you are afraid of Sir Charles and Darwin, and prefer to adhere frankly to Mr Agassiz, you have but to say so, and I am dumb. My own leaning, though not strong, is still towards them, and therefore I should be excluded from even the most modest summing up in the Atlantic, I suppose. It is not likely that I should handle the controversy vigorously—the essay would rather be an historical one—but I should have to touch it.

If you will be kind enough to send me a line, still to the care of this Legation, that I may know what to do, I shall be, as ever,

Very truly Yrs   Henry Brooks Adams.

Charles Eliot Norton Esq.

MS: MH
1. HA misdated this letter March.

To Charles Francis Adams, Jr.

London. 21 April. 1868.

My dear Charles

Just after sending my letter of last Saturday, I received your's of the 7th inst. I don't know why you sent it to Barings. The Legation is not to be closed, and until Mr Sumner or General Butler comes, the Secretaries will see to our letters, I suppose.

Your check was sensible and thoughtful. My account against you stands:

Clothes	£9.0.0	
Revue	1.5.0	
Packing-case	10.0	£10.15.0

Add to this Bridget's present and the total will be about £13. I will hold the odd £2 for further orders, if no other claims against you are brought forward.

Many thanks for Mr Ogden's letter[1] and your information about the Indianapolis and Cincinnati Railroad. Both the letter and the information are, as I expected, highly unsatisfactory.

In regard to what you say of Dwight's road,[2] I believe you are quite right. As you have no money of mine in your hands, it is scarcely worth while to discuss the question of investing. I notice that you say you shall put any small sums you receive, into it, at present rates. I beg however that you will do nothing of the kind. I wish any such small sums to be put into Boston or Massachusetts gold-paying securities, and under no circumstances whatever into anything else. This is entirely apart from any question of confidence or want of confidence in the rail-road; I should do the same though I were morally certain of its rise to par in a year. The direction, however, is positive.

In regard to politics. I was much pleased with the handsome rise I got out of you by my remark. Never salmon yet plunged more greedily at the fly. Excellent young man, I myself am guilty of the crime I charged you with. I reserve to myself as my most valued right, the privilege of attacking all parties and following none. Mutato nomine, de me fabula.[3]

At the same time, you are right in defending yourself, for your position and mine are different, and I am glad to see that you have at last chosen your side. On the whole I am glad that you have made your bed with Congress, for though I hold strong opinions in regard to that body and its proceedings; and though from an intellectual point of view I consider their arguments slightly imbecile and their policy tant soit peu canaille,[4] still from a narrower and perhaps from a lower point, I think it advisable to entertain relations with each side, and do not want to see the whole family on either. Therefore I am pleased to see that you accept the impeachment as the great triumph of law, and support Grant as President. But I have not read your letter to the Minister, for I was sure that though your policy was right, your argument would be rubbish.

Your raillery about Butler and his financial policy is very good and just. As a general thing you are clever at raillery. I advise you to cultivate it.

Send on your new article. I shall be in London, having work to do, till we sail. You can direct to the Legation.

Ever Yrs   Henry Brooks Adams.

MS: MHi

1. Presumably Edward Ogden (1808–1872) of New York City, CFA2's father-in-law.

2. Edmund Dwight (1780–1849) was a promoter, director, and from 1842 to his death president of the Western Railroad connecting Worcester, Mass., and Albany, N.Y.

3. *Mutato nomine, de te fabula:* the name changed, the tale is told of you; Horace, *Satires,* I, i.

4. *Tant soit peu canaille:* rather that of the rabble.

To Charles Milnes Gaskell

46 Rue Neuve St Augustin
Hotel d'Orient. 3 May. 1868.

My dear:

The world runs devilishing à travers. (I have *not* forgotten English, but prefer to write so.) Instead of my being back in London today as I hoped a week ago, I am as far or further from it than ever. Those imbeciles at Washington don't do anything, and are as likely as not to let the President off, after all. In which case I shall be in a nice way. I have clothes with me for one week, which is now up. I abhor Paris and am profane beyond belief in my desire to get back to London and begin work. But I see *no* chance of returning before next Saturday and perhaps not even then.

Thus far I have passed my days and nights in my room geologising.[1] I have seen no one. Your friends the Bristols passed me on the channel, as you have no doubt guessed. The Paran Stevens tribe I have not yet called upon,[2] not caring to provoke an extra visit to my mother at a time when she does not want to visit at all. If there is anyone in Paris whom I know, I have not heard of it, and I shall not stop the individual in the street.

You may tell our friends in Cadogan Place that I have executed their commissions but do not know when I shall be able to bring the plunder over to them.

I have been twice to the theatre. Once I saw Paul Forestier. I thought it very poor; the last act even worse than poor. And once to the Gymnase where little Pierson, who becomes very fat, came out as a much better actress than I ever supposed she could be. But hélas! I grow old, for I know that eight years ago the women on the stage here were the freshest young girls in life. And now they are coarse and big. Even Schneider was younger then, though she has always been coarse and fat since I've known her.[3]

Monday morning.   I kept this document back in order to obtain the information you wanted about the surgeon. But as it may be another day or two before I can satisfy myself, I decide to send.

My father is at the Brunswick House Hotel, Hanover Square. If you ever want information about my probable movements, apply to him.

Ever Yrs   H.B.A.

MS: MHi

1. Preparing his review of Lyell's *Principles of Geology.*

2. Paran Stevens (d. 1872) of Boston, a hotel magnate, and his wife, Marietta Reed Stevens (c. 1823–1895), who in the 1870s became a leader of New York society.

3. *Paul Forestier,* a new comedy by Émile Augier. Blanche-Adeline Pierson (1842–1919) moved from ingénue to more important roles after 1864. Hortense Schneider (1838–1920) made her greatest success in Offenbach's *La Grande Duchesse,* which HA had seen in 1867.

To Sir Robert Cunliffe

Pouncy's Private Hotel,
9, Holles Street, Cavendish Square,
London, 16 May 1868

My dear Robert

I use this shocking paper not because I admire Mr Pouncy's taste, but merely as the shortest way of telling you that I am master of all your chattels. I arrived here yesterday morning, having been detained in Paris longer than I expected. My people are all on their way to Italy, happily off. I have got several tons of geological books scattered over your room, but you shall have space to sit down when you arrive. Nothing but my personal friendship for you has prevented my smashing all your locks in the hopeless effort to stow away my traps, but with the blessing of God, by the time you arrive, I shall have restored order and sent off the heterogeneous mass which adorns one of your bed-rooms.

I am now known as the magnificent pauper. I have charming rooms—belonging to my esteemed friend Sir Robert Cunliffe, G.C.B. F.R.S. R.A. &c. I have a colossal and solemn servant—belonging to my father. I have excellent dinners—given to me by my large and agreeable circle of friends. Nothing that I have is my own, so that in one sense I am above fate.

The Gaskell's wrath at you has been succeeded by horror at your long silence. There is a wigging in store for you, and I proclaim loudly that you deserve it. Such is friendship and the sense of favors received!

Send me the key of your wine-cellar. I have some bottles which I want to lock up, and can't. Or rather, come yourself. We will be merry from 4 P.M. till midnight, and in the interval we will jest. We will make Sunday excursions, and will enjoy life wisely and well. I look forward with longing to the sight of my baronet's lovely countenance. And tell the youth Walter that he shall have his room whenever he wants it. I can move out as easily as I moved in. But I shall move out definitively and finally in four or five weeks, so come while I am here!

Ever Yrs   H.B.A.

MS: MHi

To Sir Robert Cunliffe

London. 19 May. 1868.

My dear Robert

Your letter arrived this morning. If Pouncy tells truth, I understand him not.

On unlocking your wine-celler I discovered an important fact, namely, as follows, to wit, viz: it wasn't locked. Or rather, to be quite correct, it *was* locked, but the inner bolts not shot. I might have opened it and it may have been opened. Nothing seemed disturbed but there was no sign of broken bottles. All was in order and if bottle has been broke, it has been removed. At all events I have put in another dozen and some few cigars, so that you may not want when you come up.

Drat your impudence! do you suppose that I had any news to tell you that was *not* about myself. As Carlo remarked last night: He was going to call on the pleasantest fellow he knew in London. "Ah! said I modestly: You are coming up to my rooms?" "To my own," he replied with equal delicacy.

I have no more to say, duty obliging me only to constate the situation of your cabaret. Tonight Carl dines with the bloody Marchioness[1] in St James's Square, goes thence to Cowper's prance and looks in to supper at Carlton House Terrace. I must go to the last also, though I would prefer to geolog at home. I am going to get some lizards and snakes up here. I find my subject requires them. Of course you won't object.

If Walter comes to town and doesn't stay here, whether I'm here or not, you and I will quarrel. Our long friendship will come to a sad end. By-the-bye, we talk of running down to Wenlock for Whitsuntide. My poor gloggy![2] I never shall do a damned line of it while you two fellows are near. And I've pledged myself to take it home with me, all complete!

Yrs ever   H.B.A.

MS: MHi
1. Lady Bristol.
2. Geology.

To Sir Robert Cunliffe

[London] Wednesday. [May 27, 1868]

Oh! my too-beloved Baronet!

Why do you come back precisely as I go away? In the first place it makes me look inhospitable. One would suppose that we had quarreled, whereas, as you know, everything in your rooms is at your service. I should have hoisted our national flags in honor of your arrival. But, hélas! Carlo waits for me at Wenlock and I am unable to wait for you here.

I have not ordered my things to be transferred to the small room because I have let my servant go to the Derby. No doubt he will come home drunk and I shall not see him again. Never mind! You have hereby plenary power of him even as myself, and he will do with my property whatever you tell him to.

I enclose the key of the wine-cellar. So far as I know, my own personal thefts from it have been limited to half a dozen of your biscuit. I don't know whether you like brown sherry, but there is a bottle open, and wanting to be drunk.

I shall be back on Monday in time to dine—I have a dinner that evening. May I hope then to embrace my Baronet! Meanwhile be not surprised if strange miscreants, friends of mine, haunt you.

I have no news for you, but look forward to much calm discussion of serious topics. You will be pleased to hear that the first half of my labors is over, but then the last is the worst.

Beloved baronet! you are anglic! that is, half angel, half anglican. My soul is impatient to resee you and I look forward to amusement.[1]

Ever Yr   H.

MS: MHi

1. After a month of leave-takings, HA joined his family and sailed from Queenstown, June 28, on the *China*. They arrived in New York, July 7.